PROBLEM SOLVING

A Structural/Process Approach with Instructional Implications

Academic Press Rapid Manuscript Reproduction

PROBLEM SOLVING

A Structural/Process Approach with Instructional Implications

JOSEPH M. SCANDURA

with co-contributions by

John Durnin, Walter Ehrenpreis, George Lowerre,
Wolfram Reulecke, Donald Voorhies,
and Wallace Wulfeck II

ACADEMIC PRESS   New York   San Francisco   London   1977

A Subsidiary of Harcourt Brace Jovanovich, Publishers

ACADEMIC PRESS, INC.
111 Fifth Avenue, New York, New York 10003

United Kingdom Edition published by
ACADEMIC PRESS, INC. (LONDON) LTD.
24/28 Oval Road, London NW1

Library of Congress Cataloging in Publication Data

Scandura, Joseph M.
Problem solving.

(Educational psychology)
Includes indexes.
1. Problem solving. 2. Psychometrics I. Title.
BF441.S267   153.4′3   77-9600
ISBN 0-12-620650-3

CONTENTS

PREFACE

Building on my earlier work on rule learning, I first considered the problems of complex human behavior in a comprehensive way in "Deterministic Theorizing in Structural Learning: Three Levels of Empiricism" (Scandura, 1971) and later in a book entitled *Structural Learning I: Theory and Research* (Scandura, 1973). In these publications, and in others that evolved from them, I introduced a deterministic partial theory that deals with content specific competence, cognitive processes, and individual differences measurement. Although *Structural Learning I* in some ways still provides the most rigorous treatment, there have been a number of important refinements, clarifications, and extensions of the basic theory during the past five years. Equally, if not more important for present purposes, little empirical work had been done specifically in the area of problem solving at the time the book was written.

In one sense, then, the present book is a progress report on my research and that of my collaborators over the past five years. In another sense, however, this volume represents our first serious attempt to help bring about synthesis in the study of human problem solving. The theory and research contained herein includes topics associated with such varied fields as artificial intelligence and computer simulation; cognitive, educational, and mathematical psychology; individual differences measurement, and educational design and development. And yet relatively little of what is included can accurately be described as belonging solely to any one area. The emphasis throughout is on those ideas, methods, and results that are either common to a number of fields or that have cross-disciplinary implications.

The various research contributions included herein were put together in one volume in the hope that this would help to reduce present barriers between the relevant disciplines—whether the primary goal involves identifying specific problem solving competencies, more general cognitive processes, individual differences measurement, or educational applications. The purposes of the book will be achieved to the extent that it helps to encourage more cooperation across disciplines, greater understanding and appreciation of the role that competing disciplines might play in solving a common problem, and more emphasis on cross-disciplinary, problem-oriented research.

Because different combinations of co-workers have contributed to the various chapters of Parts 2, 3, 4, and 5, and because portions of some of the chapters have recently appeared in scattered journals, it seemed best to retain these mostly empirical contributions in close to their original form. However, where I have felt that it might be useful to improve or make additions, I have done so. For the convenience of the reader, important changes and additions are printed in italics. Chapters 1, 2, and 15, and, in part, Chapter 14 were prepared after the others. Consequently, they should be consulted, and given greatest weight, in evaluating theoretical issues.

Although they all speak to one or more facets of a common theme, the various chapters for the most part can be read independently. The primary exception concerns the main theoretical chapter, Chapter 2, in relation to the largely empirical contributions in Parts 2 (Content), 3 (Cognition), 4 (Individual Differences), and 5 (Extensions and Educational Implications). Because of the detailed examples in the empirical chapters, the basic theory in Chapter 2 is written at a somewhat more abstract level than some psychologists and educators may be accustomed to. Nonetheless, there are no specific prerequisites—although general familiarity with the literature on problem solving, procedural thinking (e.g., computers), and/or my earlier book will be helpful. In addition, the major compendium, Chapter 15, may be helpful in this regard. It not only summarizes some of the major theoretical ideas in the book but shows how these ideas relate to current theory and research in a variety of related areas, ranging from artificial intelligence to instructional design.

The relative abstractness of the presentation in Chapter 2 should not mislead the reader into thinking that the theory is divorced from empirical reality or that it is limited in its applicability only to simple tasks of the sort used for illustrative purposes. This level and mode of presentation was used solely to facilitate explication of a number of important relationships that might otherwise have been obscured by superfluous detail. The theory is operational in its essential aspects and it specifically encompasses either in fact, or in potential, the full range of empirical work reported. In order to emphasize relationships, a short summary of relevant empirical studies, mostly reported in subsequent chapters, is provided in the last section of Chapter 2.

Because of its broad coverage, this book can be used in courses on human problem solving and seminars in cognitive psychology, human learning and development, artificial intelligence, educational psychology and instructional design, curriculum and mathematics/science education—especially where the instructor wishes to emphasize the "structural/process" point of view. In reading the book, however, one should keep in mind that I have used the term "structural" in three senses: (a) the global sense referred to above; (b) in referring to my own structural learning theory; and (c) in the modified form "structure," to refer to entities on which processes operate. Moreover, although the connotations are slightly different, the terms "rule," "procedure," "algorithm," and "process" are used interchangeably. The use in particular instances depends on continuity both with my previous writings, where rule and procedure have been favored, and with other common terminology used in areas related to particular discussions. Where intended meanings are not clear from context, the reader should consult the Glossary.

One strategy for studying the book is to begin with Chapters 1 and 15, and the introductions to the various parts of the book. Chapters 1 and 15, in particular, help to place the theory and research in a broader context. Chapter 2 might come next—but not necessarily with the aim of complete mastery and, in any case, with the intent of returning to it after reading various of the empirical chapters. Many of the ideas are subtly but importantly different from those in adjacent fields. The reader who is not already familiar with the Structural Learning Theory, particularly the empirically inclined psychologist, may find it helpful to study the rationale in Chapter 1 for testing deterministic theories and to sample from the empirical work in each part before serious study of the theory. Chapter 2, however, should probably be read before the theoretical portion of Chapter 14 on adaptive instruction. The other chapters may be read as desired.

As is the case with most books, I am indebted to many people for various kinds of help. First of all, I would like to thank my coadjutors, without whose collaboration many of the studies would never have been conducted. John Durin and Wally Wulfeck also helped by reading most of the galley proofs and identifying key words and by making helpful suggestions for improvements. Equally important, I am indebted to those funding agencies that have supported my research over the years: first the now defunct small grants and basic research programs at the USOE, then the education directorate at the NSF, and currently the NIH. Without this support very little, if any, of the work reported herein would have been possible.

In addition, various chapters of the book were read in whole or in part by Saul Amarel, Lyle Bourne, John Carr, Gerald Cason, John Feldhusen, David Hildebrandt, Felix Kopstein, Dionysios Kountanis, Robert Reynolds, and Herbert Simon. Each of them made a number of very helpful comments.

It goes without saying, of course, that not all of these reviewers would agree with all that I have said or, for that matter, that I have always agreed with their comments and criticisms. In particular, an especially important philosophical difference exists between myself and my good friend John Carr, who represents a point of view that apparently is shared by many other mathematicians (and theoretical physicists). This position holds that theories must be formulated in precise mathematical terms if they are to be taken seriously. If forced to make a choice, they would rather be precisely wrong than vaguely right. The history of recent theory building in the behavioral sciences does not convince me that this is necessarily the most productive way to deal with complex human behavior. (Indeed, if physicists held to those views during the Middle Ages, we might still be waiting for our first Copernicus.) Although I am well aware of the potential advantages of mathematical formulations in theory building, I also believe that there is merit in the converse position: that of being vaguely right rather than precisely wrong. My own working hypothesis has been that more rapid progress might be made by attending to both concerns simultaneously. That is, focus attention on the empirical requirements of comprehensive theory, while at the same time being as precise as one can be, consistent with those requirements.

Correspondingly, I have been especially receptive to criticisms of basic theoretical assumptions, to discrepancies between theoretical predictions and data, and also to specific suggestions that would improve the precision of the formulation without conflicting with my better instincts. (Mathematization almost always requires empirical compromises.) On the other hand, I am well aware that my "theory" has not yet attained a formal status. Hopefully, the present work may stimulate some mathematicians to take on this important task.

In this case, the basic challenge will be to develop a truly mathematized theory that will stand up to the breadth of empirical data, say, that is represented in this book. When someone finally does succeed in developing such a (formal) theory, I suspect that it may well have the same (conceptual) form as that proposed here.

Finally, I would like to thank those who helped me in preparing the book for publication: Tina Baker, Joe Karabinos, Natalie Nesbitt, Robert Reynolds, Alice Scandura, and Arlene Weissman, who carefully proofread the book, and prepared the camera-ready copy and the indexes; and most of all to Victoria Profy, who not only typed the original and numerous revisions of the manuscript on our word processor but who helped with the references, corrected my spelling, and in some cases my grammar—and most important of all, made the whole thing work. It is no understatement to say that without her dedication this book might well still be in draft form.

For over 10 years my wife has been encouraging me "to write a popularized version of structural learning" and I have been promising to "save her for my first best seller." After four books that would not qualify, and this one on the way, I have given up that goal. Apparently, she has given up too, for she has decided to begin studying toward a Ph.D. Given this duality of "goal shifting" (read on dear reader), and the date, I can think of no better time to dedicate this book to my dear wife Alice.

Joseph M. Scandura
February 14, 1977

PART 1

Introduction

During the early twentieth century, psychology properly
shed the cloak of logicism. Nonetheless, one can properly ask
today whether it rejected too much. On the one hand, it is
clear that an understanding of complex human behavior involves
more than just knowing the rules of logic. But, on the other
hand, it is also true that human behavior is considerably more
rational than early behaviorists thought when they first proposed that psychology restrict itself to the study of (S-R)
relationships.

In spite of the so-called paradigm shift toward cognition
generally, and information processing in particular, theories
of complex human behavior still tend to be highly restrictive.
The scientific literature is replete with theories of reading
comprehension, theories of memory, of both the permanent and
working varieties, and specialized performance theories. Only
rarely, however, do we hear much about comprehensive theories
that are both rigorous and testable. The vast bulk of research
and theory construction in behavioral science today is still
very much a matter of building from the ground up--of "bricklaying". Ever since the all too well publicized failure of
Hull's comprehensive behaviorism, attempts at theoretical synthesis in psychology have been relegated to the back burner,
and as often as not, have been ignored.

Piagetian structuralism is perhaps the only major well-
known counterweight at the present time. This approach, first
and foremost, works from the top-down. It seeks primarily to
understand the overall architecture of human cognition, including its epistemology and development. Unfortunately, however,
the resulting understanding of interrelationships (within this
tradition) has not progressed to the point where it has been

possible to make meaningful contact with the more specialized theories and results that pervade most of contemporary cognitive psychology.

Since Piaget's first monumental works became established during the 1920s and 1930s, major new logical tools have been developed which provide a potential basis for such rapproachement. Beginning with Godel's fundamental completeness and incompleteness results in logic, a number of advances have been made in both generative logic and computability that have potentially important implications for understanding complex human behavior. Interestingly enough, many of the most useful concepts seem to be associated more with the logic of computability than with computer science itself. In the latter case, the (e.g., computer) languages and results often refer to specific types of machines having features that, as often as not, conflict with corresponding characteristics of humans. (In retrospect, the latter is not surprising. Most mathematical theories, including statistics, contain as much or more that is irrelevant to psychology as is relevant.)

It is not that theories about computability and logic, in themselves, provide an adequate basis for explaining human behavior. Like all mathematical theories, they provide only logical constraints that cannot be violated in any specific more structured scientific theory of which they are a part. More to the point, basic results in these and certain other areas of mathematical foundations provide constraints (e.g., particularly with regard to scientific language) that are important in all structural/process theories of complex human behavior.

Thus, in instructional design, for example, no one who is even casually familiar with procedural logic, would suggest that in task analysis there might be a unique hierarchy for each type of task. In fact, if there is one, then it can easily be proven that there is an infinite number of others that will do the same thing. The real questions have to do with the process of how to identify those hierarchies needed to account for the behavior of given populations of subjects.

The current controversy over whether people use images in thought may be handled similarly. Although continuous quantities (images) may be represented digitally (i.e., symbolically), the fact is that it is easier to represent some things as images and other things in terms of discrete entities. Moreover, some information processors can do both (e.g., consider computers that have both digital and analog capabilities). Humans, in particular, almost certainly use images as well as discrete representations. The real questions, again, concern which kinds of things are represented in which ways, why they are represented in these ways, and most importantly, what the exact characteristics of such representations are. (This issue is one of several discussed in Chapter 15.)

Nonetheless, although the logic of computability (and certain other foundational concepts) may provide a useful starting point, the most crucial constraints in any scientific theory are independent of logic per se. Indeed, the same is true of mathematics generally. If this were not the case, there would be no need for scientific theories at all; mathematics alone would be sufficient.

Mathematical constraints aside, a major contention in this book is that there are other general constraints that must be imposed on specialized psychological theories in order that they be extendable to other phenomena. It is especially important that theory in any one area be consistent with the requirements of theory in other relevant areas. As a minimum, any viable, comprehensive theory of complex human behavior must be consistent with the requirements of specific content (problem domains), cognitive processes, and individual differences measurement. Moreover, ideally, any comprehensive theory of complex human behavior must deal with the dynamic relationship over time, between subject and environment, as well as with the details of such interaction at any given point in time. In effect, although it may have a unique identity of its own, such a theory should make contact both with general systems/cybernetic theories and with specialized theories in artificial intelligence, cognitive psychology, and individual differences measurement.

I do not claim in this book to have developed an all encompassing and complete theory of complex human behavior. In order to identify general constraints that transcend specific areas of concern (and also to identify what in mathematics may be important), it is essential that one work from the top-down. In principle, this approach, like that of Piaget's structuralism, is a never ending process, that results in successively closer approximations to "the truth". Although significant problems remain to be solved, I believe that we have learned some things about the overall relationships and constraints that must be satisfied by, and hence that may be useful in constructing, *any* specialized cognitive theory pertaining to complex human behavior. Moreover, there is reason to believe (including hard data) that these relationships and constraints may play an important role in applications, especially in education.

This is not to say, of course, that the theory and research described in the following chapters makes specialized cognitive research obsolescent. That would be presumptuous in the extreme. Rather, I believe that the present work is basically complementary to much existing theory and research in more specialized areas. Just as specialized theory and research may provide detailed understanding of specific phenomena, and may therefore supplement structural theories, the latter help provide an understanding of interrelationships, that may therefore impose constraints on the form that more specialized theories may take (i.e., if they are to lend themselves to generalization).

As a consequence, a primary goal of much empirical research in the structural tradition is to demonstrate the validity and/or importance of such interrelationships, and to illustrate the form that acceptable micro-theories of similar phenomena should take. Whereas alternative structural theories may be compared with one another in this sense, it often makes no sense to contrast them with more specialized micro-theories. The latter would be much like comparing apples and oranges. The concern of structural theory is more general--attention is focused as much with how to generate specialized micro-theories as with such theories themselves. The situation, of course, is different in the case of more specialized theories derived from global structural theories. However, even where derived micro-theories turn out to be equivalent to competing ones, it is important to recognize that whereas the former will necessarily be compatible with broader requirements, the latter often will not be (compatible).

As argued in this book, a more global level of concern is crucial in dealing with a number of perennial problems in psychology, for example, the problem of how to generalize findings in one content area to new ones, without operating at so abstract a level (e.g., difficult versus easy, meaningful versus rote) as to lose most of what is essential.

Chapter 1 provides a general introduction to the study of problem solving, including various approaches that have been taken, a general rationale for the approach taken in this book, and a brief overview of its contents. In Section 1, special attention is given to the perspectives of scientists in artificial intelligence, cognitive psychology, and individual differences measurement. In summarizing these perspectives, it is proposed that any complete understanding of the problem solving process will require a broad theoretical framework which synthesizes all three concerns.

Section 2 deals with relationships between deterministic and probabilistic theories in behavioral science. Given the (in principle) goal of understanding why individual subjects perform as they do in given problem situations, it is argued not only that deterministic theories are essential but that such theories must be tested under appropriate idealized conditions. In addition, an alternative to probabilistic theories is proposed for dealing with nonidealized "real-world" data. In this alternative a distinction is made between theoretical/structural factors, which pertain to deterministic theory, and incidental variables, which pertain to complementary observation theory.

The chapter concludes with a brief overview of the contents of the book.

Chapter 2 describes, extends, and refines the author's Theory of Structural Learning in the context of human problem solving. This theory synthesizes concerns pertaining to content, cognition, and individual differences and provides the foundation on which all of the research reported in subsequent chapters is based.

In the theory, both the competence theorist (observer) and the behaving subject play a central role. The former determines both the problem solving domain of interest and the competencies necessary for solving the problems. As in all generative theories, competence is represented in terms of rules (procedures). In the Structural Learning Theory, however, the characterization of competence differs from that in other competence theories (e.g., in linguistics and artificial intelligence) in several important ways. (1) The problems and rules are not represented at a fixed level. Rather, the level and form of representation is chosen so as to have direct psychological significance and depends both on the subject population in question and the level of behavioral (observable) detail that is of interest. (2) The individual rules are restricted in the sense that new rules, derived during the course of a given computation, may not in turn be applied during the course of the same computation. (3) The rules are assumed to operate on other rules to generate new ones, in accord with a very specific, goal switching control mechanism.

The control mechanism, and certain other cognitive constraints, are assumed to be universally available to all subjects. They determine how individual subjects use whatever specific knowledge they have (including higher-order rules) in particular problem situations. Among other things, these universals, together with specific lower- and higher-order knowledge, provide a basis for answering such questions as why it is that some people succeed in problem situations for which they do not explicitly know solution rules whereas others do not.

Finally, the theory shows how competence is related to knowledge available to individual subjects in the given population. Generally speaking, competence corresponds to the content relevant knowledge available to an idealized (prototypic) member of the target population. This competence provides a basis for identifying appropriate test items and, in turn, for the operationalization of individual knowledge. In a very real sense, the rules in a competence theory serve as "rulers" for measuring human knowledge. The last section of Chapter 2 contains brief summaries of much of the more directly related empirical research. This research involves content and its analysis, cognitive processes, individual differences measurement, and instructional applications.

Most of the basic theoretical concepts and descriptive
terms used in this book are defined in the Glossary. An effort
was made to use these concepts and terms consistently through-

out the book. Because the various chapters were written over a period of several years, however, during which time several of the basic concepts have evolved, my attempts to insure uniformity may not always have been completely successful. The terms in the Glossary refer specifically to Chapter 2 and to a lesser extent to Chapter 1 (corresponding page numbers are indicated in parenthesis). When in doubt these chapters should be given precedence.

1
Introduction, Rationale, and Overview[1]

Joseph M. Scandura

Why is it that some people can solve given problems, whereas others cannot? In one form or another this question has puzzled scholars almost from the beginning of civilization, and it lies at the heart of the problem-solving process.

Any complete answer to this question, as a minimum, will necessarily involve specification of specific problem-solving competencies *(content)*, an understanding of underlying psychological mechanisms *(cognition)*, and some way to deal with *individual differences*.

First, with regard to content, it is important to know the specific capabilities (competencies) that are needed to solve problems in given domains. Without such knowledge, one cannot intelligently study the problem-solving process, let alone train people how to solve problems. It is equally important to devise general methods of analysis. Given the limitless variety of problem domains that might be considered, such methods are needed for analyzing arbitrary domains and for combining previously analyzed domains into more comprehensive wholes.

Second, with regard to cognition, it is generally agreed that the successful problem solver must be able to understand the problems with which he is confronted (or which he defines for himself); he must be able to identify suitable subgoals; he must have at hand or be able to retrieve relevant information from memory; he must be able to distinguish relevant from irrelevant information; he must be able to derive solution procedures for each subgoal; he must be able to carry out these procedures correctly; and he must know how to verify both intermediate and terminal results. But, beyond this general outline, there is relatively little agreement on the actual nature of

[1]This chapter is based on research supported by National Institute of Health Grant 9185.

the underlying processes. What does it mean to say that a person understands a problem? And how does he do it? How does he form subgoals? Retrieve relevant information? Derive solution procedures? Or, use them?

Third, individual differences in problem-solving ability are also critical. What is a difficult problem for one person, for example, might be quite simple for another. Are these differences due to physiological capacities? Generalized physical maturation? Or, do they involve identifiable knowledge, knowledge that can be taught and learned? Undoubtedly, all three factors are involved to some extent. But where and how?

After having been largely ignored for several decades, such questions as these are being asked with increasing frequency. This reemergence of interest in problem solving and in other forms of complex human functioning can be traced to a variety of sources. Perhaps most influential has been the rapid progress over the past 15 years in computer science, particularly in the development of scientific languages suitable for describing human behavior. These developments, along with such influential books as that by Miller, Galanter, and Pribram (1960), led gradually to the whole information-processing movement that began in earnest during the late 1960s and that today characterizes much of contemporary cognitive psychology. Parallel developments took place in educational psychology with respect to more general kinds of rule learning, individual differences measurement, and curriculum design and development.

In my view, which is expounded in the following chapters, each of the above areas has something important, indeed crucial, to contribute to the understanding of human problem solving.

First, specific competencies associated with given task domains comprise much of the substance of artificial intelligence and of content analysis in instructional science. The singularly important, although superficially different, field of linguistics also has potentially much to contribute--especially with regard to general goals and philosophical underpinnings.

Second, cognitive processes have traditionally been associated with cognitive psychology, although in my opinion equally important contributions are being made by computer scientists and by educational and developmental psychologists.

Third, contemporary educational psychology has much to contribute. Criterion-referenced (performance) testing, in particular, has at least the potential of including within its scope the measurement of individual differences in problem solving. It is perhaps the potential of educational psychology, including performance testing, content analysis, and instructional science generally, that has been most overlooked.

On the positive side, there have been signs of increasing rapprochement across areas, especially in the case of artificial intelligence and theories of semantic memory where the term

cognitive science has been used. Unfortunately, however, true
synthesis has been limited. Most researchers have tended (perhaps understandably) to stick more or less exclusively with one
or another field. As a result, what cross-fertilization there
has been generally has taken the form of borrowing ideas and
applying them in new areas.

I personally do not believe that research within any one
(existing) tradition will be sufficient to understand problem
solving in any adequate sense. Nor do I believe that such
understanding will be achieved through simple union of the
various contributions. In order to achieve true synthesis, I
believe that it will be necessary to look at requirements of
the total system--the relationships among theoretical concepts
and research in the various contributing fields. In effect,
theoretical development and research within the various fields
of emphasis, if it is to contribute to the grand synthesis,
must be compatible with and complementary to related theory in
the other relevant fields.

1.   THREE APPROACHES TO THE STUDY OF HUMAN PROBLEM SOLVING

To provide further perspective on the above and some general background for later developments, let me review briefly some
traditional views and approaches to the study of problem solving.
In order to make my main points, and at the risk of some oversimplification, I have emphasized differences and limitations
and have minimized what in some cases is substantial overlap.

Content, cognition, and individual differences all play an
important and acknowledged role in understanding human problem
solving. Traditionally, however, only one or another of these
three facets have been emphasized by those most interested in
the process: (1) subject matter educators, computer scientists,
and others interested in how particular classes of problems
might be solved have emphasized the role of content; (2) psychologists interested in general laws of human problem solving
have emphasized cognitive processes; and (3) test researchers
have emphasized the role of individual differences and their
relationships to problem-solving ability.

1.1   CONTENT IN HUMAN PROBLEM SOLVING
The goals of the computer scientist interested in artificial intelligence or computer simulation, and the goals of some
subject matter (e.g., mathematics) educators and educational
technologists, center on content and/or underlying competence.
Scientists and technologists in these areas all have been concerned in one way or another with identifying specific competencies that are sufficient for solving particular classes of
problems. Depending on the field, as well as on the current

interests of the investigators, the classes of problems involved have varied, including generating grammatical sentences, ordinary arithmetic, playing chess, constructing geometric figures with compass and straight edge, answering questions, language translation, theorem proving in logic, and so on.

For the most part, although there are some exceptions (e.g., in automatic programming and educational technology), attention has been focused more on the results of analyzing such classes of problems than on the methods of analysis themselves.

At least four more or less general approaches have evolved. All of them are based on the notion that competence can be represented more or less rigorously in terms of relations and/or rules (procedures).

Two of these approaches have emphasized formal considerations, with relatively little attention to psychological processes. Although not directly related to problem solving, formal mathematical systems and formal linguistics have in some ways helped to define the nature and scope of all competence theories (e.g., Chomsky, 1957). In formal linguistics, for instance, the goal is to devise grammars (sets of rules) that account for (or recognize) language in its phonetic, syntactic, and/or semantic aspects. Whether or not such an account has psychological relevance, however, is at best of secondary concern. A simple, formal grammar *(G)*, for example, may be represented as a finite set of rules (i.e., a Post production system)

$$G = \{r_1, r_2, \ldots, r_n\}$$

Such a grammar is said to provide an account of some formal language if, given any allowable input (e.g., axiom), consecutive application of rules in *G* (to the input and successive outputs) generates an acceptable "sentence" (e.g., theorem).

From a psychological point of view, it is questionable whether either the rules or the inputs and outputs involved in such grammars are directly relevant to human knowledge or to behavior. Nor would most formal linguists make such a claim. Equally important, there is little reason to believe that people can arbitrarily compose rules (as is implicit in all formal systems).

A second formal approach has been termed *artificial intelligence*. Here one starts with a class of tasks to be accounted for and the goal is to devise an explicit procedure, usually in the form of a working computer program, whereby each task in the given class can be solved.

The primary criterion in this case is that the procedure work efficiently, relationships to human behavior being largely fortuitous. Nonetheless, artificial intelligence is concerned with the overall flow of control, as well as with the individual (component) operations themselves (as in linguistics, for instance) (e.g., Minsky & Papert, 1972). Artificial intelligence, in effect, necessarily requires attention to characteristics of some information processor, whether human or otherwise.

Two other approaches to the study of specific problem domains are more directly concerned with human behavior. Computer simulation, for example, may be defined as artificial intelligence constrained to reflect human behavior, usually in the form of protocols (verbalizations by subjects) obtained during the course of problem solving. In attempting to simulate human behavior, researchers often have incorporated (into their computer programs) experimentally determined information about human behavior. For example, most simulation programs directly reflect the limited capacity of human beings to process information (e.g., Miller, 1956).

Simulation theories developed to date, however, share a number of important limitations. A working program may reflect human behavior, at least within a limited domain, without necessarily having very much to do with underlying psychological (human) processes (see Reitman, 1965) or with problem solving in other problem domains. Furthermore, most existing computer simulation models deal primarily with performance and say little about learning (i.e., the acquisition of new procedures), motivation, problem definition, and the like (cf. Newell & Simon, 1972). There have been individual exceptions, of course. The problem is not that it is unusually difficult to model individual processes but rather that it is hard to devise models that lend themselves naturally to *all* such processes. In this regard, it is generally recognized that part of the difficulty resides in the scientific languages that have been available for representing problem situations and underlying knowledge.

Although closely tied to human behavior, the fourth approach tends to be relatively informal and often relies heavily on introspection regarding the kinds of capabilities and processes that are felt to be necessary for solving particular classes of problems. The work of Polya (1962) provides an excellent example. His analyses of problem solving, and especially his insights into the processes involved, have resulted in the identification of a number of potentially useful problem-solving heuristics. (As we shall see in Chapter 3, Polya's heuristics correspond to incompletely defined higher-order rules.) Indeed, his work has provided a foundation on which much subsequent research has been based, including work in computer simulation and artificial intelligence.

In spite of the intuitive veracity of his analyses, however, Polya's work on heuristics provides only a beginning, albeit an important beginning that has deep philosophical roots in the past. For some purposes, it may be sufficient to identify the general form of heuristics as Polya has done, but for more systematic application, whether in the design of instructional

materials, in the training of teacher educators, in computer
assisted instruction, or in computer simulation and artificial
intelligence, more precise identification of heuristics and,
indeed, methods for identifying such heuristics would be invaluable.   If such work can be closely tied in with psychological
theory, so much the better.

Until recently, relatively little attention has been given
to the processes (methods) by which the competencies underlying
given problem domains are identified. Of course one can only
speculate as to why, but at least two reasons immediately suggest themselves. First, in his early influential work on transformational grammars, Chomsky (1957) rejected as totally infeasible the goal of systematic construction of grammars (with
natural languages). This widely shared belief transferred to
scientists in parallel fields, such as computer science, so that
few seriously tried. Second, the technical problems in such
areas as automatic programming are extremely complex. Many
researchers have tried, but have become discouraged by their
relative lack of success. Undoubtedly, both factors played
some role.

Interestingly enough, probably more attention has been
given to such methods in educational psychology than anywhere
else. Given their relatively pragmatic concerns and unencumbered
by the need for formal precision, educational psychologists have
developed a variety of informal methods for analyzing content.
Such methods, for example, as task analysis (e.g., Gagne, 1970)
and content analysis (e.g., Merrill & Gibbons, 1974; Shavelson
& Geeslin, 1975) have been widely applied. With few exceptions
(e.g., Pask, 1974), however, none of the methods seem to have
an adequate theoretical foundation. Task analysis, for example,
is concerned with underlying processes in the form of learning
hierarchies but is relatively limited in scope. (Learning hierarchies correspond to single rules and successive refinements
thereof; e.g., see Scandura, 1973; Chapters 2 and 15, this
book.) Content analysis, on the other hand, is broader in scope
but lacks behavioral precision. (See Chapter 15 for a discussion
of relationships between content analysis and algorithmic/struc-
tural analysis, and the closely related issue of algorithmic vs.
propositional [relational network] knowledge. Also see Scandura,
1977b.)

1.2   COGNITION IN HUMAN PROBLEM SOLVING

The main goal of the psychologist in the study of problem
solving is to uncover the essence of the process. Traditionally,
the psychologist has been interested primarily in what is left
after the process has been stripped of what is specific to the
particular problem or class of problems at hand. Conversely,
much of what goes into solving particular problems ordinarily
will be of only secondary interest to the psychologist.

In attempting to uncover underlying processes, psychologists have employed a number of different strategies. For example, they have had subjects simply verbalize their thoughts as they attempt to solve problems (e.g., Bloom & Broder, 1950). The records then are analyzed to see if useful hypotheses can be formulated to explain how people solve problems. This approach has the advantage of tying theory directly to reality but it has some important limitations. First, it is often difficult to separate effects due to the particular problems used from effects due to basic psychological processes. Second, the approach is useful primarily for generating ideas about problem solving. Verification of such ideas, and comparison with alternative hypotheses, requires separate experimental tests under controlled conditions.

Many techniques, of course, have been used to formulate hypotheses: introspection, informal clinical observation, and previous experimental findings are just a few. Whatever the source of hypotheses, however, the vast majority of experimental studies of problem solving have attempted to deal with the process in its full complexity (e.g., Dunker, 1945). That is, most problem-solving studies have employed problem situations which involve both specific problem-solving competencies and general cognitive processes (e.g., problem definition, memory, the derivation and/or selection of solution procedures, and the use of such procedures)--usually in unknown proportion. This type of confounding has often raised questions of interpretation since it has usually been unclear to what extent various factors have been involved in any particular instance of problem solving.

Difficulties in interpretation have resulted not only because manipulated variables frequently intermix problem content and cognitive processes, but also because these factors are typically involved in varying degrees with different individuals on the same problems. To take an extreme example, solving a problem in differential equations might be a matter of direct application for an advanced student, whereas for the equally bright neophyte it might pose a serious problem requiring deep thought. In effect, traditional approaches to problem-solving research, which confound the often subtle effects of specific content, cognition, and individual difference variables, may be expected to yield only normative (i.e., averaged) information concerning general tendencies in problem solving behavior. But, they have inherent limitations when it comes to specifying the processes underlying individual behavior.

Recognizing the complexity of problem solving, and other forms of complex human learning, most psychologists properly have attempted to limit their domain of inquiry. In my opinion, however, the scope of inquiry has too often been limited arbitrarily, for example, in sometimes slavish adherence to historically defined categories (e.g., memory, simple discrimination

learning). It is becoming increasingly clear to many who have
pushed this approach to its natural limits that it is almost
impossible to study traditional psychological phenomena in iso-
lation. In recent years, for example, psychologists engaged in
research on memory have given increasing attention to the effects of learning and problem solving. In effect, while it is
important to be able to separate various psychological processes
for experimental study, such separation should be accomplished
so as to take into account overall interrelationships.

1.3 INDIVIDUAL DIFFERENCES IN HUMAN PROBLEM SOLVING

Understanding problem solving from the standpoint of individual differences amounts to identifying test measures that
correlate with problem-solving ability. Research in the area
involves searching for appropriate measures of memory, reasoning, and the like, and until very recently has been conducted
almost exclusively within the normative test tradition.

Normative testing is based on the implicit but typically
unstated assumption that complex human behavior (including problem-solving ability) has a genetic and/or diffuse intellectual
base. In attempts to determine basic (but equally diffuse)
underlying factors, numerous factor-analytic studies have been
conducted (e.g., Guilford, 1967). Moreover, individual measures
on a wide variety of factors, including various IQ, aptitude,
and other tests, have been correlated with problem-solving behavior under a wide variety of conditions (e.g., Speedie,
Treffinger, & Feldhusen, 1973).

Because of the presumed diffuse nature of human capability, the emphasis on normative comparison is quite understandable. In this view, test items are selected not primarily because they represent the kinds of problems for which predictions
are desired, although they must correlate with such problems,
but because they make it possible to distinguish among individuals and/or groups. Items that are responded to correctly by
half of the subject population discriminate maximally and are
especially sought after. In the normative view, then, test
construction is largely an empirical task.

The newer criterion-referenced test movement derives from
a quite different point of view (e.g., Glaser, 1963). Here,
problems (test items) are selected precisely because they are
representative either of specific skills considered as predictor
variables (e.g., prerequisites; see Gagne, 1970) or of the problems on which predictions are required. Distinguishing among
different individuals, or comparing individuals with groups (or
groups with groups) is not the point. In criterion-referenced
testing, each person is judged on how well he performs relative
to fixed criteria.

Because criterion-referenced testing is a relatively new
innovation, however, at least as a formal movement, many of its

aspects are incompletely understood. How many and what kinds
of items are required to test for mastery? And why? It has
become increasingly clear to those working in the area (e.g.,
Glaser, 1973) that such questions demand the development of more
adequate performance test theory. Needless to say, relatively
little problem-solving research has been done within this
tradition.

1.4   CURRENT STATUS OF THEORY DEVELOPMENT

Given our implied goal of integrating content, cognitive,
and individual differences approaches to problem solving, it is
natural to ask whether some existing theory or approach might
reasonably serve this purpose. Indeed, although each of the
above approaches tends to emphasize one or another factor, the
importance of all three is uniformly acknowledged. Computer
simulation studies, for example, have frequently placed heavy
emphasis on both problem-solving content and cognitive processes.
Simulation theories also deal with individual differences; they
refer directly to the processes used by individual subjects (on
given classes of problems). However, even though simulation
theories may share common features (e.g., the same problem
space), a different theory is needed for each individual. This
proliferation of largely independent theories poses something
of a dilemma for a public and generalized science, a dilemma
that the present development seeks to avoid.

Correspondingly, cognitive psychologists have begun to give
increasing attention to content/competence (particularly in
language). In some cases, this tendency has been so pronounced
as to equate theories with specific processes (rules/units of
knowledge) for performing particular tasks. Such processes,
however, do not necessarily refer to individuals. They are more
accurately thought of as amalgam processes that account for the
average (mean) behavior of groups of subjects, or for the average behavior of single subjects on a class of tasks.

Some educational theorists have tended to go even further
in attempting to integrate all three facets of human functioning, but they have said relatively little about potentially
complex problem solving and, with rare exceptions (e.g., Pask,
1974; Spada & Kempf, 1977), their methods have been based on
pragmatic, rather than theoretical concerns. Moreover, some of
the most promising developments are relatively narrow in scope.
For example, although criterion-referenced testing has the
potential of dealing directly with problem-solving behavior,
most contemporary approaches deal only extensionally with content (i.e., with observable inputs and outputs) and not at all
with cognition.

Although focused primarily on the early stages of human
development, Piaget's theory provides an instructive basis for
comparison with the type of theory (and general approach) that

we seek.

In agreement with our stated objectives, the theory deals with content, cognition, and, in a general developmental sense, with individual differences. Thus, the theory is concerned both with the processes (assimilation, accommodation) by which knowledge grows (through equilibration) and with content, ranging from knowledge of physical and mathematical environments to bases for moral and social behavior. Moreover, the theory emphasizes the operational character of knowledge and thought, along with global differences in human functioning over developmental stages.

Nonetheless, a Piagetian-type theory is not adequate for our purposes for some very important and basic reasons, quite apart from its emphasis on epistemology and child development. First, the theory by design deals only with the *epistemic* subject (i.e., with commonalities among subjects) and not with the individual (e.g., Furth, 1969). Although the present development shares an interest in common knowledge, a major concern is with individual behavior. The latter implies a direct interest in specific, individual knowledge. Second, in Piaget's theory the relationship between cognition and behavior is often obscure. Important features of Piaget's theory remain nonoperational in a scientific sense. To accomplish present aims, such definition would appear essential.

In effect, we do not seek a weak theory (e.g., Gestalt theory), which fails to generate empirically falsifiable hypotheses. Nor, do we want a theory of averages, a theory which says, for example, that under such and such conditions people are more likely on the average to solve such and such kinds of problems. Our goal is a theory that makes it operationally possible in principle to explain, and hopefully also to predict, the problem-solving performance of individual subjects on particular problems.

2.   RELATIONSHIPS BETWEEN PROBABILISTIC AND DETERMINISTIC THEORIZING IN BEHAVIORAL SCIENCE

2.1   PROBABILISTIC THEORIZING

Until recently, most theories and hypotheses in behavioral science were inherently probabilistic. The field was inundated with such statements, for example, as "the probability of behavior A is a function of the number of reinforcements," and "each subject learns (on each trial) with probability c." In testing such theories, the essential data have been means and other group statistics. For example, as I observed previously (Scandura, 1971, pp. 73-74):

> Consider the paradigm most typically used in testing behavioral theories. First, assumptions are made about

how individuals learn or behave. When stated in their clearest form, as in the stochastic theories of mathematical psychology, the basic assumptions are stated in terms of probabilities. Second, inferences are drawn from these assumptions yielding predictions about group statistics--that is, about characteristics of the distributions of responses made by the experimental subjects. Third, on the basis of the experimental results obtained, inferences are made about the basic assumptions.

Of course, there is no harm in this as long as it is recognized that the initial assumptions deal with probabilities and not with individual processes. But this fact has not always been made as explicit by theorists as might be desirable. What needs to be made clear with such probabilistic theories is that what any given subject ·does on a given occasion may have little or nothing to do with the particular assumptions made. For example, in stochastic models of paired associate learning it is usually assumed that each subject has the same probability of learning on each trial. Even the most superficial analysis of relevant data, however, indicates clearly that the probability of success for different subjects may vary greatly. And one cannot attribute this to the fact that the probability of learning is a random variable. This would still not explain the fundamental fact that the probability of success of many subjects tends to be either uniformly high, or low, over different trials.

More recently, a variety of stochastic models have been proposed to deal with such variation. For example, Groen (1967) has allowed for individual differences in ability and Suppes and Morningstar (1972) have introduced probabilistic automata models that reflect item difficulty. The Rasch (1960) model goes further and includes parameters that reflect both structural and individual factors (i.e., item difficulty and general student ability). This model, however, and certain extensions of it, such as the linear logistic test model (e.g., Fischer, 1977), assume local stochastic independence; effects due to prior responses are not considered. Recognizing this limitation, Kempf (1974, 1977) has extended the basic Rasch model to allow for such effects while preserving desirable characteristics with regard to parameter estimation.

Similar developments have taken place in other areas of stochastic research on learning and teaching. For example, for almost 20 years now, a number of prominent educational scientists have been attempting to build a bridge between learning and individual differences measurement in the form of aptitude-treatment interactions. Although great promise was initially held for the approach, traditional work in the area has come largely to a standstill. Leading investigators currently appear to be looking for ways of moving the approach closer to underlying cognitive reality (e.g., Snow, 1976).

Although individual differences play a central role in some recent research in mathematical psychology, such as that reported in Spada and Kempf (1977), a purely stochastic approach as a cumulative enterprise has certain important and inherent limitations. In order to account for more and more variance (e.g., more of the underlying psychological processes), stochastic models necessarily become more and more complex. This not only makes them more difficult to construct, but impractical, if not impossible, to test empirically. In order to obtain sufficient stability, literally hundreds of subjects may be required to estimate parameters (cf. Kempf, 1977; Scandura, 1977a).

Moreover, with the major exception of the Rasch (1960) family of models, and a few parameter-free models, stochastic theories infrequently *predict* new data. The data are known and are used to estimate parameters that are subsequently plugged into statistical formulas to account for the existing data. In most sciences, this goes under the rubric of "curve fitting"--a technique that is sometimes useful for selecting among or verifying empirical laws of limited generality, but that is infrequently adequate for generalized understanding or prediction.

This relative inability to use parameters obtained in one study to predict apparently compatible data in others has been particularly acute with theories, such as stimulus-sampling theory, in which little attention is given to underlying cognitive processes. In tests of such theories, estimated parameters typically reflect a range of variables, that are unspecified and/or combined in unknown ways. In stimulus-sampling theory, for example, task variables, ability variables, prior learning and memory, among other things, interact in ways that are at best only partly understood and that are left unspecified in the theory (cf. Atkinson, 1963; Bower, 1961; Estes, 1950). Even in theories of the Rasch variety, parameters derived in one structural context are unlikely to be useful in making predictions in other contexts. General environmental conditions are necessarily confounded with underlying structural and individual factors (see below; also Hilke, Kempf, & Scandura, 1977), thereby obscuring possible relationships among alternative theories and estimated parameters thereof.

2.2   DETERMINISTIC THEORIZING

In order to have any real hope of relating such theories, and thereby of achieving the type of synthesis which is (or ought to be) the goal of any theoretical science, I believe that we must adopt a different posture (cf. Kuhn, 1962). Instead of arbitrarily extending stochastic theories in ever more complex and empirically limited ways, and instead of lumping all uncontrolled factors into a single category of error variance (e.g.,

an inherently probabilistic information processor as in Rasch-
type models), I believe that a deterministic approach to human
problem solving may not only be possible but more feasible and
potentially more useful in applications. In particular, I
believe that existing developments in the area of structural
learning (e.g., Scandura, 1971, 1973) provide a foundation for
a potentially useful and comprehensive deterministic theory of
human problem solving (cf. Chapter 2).

In contrast to stochastic theories, essentially all contemporary information-processing theories have a potentially deterministic base. Such theories deal directly with specific processes and provide a potential basis for explaining and predicting what individual subjects will do in specific situations.

On the other hand, deterministic theories are intrinsically
idealizations and, hence, necessarily deal with only portions
of reality. Recall, in this regard, "that any deterministic
theory is but a partial model of reality. It deals adequately
with certain phenomenon in the sense of providing an adequate
explanation for them, but not others" (Scandura, 1971, p. 24).
In deterministic partial theories, the "other" phenomena are
simply not dealt with at all. In probabilistic theories, such
phenomena correspond to random error, which is an integral part
of such theories.

2.3 TESTING DETERMINISTIC THEORIES

In spite of this fundamental difference, the methods and
experimental paradigms that have been used to date to test most
deterministic theories have been essentially the same as those
used to test probabilistic theories. Suppose, for example, that
we want to test alternative information-processing theories, each
of which consists essentially of some hypothesized process/rule/
procedure. (These terms are used equivalently here.) In this
case, experiments are set up to determine which process best
accounts for average group behavior. Response latencies, for
example, are often used for this purpose.

This approach to theory verification has a serious limitation. Just because a theory provides a viable account of average group behavior, this says nothing definitive about how individuals perform--about individual processes. Moreover, the
very act of testing deterministic theories in this way denies
their very nature.

Whereas stochastic theories can be tested under actual behavior conditions, because the presence of random error is always assumed, this is not the case with deterministic theories.
Deterministic theories must be tested under idealized conditions
(Scandura, 1971), in situations where extraneous factors do not
enter. For example, the deterministic laws of mechanics--say
involving the inclined plane--hold only where friction, and other
peripheral factors are not involved. One could, of course, con-

ceive of alternative stochastic theories of the inclined plane, which work under various nonidealized conditions, although physicists fortunately chose not to take that route.

To make the point more poignantly, consider an example from classical physics--Galileo's famous experiments at the Leaning Tower of Pisa. Suppose, instead of dropping two iron balls of different weights, that Galileo had dropped an iron ball and a feather. How different his results would have been! Moreover, if counseled by a twentieth-century behavioral scientist--one committed to a stochastic approach to science--Galileo might have further perverted such findings (to insure reliability) by comparing the average rates of fall of 100 iron balls and 100 feathers. (Note parenthetically that the results of such an experiment in another age might well have led to an experimental rush to uncover the scientific laws governing the rates of fall of various types of droppings.)

Although such findings conceivably could have immediate interest (and possibly even practical value), it is unlikely that they would have inspired Newton in his attempts at theoretical synthesis. Of much more direct interest were Galileo's actual experiments, which were more directly analogous to what one might expect to happen under idealized conditions--say, where a feather and an iron ball are dropped in a perfect vacuum. The point is that the much simpler results associated with Galileo's actual experiments, where gravitational force was essentially uninfluenced by other forces, had far greater and longer-lived generality--far greater and longer-lived than alternative scientific laws concerning droppings. The former turned out to have implications not only for earth bound objects but for heavenly bodies as well.

One cannot help but wonder in contemporary cognitive psychology whether specific laws (rules and information-processing theories) introduced to account for unconstrained average behavior in miniature real world situations (e.g., droppings in the atmosphere) could, in the long run, have far less generality than simpler deterministic laws (determined under idealized behavior conditions). It is just possible that empirical laws of broader generality might be obtained in idealized situations.

Indeed, the fact that deterministic theories necessarily ignore certain aspects of reality did not greatly influence Renaissance physics. This was true, in part, because the effects of peripheral factors were relatively minor and/or easy to eliminate. Although friction, for example, necessarily plays some role in all systems of inclined planes, this fact did not dissuade early physicists either from constructing idealized, deterministic laws or from testing them.

The problem, of course, is to determine just what these idealized conditions might be in behavioral science. Ebbinghaus, for example, and many English-speaking psychologists after him, thought that perhaps nonsense syllables might provide a promising way to study human learning processes. It was felt, after all, that nonsense syllables ought to be equally unfamiliar (or nearly so) to all subjects and, hence, that all subjects ought to learn them in essentially the same way. After years of debate and research, it is increasingly recognized that this was a false hope. The years of prior learning and experience, which each subject brings into any learning situation, affect learning in fundamental ways, even with respect to supposedly unfamiliar material.

It is my contention that deterministic theorizing in behavioral science is not only possible, but that it is also feasible to realize idealized conditions in many behavioral situations. A deterministic theory of human problem solving is described in Chapter 2, together with the idealized (e.g., memory-free) conditions under which it must be tested. In recent publications (e.g., Scandura, 1971, 1973) and in Part 3 of the present volume, a number of experiments are described that were run successfully under idealized memory-free conditions. Under these conditions, the deterministic theory is shown to account almost perfectly for the behavior of individual subjects on specific problems.

Not all data, of course, is idealized. One of the things that most differentiates behavioral from physical theories is that it is not always possible, or at least not always feasible, to realize the idealized conditions under which deterministic theories must be tested. Thus, for example, no matter how much attention is given to ensuring that memory is *not* a factor in some instance of behavior, it will generally be impossible to exclude this possibility completely. The major question in this regard is whether idealized conditions can be approximated sufficiently closely in behavioral science research to make deterministic theorizing feasible (i.e., to make it possible to test such theories empirically).

In effect, I am under no delusions that it will ever be possible to successfully predict individual performance in really complex instances of problem solving. I take this goal as an ideal to be approached, and somewhat more realistically seek a theory that has the capability of achieving this goal in principle. I would be satisfied if deterministic prediction were possible given (1) appropriately limited empirical situations, and (2) all of the necessary information (and/or ways of determining this infomation). Actually insuring the boundary conditions, however, or determining all of the needed information in specific situations, may be extremely difficult or at best impractical.

2.4 COMPLEMENTARY OBSERVATION THEORIES
There are alternatives to probabilistic theorizing and experimentation even where idealized conditions cannot easily

be realized for purposes of experimental testing. In particular, nonidealized data can be treated (within the deterministic framework) by introducing an observation theory that complements a given deterministic theory (cf. Scandura, 1971, 1977a; Hilke, Kempf, & Scandura, 1977). By definition, an observation theory deals precisely with those factors (e.g., friction, memory) that are *not* considered within the corresponding deterministic theory and that correspond directly to deviations from the ideal.

The closer empirical conditions approach the ideal (defined by the deterministic theory), the smaller the role played by the observation theory. At asymptote, the effect is nonexistent and each datum will either tend to confirm the deterministic theory or to refute it. Conversely, nonidealized data cannot refute a deterministic theory, since both the deterministic theory and its complementary observation theory are needed to explain the data.

In effect, a deterministic theory cannot be tested independently of the total system of which it is a part, except under idealized conditions. As it was put in my original justification of deterministic theorizing (Scandura, 1971, p. 24):

Given a (deterministic) theory of this sort, probability would enter only where one wanted to make predictions in relatively complex situations where the experimenter practically speaking could not, or did not wish to, find out everything he would need to know and specify in order to make deterministic predictions. In effect, a truly adequate deterministic theory would make it possible to generate any number of stochastic theories by loosening one or another of various conditions which must be satisfied in order for the deterministic theory to apply.

As a consequence, notice that deterministic and stochastic theories cannot be compared directly. For example, it would be incorrect to argue (or to implicitly assume) that a stochastic theory is better than a deterministic theory if the stochastic theory does a better job of predicting average behavior (which it is designed to do) than a deterministic theory does of predicting the nonidealized behavior of individuals in specific situations (which it is *not* designed to do).

Clearly, any reasonable comparison of theories must be with respect to the same standards. The problem is not to determine whether one *type* of theory is better--a completely deterministic account of the same phenomena would obviously provide more complete understanding. On the other hand, (probably stochastic) assumptions concerning deviations from the ideal would appear essential to fill the inherent gap in most situations between idealizations and empirical reality. The problem is to find deterministic theories that work--that is, theories that approach deterministic predictions under idealized conditions but that include complementary observation theories and that are sufficiently robust to allow strong (probabilistic) predictions with respect to real world phenomena.

2.5 STRUCTURAL AND INCIDENTAL VARIABLES

The complementary and yet distinct roles of deterministic and observation theories impose a clear separation between structural (theoretical) variables and incidental (observation) variables. This distinction has some important implications, both theoretical and practical.

On the theoretical side, deterministic (e.g., information-processing) theories provide a basis for generating corresponding stochastic theories in a number of ways. Standard practice in the behavioral sciences has been to convert what are basically deterministic (usually information processing) theories into probabilistic theories by direct analogy. That is, deterministic statements about individuals are converted directly into analogous probabilistic statements about groups. Rather than assuming, for example, that a subject uses process A to solve particular problems in Class B (e.g., simple addition), one typically makes the weaker assumption that process A' provides the best overall account of average behavior on problems in Class B. Where individual differences are important, one similarly may assume that process A_i provides the best overall account of subject i's average behavior on problems of type B. In either case, standard statistical methods are used to compare average data with transformed but nevertheless deterministically derived predictions.

This type of conversion is implicit in a study by Ehrenpreis and Scandura (Chapter 11). Given the nonidealized training and test conditions employed, it is not likely that training on the rules and higher-order rules involved resulted in their uniform availability during later testing. Put differently, it was not reasonable to assume that the training rules were known to individuals, either perfectly or not at all. About all that one might reasonably say is that they were available with some probability. The reader may wish to compare the methods and results of the experiment reported in Chapter 11 with those of Chapters 5 and 6 where the critical rules were known in "atomic" (all or none) fashion. In the former study, initial tests of the experimental outcomes were based on the standard assumption of a normally distributed error of measurement. (A type of conversion similar to that described in the next paragraph, and implications thereof, are discussed in Chapter 11, Section 4.)

A somewhat different type of conversion is provided by the Suppes and Morningstar (1972) model for predicting performance on arithmetic computation problems (cf. Spada, 1977). In the model, the probability that a student will solve a given task is the product of the probabilities that each operation needed in the solution is carried out correctly. (Operations may be used recursively.) This model can be generated from the structural/algorithmic theory for assessing individual behavior potential (e.g., Scandura, 1973) by substituting probabilities for atomic, zero or one, assumptions regarding component rules. The probabilities in this case reflect average abilities of subjects, either individually or collectively, over problems. (The deterministic approach to assessing behavior potential is described in Chapter 2; empirical tests are reported in Chapters 8 and 9.)

Neither type of conversion, however, distinguishes data according to source. Data that may satisfy deterministic (e.g., atomic) assumptions are simply averaged in with the rest. In general, therefore, obtained deviations from deterministic predictions will reflect both inadequacies in the parent deterministic theory and deviations from assumed idealized conditions, normally in unknown proportion. Thus, for example, the probabilities assigned to component operations/rules in the Suppes and Morningstar model reflect both inadequacies in the rules themselves (structural variables) and their degrees of availability (incidental variables), along with other deviations from ideal conditions.

In cases where prior support exists for a deterministic theory (under idealized conditions), however, results obtained under nonidealized conditions provide more than just a basis for testing statistical significance. They also provide a general indication of the degree to which given empirical situations approximate the ideal. For this reason it may be useful in theorizing about complex human behavior to distinguish between variables that reflect empirically validated constructs in a deterministic theory and variables that correspond to deviations from the ideal. In the subsequent discussion, we shall refer to the former as *structural* variables and the latter as *incidental* or observational.

Rasch (1960) type stochastic measurement models have been developed by Fischer (1974), Kempf (1974), Spada and Kempf (1977) and others to deal with data similar to that considered by Suppes and Morningstar (1972). In this case, however, probabilities are replaced by (sample) parameters. There are two kinds of parameters in stochastic measurement models, those relating to items (and/or underlying competencies/rules) and those relating to individual ability. Although each type of parameter can be estimated independently of the other, however, *all* such parameters are equally difficult to interpret in the above sense. The individual parameters, for example, reflect implicit confoundings of structural variables (e.g., higher-order rules; cf. Chapter 5) and internal and external deviations from the ideal (cf. Chapter 11, Section 4). Moreover, most of the Rasch models are at best only roughly analogous to existing deterministic theories. (The subclass of stochastic measurement models[2] described in Hilke, Kempf, and Scandura, 1977, however, does

---

[2]Kempf is primarily responsible for the models themselves.

parallel certain constructs in the deterministic structural
learning theory, see Chapter 2.)

In summary, probabilities and parameters in stochastic theories, even ones that parallel corresponding deterministic theories, reflect a confounding of factors. In the absence of *direct*
empirical support for a deterministic theory, probabilities and
parameters in analogous stochastic theories necessarily reflect
in unknown proportion both structural and incidental factors.
Given prior deterministic support, however, degree of deviation
from deterministic prediction (under nonidealized conditions)
depends directly on degree of deviation from the ideal. As we
shall see below, this fact has important implications both with
regard to the construction of generalizable theories (cf. Chapter 7) and with regard to (instructional) applications (cf.
Chapter 11).

As noted previously, *integrated* theories of the above types
(cf. Chapter 10, this book; also Reulecke, 1977) have another
major limitation. In order to account for a greater variety of
psychological processes, the derivative stochastic theories
become increasingly complex and, in turn, impractical to test
empirically. For this and other reasons (which will become
clear below), it may be more desirable to retain a given deterministic theory, presumably one that works under idealized conditions, and to construct an independent observation theory.
(Notice in this regard that it is not necessary to know or to
specify incidental factors in deterministic fashion just because
the parent theory is deterministic.)

Since their main function is to complement given deterministic theories, observation theories should be as simple as
possible. In particular, in applications where generalization
to other individuals is desired, it is important to have observation theories in which the parameters are related to some defined population of subjects (in which individual differences
are ignored). Moreover, these parameters should correspond to
just those idealized behavior conditions, which are felt to be
crucial, and which are allowed to vary in given empirical test
situations. Suppose, for example, that an experiment ideally
should be run under memory-free conditions (Scandura, 1971,
1973), but that the experimental conditions nevertheless require
recall of previously learned information (with other incidental
factors playing a minor role). Then, parameters could be introduced to allow explicitly for overall "degree of availability."
Parameters could similarly be introduced where memory load, say,
or degree of understanding of given problem statements might
reasonably influence the results.

Since such parameters reflect the degree to which specific
conditions deviate from the ideal, their introduction could provide a useful basis for prediction (and explanation) in completely new empirical situations--possibly without having to use the

new data itself to estimate parameters. (Although commonly practiced in mathematical psychology, using data to estimate parameters to account for the same data has the effect of reducing "prediction" to mere curve fitting.) In particular, it might be possible to estimate, or at least order, various parameter values (e.g., availability of trained rules) in accordance with corresponding values of known or given independent variables (e.g., number of training trials). If so, known relationships (e.g., orderings) among independent variables might be used to estimate new parameter values, for example, by simple interpolation or extrapolation. Estimated parameter values, generally speaking, might be expected to have predictive value in new situations just to the extent that the independent variables accurately reflect deviations from the ideal (i.e., the parameters) and that the deterministic theory itself is adequate.

One stochastic theory that was formulated with some of the above considerations in mind was proposed initially in Scandura (1973); it is developed further in Chapter 7. In this model, the "distraction" and "chunking" parameters, α and β, refer directly to the influence of such deviations. In this case, a given external manipulation (involving coding possibilities) had expected effects on the parameters. A model proposed by Reulecke (1977; see Chapter 10, this book) to deal with "unsharpness" and other "intensity" variables (e.g., level of attention, level of activity, speed of performance, motivation, neuroticism, etc.) is also of this type. In this case, all deviations from the ideal are summarized in terms of a single parameter.

Interestingly enough, the distinction between structural (item) and incidental (individual) factors was formalized in behavioral science first by Rasch (1960), with extensions to parallel structural learning by Fischer (1974), Kempf (1974), Spada and Kempf (1977), and others in the context of stochastic measurement models (cf. Hilke, Kempf, & Scandura, 1977). Hence, the above distinction between structural and incidental factors is not unique to deterministic theories.

In both types of theory, theoretical (structural) variables must be chosen so as to apply universally. Thus, in behavioral science, deterministic variables must be such as to apply uniformly to all individuals in all specific situations. The presence or absence of a crucial unit of knowledge, for example, should be reflected in the problem-solving behavior of every individual. Correspondingly, the effects of structural/theoretical variables in stochastic theories should be independent of population and item samples (e.g., Hilke, Kempf, & Scandura, 1977). (In the latter case, effects may vary with respect to particular instances within such samples.)

Conversely, observation/incidental variables have effects that vary from individual to individual or situation to situation, or in the case of stochastic theories, from sample to sample. Thus, for example, in the former case, the effects of friction may vary from inclined plane to inclined plane and the effects of number of learning trials, from individual to individual. In the latter case, the effects of a particular method of instruction might vary from one school (sample) to the next.

In short, whereas a universal effect in a deterministic theory pertains to all individuals, a universal effect in a stochastic theory need only pertain to all samples (groups) from some given population. Conversely, whereas the individual subject may be an incidental variable in stochastic theories, the individual's role in deterministic theories is crucial (i.e., in deterministic theories that deal with individual behavior in particular situations; cf. Montague, 1974).

As a consequence, empirical support for a theoretical variable, whether deterministic or probabilistic, implies a general effect which is applicable in all associated situations. This fact is especially important with respect to deterministic theories. Strong support for a deterministic theory provides a sufficient basis for applying the results in the real world--even *without* field testing (see Chapter 11). Support for a deterministic theory under idealized conditions (where the influence of incidental factors is eliminated) means that the theory holds over *all* representative individuals and over *all* representative, idealized situations (e.g., with respect to an idealized inclined plane over all representative angles of inclination; or all representative age/ability levels and types of problem situations). Hence, a result obtained under idealized conditions holds in a probabilistically weakened sense under nonidealized conditions (i.e., where 0 or 1 assumptions/effects are replaced with probabilities, $0 < p < 1$; e.g., compare Chapter 5 and Chapter 11). Whereas the effects of incidental factors (deviations from the ideal) may ameliorate obtained deterministic effects, they cannot reverse or even completely eliminate them.

Generalization with respect to probabilistic theories is somewhat more complicated. The effects of structural variables may be expected to hold only with respect to the population (of subjects and problems) from which samples have been drawn. Thus, application to the school classroom, for example, can only be expected to the extent that classroom samples are included in that population. Hence, "field testing" is a common requisite for applying the results of basic behavioral research in education.

In contrast, tests of deterministic theories are necessarily conducted under laboratory conditions. Because it is much simpler to sample broadly over individuals/particular idealized situations than over samples, deterministic theorizing and corresponding empirical tests under idealized conditions could provide a promising new way to bridge the gap between theory and

practice.   (For further discussion of this issue, see Scandura
(1972, 1977c in press); Hilke *et al*. (1977); and Chapter 11 of
this book.)

Where theoretical and incidental (observation) factors have
not been distinguished, empirical support is never sufficient
(whether the theory is deterministic or probabilistic). Support
in one situation does not necessarily say anything about what
will happen in other situations, as the influence of the incidental factors may "wash out" hypothesized theoretical effects
(see Scandura, 1964; cf. Hilke, Kempf, & Scandura, 1977).

Unfortunately, confounding both types of factors has been
common in contemporary theory building in the behavioral sciences
(e.g., in many stochastic "learning" theories, in most educational theories, and in all stochastic analogues of unproven deterministic theories). Unlike the natural sciences, for example,
where such things as distance, mass, energy, and so on are uniformly recognized as crucial, psychologists are not even agreed
on what are the basic theoretically relevant variables. What is
a theoretical variable (e.g., number of learning trials) to one
theorist, for example, may be an artifact or mere symptom (e.g.,
of retrievability or availability in working memory) to another.

2.6   CONSTRUCTING DETERMINISTIC AND COMPLEMENTARY OBSERVATION
THEORIES

The above discussion suggests that more attention be given
to deterministic theorizing in which complementary observation
theories are as simple as possible. Unfortunately, however, it
is impossible to provide definitive prescriptions as to how this
might be accomplished. Increasing scientists' awareness of the
boundary conditions under which particular theories operate
could make deterministic theorizing in behavioral science more
common than it has been to date. As I (Scandura, 1971, pp.
25–26) first stated the argument:

> The general difficulty with most theory construction
> in psychology is that very little attention has been given
> to specifying conditions under which theories are not pre-
> sumed to hold. To date, the sole approach to this problem
> has been an *ad hoc* empirical one in which experimental
> evidence is gradually accumulated over long periods of time.
>
> It is my feeling that much can be done along these
> lines, while theories are actually being constructed. (In
> particular, I have found it useful to ask myself the ques-
> tion, "What would human behavior be like if such and such
> were not an important factor?") This does not obviate the
> need for empirical testing, of course. No one believes
> that we can ever do away with that. But I do think that
> we can do away with a good deal of it, if theorists would
> give more explicit attention in their work to identifying
> these negative conditions.

In constructing a (deterministic) theory, whether it be a mathematical theory or a scientific theory, the theorist has some model, or models, in mind at the time. These models arise basically from particular segments of reality—but more important here, they usually deal with only certain aspects of that reality. The rest is simply ignored. (In turn, theories deal only with certain aspects of models. In mathematical theories the basic entities are divorced from particular meaning, leaving a superstructure built on undefined terms.)

This approach may be a viable one in mathematics, where one aims for abstraction. One never knows where mathematical theories may ultimately prove useful, and it would undoubtedly be a mistake to tie them in too closely to any particular model, by specifying aspects of these particular models with which the theory does *not* deal.

This is *not* true in science, however, where the ultimate aim may be to devise theories which deal with more of the particular reality in question. A theorist may have many more kinds of phenomena in mind in attempting to construct a theory than he can possibly handle at one time. To get around this problem, he may purposely ignore for a time *certain* of these phenomena to facilitate constructing what might be called a *partial* theory—a theory which deals with part of the reality but not all of it.

In effect, "in constructing such a partial theory, it is critically important that the theorist do so in a way which is compatible with the broader reality he seeks ultimately to explain" (Scandura, 1971, p. 26). The ultimate aim of curriculum design, for example, is not just to analyze content. That in itself might be attempted in any number of ways (e.g., according to efficiency criteria as in artificial intelligence). What is needed is a theory of content analysis that is likely to be compatible with more encompassing theories of cognition and/or instruction (see Scandura, 1977b).

In addition to identifying those aspects of reality that a given partial theory does not consider, the theorist should have an intuitive a priori understanding of the entire model and/or reality in question (i.e., some general idea beforehand as to how the ignored aspects might fit into the overall scheme). Stated differently, the eventual introduction of critical ignored factors will be essential where the ultimate goal is more complete understanding.

If a statement derived from a deterministic theory is not supported empirically, the theorist has two alternatives. First, he can reject the theory, and try to develop a better one. Alternatively, the theorist may have reason to believe that one or more of the ignored factors played a crucial role in the supposedly idealized empirical situation used to test the theory.

In this case, the theoretical system can be maintained by assuming that not all relevant entities have been taken into account in the original empirical test(s). As noted by Hilke, Kempf, and Scandura (1977):

> Rules of correspondence in combination with (theoretical) assumptions provide a basis for deriving statements about observables. Such derived statements, however, are only logical consequents. The empirical content of any theory derives from the assumption that the assumed entities, contained in those theoretical assumptions and rules of correspondence from which the statement is derived, are the *only ones* necessary to explain the observed phenomena.

In effect, the theorist may choose to retain the theory and to explain deviations in terms of the ignored factors. Here, the theorist can take two possible courses of action, both of which might be pursued more or less simultaneously. First, he can try to set up better experiments in which the required idealized conditions are more likely to be met (i.e., where the ignored factors are "partialed out"). Second, the theorist may attempt to enrich the theory by adding new assumptions and/or rules of correspondence, which make it possible to account for the deviations. This is, in fact, what physicists had to do with respect to the force laws in arriving at the principle of linear superposition (e.g., the vector combination of forces).

Notice in this regard that strong empirical support is crucially important. Such support (in the case of deterministic theories) applies uniformly to all individuals and task situations. Hence, supported assumptions necessarily can be retained as a foundation on which a more encompassing theory may be built, thereby eliminating the need to consider alternative possibilities. (Incidental factors of either the deterministic or probabilistic variety, since they are not necessarily universal in their effects, do not have this property.)

To the extent that the negative conditions incorporated in the complementary observation theory are the crucial ones, and to the extent that the theorist has prior insight as to their relationships to the parent, deterministic theory, the job of extension will be that much easier. Notice also that as more structure is added to a (tested) deterministic theory, it will (all other things being equal) account for behavior in a broader variety of situations. Correspondingly, the complementary observation theory will play a reduced role (i.e., it will involve fewer factors of potential theoretical importance). For example, the principle of linear superposition in physics makes it possible to include such factors as friction directly into the deterministic law of the inclined plane, thereby eliminating the need for a complementary (and perhaps stochastic) observation theory.

2.7 A CONCLUDING QUESTION

Does all this mean that we need a completely new theory? New methods of empirical research? A new school of study? The answers to these questions depend on one's point of view. Clearly, we need a theory that may in some important respects differ from existing competence, cognitive, and individual difference theories, and we may need research methods that differ in important ways from more traditional ones. Nonetheless, while a true synthesis of the above concerns may require a fundamentally different perspective, I believe that it also must be potentially compatible with and serve to redirect problem-solving research in a variety of relevant areas. Does this constitute a new field or school of study, or is it simply a redirection of current energies?

3. AN OVERVIEW

3.1 MAJOR GOALS

The major goals of this book are: (1) to show how content, cognition, and individual differences in human problem solving can be synthesized in terms of the structural learning theory (Scandura, 1971, 1973); (2) to propose and illustrate new empirical methodologies for analyzing content, studying cognition, and measuring individual differences as they pertain to human problem solving; and (3) to show how the basic theory may be used to account for the findings of existing problem-solving research and to suggest new problems.

More specifically, we shall see how content, cognition, and individual differences in human problem solving may all be viewed as critical parts of a single deterministic theory that involves not only the problem solver but the observer as well. The to-be-proposed theory of content/competence is a partial theory that deals with problem solving by an idealized all-knowing (prototypic) member of some specified population of subjects. The memory-free cognitive theory deals with the behavior of individuals in the population, but only in situations where memory and processing capacity do not play a measurable role. The inclusion of processing capacity adds more structure to the theory so that it applies directly in a broader variety of situations.

The methods for assessing behavior potential (performance testing) described in Chapter 2 and Part 4 amount to "rules of correspondence" between observables and the theoretical entities of the theory, specifically between test behavior and individual knowledge. The latter is defined relative to the idealized competencies associated with the target population. The (quasi-systematic) methods proposed for analyzing arbitrary content domains complete the operational cycle; these methods define idealized competence in terms of given task domains and subject populations.

In addition, new empirical paradigms are proposed for testing various levels of the deterministic theory under idealized
conditions. Special emphasis is given to testing theories of
competence and memory-free cognition. Attention also is given
to the empirical testing of a deterministic theory of information
processing and a complementary observation theory under nonidealized conditions.

In effect, the main contents of this book provide one
group's answer to the question of how content, cognition, and
individual differences all contribute to an understanding of
human problem solving. In general form the basic theory is
relativistic and, although the notation, mechanisms, and methods
of testing differ, it has in this sense some important things
in common with the independent work of Pask (1975). Moreover,
it is not proposed as a final answer, nor does it purport to be
equally balanced in all respects. Research, for example, has
progressed further in some areas than in others. In addition,
there are some respects in which the theory is in advance of
available empirical research (and even of proven experimental
paradigms for testing the theory).

3.2   OUTLINE

In Chapter 2, many of the essentials of my Structural Learning Theory (Scandura, 1973) are reviewed as they relate to problem solving, along with recent refinements and some important
extensions. On the other hand, although perceptual phenomena
may play an important part in problem solving, detailed consideration of its role is beyond the scope of this book (even
though the foundations for such development can be found in
Scandura, 1973). Nonetheless, although some detail may have to
be inferred by the reader and/or gleaned from my earlier book
(1973), the theory described in Chapter 2 is felt to provide an
adequate basis for interpretation of the full range of empirical
studies reported--whether these involve content, cognition, individual differences, or educational applications.

Part 2 includes a series of analytic studies in which the
concern centers about content analysis (i.e., identifying sets
of processes/rules that account for given classes of problems).
In Chapter 3, a general method for analyzing task domains is
proposed and applied to the domain of compass and straight-edge
constructions in geometry. In Chapter 4 the basic method is
extended and applied to algebraic proofs.

Part 3 is concerned with the cognitive mechanisms and constraints underlying problem solving, and particularly with showing how the control mechanisms of the Structural Learning Theory
can be realized in problem-solving research with human subjects.
Although a significant beginning has been made in this direction,
we shall also see that a good deal of basic research along these
lines remains to be done, in order both to refine the theory and

to determine whether untested aspects of the theory do indeed fit the facts. Chapter 5 is primarily concerned with rule derivation (learning) in problem solving; Chapter 6 deals with the roles of retrieval, problem definition, rule selection, and combinations of such processes. Chapter 7 deals with processing constraints on the human information processor; specifically, an analytic theory is proposed and tested for determining memory loads imposed on the human processor by arbitrary rules. A complementary stochastic observation theory also is proposed and empirically tested.

Part 4 deals with the relationship between competence (content) and individual human knowledge, with special emphasis on empirical testing of the operational definition proposed in Chapter 2. Chapter 8 involves a wide variety of tasks and subject populations and is concerned with the adequacy of the approach when tested under laboratory conditions. In Chapter 9, the basic method is applied to ordinary subtraction, and is compared with other recent innovations in criterion-referenced testing that were developed on primarily pragmatic grounds. Chapter 10 deals with some statistical concerns relevant to assessing behavior potential (e.g., for evaluating alternative rule accounts of the same behavior).

Part 5 involves educational applications and some important empirical and theoretical extensions. In Chapters 11 and 12, informal versions of the structural approach to content analysis were used to construct real educational curricula. Chapter 11 involves a basic mathematics curriculum for elementary school teachers and Chapter 12 involves a "short-cut" method of analysis used in critical reading. Empirical tests of both curricula demonstrate their effectiveness. Chapter 13 extends the method of assessment to higher-order rules in the context of an experimental verification of the geometry analysis of Chapter 3. The study reported also deals with the cumulative effects of solving sequences of problems. Chapter 14 describes an important extension of the basic theory to adaptive instruction along with a computerized implementation and an empirical test of the extension.

In the concluding Chapter 15 (Part 6), the present work is summarized and related to other problem solving research. In addition, instructional implications are discussed and a number of important open problems are identified.

REFERENCES

Atkinson, R. C. Stimulus sampling theory. In R. D. Luce, R. R. Bush, & E. Galanter (Eds.), *Handbook of psychology* (Vol. 2). New York: Wiley, 1963.

Bower, G. H. Application of a model to paired associate learning. *Psychometrika*, 1961, *26*, 255-280.

Bloom, B. S., & Broder, L. J. *Problem-solving processes of college students: An exploratory investigation*. Chicago: University of Chicago Press, 1950.

Chomsky, N. *Syntactic structures*. The Hague: Mouton, 1957.

Chomsky, N. *Language and mind*. New York: Harcourt, Brace, & World, 1968.

Dunker, K. On problem solving (Translated by L. S. Lees from the 1935 original). *Psychological Monographs*, 1945, *58*, No. 270, 198-311.

Estes, W. K. Toward a statistical theory of learning. *Psychological Review* 1950, *57*, 94-107.

Fischer, G. H. *Einfuhrung in die theorie psychologischer tests*. Bern: Huber, 1974.

Fischer, G. H. Linear logistic test models. In H. Spada & W. F. Kempf (Eds.), *Formalized theories of thinking and learning and their implications for science instruction*. Bern: Huber, 1977.

Furth, H. G. *Piaget and knowledge : Theoretical foundations*. Englewood Cliffs, N.J.: Prentice-Hall, 1969.

Gagne, R. *The conditions of learning*. New York: Holt, Rinehart & Winston, 1970.

Glaser, R. Instructional technology and the measurement of learning outcomes: Some questions. *American Psychologist*, 1963, *18*, 519-21.

Glaser, R. Educational psychology and education. *American Psychologist*, 1973, *28*, 557-566.

Groen, G. J. An investigation of some counting algorithms for simple addition problems (Technical Report No. 118). Stanford, Calif.: Institute for Mathematical Studies in the Social Sciences, 1967.

Guilford, J. P. *The nature of human intelligence*. New York: McGraw-Hill, 1967.

Hilke, R., Kempf, W. F., & Scandura, J. M. Deterministic and probabilistic theorizing in structural learning. In H. Spada & W. F. Kempf (Eds.), *Formalized theories of thinking and learning and their implications for science instruction*. Bern: Huber, 1977.

Kempf, W. F. A test-theoretical approach to structural learning. In J. M. Scandura, J. H. Durnin, & W. H. Wulfeck II (Eds.), *1974 Proceedings : Fifth annual interdisciplinary conference on structural learning*. (ONR Technical Report, 1974). MERGE Research Institute, 1249 Greentree Lane, Narberth, PA., 19072.

Kempf, W. F. A dynamic test model and its use in the microevaluation of instructional material. In H. Spada & W. F. Kempf (Eds.), *Formalized theories of thinking and learning and their implications for science instruction*. Bern: Huber, 1977.

Kuhn, T. S. *The structure of scientific revolutions*. Chicago: University Press, 1962.

Merrill, M. D., & Gibbons, A. S. Heterarchies and their relationship to behavioral hierarchies for sequencing content in instruction. In J. M. Scandura, J. H. Durnin, & W. H. Wulfeck II (Eds.), *1974 Proceedings : Fifth annual interdisciplinary conference on structural learning* (ONR Technical Report, 1974). MERGE Research Institute, 1249 Greentree Lane, Narberth, PA., 19072.

Miller, G. A. The magical number seven, plus or minus two: Some limits on our capacity for processing information. *Psychological Review*, 1956, *63*, 81-97.

Miller, G. A., Galanter, E., & Pribram, K. H. *Plans and the structure of behavior*. New York: Holt, Rinehart & Winston, 1960.

Minsky, M., & Papert, S. *Research at the laboratory in vision, language, and other problems of intelligence* (Artificial intelligence: Progress report Memo 252). Cambridge, Mass.: Massachusetts Institute of Technology, Artificial Intelligence Laboratory, 1972.

Montague, R. *Formal philosophy: Selected papers of Richard Montague*. New Haven: Yale University Press, 1974.

Newell, A., & Simon, H. A. *Human problem solving*. Englewood Cliffs, N.J.: Prentice-Hall, 1972.

Pask, G. An outline of conversational domains and their structure. In J. M. Scandura, J. H. Durnin, & W. H. Wulfeck II (Eds.), *1974 Proceedings: Fifth annual interdisciplinary conference on structural learning* (ONR Technical Report, 1974). MERGE Research Institute, 1249 Greentree Lane, Narberth, PA. 19072.

Pask, G. *Conversation, cognition, and learning*. Amsterdam: Elsevier, 1975.

Polya, G. *Mathematical discovery* (Vol. 1). New York: Wiley, 1962.

Rasch, G. *Probabilistic models for some intelligence and attainment tests.* Copenhagen: Nielson & Lydiche, 1960.

Reitman, W. R. *Cognition and thought: An information processing approach.* New York: Wiley, 1965.

Reulecke, W. Statistical analysis of deterministic theories. In H. Spada & W. F. Kempf (Eds.), *Formalized theories of thinking and learning and their implications for science instruction.* Bern: Huber, 1977.

Scandura, J. M. Analysis of exposition and discovery modes of problem solving instruction. *Journal of Experimental Education,* 1964, *33,* 149-159.

Scandura, J. M. Deterministic theorizing in structural learning: Three levels of empiricism. *Journal of Structural Learning,* 1971, *3,* 21-53.

Scandura, J. M. Plan for the development of a conceptually-based mathematics curriculum for disadvantaged children: I and II. *Instructional Science,* 1972, *2,* 247-262 and 363-387.

Scandura, J. M. *Structural learning I: Theory and research.* New York: Gordon & Breach Science, 1973.

Scandura, J. M. A deterministic theory of teaching and learning. In H. Spada & W. F. Kempf (Eds.), *Formalized theories of thinking and learning and their implications for science instruction.* Bern: Huber, 1977. (a)

Scandura, J. M. Structural approach to instructional problems. *American Psychologist,* 1977, *32,* 33-53. (b)

Scandura, J. M. A deterministic approach to research in instructional science. *Educational Psychologist,* 1977, in press. (c)

Shavelson, R. J., & Geeslin, W. E. A method for examining subject matter structure in instructional material. *Journal of Structural Learning,* 1975, *4,* 199-218.

Snow, R. Aptitudes and instructional methods: Individual differences in learning related processes. In *FY 1976 Programs.* Arlington: ONR, 1976. p. 9.

Spada, H., & Kempf, W. F. (Eds.) *Formalized theories of thinking and learning and their implications for science instruction.* Bern: Huber, 1976.

Speedie, S. M., Treffinger, D. J., & Feldhusen, J. F. Teaching problem solving skills: Development of an instructional model based on human abilities related to efficient problem solving (Final Report, (OEG-5-72-0042, 509).) West Lafayette, Ind.: Purdue University, 1973.

Suppes, P., & Morningstar, M. *Computer-assisted instruction at Stanford : Data models, and evaluation of arithmetic programmes.* New York: Academic Press, 1972.

2
A Structural Learning Theory[1]

Joseph M. Scandura

Over the past several years I have been trying to develop
a unified theoretical framework (called the Structural Learning
Theory) that makes scientific contact with a broad range of
phenomena involving complex human behavior. The Structural
Learning Theory (Scandura, 1971a, 1973) deals with many of the
concerns of competence researchers (e.g., computer scientists)
and cognitive psychologists, and also attempts to explicate the
complementary relationship between these concerns in the form of
what essentially is a theory of individual differences measurement. As such, it provides a potentially useful basis for a
deterministic theory of human problem solving (cf. Chapter 1).

Although it would be presumptuous to imply that the to-be-
proposed theory has all of the desirable properties described in
Chapter 1, it is thought to be a step in this direction. In some
respects, the theory has achieved a degree of rigor and empirical support that would convince most informed critics. In other
respects, however, the theory represents hardly more than a
sketchy map and a hunting license with the promise of plentiful
game.

In this chapter, I shall describe the more significant and
relevant features of the basic theory (Scandura, 1971a, 1973),
together with some important recent extensions, all as they relate to human problem solving. To increase expository efficiency, much of the exposition is illustrated in terms of a single,
abstract example (problem domain/content). The ideas described,
however, generalize naturally over a broad range of content. To
avoid leaving the false impression that the theory applies only
to a highly restricted class of subject matters, the concluding
section provides a road map of sorts to the "real-world" examples
and relevant research reported in Parts 2, 3, 4, and 5.

[1]The research reported in this chapter was supported by National Institute
of Health Grant 9185 and the MERGE Research Institute.

1.   THEORETICAL OVERVIEW

As we saw in the last chapter, there are three general kinds of questions that may be asked concerning human problem solving:

1. *competence* (content): Given a class of tasks, however broad and general (e.g., value judgements) or narrow and specific (e.g., arithmetic computation), how can the competence required for performing these tasks best be characterized so as to reflect human behavior? Because there are an indefinitely large number of different content domains, the theory must deal with the processes by which the competence underlying arbitrary content is identified as well as with specific competence itself.

2. *cognition:* Given a specific task and the relevant knowledge available to a person, what are the control mechanisms and other constraints on the human information processor which determine how this knowledge is put to use and how new knowledge is acquired?

3. *individual differences:* What is the relationship between generalized competence and individual knowledge? Or, equivalently, how can one find out what individual subjects know relative to given content domains?

Some existing theories and technologies tend to emphasize one or another of these themes, with generally less concern for the others. For example, Polya's (1962) analyses of heuristics, artificial intelligence generally (e.g., Minsky & Papert, 1972), and task analysis (e.g., Gagne, 1970) and other forms of content analysis in education tend to emphasize question 1; many contemporary theories in cognitive psychology (e.g., Bower, 1972; Kintsch, 1970; Neisser, 1967; Hunt, 1973) and concept learning (e.g., Bourne, Ekstrand, & Dominowski, 1971; Levine, 1975) emphasize question 2; and mastery (e.g., Bloom, 1973) and other forms of criterion-referenced testing (e.g., Hively, Patterson, & Page, 1968) emphasize question 3.

On the other hand, theory and research in computer simulation (e.g., Newell & Simon, 1972), psycholinguistics (e.g., Carroll & Freedle, 1972), contemporary research on problem solving (e.g., Greeno, 1973), rule learning (e.g., Bruner, Goodnow, & Austin, 1956; Restle & Brown, 1970; Scandura, 1968, 1970) and semantic memory (e.g., Anderson & Bower, 1973; Kintsch, 1972; Rumelhart, Lindsay, & Norman, 1972; Quillian, 1968) often give more or less equal attention to both content and cognition. In addition, at a more pragmatic level, many educational and training psychologists (e.g., Ausubel, 1968; Gagne & Briggs, 1974) have been concerned with content, cognition, and individual differences measurement. With the exception of the structural learning theory (Scandura, 1971a, 1973), however, very little has been done by way of theoretical synthesis of all three concerns. (However, also see Pask, 1975. Some relationships between Pask's theory and the present work are considered in Chapter 15.)

The structural learning theory, as it has evolved over the past several years (cf. Scandura, 1971a, 1973, 1974a, 1977a) provides a unifying theoretical framework within which the concerns of the competence (e.g., artificial intelligence, linguistics, subject matter content) researcher, the cognitive psychologist, and the individual differences researcher may be viewed. In the theory, a sharp distinction is made between competence (content) and individual human knowledge, a distinction that is analogous but not identical to the one that some linguists make between competence and performance (e.g., Miller & Chomsky, 1963). (In particular, whereas *competence* refers in both cases to idealized capability, with additional restrictions in our case, *individual knowledge* is not the same as performance. The former refers to what individuals know, relative to idealized competence, independently of other cognitive constraints that influence performance, such as processing capacity.)

The theory also explicates the complementary relationship between competence and knowledge.[2] This relationship takes the form of what is essentially a performance test theory (i.e., a theory of individual differences measurement). More generally, the following sections and chapters show how theory and research in any one domain, if it is to have broader significance, is necessarily subject to constraints imposed by the requirements of theory in other domains.

In order to achieve this type of synthesis, it is not sufficient to consider just the individual (behaving) subject in interaction with a totally objective environment. The observer also plays a fundamental role in the structural learning theory; as does the relationship between the observer and the subject and environment. The observer determines the problem domain and subject population, and especially what count as the observables (e.g., problems and distinguishable solutions) and the underlying competence by which idealized, prototypic subjects in the target population might solve the problems. The current state of each individual (i.e., his knowledge), and all behavior, are always judged/measured relative to some problem domain and corresponding set of underlying competencies. The theory, in effect, is *relativistic* in nature.

In the present chapter the emphasis is on how, in this relativistic setting, one might explicate human interaction with a problem solving environment at any given stage of learning. An extension of the theory to ongoing interactions over time between subject and environment is described in Chapter 14. (For

---

[2]Although a sharp conceptual difference was made, I used the term *knowledge* in Scandura (1973a) to refer to both competence and behavioral potential (knowledge). This usage was related to the terms *competence* and *knowledge* in an epilog to Chapter 9.

an excellent discussion of relativistic theories in the latter
sense see Pask, 1975, Chapter 2, cf. p. 304.)

In the theory, both competence and knowledge are represented
in terms of rules (procedures) and the structures on which rules
operate. As indicated in the Glossary, I have preferred not to
commit myself fully to any one formal definition as to exactly
what a rule is. For present purposes, rules may be thought of
equivalently as procedures, flow diagrams, or directed graphs
(cf. Rogers, 1967; Scandura, 1969, 1970, 1972b; 1973, Chapter 5;
1976, Chapter 1). (Note: Structures include meanings and
"chunks", as described in Scandura 1973, Chapters 6 and 10, respectively. Where they recur in different settings, it is sometimes convenient to summarize structures in terms of relational
networks.) Overall, the characterization of competence in the
Structural Learning Theory differs from that in other generative
theories (e.g., in linguistics, and artificial intelligence) in
two important, related ways:

1. The way in which rules operate on other rules is constrained by a fixed mode of interaction, one that is assumed to
reflect the way in which *all* humans use their available knowledge. (This mode of interaction corresponds to Chomsky's [1968]
postulated but unspecified "fixed function" language facility
and to the kind of interaction assumed in production systems
[Chapter 1].)

2. Equally important, the constraints imposed by the assumed fixed mode of interaction, and other constraints, make
possible (quasi) systematic methods of content analysis. Characterizations in artificial intelligence are less constrained
in the former regard and, correspondingly, the methods of analysis used depend more completely on the individual analyst.

Regarding human behavior, whatever the individual learner
does and can do in any particular situation, and whatever learning takes place, are assumed in the theory to depend inextricably on what he already knows. In addition to whatever specific
knowledge may be available to an individual, the use of such
knowledge is assumed to depend on more permanent cognitive characteristics of the human information processor.

One such characteristic is realized in terms of a universal
control mechanism. This control mechanism is assumed to be
common to all people, at least beyond age seven, and to determine how available knowledge is put to use and how new knowledge
is created. Unlike other control mechanisms that have been proposed (e.g., Newell & Simon, 1972), it is not automatically assumed that people can compose available rules (whenever this is
mathematically admissible)--nor is composition the only way in
which new rules can be formed from old ones. Rather, control
is effected by a goal-switching mechanism that, among other
things, allows rules to operate on other rules and to generate
new ones. This mechanism directly parallels the form imposed

on competence theories. Among the other constraints assumed to
influence cognition are the limited capacity of working memory,
and processing speed.

In contrast to general cognitive constraints, specific
knowledge is assumed to vary over individuals. The theory shows
how competence (corresponding to an idealized prototypic member
of some population and represented at a level appropriate to
minimal capabilities associated with the population) may be used
to operationally define the knowledge had by individual subjects
in that population. In a very real sense, the rules in competence theories serve effectively as "rulers" for measuring human
knowledge.

To summarize, although the Structural Learning Theory is
concerned with a variety of different phenomena (which traditionally have been studied in different fields), it is equally
concerned with the relationships among these phenomena. Each
of these concerns: content/competence, cognition, individual
differences, and their interrelationships, is considered more
fully in the following sections. For definitions of key terms
and synonyms, the reader is encouraged to consult the GLOSSARY.
In the following sections, the first appearance of such terms
and important subsequent usages are CAPITALIZED.

2. CONTENT/COMPETENCE

As indicated above, COMPETENCE is represented in terms of
rules introduced by an observer to account for potentially observable behavior. In order to understand and to be able to
predict the problem-solving behavior of individuals in some
population of subjects, the first question that arises is what
aspects of the behavior are to be considered. Surely, if the
observer is concerned with problems in computer programming,
then whether or not a particular subject happens, in the process of solving one, to scratch his head or to get up to sharpen
his pencil is not likely to be of great import. The observer
must determine both what count as problems and the observable
conditions that must be satisfied for such problems to be solved.
As we shall see in the following sections, there is a close relationship between the way problems and solutions are represented
and the underlying rules of competence.

2.1 PRELIMINARIES
Any scientifically defensible approach to the study of
human problem solving must satisfy certain basic conditions.
Nature of Problems/Solutions: As a minimum, it must be
possible to determine through observation whether or not a given
PROBLEM has been solved. We assume, for example, that the prob-

lem situations, which actually influence relevant behavior, can
be represented externally for purposes of study (i.e., made observable) and that possible solutions can be evaluated.

No commitment, however, is made as to the sufficiency of
paper-and-pencil tests. For one thing, the problems and/or
solutions may be too complex. Problems whose solutions involve
complex value distinctions and/or moral judgement, for example,
may not always be reducible to simple verbal or iconic description (although even that has been attempted--see Kohlberg, 1971).
Similarly, the time it takes to solve a problem may be of concern as well as whether or not a given solution is correct.

For present purposes, the essential requirement is that it
must be possible to envisage, recognize, and recreate test situations in which desired problem-solving behavior can be observed.
In the case of skilled performance, for example, solution LATEN-
CIES (time to solution) often play a crucial role. Correspondingly, the given in a problem might be a complex diagram or model
representing the circulation system in man (see one of the IPN
school biology units, e.g., Eulefold, Kattmann, & Schaefer,
1975). More generally, problem situations and potential solutions may consist of observable complexes of arbitrary entities
and relations, which correspond to external counterparts of what
in contemporary memory and problem-solving research are called
relational nets (e.g., Rumelhart, Lindsay, & Norman, 1972;
Greeno, 1976). Relational nets, in turn, correspond to but
usually are not as general as internal psychological units, or
STRUCTURES (also "CHUNKS"). (Psychological) structures consist
of finite sets of elements (which correspond to nodes in relational nets); RULES and RELATIONS defined on the elements (which
correspond to relations); and HIGHER-ORDER RULES and HIGHER-
ORDER RELATIONS defined on the relations and rules (which correspond to relations between relations) (cf. Scandura, 1975, p.
509; Chapter 15, Section 3, this book). (Higher-order rules and
relations are usually missing from the relational nets used in
most contemporary memory theories; however, see Pask's 1975,
relational operators; also cf. Hays-Roth, 1974.)

It is worth noting that critical portions of even simple
problems are often only implicit (not directly observable) in
given situations. Consider, for example, the sequential task
of putting an X in the "next" slot of the external stimulus *000*.
On the first presentation, the X goes in the first slot; on the
second, it goes in the second slot, and so on, repeating the
cycle beginning on the fourth presentation. Since the external
stimulus is the same on each presentation, the only way the X
can be properly placed is by "remembering" the last response.
In effect, the effective (encoded) task input is the internalized
last placement of X superimposed on the (encoded) externally
presented *000*. Throughout our discussion, unless stated to the
contrary, PROBLEM GIVEN/INPUT means the effectively operating

(ENCODED) input, irrespective of whether all or part of it is directly observable--similarly, for PROBLEM SOLUTIONS.

The failure to take into account all relevant aspects of experimental tasks, at an appropriate level of representation (see the discussions on representation which follow), has frequently led to inconclusive and/or conflicting research findings. With regard to Piagetian conservation tasks, for example, the specific external STIMULI/RESPONSES associated directly with the tasks themselves (e.g., objects, the words "same", "different") provide only part of the critical information. It is, I think, precisely this distinction between Piaget's concern with the logical basis for a child's responding, not just the responding per se, and the exclusive concern of some experimentalists with the apparent tasks involved that has led to the plethora of claims to have proven Piaget wrong (cf. Wallach & Sprott, 1964; Scandura, 1972a). In psychological research it is easy to get carried away with the behavioral questions involved and to overlook critical characteristics/differences concerning the problems themselves--even where the problems appear to be reasonably well defined (cf. Greeno, 1973; Roughead & Scandura, 1968; Scandura, 1964, 1966, 1968). (PROBLEMS are defined as pairs consisting of PROBLEM GIVENS and SOLUTIONS. An "unsolvable problem" is not a problem in this sense.)

Although all allowable problems must lend themselves to testing (in principle), we want to avoid limiting ourselves to only "closed" systems, and do not require a priori specification of every problem. We shall require only that it be possible to determine whether or not any given problem is an INSTANCE of the PROBLEM DOMAIN (class of problems) of interest. One way to accomplish this would be simply to assign sole responsibility for such decisions to some external oracle (e.g., observer, teacher), but ordinarily one would prefer a more explicit formulation of public criteria. (In effect, we shall disallow ambiguous "fuzzy" sets for most purposes, although no commitment is made regarding how essential this exclusion is.)

Since various subsets of problems may satisfy somewhat different criteria, it is convenient for some purposes to partition problem domains into classes (e.g., see Chapter 3, where geometry construction problems are partitioned into "two-loci", "similar figures", and "auxiliary figures" problems prior to STRUCTURAL ANALYSIS). Consequently, every problem domain is assumed to be of the form

(1) $P_1 \cup P_2 \cup \ldots \cup P_n$

where each P_i is a subset of problems satisfying a corresponding set of criteria. For our purposes, these subsets need not be equivalence classes in the mathematical sense (i.e., they need not be mutually exclusive and exhaustive with respect to the problem domain). Their primary purpose is to serve a heuristic role in identifying various types of problems. (They correspond to EDUCATIONAL GOALS as used in Scandura, 1977.)

Problem Domains and Solution Rules: Since time, capacity of the human mind, and instruction are necessarily finite, one may reasonably assume in most concrete realizations that the classes P_i, and hence the entire problem domain, are COMPUTABLE FUNCTIONS (cf. Rogers, 1967). That is, in most practical applications, we may assume that each problem domain has some SOLUTION RULE (PROCEDURE). (A FUNCTION is computable if there is a RULE/PROCEDURE/ALGORITHM,[3] or equivalently a *set* of rules (RULE SET), which ACCOUNTS for it, i.e., generates the unique output associated with each input in the domain.) In view of Section 2.5 *(Rule Selection and Incorrect Knowledge),* however, the problem givens (in the problems) in problem domains may be associated with more than one solution output (including incorrect ones). Hence, in general, problem domains are better thought of as RELATIONS. In turn, rule sets that account for such problem domains may include more than one solution rule for each problem given.

Even where no such solution rules exist, however, (as has been shown to be true of complex mathematical domains, cf. Scandura, 1973, Chapter 3; Lightstone, 1964), the behavioral implications are minimal. No one has, or ever will have, complete mastery of any nontrivial problem domain (even where the problem domain may be a computable function). If all knowledge can be represented in terms of rules (equivalently, procedures/ algorithms, etc.), then the best one can hope for in these cases is to account for a relatively large portion of the domain. Alternative rule accounts of nontrival problem domains may be compared (empirically) as to comprehensiveness but they will rarely be complete.

Even where a problem domain has been or can be fully analyzed, the underlying SOLUTION PROCEDURE may be extremely complex. Where this is the case, as happens frequently in artificial intelligence research, it often is more convenient to take a *modular* approach. Here, single procedures (rules) are replaced by sets of usually simpler rules together with LAWS OF INTERACTION (CONTROL MECHANISMS in computer science), which determine how the various rules are to interact. (In fact, RULES are restricted in the STRUCTURAL LEARNING THEORY in the sense that new subprocedures cannot be derived and then applied within the same rule; see GLOSSARY. This restriction plays an important role in individual differences measurement, Section 5, and is consistent with the control mechanism postulated to govern human

---

[3]Unless otherwise specified in this book, we shall ignore formal distinction among these items (cf. Rogers, 1967; also Knuth, 1968; Nelson, 1968). I tend, however, to use the term *procedure* when internal structure is of direct concern and, *rule,* otherwise. For present purposes, the reader may think of rules/ procedures as flow diagrams. In this chapter they are represented as labeled directed graphs.

cognition, Section 4.)

For example, consider the following simple problem domain, which we will gradually expand and use to illustrate a variety of points.

(2) $\{xB\text{-}By|$ x = string of a's, y = binary numeral
representing number of a's$\}$

In this case, for example, aaaaaB-B101 is the problem (instance) corresponding to x = aaaaa, where aaaaaB is the problem given and B101 is the solution. One rule that accounts for this problem domain can be represented as

(3) START 1
STOP
2

where 1 and 2 are operations that map inputs of the form xBy into outputs of the forms $\left[\frac{x}{2}\right]$ B0y and $\left[\frac{x}{2}\right]$ B1y, respectively.
($\left[\frac{x}{2}\right]$ is a string containing a number of a's equal to the greatest integer in the number of a's in x, divided by 2, i.e., $\frac{x}{2}$.) The dot "." represents a decision-making capability that distinguishes strings of the form xBy (in which x represents an even number of a's, an odd number of a's, or zero a's) and, respectively, directs control to the operations 1 and 2, and STOP. Thus, for example, operation 1 operates on strings containing an even number of a's, and operation 2 operates on strings containing an odd number. As in (2), y is a string of 0's and 1's, but y is not necessarily a binary numeral in standard form (e.g., y could be 001 or 0101) where there are any a's to the left of B in xB (i.e., where x ≠ ∅). In the case of Rule (3), the law of combination is obvious; given any string of the form xB, apply Rule (3). For example, application of Rule (3) to aaaaaB gives (aaB1 → aB01 →) B101.

Rules

(4) r_1 = xxBy → xB0y
r_2 = xxaBy → xB1y

provide a basis for an alternative account. These rules correspond directly to operations 1 and 2, respectively, with the domains restricted as per the decision in Rule (3). That is, r_1 operates only on strings with an even number of a's, represented xx and r_2, on strings with an odd number of a's represented xxa (where x in either case can be a ∅, a, aa, aaa, ...). (Note: Throughout this book, expressions to the left of arrows are used to denote RULE DOMAINS and those to the right, to denote RULE RANGES. The arrows themselves may be thought of as OPERATIONS; see RULE. This notation should not be confused with

the replacement (substitution/assignment) operation, commonly
used in computer science, where m ← n means the value of variable m is to be replaced by the current value of n.)

In order to complete the account, we add the stipulation
(law of interaction) that these rules may be applied in sequence
arbitrarily. For example,

$$(5)\quad \text{aaaaaB} \xrightarrow{r_2} \text{aaBl} \xrightarrow{r_1} \text{aB0l} \xrightarrow{r_2} \text{Bl0l}$$

(Note: This law of interaction is basic in all formal [produc-
tion] systems [e.g., in mathematics, formal linguistics, logic].)

It takes little imagination to devise any number of trivially different accounts--e.g., progressive complications of Rule
(3) and/or Rule (4) that include redundant or unnecessary steps
(i.e., component operations/decisions). In fact, it can easily
be shown mathematically that if there is one procedure, or set
of procedures, that accounts for (i.e., generates all solutions
for all problem givens in) a given problem domain, then there
necessarily is a countably infinite number of others that do
the same thing (cf. Rogers, 1967).

On Representation: There is a close relationship between
the way problem givens and their solutions are represented
(i.e., the elementary properties and relations used to define
them) and the REPRESENTATIONS (e.g., component operations and
decisions) that may meaningfully be used to represent underlying
rules (cf. Scandura, 1973, Chapters 7 and 9, pp. 95-100,
especially p. 99).

All competence accounts (e.g., in artificial intelligence),
for example, are constrained by the level of detail introduced
to represent the problems (givens and solutions) in the associated problem domain. The minimum level of RULE REFINEMENT that
is possible depends directly on this detail (for details, see
Scandura, 1973, Chapter 5). In representing ordinary addition
problems, for example, the individual digits are typically
thought of as UNITARY. Consequently, underlying procedures for
adding numbers may be meaningfully refined only to the level of
basic addition facts. Thus, for example, an addition algorithm
can be refined only to the point that each addition fact (e.g.,
4 + 5 = 9; 3 + 2 = 5) is represented by a distinct (DEGENERATE)
component operation. More detailed counting algorithms of the
sort used by Groen and his associates (e.g., Suppes & Groen,
1967; Groen, 1967), are meaningful only when addition problems
are represented at a more detailed level, for example, when the
individual digits (numbers) are represented in terms of succes-
sors (i.e., $1 = s(0)$, $2 = ss(0)$, $3 = sss(0)$, ...). In the
latter case, for example in adding 3 + 2, one might start with
sss(0) and apply the successor operation (s) two times giving
sssss(0) (=5). The above constraints, of course, are not

limited to addition. Given any procedure there is always some
base level of detail beyond which the procedure cannot further
be refined without redefining problems and solutions (see
Scandura, 1973, Chapter 5).

Equally important, where questions of efficiency (or psychological viability) are considered, the kinds of representations that may reasonably be used depend in large part on the
content involved. Thus, for example, while symbolic representations of arithmetic problems may be sufficient for representing
computational algorithms, such representations are less likely
to provide a sufficient basis for the processes used in judging
works of art. In the latter case, for example, one might expect
analog considerations to play a more crucial role. More generally, it is hard to conceive of any mode of representation that
will be completely adequate in all situations. (Compare this
view of representation with traditional practice where fixed
standards predominate. In the latter case, for example, particular programming languages are often used for a wide variety
of purposes, if not universally. Invariably, the suitability
of the language varies greatly depending on the particular application in question. For a discussion of related issues see
Chapter 15.)

2.2 PSYCHOLOGICAL CONSTRAINTS ON CONTENT/COMPETENCE
The above considerations, of course, are largely devoid of
psychological content. Thus, for example, it would be impossible to identify all possible RULE SETS (there may be an infinite
number) that might account for a given problem domain. Moreover,
the fact that a problem domain might be represented, or accounted for, in a certain way says nothing about the psychological
relevance of any particular representation or account. Thus,
for example, whereas an observer is free to choose a level and
type (e.g., discrete/analog) of representation that meets his
needs, such representation may or may not have psychological
relevance. Given only computability considerations, representations are selected primarily to make possible distinctions that
are deemed important, and to suppress distinctions that are not.
Psychological relevance, on the other hand, refers to those
elements, relations, and operations that are behaviorally and/or
cognitively distinct relative to the population of subjects in
question.

In specifying problems in given problem domains and in devising corresponding COMPETENCE THEORIES, therefore, it is important to make a sharp distinction between the two kinds of
relevance. It is not sufficient, for example, to simply select
convenient data structures and a generally applicable computer
language (e.g., SNOBOL, LISP) since the basic linguistic elements involved may obscure psychologically meaningful entities.
Identifying the latter is an essential part of any STRUCTURAL

REPRESENTATION.

In the Structural Learning Theory, problem domains and COMPETENCE ACCOUNTS (sets of COMPETENCE RULES) are subject to two general types of constraints. First, the way specific problems and COMPETENCIES (rules of competence) are represented must be consistent with the observer's sensibilities as to the structure of the discipline and, in particular, with what an IDEALIZED, PROTOTYPIC SUBJECT in the TARGET POPULATION might be expected to know about the problem domain. As we shall see in Section 5, this requirement is essential if underlying competence is to provide an adequate basis for measuring individual KNOWLEDGE. Second, underlying competence must be represented in a way that is compatible with universal COGNITIVE CONSTRAINTS as to how competencies may interact (also see Section 2).

Population Constraints: The POPULATION CONSTRAINTS imposed by the target population are both global and local, global in the sense of overall structure of the competencies and local in the sense that the basic elements are represented at a behaviorally meaningful level of inclusiveness.

The former requirement refers to the nature of the competence rules (and structures), and particularly to the compatibility of the population constraints with these IDEALIZED (PROTOTYPIC) rules. Such rules may be thought of as being available to idealized members of the population, whether real or imagined, who have an (effectively) unlimited capacity for processing information. Accordingly, idealized individuals are assumed able to solve problems in a given domain uniformly well (or badly), and to do so without flaw or deviation from prototypic knowledge. Thus, for example, given the domain of column subtraction problems, one idealized subject might know the equal additions method for subtracting numbers and another, the method of borrowing. What would not be allowed would be for an idealized subject to know only part of a rule or to otherwise apply the rule incorrectly. (Note: Prototypic rules that systematically generate incorrect solutions are allowed. This is useful, for example, where attention is focused on systematic errors as well as on solutions.)

Although one might suspect that the number of prototypic rules would be prohibitively large, this appears not to be the case, at least not in dealing with relatively well-structured and meaningful problem domains and homogeneous target populations. Indeed, the number of basically different prototypes that need to be considered is often quite small, on the order of one or two (e.g., Chapters 3 and 4). Whether or not this also would be true of other kinds of domains is unclear at this time but the research reported in the Addendum to Chapter 12 suggests that a small number of prototypes might suffice for a wide variety of content. All other things being equal, the more realistic the content of a problem domain, the easier it appears

to be to identify the underlying competence. Because of their
idiosyncratic nature, arbitrarily organized materials, of the
sort often used in paired-associate learning, seem to cause the
most trouble (see Scandura, 1973, Chapter 10).

Locally, the problems and rules of competence must be represented at a level that has psychological relevance in the
sense that the basic elements, relations, and operations correspond to UNITARY PSYCHOLOGICAL ENTITIES (STRUCTURES). In the
case of problems and solutions, for example, it is not sufficient that the representation just satisfy the observer's concerns.
Since their main purpose is to make it possible to study other
capabilities, the ENTITIES used to represent problems must correspond to basic ENCODING CAPABILITIES that are uniformly available to all subjects in the target population. That is they
must be ATOMIC. The entities used to represent solutions must
also be atomic in the above sense. Where encoding and decoding
capabilities are not themselves the object of study they may be
designated as AUXILIARY CAPABILITIES. (Auxiliary capabilities
are discussed further below.) Although this approach may appear
to avoid questions pertaining to perception (ENCODING) and DE-
CODING, this is not entirely true. The question of how subjects
learn to perceive (i.e., to make new distinctions, to partition
the world in new ways), for example, can be viewed as combining
given GLOBAL patterns (via available encoding capabilities) so
as to make possible finer discriminations (see Scandura, 1973,
pp. 109-111).

As previously noted, the entities used to represent problems impose constraints on the underlying rules of competence.
In particular, they place a lower bound of sorts on the degree
to which given rules may be refined into components (see RULE,
REFINEMENT OF; also Scandura, 1973). In most practical applications, however, it is not maximum refinement that causes difficulties. Rules frequently can be represented at relatively
MOLAR LEVELS (i.e., at low-levels of detail/in terms of high-
level languages) relative to given problem domains without loss
of explanatory potential (see Section 5). The major requirement
is that the rules of competence must be represented in terms of
atomic (all-or-none) components that are commensurate with the
minimum ENTERING CAPABILITIES over all individuals in the target
population. A component rule is said to be atomic in this sense
if it is sufficiently elemental that it can be assumed to be
either uniformly available to individuals in the population or
not at all (see RULE, ATOMIC; also Scandura, 1971a, 1973).
Possible examples of atomic rules are rules for performing simple
carrying in subtraction, for giving the meanings of particular
words, and for reading ordinary discourse. (Assuming that the
problems are represented in appropriate detail, it is always
possible to represent the underlying rules of competence in
sufficient detail that each component acts in atomic fashion,

Scandura, 1973, Chapter 5).

In general, the level of detail (inclusiveness) that is acceptable for such purposes (i.e., the choice of primitive operations, etc.) depends on the relative sophistication (entering capabilities and/or training) of the target population. (This level also depends on the level of behavioral detail that is of interest to the observer; see Section 5.) The more molar the level of problem representation and the more sophisticated the population, the more global or encompassing the atomic elements will be. Thus, while it might be important to reduce the addition algorithm to the basic facts in dealing with a population of 8-year-olds, this presumably would not be necessary with a group of skilled accountants. Similarly, the ability to read may be atomic for educated adults but not for equally bright 6-year-olds. (In Section 2.4, we shall see schematically how one might go about identifying the competencies underlying given problem domains, including how these competencies might be represented.)

The possibility of molar representation is especially important in dealing with GLOBAL PROBLEM DOMAINS and may make possible the identification of underlying competence that might not otherwise be feasible. Consider, for example, Piagetian psychology, where the emphasis is on broad epistemological concerns. In this case, the various developmental levels correspond to different target populations. (Roughly speaking, the process of equilibration, by which children progress from one stage to the next, corresponds to the learning CONTROL MECHANISM described in Section 3.) Since the emphasis is on those competencies that are common across a wide variety of TASK (problem) domains (e.g., conservation of number, seriation, space, etc.), particular content plays a distinctly subordinate role. The effectively operating problems, the ones that are most essential to Piaget's basic stages, are extremely molar. Distinctions attributable to specific knowledge (including such bothersome phenomena as horizontal decalage; see Chapter 15, Section 3) are ignored. Entire complexes of external and internal stimulation and behavior (GLOBAL STRUCTURES) may be treated as behavioral units. Thus, to Piaget it is not so important what the child actually says in responding to a number conservation task as is the reason that the child responds in this way. The type of reasoning involved is the essential observable.

It is sufficient in this case to represent underlying competence (rule sets) in correspondingly global terms. Any further refinement of rules, while possibly relevant to more specific behavior, would be irrelevant insofar as developmental stages (i.e., observables of interest to Piagetians) are concerned. The analogy here to the inappropriateness of addition by counting procedures (see above) in doing ordinary column addition is complete, even though the tasks obviously differ in degree of

clarity and/or complexity. (Similar considerations suggest the
potential applicability of structural representations in such
heretofore largely intractable areas as job analysis; see Chapter 15, Section 3.)

In addition to directly relevant rules of competence, EN-
TERING (AUXILIARY) CAPABILITIES (COMPETENCIES) also play an
important role in conducting problem-solving research. Specifically, it is necessary to assume some capabilities on the part
of the subjects in order that they and the experimenter may
communicate with one another. Where problem definition is not
of major concern, for example, one simply assumes (and takes
precautions to ensure) that subjects can encode problem statements perfectly (see ENCODE) and can similarly DECODE obtained
solutions. More generally, it is commonly assumed, although
rarely made explicit, that all subjects can understand the
DESCRIPTIVE LANGUAGE used by the experimenter to describe problems and/or competencies (rules) in the OBJECT LANGUAGE of the
problem domain. For example, the statement "xxBy → xB0y" can
be viewed as a description (in the descriptive language) of rule
r_1 (4), which itself is an entity in the object language. Generally speaking, logical-reasoning abilities also are commonly
assumed. Similarly, readers of this book will surely have the
ability to read and extrapolate from standard scientific English.

Unless a rule of competence is itself the subject of study,
nothing of behavioral significance is gained by detailing the
component operations and decisions. Hence, in experimental
studies, auxiliary competencies are simply assumed to be available to subjects in the target population (and to the experimenter). Nonetheless, such competencies play a critical role.
They constitute assumptions about the target population that,
if found empirically not to hold, invalidate any experimental
results based thereon.

In summary, I would like to emphasize the relativistic
nature of competence, something that should be kept in mind in
evaluating (and/or constructing) alternative accounts of semantic memory, language, and artificial intelligence generally.
Rules of competence depend not only on the problem domain involved but on the subject population and, insofar as detail is
concerned, also on the standards used by the observer to evaluate behavior. Thus, the limits imposed on the rules of competence by the way problems are represented, is not just a formal
consideration but may be behaviorally meaningful as well. If
one is interested solely in whether or not a problem solution
is correct, for example, then there is no need to consider, say,
LATENCY in representing competence. Similarly, where global
standards are used, the underlying rules of competence will be
global also. Moreover, as we shall see in the section on individual differences measurement, classes of competence accounts
may all make the same predictions on problems in a given domain.

They may be distinguished only by means of extra-domain considerations.

Universal Constraints: The constraints imposed specifically by the observer (depending on the level of behavioral detail of interest) and by the target population of subjects have their effect at the level of inputs, outputs, and individual rules (and structures). For purposes of modeling PERFORMANCE (see RULE ACCOUNT), or where single SOLUTION PROCEDURES otherwise suffice, these are the only constraints involved. Thus, for example, solution procedures for some simple problem domains (e.g., column subtraction problems) are well known and characteristic of easily defined populations (e.g., borrowing for most American school children). Most BEHAVIORAL OBJECTIVES in education are of this type (see PROBLEM DOMAIN; also Scandura, 1971a, 1977a).

The competence underlying many, perhaps most problem domains does not lend itself to representation in terms of single solution procedures. Even where a single procedure is known to exist, it may be impossible or impractical to identify one directly (e.g., the analyst may not be clever enough to pin it down, or he may not have the time, energy or money to do so). Alternatively, it may be possible to devise solution procedures that work, but that have little to do with any reasonable target population of humans. General resolution methods for theorem proving (e.g., Nilsson, 1971) are of this type.

Nonetheless, such domains frequently yield at least partially to modular approaches. In particular, it may be possible to represent the competence underlying given problem domains in terms of finite sets of rules, or modules, together with laws governing their interaction. There are, of course, any number of ways in which this might be accomplished. In artificial intelligence, for example, the major constraints involve efficiency considerations (as well as characteristics of the computers themselves).

In the structural learning theory, interactions among rules take place in a very specific way, a way that is assumed to be compatible with human cognition. (This promissory note is discharged in Section 4, and Part 3, this book.) In particular, in accounting for problem domains we assume that arbitrary rules, in the associated competence account (rule set), may operate on other rules (i.e., structures including rules), at arbitrary levels, and that derived rules in turn may be used in generating solutions to given problems (see HIGHER-ORDER RULE). Rules that operate on other rules in the process of generating a given problem solution are said to be of relatively higher-order (in that derivation). In ordinary discourse we shall speak loosely of *higher-order rules*.

The following discussion illustrates some of the kinds of higher-order rules that may underlie problem domains (also see

Scandura, 1973, Chapter 5) and helps to clarify the assumed laws of interaction. (The "academic grapevine" has it that this type of interaction has been partially formalized in an as yet unpublished paper in mathematical logic, but I have not seen the paper and cannot judge its immediate relevance.) Consider problem domain (2) once again, this time with respect to the rule set (competence account)

(6) $A = \{r_1, r_2, *\}$

where r_1 and r_2 are defined as in (4) above and $*$ is a (modified) HIGHER-ORDER COMPOSITION RULE that operates on pairs of COMPATIBLE RULES (defined below) that are either in A or can be derived from rules in A (as described below) and such that the RANGE of one of the rules is contained in the DOMAIN of the other. The higher-order rule $*$ generates COMPOSITES of its domain rules. For example, $*(r_1, r_2) = r_1 r_2$ where $r_1 r_2$ means apply r_1 and then r_2. Although binary composition in its usual sense does not satisfy the above domain conditions, the rule compatibility condition may be modified just sufficiently so that $*$ can operate on itself; e.g., $*(*,*) = **$ where $**$ operates on triples of rules--e.g., $**(r_1, r_2, r_1) = r_1 r_2 r_1$. (Optional Note: To accomplish this we might define the rule compatibility condition as follows: Two rules r and r', in or derivable from a given rule set, are said to be compatible if $\langle Ran_S\ r, S\ \rangle \subset Dom\ r'$ where $Ran_S\ r$ is Ran r restricted to type S, and S is a structure defined on the (finite) rule set (e.g., A) or on one of its derivatives (i.e., A^n) and/or on a given to-be-accounted for problem in the associated problem domain. In the illustrative case $\langle Ran_S\ *, S\ \rangle \subset Dom\ *$ [i.e., $*$ is compatible with itself and hence can be operated on by $*$] when S is a rule in A such that: (a) $S = r_1$ or r_2 if and only if $Ran_S\ *$ consists of composites of rules r_1 and r_2 or (b) $S = *$ if and only if $Ran_S\ *$ consists of composites of $*$. [Where r and r' are composites of r_1 and r_2, restrictions also must be placed on $Ran_S\ r$, relative to Ran r, if r and r' are to be compatible in this sense.] The mathematically inclined reader should notice that, unlike binary composition in mathematics, $*$ is not uniformly applicable. Its effective domain is restricted to pairs of rules [in A and derivative rule sets thereof; see (7) below] that are compatible in the above sense.)

Without loss of generality, A is said to account for problem domain (2) if for each problem (instance) in (2) (e.g., aaaaaB-B101) either there is a rule in A that generates the solution or such a rule may be derived by application of rules in A to other rules in A. For example, consider the pair aaaaaB-B101. In this case, $*$ applied to itself gives $*(*,*) = **$. In turn, double composition $**$ applied to r_2, r_1, and r_2 gives $**(r_2, r_1, r_2) = r_2 r_1 r_2$). Finally, $r_2 r_1 r_2$ applied to aaaaaB gives

$$aaaaaB \xrightarrow{r_2} aaBl \xrightarrow{r_1} aB0l \xrightarrow{r_2} B10l$$

More generally, a rule set R = R' is said to ACCOUNT for a problem (instance) if there is a finite number n such that there is a rule in R^n that generates the solution. R^n is a rule set that is obtained recursively by letting all the rules in R^{n-1} operate on the given problem and the Rules in R in all allowable ways. For example, with respect to (6) we get

$$(7) \quad A = \{*, r_1, r_2\}$$
$$A^2 = A(A) = \{*, r_1, r_2, **, r_1r_1, r_1r_2, r_2r_1, r_2r_2\}$$
$$A^3 = A^2(A) = \{*, \ldots, r_2r_2, ***, r_1r_1r_1, \ldots, r_2r_2r_2\}$$
$$\cdot$$
$$\cdot$$
$$\cdot$$
$$A^n = A^{n-1}(A)$$

With respect to the instance aaaaaB-B10l, for example, the rule $r_2r_1r_2$ in A^3 serves this purpose. As a second example, notice that rule r_2r_2 in A^2 accounts for the pair aaaB-B1l.

Although this formulation illustrates the general mode of interaction, it is overly restrictive. Specifically, newly generated rules in A^n may be applied only to rules in A; hence the notation $A^n(A)$. The following more general form of rule interaction allows for the derivation of new domain rules (as seems to be involved in cognition; see Chapter 6).

$$(8) \quad A^n(A^m)$$

Rule set (8) includes every rule that can be derived by applying rules in A^n to rules in A^m. Formulations (7) and (8) are mathematically equivalent to (3) and (4) insofar as computing power relative to problem domain (2) is concerned.[4] Hence, in one sense we have nothing new. Mathematical equivalence, however, does not necessarily (or even often) imply psychological equivalence. For one thing, as noted above, * is not universally applicable. In general, people may be able to compose some things but not others. Even more important, whereas (7) and (8) are assumed to be compatible with the to-be-postulated cognitive CONTROL MECHANISM, arbitrary composition of Rules r_1 and r_2, as in (4), is not. Empirical support for both contentions are reported in Chapter 5. Cognitive control mechanisms, corresponding to the modes of rule interaction implicit in (7) and

---

[4]Given the simplicity of this rule set, it is easy to avoid composition (*) altogether by allowing recursion on r_1 and r_2. Thus, assuming suitable decision-making capabilities, the rule denoted

$$\text{START} \underset{r_2}{\overset{r_1}{\circlearrowleft}} \text{STOP}$$

has the same computing power as the collection of sets A^n (n = 1, 2, ...).

(8) are assumed to be compatible with the to-be-postulated cognitive CONTROL MECHANISM, arbitrary composition of Rules r_1 and r_2, as in (4), is not. Empirical support for both contentions are reported in Chapter 5. Cognitive control mechanisms, corresponding to the modes of rule interaction implicit in (7) and (8), are discussed below in Sections 4.1 *(Goal Switching)* and 4.2 *(Extensions)*, respectively, on cognitive processes.

Formulations (7) and (8) also are overly simple in the sense that composition is not the only type of higher-order rule that might be included in a rule set. For example, consider the higher-order rule

(9) $r_a \Rightarrow r_b$

This rule operates on (certain) rules involving a's and converts them into corresponding rules involving b's (e.g., $r_a \Rightarrow r_b(r_1)$ = x'x'By → x'BOy where x' is a string of b's). The addition of just this one rule to rule set A would double its generating power to include an equivalent set of problems (instances) involving b's (along with those involving a's). Further, every time a new rule involving a's is added to the rule set, overall generating power is increased to include not only the corresponding problems involving a's but a parallel set of problems involving b's. (Concrete examples of "analogy" and other non-composition higher-order rules are given in Chapters 3, 4, 5, and 11.)

In talking about rule sets we have glossed over a number of questions, one of the most basic of which is how STRUCTURES fit in. In brief, structures are implicit in the rules. They may be defined as those complexes of entities that satisfy conditions contained in the competence rules. These conditions effectively define the essential characteristics of specific structures. (The neutral term "complex" is used to emphasize that the structures are arbitrary as to type; they may be simple sets, ordered sets, semi-groups, or whatever; cf. Scandura, 1973, Chapter 6; Chapter 7, this book.)

Structures are the things on which rules operate. As will become clear in Section 5, the conditions that define structures (and hence the structures themselves) must be ATOMIC if they are to provide an adequate basis for assessing behavior potential. They correspond roughly to (generalized) "chunks" in Miller's (1956) sense and to "frames" as the term has been used by Minsky (1975). In the case of frames, however, the structures typically are not atomic but rather refer only to global cognitive ideals. They cannot, therefore, be used for assessment purposes (e.g., see Chapter 15, Section 3).

In the case of SIMPLE RULES, the defined structures correspond to encoded STIMULI or, more generally, to SUBSTIMULI (ATOMIC STRUCTURES) in the sense of Scandura (1973, Chapter 10;

also see Chapter 7, this book). In the case of higher-order
rules, the defined structures include the complexes of rules
being operated upon. Relative to higher-order composition rules,
for example, the corresponding structures include pairs of compatible rules. More generally, some complexes of rules (and
other elements) may recur in a variety of contexts and, thereby,
may take on a distinctive character. These are the structures
that are frequently elaborated and discussed in the semantic
memory literature where they are called semantic nets or rela-
tional/propositional networks (cf. Chapter 15, Sections 2 and 3).

The basic difference between DEGENERATE (atomic) structures
and (nondegenerate) structures, that include nondegenerate (nonatomic) rules, is that the elements in the former are ATOMIC.
They may be operated upon but never themselves operate (on anything). The digits, the columns, and the partial sums in the
addition problem (structure)

    457
    +273

are atomic in this sense. As noted above, higher-order rules
play a crucial role in defining (nondegenerate) structures of
the latter type. For an example that deals with trigonometric
identities and the Pythagorean Theorem see Chapter 15, Section
3. (Note: What counts as atomic is a relative matter, of
course, and depends on the level and type of detail that one is
interested in. In the above addition problem, for example, the
relations among the various digit locations could be expressed
in terms of rules, say, for generating new locations from given
ones. Moreover, such rules might be applicable in arbitrary
arrays, not only with respect to column addition problems. But,
they would likely be of interest, for example, only where attention is focused on the processes by which such arrays are
constructed.)

Another matter that has been glossed over concerns the possible role of a problem (instance) itself in the derivation of
a rule that accounts for it. Although it was mentioned only
incidentally in the above discussion, rules may act on instances
as well as on other rules. In effect, any given instance,
strictly speaking, is an integral part of the rule set characterizing underlying competence. The rationale for this inclusion will become clear in the discussion of corresponding cognitive processes (Section 4). (In brief, the problem givens and
solutions in the instances correspond to problems (givens) and
goals, respectively. During problem solving, givens and goals
are assumed to be active in the human information processor
along with some finite set of rules.) The importance of instances in competence accounts is also alluded to again in the
discussion of rule selection.

2.3 FURTHER COMMENTS

Semantics: The reader should not be misled by the syntactic character of our examples. In principle, the proposed type of competence theory can be used to handle meaning as well (cf. Scandura, 1973, Chapter 7, Section 6; Suppes, 1974).

Thus, for example, one could extend problem domain (2) to include a partial language, L, for describing rules in $A^n(A^m)$. Specifically, correspondences (input-output pairs) could be established between such expressions as "xxBy" and their symbolic meanings (in the object language L_O). In the case of "xxBy", for example, the meaning is the domain of rule r_1 (i.e., the set of all strings containing an even number of a's, followed by a B, followed by a string of 0's and 1's). Correspondingly, the meaning of the expression "xxBy $\to$ xB0y" is rule r_1; that is, the above domain, the operation that maps strings in the domain into corresponding strings in the range, and the range (i.e., the set of strings associated with the meaning of xB0y). Correspondences of this type, between symbol expressions and meanings, could presumably be generalized and expressed as rules of interpretation. Such rules would operate on expressions and generate structures that represent their meanings.

In a similar manner, strings involving a's in the object language could, in turn, be treated as elements that denote still more concrete objects. For example, each syntactic rule in L_O might denote a semantic rule that operates on unarranged piles of concrete objects (e.g., sets of 3-inch wooden dowels) and regroups them as a base 2 concrete embodiment of the corresponding binary numeral (e.g., see Dienes, 1960; Scandura, 1971b). For example, the syntactic rule $r_2r_1r_2$, as applied to the input aaaaaB gives

$$\text{aaaaaB} \xrightarrow{r_2} \text{a'a'Bl}_a \xrightarrow{r_1} \text{a"B0}_a\text{l}_a \xrightarrow{r_2} \text{Bl}_a\text{"}_a\text{0}_a\text{l}_a$$

where primes and subscripts are used to indicate that the meanings of the a's depend on the context in which the a's appear. The corresponding semantic rule $rs_2rs_1rs_2$ regroups objects (e.g., five 3-inch dowels) at each step into sets of size 2^n, where n is the number of 0's and/or 1's in the corresponding syntactic input. Thus

$$///// \xrightarrow{rs_2} //\ // \not\phi \xrightarrow{rs_1} ////\ \circ\ \not\phi \xrightarrow{rs_2} /\!/\!/\!/\ \circ\ \not\phi$$

Notice that the a's in the initial input (aaaaaB) denote single ($2^0 = 1$) objects (e.g., 3-inch dowels). Each a' in the string derived by application of rs_2 denotes two ($2^1 = 2$) objects and the l_a to the right of B denotes one single element set, denoted $\not\phi$ (e.g., a 3-inch dowel with a rubber band around it). In the third string, the a" denotes four ($2^2 = 4$) ungrouped objects and the "0_a'" to the right of B denotes no sets containing two objects (denoted ⌀). Similarly, the 1_a" just to the right of B in the final output denotes one set of four ($2^2 = 4$) objects (denoted ~~///~~).

In short, each input/output element (whether terminal or intermediary), as well as each of the rules in our syntactic example, may be assigned a semantic meaning. The a's denote piles of objects, the sizes of the piles depending on the number of digits to the right of B. The digits 0 and 1, similarly, denote sets of size 2^n (e.g., groups of dowels with rubber bands around them). The "B" serves a strictly syntactic purpose, similar to that of the comma in ordinary English, and makes it easier to interpret each string.

Global Competence: A few additional remarks are also in order concerning global problem domains (e.g., Piagetian con- servation tasks, logical reasoning, value-laden decision-making). Generally speaking, the competencies underlying such domains may be relevant to a wide variety of different, more specific prob- lem domains. In this sense, they are more aptly thought of as general characteristics of given target populations or cultures rather than as competencies associated with specific content. Logical reasoning and cultural values, for example, tend to have this characteristic, in that they may enter into a wide variety of more specific behavior, and are constrained primarily by the population "culture" (including such normative factors as sex, stage of development, ethnic heritage, etc.).

In effect, molar competencies tend to be at once relatively independent of and potentially relevant to particular content domains. Once identified, competencies of this type might well play a role in competence accounts of a wide range of more spe- cific problem domains, either by becoming an integral part of such accounts and/or by imposing additional constraints on their form.

As noted above and in Chapter 1, for example, global/molar competence is analogous to Piagetian epistemic analysis. Epi- stemic competence is complementary to that emphasized in this book in that it deals primarily with general features of broader domains and populations and not with unique or idiosyncratic aspects of particular problem domains. Once specified, however, global/epistemic competence, for example that associated with various developmental stages, could provide additional con- straints on structural analysis. Although it is beyond the scope of this book to consider the implications in detail, as shown in the next section, such constraints could help to in- crease the cognitive verity of competence accounts. Notice also that many higher-order rules, especially simple ones, tend to have this global character. Thus, for example, higher-order composition and analogy rules appear to play a central role in a wide variety of specific problem domains (cf. Chapters 3, 4, 5, 6, 11, 13, and 14 of this book). Where attention is focused on broader domains, therefore, the scope of the domains of such rules might be increased accordingly. (As shown in Section 5, however, such changes could not be detected by testing within the scope of any specific domain.)

2.4 STRUCTURAL ANALYSIS OF PROBLEM DOMAINS

Specifying the form that a rule set must have provides useful information. In fact, form together with examples are about all that are provided by contemporary competence theories. As previously mentioned, however, specifying the way in which competence is to be represented tells only part of the story. Because there are arbitrarily many different problem (content) domains, a complete theory of competence must include a systematic method for identifying the competence underlying any given domain. (Note: Although global competencies may be common over a variety of problem domains and subject populations, Piaget's work clearly shows that even logical reasoning, for example, is constrained by developmental level.)

At the present time, we are a long way from having developed a strictly algorithmic approach to STRUCTURAL ANALYSIS. It may even be impossible to develop a method that would be adequate for analyzing arbitrary domains (e.g., such as natural languages, cf. Chomsky, 1957). In general, moreover, it is unlikely that any rule set will be completely adequate (just as in linguistics there are no perfect grammars for natural languages).

Nonetheless, the population and universal constraints described above tend to force structural analysis in certain directions so that some progress has been made toward systematization. The rule sets described in Chapters 3, 4, and 14, for example, were identified in a quasi-systematic and to some extent self-correcting manner that takes higher-order relationships (universal constraints) into account. As presently practiced, however, the behavioral viability of any given structural analysis (e.g., see Chapters 11 and 13) still depends largely on the perspicuity of the structural analyst/observer, and specifically on his familiarity with both the problem domain and the relevant culture (developmental level, school curriculum, etc.) of the target population.

The basic method of structural analysis is described in the next two sections, both as it is practiced today and as it might be refined and extended. The emphasis is on those aspects of structural analysis that can be objectified and tied in with the aforementioned constraints. Some feeling for the intuitive judgements that need to be made in particular situations can be gleaned from the more concrete analyses reported in Chapters 3, 4, and 14. For illustrative purposes, the present discussion

takes place in the context of the following "symbol" problem
domain

(10) $\{xB\text{-}By\ |\ x =$ string a's; $y =$ binary numeral (a's)$\}$
   $\cup\ \{x'B\text{-}By'\ |\ x' =$ string b's; $y' =$ binary numeral (b's)$\}$
   $\cup\ \{wT\text{-}Tz\ |$ number a's in $w =$ number b's in $z\}$
   $\cup\ X$ (a complementary partially defined "fuzzy" set
      involving a's, b's)

The first step in analyzing a problem domain is to decide
on a suitable way to represent the problem givens and solutions
associated with the domain. In general, the representation
chosen must satisfy two types of constraints. One, the representation must make it possible to distinguish those aspects of
the environment (i.e., problem givens and solutions) that are
of interest to the observer. Two, the elements, relations, and/
or operations used to represent the observables must be atomic,
both perceptually and decoding-wise, relative to the target
population. In the present case, the symbols "a", "b", "B",
"0", and "1" serve as the basic elements and the relevant concepts (expressible as relations) include such things as "to the
left/right of", the whole numbers, even (number), odd, and binary numeral. Unless problem definition and/or decoding skills
are of direct interest, which they are not here, these elements
and relations may be assumed to be encodable and/or decodable
by the subjects in question. Such skills are said to be ATOMIC.
With at most a few minutes instruction/review (e.g., on binary
numerals) these problems and solutions are perfectly understandable to readers of this book so we take this as our target
population.

None of this, of course, says how one might choose an
appropriate representation in general. At present, I know of
no answer to this important question other than to use one's
own good judgement. In general, this will depend on what things
are important to the observer and whether those things are likely to be atomic with respect to the target population. Where
questions arise, one can check the atomicity assumptions informally, preferably with weaker (performing) members of the target
population. Experience suggests that this is a relatively
straightforward task where the observer/analyst shares a common
"culture" with members of the target population. Where this is
not the case, the observer would do well to determine directly
what the targeted subjects can do. As Piaget's well known research shows, for example, it is often difficult for the adult
to recapture the conceptual innocence of the child.

Although empirical observation of human subjects may play
an important role (at several points) in structural analysis,
the purpose of such observation is quite different than in the
case of traditional information processing theories. Experi-

mental data of the sort motivated in the latter case, not only
are not necessary but may be seriously misleading (with respect
to our goals). Whereas traditional information processing theories are concerned with accounting for actual, though average,
human behavior (see Chapter 1), competence is concerned with
IDEALIZED PROTOTYPES (also see COMPETENCE RULE). In order to
provide a useful basis for assessing individual knowledge these
prototypes must, in addition, be represented in terms of atomic
components (see Section 5).

   To summarize, the main purposes of behavioral observation,
insofar as structural analysis is concerned, are to identify
prototypic rules (see below), with such things as memory and
processing capacity "partialed" out, and levels of representation, that act in atomic fashion. Although discussion of the
issue is postponed until Chapter 15, the present form of the
Structural Learning Theory (like mathematics) is neutral with
respect to the issue of analog (continuous) versus discrete
(verbal/symbolic/propositional) representations (e.g., Kosslyn
& Pomerantz, 1977). In brief, although continuous quantities
can be represented in discrete terms, this is not the main
consideration. Depending on what aspect of what is being represented, either discrete or analog representations may allow processing that is more efficient and/or compatible with human
capabilities. Nothing in the theory disallows either form of
representation; the same principles apply in either case.

   The second step in structural analysis is to select a representative (finite) sample of instances from the problem domain.
The sample need not be exhaustive, although in practice it is
desirable to include all problems (instances) that the analyst/
observer deems both important and in some sense qualitatively
different (from other problems). Normally, a sample should
include at least one problem-solution pair (problem) from each
definitive subtype (subclass) of the domain.

   Although it is beyond the scope of this book to detail
appropriate procedures by which such selection might be accomplished, the representation chosen might play an obvious role.
Thus, the sample of problem-solution pairs might be chosen so
as to include all of the basic elements (e.g., a, b, B, 0, and
1) and relations (e.g., odd, even). In the present case, suppose we select

       aaaaaB-B101
       aaB-B10
       bbbB-B11
       bbbbB-B100
       aaT-Tbb

The third step is to devise methods for solving the sampled
problems that are consistent with how idealized subjects in the
target population might be expected to solve them. Thus, in

general, the solution method associated with a given problem (instance) will account for (sub)classes of problems in the domain, not just the sampled problem. For example, the emphasis in this case might be on how particularly successful subjects in the population solve the problems. As noted previously, prototypic solution methods used by individuals may be more significant than experimentally derived procedures that account for average behavior. The theory, however, is relatively neutral as to how the solution methods are actually identified: depending on the circumstances, simple introspection, subject matter intuition, informal observation of typical subjects, or more systematic experimental methods may serve a useful role. One major constraint is that all components must be atomic relative to the subject population. As we shall see in Section 5, this constraint plays a crucial role in assessing the behavior potential of individual subjects in the target population (i.e., in operationalizing individual knowledge). (Such solution methods need not satisfy the constraints imposed on RULES [i.e., where new subrules may not be both generated and used in a single application], as long as all rules in some derived rule account are RULES [see below].)

Since the inclusiveness of atomic units varies directly with population sophistication, the complexity of procedures cannot be determined in the abstract. For example, on the one hand, it might be difficult to detail the competence underlying a particular job analysis (in training) in sufficient detail for an unselected group of individuals. On the other hand, it might be a relatively straightforward undertaking for an adequately prepared group of trainees.

Admittedly, the judgements required impose a heavy responsibility on the structural analyst. If we are to deal rigorously with both specific problem domains and individual behavior, however, I see no viable alternative. Hopefully, as we identify more and more constraints and subsequently incorporate them into the method of structural analysis, progressively less intuitive judgement will be involved. Some progress has already been made in this direction (e.g., Chapters 3, 4, 11, and 14).

Given the five instances above, of course, the analysis is almost trivial. On the assumption that rules r_1 and r_2 are atomic, the number of feasible solution rules (i.e., solution rules that are potentially compatible with population requirements) is sharply limited (see RULES OF COMPETENCE). One feasible set of solution rules can be represented

(11) $K = \{r_2 r_1 r_2,\ r_1 r_2,\ r_2' r_2',\ r_1' r_1' r_2',\ r_{ab}\}$

where r_1, r_2 are as above, r_1' and r_2' parallel r_1 and r_2 with a's replaced by b's, and r_{ab} replaces each a to the left of T in the input with one b to the right of T in the output.

Clearly, K accounts for some of the problems in problem domain (10), but not all of them. In particular, K consists exclusively of special purpose rules (whose domains are highly restricted in scope) that apply only to the sampled problems themselves. The rule set, for example, does not account for bbbbbB-B101. Such limitations can be overcome in two basic ways. One can either add new solution rules or search for more basic rule sets from which both original and new solution rules may be derived. (Such rule sets have been called *innate bases,* Scandura, 1973.) The decision as to which direction to go will depend on such criteria as atomicity, assumed entering capabilities, and scope of the intended problem domain. For example, if a problem domain appears limited to the originally sampled problems, plus a small number of additional types (with one solution rule per type), it would likely be sufficient and most convenient to simply add the corresponding new solution rules.

With more complex problem domains it will ordinarily be necessary to take the latter route (step four). In order to identify an innate basis for the initial (solution) rule set, the main things to look for are parallels among the initial solution rules. The parallels may involve identical components, analogies (e.g., identical forms, different components), greater/lesser generality (e.g., of domains), and possibly other as yet unidentified relationships among the rules (involving their component operations, domains/decisions, and/or overall forms). These parallels are typically reflective of higher-order rules. The identification of such higher-order rules, in turn, often makes it possible to specify the simpler rules (structures) on which the former must operate (i.e., by "backtracking" from the solution rules; cf. Scandura, 1973, especially p. 99). For example, notice the central role in rule set K played by composition and the fact that all of the solution rules are sequences consisting of a common set of simpler rules. Recalling the generative capacity of generalized composition (*), we get

(12) $K' = \{*, r_1, r_2, r_1', r_2', r_{ab}\}$

Rule set K' serves as an innate basis for K. That is, $K \subseteq (K')^n$ for some finite number n (Scandura, 1973). By analogy to equations (7), it is easy to see that $(K')^n$ contains all allowable m-fold composites $(m \leq n)$ of $*$, r_{ab}, r_1, r_2, r_1', r_2', and r_{ab} (e.g., $r_2 r_2$, $r_2' r_1' r_2'$).

Rule set K' is clearly far more powerful than K in that it accounts for more of problem domain (10). It accounts for bbbbbB-B101, for example, since solution rule $r_2' r_1' r_2'$ can be derived from K'. Nonetheless, K' still has important inadequacies. For example, it does not even account for as simple a problem as bbT-Taa.

Noticing that rules r_1' and r_2' are directly analogous to r_1 and r_2, respectively, potential generating power can be further increased by introducing the higher-order rule $r_a \Rightarrow r_b$

which operates on rules involving a's and generates corresponding rules involving b's.   In so doing, rules r_1' and r_2' can be
eliminated as redundant.   This gives the second generation
innate basis.

$$K'' = \{*,\ r_1,\ r_2,\ r_{ab},\ r_a \Rightarrow r_b\}$$

(Note: $r_a \Rightarrow r_b$ corresponds to "substitution" as used by logicians
but need not apply universally to all rules involving strings
of a's.   The specific problem domain and/or rule set in question
may impose additional constraints on the domain of this rule
just as it does with the higher-order composition rule [*] above.
For this reason, if no other, $r_a \Rightarrow r_b$ and * may not be equated
with their mathematical counterparts.)   A simple check (step
five) will show that K'' not only accounts for everything that
K' does but that it accounts for all problems of the form zT-Tw
(where z is a string of b's and w is an equal string of a's).
Further, the addition of any new rule involving a's is tanta-
mount to also adding a corresponding rule involving b's.   In
effect, rule set K'' makes a measurable dent in set X in (10),
the complementary (i.e., nonoverlapping), only partially defined
set involving a's and b's.

Along with the overall increase in potential computing
(generating) power obtained in this manner, notice that greater
simplicity of individual rules also has been achieved.   Whereas individual rules in K are composed of several atomic (unitary) rules, those in K'' are all atomic.

Incidentally, notice that higher-order rules need be no
more complicated than simple ones; indeed, they may be quite
simple (in the colloquial sense).   In effect, one can envision
extending an analysis of this sort far enough (given enough
detail concerning the problem domain) so as to ensure compatibility with the most naive subject populations.   All but the
most confirmed environmentalists believe that people come into
the world "wired in" with some capabilities (instincts, general
arousal levels, basic perceptual capabilities, and the like).[5]
Following the present thesis to its natural conclusion, it is
my current position that such capabilities provide the innate
bases on which knowledge grows by interacting with the environment (see Chapters 13, 14, and 15).   (Note, however, that this
position is neutral as regards maturation.   It is certainly
reasonable to suppose that new and/or modified capabilities may
come about as a result of physical maturation, rather than
learning.   The present theory is silent on the issue.)

On the other hand, notice that the more complex rules in K
have more *direct computing power* than those in K'' in the sense

---

[5]In the structural learning theory, such capabilities are assumed to be
over and above the control mechanism of the section on cognitive mechanisms,
which is hypothesized to determine the way in which available rules interact.

that they can be used directly (i.e., without the intermediate
generation of new rules) to solve more complex problems (cf.
Scandura, 1973). (Note: In the strict sense of Scandura, 1973,
K does not quite have more computing power than K" since r_1 and
r_2 in K" [but not in K] account for the special cases B-B0 and
aB-B1, respectively.) In Section 4 on cognitive mechanisms, we
shall see that direct computing power corresponds to the capability of responding in problem situations directly on the basis
of available knowledge/rules (as opposed to first having to
generate new rules; i.e., *rules* in the restricted sense of this
book).

In general, the appropriate level of rule analysis, for a
given subject population, is one at which all rules are either
atomic or uniformly available to members of the population (or
at which no further behavioral/observable distinctions can be
made within the scope of the problem domain; see Section 5 on
assessing behavior potential). Accordingly, structural analysis
is to some extent *self-correcting*. Thus, one could start with
a variety of different samples of problems from problem domain
(10) (ignoring set X). As long as the sample is equally representative, and under similar assumptions of atomicity, etc., one
would have a good chance of arriving eventually at the same rule
set K". (The interested reader may wish to check the sample
aaaaB-B100, aaaB-B11, bbbbbbB-B110, and aaaT-Tbbb. In this case,
the initial rule set is

$$\{r_1r_1r_2,\ r_2r_2,\ r_1'r_2'r_2',\ r_{ab}\}.)$$

Structural analysis also is robust with respect to types
of solution rules. Irrespective of which problem sample is
selected, for example, suppose that the initial set of solution
rules had consisted of Rule (3), an analogous recursive rule
involving b's, and r_{ab}. In this case, Rule (3) solves any problem in SUBDOMAIN

$$\{xB\text{-}By \mid x = \text{string a's; } y = \text{binary numeral (a's)}\}$$

the analogous rule solves any problem in

$$\{x'B\text{-}By' \mid x' = \text{string b's; } y' = \text{binary numeral (b's)}\}$$

and r_{ab} solves any problem in

$$\{wT\text{-}Tz \mid \text{number a's in } w = \text{number b's in } z\}$$

The rule set is equally limited, however, with respect to the
complementary, "fuzzy" subdomain X. For example, the rule set
cannot account for problem bbT-Taa.

In this case, the parallels between Rule (3) and its analog

involving b's again leads to higher-order rule $r_a \Rightarrow r_b$ (by which the latter can be derived from the former). Eliminating redundant rules, the introduction of this higher-order rule gives the innate basis

$$\{\text{Rule (3)}, \; r_{ab}, \; r_a \Rightarrow r_b\}$$

This rule set is comparable in generating power to K" with one major exception. The direct availability of *, r_1, and r_2 in the case of K", rather than just Rule (3), allows more flexibility. For example, in the case of K", the addition of new rules r_1'' and r_2'', say, involving c's (but otherwise parallel to r_1 and r_2) could provide a sufficient basis for solving any parallel problem involving c's. In effect, the domain of * may include pairs of rules other than just those involving a's or b's whereas Rule (3) (together with $r_a \Rightarrow r_b$) is limited to the latter types exclusively. The above rule set can be made equivalent to rule set K" by breaking recursive Rule (3) into its components and adding a higher-order "recursion" rule (Rec), that operates on pairs of rules whose domains are both disjoint and exhaustive (as are r_1 and r_2) and generates corresponding recursive rules.

$$\{\text{Rec}, \; r_1, \; r_2, \; r_{ab}, \; r_a \Rightarrow r_b\}$$

For present purposes it is not necessary to detail Rule Rec but simply to recognize that it would not be difficult to devise such a rule and that Rec is equivalent to * on problem domain (10).

In effect, in addition to illustrating the self-correcting nature of structural analysis, this example illustrates a second important principle. Within a given problem domain it may be *impossible* to distinguish behaviorally between alternative accounts such as rule set K" and that above, even where they might otherwise be quite different. As shown in Section 5, in order to make such distinctions the problem domain used for reference (testing) purposes must be modified, refined, and/or extended.

2.5   EXTENSION OF THE BASIC METHOD

The preceding discussion sloughs over several matters that have considerable practical as well as theoretical importance.

Rule Selection: The possibility was mentioned (in Section 2.1) that one problem (input) in a domain might be associated with more than one distinguishable solution. In this case, the corresponding competence account would have to include rules for generating each of the (finite number of) distinguishable solutions. In the simplest case, two or more solution rules would be associated with the same problem input, each generating a different solution.

In the previous section, however, no two of the (problem-solution) instances selected by the observer/analyst involved the same problem input. To each input, there was one and only one solution associated with it. This does not have to be the case. An observer may for some purposes want to distinguish among alternative solutions. Thus, for example, in multiplication by powers of ten (10, 100, 1000, etc.), the arithmetic teacher might want to distinguish between arithmetic products generated via the usual multiplication algorithm and via short-cut procedures for multiplying by 10, 100, etc. The basis on which such distinctions are made is immaterial; the distinctions may involve speed as well as accuracy, or written traces of the processes used (as when the teacher has pupils show their work). The important thing is that the alternative solutions must be distinguishable and represented in terms of ATOMIC DECODING CAPABILITIES. These representations, for example, may involve latency considerations and/or analog/continuity as well as discrete/verbal/propositional considerations (see Chapter 15). This requirement is essential if desired distinctions are to be observed reliably.

It is equally important to notice that the observer may simultaneously also be interested in instances consisting of individual problem inputs and *all* of their solutions collectively (i.e., less detailed representations of solutions). Thus, in addition to being able to distinguish between different solutions, the observer at another level may also be interested in simply determining whether (any) solution has been generated, irrespective of type. (Note: In the present formulation, observable solutions [indeed problem inputs as well] are effectively equivalence classes of solutions [inputs] [cf. Scandura, 1968/69, 1970, 1972b], equivalence classes defined by the representation selected by the observer. What higher-level representations [as above] do is to allow the observer to represent solutions at more than one level simultaneously. In this regard, it is worth emphasizing, that in the structural learning theory, the level of observation may be more global than the atomic entities used to represent solutions, but not vice versa.)

This dual concern with specific solutions, on the one hand, and generalized (more abstract) solutions, on the other, imposes new constraints on competence. In particular, it is not sufficient in a complete competence account (rule set) to allow for generating each of the alternative specific solutions. Thus, in the case of an instance involving a problem input and a generalized solution, one of the specific solutions will be generated but it will not be possible on the basis of the competence account to tell which one(s). A complete account ought not only provide solution rules for generating each of the possible solutions but also a rule for determining when each can be used (for details, see Chapter 6).

For present purposes, the important point is that parallel
pairs (or triples, etc.) of solution rules may account for corresponding problems. In the previous section, for example, two
alternative kinds of solution rules were identified for solving
a variety of problems in symbol domain (10). Thus, the problem
aaaaaB-B101, for example, might variously be solved by Rule (3),
$r_2 r_1 r_2$, or a direct association (DEGENERATE RULE) connecting the
problem (aaaaaB) with its solution (B101). Analogously, the
problem bbB-B10 might be solved via the b analog of Rule (3),
$r_1 r_2$, or a direct association.

Where parallels among various (sampled) pairs of rules are
observed, HIGHER-ORDER SELECTION RULES may be constructed, that
operate on a domain including such rule pairs (triples, etc.)
and select one among them. (In general, of course, higher rules
may allow simultaneously for more than one process, such as
derivation and selection.) In the above, for example, the
selection rule "Choose the simplest rule" (e.g., the rule that
has most properties in common with the given problem) might
suffice.

Although the type of selection involved in the above example may seem rather artificial, nothing essential (other than
the particular rules) would change if the alternative pairs of
rules, and the solutions they generate, referred to alternative
types of activities (e.g., cooperative versus competitive games),
and the selection rules referred to motivational tendencies to
select one or another type of activity. In effect, selection
rules provide a basis for explaining what is commonly referred
to as *motivation* (cf. Scandura, 1971a, 1973, Chapter 8).

As with other higher-order rules, there is as yet no systematic method for identifying selection rules. About all one
can say, in general, is that the structural analyst must be generally sensitive to differences in the ways subjects solve given
problems and to parallels among such differences. In the case
of selection rules it also is worth noting that the critical
parallels are not among individual solution rules but among pairs
(triples, etc.) of solution rules associated with given problems.
Hence, the parallels may involve identical relationships between
the individual pairs of rules, or analogies or other relationships among the pairs.

Breaking Problems into Subproblems: A second major concern
has to do with whether the sampled problems are UNITARY (ATOMIC)
in the sense that they can be solved either by a rule in the
associated rule set or by a solution rule derivable directly via
the rule set. In effect, the sampled problems in a domain, from
which the corresponding rule set is derived as above, are atomic
in this sense. Atomic problems, then, represent the important
types. All other problems in the problem domain (DERIVATIVE
PROBLEMS) can be represented as finite sequences of the atomic
problems. In the present context, for example, the problem

(instance) aaaaaB-B101 would be unitary, whereas the problem
aaaaaB-2 would not be. This statement would seem to hold even
(especially) if we are told that the solution "2" denotes the
number of 1's in the binary numeral representation of the number
of a's. It seems more natural to think of the latter problem
in terms of the pair (sequence): aaaaaB-B101, B101-2. Thus, for
example, if presented with aaaaaB and asked to find the number
of 1's in the binary numeral representation (of the number of
a's), most people would break the problem into a pair of subproblems: first find the binary numeral representation, and
then count the number of 1's (in the binary numeral).

Because the problem aaaaaB-2, and the corresponding pair
of subproblems, may both be included in a given problem domain,
and because the relationship between them may be shared between
other problems (and subproblems), it is natural to think in terms
of rules that operate on problems and generate other problems
(e.g., pairs of subproblems). For example, any problem of the
form xB-z (number of 1's in the binary numeral representation
of the number of a's in x), where x is a string of a's, or of
the form x'B-z, where x' is a string of b's, may be broken,
respectively, into the pairs ⟨ xB-By; By-z ⟩ and ⟨ x'B-By; By-z ⟩.
The rules operating in this case have the effect of introducing
binary numeral representations of the number of elements (e.g.,
a's or b's) in given strings (i.e., By) as explicit outputs/
inputs. Notice that these outputs/inputs are implicit in the
definition of given problems (i.e., z is the number of 1's in
the binary numeral representation of the number of elements in
some string). In discussing cognition, we shall see that such
rules correspond to problem definition rules, or rules for
breaking PROBLEMS (in the cognitive sense, see Glossary) into
subproblems.

In order to devise a competence account, that takes subproblems into account, careful attention must be given to the
procedures that idealized subjects in the target population
might use to solve the sampled problems. Thus, in step three
of the previous section, the analyst must pay particular attention to whether knowledgeable (prototypic) subjects tend to
solve parts of given problems, before attacking other parts, or
whether they solve them as a whole (e.g., proceeding without
significant pauses once a problem solution process has been
initiated). (In view of the above comments on rule selection,
of course, idealized subjects might be able to do both.) The
former strategy corresponds to breaking problems into subproblems.
The latter corresponds to sudden (not necessarily immediate) insight. As with higher-order rules, parallels in the ways various problems are broken down are viewed as manifestations of
underlying subproblem rules. (Rules that break problems into
sequences of subproblems are called SUBPROBLEM RULES.) In the
present case, presumably, these parallels will depend on the

nature of the problems involved (e.g., common elements or forms, etc.).

Because higher-order derivation/selection rules and sub-problem (PROBLEM DEFINITION) rules may both enter into an account of any given problem, let me try to make the distinction between them sharper and more operational. In attacking a problem, where knowledgeable (idealized) subjects attempt to derive total solution procedures before actually applying them, higher-order derivation rules are assumed to be operating (in the present theory). On the other hand, where such subjects actually solve part of a problem before attempting to derive a solution procedure for the rest, subproblem rules are involved. Given the problem aaaaaB-2, for example, a subject of the former type would attack the task by generating a "binary numeral" rule (e.g., Rule 3) and combining it (implicitly or explicitly) with a "digit counting" rule before actually applying any part of the derived rule to the input aaaaaB. A subject of the latter type, on the other hand, would first generate a binary numeral rule, then apply it, yielding B101, before attempting to find the number of 1's in the binary numeral. (Note: Higher-order rules may be needed to generate solution rules for given subproblems.)

It should be clear that either type of account may be simulated by the other so that there are no differences between them with regard to generative power. The advantages of using both types stem from greater flexibility insofar as accounting for more of the detail of human cognition (e.g., see Section 5, Stage Equivalence), and not just end results.

Structures: As mentioned earlier, STRUCTURES are defined in terms of rules (i.e., they are the DATA STRUCTURES on which rules operate). Since they satisfy conditions inherent in the definitions of rules, the question of how to identify them reduces to the problem of how to identify (and represent) the conditions in rules. If a rule is to be compatible with a given subject population, as required in the Structural Learning Theory (to allow for the operational definition of individual knowledge, see Section 5), then the CONDITIONS must be ATOMIC. A CONDITION is said to be ATOMIC if all subjects in the target population are able to distinguish perfectly between entities that satisfy the condition and those that do not. Clearly, atomic conditions, in the terminology of experimental psychology, are nothing more than concepts that have been learned perfectly (by everyone in the target population).

As is the case with atomic rules, it is always possible in principle to refine a given rule sufficiently (e.g., to represent the conditions at a basic enough level) that the conditions are atomic with respect to a given population. In particular, the conditions may be sufficiently basic that they correspond to ATOMIC STRUCTURES (i.e., indivisible elements) (cf. Scandura, 1973, Chapter 5). (Note: Atomicity of conditions is not de-

fined in terms of uniformly good or bad performance, as with
ATOMIC RULES, because such a criterion would imply random responding for subjects who have not mastered the condition.
Rules represented in terms of unmastered decision-making capa-
bilities/conditions would not lend themselves to assessing behavior potential (see Section 5). (A "lucky" success on one
item (problem input) to which a PATH of a rule applies, for
example, would not necessarily imply success on any other item
to which that path applies; see Section 5. Random performance
is to be expected prior to concept [condition] learning just as
uniform failure is to be expected prior to nonDEGENERATE rule
learning. In earlier publications (e.g., Scandura, 1968, 1970),
concept learning has been shown to be just a special case of
rule learning with learning in both cases taking place according
to the same principles, cf. Section 3.)

As with atomic rules, atomic conditions may be identified
via intuition, observation of subjects in the target population,
and/or formal testing. In any case, the specification of such
conditions is an important ingredient of step three of structural analysis, as outlined above. The basic significance of
the whole issue of atomicity is considered further in Section 5.

Molar Domains: With many problem domains, including many
in the field of artificial intelligence (e.g., chess, Tower of
Hanoi, theorem proving), the basic elements, operations, and
relations are relatively easy to identify. For example, in
ordinary subtraction, the basic entities include the digits 0-9,
in chess they include the pieces, in the Tower of Hanoi, disks
and in theorem proving, the basic constants, variables, functions, and relations. Such domains may be referred to as
STRUCTURED.

With molar problem domains, on the other hand, identifying
the critical elements, operations and relations may be more difficult. The critical aspects of the observables may be relatively complex and/or ill-defined and identifying them may
require considerable insight.

Nonetheless, such identification can and has been accomplished, in many cases rather routinely. We do this, for example, whenever we construct a map of some reality, or a diagrammatic representation of some real phenomenon (e.g., the
circulatory system in man, Eulefeld, Kattmann, & Schaeffer,
1975). In any iconic representation, we extract relevant features (i.e., features of interest) and ignore others (cf.
Scandura, 1970, 1973, Chapter 7).

More generally, what makes the representation of molar
domains feasible, indeed just as feasible as with many so-called
structured domains, is that normally only (a small number of)
molar elements/operations/relations need to be represented. An
important point that is often overlooked in analyzing human behavior is that the levels of input and output representation

must be compatible. Thus, given only a molar representation of a problem, it is unrealistic to expect a detailed accounting of the solution. Conversely, if one is interested only in a molar measure of solutions (e.g., one-to-oneness) then an overly detailed representation of problems would be at best wasteful and at worst misleading.

These principles would apply, for example, in analyzing Piagetian conservation domains. Thus, in number conservation, the essential elements of each problem (insofar as conservation is concerned) are a pair of sets of elements and the correspondence relation (e.g., many-to-one, one-to-one) between them. The set elements may be anything at all, although attention normally is restricted to small, easily manipulated objects. The arrangement of the objects is also arbitrary, subject only to a suitable working area for experimental purposes.

Similarly, the critical aspects of observable solution behaviors are those that indicate whether or not the subject can distinguish one-to-oneness from its absence. It is not sufficient, in this case, that the subject give the correct verbal answer ("same", "more", etc.) to a particular display (problem) but whether the child can do this consistently, and even more important, whether the child knows why each answer is correct. Piagetian researchers have attempted to determine the bases for children's responses by such techniques as asking the child if he is sure, trying to talk the child "out of" his answer, surreptitiously adding or removing elements when the child is not looking, etc. (cf. Scandura, 1972b).

Again, there are no easy prescriptions as to how to represent molar problems and their solutions. Suffice it to say that the basic elements must remain invariant under certain kinds of changes (transformations) in problems/solutions (e.g., simple rearrangements in number conservation). That is, allowable transformations must not affect crucial properties of the problem representations. In number conservation (above), examples of such transformations include replacing one set of objects with another and rearranging given sets of objects in various ways. Such transformations form a group (i.e., they satisfy such group axioms as closure, associativity, and existence of identities and inverses; cf. Scandura, 1973, Chapter 6).

In trying to devise a suitable representation, the observer/analyst must ask what is essential about the problems (solutions) and what is irrelevant (cf. Chapter 14 in this volume). In this regard, recall the limits imposed by the level of problem representation on the minimal size of atomic rules in the underlying competence account. Accordingly, the more processing detail the observer/analyst wishes to take into account, the more detail concerning the problems and solutions must be represented. All other things being equal, for example, more detail would have to be represented where solution latencies are of

concern than where simple correct/failure information will
suffice. Conversely, where a molar level of description is
sufficient (e.g., as with Piagetian conservation tasks), underlying competence also can be represented at a molar level. In
effect, structural analysis may be feasible even though molar
domains frequently appear to be relatively complex and/or ill-
defined.

    Incorrect Knowledge: Implicit throughout the above dis-
cussion is the assumption that competence is concerned exclusively with successful problem solving. Rules of competence
either generate correct solutions or they do not. No explicit
provision has been made for systematic errors.

    This is a potentially serious limitation because with many
problem domains and subject populations there are various patterns of errors. A particularly important type of error results
from using the right rule on the wrong problem (i.e., a solution
rule that works in some situations may be inappropriately applied). More precisely, the errors occur in this case because
the domain of the competence rule includes inappropriate as well
as appropriate items. In learning rules of grammar, for example,
young students often fail to learn all of the relevant exceptions and thereby to appropriately restrict the corresponding
rule domains.

    More generally, it is often easier to identify (or learn)
the operation of a rule than the domain of applicability. This
is particularly true of higher-order rules, more informally
called "heuristics". Consider the higher-order generalization
(induction) rule shown in Figure 1 of Chapter 5. Although the
operational aspects of this rule are specified, the domain
strictly speaking is not. In the studies reported, the experimental inputs were triples of instances such as

$$1 \rightarrow 3$$
$$4 \rightarrow 12$$
$$5 \rightarrow 15$$

The higher-order rule identified operates on such triples and
generates as outputs rules of the form $n \rightarrow an + d$. But, this
higher-order rule will not work with all such triples. For
example, consider

$$1 \rightarrow 1$$
$$4 \rightarrow 16$$
$$5 \rightarrow 25$$

In order for the rule to succeed universally the domain would
have to be limited to triples of the form

$1 \to a + d$

$m \to am + d$

$m + 1 \to am + a + d$

Whereas it would be possible to limit the domain of the rule in this case, and in others even more complex, I do not believe for the most part that human knowledge is that algorithmic. In general, I believe that human knowledge, especially of the higher-order variety, consists of rules with only more or less accurate domains.

Nonetheless, the responses associated with various error patterns are frequently quite predictable and rules that generate them in pure form can often be identified. Given the problem 1/2 + 2/3 = ?, for example, many children will respond

$1/2 + 2/3 = 3/5$

What they seem to be doing in this case is overgeneralizing ordinary addition of natural numbers to pairs of such numbers (namely those pairs used to define fractions, see Scandura, 1971b). Other children may respond

$1/\not2 + \not2/3 = 1/3$

Such children appear to be overgeneralizing the notion of "cancelling" as it applies to multiplication of fractions. Although it is impossible to say why these types of errors are so common, one reason may be the relative simplicity of these error rules (operations) in comparison with those for generating correct solutions. This comparison is easy to see in terms of the algebraic analogs

$a/b + b/c = a+b/b+c$

$a/\not b + \not b/c = a/c$

$a/b + b/c = ac+b^2/bc$ (correct)

In effect, problem domains which include errors as well as correct solutions constitute an important special case of those problem domains in which two or more solutions are assigned to the same problem inputs (cf. *Rule Selection* above). In accounting for such domains, in general, a major task may involve identifying appropriate higher-order selection rules. Where subjects have not been exposed explicitly to either error or correct solution rules, however, this task may be relatively straightforward. Thus, for example, if a subject on his own generalizes cancellation to addition of fractions in one case then, in the absence of negative feedback, he will be very likely to use it in other cases as well. The correct rule is not likely to compete because the subject has not been exposed to

it. (In addition, the subject is not likely to generate a
correct rule on his own because of its relative complexity.)
In this case, the error rule may serve as a prototype for that
subject and others like him. In effect, error and solution rules
may initially (i.e., before learning) correspond to different
subpopulations.

After learning, of course, or where subjects have been exposed to both error and correct solution rules, subjects may
know both kinds of rules. In this case, the situation involves
the same kinds of considerations as in identifying other selection rules. Thus, in identifying (terminal) competence associated with unrestricted domains (including both correct and incorrect solutions), particular attention must be paid to the
conditions under which one or the other of the alternative rules
is apt to be used. For example, using an overgeneralized rule
for multiplication of fractions may be less likely on problems
that do not provide opportunities for cancelling. Hopefully,
future research will address itself to this problem (also see
Chapters 6 and 13).

Combining Competence Analyses: Structural analysis of
problem domains may reasonably be expected to be a cumulative
enterprise. Thus, where separate analyses of different domains
pertain to the same subject populations, it is possible to combine them more or less directly. The first step would be to
form a simple union of the component rule sets. The analysis
would, then, proceed by seeking out parallels among the rules
as with any other rule set (see *Structural Analysis* above).

With closely related domains, moreover, it is reasonable
to expect a significant number of common rules. Commonalities,
particularly of the higher-order variety, have been observed
even where the domains are quite different (see Chapters 3, 4,
and 11). In general, therefore, the rule sets associated with
combined domains will contain at most no more rules than the
union of the sets of rules associated with the component domains.
To turn a phrase, the sum of the whole may be less than the sum
of its parts. On the other hand, extending a given domain may
require additional and more exacting analysis (cf. discussion
in Section 5).

Concluding Comment: By way of conclusion, I would like to
emphasize my considered belief that structural analysis is not
limited in its application to highly structured content. Indeed, I believe that anything that can be learned at all, can
potentially be formulated in structural terms--moreover, that
as a result of such analysis one can do a better/more efficient
job both of diagnosis (the identification of what individual
subjects do and do not know) and of instruction.

3.   THE LEARNER

The competence associated with a given problem domain and subject population may be thought of as representing the knowledge (relative to the domain) available to idealized members of the respective population.

What a particular learner does and is able to do in a given problem situation, however, depends not on some ideal but inextricably on what the learner knows at the time. More specifically, in the present theory (Scandura, 1971a, 1973) individual behavior is assumed to depend on: (1) General, relatively universal constraints on the use of knowledge (performance, acquisition, etc.) that stem from the basic nature of man as an information processor, and that have a more or less permanent and possibly physiological base (e.g., limited capacity for processing information, Miller, 1956; time to encode information [about 5 seconds]; etc.).   (2) Specific knowledge that is both available to the individual and relevant to some given problem domain and/or subject population.

3.1 BACKGROUND

Information-processing psychology in general is predicated on the belief that human cognition can profitably be represented in terms of processes/rules/procedures.   Given a class of tasks, an information processing/cognitive theory (relative to that task domain) consists of a procedure that accounts for various facets of human behavior on these tasks.   In computer simulation, for example, cognitive theory is equated with computer programs that reproduce the behavior of individual subjects on given classes of tasks (e.g., chess).   For the most part, information processing research in contemporary experimental psychology deals with simpler discrimination and short term memory tasks (e.g., Levine, 1975; Sternberg, 1969).   Latency provides one of the favorite indices of process form and complexity.

In many cognitive theories, the above distinction between universal constraints and specific, learnable information is often suppressed.   In computer simulation theories, for example, various parts of the programs (process theories) correspond to content specific knowledge (and/or particular subpopulations of subjects) whereas other features correspond to more universal characteristics of the processor.   In some cases, however, what counts as what is as much a function of the computer languages used as of characteristics of the human information processor. Production systems, for example, implicitly assume a particular type of control (see Chapter 5).   Indeed, the distinction between process and control is arbitrary, in the same formal sense that there is a logical equivalence in computer science between program and hardware (Gorn, 1973).   Whatever theoretical value any particular distinction might have in the present context must necessarily derive from its utility in explaining, predicting, and/or controlling human behavior.

As we shall see, the distinctions proposed below provide a basis both for studying cognitive universals independently of specific knowledge and for assessing the specific behavior potential of (knowledge available to) individual subjects. Thus, for example, the possibility of direct deterministic tests of such universals (see Chapter 1) depends heavily on this distinction, and in particular on the experimental manipulation of specific knowledge. Individual knowledge, in turn, is operationally defined relative to given problem domains and, in principle, can be determined at any given point in time (e.g., the start of an experiment). Collectively, then, individual knowledge and cognitive universals provide a basis for determining what individuals will do in particular problem situations. Unlike most contemporary cognitive theories (Levine's, 1975, probe technique is a notable exception), for example, individual differences are an integral part of the theory rather than a bothersome fact of life to be "partialed out" or otherwise ignored, wherever possible (see Chapter 1). Also, unlike simulation theories, individual differences are always judged relative to a common base (i.e., competence theory) so that one is not put in the bind of having to develop a new theory for each individual.

In Section 4.1 a (possibly innate) control mechanism, that is assumed to govern the way in which known rules interact in producing behavior, is described and illustrated. This mechanism is just one of probably many "hardware" characteristics of the human information processor, and is assumed to operate with respect to arbitrary domains of knowledge and all subpopulations of subjects. In turn, this mechanism is shown to account at a schematic level for simple performance, insight learning (rule deviation), motivation (rule selection), subgoal formation (defining problems), and retrieval. Directly relevant empirical data is presented in Part 3.

Section 4.2 deals with two other presumed "hardware" characteristics, the limited capacity for processing information and characteristic processing speed. An enriched theory is proposed that deals with the question of what counts as a unit of memory load, or chunk, in processing available rules and how processing capacity interacts with control in human cognition. Relationships to processing speed are also considered. Relevant empirical evidence and a stochastic extension of the deterministic theory, that allows for deviations from idealized test conditions, is described in Chapter 7.

Section 5 is concerned with the operational definition of individual knowledge. The theory shows how needed TEST ITEMS (problems) can be determined via competence associated with given problem domains. Related empirical work and some evaluation techniques are presented in Part 4.

3.2   REPRESENTATION OF KNOWLEDGE

In the structural learning theory, individual rules of knowledge are represented in the same way as competence, that is, in terms of rules/procedures (and implicitly the structures on which they operate). The term knowledge, however, refers to a potential for actual (individual) behavior, relative to a given problem domain, rather than to a rule account of the domain tailored to idealized prototypes (associated with the target population). Moreover, knowledge rules may be used to explain/predict individual behavior in particular situations rather than just to account for group behavior, as is frequently the case in existing information processing theories in psychology.

In the Structural Learning Theory, *all* knowledge is assumed to denote a potential for behavior. Moreover, all such potentials are assumed to be representable in terms of rules (e.g., labeled directed graphs, Scandura, 1971c, 1973). For present purposes (where perceptual and decoding processes are largely ignored, however, see Scandura 1973, Chapter 5), concern is limited to two major components of rules, operators (arrows) and decisions (nodes). The former tell what to do and the latter, which to do. (In the present formulation, decision-making capabilities may involve any finite number of predicates/classifications, see Scandura, 1973, p. 93. A partition of strings into those that contain zero elements, an even number of elements, and an odd number of elements provides an example of a ternary decision.)

As noted parenthetically in Section 2.1, RULES allowed in the structural learning theory also are restricted in another way. All operations within any given rule act at the same level: Specifically, operations in a rule may not be used to generate new rules (SUBROUTINES) that are applied later during the course of the same computation. Justification for this restriction derives from the control mechanism discussed below. This mechanism is assumed (on the basis of empirical evidence, see Part 3) to be universally available to human subjects. Thereby, in the formulation of individual rules, that part of the flow of control that may be accounted for in terms of the mechanism may be eliminated. As we shall see in Section 5 (especially 5.6), the latter restriction plays an important role in assessing behavior potential.

Where component operations/decisions and internal structure are not of special interest, rules may be represented by single arrows between two nodes. In any case, the domains and ranges of rules play a crucial role in determining their applicability (cf. Newell & Simon, 1972). In this regard, recall that any given rule may serve either of two distinct roles. Rules may act on other elements (structures), in which case they serve as *operators;* or, as parts of structures, they may be operated on, in which case they serve as *states.*

4. COGNITIVE CONSTRAINTS

As we saw in Section 2, the only universal invariants with respect to structural analysis are the LAWS OF INTERACTION (RULES OF COMBINATION). Such rules of combination, recall, were assumed to be compatible with the way in which human information processors use their available knowledge (i.e., with human control mechanisms). Accordingly, since structural analyses apply to entire subject populations, individual behavior (i.e., the use of knowledge) in the present theory is assumed to be governed by a single, universal, cognitive control mechanism.

It is critical, therefore, to know whether there is a realistic control mechanism that both parallels the assumed rules of combination and might reasonably account for the variety of complex psychological phenomena of which humans are known to be capable. Even more important, it is essential to know whether the mechanism is consistent with actual human behavior. In view of the discussion of deterministic theorizing in Chapter 1, such a mechanism must be tested under IDEALIZED CONDITIONS that parallel those assumed in checking generative (computational) adequacy of rule sets. That is, all rules of knowledge should be fully known and available to the learner; the learner's processing capacity should not be overtaxed; the learner should have all of the time necessary for responding, and the learner should understand and be fully motivated to solve each problem posed. (Note: The "problems" themselves may involve defining problems.)

The influence of memory, processing capacity, motivation, and time, of course, are undoubtedly important in most "real" problem solving. Hence, any complete characterization of the learner will necessarily involve more than just available knowledge and a universal control mechanism. Nonetheless, as shown in Chapter 1, it is not necessary to field test implications of deterministic theories that have been successfully tested under idealized conditions. Results obtained under idealized conditions in the laboratory, for example, are equally as applicable, although only probabilistically so, in real educational settings (e.g., see Chapter 11).

To date, the only other major constraint specifically considered and tested with respect to the theory involves the generally recognized, strict limitations on human information processing capacity (cf. Miller, 1956; Nahinsky, 1974; Scandura, 1973, Chapter 10). Among the constraints that might but have not yet been considered are inborn instincts (e.g., general arousal level, Farley, 1974), processing speed, and encoding and decoding latencies (e.g., Newell & Simon, 1972) characteristic of various body receptors and effectors (e.g., eyes, hands). In effect, although such considerations are beyond the scope of the present theory, the theory does not purport to deny

an important role for human physiological psychology. Indeed,
the existing partial theory acts as a potential "place holder"
of sorts, which may be elaborated via relevant behavioral findings attributable to human biology.

In this regard, I am not committed to the view that all
individual differences are caused by environment. To the contrary, for example, although effective processing capacity apparently can be manipulated via training (e.g., by teaching
more efficient processing procedures, see Chapter 7), I suspect
that each individual may usefully be assumed to have a fixed,
relatively permanent underlying capacity (compare, e.g.,
Pascual-Leone, 1970). Moreover, individual differences in processing capacity may have a large cumulative effect on learning
and behavior over the years. All other things being equal, for
example, subjects with low processing capacities may be forced
to rely more on and thereby to further develop higher-level processes, a possibility that runs counter to prevailing wisdom in
intelligence testing (Scandura, 1974d). Nonetheless, given data
accumulated to date, I take no firm position on whether particular capacities develop in the womb (i.e., are innate), or after
birth, as a result of maturation or learning.

4.1 CONTROL MECHANISMS

Consider first the question of control. The approach is
straightforward and rather commonsensical. When a person is
confronted with a problem that he does not know how to solve,
we assume that he tries to figure out some way to attack it.
The basic assumption is that human beings are goal-directed
information processors, and that control shifts, among higher-
and lower-level goals, automatically in a fixed, predetermined
manner. The theoretical problem, of course, is to specify just
what this means.

The mechanism may be thought of informally as follows:
Given a problem for which the learner has a solution rule immediately available, the learner will apply the rule. (Although
this statement appears almost tautological, it is an assumption.
Rule use does not follow logically from availability.) Where
no such rule is available, control is assumed to automatically
switch to a HIGHER-LEVEL GOAL, one satisfied by rules that do
apply. With a higher-level goal in force, the subject presumably selects from among available and relevant rules in the same
way as he would with any other goal: If the subject has an
applicable higher-order rule available, then he will use it.
(Note: Rules that satisfy higher-level goals ordinarily operate
on other rules, more accurately, on structures that contain
rules. In this case they are of relatively higher-order and are
called HIGHER-ORDER RULES.) Where no such higher-order rules
are available, the theory assumes that control moves to still
higher-level goals. Conversely, once a higher-level goal has

been satisfied by application of some rule, control is assumed to revert to the next lower level.

This mechanism is deceptive. Although extremely simple, it is potentially quite powerful and, when suitably generalized, it provides a schematic basis for explaining a wide variety of psychological phenomena, ranging from simple insight learning, to memory, to motivation, to breaking problems into subproblems. (The mechanism was first proposed in Scandura, 1971a. A somewhat more formal, but slightly less general, statement of the mechanism is given in Scandura, 1973, Chapter 9.)

A major goal is to find one control mechanism which applies in all problem solving situations and which may be assumed to be available to human beings, at least from about the age of seven. (Although we have run some younger subjects, see Addendum to Chapter 5, most of our experimental subjects have been seven or above.) We start with the "FIRST APPROXIMATION" MECHANISM introduced in Scandura (1974b) and systematically consider changes required in various types of problem-solving situations.

Throughout, I have tried to make it clear that there are a variety of possible control mechanisms. Some alternatives can be eliminated on purely analytic/structural/computational grounds. Thus, for example, the "first approximation" mechanism described below accounts for simple insight learning/rule derivation, but it is inadequate for motivation/rule selection. In succeeding sections, parsimonious modifications are proposed that account both for new and previously considered phenomena. Sometimes the differences are subtle but they are nonetheless important, especially in any theory that purports to provide a rigorous account of human problem solving.

The behavioral adequacy of these mechanisms is demonstrated empirically in Chapters 5 and 6.

Insight Learning/Rule Derivation: To see how goal switching might bring about insight learning (see DERIVATION RULE under HIGHER-ORDER), consider the following "first approximation" mechanism.

Given a problem/GOAL SITUATION (S,G) (Glossary; for further discussion see Scandura, 1973, Chapters 7 and 9), the subject tests to see if a problem SOLUTION is immediately available (i.e., if he knows the solution, an element that satisfies [S,G]). If not, control automatically shifts to the higher-level SOLUTION GOAL (G2 = SG), a goal that is satisfied by potential solution rules. A rule r is a potential SOLUTION RULE if r includes S in its domain (S $\in$ Dom r) and the range of r contains the goal ([S,G] $\subset$ Ran r). (More generally, S x e $\in$ Dom r where e may be any available entity [structure], e.g., assumptions that enter into a problem solution [and are specified by the conditions in some available rule].) The subject then tests each of his available rules (r) to see if these conditions are met (i.e., to see if r satisfies G2). If such a rule is found, control reverts automatically to the original goal G, and the rule is applied to S (possibly supplemented by other available entities, e).

If not, control shifts to the higher-level goal (G3 = HG) satisfied by higher-order rules (h) whose ranges contain G2 (the set of potential solution rules). With G3 in force, the subject is assumed to test his available rules as before. The only essential difference is that a rule h need not operate on the given S in order to be applicable. In principle, its domain may include any class of available structures (e.g., complex of available rules), denoted $\{s \mid s \in \text{Dom } h\}$. If such a rule is found (i.e., if G2 $\subset$ Ran h and there is an available s $\in$ Dom h) control reverts to G2, and rule h is applied to structure s. In the process, h may generate a new solution rule. The new rule is automatically added to the set of available (knowledge) rules. In turn, if G2 = SG is satisfied by the new solution rule, control reverts to the original goal G and the new rule is applied to S. The problem is solved if the output generated satisfies the given problem situation (S,G). (The serious reader should compare this description with that given in Scandura, 1973, Chapter 9. More details and concrete examples are given below and in Chapter 5.)

It should be emphasized that testing, goal shifting, and rule application are essentially the same at all goal levels. In general a rule (r) satisfies a goal (Gn) if there is an available structure (s) such that s $\in$ Dom r and Gn-1 $\subset$ Ran r. Furthermore, higher-order rules are formally identical to other rules and obey the same laws of behavior. The descriptor *higher-order* refers to the use a rule is put in a particular instance of problem solving, not to its basic nature. In computer science, this flexible, nonhierarchical use of rules is often referred to as *unstratified,* or heterarchical control.

For illustrative purposes, suppose a naive learner is confronted with the problem input bbbbbB and is asked to find the binary numeral that represents the number of b's. The problem (goal) situation (S,G) in this case may be represented by

(12) (S,G) = $\{$By $\mid$ binary no. y = no. b's in bbbbbB$\}$

Assume that the only relevant rules available to the learner are Rule

(3) 1

2

where Dom Rule (3) = $\{$xB $\mid$ x = string of a's$\}$ and Ran Rule (3) = $\{$By $\mid$ y = binary numeral$\}$, and Rule

(13) $r_a \Rightarrow r_b$

where Dom $r_a \Rightarrow r_b$ consists of rules involving a's and Ran $r_a \Rightarrow r_b$ consists of rules involving b's.

In this case, the subject does not know the solution (B101) so control automatically shifts to

G2 = $\{r \mid$ bbbbbB $\in$ Dom r; (S,G) $\subset$ Ran r$\}$

Neither of the available rules satisfy G2. (Rule 3 applies to strings involving a's rather than b's and Rule 13 applies only to rules.) Hence, control goes to

G3 = $\{r \mid$ There is a structure s $\in$ Dom r; G2 $\subset$ Ran r$\}$

Rule (13) satisfies G3 since the rule includes Rule (3) in its domain and G2 in its range. (G2 is satisfied by rules r such that bbbbbB $\in$ Dom r and (S,G) $\subset$ Ran r.) Thus, control reverts to G2 and Rule (13) is applied to Rule (3) (the only available rule to which it applies). This generates Rule

(3')

$\qquad$ 1'

$\qquad$ 2'

where 1' and 2' operate on strings involving b's but in every other way are identical to operations 1 and 2 in Rule (3). Rule (3') satisfies G2 (i.e., bbbbbB is in the domain of Rule (3') and its range includes [S,G]). Hence, control reverts to the original goal situation (S,G) and Rule (3') is applied to bbbbbB. Since the output B101 satisfies (S,G), the problem is solved. In the process, the subject is assumed to have learned the new Rule (3').

As a second example, consider the situation where a learner knows a number of special rules like

(14) $r_2 r_2 r_2$
$\qquad r_1 r_2$

After having learned a number of such rules (e.g., after having solved a number of specific tasks of this type), it is reasonable to suppose that some learners may discover/induce a general method/rule for solving any such task.

To see how this might come about, suppose the learner also knows Rule h. Rule h operates on discrete rules, that are composed of pairs of rules, like r_1 and r_2, in which the domains are complementary (i.e., where exactly one applies to each element in a given universe of elements--say, to strings of a's), and generates general recursive rules. I shall not attempt to precisely formulate such an h but rather shall leave that as an exercise for the interested reader. (For hints see Chapter 5, Experiments II-IV. As a minimum, when applied to special rules like those in (14), which are compositions of r_1 and r_2, Rule h should generate a recursive binary numeral generator. Rule (3) is one such generator.

In addition to suggesting how induction may enter into the theory, this example suggests how formerly discrete rules may be integrated into more comprehensive wholes.[6] (For further discussion concerning the related processes of generalization, induction, discovery, and analogy, see Scandura (1973) and Chapters 3 and 4. Earlier analyses of discovery learning are given in Scandura (1964, 1968, 1969) and Roughead and Scandura (1968). In artificial intelligence, a series of parallel dissertations dealing with learning by induction have been completed under John Carr.

Motivation/Rule Selection: A person is said to be motivated if, given a choice, the person engages in some activity of his own free will. Indeed, theoretically speaking, human motivation can be formulated either in terms of goal selection or of rule/activity selection (Scandura, 1973, Chapter 8; cf. Taylor, 1960; Simon, 1967). Adopting one of a set of alternative goals is equivalent to selecting from among alternative rules for achieving them.

As formulated, the "first approximation" mechanism tells what happens when a person has at most one rule available for achieving a given goal. But, it leaves open the question of what happens where two or more rules apply at a given goal level. Which of the alternatives will the person be motivated to select? In accordance with the "first approximation" mechanism selections are made on a NONDETERMINISTIC basis (see Scandura, 1973, Chapter 8). That is, one of the rules will be selected but the "first approximation" mechanism (irrespective of the particular rules involved) does not allow one to distinguish between them.

Fortunately, the "first approximation" mechanism can easily be modified to account for motivation/rule selection. In particular, an additional constraint is added to the mechanism so that control reverts to next lower-levels and rules are applied only where *exactly* one rule satisfies the corresponding goal conditions. If two or more rules satisfy a goal, control is assumed to move to a higher-level goal just as when no rule does (satisfy a goal). (In addition, a basic test condition (i.e., Gn ⊂ Ran r) used to determine the applicability of particular rules must be modified slightly. Because discussion

---

[6]To my mind, one major open question concerning the goal-switching mechanism involves the possible relationships in testing between *Ran r* and G_n. In my original formulation (Scandura, 1973a), I had postulated that *Ran r* ⊂ G_n. Subsequent analysis, however, showed this condition is not fully adequate. For example, requiring the range of a composition rule to be contained in a goal is overly restrictive because the range of any realistic composition rule will include a wide variety of composite rules, including composite rules that have nothing to do with the task in question.

involves the internal structure of rules, however, discussion
is postponed until a later section; see *Goal Structure.)* Otherwise, the mechanism is assumed to work as before.

To see the implications of this modification, notice that
higher-order rules may act on structures, consisting of (sets
of) two or more rules, and output one of the rules. Higher-
order rules that operate in this way have been called SELECTION
RULES (Scandura, 1973). As a simple example, consider problem
(12) above. Assume further that the student knows Rule (3')
and Rule

(15) g_1

g_2

where g_1 and g_2 are generalizations of operations 1 and 2, respectively, which apply not only to stimuli involving strings
of a's but to strings of arbitrary letters in the English alpha-
bet (e.g., bbB, cccccB). As before, the node represents a decision-making capability for distinguishing between strings containing odd and even numbers of elements. In this case, Rules
(3') and (15) both satisfy G2 in the previous section (i.e.,
both rules apply to aaaaaB and have ranges that contain G).
Hence, control presumably would shift to G3 (previous section).

To enable the subject to make a choice at this level, some
selection rule would have to be available. A simple selection
rule that would serve this purpose can be described loosely as
"use the least general rule" (i.e., check the domains and if
one domain is contained in the other, select that more specific
rule). As this example makes clear, selection rules may apply
to potentially broad classes of rule pairs. This fact, together
with available empirical evidence (Chapter 6 in this book; cf.
Scandura, 1971a, 1973, Chapter 8), suggests that selection rules
may provide a useful basis for explaining human motivation.

Rule Retrieval: Perhaps surprisingly, retrieval from memory in the present formulation requires no essential change in
the above (modified) mechanism. In the structural learning
theory, learning and retrieval both involve using higher-order
rules in accordance with the modified mechanism to generate
other rules. (Although the "first approximation" mechanism also
is adequate in this case, our ultimate theoretical objective is
a single goal switching mechanism that allows for all cognitive
processes. Our discussion leads in that direction.)

There is, however, a connotative difference. LEARNING
corresponds to operating on given rules (structures) and generating new ones. The term RETRIEVAL, on the other hand, refers
to operating on (usually) more complex structures and extracting
parts of them. (In most studies of memory the retrieved entity

is typically a simple element or a degenerate rule/S-R association.)[7] Thus, although goal switching operates in the same way,
there is a difference as to whether the to-be-generated entity
(structure) represents a unit of new knowledge (i.e., a new rule
in the rule set) or is part of, and hence implicit in, an available and more comprehensive cognitive unit (STRUCTURE).

In an IDEALIZED MEMORY-FREE context, where working memory
may be assumed to have an effectively unbounded capacity (cf.
Chapter 1; Section 4.2 of this chapter), retrieving a substructure (e.g., simple element/rule) amounts simply to applying a
retrieval rule to some more encompassing structure (e.g., rule
or complex thereof). Interactions among rules are determined
as before. It is important to emphasize, however, that the
to-be-retrieved item may itself be a rule or other nondegenerate structure. Moreover, retrieval may simply be part of a more
complex process of problem solving. In particular, a retrieved
rule may enter into the solution of a more encompassing problem.

For example, suppose that a person has available rule

$$r_2 r_1 r_2$$

(which will serve in this instance as a structure) and is presented with the task of generating the binary numeral representing the number of a's in aaB? What additional information
(retrieval rule) would the person need in order to succeed?
One possibility (not necessarily compatible with human behavior)
would be a (higher-order) retrieval rule that operates on chains
of atomic rules and extracts subchains. Such a rule might, for
example, check the domains of each component in turn to see if
the given stimulus (aaB) is in its domain and, if so, remember
it while checking the ranges of following components until there
exists either a mismatch or the range contains the desired goal.

The situation with less clearly structured subject matters
is more ambiguous because encoding and decoding processes often
play a more crucial role (not only in retrieval but in storage
in memory as well, see next section). Consider, for example,
traditional studies of paired-associate learning. As with more
structured content the goal is normally unambiguous (there is
usually general agreement on whether or not an item has been
retrieved). The main questions tend to concern what constitutes
the effective cue (i.e., the problem given) for retrieval, the

---

[7]In most information-processing theories of memory (e.g., Anderson & Bower,
1973; Kintsch, 1972; Rumelhart, Lindsay, & Norman, 1972), memory is also represented in terms of relational (semantic) nets, with retrieval being viewed as
searching through the nets. In the present view, this corresponds to a situation
where a rule (directed graph) is in the processor and the desired element is a
node in that graph. Retrieval is similar to that in the Rumelhart, Lindsay, and
Norman (1972) theory in which items (nodes) are "reconstructed" via higher-order
nodes (which correspond to subrules). The structural learning theory, however,
explicitly allows for the retrieval of nondegenerate subrules.

PARENT STRUCTURE (what is stored), and the retrieval rule.

In such studies, for example, the answer to these questions is not always clear since the effective stimuli (retrieval cues) are not always identical to the nominal (training) stimuli (e.g., nonsense syllables). Consequently, the effective associations, which constitute the parent memory structures, usually are not between the nominal stimuli and responses but rather between their effective (encoded) counterparts. The retrieval rules similarly operate on the effective stimuli and associations. What constitute the effective stimuli in serial (list) learning is even less clear, especially since the answer undoubtedly depends in part on the specific content. Nonetheless, some psychologists still feel that this is an important problem for research and the issues are still being debated after decades of research in the area (e.g., what constitutes the effective stimulus: position, the preceding item, or all of the preceding items acting as a unit).

For further discussion of the issues, see Scandura (1973, Chapter 10). Also see Chapter 6 of this book.

Rule Storage: Although no changes in the control mechanism are required, storage in memory involves a few new twists. In the present view, storage can be conceptualized as follows. When presented with an item of information to-be-stored, whether it be a simple element (degenerate structure), a more complex structure, or a rule, the item is necessarily presented in some context, whether external and/or internal. Storage involves deriving a (retrieval) rule that relates some portion of the context (effective retrieval cue) with the to-be-stored item. In this view, the effective goal during storage (i.e., in trying to memorize something) is to derive a rule that takes the context as input and contains the to-be-stored item in its range. Hence, when a subject succeeds in deriving a rule that connects a given context (e.g., aaaaaB) with a to-be-remembered item (e.g., B101), he has effectively stored the item with respect to that context. In order to retrieve the item, then, the learner must apply the derived rule (in the context of the retrieval cue) to retrieve the item.

In the real world, of course, things are not always so simple. For one thing, contexts (retrieval cues) and retrieval goals (i.e., the relations to-be-satisfied in the retrieval/ problem situation) may differ subtly from situation to situation. Unless cues and goals are unambiguously specified, the retrieval rules derived during storage may or may not apply during attempted recall. In memorizing a poem or a joke, for example, any number of retrieval rules might be formed during storage, and each might operate on different cues. (For further discussion, see Scandura, 1973, Chapter 10; also Chapter 6, this book.)

Equally important, the to-be-recalled item (e.g., joke) might not be represented in a way that is compatible with the

goal presented during retrieval. Thus, for example, suppose
one friend asks another, "Tell Alice the joke you heard at the
last APA convention." In this case, the other might reply,
"What joke?" or "What was the joke about?" Assuming that the
joke was represented during storage in terms of its content,
the response might have been quite different if the original
question had been "Tell Alice that joke about ...." In either
case, according to the present theory, successful recall would
require as above that the presented goal be contained in the
range of the rule derived during storage. (Otherwise, the rule
derived during storage, i.e., the retrieval rule, would not be
applied.)

In addition, under nonidealized/nonmemory-free conditions,
the retrieval rule might not be directly available in the processor (see Section 4.2). In this case it would have to be
rederived, only this time in the context of the retrieval goal
(rather than the to-be-recalled entity). Whether or not any
specific to-be-recalled entity will be retrieved, of course,
will necessarily depend on the exact nature of the goal (i.e.,
its representation) and the available rules.

As noted above, such complications appear to be more common
in research involving materials like nonsense syllables and
lists of common words, than in research involving more structured materials (also see Scandura, 1973, Chapter 10).

Defining Subproblems: In discussing learning, motivation,
and memory, it has been assumed implicitly that all learners
attempt to solve problems exactly in the form (i.e., $[S,G]$) they
are given. People do not always do this.

In particular, humans may solve problems either through
sudden insight or in stages. This distinction corresponds to
whether or not a given problem is solved as a whole (i.e., in
the form $[S,G]$) or is broken into subproblems. Whereas the
former Gestalt-type view has traditionally played an important
role in explaining the results of earlier problem-solving research (witness "the insight" showed by Kohler's apes), the
latter has played a central role in much contemporary problem-
solving research (cf. the subgoal hierarchies of Newell &
Simon, 1972).

The basic question here is whether the proposed control
mechanism allows for such distinctions and, if not, whether it
can be modified so as to provide an adequate explanation. For
a long time, I was deeply puzzled about this problem (much as
was the case initially with motivation, cf. Scandura, 1973,
Chapter 8). From the beginning, it seemed fairly clear that
the process of forming subproblems could be represented in terms
of higher-order rules. What was not clear was why a problem
solver would sometimes first break problems into subproblems
and, at other times, attempt to solve them as wholes (cf.
Scandura, 1973, p. 348). This question would appear to be

particularly crucial in situations where the problem solver has
sufficient knowledge available for doing both. Arguments can be
made for assuming either of the two possible orders of priority.
    Alas, it appears to me now that making such a choice may
be unwise. People almost certainly can proceed in either order.
Given the choice, a subject can either break problems into subproblems or attack them as wholes. Presumably, whatever choices
need to be made can be accomplished via the previously described
selection mechanism. In fact, it appears most parsimonious to
maintain the above control mechanism largely as is (see Chapter
6). Only the following changes seem necessary: (1) Introduce
higher-order rules for breaking problems into sequences of subproblems (i.e., *plans* for attacking problems, cf. Miller,
Galanter, & Pribram, 1960). (2) "Sensitize" goal switching
(control) so as to include SOLUTION PLANS as well as explicit
solution procedures (i.e., so that solution plans may satisfy
goals as well as solution rules).
    Consider for example, the problem of finding the number of
1's in the binary numeral representation of aaaaaB. (If C denotes the number of 1's; B, the binary numeral representation;
and A, the stimulus aaaaaB; then the problem (goal situation)
may be represented $[A, C = f(B)]$. The function f does not
necessarily have to be specified; $C = f[B]$ indicates simply that
the desired goal C is a function of some variable B [e.g.,
binary numerals] that is specified in the goal situation.) To
make the situation more specific, assume that the subject does
not know an explicit solution rule or plan for solving the
problem. In this case, after searching his available rules and
plans, and not finding one that will solve the problem (i.e.,
G2 is not satisfied), control moves to a higher-level goal (G3).
The proposed modification (i.e., "sensitization" of goals to
plans) allows G3 to be satisfied by either a solution rule or a
plan for attacking the original problem.
    Let us suppose, for the sake of further argument, that the
subject knows a SUBPROBLEM formation (i.e., PLANNING) rule that
operates on problems of the form (A, C = f(B)) and generates
solution plans of the form $[(A, B), (B, C)]$. The solution plan
$[(A, B), (B, C)]$ means solve subproblem (A, B) and then solve
subproblem (B, C). In this case, control shifts downward (to
G2) and the subproblem rule is applied yielding the plan: Solve
(aaaaaB, binary numeral representing number of a's) and then
solve (binary numeral, number of 1's in binary numeral). This
plan then is tested against the goal G2.
    Since the domain and range have the necessary properties,
control goes to the original goal (G) and the plan is put into
action. That is, the subject first tries to solve subproblem,
(A, B) = (aaaaaB, binary numeral representing number of a's),
using the basic control mechanism. If successful, the subject
goes on to the second subproblem, (B, C) = (binary numeral,

number of 1's in binary numeral).

Lest there be any confusion on the point, note that subproblems may be redefined at each stage leading to hierarchies
of subproblems. The first subproblem above, for example, can
be broken down into a series of subproblems of the form "reduce
the number of a's to the left of B."

Relationship to Goal Hierarchies: Although they use different mechanisms, both Ernst and Newell's GPS (General Problem
Solver) (1969) and Newell and Simon's (1972) production systems
allow similar (they call them *goal*) hierarchies. Moreover, any
class of problems that can be ACCOUNTED FOR by these formulations
can also be accounted for by ours, and vice versa. There is
another key feature of problem solving, however, that is not so
easily captured by these other formulations. They do not seem
to allow for learning new solution rules (via derivation), at
least not in a way that appears to be as general as goal switching. For one thing, in the state space approach, on which these
formulations are based, solution rules are always composites of
given (atomic) rules (cf. Banerji, 1974).

It is not clear, for example, how one would allow for learning in these other formulations where generalization or analogy
are involved. For example, suppose a person is presented with
the problem of finding the binary numeral representing the number of b's in bbbbbB but that he does not know any rules that
operate on strings involving b's. Assume that he only knows
rules that operate on strings involving a's and analogy rule
$r_a \Rightarrow r_b$. Solving this problem in the present view would follow
directly. Whereas such a problem can also be solved by breaking
the problem down into subproblems, it is not clear how or why
this might be done given the same information (i.e., rules).
Thus, in the GPS formulation, which is based on reducing successive differences between the problem given and the goal, the
problem could be broken into the following sequence of subgoals:
(1) convert bbbbbB into aaaaaB, (2) find the binary numeral which
represents the number of a's in aaaaaB, (3) assign the same
numeral to the b's in bbbbbB. However, in this case, the rationale as to why aaaaaB or aaB1 (obtained by applying r_2 to
aaaaaB), for example, should be defined as being closer to the
binary numeral for bbbbbB than the original stimulus itself is
not entirely clear (to me). Presumably one could intuitively
reason backward from the analogy rule $r_a \Rightarrow r_b$, but then that
would tend to support the present position (where $r_a \Rightarrow r_b$ is made
explicit).

One additional point may be worth mentioning. In empirical
studies, it has commonly been observed that when the same problems are presented repeatedly over a series of trials, subjects
tend to break them into progressively larger subproblems (cf.
Harlow's 1945 classic study on "insight" training). This seems
to be particularly true on well-defined tasks where the atomic

rules are specified to the subject in advance (cf. The Tower of
Hanoi, e.g., Klix & Sydow, 1968; missionaries and cannibals,
e.g., Thomas, 1974; Greeno, 1973). As subjects gain experience
with a given problem, it appears on succeeding trials that they
tend to convert more and more tentative solution plans into
concrete solution rules for the various subproblems. Correspondingly, the size of the subproblems identified on succeeding trials may be expected to increase (and the number of such
subproblems to decrease).

Problem Definition: Presenting a subject with a statement
or description of a problem is no guarantee that it will be interpreted as intended. In many situations, PROBLEM DEFINITION
(under RULE) is an important aspect of problem solving. Indeed,
before a problem (goal situation) in the above sense can reasonably be attacked, the problem statement/description must be
understood. In the present view, this means that the semantics
of the problem itself must be properly represented.

In cases where it is reasonable to assume that all subjects
properly understand the language in which problems are stated
(presented), the distinction between syntax and semantics may
be suppressed. Where the encoding PROCESSES (problem definition
rules) involved are more complex, however, or where they are
otherwise of special interest, these processes must be represented in finer detail just as with any other process of concern.
In order to accomplish this, two levels of representation must
be distinguished. One level is based on the DESCRIPTION LANGU-
AGE used to represent the important syntactic features of written and/or spoken (problem) statements (e.g., even generalized
environmental stimulation upon which scientific problems are
based). The other level is based on the OBJECT LANGUAGE used
to represent the corresponding problem of semantics. (The
syntax of problem statements has been ignored for the most part
in previous discussions. Even the representations used in our
"syntactic" example refer to the object language and, hence,
are semantic.) Syntactic representations of given written and/
or spoken problem statements, then, constitute the effective
inputs of problem definition rules. The semantics of the problem (goal) situations constitute the effective outputs.

We do not attempt in this book to detail particular processes by which various types of problems might be defined
(e.g., problem statements interpreted). One might envisage, for
this purpose, some modification or extension of a question-answer
system in artificial intelligence, such as Winograd's (1972) or
Schank's (1973). However, the structural learning formulation
does *not* require the same degree of specificity (in order to be
useful) as is required in operating computerized question-answer
systems. It is necessary only that the component operations
and decisions of problem definition rules be atomic relative to
the target population. Consequently, relatively molar analyses

may still serve quite adequately insofar as behavioral predictions are concerned (see Section 5). The analysis of critical reading in Chapter 12 is of this type.

The important thing for present purposes is to show schematically how the postulated control mechanism provides a basis for problem definition. Given any problem statement, subjects invariably break them (i.e., the *syntactic problems* implicit in the statements) into pairs of subproblems; a DEFINING PROBLEM, which involves going from syntax to semantics (i.e., to the underlying problem), and a SOLVING PROBLEM, which is the underlying (semantically represented) problem itself. Indeed, perhaps one of the first things that a young child must learn in communicating with an adult about problem solving is that such statements as "solve the following problems" must be interpreted to mean: Interpret each of the following problem statements and, in turn, solve the problems so defined. For example, consider the problem statement: "Find the binary numeral represented by the number of a's in aaaaaB." The word "find" in the statement is a sure cue that the subject is to break the given problem statement (viewed as a syntactic problem) into a pair of subproblems; first define the problem described by the problem statement (i.e., construct a semantic representation of the problem given a syntactic representation of the problem statement), and then solve the problem.

How is this accomplished? In the present view, human beings characteristically interpret more or less broad varieties of environmental situations as (syntactic) problems to be solved. Some such situations involve specific problem statements, such as those above, in which the cues (e.g., "find") are easily identified. Others involve cues that are far more subtle, for example, consider the kinds of incongruities in the world requiring resolution to which research scientists gradually became sensitized. Usually, these incongruities are not in the form of nice neat descriptions of problems to be solved nor need they be represented syntactically (at least not in the usual sense), but they nonetheless serve essentially the same purpose. Problems involving incongruities of this sort must be defined (i.e., the incongruities to be resolved/relations to be achieved must be represented) in a form that they can be dealt with. (One might speculate that at least some incongruities result from the relative ease with which various structures may be represented in discrete versus analog terms. Thus, for example, it is sometimes possible to "picture" a whole before crucial interrelationships among the elements [e.g., the problem] can be made explicit. For a discussion of discrete/analog representations see Chapter 15, Section 2.3.)

Whatever type of "syntactic" problem is involved, control according to the Structural Learning Theory automatically moves as before to the higher-level goal of finding a solution rule or plan (in this case usually a plan) for solving the problem. Here is where the above sequence of subproblems comes in. What I have said, in effect, is that these are the kinds of solution plans that are characteristically derived; these solution plans are sequences consisting of a defining problem followed by a solving problem. What I have not done is to specify particular subproblem rules that might be involved in deriving specific solution plans for various classes of "syntactic" problems. It is particularly important to notice in this regard that individuals may differ, for any given problem statement, as to just what constitutes the defining problem. For one subject, a problem may be adequately defined whenever the problem given and goal have been formulated in a way that captures the meaning of certain key words (even though not all of the essential relationships are represented). For another, a well-defined problem may involve a certain type of logical consistency among the parts as well. (Incidentally, notice that the process of understanding a problem statement may yield a defined problem that has no solution, e.g., find an albino with brown eyes.)

We shall not attempt to specify specific rules for interpreting problem statements, although this is an important task for future research. (Indeed, Simon and others at Carnegie-Mellon University are currently working on this problem.) It is sufficient here to simply point out that from the present point of view such research must: (1) specify subproblem rules for breaking given classes of problem statements (or, e.g., incongruities in the world) into corresponding solution plans (i.e., sequences of what are called above defining problems and solving problems) and (2) specify PROBLEM DEFINITION rules for defining (i.e., solving) the defining problems.

In summary, I have argued that: (3) problem statements are invariably broken down into pairs of subproblems, both of which constitute important aspects of problem solving, and (4) the overall process is governed by the control mechanism described above.

Encoding (Decoding) the Environment: Although perceptual (decoding) phenomena are beyond the scope of the present development, I should perhaps note that in the structural learning theory new DECODING SKILLS are assumed to be generated from more primitive ATOMIC ones (via rules that operate on them). Presumably such basic perceptual distinctions (decoding skills) as motion/no motion, light/dark, topologically closed/open, etc. are the basic building blocks for all perceptual learning; the finer discriminations come later.

Although complex percepts (e.g., arrangements of blocks) in most artificial intelligence theories of perception (e.g., Winston, 1972) as well as in traditional theories of concept attainment (e.g., Bruner, Goodnow, & Austin, 1956), also are generated from more primitive ones, the emphasis to date has

been on identifying procedures for recognizing complex percepts (concepts). Relatively little attention has been given
to how such procedures are learned, or to how newly learned
UNITARY ENCODING CAPABILITIES become automated (i.e., ATOMIC/
a highly skilled part of the learner's perceptual machinery).
Interestingly enough, these aspects of perceptual learning
appear to be explicable in terms of the same mechanisms that
govern other learning (Scandura, 1973, Chapter 5, especially
pp. 104 & 109-111; also see Section 4 in this chapter).

Skilled (Automatic) Performance: In the Structural Learning Theory, the rules corresponding to skilled performance are
assumed to be acquired (derived/learned) according to the same
mechanisms as other rules. Consider, for example, the procedure
$r_2r_1r_2$, for solving the problem
  (aaaaaB, binary numeral representing number of a's)
along with a class of similar procedures of the same type (e.g.,
r_2r_2 for solving [aaaB, binary numeral]). In this case, it is
easy to conceive of higher-order rules that operate on the
relatively complex solution procedures and eliminate redundant
or unnecessary steps (cf. the higher-order "elimination" rules
in Scandura, 1973, p. 104).

One such higher-order rule might operate on multi-step
procedures, such as those above, together with their solutions,
and generate the corresponding instances (i.e., problem given-
solution pairs). These new instances, then, could serve as
(DEGENERATE) rules (or associations) for solving the corresponding problems in a skilled/automatic manner. For example, once
having solved the above problem, presumably via the procedure
$r_2r_1r_2$, the solution B101 (also a DEGENERATE rule) would be
added to the rule set.

Suppose, then, on subsequent presentations of the (above)
problem, that the subject is required to respond as "quickly
as possible", or within specified time limits. Under these
conditions, the original solution procedure $r_2r_1r_2$ would no
longer be applicable so that control would move to the higher-
level goal. Given the availability of the above higher-order
rule and the solution B101, the subject would then derive the
"automatic" rule (association) aaaaaB-B101. From that point on,
presumably, performance on the problem would qualify as "skilled".

Clearly, this simplified account deals only with the idealized, memory-free case where processing capacity is not considered (see Section 4.2). In addition, it ignores the possible
influence of nonatomic encoding/decoding capabilities. Nonetheless, for reasons detailed in Chapter 1, it is often desir-
ably, as well as feasible, to build on a proven deterministic
base in dealing with "real world" phenomena. I would propose,
in this case, that the above account might provide a useful
starting point in explaining the acquisition of various (particular) kinds of skilled performance. Although none of our

own empirical work deals with this issue directly, some potentially relevant research has been reported in the literature (most
notably that of Groen and his associates). This issue is discussed further in Section 5.

Extension to Domain Goals: In all versions of the control
mechanism described above, it is assumed at each goal level
that the domains and ranges of rules (and plans) are tested
simultaneously. There are, however, many situations where this
is not possible. Thus, whereas the above mechanism implicitly
assumes that all of the information needed to solve problems is
immediately available, this is not always the case. Needed
information may be given only implicitly or not at all. In
proving theorems, for example, critical information may vary
widely and identifying it is often as difficult as using it
(cf. "key first steps" in the existence proofs of Chapter 4).
Generally, almost everyone has experienced situations where one
knows how and could solve a problem, if only one could remember
some missing fact. In current terminology, an adequate (possibly higher-order) rule is available (its range contains the
goal) but some of the needed domain elements on which the rule
operates are not (immediately available).

The mechanism can be generalized to account for such situations by requiring that the tests are performed in series.
Specifically, we assume that higher-level goals are satisfied
by rules whose ranges contain the next lower-level goals: For
any given n, a Rule r is said to be contained in $Gn(r \in Gn)$ or
to satisfy

$$Gn = \{r \mid Gn\text{-}1 \subset Ran\ r\}$$

if $Gn\text{-}1 \subset Ran\ r$, where G1 is the given problem (S_o, G). (Note:
The SITUATION S is subscripted to emphasize its status as a
constant, as a problem given. In the subsequent discussion S
is a variable which defines the domain from which S_o is drawn.
For example, in the foregoing we have implicitly assumed that
aaaB, for example, is drawn from the domain xB where x is any
arbitrary string of a's. The following discussion is constructed so as to allow the general reader to ignore these subtleties
without serious loss of comprehension.)

Once a rule has been identified that satisfies a goal at
any level (in the context of a given goal situation), control
transfers to the corresponding DOMAIN GOAL. The domain goal
associated with rule r (which satisfies Gn) in the context of
(S_o, G) may be denoted $Dom\ Gn(r) = [(S_o, G), Dom\ r]$. (Note:
In Dom Gn(r), the domain of r, Dom r, plays a role analogous to
G in problems [i.e., initial goal situations] denoted $[S_o, G]$.
The $[S_o, G]$ in Dom Gn(r) similarly corresponds to S_o. Thus,
Dom r specifies the form of the structures that satisfy
Dom Gn(r) and problem $[S_o, G]$ specifies which structures of

that form are acceptable. Spelling out the details involved in
any particular case depends on the particular representation
chosen for the problem domain and cannot be considered here.
However, see below.)

Where a structure in a domain goal is immediately available, the Dom Gn(r) is satisfied directly. Where this is not
the case, subsequent shifts to higher- and lower-level domain
goals are assumed to take place as with any other initial goal.
(In general, mth level domain goals may be denoted

$$\text{Dom Gn}^m(r) = \{r \mid \text{Dom Gn}^{m-1}(r) \subset \text{Ran } r\}$$

where Dom $\text{Gn}^1(r)$ = Dom Gn(r).) Once a domain goal (at any
level) has been satisfied, control reverts to the next lower-
level, the identified rule is applied to the derived domain
elements, and the process continues.

For example, consider the problem (bbB, binary numeral)
where only the following rules are available: $r_a \Rightarrow r_b$, Rules (14)
and Rule h (a rule that generates general recursive rules, like
Rule (3), from specialized rules, like Rules (14)). In this
case, $r_a \Rightarrow r_b$ satisfies higher-level goal G3 in the sense that
its range contains the set of potential solution Rules (G2).
Hence, control is assumed to shift to the domain goal,
Dom G3($r_a \Rightarrow r_b$), satisfied by those rules (involving a's) in the
domain of $r_a \Rightarrow r_b$ that are compatible with the goal situation
(bbB, binary numeral). Compatibility in this case means that
the rules operate on strings and generate corresponding binary
numerals. (Note: More concrete instances of compatibility may
be gleaned from the experimental procedures described in Chapter
5, Experiment II, involving the derivation of general rules compatible with given instances [part of the goal situation], and
Chapter 6, where domain goals are considered directly.)

Rule (3) would satisfy Dom G3 ($r_a \Rightarrow r_b$) but it is not directly available. Thus, control goes to Dom $\text{G3}^2(r_a \Rightarrow r_b)$ (as with
any other upward goal shift). Goal Dom $\text{G3}^2(r_a \Rightarrow r_b)$ is satisfied
by generators of rules in Dom G3($r_a \Rightarrow r_b$). Rule h serves this
purpose, so control reverts to Dom G3($r_a \Rightarrow r_b$), and it is applied.
(Needed domain elements, Rules (14), are available by assumption.) The output Rule (3) satisfies Dom G3($r_a \Rightarrow r_b$) so control
returns to G2, and $r_a \Rightarrow r_b$ is applied to Rule (3), giving Rule
(3'). Rule (3') satisfies G2, and the process continues as
before.

Clearly, the above generalization makes it possible to
handle a broader variety of problem situations, including complex problem situations that involve two or more different processes (see Chapter 6). In the above illustration, for example,
Rule (3) must be "retrieved" before the available higher-order
rule (h) can be applied to derive solution Rule (3'). It is
impossible to say definitively, at the present time, whether

this control mechanism is sufficiently general to account for all problem solving (i.e., specific knowledge aside). It appears, however, to have desirable recursive properties and, so far, I have not found any basic limitations in this regard. I cannot make a similar statement regarding the precise nature of the tests required at various goal levels. Further refinements may be needed in this direction (cf. Scandura, 1973, pp. 205-213, 293-296; 1974a, p. 77; and the following section).

Incidentally, notice that the above mechanism reduces essentially to the earlier one in situations where needed domain elements are immediately available. In this case, domain goals are satisfied directly; no derivation is required.

Goal Structure: Throughout the above, it is implicitly assumed that goals are structureless; that they represent ATOMIC TESTS with no internal structure. It is not hard to identify limitations of UNITARY, unanalyzed GOALS of this type in real problem solving. For one thing, broader contexts (both external and internal) were ignored in previous sections. Consider, for example, a bizarre situation in which Goldfinger has placed James Bond on a ledge just above a snake pit and has presented him with the challenge of solving a difficult mathematical problem. If he succeeds, he goes free, else....

While he is attempting to solve the problem, James must be extremely wary. His goal is a composite one; solve the problem but maintain good health in the process. Any rule used under such circumstances would likely have more to it than just mathematics; it would include among its decision-making capabilities a safety valve of sorts. If at any point a certain danger threshold is reached, Bond presumably would forget about the problem for a moment and avoid striking fangs. Perhaps a more common (and peaceful) occurrence is a situation in which many scientists often find themselves--thinking about a problem while driving one's car to or from work. Under ordinary driving conditions, it is often possible to make reasonable progress. But, in an emergency this would be rare indeed.

More generally, it would appear that shifts in attention may be accounted for in terms of composite goals, in particular goals where specific goals act jointly with more global ones. In addition to the above examples, where shifting attention depends on real-world events over which the person has little control, there are other situations where the triggering events may be a direct result of stimuli produced by the person himself. Changes in internal stimulation, for example, presumably account for such common observations as a person stopping in the middle of a task because of fatigue or hunger. Similarly, new information obtained as a result of active searching or responding may lead a person to suddenly take a new tact.

Where general predispositions are involved (e.g., resistance to fatigue), individuals may be expected to react in much the same way in broad classes of problem situations. Thus, general predispositions/avoidance tendencies, for example, may correspond to global decision-making capabilities that are common to a variety of solution rules. Stable individual differences in such cases, presumably, could provide a useful basis for explanation, prediction, and to some extent, control.

More generally, the global level of representation used to represent goals in the previous sections precludes the possibility of specifying interrelationships among various goals. In the above examples, the goals are best viewed as composites of other goals. Specifically, the composite goals were intersections of two goals, one specific and the other global. In the James Bond example, for instance, the specific goal Gs pertains to the mathematical problem and the GLOBAL goal Gg, to staying alive. The effective goal, G, then, may be represented G = Gs $\cap$ Gg.

Defining composite goals in terms of other goals is particularly important where rule selection is of interest. In the section on *rule selection,* recall, the point was made that the test condition, Gn $\subset$ Ran r, used to determine rule applicability, had to be modified somewhat. Although the example used in that section avoids the issue, useful distinctions can often be made between solutions generated by different solution rules (e.g., the solutions may be generated more quickly or otherwise have slightly different properties). These distinctions derive from the relations that define the corresponding goals.

To see how such distinctions may be represented, and their influence on the above test condition, consider, for example, the problem of designing a house given certain dimensions, costs, etc. A corresponding problem, in this case, one with a more prescribed (discriminating) goal, might involve designing a *brick* house (given similar constraints). Another such problem might involve designing a *wood frame* house. If we let (S, Gb) represent the problem of designing a brick house, and (S, Gf), the problem of designing a frame house, then the initial problem (of designing a house of unspecified type) may be represented (S, Gb $\cup$ Gf), where Gb $\cup$ Gf is simply the union of Gb and Gf.

With regard to the above test condition, notice that the range of solution rule r_b (Ran r_b) for problem (S, Gb) need not contain the more global problem (S, Gb $\cup$ Gf). Given this global problem, therefore, rule r_b need not satisfy the above goal condition (i.e., it is not necessarily the case that [(S, Gb $\cup$ Gf) $\subset$ Ran r_b]). Accordingly, rule r_b would be rejected as a possible solution rule whereas our analysis of rule selection indicates that it should be one of possibly several solution rules. With this in mind, the critical test conditions used in goal switching must be modified. In the case of rule selection (at least of the type we have considered), it is sufficient to simply require that *some* identifiable subset of the goal (there exist only a finite number of such subsets) be contained in the range of a candidate rule. In this case, rule r_b would satisfy goal G2 (associated with problem $[S, Gb \cup Gf]$) because $(S, Gb) \subset Ran\ r_b$.

Clearly, forming intersections and unions of given goals are only two ways in which new goals may be defined in terms of existing ones. One might, for example, also define new goals by taking complements of given ones. Rather than constructing a plane figure that is a triangle, for example, one might pose the problem of constructing a plane figure that is not a triangle.

In addition to defining new goals extensionally in terms of logical connectives (and given goals), new goals may be defined in terms of internal relations used to define existing goals. For example, consider the problem

$$(aaB, binary\ numeral)$$
$$= \{By \mid binary\ numeral\ y = no.\ a's\ in\ aaB\}$$
$$= \{By \mid R(aaB, By)\}$$

where R is the defining relation. Then, problem

$$\{z \mid z = no.\ 1's\ in\ binary\ no.\ a's\ in\ aaB\}$$

can be represented as

$$\{z \mid R'(R(aaB, By), z)\}$$

where relation R' refers to the number of 1's in binary numerals. Further examples of this type, in the context of geometry construction problems, are given in Chapter 14.

It remains simply to note that each of the (in general, n-ary) relations comprising the internal structure of a goal corresponds to an (n-1 ary) atomic rule for achieving it (more exactly, each such relation corresponds to a particular atomic rule in the class of functions/atomic rules it defines). These relations are assumed to have uniform behavioral effects and to be universally available to all subjects. Were it otherwise, there could be no guarantee that problems represented at this level would be understood by subjects in the target population.

Conclusions: As simple as it appears, the control mechanism elaborated above appears to provide a potential basis for explaining a wide variety of cognitive phenomena: "insight" learning, motivation, breaking problems into subproblems, problem definition, and storage and retrieval from permanent memory. There are many fine points that are still unresolved, of course, and the mechanism itself provides only a general cognitive schema. The control mechanism, presumably, constrains the use of specific rules, involved in particular applications, but it

says nothing itself about what the specific rules are. (As we
saw in Section 2, however, these constraints play a crucial role
in identifying specific rules of competence. In Section 5, we
shall see how these rules, in turn, provide a basis for identifying the specific rules of knowledge available to individual
subjects.)

Moreover, the question of how to isolate the proposed control mechanism(s) for empirical study poses problems not unlike
those confronted in contemporary research on memory. When a
subject performs on a memory task, for example, it is not always easy to determine whether or when information comes from
short-term or long-term store (cf. Atkinson & Shiffrin, 1968;
Waugh & Norman, 1965), or equivalently from the processor/work-
ing memory or prior store/permanent memory (Scandura, 1973,
Chapter 10). Similarly, in most real-world environments, unless
special precautions are taken, it is difficult to determine unambiguously which aspects of behavior may be attributed to the
proposed control mechanism, which to specific learnable knowledge and, as we shall see in the next section, which to a person's limited capacity for processing information.

As suggested in Chapter 1, the approach my collaborators
and I have taken has been to study behavior under idealized
conditions, where it was known in advance exactly what relevant
rules the subject knew and had immediately available and where
explicit provision was made to ensure that the subject's processing capacity was not exceeded (e.g., where the subject had
all of the time he needed and/or where paper and pencil or other
aids were available for aiding memory and/or recording intermediate results). Relevant research is cited in the concluding
section and is described at greater length in Part 3.

4.2 MAN: A LIMITED-CAPACITY INFORMATION PROCESSOR

Throughout the above discussion, it was assumed that all
rules and other elements known to a subject are uniformly and
immediately available during cognition. In effect, it was implicitly assumed that human capacity for processing information
is essentially unbounded. Although the former assumption is
reasonable under idealized conditions (cf. Chapters 5 and 6 of
this book), one need hardly refer to the massive literature on
information processing to conclude that the ability of humans
to cope with problems depends in substantial part on the memory
load imposed. Man is unquestionably a limited-capacity information processor.

In this section we consider the question of how processing
capacity might interact with the proposed control mechanism in
generating behavior. Incidentally, we also consider possible
relationships between capacity and processing speed. If the
memory load imposed by a task is too great, the task may exceed
the subject's capability, even where the subject knows *how* to

solve the task. But just what constitutes memory load, and how
is it determined?

Memory Load/A Global Analysis: As a first approximation,
memory load would seem to depend on the number of entities
(e.g., structures, rules, goals) that must be kept in mind during processing. For illustrative purposes, recall once again
our standard example: Let S be bbbbbB and G, the binary numeral
goal; assume also that the subject knows and has available both
Rule (3) and higher-order rule $r_a \Rightarrow r_b$. Upon initial presentation
of the problem (S,G), the subject must keep in mind each element
in set

$$A = \{S,\ G,\ (S,G),\ \text{Rule (3)},\ r_a \Rightarrow r_b\}$$

Since no solution rule is available, the control mechanism introduces the higher-level goal G2, thereby increasing memory
load. With G2 in control, the individual elements in set A are
again tested. Since none satisfies G2, control shifts to G3,
with G3 presumably adding further to memory load. Since G3 is
satisfied by $r_a \Rightarrow r_b$, control moves to the domain goal associated
with $r_a \Rightarrow r_b$. The domain goal may be assumed to replace G3, with
memory load remaining constant. With the domain goal in control,
the available rules are again tested, this time singling out
Rule (3). Control then goes to G2, making it unnecessary to
retain the domain goal in the processor, and $r_a \Rightarrow r_b$ is applied
to Rule (3). (In the case of rule application, overall memory
load depends on the complexity of the computation, cf. below,
Chapter 7.) The output Rule (3') satisfies G2 so it is added
and G2 is eliminated from the processor, and control returns to
(S,G). Finally, Rule (3') is applied and the generated solution
is tested against the problem goal (S,G).

This example provides a general, qualitative account of
how memory load might change during processing. It provides,
therefore, some basis for determining whether or not a given
derivation might be carried out by a particular subject. The
major requirement is that the subject's processing capacity be
known in advance and compared with the memory load at each
stage of processing. This account, however, lacks detail and
precision because it deals exclusively with atomic goals and
structures, and with RULE EXTENSIONS, rather than with their
internal structure.

As Miller (1956) argued earlier, memory load is not a simple function of the number of nominal elements that must be
retained but rather of the number of "chunks" involved. Although there are many examples of chunks in the literature
(e.g., digits, letters, words, base 10 equivalents of binary
numerals, etc.), however, it is not clear exactly what a chunk
is, or, to put it differently, how to determine what counts as
a chunk in computing memory load.

In the structural learning theory, any structure, rule, or goal (relation), or any part thereof, may count as a chunk under certain circumstances (cf. Scandura, 1973, Chapter 10; Nahinsky, 1974). To see this, notice first that all rules operate on structures and substructures thereof (e.g., the addition algorithm operates on column addition problems, columns, digits, etc.). What counts as a structure or substructure in each case depends directly on the rule involved, and specifically on how the relations inherent in the rule happen to carve up (i.e., structure) the internal/external inputs. (This idea corresponds to the view that we perceive what we want to perceive--or more generally that cognitive units/structures are determined by cognitive processes, cf. Neisser, 1967.) The effective structures at any given stage of a process (rule), then, are precisely those that enter into the process at that stage as a STATE. In ordinary addition, for example, any or all of the following might serve effectively as structures: digits, columns of digits, the relation ≥ 10 (e.g., to determine whether or not to "carry"), and partial sums.

More generally, COGNITIVE PROCESSING may be under the control of: (1) rules, which operate on and control the generation of structures, (2) goals, which operate on rules and control testing, and (3) the control mechanism, which operates on goals and controls shifts among them. Just as rules determine effective structures, then, the relations that comprise given goals determine which aspects of rules are essential during testing. Similarly, the control mechanism may either eliminate goals or generate new goals from given ones; in this case, the goals are treated globally.

In effect, the number of critical cognitive units (structures, rules, goals) is computed relative to what process is in control (i.e., rule, goal, mechanism) at each moment. For example, given a rule that is undergoing processing, the number of critical substructures is determined as follows. At each stage of a computation (i.e., at each stage of application of a rule) certain substructures (elements) must be retained in order to determine future outputs and operations. At the conclusion of any given stage, it may be possible to eliminate certain of the elements required at a preceding stage, and new elements may be added. In adding 45 + 71, for example, it is necessary to remember the two unit digits 5 and 1 before summing them, but afterwards only the partial sum 6 must be retained (for details see Chapter 7; also see Scandura, 1971, 1973).

In the Extended Structural Learning Theory, it is assumed that each individual subject has a fixed capacity for processing information, usually on the order of 5 to 9 "chunks". Thus, given an independent assessment of processing capacity, and the memory load associated with any given instance of cognitive processing (e.g., application of a known rule; see Chapter 7), it is possible to determine whether or not the subject will be successful on that instance. As we shall see below, it also should be possible to determine the LATENCY associated with any instance of successful performance.

What is a "Chunk": Knowing the number of COGNITIVE UNITS (i.e., structures, rules, goals) that enter into given cognitive stages, of course, says nothing directly about the memory load imposed by these units. Some units may impose minimal load on the processor whereas others may impose a heavy load. In order to serve a useful function in psychological theory, some way must be found to translate cognitive units into memory load. One possibility might be to introduce some measure of complexity on the units (perhaps via empirically based parameter estimation methods). Although complexity measures might have pragmatic value, however, it is doubtful that they would have more than normative significance (i.e., they would pertain only to average behavior).

In the structural learning theory, a basic goal has been to identify underlying causes. Thus, rather than taking cognitive units as is and imposing complexity measures on them, an attempt has been made to identify the basic conditions that must be satisfied in order that different cognitive units impose the same memory loads, that each cognitive unit serves as a CHUNK. Under what conditions, for example, would partial sums and columns in ordinary addition problems impose the same loads as the individual digits of which they are composed? Composite rules (e.g., subtraction algorithm) impose the same load with respect to higher-order rules as their component rules?

As a first approximation, each of a set of cognitive units might reasonably be assumed to impose the same processing load (act as chunks) in cases where they are responded to with equal ease by any given subject. The problem, of course, is to specify just what constitutes equal ease. Consider, for example, the task of subtracting numerals via one of the standard algorithms (see Chapter 9). In all such algorithms, one step invariably involves the use of the basic subtraction facts up to $18 - 9 = 9$ (i.e., $1 - 1 = 0$, $2 - 1 = 1$, $3 - 1 = 2$, ... $9 - 5 = 4$, ... $18 - 9 = 9$). Although each of these facts may be learned separately, they are typically grouped together as a single atomic rule in representing subtraction algorithms. Moreover, the data reported in Chapter 9, for example, suggests that this is probably a reasonable simplifing assumption to make with students, all or almost all of whom have learned these facts.

On the other hand, BEHAVIOR EQUIVALENCE does not necessarily mean that generating each fact (i.e., difference) imposes the same processing load, or that they take the same time to perform. With many subjects, for example, performing $3 - 2 = 1$ is apt to be a more automatic skill then subtracting 6 from 15.

Thus, in the latter case, the additional input digits (3 versus 2) and the increased likelihood of finding the difference in stages (e.g., take away 5 from 15, giving 10, before subtracting the remaining 1 from 10) could result in an increase in both memory load and processing time.

The generalizability of any theory about memory loads, therefore, or what counts as a "chunk", will depend on appropriate simplifying assumptions. In the EXTENDED STRUCTURAL LEARNING THEORY, where PROCESSING CAPACITY is a factor, this is accomplished by taking PROCESSING SPEED into account. It is assumed that the minimal components (processes) of which rules are composed must, for any given individual, all take the same minimal unit of time to perform, irrespective of inputs (to the components). Such rules are said to be PROCESS ATOMIC (see Section 5.9). Thus, for example, if the above atomic rule were process atomic, then individual subjects not only would respond in equal time to basic subtraction problems, like 3 - 2 and 15 - 6, but also would respond equally as fast with respect to every other process atomic rule.

Whether or not such a detailed level of representation can be guaranteed to exist is problematical. Such an assumption, however, would seem reasonable to the extent that human physiology parallels the digital computer. In the latter case, all processes can be broken down ultimately into physically equivalent binary decisions. (As we shall see in Section 5.9, the assumption of PROCESS ATOMICITY plays a central role in assessing BEHAVIOR POTENTIAL up to PROCESS EQUIVALENCE [see, ATOMICITY, PROCESS].)

When the representation of a rule is PROCESS ATOMIC (i.e., when the component processes all have the same characteristic, minimal processing speed), then the structures defined by the rule are assumed to act as CHUNKS (i.e., to impose one unit of memory load on the information processor). This would be true whether a given chunk consisted of a simple element (e.g., digit) or was composed of a complex of rules (e.g., those involved in deriving certain trigonometric identities, see Chapter 15, Section 3). (Just because a rule is process atomic, of course, it does not follow that overall latencies should be identical. Thus, one task might be performed directly whereas another might be accomplished over several stages, each of which takes the same time to perform.) For the structures defined by a rule to act as chunks, then, it is *not* sufficient that the component processes be atomic in the sense that individual subjects can use them (or some computational equivalent) either perfectly on all items to which they apply, or not at all. (In Section 5 this type of atomicity is referred to as BEHAVIORAL or SUCCESS/FAILURE ATOMICITY.) According to the above, all of the knowledge rules available to any given individual must be represented in terms of component processes that, in addition to behavioral atomicity, all take the same time to perform (cf. Scandura, 1973, particularly pp. 99-100, 109-111, 183; 1976, Chapter 1).

In realistic applications, fortunately, it may not be necessary (or even desirable) to require that component processes be process atomic in the most restrictive sense (i.e., be minimal and equal over *all* conceivable component processes). Indeed, it is hard to see how this could ever be guaranteed (i.e., operationalized). In order to insure that each structure defined by a rule imposes the same load on the processor, it may be sufficient to assume only that the component processes be process atomic *relative* to the problem domain in question. "What is a chunk", therefore, will necessarily be relative (to some problem domain). Defined in this way, processing capacity and UNIT LATENCY are allowed to vary from problem domain to problem domain. By an extension of the arguments in Section 5, however, it follows that one could never detect such differences *within* any given problem domain. More important, with all but the simplest problem domains, individual processing capacities and unit latencies are likely to be so close to asymptote, i.e., to their true universal values, that the differences might be ignored for most practical purposes.

Nonetheless, the assumption, that each component process takes the same time to perform for every input in its domain, places important constraints on the level of molarity at which such processes can be represented. Specifically, any given rule that is LATENCY EQUIVALENT (i.e., takes the same time to perform) with respect to its domain can be refined at most into a finite number of distinct component processes which are applied consecutively to each input. If "looping" were involved (i.e., iterative reapplication of component processes), then the latencies associated with different inputs would differ and the rule could not be latency equivalent (cf. Scandura, 1973, pp. 99 & 333-334).

One could reject the above assumptions, of course, and argue in favor of other alternatives. Thus, some psychologists might argue that it seems unlikely in human cognition that the latencies associated with all component rules, no matter how MOLECULAR the level of representation, would *all* be equal (even within subjects). Thus, although one can break rules (processes) down into minimal components, it may not be feasible simultaneously to equate the number of structures that enter into any given component process. In adding the numerals 5 and 7, for example, the load might be two, one for each digit. On the other hand, if these same digits were part of the (partially solved) column addition problem

$$\begin{array}{r} 54 \\ +72 \\ \hline 6 \end{array}$$

the corresponding load (for the same processes) might be four,
two for the 5 and 7, one for the column, and one for the partial
sum (cf. Chapter 7).

Although the basic processes are minimal in both cases
(relative to the indicated level of representation), it clearly
is problematical (i.e., an empirical question to determine)
whether one can assume equal latencies under these circumstances.
In fact, the results of research by Sternberg (1969) and others
suggests that perhaps latency might be a linear function of
memory load. To the extent that we can believe Sternberg's results in the present context, latencies might not be equal within given minimal processes. The respective latencies, however,
might still be linearly related to the corresponding memory
loads for each subject. More particularly, one could assume
that each chunk contributes equally to latency. In this case,
the latency associated with each minimal component process would
equal a sum of unit latencies, one for each chunk associated
with that process.

Although it might appear to fit the "facts", I would be
skeptical of such an assumption for several reasons. First,
Sternberg's results are based on normative data, cf. Chapter 1,
and may not deal adequately with individual processes. In particular, in the present view it would make a big difference
whether or not the processes in question (e.g., those used to
identify the target items used in the Sternberg task) are well
learned. For example, where correspondences between targets
and entire memory sets are well learned, the search processes
used would tend to be relatively automatic (see *Skilled Performance*). Hence, one would expect processing speed (LATENCY)
to be relatively independent of the size of the target set. On
the other hand, where correspondences between individual items
in the target and memory sets vary over test items, the search
processes would be less automatic so that processing speed would
almost certainly depend on target set size (cf. Schneider &
Shiffrin, 1977). Second, the data itself suggest that the
rules/processes themselves are not process atomic. Certainly
the identified component processes took differential amounts of
time. (Whether this could be overcome via training *is* an empirical question.) Third, such an assumption would complicate
life (although not unbearably so). I have found on several key
occasions in my own theoretical work that the simplest assumptions often turn out to be the best empirically (cf. Scandura,
1973, pp. 266-271).

Memory Loads Associated with Arbitrary Rules: Assuming
that the above conditions are satisfied, the latency associated
with an entire COMPUTATION would be the sum of the latencies
associated with the individual processes (process atomic rules).
Moreover, the memory load associated with such a computation
would be the maximum number of chunks associated with the vari-

ous stages of the computation. Details as to how memory loads may be determined with respect to individual rules, together with related empirical support, are given in Chapter 7 (also see Scandura, 1973) and are not repeated here. A stochastic extension of this theory, which applies under nonidealized conditions, also is described in Chapter 7.

To my knowledge, no directly relevant empirical work along these lines has been done with respect to higher-order rules, or where processing is under the control of goals (testing) or the goal-switching control mechanism. In view of the above, it nonetheless seems reasonable, in the case of higher-order rules, to expect memory load to depend on the amount of internal structure of the input rules/goals that must be taken into account in carrying out the higher-order decisions and operations. The more the individual input rules act as units (i.e., chunks), the lower the memory load. Conversely, where explicit attention is given to chunks that are embedded in such rules, memory loads should be relatively high.

Similar comments would apply to testing with respect to goals, and to goal switching with respect to the control mechanism. In the initial illustration concerning the control mechanism, for example, the rules were treated as wholes. No mention was made of internal structure.

Although we shall not attempt here to delve into the matter, the previously described distinction between unitary and composite goals may have some relation to the notion of "intensity of concentration." In particular, the more unitary a goal, the greater the degree of concentration that may be possible, presumably as a result of the lower load imposed by the goal on the processor. In intense situations, however, a person's behavior is apt to be less flexible. Perhaps this has something to do with the phrase "single-minded". For further discussion of related issues see Scandura (1973, Chapter 10; 1974c). Also see Chapter 7.

To summarize, two basic assumptions in the structural learning theory are that each individual subject may be uniquely characterized by a fixed processing capacity and a fixed processing speed. Moreover, I have suggested above that may be a close relationship between memory load and processing speed--specifically, that the structures associated with a rule act as chunks (i.e., impose a unit load on the processor) in cases where the rule is represented in terms of process atomic components. As noted above, this assumption may be interpreted in either an absolute or a relativistic sense. In addition, as observed in Section 5.9, this assumption (interpreted in the latter sense) also provides a basis for operationally defining "what is a chunk", and hence behavior potential (individual knowledge), in situations where processing capacity and response latency are taken into account.

Presumably, the fixed capacities and speeds that are assumedly associated with various individuals, as well as the proposed relationship between memory load and processing speed, are fundamental characteristics that may be expected to apply universally over all tasks and individuals. Although these assumptions have yet to be subjected to definitive empirical test, and are clearly speculative, they are not entirely arbitrary. In particular, some variant of these assumptions would appear necessary in any "enrichment" of the proposed theory that maintains essential relationships among content, cognition, and individual differences (cf. Sections 2.2 and 5.9 in this chapter). In any case, the assumptions potentially could have far reaching consequences. Both theory and implications derived therefrom should be subjected to extensive experimental testing.

The research reported in Chapter 7 constitutes only a small first step in this direction. In particular, after fairly extensive training designed to bring processing speed (on component processes) to asymptote, each subject was allowed to process composite tasks at his own rate, a rate that was constant over component processes but, nevertheless, was "comfortable" to him. Presumably these rates approached asymptote and satisfied at least some of the above conditions. The composite tasks involved such things as ordinary addition and repeating lists of digits. Among other things the results suggest that various individuals may in fact have different, yet fixed processing capacities, that generalize across different classes of problems.

5. INDIVIDUAL DIFFERENCES MEASUREMENT/ASSESSING BEHAVIOR POTENTIAL

In Section 2, on competence, we saw how arbitrary problem domains can be analyzed to determine the underlying (higher- and lower-order) competence rules characteristic of given subject populations. In Sections 3 and 4, we discussed certain (assumedly) universal characteristics of the human information processor and showed how they provide a comprehensive framework for viewing much of human cognition. The specific cognitive content (knowledge rules) available to individual subjects was assumed.

It is one thing, however, to say that behavior depends on the relevant knowledge available to a learner, and quite another thing to measure (identify) such knowledge. Because of its sheer magnitude, it is obviously impossible to measure all of any individual's knowledge. It is equally impossible to measure all possible individual variations, even with respect to problem domains of modest size.

A basic assumption in the structural learning theory is that this is not necessary; it is necessary only to measure knowledge with enough precision to distinguish the observables (i.e., problems, solutions) of interest. Indeed, in a "top-down" theory, that purports to deal with overall interrelationships, too much attention to detail may obscure essential distinctions. Individual differences measurement, in effect, is necessarily *relative* to some problem domain and subject population. The precision, efficiency, and reliability of such measurement, with respect to individuals, depends on the adequacy of competence assumptions concerning: overall compatibility of competence rules with target populations, atomicity of component rules (cf. Scandura, 1973, Chapter 5), assumed entering capabilities, context, and level of analysis.

To see how these assumptions enter, we first review the structural approach to individual differences measurement as it applies to single rules (Scandura, 1971a, 1973; Chapters 8 and 9, this book). Then we consider various extensions of the approach (e.g., to provide a basis for determining entering abilities with respect to NONTRIVIAL PROBLEM DOMAINS). The general approach to individual differences measurement, which is described below, effectively constitutes a "law of correspondence", which operationally defines individual knowledge (a theoretical construct) in terms of observable behavior (cf. Hilke, Kempf, & Scandura, 1976; Chapter 1, this book).

We begin with some general background.

5.1 BACKGROUND

Contemporary information processing research relevant to the problem of identifying cognitive processes tends to fall into two categories: (1) Most experimental/cognitive psychologists have concentrated largely on attempts to identify processes that provide the best overall account of *group* (sample) performance on given classes of tasks. (2) Others, primarily in the area of computer simulation, have been more concerned with identifying the processes used by particular *individuals*.

In the former case, alternative rules/processes are postulated, predictions based on the various processes are made, and the predictions are compared with respect to averaged data, usually averaged over items and groups, although sometimes over items within individuals (cf. Scandura, 1973, Chapter 8). This approach necessarily ignores differences involving individuals, items, or both. For example, suppose that we identify two processes by which the binary numeral representing the number of a's in xB (where x is a string of a's) might be generated-- namely Rule (3)

and, collectively, r_1, r_2, *. In each case, stochastic parameters can be introduced to represent the times required to perform various components of the respective processes. For example, let α, β, and γ be parameters representing the times required to carry out r_1 (or Operation 1), r_2 (or Operation 2), and *, respectively. Ignoring the time required to determine whether the number of a's is odd or even (which could involve an additional parameter, see Section 4.2), the time required to apply Rule (3) would be $x_1\alpha + x_2\beta$, where x_1 and x_2 denote the number of applications of operations 1 and 2, respectively. In generating the binary numeral associated with aaaaaB, for example, $x_1 = 1$ and $x_2 = 2$. By adding suitable parameters, one could also derive an expression to represent latencies involving interactions among rules r_1, r_2, and *. Estimates of such parameters can be obtained by standard regression methods, both in the case of data averaged over items and groups (Suppes & Groen, 1967) and over items within individuals (Groen, 1967; cf. Scandura, 1973, Chapter 8).

The relative adequacy of alternative theories (processes), then, can be determined by substituting the obtained parameter estimates into the latency expressions and comparing the resulting latency predictions with the obtained average data. Normally, of course, one would prefer the process that provides the best overall fit. (For actual studies along these lines, see Suppes & Groen, 1967; Groen, 1967.)

The main limitation of this approach is that individual processes may be obscured by group data. The fact that a process provides the best overall account says nothing directly about the processes used by individuals (Chapter 1). As became so clear as a result of the controversy concerning all-or-none versus incremental learning during the early 1960s, for example, completely contrary statistical assumptions may lead to essentially the same predictions regarding average behavior. Estimating separate parameters for each individual, of course, may help to minimize this problem but will not eliminate it entirely. Uncertainty as to which process individuals are actually using will exist just to the extent that the constraints discussed in Section 4.2 (as well as others) have not been satisfied. For further details and discussion along the lines of our example, see Scandura (1973, pp. 259-262; 1967).

The second approach is perhaps best typified by research on computer simulation. In computer simulation of human performance the goal is to devise explicit computer programs (rules) that solve given classes of tasks (e.g., arithmetic, chess) in the same way as individual subjects. That is, a given program may be thought of as representing the knowledge had by a particular subject relative to a given task domain.

Although there is no entirely systematic method for devising simulation programs, a basic approach is not unlike the initial steps of structural analysis described in Section 2. That is, individual subjects may be observed while solving a variety of representative problems, and programs may be devised to parallel the observed processes. In existing simulations, the programs frequently incorporate general performance constraints such as a limited capacity for processing information (cf. Newell & Simon, 1972). In turn, the outputs of trial programs are compared with new behavior, with subsequent refinements and evaluation where necessary.

To date, the approach seems to be useful primarily as a means of modeling complex human performance. Relatively little progress, for example, has been made in dealing with learning. Nonetheless, computer simulation research perhaps more than any other single movement is responsible for the mass shift in experimental psychology toward information processing.

From the present point of view, the simulation approach has two major limitations. First, it is relatively inefficient. Thus, whereas rules designed to deal with averages often fail to account for individual behavior, simulation rules/programs too often fail from the other end. A simulation program may adequately represent the knowledge of particular individuals but not that of others in the population. In general, simulation programs must be constructed anew for each subject (although the same state space can often be used, cf. Newell & Simon, 1972; Chapter 15, this book). Second, simulation programs generally confound control mechanisms with specific knowledge. Even where separable (e.g., Newell & Simon's [1972] production systems; Minsky & Papert's [1972] heterarchical systems), there is little direct evidence or justification to suggest that

the control mechanisms used are characteristic of human processors. As described in Section 4 on cognitive mechanisms, clearer
separation (of control and knowledge) could have important advantages in accounting for cognitive activities, such as learning
and motivation, other than simple performance.

5.2 SIMPLE PROBLEM CLASSES/SINGLE RULES

The structural learning theory combines many of the advantages of both of the above methods. Competence rules are used
as an instrument of sorts with which to measure individual human
knowledge. More specifically, the theory tells how, via finite
testing procedures, one can identify which parts of given rules
in a competence theory individual subjects know--that is, which
rules or parts thereof accurately represent their behavior potential. The rules in a competence theory, in a very real
sense, serve as rulers of measurement, and provide a basis for
the operational definition of human knowledge.

Refinement of Rules: Consider the assessment problem first
with respect to simple problem domains (classes), specifically
where success/failure constitutes the essential behavior and
where idealized performance may reasonably be assumed to be
governed by a single rule (e.g., simple addition in contemporary American schools). In this case, the population may be
assumed to share a common "culture" with respect to the given
class of problems.

Recall in this regard that rules may be represented as
labeled directed graphs, and that the various arrows (operations) and nodes (decisions) can always be broken down (REFINED)
into simple enough components so that each learner in a given
population is able to perform each component perfectly or not
at all. In short, any rule can be represented in terms of
ATOMIC rules. (For arguments to this effect, see Suppes, 1969;
Scandura, 1970, 1973, 1976.)

In general, a PATH through a rule acts in atomic fashion
if and only if each component acts in atomic fashion. The chain,
in effect, is only as strong as its weakest link. Given the
assumption of atomicity, there are only a finite number of distinct paths through any given rule (i.e., there is no need to
distinguish paths according to the number of repetitions of
loops). For illustrative purposes consider the class of tasks
(1) above and solution Rule (3).

(3)

There are three distinct paths through Rule (3), represented by

(3a)  $\circlearrowleft$ 1   (3b)  $\circlearrowright$ 2   (3c) 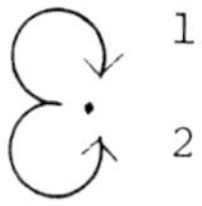 $\{\circlearrowleft$ 1 $\circlearrowright$ 2

Paths (3a) and (3b) are obviously atomic, since each involves only a single atomic rule. Path (3c) is also atomic since each of its components is atomic.

Using Refined Rules for Testing: Collectively, the paths of a rule impose a partition on the domain of problem situations to which the rule applies. That is, each path makes it possible to generate responses to a uniquely specified equivalence class of problems and to no others. For example, Path (3a) applies to all strings that contain a number of a's equal to some power of 2 (if we ignore, for argumentation purposes, the final step of generating a "1" to the left of a string of 0's [e.g., aaaaaaaaB has 2^3 a's]). Path (3b) applies to all strings that contain a number of a's equal to some power of 2 minus 1, 2^n-1 (e.g., aaaB, aaaaaaaB). Path (3c) is superordinate to the others and applies to all strings.

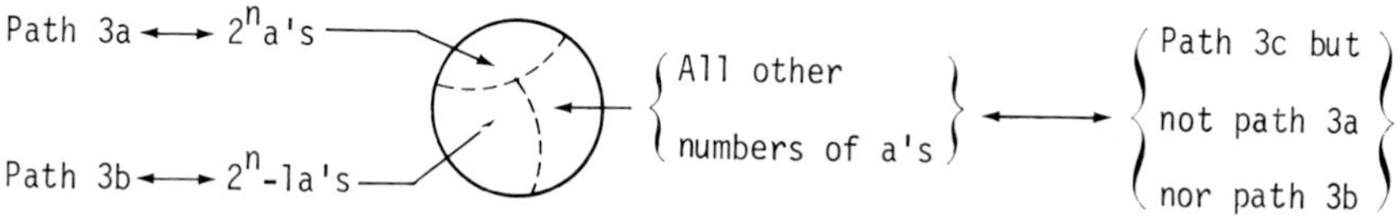

Path 3a $\longleftrightarrow$ 2na's —   { All other numbers of a's } $\longleftrightarrow$ (Path 3c but not path 3a nor path 3b)

Path 3b $\longleftrightarrow$ 2^n-1a's —

Figure 1. Representation of the partition imposed on the problem domain {xB - By} by paths 3a, 3b, and 3c. Problems in the three equivalence classes can be computed (solved) by the indicated paths.

The fact that the paths of a rule partition its domain makes it possible to pinpoint, via a finite testing procedure, what individuals in the corresponding population know relative to that rule. On tasks where the probability of guessing is low, it is sufficient, according to the atomicity assumptions, to test each person on just one item (problem) selected randomly from each mutually exclusive (nonoverlapping) equivalence class. Success on any one item implies success on any other item drawn for the same equivalence class, and similarly for failure. Correspondingly, individual knowledge is represented in terms of rules, specifically in terms of subrules of given rules of competence.

Suppose, for example, that a person is tested on strings aaaaaaaaB, aaaB, and aaaaaB, corresponding to Paths (3a), (3b), and (3c), respectively. Also assume that the testee is successful on the first item but not on the second or third. In this case, the testee's knowledge would be represented by Subrule (3a).

Although this example is a bit too simple to illustrate the point, it is important to note that the level of REFINEMENT

OF A RULE into components is critical in determining test efficiency. If a rule is refined too much (i.e., if the components
are too molecular relative to the entering capabilities of subjects in the target population), testing may be unnecessarily
inefficient (see Chapter 15). More test items may be required
than necessary. On the other hand, if the components are too
molar (e.g., if Rule (3) itself were assumed to be atomic), the
assumption of atomicity may not hold, and testing may be correspondingly imprecise. The critical assumption for purposes of
measurement is that the level of rule refinement (as well as the
form of the rule) must be appropriate to the population. This
level ordinarily will be more molar than the maximum refinement
possible. Moreover, the more "sophisticated" the population the
more molar this level will be (cf. Scandura, 1970, 1973, 1976,
1977b; Chapter 15, this book).

In testing and constructing subrules to characterize individual knowledge, it also is important to keep in mind hierarchical relationships among the various paths. A path (e.g., Path
3c) is said to be superordinate to another if the associated
equivalence class includes the equivalence class associated with
the other path (e.g., Path 3a). Thus, success on a problem
associated only with a superordinate path necessarily implies
success on problems associated with corresponding subordinate
paths. For example, success on aaaaaB, which is uniquely associated with Path (3c), necessarily implies success on aaaB.
(The formulation in Scandura, 1973, and Chapters 8 and 9 of
this book, are equivalent, although slightly different.)

According to the theory, testing on a subordinate path is
necessary only where a person fails on all paths superordinate
to it. Hence, the number of test items required to measure
individual knowledge may be reduced accordingly through *sequential* testing. For example, if a testee succeeds on a test item
corresponding only to Path (3c), it can be assumed (on the basis
of atomicity) that the testee will also succeed on items associated with Paths (3a) and (3b). This follows because Path (3c)
(now viewed as a rule) also applies to items associated with
Paths (3a) and (3b).

Success on Paths (3a) and (3b), on the other hand, does
not necessarily imply success on Path (3c) because it is possible to learn repeated application of Operation 1 (Path 3a) and/
or repeated application of Operation 2 (Path 3b) without necessarily having mastered the overall structure of Path (3c), including the critical decision-making capability (node). Hence,
the individual knowledge of a person who knows Paths (3a) and
(3b), but not Path (3c), would be represented by a discrete pair
of rules (i.e., the two paths viewed as rules of knowledge).
A testee who also knows Path (3c) might be summarized by Rule
(3) (corresponding to Path 3c).

In effect, the question of whether to represent knowledge

in terms of discrete paths (subrules), or in terms of integrated graphs, depends on how the testee's performance relates to the hierarchical relationships among the various paths. If a testee is successful on a superordinate path, then his knowledge may be represented in terms of the corresponding, integrated subgraph. Success on only unrelated subordinate paths implies discrete representation. (Note: The hierarchical arrangement of paths, and of components thereof, corresponds roughly to learning hierarchies, Gagne, 1970. Indeed, the above rationale provides theoretical justification for learning hierarchies, which traditionally have been based on primarily pragmatic considerations, cf. Chapters 8 and 9.)

Summary: It is important to emphasize that the knowledge attributed to different individuals may vary even though only one rule of competence may be involved. The idea is directly analogous to measuring different distances with the same ruler.

The proposed, relativistic approach to measurement has important advantages in comparison to the methods of averages and of computer/behavior simulation. Unlike the method of averages, for example, where information-processing models (rules) are designed to reflect average performance, rules of competence are designed to reflect idealized performance (prototypes), which in some sense reflect the ultimate to be expected of subjects in the target population. The latter approach provides a deterministic basis for assessing individual behavior potential, which holds under idealized test conditions. Moreover, although accounts of average behavior may be useful for some purposes (e.g., under nonidealized test conditions), the structural approach, even here, is suggestive of more detailed characterization along the lines of diagnostic testing. Thus, for example, rather than summarizing the average behavior of a sample of subjects in terms of a single rule one might summarize the average behavior of various subsamples in terms of various subrules. More refined characterization of this sort would be especially useful where there are identifiable differences in ability relative to the tasks in question.

In computer simulation, on the other hand, a different rule may be required to represent the behavior potential of each individual. Moreover, there is no "theory" as to how the various rules are related. The structural theory deals directly with this problem and, consequently, is more efficient. One competence rule may be adequate to characterize the knowledge of all individuals in a given population. The idea is roughly analogous to using the same problem/state space in artificial intelligence (see Nilsson, 1971), except that problem spaces deal with logical possibility rather than cultural constraints (on competence rules) as in the present theory (see Chapter 15).

Nonetheless, the above (structural) approach to individual differences measurement is inadequate in its simplest form. In the following sections we shall consider particular inadequacies of the approach and extensions that have been designed to deal with them.

5.3 SIMPLE PROBLEM CLASSES/TWO OR MORE RULES

Where two or more distinct "cultures" are combined in the same population, two or more distinctly different rules may be required to adequately represent the underlying competence. Ordinary subtraction, for example, is often carried out by quite different methods (rules), depending on the culture in question. In contemporary American schools, for example, the "borrowing" method is almost universal, whereas in European schools the "equal additions" method seems to be favored.

One extension of the above method is concerned with assessing behavior potential with respect to simple classes of problems (e.g., ordinary subtraction) in cases where all problems in the class can be solved via two or more rules (at most a finite number), each of which is potentially compatible with the target population. This extension is detailed in Scandura (1973) and Chapter 9 of this book.

The basic idea is straightforward. Each rule imposes a partition on the class of problems as above. Since these partitions ordinarily will differ, they collectively impose a new "intersection" partition on the class. In general, each equivalence class in the intersection partition is an intersection of equivalence classes, one from each of the partitions associated with the various underlying rules.

The intersection equivalence classes are homogeneous with respect to each rule. Hence, given the adequacy of the initial atomic assumptions, it is always sufficient for testing purposes to select one test item (problem) from each of the intersection equivalence classes.

Moreover, given the alternative rules it is often a simple matter (and always possible) to construct a single rule associated with the intersection partition (i.e., a rule that imposes the same partition on the domain as do the alternative rules collectively). An example based on ordinary column subtraction is given in Chapter 9. In this case, the "borrowing" and "equal additions" algorithms serve as alternative rules.

It would appear, therefore, that one can always replace two or more rules, which underlie the same class of problems, by a single rule. But, this is true only as long as attention is limited to the problem class in question. In Section 5.6, we consider a more general case where extra-domain problem solving also is of concern.

5.4 IDIOSYNCRATIC INDIVIDUAL DIFFERENCES

The above argument makes it possible, in principle, to allow for any finite number of different prototypes (competence rules) with respect to a given problem domain and subject population. Nonetheless, there are some situations where individual differences are so idiosyncratic that it may be impractical to take into account all variations. In experimental psychology, for example, perhaps the prime example of this type involves paired-associate and serial learning in its various formats (where the "problems" consist of simple stimulus-response (S-R) associations, cf. Scandura, 1970, 1973, Chapter 10).

Ironically, in view of the motivation underlying traditional S-R learning experiments, the more complex and highly structured a problem domain, the less idiosyncratic individual differences tend to become. That is, although individual differences in knowledge may vary considerably with respect to given rules, the number of different rules of competence required to measure this knowledge (to some acceptable level of precision) is typically quite small.

In testing on simple problem classes, unacceptable reliability/precision may stem from two basic sources. First, individuals in the population may attack the problems in so many different ways that the analyst might have to introduce almost as many rules of competence (prototypes) as individuals. In this case, practically speaking, the analyst might be willing to compromise and to select only those rules that are compatible with (i.e., can be used to measure) the knowledge of a significant percentage of subjects. The other would be ignored. The number and types of rules, which may safely be ignored in any specific application, will depend on the desired level of precision.

A second major source of imprecision stems from attempts to say more about individual behavior than the level of analysis allows. Thus, for example, Piagetian theory appears to provide a general basis (GLOBAL rules) for classifying a child as a conserver, nonconserver, or transitional but not necessarily for specifying the particular stage associated with specific types of conservation tasks. Thus, behavior on a sample of conservation tasks may be sufficient for identifying developmental stage globally, but behavior on one type of conservation task may not always be sufficient for identifying stages with respect to other types of conservation tasks (see "horizontal decalage" in Chapter 15, Section 3.6). Similarly, it might be possible to predict the general quality of a contractor's work but not the quality of any particular building. In effect, it may be possible to eliminate some behaviors as unlikely (e.g., inefficient floor plans), and to identify others as possibilities, but not to specify which of the possibilities will actually be produced. Where no theoretical distinctions exist between otherwise distinguishable alternatives the predictions are called NONDETERMINISTIC (cf. Scandura, 1973, Chapter 8).

Relative to the more detailed level at which problem solu-

tions are represented, global rules of the above sort correspond
to heuristics or "fuzzy algorithms" (e.g., Landa, 1974; Pask,
1975; also see Chapter 3, this book). Roughly speaking, the
latter correspond to rules (algorithms) that have not been sufficiently well specified to precisely predict individual behavior on specific problems. In present terminology, a rule would
be considered heuristic in Landa's (1974) sense if some of the
components of which it is composed are not atomic, relative to
the prespecified problems/solutions. (Note: The components
may, nonetheless, be atomic relative to a more global level of
representation of problems/solutions.)

5.5 TESTING BY DESCRIPTION ("TEACHBACK")
    Since competence has a syntactic as well as a semantic
component, it is not always necessary to assess individual
knowledge directly. Testing can also take place with respect
to some agreed on LANGUAGE of discourse. That is, instead of
having the subject solve problems associated with given rules
of competence, the subject might be asked to describe that
competence.
    At a minimum, the language of communication between the
observer and the subject, insofar as the observer influences
the subject's problem environment, must provide a basis for
posing problems and for describing processes. It must, in effect, be a command-and-question language, as well as a declarative one. The language of discourse, for example, could be some
natural language. Ordinarily, however, the language must be
restricted and/or extended to conform to the subject population
and problem domain. In particular, the language must be understandable to the subjects, if they are to comprehend given information, and it must be usable by them, if they are to be able
to describe what they know.
    Unless the competence associated with the language itself
is a subject of concern, it will normally be desirable, for
purposes of study, to keep the language as simple as possible
and the level of (language competence) analysis as molar as
possible (cf. Chapter 12). In the theoretically-motivated empirical research, that is reported in this book, care was taken
to insure that subjects in the target population could interpret
and/or use the language involved (see Chapters 5 and 6). That
is, the required language competencies were AUXILIARY (see EN-
TERING CAPABILITIES).
    Notice, however, that the previously described methods for
measuring individual knowledge directly could be applied equally
to communication competencies. Thus, where language production
and interpretion competencies cannot be uniformly assumed of all
subjects, these competencies may be represented in terms of
atomic processes to provide a basis for testing. For examples,
see the Addendum to Chapter 12 (Section 8) and a computer program

designed by Carroll (1975) for speech production. One can also
imagine adapting for this purpose one of the recent question-
answer systems in artificial intelligence (e.g., Winograd, 1972;
Schank, 1973).

There is, however, a major difference between the present
approach and those based on computer programs. Whereas computer
programs in the latter case are represented at a fixed (usually
molecular) level of detail, determined by the computer language
in question, competence rules in the former case need only be
represented in sufficient detail to account for the prescribed
behavior of subjects in the target population. Ordinarily,
rules of competence may be represented in relatively molar terms,
with no loss of predetermined behavioral precision and an increase in test efficiency (see Chapter 15, Sections 3.2 and 3.3).

In overall form the proposed approach is similar to Pask's
(1975) use of "teachback" in his theory of conversations. His
emphasis, however, seems to be on ensuring the availability of
a language in terms of which participants in a dialogue may
communicate. Although communication may take place by showing
(i.e., solving problems), for example, as well as by describing,
it is not clear whether or how conversation theory purports to
deal with the corresponding questions of problem homogeneity/
heterogeneity (i.e., equivalence classes).

Incidentally, Pask makes a useful distinction between two
roles of the observer/teacher (agent/other participant). One
role is that of the analyst who specifies problems and identifies underlying competence. The second role is that of the
"other" participant in a dialogue, the environment, discussant,
or teacher with whom the subject interacts. Although important,
this distinction has been suppressed in this chapter because the
emphasis is on the detailed analysis of single-problem episodes
(where only the former plays a central role). The distinction
is reintroduced in Chapter 14 where the concern shifts to the
dynamic interaction between teacher and learner over time (i.e.,
over sequences of problems). Conversation theory is concerned
primarily with this dynamic relation, with correspondingly less
attention to the mechanisms governing each episode thereof.

5.6 NONTRIVIAL PROBLEM DOMAINS

As observed in the previous sections on competence, it is
not always feasible to identify directly a single procedure that
accounts for a given problem domain. (Problem domains with this
characteristic are called NONTRIVIAL.) In general, then, the
competence underlying any given problem domain may involve more
than just one rule. To determine the associated knowledge in
this case, it might appear sufficient, on first thought, to
simply test for each rule separately as described in Section
5.1-5.3. Alternatively, the rules of competence (finite in
number) might be combined to produce a single, comprehensive

procedure that accounts for the problem domain in its entirety, or at least as much of it as do the component rules collectively. (In addition to the initial rules, such a procedure would necessarily incorporate some equivalent of the postulated control mechanism.)

Deeper reflection, however, suggests that neither approach in itself would be entirely satisfactory. Testing each rule separately would be unnecessarily inefficient, for instance, because there is no unique level of structural analysis. Hierarchical relationships among the various levels of structural analysis must be considered in any complete specification of individual differences. Specifically, recall that a given level of structural analysis is appropriate for a subject population only if one of two conditions is satisfied: (1) the rules in the corresponding rule set are essentially atomic (whereas at preliminary levels of analysis the rules are not atomic) or (2) the individual rules are represented in terms of atomic rules and the rule set itself (fully) accounts for the problem domain. (In case 2 any further extension of the analysis cannot be distinguished with respect to the domain, cf. Section 5.8.) If one tests only on rules associated with a preliminary level of analysis, then failure with respect to a particular rule (or path thereof) may be due to failure on just one of the component (e.g., atomic) rules or on all of them. Thus, a subject might fail on items associated with composite rules, but it would be impossible to determine the sources of such failure. No distinctions among unsuccessful testees would be possible.

The essential point is that testing with respect to the SOURCE RULES associated with deeper levels of structural analysis may make such distinctions possible. Thus, in assessing transfer potential (to problems that cannot be solved via a single rule of competence; see ATOMICITY, TRANSFER) it may be important not only to know whether a subject has a complex capability (rule) relative to the given problem domain, but whether he also has the potential for deriving parallel rules as well (i.e., the potential for transfer). Any given source rule may be involved in the derivation of any number of more complex rules. Where this is the case, testing for distinctions among source rules may be critical. Indeed, testing with respect to various levels of structural analysis is especially important where one is concerned with the cumulative effects of learning over time. (The important issue of cumulative learning is purposely avoided in this chapter; for details see Chapter 14.) In our basic illustration, for example, it makes a difference whether a person uses rule $r_2 r_1 r_2$ to solve the problem aaaaaB-B101, or whether the solution is derived from more basic source rules (e.g., r_1, r_2, *). The latter case implies a potential for transfer (e.g., to aaB-B10) that the former does not. (Note: Testing with respect to higher-order rules is

accomplished according to the same principles used with other
rules. Specifically, the inputs and outputs are descriptions
of lower-order rules. In testing *, for example, the inputs
are pairs of rules and the outputs are composite rules. More
details and realistic examples are given in Chapter 5, Experiments III & IV, and Chapter 13.)

Nonetheless, testing with respect to preliminary levels of
analysis may serve to increase the efficiency of testing, much
as with superordinate paths of individual rules. For example,
if a preliminary rule set is otherwise sufficient (i.e., if it
accounts adequately for the given problem domain), then testing
with respect to more basic source rules (deeper-levels of structural analysis) could increase the number of required test items.
(I do not know whether this statement is true in general, or
what specific conditions would need to be satisfied for the
statement to be true in all cases.) Moreover, any further information obtained via testing on source rules in this case
would be immaterial insofar as the problem domain itself is
concerned.

There also are difficulties in using a single comprehensive
rule of competence for testing purposes. Perhaps the major difficulty is definitional in that such rules necessarily involve
more complex interactions among components than is allowed in
the theory (see Section 2.1). The point can perhaps be made
most simply by observing that the interactions involved in
accounting for nontrivial problem domains might well involve
the generation of new rules and their subsequent use during the
course of a given computation (i.e., during the application of
a single, comprehensive rule). In the structural learning theory, behavior potential is defined with respect to more restricted kinds of rules (i.e., rules that do not involve the above
type of interaction). Moreover, it is not at all clear that
behavior potential can be defined in any reasonable or efficient way with respect to comprehensive rules that involve the
above type of interaction. For one thing, the number and complexity of the needed test items would almost certainly be greater than with the restricted kinds of rules allowed in the theory.

To summarize, testing with respect to nontrivial problem
domains, may involve various levels of structural analysis
(i.e., rule sets at various levels). Thus, testing with respect
to source rules (including higher-order source rules) may be
crucial, especially where the preliminary rule sets (from which
the source rules are identified via structural analysis) are
not adequate to account for the corresponding problem domain in
its entirety. However, where a rule set is sufficient in this
sense any further reduction of the rule set may not only be unnecessary but may result in unnecessarily inefficient testing.

5.7 SUMMARY: INDIVIDUAL DIFFERENCES MEASUREMENT TO BEHAVIORAL EQUIVALENCE

In the preceding sections we have considered how to assess individual behavior potential in three kinds of situations: (1) simple problem domains where there is only one feasible underlying rule of competence; (2) simple problem domains where two or more rules (possibly including error rules) account for the domain and also serve as cognitive prototypes for various subpopulations of subjects, and (3) nontrivial domains where the underlying competence consists of finite sets of rules taken collectively. We also sketched how one might test by description

In each case, testing is assumed to take place under appropriate memory-free conditions: Relevant rules of individual knowledge (not competence) are assumed to be uniformly available to testees; precautions are taken to insure that processing capacity is not overloaded; unlimited time is provided for responding; the test problems (given and goals) are both known to and properly encoded by the testees. (As shown in Table 1, these boundary conditions may be relaxed somewhat, where testing is tailored to the enriched structural learning theory outlined in Section 4. See Section 5.9 for discussion of Stage, (Latency), and Process Equivalence.)

Table 1
Types and Nature of Equivalence

Type	External Measure	Assessment Assumptions	Test Boundary Conditions	Bases For Predicti
Behavior	Success/ Failure	Compatibility of Competence, Behavioral Atomicity of Competence Rules	Uniform Availability (or Lack) of Knowledge Rules/Unlimited Time/ Capacity/Problem (Subject's Goal) Known/Encoding & Decoding Assured	Control Mechanism
Stage (Latency)	Above +Intermediate Stages (Latency)	Above +Externalizability of Intermediate Stages +(Fixed Latencies for Each Subject and Each Atomic Rule, Goal Switching, etc.)	Above	Control Mechanism (Latency Atomicity)
Process	Latency	Above +Unit Latencies, Minimal and Equal for Each Subject for All Atomic Processes	Problem (Subject's Goal) Known/Encoding & Decoding Assured	Control Mechanism + Processing Capacity Unit Latency

Although all three variations rely on specific rules (in an underlying competence theory) to identify needed test items, such testing does not uniquely identify individual processes. Rather, individual differences are identified only up to equiva-

lence classes of processes--in particular, equivalence classes
within which processes can not be distinguished insofar as the
behavior they generate is concerned. Thus, while two processes
in a given equivalence class may differ in detail, they impose
identical partitions on the problem domain to which they apply.
Consequently, they yield precisely the same predictions on the
given problem domain with regard to success/failure. In effect,
individual differences in specific knowledge may be identified
by the above techniques only up to what we shall call BEHAVIOR
EQUIVALENCE.

5.8 NONEQUIVALENCE OF DIFFERENT PROBLEM DOMAINS

As noted in Section 5.6, identical behavior (success/fail-
ure) predictions with respect to a given problem domain may be
generated via any number of rule sets. Where behaviorally
equivalent alternatives exist one can never be sure after testing, for example, whether a subject performed successfully because he knew a solution rule prior to testing, or because he
derived a new one during the testing. Successful test behavior
could occur either as a result of direct performance or of learning. In effect, given a problem domain, distinctions among performance, learning, or other alternative rule accounts might be
immaterial. Precisely the same success/failure predictions
might be made in each case.

Such predictions, however, would not necessarily be equivalent with respect to more comprehensive problem domains (or, as
we shall see in Section 5.9, with respect to given domains where
finer grained response measures are introduced). Thus, in testing on a problem domain that is larger than the original one,
the potential to learn might reflect itself in considerably
broader behavior potential. Consider, for example, problems of
the form xB-By and x'B-By where x is a string of a's, x' is a
string of b's, and y is the binary numeral representing the number of a's or b's in the corresponding input. Let the problems
involving a's as inputs constitute the original domain of primary interest. In this case, Rule (3) provides a direct PERFOR-
MANCE (RULE) ACCOUNT. An alternative LEARNING/TRANSFER (RULE)
ACCOUNT of this problem domain is provided by Rules r_1, r_2, and
a higher-order recursion rule that operates on rules like r_1 and
r_2 and generates recursive combinations of components (like
Rule 3).

Clearly, any BEHAVIOR PROFILE associated with the original
domain can be accounted for either in terms of Rule (3), the
performance account, or in terms of the alternative account
based on learning. These alternative accounts, however, are not
equivalent with regard to behavior on the larger problem domain
which includes problems of the form x'B-By. Testing with respect to the latter account, for example, provides information
regarding transfer potential that the former does not. Thus,

for example, predictions concerning the x'B-By problems in the larger domain can be made in relation to subjects who are tested with respect to the learning account and then are trained on Rules r_1' and r_2' (which correspond to r_1 and r_2 and apply to inputs involving b's). This would not be possible where subjects are tested only with respect to Rule (3) (and then trained on r_1' and r_2'). Suppose, for the sake of argument, that the higher-order recursion rule is atomic and applies to rules involving a's or b's. Then, in the former case, but not the latter, success would be expected on any input x'B, involving the same number of b's as some success input involving a's (and similarly for failure). As the reader may verify for himself, different success/failure profiles on transfer tasks may be obtained by assuming different patterns of availability of initial subrules.

(Notice parenthetically that the above transfer account could be simulated by a single, combined procedure, that takes as inputs strings of a's or b's together with one or more rule involving a's or b's. As indicated above, however, such a simulation procedure would amount to combining the postulated learning mechanism with lower- and higher-order rules, and would not lend itself readily to individual differences measurement.)

The same type of analysis can be applied where two or more rules might reasonably account for a given class of problems. Although their joint effects may be determined by testing with respect to the corresponding intersection partition, as indicated in Section 5.3 (also see Chapter 9), this approach may result in a loss of predictive power with respect to larger domains. For example, consider the illustrative (original) domain above together with Rule (3) and, say, the degenerate special Rule r, which operates on aB, aaB, and aaaB, and which generates the outputs B1, B10, B11, respectively. In this case, the introduction of higher-order selection rules for testing purposes may have important implications for performance beyond the original problem domain. To see this, suppose in the above example that the selection rule is defined by "select the more specific rule," and envision Rule r' and Rule (3'), which involve b's as inputs and which correspond, respectively, to Rules r and (3). Assume also that solving the above items via Rule r is somehow preferable (e.g., it may be faster) to Rule (3). In this case, testing with respect to higher-order selection rules may provide not only a basis for predicting transfer on new problems but also for predicting more detail concerning solutions (e.g., latencies). Thus, whereas the two rules are equivalent insofar as the outputs B1, B10, and B11 themselves are concerned, they might not be equivalent when latency, say, is also considered.

In order to distinguish latencies, as well as correct and incorrect solutions, it is not sufficient to base testing on a composite of alternative rules. The bases for selecting among

one or another of the rules must also be determined. That is,
it is necessary in this case to test with respect to selection
rules as well as the alternative rules (e.g., Rules r and 3) on
which they operate.

Although this discussion gets somewhat ahead of our main
development (see Section 5.9), including it here provides an
instructive basis for comparison. Thus, for example, errors
may be distinguished in a similar manner. Error and solution
rules, recall, may apply to the same stimuli and generate different responses--for example compare

$$\frac{3 + 2}{6} = \frac{\cancel{3}^{1} + 2}{\cancel{6}_{2}} \text{ (incorrect cancellation)} = \frac{1 + 2}{2} = \frac{3}{2}$$

with

$$\frac{3 + 2}{6} = \frac{5}{6}$$

Since subjects may know error rules as well as solution rules,
rules of both types may properly be included in competence accounts (see Section 2.5). Notice, moreover, that distinguishing
among alternative kinds of errors (or errors and solutions) is
directly analogous to distinguishing among different correct
solutions (e.g., according to latencies).

In order that testing allow for differential error prediction, therefore, selection rules must be taken into account.
It is interesting to note, also, that one could conceivably
account for "careless errors" in these terms. Thus, people frequently know both solution rules and error rules. In learning
mathematics, or in almost any field, people (some more than
others perhaps) may form premature closures (e.g., learn rules
that work only on the tasks of immediate interest, and that do
not readily generalize). Premature learning of this type may
interfere with subsequent performance on new tasks--even after
the corresponding, broader class of tasks has been mastered.
Arithmetic and spelling provide probably the best known examples.
Presumably, detailed analysis of the selection rules governing
behavior in these cases could be instructive, and might even
provide some insight as to how careless errors might be avoided.

The same principles would apply with respect to rule sets
involving other kinds of higher-order rules (e.g., subproblem
and retrieval rules). For example, it might not make any difference within a given domain whether a problem is solved directly or by breaking it into subproblems and solving the subproblems. Transfer potential, on the other hand, might be directly dependent.

5.9 OTHER KINDS OF EQUIVALENCE

As suggested above, behavior equivalence may not be sufficient for some purposes. In addition to success/failure, for

example, the behavioral scientist may be interested in saying more about the processes subjects use in solving problems.

Stage Equivalence: One obvious way to identify processes more precisely is to consider the stages subjects go through in solving problems. Specifically, rule sets may be required to account not only for final solutions but also for interim steps. A particularly interesting case involves the relationship between higher-order derivation and subproblem rules. Consider, for example, problems of the form xB-n (where n is the number of 1's in the binary numeral representation of x). Each such problem can be solved by composing Rule (3) with a simple counting rule, via a higher-order derivation rule, or by breaking the problem into subproblems and solving each in turn. The same equivalence classes of terminal behaviors would be generated in both cases.

In the former case, however, a composite rule is derived first and then applied. In the latter case, Rule (3) is selected and applied, followed by the counting rule. The two cases might be distinguished, therefore, by keying on intermediate stages. Operationally, this might be accomplished, for instance, by requiring subjects to manipulate physical representations of rules (cf. Chapter 5), or by determining natural pauses in responding (cf. Section 2). (Latency is used below in a more direct way.)

In spite of its apparent similarities, one should not confuse stage equivalence with the practice of using protocols to evaluate computer simulation theories (also see Bloom & Broder, 1950). In the former case, the rules of competence refer to prototypic (idealized) subjects and not to real ones. As before, individual knowledge is assessed relative to how subjects would solve the problems, if one knew a prototypic rule perfectly.

Although stage equivalence has not been used, as such, in testing the Structural Learning Theory (partly because this aspect of the theory had not been developed at the time the studies in Part 3 were conducted), such equivalence could in some ways provide a more exacting test than behavioral equivalence of the hypothesized control mechanism (or alternatives).

An alternative, indirect way to identify individual knowledge (processes) more precisely would be to use more detailed response measures. In view of its dominant role in cognitive psychology, let us consider the requirements that would have to be met in the case of latency. Here, in addition to behavioral atomicity, the major requirement would appear to be LATENCY ATOMICITY (not necessarily process atomicity as defined in Section 4; cf. next section). Not only must each atomic rule be homogeneous over inputs with respect to success/failure but, in the case of successes, the time required to carry out each atomic process, *for any given subject,* also must be constant on

its domain of applicability. (Note: The various atomic processes, however, need not have the same latency as in the case
of process atomicity.)

As noted previously, the requirement of constant latency
imposes an important constraint on atomic rules: They must not
lend themselves to refinements (i.e., more detailed representations) that involve "loops" (i.e., iterative reapplication of
component processes). Otherwise, some component operations of
the atomic rules would be involved different numbers of times,
with different inputs, so that an assumption of constant latency
would be untenable (cf. Scandura, 1973, pp. 99 & 333-334).

Refinement of a rule into atomic processes that satisfy
this condition is always possible (cf. Scandura, 1970; Suppes,
1969). This degree of refinement, however, may involve a relatively molecular level of rule representation. In turn, a relatively large number of atomic processes could normally be involved in responding to test items (e.g., in comparison with testing
under conditions of behavioral atomicity). Since errors of measurement would be compounded, probabilistic approximations would
seem reasonable in all but the most exacting tests.

In fact, this is precisely what a number of investigators
have done in order to account for latencies on tasks that subjects are otherwise able to perform (see Section 5 for a simple
example). Thus, Groen, Suppes and their associates developed
analogous probabilistic models where the latency parameters were
random variables corresponding to the various components of
simple addition algorithms. The parameters in the case of
Suppes and Groen (1967) referred to groups of subjects. As per
a suggestion made by Scandura (1967), Groen (1967) conducted a
parallel study in which the parameters referred to individuals.
For further discussion, see Scandura (1973, pp. 260-261) and
Suppes and Morningstar (1972; cf. Chapter 1, this book).

To summarize, in assessing behavior potential up to stage
equivalence the goal is to identify individual knowledge (relative to underlying competence) up to prespecified critical
stages. That is, knowledge must be specified in sufficient detail that it is not only homogeneous with respect to success/
failure but, in cases of success, also with respect to prespecified stages. In general, however, components of the underlying
rules may differ as to the relative ease with which they can be
performed. In particular, the corresponding processes may take
various times to perform.

Process Equivalence: The previous discussion in Section 5
deals almost exclusively with the operationalization of individual knowledge under "memory-free" conditions. It is assumed
that all relevant knowledge is immediately available to the
testee and that the testing conditions are such as to eliminate
effects due to the human processor's limited capacity for processing information.

The discriminating reader of Section 4 may anticipate what
is coming. Thus, although behavior and stage equivalence provide a basis for specifying the operational aspects of what is
known, data of this type does not say anything about the psychological significance of the entities being operated on.

PROCESS EQUIVALENCE provides an admittedly speculative
remedy for this limitation; it provides a potential basis for
the operational definition of "what is a chunk". As argued in
Section 4, the structures defined by a rule (or a goal, or the
control mechanism) act as chunks (i.e., impose a uniform measure,
or unit, of memory load on the information processor) only where
the corresponding rules (testing, control) are represented in
terms of process atomic processes (i.e., where each process is
asymptotic in the sense that it imposes minimal strain on each
subject). The associated latencies recall, need not be identical for all subjects. Rather, the structures defined by a rule
(i.e., the entities being operated on) count as chunks if each
component processes contribute the same amount to latency, irrespective of the particular inputs. A rule represented at this
level of detail is said to be PROCESS ATOMIC. The latency associated with any given process atomic rule, therefore, is assumed
to be a sum of UNIT LATENCIES, one for each component process,
where each subject may have a different characteristic processing time (i.e., unit latency). (Assumedly, the other basic
parameter characterizing individual cognition is a fixed processing capacity.)

In effect, the structures defined by a rule count as chunks
where observed latencies can be accounted for in terms of a
single latency parameter for each subject. As with stage equivalence, of course, it makes sense to talk about what chunks are
involved only where subjects are successful (and behavior and
stage equivalence are otherwise satisfied). Again, the basic
question is one of detail, the precision with which individual
knowledge can be determined.

It is not at all clear, of course, that the proposed operational definition is a good one, or whether it is even feasible
to account for observed latencies in terms of a single parameter.
(Its apparent simplicity is appealing but unfortunately the
world does not always turn out as one might like.) Moreover,
the proposed operational definition may or may not be consistent
with the assumption that individual subjects have a fixed capacity for processing information (see Section 4.2). More specifically, although this operational definition provides a potential basis for identifying the number of chunks (of memory load)
associated with any given computation, there can be no a priori
guarantee that the memory loads so determined will be consistent
with the assumption that each subject has a fixed capacity for
processing information, one that holds over all tasks (in the
associated problem domain). The data reported in Chapter 7 are

suggestive in this regard, but not definitive.

To the extent that these assumptions are good ones, they have potentially interesting implications for the representation of knowledge. They imply, for example, that both digital/discrete and analog/continuous representations may play a crucial role. Latency, for example, is an inherently continuous measure (although time can be approximated less efficiently in digital form), whereas chunks are inherently discrete. The general issue of digital versus analog representation is discussed further in Chapter 15.

One additional point should be made in view of our previous comments to the effect that individual knowledge may only be identified relative to some common standard. In the case of behavior equivalence, recall, the only cognitive assumption involves the control mechanism. This assumption of universal control is essentially a marriage of convenience because any rule account, involving such control, can be simulated insofar as success/failure is concerned by an alternative (unrestricted) procedure that includes both rules and control. The introduction of universal control, however, makes it possible to impose restrictions on the form of rules, and this in turn makes it possible (feasible) to assess individual behavior potential relative to given problem domains. The fact that goal switching control appears to be uniformly available to humans from a very early age (cf. Chapters 5 and 6) is an added benefit.

PROCESS EQUIVALENCE on the other hand, in principle, may be defined independently of particular problem domains (aside from that containing all human knowledge, real or potential). In this case, unit latencies might be assumed to hold over *all* (process atomic) rules so that *all* simulating rules would necessarily lead to identical predictions (e.g., including success/failure and latency) on the whole of human behavior. Indeed, it is hard to see how a level of *cognitive* detail beyond that inherent in process atomicity might have direct behavioral implications. Presumably further reduction would force one to consider the correlated physiological mechanisms that underlie process atomicity.

Nonetheless, even assessing individual knowledge up to process equivalence would not allow complete explanation, or perfect prediction, in all real world situations. Although it might potentially provide for a level of detail which exceeds anything that is presently available, it would not in itself, for example, take encoding or decoding into account. Presumably, any enrichment of the present theory, that incorporates encoding and decoding, would have to deal with both the form and characteristic latencies associated with these processes.

Nonetheless, being able to specify the structural (what is a chunk), as well as the operational, aspects of knowledge helps to fill a void in earlier versions of the structural learning theory (cf. Scandura, 1971a, 1973, Chapter 10; 1976, pp. 315-316). Given the processing capacity and unit latencies associated with an individual (along with the assumption of universal control), and most importantly the representation of competence rules at a level of PROCESS ATOMICITY, it is theoretically possible to operationally define individual behavior potential in a way that is sensitive to memory load. (Compare this situation with testing to behavioral equivalence where *all* relevant knowledge is assumed to be available.) In particular, it would be possible to assess and then to predict both responses and latencies where internal and/or external *context* is allowed to vary as well as the problem input. In Chapter 7, we show how this might be done in the context of particular rules. In the studies reported, rules were represented at a level that approximates process atomicity. These rules provided a basis for defining the memory load in chunks at each stage of processing. Because the memory loads involved could be compared with independently determined processing capacities of individual subjects, behavioral predictions were possible on specific items.

The same general ideas, presumably might be used where goals are in control during testing (to determine rule applicability) or the control mechanism, during goal shifting (cf. Section 4.2). For example, if a subject is presented with a novel problem after solving a series of problems of a misleadingly similar type, he may fail even where he might otherwise succeed. The water jar problems of Luchins (1942) provide a well-known prototype. After solving a series of such problems using one rule, Luchins' subjects failed to see another simpler mode of solving a new water jar problem. (Although Luchins did not run a parallel condition of testing on the novel problem before the initial series of problems was presented, it seems likely from an analysis of the problem that the novel one would have been easier under these conditions.)

The obvious explanation for such context effects is that the control processor (working memory) may be filled with rules that generate solutions, either efficiently or inefficiently. Thus, after solving the given series of tasks, the working memories of Luchins' subjects were likely to have been filled with relatively inefficient rules. Because the previously used rule was adequate for solving the new problem, the subjects were not motivated to derive a more efficient rule.

The contents of working memory, of course, may also be influenced directly by the immediate context in which a problem is presented. Suppose, for example, that a subject is shown how to cover a 3 x 3 array of dots with five strokes (lines) of a pencil, without lifting the pencil off the paper (see Figure 2)--and then is asked to do the same thing with only four strokes.[8] (If you do not know the answer, try the problem before reading footnote 8.)

[8]Hint: Try the problem allowing some of the strokes to extend beyond the boundary of the dot array.

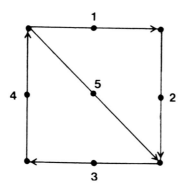

Figure 2. Five stroke solution to dot problem.

To summarize, the operational definition of what is known, up to process equivalence, could provide a potential (but as yet unrealized) basis for predicting individual behavior on specific (new) problems. Moreover, the corresponding enriched version of the structural learning theory might apply in a broader variety of (idealized) situations, specifically in situations where processing capacity (but not, e.g., encoding or decoding) may be involved, and with more precision (e.g., including latencies). Among other things, it might be possible to specify what individuals know in sufficient detail that predictions might be made in situations where the internal context (what is available in the processor) may vary as well as externally given problems. In particular, it might be possible (at least in principle) not only to specify the operational aspects of rules available to individuals but also the "chunks" on which these operations operate. Thus, given the problem adopted by a subject, and what other information is available at the time (e.g., determined by the prior context), not only might predictions be made as to success/failure but, in the case of success, as to latencies as well. It is important to emphasize that such predictions might be possible even where solving the problems in question might involve goal switching (e.g., the derivation of new solution rules).

The possibility of such prediction, of course, does not come free. Such predictions can only be realized where severe additional restrictions are imposed on the representation of competence. All competence rules (and their components) must be process atomic.

Summary and Concluding Remarks: The major considerations involved in measuring individual differences up to the above types of equivalence are summarized in Table 1. In addition to compatibility of competence rules with the subject population, the major assumption in the case of behavioral equivalence is the representation of competence rules in terms of atomic units. Given these assumptions, and assuming the indicated boundary

conditions during testing, the obtained profile of success/fail-
ure should provide an adequate basis for assessing individual
knowledge up to behavior equivalence. In stage equivalence, it
is important that competence also account for various stages of
problem solving. Assessing behavior potential (individual
knowledge), in this case, can be accomplished either through
direct observation of the steps taken in solving test problems
or indirectly in terms of latencies (or perhaps other more precise response measures).

In process equivalence, component rules must be process
atomic as well as atomic in a behavioral/stage sense. Just as
assuming atomicity (and population compatibility) provides an
operational basis for assessing what rule is known, assuming
process atomicity provides an operational basis for assessing
what count as psychologically meaningful units, or "chunks" (cf.
the node labeled graphs of Scandura, 1973, Chapter 7). In effect, a major distinction between behavior/stage equivalence and
process equivalence stems from the nature of the underlying theory. Behavior equivalence, for example, refers only to the memory-free theory; stage equivalence imposes additional constraints
on observables, with no concurrent enrichment of the theory per
se. (In both cases, the sole constraint imposed by cognitive
universals involves the control mechanism.) Process equivalence,
on the other hand, is consistent with behavior/stage equivalence
with regard to the operational aspects of rules but reflects
also the entities (chunks) on which they act. Relatively little
research has been done with respect to either stage or process
equivalence. It is instructive, nonetheless, to compare the
work by Groen, Suppes, and their associates, where individual
knowledge has been measured up to stage equivalence, and that
reported in Chapter 7 of this book where knowledge is measured
to (an approximation of) process equivalence.[9]

Even strong empirical support for untested assumptions,
pertaining to the enriched theory, however, would not be sufficient. Thus, for example, although a valid operational definition of "what is a chunk" would be crucial, the enriched theory
described in Section 4.2 does a better job of specifying how new
chunks are activated (added to working memory) than it does of
specifying which ones are eliminated (e.g., where capacity would
otherwise be overloaded). As argued in Scandura (1973, pp. 321-
324; also 1976, pp. 315-316), partial resort to stochastic approximations may be necessary at this level.

Even if a satisfactory deterministic solution to this prob-

---

[9]Notice that the assumptions on which individual differences measurement
is based correspond to the idealized boundary conditions under which different
levels of the deterministic cognitive theory must be tested. In the latter case,
rules must be "built in" via training (cf. Part 3). In situations where behavior
potential must be measured through testing (even given a perfect deterministic
theory), behavioral predictions will be accurate just to the extent that the
corresponding assessment assumptions are valid.

lem were found, however, the theory itself would still be incomplete in at least two important senses. First, explicit attention would have to be given to encoding and decoding processes. The mind, in effect, would have to be placed in the body. My associates and I have done almost nothing in this direction, with the exception of the discussion in Scandura (1973, pp. 109-111). This discussion deals primarily with the hypothesis that new encoding and decoding capabilities may be derived according to the same principles as with cognitive knowledge.

Second, a complete characterization of complex human behavior would have to deal with the dynamic interaction over time between the subject and his (external or internal) problem environment, that is, between what the subject knows at a given point in time and the problems he either considers himself or is presented with by some external agent (e.g., teacher). This problem is considered (in a limited sense) in the first half of Chapter 14.

In the present chapter, attention has been focused primarily, on what happens at any given stage of such interaction. As we shall see in Chapter 14, however, recursive structural analysis, and taking different levels of such analysis into account in assessing behavior potential, play an important role (in DYNAMIC INTERACTION).

6.   A BRIEF SUMMARY OF DIRECTLY RELATED RESEARCH

The proposed theory provides intuitively simple mechanisms by which individuals may be assumed to bring the knowledge they have to bear in problem solving. It also provides a basis for identifying the specific competencies underlying given problem domains, and associated with given subject populations. Finally, the theory provides a basis for using such competencies to determine the relevant knowledge available to particular individuals (in the given population).

To avoid the impression that the structural learning theory is purely speculative, some of our more directly related empirical research is briefly summarized below. In subsequent chapters, we shall see how the theory may be realized in more concrete situations. Part 2 deals with the analysis of real subject matters; Part 3 involves experiments with human subjects, and Part 4, with the measurement of individual differences. Part 5 includes educational applications and theoretical extensions to solving sequences of problems. Relationships to other research, practical implications, and future directions are considered in Part 6.

6.1   CONTENT ANALYSIS (INCLUDING EDUCATIONAL APPLICATIONS)
The structural analyses, that have been completed to date,

strongly suggest that the proposed approach is practicable and; in fact, the method of analysis and empirical work have developed hand in hand. The first such attempt by Ehrenpreis and Scandura (Chapter 11, this book) had a largely practical purpose, to determine the feasibility of identifying the rules and higher-order rules underlying standard text material. In particular, my text *Mathematics: Concrete Behavioral Foundations* (1971b) was systematically analyzed to determine, in turn, the implicitly defined tasks, corresponding rules, and higher-order rules. As it turned out, this was not only possible, but the results were used as a basis for a commercial workbook paralleling the text (Scandura, Durnin, Ehrenpreis, & Luger, 1971).

At about the same time, a separate analysis was conducted of critical reading by Lowerre and Scandura (Chapter 12, this book) using an approximation method. In this case, paragraphs were categorized along various dimensions in a way that parallels more strictly rule-based analyses. The materials developed for this purpose were shown to provide a sound basis for both diagnosis and instruction (see Chapter 12, this book). These materials too have since been extended into a series of four school workbooks (Scandura, Lowerre, & Scandura, 1974).

Scandura, Durnin, and Wulfeck (Chapter 3, this book) undertook a more intensive analysis of geometry (straight-edge and compass) construction tasks. Among other things, this study demonstrated that heuristics (e.g., Polya, 1962) can be made sufficiently precise that they can be programmed on a computer and, moreover, so that it is possible to determine analytically in which behavioral situations a given heuristic may be used and in which situations it can not be. Moreover, unlike the Ehrenpreis and Scandura study (Chapter 11, this book), where the introduction of higher-order rules served only to eliminate (then) redundant (lower-order) solution rules, the lower-order rules in the second order rule sets of Chapter 3 were considerably simpler than the solution rules from which they were derived. Wulfeck (reported in Chapter 14, this book) later extended this analysis to provide a basis for his dissertation on instructional sequencing.

The above results and method of analysis used by Scandura, *et al.* (Chapter 3, this book) were limited in three important ways: no attempt was made to include logical inference; all of the higher-order rules had the effect of composing rules (no other kinds of higher-order rules were considered); and no distinctions were made between rule derivation and breaking problems into subproblems. A subsequent study by Scandura and Durnin (Chapter 4, this book) dealt specifically with these limitations. In particular, a total of 24 lower-order, derivation, and problem definition rules were shown to be adequate for proving over 130 theorems and proof exercises (along with an undetermined number of others) in an experimental high school text on algebraic number systems.

Structural analyses have also been used in a study that Haussler (personal communication) in West Germany is planning in physics education. This study should provide useful information concerning the effectiveness of teaching generalization rules in discovering functional relationships.

To date, however, none of the structural analyses have taken into account "motivation" (i.e., choosing alternative rules), nor has any serious attempt been made to analyze social or other molar domains. The furthest we have gone in this direction is a preliminary analysis of number conservation (Scandura, 1972b) and a rule-based extension of the Lowerre and Scandura study (see Addendum to Chapter 12, this book). Perhaps the single most important problem in the area of structural analysis, however, is that several important aspects of the method depend heavily on intuition. Hopefully, future research in this area will lead to greater systematization.

6.2 COGNITIVE MECHANISMS

In the cognitive domain, studies have been conducted both in the laboratory under idealized, "memory-free" conditions, and as an adjunct to some of the structural analyses. For example, Scandura (Chapter 5, this book) found that under idealized conditions the "first approximation" control mechanism, as it applies in rule derivation, can be assumed to be universally available to essentially all learners, at least from about the age of 7. Moreover, in an Addendum to Chapter 5, this mechanism was also shown to be universally available to 4-, 5-, and 6-year-old children. The data reported in Chapter 5, however, are not consistent with other control mechanisms that have been proposed (e.g., the cyclical "stack-type" control mechanism implicit in the production systems of Newell & Simon, 1972; cf. Chapter 5, this book).

The adequacy of generalized goal switching control was demonstrated in a later study (Scandura, Chapter 6, this book) in the case of retrieval, rule selection, and breaking simple problems into subproblems. Similar results were obtained with respect to domain control. In studying more complex problem solving, however, it became increasingly difficult to approach idealized conditions. The influence of processing capacity appeared to play a somewhat bigger (although not yet critical) role, despite attempts to eliminate its effects.

Attempts have also been made to test a memory-load model (Scandura, 1973) under corresponding idealized conditions (e.g., where process atomicity may be assumed, cf. Table 1). Given constraints on time and resources, however, such conditions could only be approached. Correspondingly, while the results were highly consistent with the model in the standard (stochastic) sense, they deviated significantly from the deterministic

ideal. A stochastic extension of the deterministic model
(Scandura, 1973), however, which explicitly allows for distractions ("unsharpness") and unwanted "chunking", provided a close
fit to the data (Voorhies & Scandura, Chapter 7, this book).

In educational applications, these results have held up
extremely well. In a study by Ehrenpreis and Scandura (Chapter
11, this book), for example, one group of students was taught a
total of about 300 rules for solving a comparable number of
tasks, one rule for each task. A second group was taught 5
higher-order rules together with a reduced list of about 160 of
the original rules. Interestingly enough, the second group did
just as well as the first (in an absolute sense) on tasks on
which only the first group had been trained. In addition, the
second group performed significantly (about 33 percent) better
on tasks for which neither group had been trained. Moreover,
the results of this study were relatively unaffected by memory,
suggesting that the theory may be relatively robust concerning
this type of deviation from the ideal. Finally, in an Addendum
to the chapter, it is shown that the degree of transfer can be
predicted within one percentage point, based solely on the
availability of the corresponding lower- and higher-order rules
(i.e., based on the degree of deviation from the ideal, cf.
Chapter 1, this book).

The viability of the proposed control mechanism is shown
further in Chapter 14 by Wulfeck and Scandura. In this study,
the data are consistent not only with the cumulative effects
of learning over time, as predicted via the control mechanism,
but also with the expectation that solution time should be a
function of the level of derivation (required for solution).

Among the more critical open questions at the present time
are the following: Is the control mechanism innate? Or, does
it develop slowly as the child matures? And, if the latter,
what is the source of the developmental changes? Is the proposed operational definition of what is a chunk a good one--
that is, is it consistent with the assumption of a fixed capacity processor? And, if so, does the corresponding enriched
theory provide a useful and efficient basis for explaining and/
or predicting human problem solving behavior? The results reported in the Addendum to Chapter 5 suggest that the answer to
the first three questions must be sought below the age of 4.
The remaining questions are considered but not fully resolved
in Chapters 7 and 15.

6.3   INDIVIDUAL DIFFERENCES

In the area of individual differences, there have been two
major studies by Durnin and Scandura. The first study demonstrated the basic viability of the proposed approach to assessing behavior potential. In this study, the underlying atomic
rules were actually built into the subjects and the testing it-

self was individualized and conducted under close-to-idealized conditions. Under these (near idealized) conditions, with testees ranging from elementary school students to Ph.D. candidates, it was possible to predict performance on new items, given performance on initially selected test items, with over 96 percent accuracy (Scandura & Durnin, Chapter 8, this book).

In the second study, where testing took place under ordinary classroom conditions, and where judgements had to be made concerning the atomic rules, the predictions were accurate in about 84 percent of the cases (Durnin & Scandura, Chapter 9, this book). In this study the structural approach also was compared with other forms of criterion-referenced testing (e.g., item forms, Hively, *et al.*, 1968). The structural approach not only provided superior prediction but it accomplished this with many fewer test items.

In Chapter 10, by Scandura and Reulecke, consideration is given to the question of how to determine which of several alternative rules provides the best overall fit for a given set of (nonidealized) data. Further discussion of the distinction between structural and incidental variables also is included. In addition, the validity of the structural approach to diagnostic testing (and remediation) has been demonstrated in the case of higher-order rules in studies by Scandura (Experiments III and IV, Chapter 5) and Scandura, Durnin, Wulfeck, and Ehrenpreis (Chapter 13, this book).

One major open question, pertaining to individual differences measurement, involves testing with respect to nontrivial domains where underlying competence consists of sets of rules considered collectively. Work in this area could help to bridge the current gap between normative and criterion-referenced testing and could have important practical applications.[10] A second important problem area involves the application of the structural approach to testing with respect to molar problem domains. Testing up to process equivalence is a third important area for future research, one that is almost completely open.

---

[10] In a forthcoming paper, I plan to discuss relationships between structural and normative approaches to testing, and to suggest some empirical comparisons that should be undertaken. To my knowledge, that work remains to be done.

REFERENCES

Anderson, J. R., & Bower, G. H. *Human associative memory.* New York: Halsted-Wiley, 1973.

Atkinson, R. C., & Shiffrin, R. M. Human memory: A proposed system and its control processes. In K. W. Spence & J. Spence (Eds.), *The psychology of learning and motivation: Advance in research and theory* (Vol. 2). New York: Academic Press, 1968.

Ausubel, D. P. *Educational psychology: A cognitive view.* New York: Holt, Rinehart, & Winston, 1968.

Banerji, R. B. A formal approach to knowledge in problem solving. In J. M. Scandura, J. H. Durnin, & W. H. Wulfeck II (Eds.), *1974 Proceedings: Fifth annual interdisciplinary conference on structural learning* (Office of Naval Research Technical Report, 1974). MERGE Research Institute, 1249 Greentree Lane, Narberth, PA 19072.

Bloom, B. S. Recent developments in mastery learning. *Educational Psychology,* 1973, *10,* 53-57.

Bloom, B. S., & Broder, L. J. *Problem-solving processes of college students: An exploratory investigation.* Chicago: University of Chicago Press, 1950.

Bourne, L. E., Ekstrand, B. R., & Dominowski, R. L. *The psychology of thinking.* Englewood Cliffs, N.J.: Prentice-Hall, 1971.

Bower, G. H. A selective review of organizational factors in memory. In E. Tulving & W. Donaldson (Eds.), *Organization of memory.* New York: Academic Press, 1972.

Bruner, J. S., Goodnow, J. J., & Austin, G. A. *A study of thinking.* New York: Wiley, 1956.

Carroll, J. B. Towards a performance grammar for core sentences in spoken and written English. *Journal of Structural Learning,* 1975, *4,* 189-198.

Carroll, J. B., & Freedle, R. O. (Eds.). *Language comprehension and the acquisit of knowledge.* Washington, D.C.: Winston, 1972.

Chomsky, N. *Syntactic structures.* The Hague: Mouton Press, 1957.

Chomsky, N. *Language and mind.* New York: Harcourt, Brace, & World, 1968.

Dienes, Z. P. *Building up mathematics.* London: Hutchinson, 1960.

Ernst, G. W., & Newell, A. *GPS (General Problem Solver): A case study in generality and problem solving.* New York: Academic Press, 1969.

Eulefeld, G., Kattmann, U., & Schaefer, G. *Three approaches for restructuring school biology.* Technical Report for Institut fur die Padagogik der Naturwissenschaften an der Universitat Kiel, 1975.

Farley, F. Basic process individual differences. Talk given at American Educational Research Association Annual Meeting, Chicago, April, 1974.

Gagne, R. M. *The conditions of learning* (2nd ed.). New York: Holt, Rinehart, & Winston, 1970.

Gagne, R. M., & Briggs, L. J. *Principles of instructional design.* New York: Holt, Rinehart, & Winston, 1974.

Gorn, S. On the conclusive validation of symbol manipulative processes: How do you know it has to work. *Journal of the Franklin Institute,* 1973, *296,* 499-518.

Greeno, J. G. The structure of memory and the process of solving problems. In R. Solso (Ed.), *Contemporary issues in cognitive psychology: Loyola symposium.* New York: Halstead-Wiley, 1973.

Greeno, J. G. Cognitive objectives of instruction: Theory of knowledge for solving problems and answering questions. In D. Klahr (Ed.), *Cognition and instruction.* Hillsdale, N.J.: Erlbaum Associates, 1976.

Groen, G. J. *An investigation of some counting algorithms for simple addition problems* (Technical Report No. 118). Stanford, Ca.: Institute for Mathematical Studies in the Social Sciences, Stanford University, 1967.

Harlow, H. F. The formation of learning sets. *Psychological Review,* 1949, *56,* 51-65.

Hays-Roth, F.   Representation, abstraction, and recognition of structured events.
    In J. M. Scandura, J. H. Durnin, & W. H. Wulfeck II (Eds.), *1974 Proceedings:*
    Fifth annual interdisciplinary conference on structural learning (ONR
    Technical Report, 1974).   MERGE Research Institute, 1249 Greentree Lane,
    Narberth, PA 19072.

Hilke, R., Kempf, W. F., & Scandura, J. M.   Deterministic and probabilistic
    theorizing in structural learning.   In H. Spada & W. F. Kempf (Eds.),
    Formalized theories of thinking and learning and their implications for
    science instruction.   Bern: Huber, 1977.

Hively, W., II, Patterson, H. L., & Page, S.   A "universe defined" system of
    arithmetic achievement tests.   *Journal of Educational Measurement*, 1968,
    5, 275-290.

Hunt, E. B.   The memory we must have.   In R. C. Shank & K. M. Colby (Eds.),
    Computer models of thought and language.   San Francisco: Freeman, 1973.

Kintsch, W.   *Learning, memory, and conceptual processes.*   New York: Wiley, 1970.

Kintsch, W.   Notes on the structure of semantic memory.   In E. Tulving & W.
    Donaldson (Eds.), *Organization of memory.*   New York: Academic Press, 1972.

Klix, F., & Sydow, H.   The organization of information processing in problem
    solving behavior.   *Publications of National Center for Scientific Research*,
    15 Quai Anatole-France, Paris, 1968.

Knuth, D. E.   *Fundamental algorithms.*   Reading, Mass.: Addison-Wesley, 1968.

Kohlberg, L.   From is to ought: How to commit the naturalistic fallacy and get
    away with it in the study of moral development.   In T. Mischell (Ed.),
    Cognitive development and epistomology.   New York: Academic Press, 1971.

Kosslyn, S. M., & Pomerantz, J. R.   Imagery, propositions, and the form of
    internal representations.   *Cognitive Psychology*, 1977, *9*, 52-76.

Landa, L. N.   *Algorithmization of learning and instruction.*   Englewood Cliffs,
    N.J.: Educational Technology, 1974.

Levine, M. A.   *A cognitive theory of learning: Research on hypothesis testing.*
    Hillsdale, N.J.: Erlbaum Associates, 1975.

Lightstone, A. H.   *The axiomatic method.*   Englewood Cliffs, N.J.: Prentice-Hall,
    1964.

Luchins, A. S.   Mechanization in problem solving: The effect of Einstellung.
    Psychological Monographs, 1942, *54*, No. 6, (Whole No. 248).

Miller, G. A.   The magical number seven, plus or minus two: Some limits on our
    capacity for processing information.   *Psychological Review*, 1956, *63*, 81-97.

Miller, G. A., & Chomsky, N.   Finitary models of language users.   In R. D. Luce,
    R. R. Bush, & E. Galanter (Eds.), *Handbook of mathematical psychology*
    (Vol. 2).   New York: Wiley, 1963.

Miller, G. A., Galanter, E., & Pribram, K. H.   *Plans and the structure of*
    behavior.   New York: Holt, Rinehart, & Winston, 1960.

Minsky, M. L.   *Computation: Finite and infinite machines.*   Englewood Cliffs,
    N.J.: Prentice Hall, 1967.

Minsky, M.   A framework for representing knowledge.   In P. Winston (Ed.),
    The psychology of computer vision.   New York: McGraw-Hill, 1975.

Minsky, M., & Papert, S.   *Research at the laboratory in vision, language, and*
    other problems of intelligence (Artificial Intelligence Progress Report,
    Memo 252).   Cambridge, Mass.: Massachusetts Institute of Technology,
    Artificial Intelligence Laboratory, 1972.

Nahinsky, I.   Going by rules, a review of *Structural learning I: Theory and*
    research by J. M. Scandura.   *Contemporary Psychology*, 1974, *19*, 414-416.

Neisser, U.   *Cognitive psychology.*   New York: Appleton-Century-Crofts, 1967.

Nelson, R. J.   *Introduction to automata.*   New York: Wiley, 1968.

Newell, A., & Simon, H. A.   *Human problem solving.*   Englewood Cliffs, N.J.:
    Prentice-Hall, 1972.

Nilsson, N. J.   *Problem-solving methods in artificial intelligence.*   New York:
    McGraw-Hill, 1971.

Pascual-Leone, J.   A mathematical model for the transition rule in Piaget's
    developmental stages.   *Acta Psychologica*, 1970, *63*, 301-345.

Pask, G. Conversational domains and their structure. In J. M. Scandura, J. H.
    Durnin, & W. H. Wulfeck II (Eds.), *1974 Proceedings: Fifth annual inter-*
    disciplinary conference on structural learning (Office of Naval Research
    Technical Report, 1974). MERGE Research Institute, 1249 Greentree Lane,
    Narberth, PA 19072.
Pask, G. *Conversation, cognition, and learning.* Amsterdam: Elsevier, 1975.
Polya, G. *Mathematical discovery* (Vol. 1). New York: Wiley, 1962.
Quillian, M. R. Semantic memory. In M. Minsky (Ed.), *Semantic information*
    processing. Cambridge, Mass.: M.I.T. Press, 1968.
Restle, F., & Brown, E. Organization of serial pattern learning. In G. H.
    Bower (Ed.), *The psychology of learning and motivation: Advances in*
    research and theory (Vol. 4). New York: Academic Press, 1970.
Rogers, H. J. *Theory of recursive functions and effective computability.* New
    York: McGraw-Hill, 1967.
Roughead, W. G., & Scandura, J. M. "What is learned" in mathematical discovery.
    Journal of Educational Psychology, 1968, *59,* 283-289.
Rumelhart, D. E., Lindsay, P. H., & Norman, D. A. A process model for long-term
    memory. In E. Tulving & W. Donaldson (Eds.), *Organization of memory.* New
    York: Academic Press, 1972.
Scandura, J. M. An analysis of exposition and discovery modes of problem-solving
    instruction. *Journal of Experimental Education,* 1964, *33,* 149-159. (Re-
    printed in P. C. Burns & A. M. Johnson (Eds.), *Research on elementary school*
    curriculum and organization. Boston: Allyn & Bacon, 1969.)
Scandura, J. M. Prior learning, presentation order, and prerequisite practice
    in problem solving. *Journal of Experimental Education,* 1966, *34,* 12-18.
Scandura, J. M. An alternative approach to research in mathematics learning--a
    reaction to Suppes' paper. *Journal of Research and Development in Education*
    1967, *1,* 33-43.
Scandura, J. M. New directions for theory and research on rule learning: I. A
    set-function language. *Acta Psychologica,* 1968, *28,* 301-321. II. Empirical
    research, and III. Analyses and theoretical direction, *Acta Psychologica,*
    1969, *29,* 101-133, 205-227.
Scandura, J. M. The role of rules in behavior: Toward an operational definition
    of what (rule) is learned. *Psychological Review,* 1970, *77,* 516-533.
Scandura, J. M. Deterministic theorizing in structural learning: Three levels
    of empiricism. *Journal of Structural Learning,* 1971, *3,* 21-53. (a)
Scandura, J. M. *Mathematics: Concrete behavioral foundations.* New York:
    Harper & Row, 1971. (b)
Scandura, J. M. A theory of mathematical knowledge: Can rules account for
    creative behavior? *Journal of Research in Mathematics Education,* 1971,
    2, 183-196. (c)
Scandura, J. M. Plan for the development of a conceptually based mathematics
    curriculum for disadvantaged children. Part I: Theoretical foundations,
    Part II: Applications. *Instructional Science,* 1972, *2,* 247-262; 363-387. (a)
Scandura, J. M. What is a rule? *Journal of Educational Psychology,* 1972, *63,*
    179-185. (b)
Scandura, J. M. *Structural learning I: Theory and research.* New York: Gordon
    and Breach, 1973.
Scandura, J. M. Human problem solving: Synthesis of content, cognition, and
    individual differences. In J. M. Scandura, J. H. Durnin, & W. H. Wulfeck II
    (Eds.), *1974 Proceedings: Fifth annual interdisciplinary conference on*
    structural learning (Office of Naval Research Technical Report, 1974). MERGE
    Research Institute, 1249 Greentree Lane, Narberth, PA 19072. (a)
Scandura, J. M. The role of higher order rules in problem solving. *Journal of*
    Experimental Psychology, 1974, *120,* 984-991. (b)
Scandura, J. M. The structure of memory: Fixed or flexible? (University of
    Pennsylvania, Structural Learning Report 73, 1973). *Catalog of Selected*
    Documents in Psychology, Spring, 1974. (c)
Scandura, J. M. Creative problem solving. Unpublished talk given to the
    American Psychological Association, August, 1974. (d)

Scandura, J. M. How does mathematics learning take place? *Educational Studies in Mathematics*, 1975, *11*, 375-385. (*Educational Studies in Mathematics*, 1975, *11*, 111-222).

Scandura, J. M. *Structural learning II: Issues and approaches*. London/New York: Gordon and Breach, 1976.

Scandura, J. M. A deterministic theory of teaching and learning. In H. Spada & W. F. Kempf (Eds.), *Formalized theories of thinking and learning and their implications for science instruction*. Bern: Huber, 1977. (a)

Scandura, J. M. Structural approach to instructional problems. *American Psychologist*, 1977, *32*, 33-53. (b)

Scandura, J. M., Durnin, J. H., Ehrenpreis, W., & Luger, G. *An algorithmic approach to mathematics: Concrete behavioral foundations*. New York: Harper & Row, 1971.

Scandura, J. M., Lowerre, G. F., & Scandura, A. M. *Critical reading series* (A self-diagnostic and instructional series of workbooks for teaching critical reading based on logical inference). Worthington, Ohio: Ann Arbor Publishers, 1974.

Schank, R. C. Identification and conceptualization underlying natural language. In R. C. Schank & K. M. Colby (Eds.), *Computer models of thought and language*. San Francisco: Freeman, 1973.

Schneider, W., & Shiffrin, R. M. Controlled and automatic human information processing: I. Detection, search, and attention. *Psychological Review*, 1977, *84*, 1-66.

Simon, H. A. Motivational and emotional controls of cognition. *Psychological Review*, 1967, *1*, 29-39.

Spence, K. W. An experimental test of the continuity and non-continuity theories of discrimination learning. *Journal of Experimental Psychology*, 1945, *35*, 253-266.

Sternberg, S. Memory-scanning: Mental processes revealed by reaction-time requirements. *American Scientist*, 1969, *57*, 421-457.

Suppes, P. Stimulus-response theory of finite automata. *Journal of Mathematical Psychology*, 1969, *6*, 327-355.

Suppes, P. The semantics of children's language. *American Psychologist*, 1974, *2*, 103-115.

Suppes, P., & Groen, G. J. Some counting models for first-grade performance data on simple addition facts. In J. M. Scandura (Ed.), *Research in mathematics education*. Washington, D.C.: National Council of Teachers of Mathematics, 1967.

Suppes, P., & Morningstar, M. *Computer-assisted instruction at Stanford: Data, models, and evaluation of arithmetic programmes*. New York: Academic Press, 1972.

Taylor, D. W. Toward an information-processing theory of motivation. In M. R. Jones (Ed.), *Nebraska Symposium on Motivation*. Lincoln: University of Nebraska Press, 1960.

Thomas, J. C. An analysis of behavior in the Hobbits-Orcs problem. *Cognitive Psychology*, 1974, *2*, 257-270.

Wallach, L., & Sprott, R. Inducing number conservation in children. *Child Development*, 1964, *35*, 1057-1071.

Waugh, N. C., & Norman, D. A. Primary memory. *Psychological Review*, 1965, *72*, 89-104.

Winograd, T. Understanding natural language. *Cognitive Psychology*, 1972, *3*, 1-191.

Winston, P. H. *Summary of selected vision topics* (Flash 30). Cambridge, Mass.: Massachusetts Institute of Technology, Artificial Intelligence Laboratory, July, 1972.

GLOSSARY

Because Chapter 2 provides the most definitive statement
of the Structural Learning Theory, the Glossary is keyed to this
chapter (supplemented with a few technical terms from Chapter 1).
In addition to the major entries, however, various close synonyms
also are included. Hence, the Glossary should be helpful
throughout this book and the reader is encouraged to review it,
at least briefly, before commencing a serious study of the field.
(Although the descriptions included are suggestive, they are not
intended as formal mathematical definitions and should not be
so construed.)

Terms in the Glossary are capitalized both where they first
appear in Chapter 2 and/or where they are defined or discussed
in some detail.

ACCOUNTED FOR   see COMPETENCE ACCOUNT (p. 92)

ATOMIC (DEGENERATE/UNITARY) STRUCTURE (SOMETIMES DATA STRUCTURE/
    ENTITY/SIMPLE ELEMENT/SUBSTIMULI)   a structure that is
    represented in terms of a single indivisible element.
    Atomic and UNITARY structures correspond to inputs and out-
    puts that are assumed to be so basic that all subjects in
    the target population can encode/decode them uniformly
    well. UNITARY structures, however, need not be represented
    in terms of a single indivisible element (p. 99). Elements
    viewed as atomic may be operated upon but never themselves
    operate (on anything). (pp. 51, 57, 58, 70, 72) (Also
    see CHUNK.)

ATOMIC (UNITARY) ENCODING/DECODING CAPABILITY (ATOMIC CONDITION/
    TEST/RELATION)   in reference to level of representation
    refers to an encoding/decoding capability that is uniformly
    available to all subjects in the target population. Where-
    as ATOMIC also implies an "automatic", highly skilled capa-
    bility, UNITARY need not (see p. 99). (pp. 72; encoding,
    51; decoding, 51, 69, 95, 96)

ATOMIC GOAL   see GOAL, UNITARY/ATOMIC

ATOMIC RULE   see RULE, ATOMIC

ATOMIC TESTS   refers to testing entities to see if they satisfy
    atomic (unitary) goals. (p. 99)

ATOMICITY (BEHAVIOR EQUIVALENCE)   refers to representation of a
    rule at a level such that behavioral distinctions due to
    further refinement cannot be detected via testing with re-
    spect to given criteria. (p. 125)

___, BEHAVIORAL (BEHAVIOR EQUIVALENCE/SUCCESS-FAILURE ATOMICITY)
    representation of a rule in terms of atomic, all-or-none
    rules that are behaviorally equivalent (homogeneous) with
    respect to success/failure (i.e., further refinement of the
    rule itself cannot be detected relative to success/fail-
    ure). (pp. 105, 106, 125)

___, LATENCY   representation of a rule in terms of operations
that are behaviorally equivalent (homogeneous) with respect to LATENCY. (pp. 108, 128)

___, PROCESS   representation of a rule in terms of atomic rules
that are not only homogeneous with respect to latency (and
success/failure) but with respect to each other (i.e., the
associated latencies are fixed for any given subject, and
independent of the particular atomic rule). A rule represented at this level is said to be PROCESS ATOMIC and provides a basis for assessing BEHAVIOR POTENTIAL up to PRO-
CESS EQUIVALENCE. (Note: The components of process atomic
rules are necessarily PROCESS ATOMIC.) (pp. 106, 130, 131)

___, RULE   see RULE, ATOMIC

___, STAGE (LATENCY)   representation of a rule in terms of
atomic rules that not only are homogeneous with respect to
success/failure but to the (externalized) stages one goes
through in solving the problem. (Stages may be determined
indirectly via latencies, i.e., there is a fixed latency
associated with each atomic rule.) Further refinement of
the rule itself cannot be detected relative to observable
responses corresponding to respective atomic rules. The
integrity (form) of such a rule is said to be preserved by
stage equivalence. (p. 128)

___, TRANSFER (TRANSFER EQUIVALENCE)   refers to behavior (suc-
cess/failure) equivalence with respect to problems whose
solutions may require more than one rule. (p. 122)

AUXILIARY CAPABILITIES   see ENTERING CAPABILITIES

BEHAVIOR EQUIVALENCE   see ATOMICITY

BEHAVIORAL OBJECTIVE   an educational goal such that each problem
in the class can be solved by (at least one) easily specified rule. (p. 54)

BEHAVIOR POTENTIAL   see RULE, KNOWLEDGE

BEHAVIOR PROFILE   pattern of successes and failures on a test.
Used with respect to items selected from EQUIVALENCE
CLASSES of a PARTITION on a class of problems. (p. 125)

CHUNK (SUBSTIMULUS)   a structure that imposes a unit of memory
load on the human information processor. (pp. 44, 57, 105,
106)

COGNITIVE CONSTRAINTS, UNIVERSAL   refers to characteristics of
the human information processor that apply universally,
irrespective of the specific knowledge that an individual
might have. These characteristics are assumed to have a
more or less permanent character. The three major cognitive constraints considered are: goal switching control
(see CONTROL MECHANISM), PROCESSING CAPACITY, and processing speed (see LATENCY). (p. 50)

COGNITIVE PROCESSING   may be under the control of: (a) rules,
which operate on and control the generation of structures,
(b) goals, which operate on rules and control testing,

(c) goal switching control, which operates on goals and controls shifts among them. (p. 104)

COGNITIVE UNIT   see STRUCTURE

COMPATIBLE (PAIRS OF) RULES   roughly speaking, a pair of rules such that the outputs of one serve as (possibly only one of) the inputs to the other. (Especially, see p. 55) (also see HIGHER-ORDER COMPOSITION RULE)

COMPETENCE ACCOUNT (COMPETENCE THEORY/COMPETENCE/RULES OF COMPETENCE)   a finite set of competence rules that collectively ACCOUNT FOR a problem domain that is compatible with some target population. COMPETENCE is sometimes used to refer to rule sets and/or competence rules, with intended meaning implied by the context. (pp. 43, 49, 50, 53, 64)

COMPETENCE, GLOBAL/MOLAR   a competence account associated with problems (in a domain) that are represented in terms of higher-level (global) properties. (pp. 43, 49)

COMPETENCE RULE (PROTOTYPIC/IDEALIZED RULE/COMPETENCY)   a rule of competence that corresponds to the way some idealized subject in the target population would solve problems in the associated class, ignoring memory load and other processing constraints. In some cases, may be identified by observing behavior of prototypic (e.g., successful) subjects. (To minimize the effects of processing capacity, preference is given to relatively simple problems in the class.) (pp. 50, 63)

COMPUTABLE FUNCTION   a function (in the mathematical sense) for which there exists a rule that when applied to any given input generates the corresponding output. (p. 46)

COMPUTATION (ASSOCIATED WITH A RULE)   a sequence of structures (states) generated on application of a rule to a given input. (p. 108)

CONTENT   see PROBLEM DOMAIN

CONTROL MECHANISM   a basic mode of functioning that characterizes an information processing system and determines how specific capacities (e.g., rules) are put to use. (pp. 46, 52, 57) (Compare with LAWS OF INTERACTION/RULES OF COMBINATION which parallel control mechanisms in the case of competence. (pp. 81, 82) (also see COGNITIVE PROCESSING)

___, GOAL SWITCHING   a possibly innate, possibly learned control mechanism that is assumed in the Structural Learning Theory to be universally available to all human information processors, and to determine how all rules of knowledge interact (rules are unstratified with respect to goal switching control). (pp. 83-99)

___, "FIRST APPROXIMATION"   a simplified "first approximation" to goal switching control that provides a basis for explaining simple human performance and "insight" learning (i.e., the derivation of new solution rules). (pp. 83-86)

DECODE refers to constructing an observable corresponding to an
internal structure. Also, used in reference to constructing
a syntactic representation of a semantically represented
structure (e.g., of a problem solution). (pp. 51, 53, 95)
(cf. "extracting" an external representative of an internal
equivalence class, Scandura, 1973.)

DEGENERATE   see DEGENERATE under RULE (e.g., p. 70) or STRUCTURE
(p. 58) as appropriate.

DETERMINISTIC (BEHAVIOR) THEORY   a theory that makes it possible
under appropriate conditions to explain/predict what individual subjects can/will do in particular problem
situations.

DYNAMIC INTERACTION   refers to the interaction between subject
and (problem solving) environment (e.g., teacher) over
time, and to the continual growth of knowledge as a result
of such interaction. (Note: The theory described in Chapter 2 deals with what happens at each stage of such interaction. Chapter 14 builds on this foundation and emphasizes interaction over time.) (p. 135)

EDUCATIONAL GOAL/CURRICULUM   see PROBLEM DOMAIN   (p. 46)

ENCODE (PERCEIVE)   refers to internalizing external stimulation
(e.g., problem given). Also, used in reference to constructing a semantic representation of a syntactically
represented structure (input) (e.g., of a problem statement). (pp. 45, 51, 53) (cf. inserting external, sensory
stimulation into equivalence classes; i.e., the encoded
percepts, Scandura, 1973, pp. 96-98.)

ENTERING (AUXILIARY) CAPABILITIES (COMPETENCIES) rules (e.g.,
encoding/decoding capabilities) assumed to be uniformly
available to all subjects in the target population. (pp.
51, 53, 120)

EQUIVALENCE CLASS (of problems)   a class of problems solvable
via a given path of a rule. (p. 115)

"FIRST APPROXIMATION" MECHANISM   see CONTROL MECHANISM

GIVEN/STIMULUS SITUATION/INPUT (also EFFECTIVE STIMULUS/EFFEC-
TIVE CUE)   unless stated otherwise, refers to encoded
stimulation (appropriately represented) from the external
environment (i.e., a structure). (The encoded representations constitute STRUCTURES in the present sense; they are
psychologically meaningful entities that consist of a basic
set of elements, rules, and relations on this set, and/or
higher-order rules and relations.) (p. 44)

GLOBAL   see MOLAR/GLOBAL

GOAL (PREDICATE/RELATION/CRITERIA/PROPERTY)   a relation or relations (criteria) to be satisfied. In problem solving context, goals define sets of possible solutions. (p. 90)

___, DOMAIN associated with a rule r (which satisfies Gn) in
the context of problem (S_0,G). May be denoted Dom Gn(r) =
$[(S_0,G)$, Dom r$]$. In Dom Gn(r), the domain of r, Dom r,

plays a role analogous to G in problems (goal situations, denoted $[S_0,G]$). (S_0,G) in Dom Gn(r) similarly corresponds to S_0. Thus, Dom r specifies the form of the structures that satisfy Dom Gn(r) and (S_0,G) specifies which structures of that form are acceptable. (p. 97)

___, HIGHER-LEVEL (e.g., SOLUTION) goals satisfied by rules whose ranges contain given goals (defined as sets). Denoted Gn where n is the level. Gn is defined automatically in terms of Gn-1 (n > 0). (pp. 82, 86)

___, UNITARY/ATOMIC a goal that is represented in terms of an atomic (unanalyzed) relation. (p. 99)

GOAL SITUATION/PROBLEM (TEST ITEM) a goal constrained to reflect a given stimulus situation (input). A PROBLEM in the cognitive sense; sometimes TEST ITEM in assessing behavior potential. Represented (S,G) or (S_0,G) = Gl. (p. 83)

___, MOLAR (GLOBAL) a problem (goal situation) represented at a global level (i.e., in terms of a higher-level description language). Appropriate where only global aspects of a problem are of interest.

HIGHER-ORDER RULE a rule that operates on structures that contain rules. Loosely speaking, higher-order rules are often said to "operate on rules". (pp. 44, 54, 82)

_____ COMPOSITION RULE (*) a higher-order rule that operates on pairs of compatible rules and generates their COMPOSITES (i.e., one of the rules followed by the other). (p. 55)

_____ DERIVATION RULE a higher-order rule that operates on rules (in or as structures) and generates (derives) new rules. Deriving a rule in this way corresponds to INSIGHT, and problems solved via RULE DERIVATION are said to involve INSIGHT LEARNING. (p. 83)

_____ SELECTION RULE a higher-order rule that operates on non-degenerate structures (e.g., pairs of rules) and selects (generates) one of the rules as outputs. (p. 70)

_____ RELATIONS see RELATIONS, HIGHER-ORDER

IDEALIZED CONDITIONS boundary or test conditions that must be satisfied if an empirical situation is to provide an adequate basis for testing a deterministic behavior theory. (p. 81)

___, MEMORY-FREE idealized conditions that are appropriate for testing the memory-free (non-extended) Structural Learning Theory (i.e., that part of the theory that assumes goal switching control, but without constraints on processing capacity or speed). (p. 88)

IDEALIZED (PROTOTYPIC) SUBJECT an idealized subject who has unbounded processing capacity (speed). Used in reference to rules of competence that serve as prototypes relative to which the rules of knowledge (behavior potential) of real subjects are compared. (p. 50)

INCIDENTAL VARIABLES (OBSERVATION FACTORS) refer to entities associated with a complementary observation theory. (Chapter 1)

INSIGHT see HIGHER-ORDER DERIVATION RULE

INSTANCE (PROBLEM) a solved problem including the given/stimuli and response/solution, represented S-R. (p. 45)

KNOWLEDGE see RULE, KNOWLEDGE

LANGUAGE

____, DESCRIPTION language used to represent problem statements. (pp. 53, 93, 115, 120)

____, OBJECT language used to represent problems (givens, goals) and rules. (p. 53)

LATENCY processing speed, in experiments usually is operationally defined as the time between the onset of stimulus (input/problem statement) and the desired corresponding behavior response (output/behavior/solution). (pp. 53, 105, 106)

____ EQUIVALENT see p. 107

____, UNIT a minimum latency attributable to component processes of all process atomic rules. May vary over individuals but assumed to be a (relatively) fixed parameter of individual subjects. (See ATOMICITY PROCESS.) (pp. 130, 131, 132)

LAWS OF INTERACTION (RULES OF COMBINATION) depending on context, used both in general reference to the fact that rules of competence necessarily interact in accounting for associated problem domains and to the specific form of interaction specified in the Structural Learning Theory. (p. 81)

LEARNING adding new rules to a rule set by applying available (higher-order) rules to other rules (structures). (p. 87)

LOWER-ORDER RULE a rule that operates on structures that do not themselves contain rules.

MOLAR/GLOBAL (level) refers to representation in terms of a high-level language, i.e., a low-level of detail. (pp. 51, 103, 119)

MOLECULAR (level) the opposite of MOLAR. (p. 107)

MOTIVATION refers to selecting one rule (course of action) from among (a structure containing) several, via a higher-order selection rule. (pp. 86-87)

NONDETERMINISTIC THEORY (PREDICTION) a theory that makes it possible under appropriate conditions to explain/predict that individuals can/will do one of a finite number of things in particular problem situations but where the predictions are neutral with regard to further distinctions. (pp. 86, 119)

OBSERVATION THEORY a theory that complements a given deterministic theory. Deals with deviations (discrepancies) from deterministic predictions attributable to deviations from idealized boundary conditions. (Chapter 1)

PARTITION   a partition of a class of problems solvable via a rule into equivalence classes associated with the paths of the rule. (p. 115)

PATH (of a rule)   an equivalence class of computations associated with a rule in which the individual computations differ at most in terms of number of repetitions of particular subsequences of structures. May be thought of as a "trace" through a directed graph (flow diagram) representation of a rule which ignores the number of times a "loop" is traversed. (pp. 73, 114)

POPULATION COMPATIBILITY   the degree to which a competence account provides a precise basis for assessing the behavior potential (identifying/measuring the generative potential) of individual subjects in some specified population. (p. 50)

_____ CONSTRAINTS   refer to constraints imposed on the representation of competence by idealized prototypes associated with the target population. (p. 50)

PROBLEM (SITUATION)   used in two ways. In context of problem/domain/competence, is an INSTANCE (i.e., a problem GIVEN-SOLUTION pair). In context of cognition/knowledge (individual differences measurement), a problem situation (GOAL SITUATION/TEST ITEM) is a pair consisting of a problem GIVEN and a GOAL. "PROBLEM" also is sometimes used informally to indicate the problem GIVEN (e.g., as in "find the SOLUTION to the PROBLEM"). (pp. 43, 45, 79) (Also see DEFINING PROBLEM and SOLVING PROBLEM, pp. 94 and 95.)

___, DERIVATIVE   problem that can be represented as a finite sequence of atomic problems. Atomic problems are problems that can be accounted for without reference to SUBPROBLEM RULES. (p. 70)

PROBLEM (TASK) DOMAIN (also EDUCATIONAL GOAL/CURRICULUM)   a class of problems. In education, a finite set of goals, each of which itself is a class of problems. (CONTENT is sometimes used in referring informally to problem domains.) (pp. 45, 52, 54, 69)

___, GLOBAL   a problem domain in which the problems are represented at a global/molar level. (p. 52)

___, NONTRIVIAL   a problem domain for which one cannot easily identify a single solution rule. (pp. 111, 121)

___, STRUCTURED   a problem domain in which the basic elements, relations, and operations are relatively easy to identify.

___, SUB   a subset of problem domain. (pp. 67, 73, 91)

PROCESS EQUIVALENCE   see ATOMICITY, PROCESS (pp. 106, 130-134)

PROCESSING CAPACITY   refers to the number of chunks (e.g., simple elements, rules, goals) that a human information processor can maintain in working memory at one time. (p. 106)

PROCESSING SPEED   see LATENCY

PROCESSOR, HUMAN INFORMATION   the machine (human) responsible for encoding/decoding environmental stimulation and for using rules to process the internalized structures. The

universal constraints under which the human processor
operates are a major focus of study in the Structural
Learning Theory (Section 4).

RELATIONS   sets of ordered n-tuples of elements in some description or object language. (pp. 44, 46)

___, HIGHER-ORDER   sets of ordered n-tuples of relations/rules.
(p. 44)

REPRESENTATION   representation of a problem (given/solution,
goal, rule, structure, etc.) in terms of the OBJECT
LANGUAGE, or of a statement or description in the DESCRIP-
TION LANGUAGE. (p. 48) (Also see LANGUAGE.)

___, STRUCTURAL   representation of problem domains and underly-
ing competence in a way consistent with the Structural
Learning Theory.

RETRIEVAL   refers to extracting rules/structures from available
structures via some (retrieval) rule. (p. 87)

RULE   (PROCEDURE/ALGORITHM/PROCESS)   roughly speaking, a restricted type of mechanical procedure that can be applied
to any problem in a given class and that generates a corresponding output (Rogers, 1967). May be thought of as a
flow diagram (or labeled directed graph, Scandura, 1973)
restricted so that it is not possible to both generate a
new (sub)rule and to apply that (sub)rule within the same
flow diagram (i.e., flow of control within a rule is stratified, cf. unstratified control of postulated goal switching CONTROL MECHANISM). Each rule has associated with it
a prespecified domain and range.

Alternatively, a rule is a fixed finite sequence of
explicitly given operations and decision-making capabilities at a given level that are applied in order. (Notes:
(1) In the memory-free theory, the entities on which rules
operate, whether they derive ultimately from observables
in the environment or from memory, are assumed to be uniformly available. (2) Rules are like Post's productions
except that the former explicitly include decision-making
capabilities; they are intermediate between productions
and production systems (e.g. see Minsky, 1967, pp. 230-232;
cf. Scandura, 1973, pp. 65-67 & 119). (3) Although defined
in terms of discrete entities, no commitment is made in
this regard. The theory is oriented toward a definition
of rules that would include analog processing, cf. Chapter
15, Section 2.3.)

The term "rule" is used most generally, especially
where internal structure of the referent (e.g., individual
operations and decision-making capabilities) is not essential (p. 78); "procedure", where internal structure is
essential; "algorithm", where the procedure/rule necessarily terminates in a finite number of steps; "process", where
the referent is used in context of cognitive psychology.
(pp. 46, 47, 64, 80)

____, ATOMIC (ALL-OR-NONE) a rule that is represented in terms of an indivisible domain (condition) and operation. Such rules correspond to single operation productions in the sense of Newell and Simon (1972). In the context of human behavior, atomic rules can either be applied successfully to all structures in their respective domain or not at all --by each member of some subject population. The implication is that the rule is so simple/basic relative to the TARGET POPULATION that it would be impossible to teach a subject only part of it without also teaching the rest. Psychologically speaking, atomic rules may be equated with their extensions (i.e., the corresponding functions between inputs and outputs). (pp. 51, 73, 114)

____(s), COMPUTATIONALLY EQUIVALENT two or more rules that have the same domains and that generate the same outputs for each input. (p. 68)

____, DEGENERATE a special case of a rule. May be a concept (i.e., a class of inputs each of which is mapped by the rule into one of two responses called exemplars and non-exemplars), a simple stimulus-response (S-R) association (i.e., a rule with one element in its domain), or even a simple indivisible element. Note: Indivisible elements may be thought of as special, degenerate cases of both rules (i.e., 0-ary rules, or functions) and structures (i.e., structures consisting of a one element set and no relations or rules). (pp. 70, 73, 96)

____ DOMAIN (DOM) the set of structures (the given) to which a rule applies. The rule may or may not generate acceptable solutions for all givens in its domain. (pp. 47, 55)

____, ERROR a rule that generates incorrect solutions with respect to some problems in its domain. Used in connection with prototypic rules of competence that account for systematic errors. (p. 121, 124)

____ EXTENSION the class of problems that the rule solves. (p. 103)

____ OF KNOWLEDGE (KNOWLEDGE RULE/BEHAVIOR POTENTIAL) a rule that represents part of the generative potential of some subject (referred to as the subject's BEHAVIOR POTENTIAL). (pp. 41, 80)

____, MOLAR LEVEL OF schematic representation of a rule (i.e., representation of the operations and decisions in terms of a high-level language only). (p. 51)

____, PROBLEM DEFINITION see RULE, SUBPROBLEM

____, PROCESS ATOMIC a rule that is both atomic with regard to success/failure and whose application requires one minimal unit of latency over its entire domain. This same unit latency is common across all process atomic rules for any given subject. (pp. 124-127)

____, PROTOTYPIC/IDEALIZED see COMPETENCE RULE

_____   RANGE (RAN)   the set of structures (solutions) associated with a rule.   In general, a rule is characterized as a triple consisting of a domain, an operation, and a range. (pp. 47, 55)

_____, REFINEMENT OF   representation of the individual operations and decisions of a rule in relatively more detail (e.g., in terms of a lower-level language).   (pp. 48, 51, 115)

_____, SELECTION   see HIGHER-ORDER RULE   (p. 87)

_____, SIMPLE   a rule that operates on entities (i.e., structures) that do not themselves contain rules.   (p. 57)

_____   (PROCEDURE), SOLUTION   descriptive term for a rule in reference to a class of problems (instances) that can be solved (accounted for) by the rule.   Alternatively, a rule that contains given elements in its domain and the goal in its range.   (pp. 46, 54, 62)   (Also see SOLUTION METHOD (pp. 63-64.)

_____, SOURCE   a rule that enters into the derivation of a given rule or set of rules   (p. 122)

_____, SUBPROBLEM (PLANNING)   a rule (not necessarily higher-order) that operates on problems and generates solution plans (sequences of subproblems).   Sometimes used synonomously with PROBLEM DEFINITION RULES (p. 72), although the latter strictly speaking, are rules which operate on syntatic representations (e.g., of problem statements) and generate semantic representations (e.g., of problems themselves). (pp. 71, 93) (Also see DEFINING PROBLEMS and SOLVING PROBLEMS on pp. 93-95.)

RULE ACCOUNT   a rule set whose rules collectively make it possible to generate solutions to each problem in some problem domain.   Also, a rule is said to "account for" a problem (given-solution/instance) (p. 117).   Where problem domains cannot be accounted for by any known rule, rule sets that account for a significant portion of the domain are loosely referred to as (partial) rule account.   A rule account may or may not be compatible with an associated target population.   (pp. 46, 54, 56)

_____, LEARNING/TRANSFER   a rule account involving the derivation (learning) of solution rules.   (p. 125)

_____, PERFORMANCE   a rule account involving a single rule.   (p. 125)

RULE SET   a set of rules.   Unless stated otherwise, contains a finite number of rules.   (pp. 46, 49, 56)

RULES OF COMPETENCE   see COMPETENCE ACCOUNT/COMPETENCE RULE

_____, FEASIBLE   a competence account that is potentially compatible with the target population.   (p. 64)

SOLUTION (PROBLEM SOLUTION/RESPONSE/OUTPUT)   unless otherwise stated, refers to a nondecoded (i.e., internal) output structure.   (pp. 45, 83, 90)

SOLUTION PLAN   a sequence of subproblems such that the given of the first subproblem is the given of the associated problem and the goal of the last subproblem is the goal of the problem. (p. 91)

SOLUTION GOAL   a goal that is satisfied by potential solution rules. Usually denoted SG = G2. (p. 83)

SOLUTION RULE   see RULE, SOLUTION (p. 83)

STAGE EQUIVALENCE   see ATOMICITY, STAGE

STIMULUS (RESPONSE)   external, directly observable counterparts of inputs or problem givens (outputs or problem solutions). (STRUCTURE is more general and refers to any encoded input/ output.) (pp. 45, 57)

STORAGE   deriving a rule that operates on retrieval cues and generates to-be-retrieved entities. (pp. 89-90)

STRUCTURAL (THEORETICAL/DETERMINISTIC) VARIABLES/FACTORS   refer directly to entities in a deterministic theory of behavior. (Chapter 1)

STRUCTURAL ANALYSIS (sometimes STRUCTURAL METHOD OF ANALYSIS)   a more or less systematic method of identifying and representing the rules of competence (rule set) associated with a given problem domain and subject (target) population (p. 61). Used loosely to refer both to present informal methods of analysis and to what the method might ultimately become. May be applied recursively (iteratively), each time resulting in a *deeper level* of analysis (i.e., further *reduction* of the rule set obtained at any given level of analysis). Resulting rules may be called SOURCE rules (the latter may be used to derive rules at *preliminary* levels of analysis). (pp. 45, 61, 122)

STRUCTURAL LEARNING THEORY   the particular theory of structural learning on which this book is based, not THE only theory that purports to deal with similar phenomena. A "top-down" theory in the sense that emphasis is on overall interrelationships first, detail second. Theories associated with particular fields (artificial intelligence, cognitive psychology, testing) tend to be more specialized but some are potentially compatible. (p. 46)

___, MEMORY-FREE   that part of the Structural Learning Theory that assumes an information processor with goal switching control but without constraints on processing capacity or processing speed.

___, EXTENDED (ENRICHED)   an extension of the Memory-Free Structural Learning Theory that assumes a fixed processing capacity and/or processing speed. (p. 106)

STRUCTURAL REPRESENTATION   the type of representation of competence obtained as a result of Structural Analysis. (p. 50)

STRUCTURE (PSYCHOLOGICAL STRUCTURE) (also UNITARY or PSYCHOLOGI-' CAL ENTITY/STATE or COGNITIVE UNIT/ENCODED COMPLEX)   a n-tuple consisting of a finite set of elements (either

indivisible or themselves rules), and relations and rules
(functions in the mathematical sense) that are defined on
the elements, and higher-order relations and higher-order
rules (defined on the relations and rules). Act as unitary
psychological entities on which rules operate--e.g., a set
of rules is a structure. (In earlier formulations, structures were sometimes referred to as "sets of rules" or
complexes.)

Structures are defined by rules; they are the entities
(DATA STRUCTURES) on which rules operate. Where the basic
elements in structures are not themselves rules and/or
where rules (i.e., operations) and higher-order relations/
rules do not play an important role, structures may be
represented in terms of relational networks. (Psychological) structures correspond to structures in the mathematical
sense except for the finite restriction on the basic sets.
The former also routinely include higher-order rules/rela-
tions on rules/relations. COGNITIVE UNIT is sometimes used
to emphasize that the structures that are being operated
on may consist of rules and/or goals (p. 105). (Note:
Problems and rules of competence must be represented at a
level that has psychological relevance in the sense that
the basic elements, relations and operations correspond to
atomic psychological entities.) (pp. 44, 57, 72, 88)

___, DEGENERATE (ATOMIC/SIMPLE) a special case of a structure
(e.g., a simple input/output element). (pp. 58, 73)

___, MOLAR/GLOBAL a structure that is represented at a MOLAR
level. (p. 52)

___, PARENT a structure from which another has been somehow
derived (e.g., a to-be-retrieved rule may be embedded in
a parent structure). (p. 89)

STRUCTURED DOMAINS problem domains in which it is relatively
easy to identify the basic elements, operations, and relations. (p. 73)

SUBRULE (SUBGRAPH/SUBROUTINE) a portion of a rule, used generally to include cases where the subrule retains the initial
node and an exit node and where it does not (e.g., a path
is of the former type). Where important, distinctions are
made in context. Thus, SUBROUTINE often refers to rules
(subrules) derived during the course of a computation. In
the restricted sense of RULE used in this book, such subroutines may not in turn be applied within the same computation. (pp. 80, 111)

TARGET (SUBJECT) POPULATION the population of subjects with
which the theorist/competence analyst is concerned. In
order to have behavioral relevance, rules of competence
must not only account for given problem domains but must
do so in a way that is compatible (see above) with the
target/subject population. (p. 50)

TEST ITEM   see PROBLEM (GOAL) SITUATION

UNITARY   equivalent to ATOMIC under RULE (e.g., p. 48) and
 GOAL.   In the case of STRUCTURES and ENCODING/DECODING
 CAPABILITIES, however, UNITARY is not the same as ATOMIC.
 (See ATOMIC [UNITARY] ENCODING/DECODING CAPABILITIES.)
 In particular, while "unitary" refers to encoding/decoding
 capabilities (and structures determined by them) that are
 uniformly available to subjects in the target population,
 they need not consist of single indivisible elements.
 (p. 48)

PART 2

Content Analysis (Competence)

In Part 2, we adopt the perspective of the competence theorist. The overall aim is to demonstrate the viability of a particular type of competence theory as a means of representing the knowledge needed to solve problems in given problem domains. Rather than having rules (in rule sets) interact as in formal systems in mathematics, or as in generative grammars in linguistics (cf. Chapter 1), they are allowed to operate on and to generate new rules in accounting for particular instances of problem solving. Unlike computer systems in artificial intelligence, on the other hand, where the programmer generally has complete freedom to do whatever he thinks might be useful (however, see Chapter 15), the rules in such rule sets are required to interact in a very specific way.

Furthermore, unlike linguistic theorists who are more or less agreed on a content area (e.g., the production and comprehension of grammatical discourse, with or without semantics), theorists interested in competence, more generally, must adopt somewhat different goals. Rather than concentrating solely on competence accounts of certain specific domains of problems, equal attention must be given to the *general processes* by which viable accounts of *arbitrary* domains may be devised.

The two chapters in Part 2 are concerned primarily with the analysis of problem domains. In addition to identifying underlying competence (rule sets), however, the reported research also illustrates *how* arbitrary problem domains may be analyzed. Many workers in artificial intelligence, and also in linguistics, are committed to the idea that the analysis of problem domains is primarily an artistic endeavor; that any attempt to systematize the identification of rule sets will surely fail (cf. Chomsky,

1957). I agree that a major portion of competence analysis may necessarily depend on the perspicacity of the analyst. On the other hand, I believe that the requirement of compatibility with cognitive universals and given subject populations imposes important constraints on structural analysis, both as to results (rule sets) and method (see Chapter 2).

In the following chapters, the only cognitive universal that is considered involves the manner in which rules are assumed to interact. This constraint makes it possible to adopt a prespecified modular approach: (1) solution rules are identified for representative sets of clearly delineated problems in the given domains, (2) various kinds of parallels among these solution rules are identified, represented as higher-order rules, and incorporated into second order rule sets. (In principle, derived rule sets may be analyzed further in the same way, i.e., recursively. Each time this is done a set of rules is obtained in which the individual rules are simpler and the set as a whole has greater generating power (than the original rule set) relative to the problem domain. See Chapter 14 for an example. In Scandura, 1973, rule sets derived in this manner are referred to as "innate bases".)

For the most part, in Chapters 3 and 4 the constraints imposed by particular subject populations were applied informally, largely on the basis of intuition. Thus, whereas detailed observations of prototypic subjects under idealized conditions might be better, many important rule characteristics can often be identified via introspection--at least where the analyst shares or is familiar with the subject populations in question. In accounting for ordinary subtraction, for example, a rule based on the method of complements (widely used in parts of Europe) would not be appropriate for use with American children. The latter are typically trained in the borrowing method. In general, of course, the more that is known about the competences characteristic of a given population, the more *a priori* constraints that can be placed on the method of analysis. (Irrespective of how rules are identified, of course, the final test of their adequacy is empirical--i.e., is their utility as a basis for assessing the behavior potential of individual subjects.)

In view of its importance, it is instructive to contrast this compatibility requirement with the notion of epistemic knowledge as used by Piaget. Piaget is not concerned with competence that is compatible with the knowledge had by *individual* subjects. Rather, he is concerned with that knowledge which may reasonably be assumed to be common to human beings generally at various stages of development (see Furth, 1969). Correspondingly, in the present vernacular (cf. Chapter 2, Sections 2.3 and 2.5), Piagetian stage theory may deal veridically only with global/molar aspects of behavior. According to the structural learning theory, the only thing that *all* humans have in common in all situations is the postulated control mechanism described in Chapter 2; the rest of cognitive potential consists of knowledge specific rules. The latter are always judged relative to some problem domain, whether highly specific and prescribed or general and molar. Of course, as individuals mature and develop, particularly within given cultures, they presumably grow to share more in common. In this sense, the two approaches are complementary. Global competencies/rules, associated with Piagetian tasks, may be expected to enter directly or indirectly into the analysis of any number of problem domains where the subject populations correspond to various developmental stages. Indeed, these competencies could impose useful constraints on structural analysis. A major prerequisite to identifying such constraints would be a prior structural analysis of Piagetian theory. Undertaking such an analysis would be a major but potentially important task. Hopefully, someone may be motivated to take it on.

In Chapter 3 the general method of analysis is detailed and illustrated with the domain of compass and straight-edge geometry construction problems. Higher-order rules were constructed for the two-loci, similar figures and auxiliary figures problems identified in Chapter 1 of Polya (1962). The higher-order rules are precise, compatible with Polya's heuristics, and seem to reflect the kinds of relevant knowledge that successful teenagers might possess. Limitations of the obtained analysis also are discussed and directions for future research are suggested. In particular, the analysis in Chapter 3: (a) is restricted to higher-order rules that form compositions of given rules, (b) does not take into account the role of logical inference, and (c) does not distinguish between the derivation of new rules and breaking problems into subproblems.

162   PART 2

The above gaps are filled in Chapter 4 where a partially
generalized form of structural analysis is used to analyze the
domain of algebraic proofs in the Ball State Algebra I course.
In this case, the problem inputs are the theorems in this proof-
oriented text and the outputs (problem solutions) are the proofs.
Among other things, the analysis shows that first steps in the
various proofs can be generated independently of the particular
number systems (e.g., natural numbers, rational numbers) involved
and depend exclusively on the general form of the theorem statement (e.g., whether and which quantifiers it involves). Generating the remaining steps of a proof, however, given the first
step, depends also on the system within which one is working.
Also identified as a result of the analysis were higher-order
rules that can be used for purposes of both generalization and
restriction (e.g., analogy).

Chapter 4 STRUCTURAL (ALGORITHMIC) ANALYSIS OF
           ALGEBRAIC PROOFS   201

Although the analyses in Chapters 3 and 4 demonstrate the
potential value of structural analysis, neither the forms of
structural analysis used nor the results of the analyses themselves exhaust the possibilities inherent in the theory described in Chapter 2. For one thing, the methods used were not as
systematic, strictly objective or general as might be desired.
No attempt, for example, was made to incorporate selection rules
in the analyses, to explicitly identify the structures involved
(cf. Chapter 4, last page), or to apply structural analysis
recursively (however, see Chapter 14). Moreover, all of the

structural analyses to date refer exclusively to the idealized (memory-free) theory (cf. Chapter 2). In future research more explicit attention needs to be given to motivation (i.e., selection from among alternative rules), goal definition (i.e., procedures by which problem statements are interpreted), and memory. Perhaps even more obvious, structural analysis (even in its present incomplete form) should be applied to a wider variety of subject matters. The analysis in Chapter 12, especially in the Addendum, is suggestive of broad applicability but more detailed analyses are needed.

REFERENCES

Chomsky, N. *Syntactic structures*. The Hague: Mouton, 1957.
Furth, H. G. *Piaget and knowledge: Theoretical foundations*.
    Englewood Cliffs, N.J.: Prentice-Hall, 1969.
Polya, G. *Mathematical discovery* (Volume 1). New York: Wiley,
    1962.
Scandura, J. M. *Structural learning I: Theory and research*.
    London/New York: Gordon & Breach, 1973.

3
Higher-Order Rule Characterization
of Heuristics for Compass and Straight-Edge Constructions in Geometry[1]

Joseph M. Scandura   *John H. Durnin[2]*   *Wallace H. Wulfeck II*

According to Polya (1962), perhaps the greatest value to be gained from the study of mathematics is the ability to solve problems. In spite of its importance, however, relatively little is known about how to teach people to solve problems, or how to program computers to do so. Specifically, one of the great mysteries of our time is why some problem solvers (human or computer) succeed on problems for which they have all of the necessary component skills (operators) whereas others fail.

In dealing with this question, most research in artificial intelligence (AI) has been concerned with the construction of powerful computer programs that can solve more or less diverse classes of complex problems. In computer simulation, an attempt is made to also parallel human performance on such problems. In general, such systems (e.g., Newell & Simon, 1972; Minsky & Papert, 1972) have been comprehensive in scope; they have been concerned with problem definition (the construction of subgoals), memory, the derivation of solution procedures, and the use of such procedures.

The present research has adopted a somewhat different strategy. It seeks understanding by dealing separately with the various aspects of problem solving (e.g., the derivation of solution procedures). In particular, this research was concerned with the specification and testing of general, potentially useful heuristics for constructing procedures for solving compass and straight-edge construction problems in geometry. The research was also concerned with developing and determining the feasibility of a general method by which heuristics may be identified in arbitrary

[1]This research was supported by National Science Foundation Grant GW 6796 to the first author.

[2]Now at Villanova University.

165

problem domains.

One general point of departure was Polya's (1962) work on
heuristics for geometry construction problems. These heuristics
are purposely cast in a form designed to parallel human thought
processes in much the same way as are such general heuristics
as means-ends analysis (e.g., Newell & Simon, 1972). Human
processing presumably is highly efficient in many situations,
and the importance of paralleling human processing in AI, as
well as in computer simulation, has become increasingly well
recognized as a means of significantly reducing processing time.
Winston (1972), for example, has noted how constraining syntactic procedures to reflect underlying semantics in the recognition
of block scenarios can drastically reduce the number of possibilities that must be considered.

In spite of the broad acclaim for Polya's work generally,
however, and the intrinsic support for his notion of heuristics
specifically, it has sometimes been difficult to capitalize on
these ideas as fully as might be desired. Although often useful,
his heuristics are frequently little more than general hints,
and leave much to be desired insofar as pinpointing what a human
or computer must know in order to solve specific kinds of problems. In order to lend themselves to technological treatment,
heuristics must be transformed or incorporated into strictly
mechanical procedures that can be more or less readily implemented on computers. Ideally, one might desire reduction of
heuristics to algorithms; witness the alpha-beta "heuristic"
(e.g., Nilsson, 1971).

Since heuristics tend to be specific to problem domains,
the potential value of more-or-less general and systematic
methods for specifying heuristics in arbitrary problem domains
seems fairly clear. Our approach to this problem was designed
to be compatible with Scandura's (1973) theory of structural
learning, and is an extension of a method used earlier by
Ehrenpreis and Scandura (Chapter 11). That portion of the theory, with which this research is most concerned, has been shown
empirically to reflect the behavior of individual subjects in
particular situations where problem definition and memory do not
play an important role. Furthermore, this idealized theory has
been shown with some empirical verification (Scandura, 1973,
1974) to be extendible to situations involving memory and, also,
apparently, problem definition and perception (Scandura, 1973,
p. 348, Chapter 5, res.), without essential change. The structure
of the theory must be enriched in these cases but without affecting its basic character (i.e., underlying behavior mechanism).
This research is based directly on one part of the idealized
theory, in particular that part that is concerned with compe-
tence--the specification of rule sets that account for classes
of problems. In this theory, a rule set is said to account for
a class of problems, roughly speaking, if for each problem in

the class, (1) there is a solution rule (operator) in the rule set that has the problem in its domain and whose range contains the solution to the problem or, (2) there is a higher-order rule in the rule set that applies to rules in the set and generates a solution rule. In such a rule set, higher-order rules correspond to heuristics. (For a more general and formal formulation, which allows for any number of levels of derivation, see Scandura, 1973, Chapter 9; and compare it with the still more general formulation in Chapter 2, this book; also Scandura, 1974.)

It seems unlikely, of course, that strictly algorithmic methods can be found for devising nontrivial rule sets or heuristics for arbitrary problem domains. Indeed, as Chomsky (1957) has argued in the case of linguistics, no such method exists for dealing with observables as complex as language. Work in automatic programming, on the other hand, while it is quite far at present from a satisfactory solution, is proceeding, as the authors[3] understand it, on the assumption that significant progress in this direction can be made.

In the present research, the task of specifying heuristics is made simpler in at least two ways. First, and most important, the type of competence theory proposed imposes important constraints on the nature of allowable rule sets, and in turn on the form of the heuristics (higher-order rules). In particular, higher-order rules are assumed to operate on component (lower-order) rules to generate integrated problem solution rules (procedures). These rules may simply compose component rules but may also modify them, for example, via generalization or restriction rules (Scandura, 1973).

Second, restricting the level of analysis to that of flow diagrams, rather than computer programs, makes it natural to represent the constituent operations and decision-making capabilities at whatever level seems to most adequately reflect human knowledge rather than at a level predetermined by some programming language. (We do not mean to minimize the importance of devising working programs. In fact, parts of this analysis have been implemented by one of the authors.) While no general assurance can be given with regard to any particular method, it would seem that a method that results in heuristics and simple operators that appear consistent with human thought, would have a reasonable chance of having general value.

---

[3]The authors do not profess to be experts in artificial intelligence or in computer simulation as such, but rather in the adjacent, and, we think, complementary, domain of structural psychology, which is, in our view, considerably broader than contemporary cognitive and information-processing psychology.

1. METHOD OF (STRUCTURAL) ANALYSIS

Our method of analysis went something as follows. First, we attempted to set some reasonably explicit bounds on the class of geometry construction problems to be considered. In particular, we considered only those problems in, or like, those of Chapter 1 of Polya (1962).

Our next step was to classify these problems on heuristic-intuitive grounds. Our aim was to place similar problems in the same categories, in accordance with the general form of their solutions. We were one step up in this regard, since Polya had already done part of the categorization for us. All of his problems can be solved according to some variant or combination of the three general heuristics he describes: (1) the pattern of two loci, (2) the pattern of similar figures, and (3) the pattern of auxiliary figures (cf. Chapter 2, Structural Analysis).

After a broad sample of tasks had been classified, we made sure that the domains and ranges of each task were fairly explicit. Then we identified explicit procedures for solving each type of task. Care was taken to insure that these procedures reflected our intuitions as to how intelligent high school students might go about solving the problems. In some cases it was possible at this point to subclassify some of the tasks.

The most critical step was to identify general parallels among the procedures developed for the sampled problems, within each of the various classifications, and even more important, to devise higher-order rules (operator combination methods) that realized these parallels as relatively formal, but still general, procedures. The higher-order rules so identified (together with the component lower-order rules on which they act) provided a general basis for constructing solution rules for the sampled problems.

Then we attempted to refine the resulting higher-order rules with regard to specific sampled problems. This was done systematically: where a higher-order rule failed to yield an adequate solution rule for a sampled problem, appropriate modifications in the higher-order rule were made. A serious attempt was also made to insure that the higher-order rules were compatible with human knowledge.[4]

[4]The only really adequate way of determining whether a rule is compatible with human behavior is to effect a behavioral test; that is to see whether a rule provides an adequate basis for assessing the behavior potential of individual subjects, thereby making it possible to predict the behavior of individual subjects on new instances of the rule. (The theoretical foundations for such tests have been worked out and tested empirically [Scandura, 1971; 1973a; Chapter 10; Chapter 11]. The basic idea is to determine each subject's behavior potential with respect to each rule in an identified rule set, and then to use the theory as a basis for making predictions concerning performance on problems which require interactions among the rules. The closeness of fit between the predictions and observed behavior would provide a direct test of the adequacy of the rule set. A study reported in Scandura [1973a] on rule

2. PATTERN OF TWO LOCI

Our first step was to select a broad sampling of two loci problems, and to devise procedures for solving each. For example, consider the problem: "Given a line and a point not on the line, and a radius R, construct a circle of radius R that is tangent to the given line and that passes through the given point." This problem can be solved according to the following procedure: "Construct the locus of points at distance R from the given point; construct the locus of points at distance R from the given line; construct a circle using the intersection point of the two loci as center, and the distance R as radius."

This solution rule clearly involves the pattern of two loci. In this case, as with all of the problems in Polya's first category, the tasks may be characterized according to the form of their solution procedures: Two loci are determined one after the other; the point of intersection of these loci, in turn, makes it possible to construct the goal figure.

Further analysis of the class of two-loci problems, however, revealed differences in the ways problems are solved. In many solution rules, for instance, like the example above, the two loci can be found independently, in either order. Furthermore, at no point in the course of applying the solution rule is it necessary to measure a distance. Some form of distance measurement, however, is required with other tasks. Some of the sampled tasks require measurement in order to construct the goal figure; the solution rule for another problem involves measurement before the second locus can be found. In still another task, one of the loci is actually given, or, equivalently, can be thought of as obtained by applying an identity rule. The goal figure in still another task is simply the point of intersection of the two loci.

2.1 AN INITIAL CHARACTERIZATION

As a first step in characterizing a two-loci higher-order rule, we systematically went through the various solution rules for the pattern of two-loci tasks and identified all of the different component rules that appeared in our sample problems, either: (1) in constructing one of the loci, or (2) in constructing a goal figure. The lower-order rules we identified were mostly common constructions (e.g., perpendicular bisector, circle, parallel line). Some of the lower-order component rules were used to construct a needed locus, others were involved in constructing goal figures, and some served both functions.

The higher-order rule in Figure 1 shows schematically how

generalization was of this type.) Since this was impractical in the present study, we adopted the weaker and less rigorous criterion of requiring that the rule sets be compatible with our intuition (cf. Chomsky, 1957).

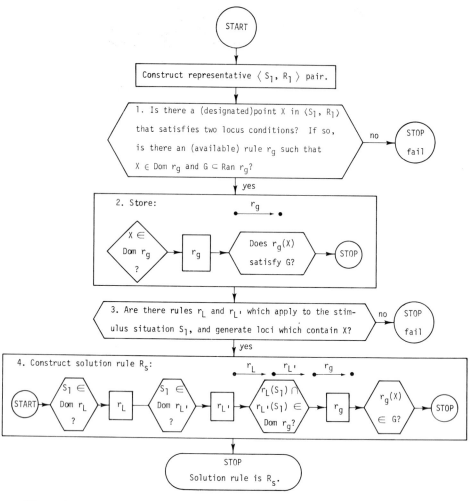

Figure 1.   Two-loci higher-order rule.

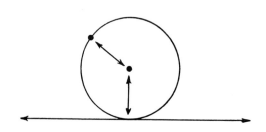

Figure 2.   Sketch of a two-loci problem.

the various solution rules may be constructed from the component
rules. The higher-order rule in Figure 1 applies to the problem
(i.e., the stimulus situation, S_o) and to the goal (G) itself,
as well as to the lower-order component rules.[5]

First, an arbitrary representation $\langle S_1, R_1 \rangle$ analogous to
the solved problem is constructed. In our illustrative task,
a sketch like Figure 2 would serve this purpose. Note that constructing such a representation is *not* the same as either solving
the problem, or constructing a solution rule for the problem.
The sketch in Figure 2, for example, can easily be generated by
first drawing an arbitrary circle, then drawing an arbitrary
line tangent to it, and placing an arbitrary point on it. More
generally, an arbitrary representation (R_1) of the goal figure
(R_o) is constructed first. Only then is a representation (S_1)
of the information given in the stimulus situation (S_o) constructed in relation to the representation of the goal figure.
In effect, the first operation on the higher-order rule amounts
to representing geometrically the meanings of goal situations
(i.e., goals plus stimulus situations) by a "sketch", or some
equivalent representation.[6]

The second step is the question: "Is there a point X in
$\langle S_1, R_1 \rangle$ that satisfies two locus conditions--and, if so, is there
a goal-constructing rule (r_g) such that point X is contained in
the domain of r_g (Dom r_g) and such that the goal G, is contained
in the range of r_g (Ran r_g)?"

As shown in Scandura (1973) decision-making capabilities
can be characterized as partitions on a class of input situations; in the present case, each representation $\langle S_1, R_1 \rangle$ either
contains a point X that satisfies two locus conditions or it
does not. If it does satisfy two such conditions, and there is
a rule r_g in the rule set (as above), then the following opera-

[5]Strictly speaking, human subjects are presented with statements of
problems as stimuli. Throughout this, and our subsequent analyses, we assume
that the subject's initial subgoal is to interpret the goal statement (i.e.,
determine its meaning). The second subgoal is to solve the problem. In effect,
the initial goal is divided into a pair of subgoals to be achieved in order.
Our analysis is limited to the second part of this task, and then only on the
assumption that there is no further division of the problem into subgoals. We
also assume that the given problem statements can be uniformly and correctly
interpreted.
    Although we do not pursue the question here, we have reason to believe
that forming subgoals is closely related to the question of (problem) representation (cf. Amarel, 1968).

[6]Other representations would probably be more efficient for computer implementation, since graphic systems are relatively complex to implement. For example,
some sort of naming system for points, lines, etc., could be devised, together
with appropriate interpretive routines to identify relations of interest among
elements. In fact, the naming system for triangles in common use evolved for
just this purpose--names for sides, vertices, medians, etc.--if correctly interpreted, carry much information about relative position, intersections, etc.

tion simply stores r_g for later use.

Next, the available component rules are tested to see whether there are two of them that apply to the represented stimulus (S_1) and generate loci that contain the point X. Given that such locus rules exist, the next operation constructs the solution rule R_S, in which first one locus rule r_L is applied, then the other r_L', and finally the goal construction rule r_g.

2.2 A MORE RIGOROUS ANALYSIS

This level of description is sufficient to give one an intuitive feeling for how the higher-order rule operates. But the rule is ambiguous, especially for computer implementation purposes. In the first decision-making capability, for example, it is not clear just what constitutes a locus condition. Similarly, in the second decision-making capability the notion of a rule applying to a stimulus situation is something less than precise.

Closer perusal of the individual tasks made it possible to overcome these ambiguities. In many cases, the desired point X is a given distance from one or two given points and/or lines. In the example above, for instance, the point X is a distance R from the given point and from the given line. This suggested the following more rigorous characterization of the first decision-making capability: Does there exist a point X in $\langle S_1, R_1 \rangle$, such that X is a given distance from one or two given points and/or lines, and if so, is there a rule r_g such that (X, E) is contained in the domain of r_g where E is a given distance, and the goal is contained in the range of r_g (G $\subset$ Ran r_g)?

A similar analysis suggested reformulating the second decision-making capability as: Is there a rule r_L such that a pair consisting of given points, lines, and/or distances in S_1 is in the domain of r_L (Dom r_L) and such that X is a member of L (i.e., a point on L) where L is contained in the range of r_L (X $\in$ L $\in$ Ran r_L)?

A similar characterization is required for r_L'.

A higher-order rule incorporating these refinements can be used to generate solution rules for many two-loci problems. For example, in the illustrative problem there is certainly a point X in the representation $\langle S_1, R_1 \rangle$ that is at the given distance R from a given point and from a given line in S_1. It is also true that there is an r_g rule that applies to the pair consisting of the point X and the given distance, and whose range consists of circles and is thereby contained in the goal.

Unfortunately, as it stands, the modified higher-order rule does not provide an adequate means for characterizing solution rules for other sampled two-loci tasks. In certain tasks, for example, no distance is given. The important requirement in such cases is often that the point X be equidistant from a given pair of elements, points and/or lines, in two different instances (i.e., for two given pairs of elements). Thus, in the task, "Inscribe a circle in a given triangle," the desired point X is equidistant simultaneously from two different pairs of sides of the triangle, or equivalently, the point X is equidistant from the three sides.

Still other tasks involve the lower-order rule for constructing the locus of vertices of an angle of given measure subtending a given line segment. The task, "Given side a of a triangle, the median M_a, and the measure of angle A opposite side a, construct the triangle," is of this type. The locus of vertices, in this case, is an arc, but the points on it are not at a fixed distance from any point on the given segment. Nor are the points of the locus equidistant from any two particular points on the line segment.

In order to take these possibilities into account, the decision-making capability was generalized so that the point X could be equidistant from pairs of points or lines, or could serve as vertices of an angle of given measure whose sides subtend (i.e., pass through the endpoints of) a given segment. Decision-making capability (3) (Figure 1) was also enriched so that pairs consisting of angle measures and/or segments could be in the domain of a locus rule.

Further, in the problem, "Given three intersecting lines, not all intersecting at a common point, construct a circle that is tangent to two of the lines and whose center is on the third," we have a situation where one of the loci, the line containing the point X, is already given. To handle this possibility we simply assume an "identity" lower-order rule, one that identifies a given line as a required locus.

With these modifications, the higher-order rule handled almost all of the pattern of two-loci tasks we had sampled. We ran into difficulty, however, with another task: "Given two parallel lines and a point between them, construct a circle that is tangent to the two lines and passes through the point." This difficulty involved the second decision-making capability (3). There is a pair of lines in the domain of one of the locus rules--one that constructs the locus of points equidistant from the two given parallel lines. The second locus rule, however, requires that we first measure a distance between two parallel lines, one of which is not present in the stimulus S_0 until after the first locus rule is applied. That is, we need to determine the distance between one of the parallel lines and the locus of points equidistant from the two given parallel lines. This distance serves as the desired radius.

Application of the higher-order rule in this case results in failure at decision-making capability (3). Fortunately, it is easy to modify the higher-order rule to take this possibility into account. Furthermore, as we shall see, this modification serves an important purpose in dealing with the larger class of construction problems solvable either by the pattern of two loci or by the pattern of similar figures.

Instead of stopping when the second decision fails, we simply add another group of tests (A–C). Tests A and B duplicate (1) and (2) of Figure 1 except that X must satisfy only one specific condition. Test C asks: "Is there one component rule such that a pair of given points and/or lines is in the domain of that rule and is there a locus L such that the point X is part of L and L is contained in the range of r_L?" If the answer to this is no, we stop, but if the answer is yes, we can ask whether there is another locus rule r_L', such that the represented stimulus situation S_1, together with the preceding locus $r_L(S_1)$, contains a pair of given points and/or lines that are in the domain of r_L'. A revised higher-order rule that incorporates all of these modifications is shown in Figure 3. (The abbreviated description in Step 1 should be interpreted as in 2.2. Steps A and B are unnecessary here but are included for comparative purposes, cf. Figure 4.)

In checking this higher-order rule, we found that it provided an adequate account, not only of all of the pattern of two-loci problems sampled, but others as well. For example, consider task A: "Given sides a, b, and c of a triangle, construct the triangle." In this case, application of the higher-order rule generates the solution rule. This solution rule involves: (1) application of the rule, "Construct the locus of points at a given distance from a given point," to the endpoint of one line segment, using another side as distance, followed by (2) another application of the rule to the other endpoint, using the remaining side as radius. Then, the triangle rule, "from a point not on a given segment, draw segments to the endpoints of the given segment," is applied to the intersection of these two loci to obtain the desired goal figure.

In some cases, of course, different lower-order (component) rules were involved. For example, consider task B, "Given two intersecting lines and a point of tangency on one of the lines, construct a circle that is tangent to the two lines and that passes through the given point of tangency." In this case the locus rule for constructing perpendiculars to lines through points on the given lines had not been required with any of the sampled problems.

2.3 DISCUSSION

Aside from the possibility that new two-loci problems may require additional lower-order rules, the (modified) higher-order rule appears adequate. In particular, the higher-order rule not only generates solution rules for each of the sampled two-loci problems, but also seems compatible with human knowledge.

As the form of the higher-order rule suggests, the component decision-making capabilities play a crucial role in deriving solution procedures. These decision-making capabilities are designed to reflect the underlying semantics of the problem

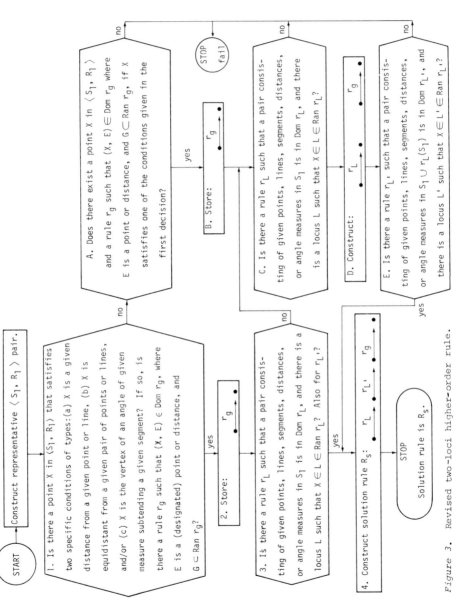

Figure 3. Revised two-loci higher-order rule.

situations by referring directly to figural representations of semantic information implicit in the problem descriptions. In general, parts of a figural representation S_1, R_1 will represent the meaning of a task statement and reflect the relation between the given stimulus (S_0) and the goal figure (R_0). Notice that while the relation between S_1 and R_1 will be the same as between S_0 and R_0, S_1 and R_1 will not, in general, be the same as S_0 and R_0, respectively.

For purposes of our analysis, the decision-making capabilities were viewed as atomic although they can also be analyzed into more basic components. The first decision-making capability in the second two-loci higher-order rule, for example, involves both a conjunction and disjunctions of a number of simpler conditions. This decision-making capability could be subdivided, for instance, into several decisions, including: (A) Is there a point X that is a given distance from a given point and/or line? (B) Is there a point X equidistant from a pair of given points or lines? Instead of having one decision-making capability involving conditions A, B, etc., then, we could have one decision-making capability involving A, one B, and so on.[7]

In addition to its purported compatibility with human knowledge, the higher-order rule is also sufficiently precise to be mechanizable. One of the authors (Wulfeck) has recently written a program in SNOBOL 4 that uses an intermediate version of the two-loci higher-order rule to generate solution procedures for many of the problems we sampled. A naming system replaced the figural representation described above (see footnote 6). Routines corresponding to many of the lower-order rules were also written.

Granting the adequacy of the higher-order rule for purposes of our analysis, we wish to comment briefly on some limitations in regard to the compatibility of the lower-order rules with human knowledge, although the specification of component rules is not our central concern. These limitations are all variants on a common theme: The lower-order rules we have identified can be constructed from more basic components. This fact is reflected in at least three ways.

First, many of the simple rules have components in common. Several rules, for example, all involve constructing a locus of points (circle) at some distance from some point. The differences lie in whether or not the distance and/or center points are given directly or must be determined first. The construction rules needed to determine these distances and/or center points are quite basic and are apt to be useful in a wide variety of construction situations. Any reasonable account, designed to

---

[7]For a discussion of how new decision-making capabilities are learned from simpler ones, see Scandura (1973a). Such refinement may be useful in the assessment of behavior potential (Chapter 8), specifically in increasing the precision of diagnostic testing.

deal with a wider variety of problem situations, would undoubtedly include these construction rules directly in the rule set.

Second, certain of the identified lower-order rules, particularly the rule for constructing the locus of vertices of an
angle of a given measure subtending a given line segment, are
complex in themselves and cannot automatically be assumed to be
available to many problem solvers.

A third limitation is closely related to the first and was
mentioned earlier: The lower-order rules are to some degree
specific to the tasks we have identified. To some extent, this
specificity may be unavoidable because there are always certain
problems that require "trick" solutions. It would be desirable,
of course, to keep this specificity to a minimum. In this regard, it should be emphasized that the simpler the lower-order
rules the greater the problem-solving flexibility.

One way to modify our characterization in order to handle
these limitations would be to "reduce" the lower-order rules
into their components and, correspondingly, to "enrich" the
higher-order rule by adding subroutines for constructing the
needed locus (r_L) and goal, (r_g) rules.[8] Such rules would correspond to the type of knowledge that a person, just having been
taught the basic construction rules, would need to have in order
to generate solution rules directly.

For example, consider the rule: "Determine the distance
between a given point and a given line and then construct the
locus of points at the obtained distance from the given point."
This rule can be divided into two subrules: (1) "Determine the
distance between a point and a line," and (2) "Construct the
locus of points at a given distance from a given point." To
compensate for the reduction in the latter case, the higher-
order rule could be "enriched" so that more complex r_L and r_g
rules can be generated where needed. Specifically, instead of
selecting a composite rule directly, when it meets certain prescribed conditions, as we have done so far, we include in the
higher-order rule a simple subroutine for combining component
lower-order rules. Such a subroutine for example, might select
subrules until one is found whose domain includes a pair consisting of a point and a line (e.g., the distance measuring rule
[1]), and another (e.g., the circle rule [2]) such that its range
consists of circles (loci). To make the search more efficient,
it is natural to add the requirement that the range of the former

---

[8] In evaluating alternative rule-based accounts for a given class of tasks,
decisions must always be made concerning exactly how the computational load
should be apportioned to the higher- and lower-order rules. Any number of
alternatives exist; at one extreme, the lower-order rules may do all of the
computation, in which case a separate rule would be needed for each type of
problem, and, at the other extreme, the component lower-order rules may be of
minimal complexity with the higher-order rule assuming most of the computational
burden. The requirement of compatibility with human knowledge, of course,
substantially reduces the number of plausible characterizations.

be contained in the domain of the latter. After the component
rules have been identified, the subroutine would form the composite of these rules, and finally, would test the composite
against the condition in the initial higher-order rule.

As attractive as this possibility might appear at first,
a little thought suggests its implausibility as a way of modeling human knowledge. This can be seen by noting that all geometric constructions with straight-edge and compass are generated by just three basic operations: (1) using a straight-edge
(e.g., to draw a line, ray, or segment through two given points,
or through one point, or intersecting a line, etc.); (2) drawing
an arc, given a compass set at some fixed radius; and (3) given
two points, setting a compass to the distance between those
points.

As we have seen, many of the lower-order rules are really
quite complex. Requiring a higher-order rule, designed to reflect human knowledge, to generate such rules from elemental
components, is unrealistic. It is unlikely that a subject who
is only able to perform the three indicated operations above
would also have at his command a rather complex and sophisticated higher-order rule. The acquisition of such complex capabilities by naive subjects, whether of a higher- or lower-order,
would almost certainly have to come about gradually through
learning, presumably by interacting with problems in the
environment (see Chapter 14).[9]

3.   PATTERN OF SIMILAR FIGURES

3.1   THREE CLASSES OF SIMILAR FIGURES PROBLEMS

The pattern of similar figures problems was analyzed in
similar fashion. Again, we began with a broad sampling of problems from Polya (1962). One of the problems identified was,
"Given a triangle, inscribe a square in it such that one side
of the square is contained in one side of the triangle and the
two other opposite vertices of the square lie on the other two
sides of the triangle." The second step was to identify a solution rule for each of the problems. For the problem above the
solution rule was, "Construct a square of arbitrary size such
that one side is contained in the side of the triangle that is
to contain the side of the goal square, and such that one vertex
is on another side of the triangle. Draw a line through the
point of intersection of those two sides of the triangle and
through the fourth vertex of the arbitrary square. From the
intersection of this line and the third side of the triangle
(which is the fourth vertex of the goal square), construct a
segment perpendicular to the side of the triangle that is to

---

[9]See Section 6 on future directions.

contain a side of the goal square. Complete the goal square
using the length of the perpendicular segment as the length of
the sides."

Similar figures problems, like the example task above, may
be characterized as those whose solution procedures involve a
similarity mapping process: From some center point of similarity, a figure or set of points is mapped onto another. Further,
the solution procedures always involve constructions according
to geometric invariants under similarity mappings, either parallel lines, since parallelism is preserved, or equivalently,
"copying" angles, since similarity maps are conformal.

Further analysis of the similar figures problems revealed
three relatively distinct classes of solution rules. In the
sample problem above, and in other problems in the same class,
the solution rules all involve first constructing a square of
arbitrary size that is in the same orientation as the desired
goal square, and that meets as many of the task conditions as
possible. (Rules of this type for constructing similar figures
are denoted by r_{gs}.) The second step in each solution rule uses
two pairs of corresponding points in the goal and similar figures
(i.e., in $\langle S_1, R_1 \rangle$ superimposed with the similar figure) to determine the point of similarity (P_s), and then, constructs a
line through the point of similarity and a point on the similar
figure which corresponds to a needed point of the goal figure.
(Point of similarity rules are denoted r_{ps}.) Finally, the obtained point on the goal figure is used as a basis for constructing the goal square.

The second class is well represented by the problem, "Given
angles B and C of a triangle, and the median M_a to side a, construct the triangle." The corresponding solution rules begin
similarly by applying a similar figures rule (r_{gs}) to two given
angles to construct an arbitrary-sized triangle similar to the
goal triangle, with medians, altitudes, etc., as required. Then
a modified point of similarity rule (r_{ps}) is used to determine
the point of similarity (P_s, the vertex of the nongiven angle),
and to construct the given segment (e.g., M_a), such that one
endpoint of the segment is the point of similarity, and such
that the segment coincides with the corresponding segment in
the similar triangle. Finally, a line is constructed, through
the other endpoint of the constructed segment parallel to the
side of the similar triangle that is opposite to the point of
similarity. The remaining sides of the goal triangle are obtained by extending two sides of the similar triangle to intersect the constructed parallel line.

The solution rules for the third class of problems differ
in that the first step in each is to use an r_L rule to construct
a locus of points that contains a critical point, specifically
the center of the goal circle. In the problem, "Given a line
and two points (A and B) on the same side of the line, construct

a circle tangent to the line that passes through the two given points," for example, the locus of points (L) equidistant from the two given points contains the center of the goal circle. Also, the point of similarity is the intersection of the locus and the given line. The second step is to construct a similar figure (circle, C_1), which satisfies part of the goal condition. In our example, a circle is constructed with its center on the constructed locus and tangent to the given line. Next, another version of the point of similarity rule is applied; this time the point of similarity (P_s) and a given point on the goal figure (e.g., B) are used to determine a corresponding point (B') on the similar circle. Then parallel lines involving corresponding points are constructed to determine the center of the goal circle. Finally, the goal circle is actually constructed.

3.2   THE SIMILAR FIGURES RULE

The higher-order rule shown in Figure 4 (together with a set of applicable lower-order rules) provides a sufficient basis for solving all of the sampled pattern of similar figures problems. Furthermore, the higher-order rule appears to reflect the underlying semantics. For example, let us see how a solution rule for the first illustrative problem above (inscribing a square in a triangle) can be generated by application of the higher-order rule. The first decision-making capability (A) asks, essentially, whether a point X is needed to serve as the center for a goal circle. As the goal figure is a square, the answer is obviously no. Decision-making capability J then asks if there is a goal similar figures rule (r_{gs}) that applies to representing stimulus S_1 and generates squares that satisfy part (G_s) of the goal condition (i.e., G_s is contained in the range of r_{gs}, where G_s in turn contains G--equivalently, anything that satisfies G, satisfies G_s, but not necessarily conversely). The lower-order rule, "Construct a square in a triangle with one side coincident with one side of the triangle and one vertex on another side of the triangle," satisfies these conditions, so the rule is retained as indicated in operation K.

Decision-making capability L asks two things: (1) Is there a point X_s in the similar figure that corresponds to a missing point X in the goal square (that can be specified via r_{ps})?   (2) Is there a rule r_g such that the given stimulus S_1, supplemented with the point X (i.e., $X \cup S_1$), is in the domain of r_g, and r_g generates a goal-like figure (G $\subset$ Ran r_g).   In short, is there a point X_s in the similar square that corresponds to a point X from which the goal square may be constructed?   Clearly, there is such a point, X_s, and the rule, "Determine the distance from a point to a given line segment and construct a square with sides of that length" satisfies the necessary conditions.   Operation M forms the solution rule consisting of the two rules above with the point of similarity rule between them.

To see how the higher-order rule works with the second

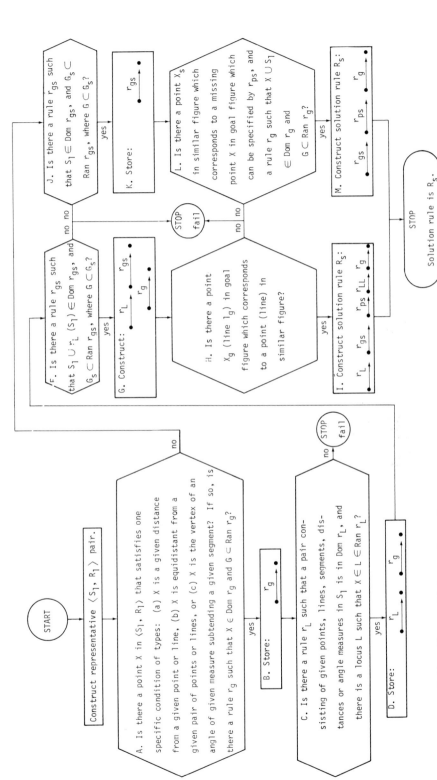

Figure 4. Similar figures higher-order rule.

class of problems, consider the second illustrative problem
above (constructing a triangle, given two angles and a median).
In this case, the answers to decision-making capabilities A and
J are again "no" and "yes", respectively. Here, r_{gs} is, "Construct a triangle of arbitrary size using two given angles and
add parts corresponding to given segments." At decision-making
capability L, there is a point X in the goal figure, the endpoint
of median M_a, which can be specified by r_{PS}. Operation M again
forms the solution rule.

Notice that the first two classes of problems involve the
same path in the higher-order rule. Each solution rule requires
a goal similar figure rule (r_{gs}), the point of similarity rule
(r_{PS}), and a goal constructing rule (r_g). The only difference
is whether the goal and similar figures are squares or triangles,
with all that implies for the particular r_{gs} and r_g rules required. In short, this example illustrates how what may appear
initially to be basically different kinds of problems may turn
out to have a common genesis.

The third problem (constructing a circle tangent to a given
line and passing through two given points) illustrates the other
path through the higher-order rule. In this case, if we knew
the center (X) of the desired circle, we could solve the task.
Furthermore, this missing point X is on a locus, namely the locus
of points equidistant from the two given points. Hence, decision-making capabilities A and C are satisfied, and we retain
the circle constructing rule (r_g) and the perpendicular bisector
rule (r_L). Decision-making capability F asks if there is a rule
(r_{gs}) that applies to the stimulus S_1 as modified by the output
of the locus rule (i.e., $S_1 \cup r_L(S_1)$). Condition F is satisfied
by a rule that generates circles with centers on a given line
(the locus) and tangent to another given line. The answer to
the decision-making capability H is also yes. The two given
points on the goal figure obviously correspond to two points on
the similar circle. By operation I (Figure 4), the solution
rule follows directly: "Construct the locus of points equidistant from the two given points (i.e., use r_L); construct a circle with center on that locus tangent to the given line (i.e.,
use r_{gs}); apply the point of similarity rule (r_{PS}), and then
the parallel line rule (p_{LL}) to determine the center of the
goal circle; construct the goal circle using this center and
the distance between it and a given point as radius (r_g)."

It should be noted that in one of the sampled tasks the
"locus" is given. The easiest way to handle this special case
is to simply add an identity-locus constructing rule as before.
It would also be a simple matter to modify the higher-order rule
to take this possibility into account by asking, prior to, or
at decision-making capability C, whether there is a line in S_1
that contains X.

3.3 COMBINED RULE FOR TWO-LOCI AND SIMILAR FIGURES PROBLEMS

It would appear from our analysis that the two higher-order rules, together with the necessary lower-order rules, would provide an adequate basis for solving the sampled two-loci and similar figures problems and others like them. Indeed, there are two possible modes of solution in the case of one of the sampled similar figures tasks: "Inscribe a square in a right triangle so that two sides of the square lie on legs of the triangle, and one vertex of the square lies on the hypotenuse." Instead of using the pattern of similar figures, as illustrated in our first example, the pattern of two-loci rule can be used to construct the bisector of the right angle. The intersection of this locus with the hypotenuse (the other locus) is the missing point X and provides a sufficient basis for constructing the goal square.

Although it is not always critical to distinguish between different modes of problem solving, any complete account designed to reflect human behavior must specify why one mode of solution is preferred over another (cf. Scandura, 1973, Chapter 8). In the present case, there are two possible ways of handling this problem. First, we can add a higher-order selection rule to the rule set that says simply: "If both higher-order rules apply, select the pattern of two loci." The rationale is that the pattern of two-loci rule will generally yield a simpler method of solution.

A second way to handle the problem is to devise a single higher-order rule that combines the advantages of both higher-order rules. The higher-order rules in Figures 3 and 4 can be combined to yield the higher-order rule depicted in Figure 5. The path in this higher-order rule designated ⟨1,2,3,4⟩ corresponds to that path of the two-loci higher-order rule that deals with those cases where the two loci may be found in either order. The path ⟨1,2,3,A,B,C,D,E,4⟩ deals with those two-loci problems where one locus must be found before the other. The other two paths correspond to the similar figures higher-order rule.

4. PATTERN OF AUXILIARY FIGURES

Not all compass and straight-edge problems can be solved via the pattern of two loci or the pattern of similar figures. In this section, we describe a higher-order rule for dealing with the third class of problems identified by Polya (1962), the pattern of auxiliary figures. We also show how the combined higher-order rule (above) may be extended to account for essentially all of the construction problems identified by Polya (1962).

4.1 AUXILIARY FIGURES HIGHER-ORDER RULE

Our initial analysis was based on a sample of five diverse auxiliary figures problems. One of the problems used was, "Given

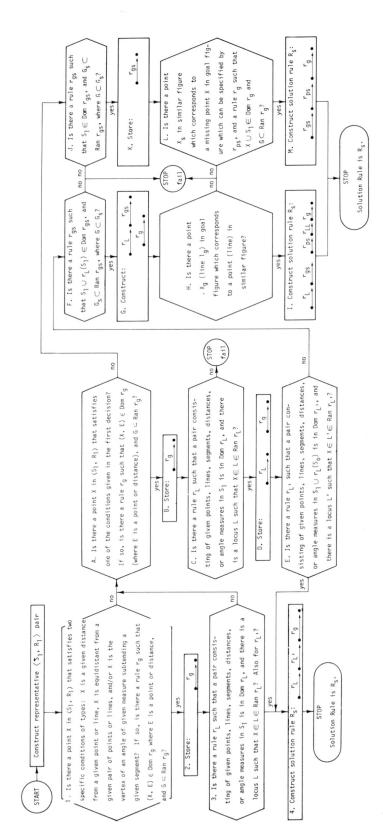

Figure 5. Combined two-loci, similar figures higher-order rule.

the three medians of a triangle, construct the triangle."
The analysis proceeded as before. First, we identified a
procedure for solving each problem. Then, we looked for similarities among the solution rules and identified the component
rules involved. In general, the required goal figures were not
constructable via either the two-loci or similar figures higher-
order rules. However, in each case the goal figure could be
obtained from an auxiliary figure that was constructable from
the given information. In the problem above, for example, a
triangle can be constructed from segments one-third the lengths
of the given medians. The goal figure is obtained by extending
two of the sides of this auxiliary triangle to the respective
median lengths and drawing lines through the resulting endpoints.
The analysis resulted in the auxiliary figures higher-order
rule shown in Figure 6. This higher-order rule generates a
solution rule for the illustrative task above as follows. First,
an arbitrary representation for the solved problem $\langle S_1, R_1 \rangle$ is
constructed. In this case, an arbitrary triangle is sketched,
and its medians are represented on it. The first decision depicted in Figure 6 asks whether there is (1) an auxiliary figure,
and (2) a rule r_q that operates on the auxiliary figure and generates the goal figure. In this task, there is such an auxiliary
figure, a triangle having sides one-third the lengths of the
given medians.[10] In addition, the rule, "extend the constructed
segments to their given lengths and draw lines through their
endpoints," satisfies the second condition. The next decision
(III) depicted in Figure 6 asks whether or not a point is needed, in addition to the auxiliary figure, to construct the goal.
Here, the answer is no; no other point is needed. Finally, decision IV asks if there is an auxiliary figure construction rule
(r_a) available whose domain contains S_1 ($S_1 \in \text{Dom } r_a$) and whose
range contains the auxiliary figure (i.e., $\{A|A \text{ is like}$
$A \cup X\} \subseteq \text{Ran } r_a$). In this case, the rule, "Construct a triangle
from segments one-third the lengths of three given segments
(medians)" satisfies these conditions and operation 5 constructs
the solution rule, "Construct a triangle having sides one-third
the length of the given medians; extend two segments of the constructed triangle to the respective median lengths, and draw
lines through the endpoints of the medians to construct the goal
triangle."
The other path through the higher-order rule may be illus-

----

[10]We do not attempt to spell out the procedures necessary for finding
auxiliary figures. However, in all of the sampled auxiliary figures problems,
it was necessary to construct a line parallel to some distinguished line through
some distinguished point not on that line. Such procedures also frequently
require special knowledge--for example, that medians intersect at a common point
that is two-thirds of the distance from the respective vertices to the midpoint
of opposite sides. Such knowledge is frequently logically deducible, but for our
purposes, may be represented in terms of simple associations--for example,
between triangles with their medians and the common intersection property.

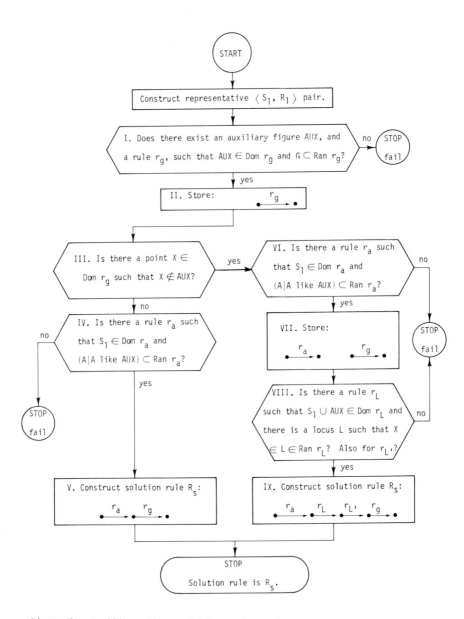

Figure 6. Auxiliary figures higher-order rule.

trated using the task, "Given the four sides a,b,c,d of a trapezoid (a < c), construct the trapezoid." Again, the answer to
decision I is yes. (Where the answer is no, the higher-order
rule fails.) The triangle with c-a, b, d as sides, serves as
the auxiliary goal figure and the goal rule, "Through corner
points of an auxiliary figure and through another point not in
the auxiliary figure, draw segments to complete the goal," is
selected. Unlike the first path, however, the answer to decision III is "yes" since the goal rule (r_g) acts on pairs
(X, AUX) consisting of an auxiliary figure and a critical point
X. The next decision (VI) asks if there is a rule r_a that constructs the auxiliary figure from given information. This condition is satisfied by the r_a rule that constructs the auxiliary
triangle from the sides of a trapezoid. Decision VIII asks
whether there are two locus rules $(r_L$ and $r_{L'})$ that apply to the
auxiliary figure and/or other given information (S_1) and whose
ranges contain X. The circle rule (r_C), applied to different
portions of $S_1 \cup$ AUX, plays the role of both locus rules. The
solution rule (Operation IX) is a concatenation of the component
rules.

4.2   COMBINED TWO-LOCI, SIMILAR AND AUXILIARY FIGURES HIGHER-ORDER RULE

Taken collectively, the three higher-order rules described
above can be used to construct solution procedures for a wide
range of geometry construction problems. Furthermore, they appear compatible both with human behavior and with the heuristics
originally identified by Polya (1962).

This is not meant to imply, however, that the three higher-
order rules are unrelated to one another. Both the needed point
X in the pattern of two-loci, and the similar figure in the
pattern of similar figures can be regarded as special auxiliary
figures. Indeed, one could modify the auxiliary figure higher-
order rule so that it, together with the relevant lower-order
rules, would account for all three classes of problems. In
addition, the similar and auxiliary figures higher-order rules
may be viewed as progressive generalizations of the two-loci
higher-order rule. It is not difficult to conceive of third-
level higher-order generalization rules that have the two-loci
higher-order rule and a similar or auxiliary figure as inputs,
and a more general higher-order rule in which a similar or
auxiliary figure is substituted for the missing point X, as the
corresponding output.

Alternatively, the combined two-loci, similar figures
higher-order rule (Figure 5) can be extended to include auxiliary
figures. In addition, the extended higher-order rule depicted
in Figure 7 allows recursion on the higher-order rules. To see
this, notice that the higher-order rule shown in Figure 6 can
terminate at several points without finding a solution rule.

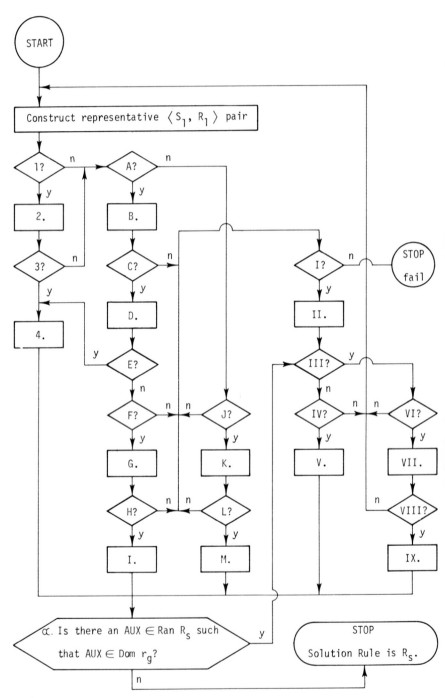

Figure 7. Combined two-loci, similar and auxiliary figures higher-order rule.

In some problems this is unavoidable; there may not be an
auxiliary figure from which the goal figure can be constructed.
Sometimes, however, there is an auxiliary figure, but one that
is not directly constructable from the given information. Such
auxiliary figures can often be constructed via the pattern of
two loci, the pattern of similar figures, or the pattern of
auxiliary figures itself. In those cases where such an auxiliary
figure exists, we allow for this possibility by returning control
to the start of the combined higher-order rule in order to derive an r_a rule for constructing the auxiliary figure. Once an
auxiliary figure (r_a) rule has been derived, the original procedure resumes.

  To see how this higher-order rule works, consider the following task, "Construct a trapezoid given the shorter base a,
the base angles A and D, and the altitude H_t." As in the trapezoid example given earlier, the needed auxiliary figure is the
triangle having sides c-a, b, and d. But, this triangle is not
directly constructable from the given information. None of the
assumed lower-order rules is adequate, so the higher-order rule
breaks down at step VI. The flow of control therefore returns
to step 1 with the aim of constructing the auxiliary figure.[11]
Beginning here, the problem of constructing this auxiliary figure
is a straightforward similar figures task, one, in fact, that
we had sampled.

  The higher-order rule of Figure 7 also generates solution
rules for even more complex problems, provided we assume the
necessary component rules. For example, consider the problem
in Figure 8, "Given three noncolinear points A, B, and C, construct a line XY that intersects segment $\overline{AC}$ in the point X and
segment $\overline{BC}$ in the point Y, such that segments $\overline{AX}$, $\overline{XY}$, and $\overline{YB}$
are all of the same length."

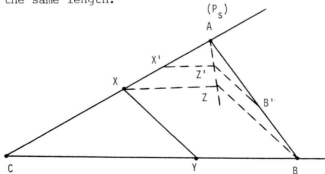

Figure 8. Sketch of a combined two loci, similar and auxiliary figures problem.

  The reader may wish to derive the solution rule for this
more difficult problem himself. (Hint: Several recursions are
required. See Polya, 1962.)

_____
[11]This involves memory and is not indicated in the flow diagram.

5. DISCUSSION

5.1 SUMMARY

In summary, a quasisystematic method for characterizing heuristics involved in problem solving was proposed and illustrated with compass and straight-edge constructions in geometry. Higher-order rules, together with corresponding sets of lower-order rules, were constructed for the two-loci, similar figures and auxiliary figures problems identified by Polya (1962). First, the two-loci heuristic of Polya was made precise. We saw how decision-making capabilities (decisions), and particularly the conditions used to define decisions, play a central role in higher-order rules. The similar figures and auxiliary figures heuristics were similarly formulated. We also showed how the two-loci and similar figures higher-order rules could be combined to form one higher-order rule, which (together with appropriate lower-order rules) provides a basis for solving both kinds of problems. Finally, a combined two-loci, similar and/or auxiliary figures higher-order rule was constructed. This higher-order rule allows recursive returns to components of the higher-order rule, corresponding to the individual higher-order rules, and was considerably more powerful than the others. Its use on some complex problems was illustrated.

Overall, the analyses demonstrated the viability of the analytic method. The higher-order rules identified were precise, compatible with the heuristics identified by Polya, and intuitively seemed to reflect the kinds of relevant knowledge that successful problem solvers might have.

The central role played by semantics in the analysis should be emphasized. The meaning of each task was represented by a goal figure $\langle S_1, R_1 \rangle$ representing the given goal situation $\langle S_0, R_0 \rangle$. The relations among, and properties of, the elements of these figures, together with the domains and ranges of individual rules, were reflected directly in the higher-order rules. Although little attention was given to the formal representation of semantic features, the goal figures clearly placed powerful constraints on the rules selected at each stage in applying the higher-order rules. Representation in terms of some arbitrary (e.g., random) syntax, unconstrained by goal figures, would have necessitated backup capabilities and, in principle, could easily increase the number of possible construction rules at each stage beyond any reasonable computational capability. That is, without the constraints imposed by the goal figures, the number of possible points, arcs, and lines that might be constructed could be almost unlimited. The effect of using goal figures is very much the same as that referred to by Winston (1972) in a recent paper on vision. He argued that although the number of possible combinations of vertex types (Guzman, 1968) is very large, the number of types that yield real figures is much smaller.

5.2 LIMITATIONS

Nonetheless, the present study has certain limitations that, in principle, could be overcome. First, all of the higher-order operations were limited to compositions of rules. In future research, more attention should be given to other kinds of operations. Generalization, restriction, and selection rules (e.g., Scandura, 1973), for example, might well be expected to play an important role in problem solving.

There are a variety of ways in which such rules might enter. First, in discussing the two-loci higher-order rule, we have already seen how the scope of a decision-making capability may be generalized to generate solution rules for a broader range of problems. In particular, we saw how the first decision, which was initially restricted to situations where the desired point X was a given distance from two given points, could be generalized, for example, to allow the point to be the same distance from two given points. It is not hard to envisage a generalization rule by which such shifts might be made. The relationships observed previously between the missing points X, and the similar and auxiliary figures, suggest another kind of generalization involving the identified higher-order rules.

Second, there are a wide variety of construction problems that might require the independent derivation of more than one missing point X, similar figure, or auxiliary figure. As a simple example, consider the task of constructing two circles, one of which is to be inscribed in a given triangle and the other, to pass through its vertices (i.e., to circumscribe the triangle). In this case, the problem can be solved by applying the two-loci higher-order rule twice. The higher-order derivation rule here can be thought of as a generalization of the two-loci rule in which two or more applications (i.e., recursions) may be allowed. One can easily conceive of a simple higher-order generalization rule that operates on rules and generates corresponding rules that are recursive. The combined two-loci, similar and auxiliary figures higher-order rule is one possible consequence of applying some such higher-order rule.

Third, if we had allowed unsolvable variants of the problems considered, truly viable solution rules would have to be appropriately restricted. The solution rule for constructing a triangle with sides of predetermined length, for example, works only when the sum of each pair of sides of the triangle is greater than the third. A completely adequate solution rule would have to test this possibility. It is possible to conceive of higher-order rules that operate on rules of various kinds together with special restrictions (e.g., the triangle inequality) to generate correspondingly restricted rules.

Fourth, it is also possible to conceive of three-dimension-

al analogues of compass and straight-edge constructions.   In
this case, the higher-order rules would operate on the usual
two-dimensional construction rules and would generate their
three-dimensional analogues.   For example, a rule for constructing the locus of points equidistant from a given line (i.e., a
pair of lines) corresponds to a three-dimensional rule that
constructs a cylinder about the line.[12]

A second general limitation is that nowhere did deduction
play a role in our analysis.   In solving constructions, real
people frequently attempt to justify, logically, the various
constructions they make.   Constructing a triangle given its
three medians, for example, requires that a person know or deduce
the fact that the medians intersect at a point two-thirds of the
way from each vertex to the opposite midpoint (see footnote 10).
To this extent, our analysis is limited and may not adequately
reflect human knowledge.   Our rules reflect semantics, but not
inference.   Extension of the proposed analysis to deduction
should be a first order of business.   It is likely that existing
geometry theorem-proving systems (e.g., Gelernter, 1963) may be
useful in this regard.

A third major limitation of this research is that cumulative effects of learning were not considered: each problem in
our analysis was considered as *de novo*.   If one wishes to characterize solutions to problems in a given class (e.g., the two-
loci tasks) relative to a fixed, self-sufficient set of rules,
some fairly complex rules (e.g., the angle vertices rule) must
be included.   Furthermore, and in many ways more important, such
characterizations, at any particular level of analysis in a task
domain, tend to lack flexibility.   The atomic elements are so
large, relatively speaking, that there are many intermediate-
level problems that cannot readily be solved using such rule
sets exclusively.   Also important from the standpoint of behavioral analysis, it is doubtful that such lower-order rules would
adequately reflect the knowledge had by most subjects, assumed
to know the identified higher-order rules.   Such subjects would,
almost certainly, also know a wide variety of simpler construction rules, even though they might not be included explicitly
in a rule set determined by sampling complex problems of the
sort we used.   Future work is planned that is designed to meet
many of these objections (see Chapter 14).

---

[12]Implicit in these examples is another limitation to which we have indirectl
referred previously.   Our original analyses were limited almost exclusively to
single higher-order rules.   In no case did we attempt to identify rules that may
operate on higher-order rules, although our examples make it clear that we could
have done so.   The problems involved in accomplishing this would be practical
rather than theoretical.

6.   UNDERLYING THEORY AND FUTURE DIRECTIONS

The method of (structural) analysis used in the present research is based on Scandura's (1973) theory of structural learning, more particularly on those aspects of it that deal with competence. The aim of the latter is to specify (hopefully mechanizable) procedures that characterize the knowledge underlying given classes of behaviors (e.g., problem solutions) that one might wish to attribute to an idealized knower. As noted, our approach to this problem involves the invention of finite sets of rules (including higher-order rules that may operate on other rules as well as on data elements) that can be applied as indicated, for example, to generate problem solutions.

This level of theory, of course, applies only at an analytic level in the sense that generative grammars account for language behavior. The relevance of the theory to actual human behavior, or, for that matter, to the design of artificial intelligence systems, depends fundamentally on our ability to specify mechanisms by which such rules are to interact in specific situations, and to specify what effect if any such interaction has on the nature of the rule set itself.

The structural learning theory (Scandura, 1973) is partly concerned with the specification of such mechanisms. The theory rests on the fundamental and widely held assumption that, in problem solving, people are attempting to achieve some goal. In the simplified version of the theory considered here, the basic mechanism that governs the use of available rules is as follows:

(A) The subject tests his available rules (r) to see if one (or more) of them satisfies the given goal situation (i.e., if $S_o \in$ Dom r and Goal $\subset$ Ran r). If so, the subject will apply it.

(B) If a subject does not have a rule available for achieving a given goal, then control automatically shifts to the higher-level goal of deriving a procedure that will satisfy the original goal.

(C) If a higher-level goal has been satisfied (i.e., if some new rule has been derived that contains the stimulus situation in its domain and whose range contains the original goal), the derived rule is added to the set of available rules and control reverts to the previous goal.

The third hypothesis allows control to return to lower-level goals once a higher-level goal has been satisfied. (For more general and rigorously formulated sets of hypotheses, see Scandura, 1973; latest version is given in Chapter 2, this book.)

Putting all this together, we see that if an appropriate higher-order rule is available when control shifts to a higher-level goal, then the higher-order rule will be applied and control will automatically revert to the original goal. The subject

will then apply the newly derived rule and solve the problem.
If the subject does not have a higher-order rule available for
deriving a procedure that works, then control is presumed to
move to still higher levels (e.g., deriving a rule for deriving
a rule that works). Although this process is assumed to go on
indefinitely in the idealized theory, memory places strict limits in actual applications.

Even this simple assumption provides an adequate basis for
generating predictions in a wide variety of problem-solving
situations. Consider the problem of converting a given number
of yards into inches. There are two possible ways in which a
subject might solve the problem. The first is to simply know,
and have available, a rule for converting yards directly into
inches: "Multiply the number of yards by 36." In this case,
the subject need only apply the rule according to hypothesis A.
The other way is more interesting, and involves the entire
mechanism as described above. Here, we assume that the subject
has mastered one rule for converting yards into feet, and another
for converting feet into inches. The subject is also assumed
to have mastered a higher-order composition rule.

In the second situation, the subject does not have an application rule that is immediately available, and hence, according to hypothesis (B), he automatically adopts the higher-level
goal of deriving such a procedure. Then, according to the simple
performance hypothesis (A), the subject applies the higher-order
composition rule to the rules for converting yards into feet
and feet into inches. This yields a new composite rule for converting yards into inches. Next, control reverts to the original
goal by hypothesis (C) and, finally, the subject applies the
newly derived composite rule by hypothesis (A) to generate the
desired response.

Moreover, this mechanism provides a basis for an efficient
characterization of learning, since, according to hypothesis (C),
newly derived rules are added to the knowledge base (rule set).
Such additional rules are in no way distinguished from any others
in the rule set; for example, they may serve as component rules
in new higher-order rule applications. (Also, it should be
noted that derived rules may themselves be of higher-order and
may, thus, be used to satisfy future higher-level goals.)

To see how knowledge may cumulate according to this mechanism, let us assume that the learner initially knows rules for
converting miles into yards, yards to feet, feet to inches, and
the higher-order composition rule above. Suppose also that the
learner is first presented with the problem of converting miles
to inches. In this situation, the learner will fail to solve
the problem, since the composition rule we specified above applies only to pairs of rules. (We assume that it does not apply
to itself.) However, if the problem of converting yards to
inches is presented first, the subject will solve it as before,

and derive a yards to inches rule in the process. Further, if
the miles to inches problem is then presented, it can be solved
using the derived yards to inches rule and the miles to yards
rule as components. Although this example is obviously very
simple, it does illustrate the potential importance of problem
sequence in a growing (learning) system.

Although other investigators have made use of similar
notions in varying degrees, the type of mechanism proposed appears to make more general use of rule and higher-order rule
constructs. Frequently, for example, procedures that are allowed
to operate on procedures are not themselves part of the knowledge
base; they are viewed as control processes. (In the present
case, only the learning mechanism itself acts as a control process.) Nor are newly derived solution procedures often added
to the set of available procedures. Newell and Simon (1972,
p. 135), for example, allow the Logic Theorist to add proved
theorems to an initial set of axioms, but this is essentially
at the level of data, upon which proof generation procedures
operate, and not at the level of the procedures themselves.
Viewing learning as "debugging" (e.g., Minsky & Papert, 1972)
or as "means-ends" analysis (Newell & Simon, 1972) is essentially analogous to the introduction of higher-order rules except
that in these cases implicit restrictions are imposed on the
allowable higher-order rules.

In any case, most investigations in artificial intelligence
have involved some kind of state space representation (e.g.,
Nilsson, 1971), with problem solving involving some type of
search. No generally agreed-on way of representing learning
seems to have emerged, however. Sometimes, learning is treated
as the modification of parameters in evaluation functions that
select promising nodes for expansion (e.g., Samuel, 1959). In
other cases, learning systems have been devised to reflect
stimulus-response principles in psychology (e.g., Feigenbaum,
1961; Bower, 1972). Where considered by information-processing
psychologists who have adopted this point of view (e.g.,
Rumelhart, Lindsay, & Norman, 1972), learning involves the transformation of one state space to another (Scandura, 1974).

Though the proposed representation may be formally equivalent, it is our belief, based on a variety of studies with
human subjects (e.g., Scandura, 1973), that it is not psychologically equivalent. For one thing, the search for basic psychological mechanisms (e.g., of learning), which reflect commonalities in human behavior, differs in important ways from the
goals of computer simulation, where the essential goal is to
parallel overt human behavior in complex instances of problem
solving and where the basic mechanisms (e.g., means-ends analysis) are judged on more immediately pragmatic grounds.

Irrespective of one's opinion on the issue, the assumption,
that laws that govern the interactions among individual rules

are fixed once and for all, has potentially important implications for computer implementation. In particular, the fixed
mode of interaction would make it possible, in principle, to
modify and/or extend an artificial intelligence system rule by
rule, without having to worry about the effects of these changes
on other parts. (This latter property appears, to some extent,
to be shared by Newell and Simon's [1972] production systems.)

One of the major complications in current artificial intelligence research is that even minor changes in one part of
a system may have unpredictable effects that may require compen-
sating changes elsewhere. The switch to heterarchical systems
(e.g., Minsky & Papert, 1972), in which control may shift among
individual programs in some predetermined manner, does not appear to alleviate this problem. In contrast to the above mechanism, the mode of control in heterarchical systems may vary
from system to system, and worse, from the standpoint of debugging, may interact with the individual programs themselves. In
short, the important point for artificial intelligence research
is the possible advantage for implementation of a fixed mode of
interaction, such as that specified in the structural learning
theory.[13]

Whether or not the mode of interaction is restricted to
the method proposed here is not the most crucial point. To
the extent that artificial intelligence research may benefit by
taking account of such mechanisms, psychological research aimed

---

[13]Scandura's (1974) comments regarding relationships between the structural
learning mechanism, and the notion of heterarchical control in systems of artificial intelligence (Minsky & Papert, 1972) may be relevant here.

For a time artificial intelligence systems were viewed as wholes, as frequently complex programs. As work in the area progressed, the difficulties of
building upon earlier work became increasingly clear because of the close interrelationships among various parts of such systems.

To overcome this limitation, *heterarchical,* or modular planning has been used
(e.g., Minsky & Papert, 1972). Heterarchical systems consist of sets of programs
(modules) pertaining to syntax, semantics, line detection, and so on, together
with an heterarchical executive which switches control among these "modules" in
accordance with a predetermined plan.

Modules in heterarchical systems correspond essentially to rules in the
structural learning theory; the executive control structure corresponds to the
basic mechanism. There is, however, an important difference between the two. In
heterarchical systems, the basic goal is pragmatic. Such systems make it easier
to modify and build upon previous work. No one seriously means to imply that
heterarchical control reflects the way people perform, although in developing
artificial intelligence systems intuitive judgements are sometimes made with this
in mind.

In contrast, the structural learning mechanism is assumed to be built into
people (presumably from birth); *it is not learned and need not be taught.* While
the rules a person knows may increase from time to time, the mechanism is assumed
to remain constant.

This is a strong claim, something which no responsible person would make
concerning executive systems currently used in heterarchical systems. Among other
things, it is very unlikely that an existing control system would be useful in
systems other than the one for which it was designed. It is my contention that
benefits might accrue in artificial intelligence and, of course, in simulation if
structural learning like control structures were used (pp. 42-43)

at discovering what these mechanisms are would appear to be a
first order of business for those interested in human thought
(see Chapters 5 and 6).

With the foregoing in mind, an alternative, that we are
now pursuing is to begin initially with rule sets composed of
simpler rules, and to allow these rule sets to grow gradually
by interacting with a problem environment.[14] In the present
case, only three atomic operators (lower-order rules) will be
introduced initially: (1) setting a compass to a given radius,
(2) drawing a straight line (segment), and (3) using a set compass to make a circle. It is not immediately clear what the
higher-order rules should be but, presumably, any reasonably
satisfactory rule set would include some types of simple composition, conjunction, and generalization higher-order rules, together possibly, with variants of the two-loci and other higher-
order rules identified above. It should be emphasized in this
regard that the initial selection of rules would not, in itself,
be sufficient; the choice and sequencing of to-be-solved problems
may also be expected to have important effects on both the rate
and type of knowledge acquisition. For obvious reasons, computer
implementation seems almost essential in this research and is
the course we are pursuing. (The results of this research are
described in Chapter 14.)

7.   IMPLICATIONS

7.1   ARTIFICIAL INTELLIGENCE

The present research appears to have three general implications for work in simulation and artificial intelligence.

First, the rules we have identified may be implemented
relatively easily (some already have). As such, they would be
useful either directly in systems concerned with geometric
figures and constructions, or indirectly in research having more
encompassing aims as described above.

Second, the results are suggestive of how the construction
of at least certain artificial intelligence systems might be
partially systematized. In this regard, the topic of compass
and straight-edge constructions is not nearly as important as
is the fact that the analysis serves as a prototype for the proposed method of analysis. At the present time, this method is
being used to analyze the proofs contained in an experimental,
introductory algebra high school text based on axiomatics.
(See Chapter 4.)

Third, our use of flow diagramming as a mode of representation of individual rules suggests that perhaps such representa-

[14]Such rule sets have been called *innate bases* (Scandura, 1973a, Chapter 5).
In general, innate bases lack the immediate, direct computing power of comparable
rule sets composed of more complex rules but, theoretically at least, can grow to
become more powerful.

tion might play a somewhat larger role in the exposition of
future artificial intelligence research. The routine use of a
large number of different and highly technical programming
languages is often enough to turn away outsiders (such as ourselves) who might otherwise be interested.[15] The limitations
of flow diagrams with regard to memory considerations may be a
small price to pay for a more neutral and familiar form of representation. Furthermore, flow diagrams have a flexibility as
to the level of representation that is not shared by particular
programming languages. This makes it possible to more readily
represent basic components at a level of atomicity tailored to
immediate needs, and to psychological reality (cf. Scandura,
1973), rather than to basic components determined by some programming language. These comments, of course, apply only to
psychological and expository considerations and say nothing of
the more strictly technical problems of representation that must
be dealt with in computer implementations. (See Chapter 14.)

7.2 EDUCATION

The results of this study also have both long-range and
immediate implications for education. The promising nature of
the results attests to the practicability of the proposed approach as a means of identifying the knowledge underlying reasonably complex kinds of problem solving. In addition to serving
as a prototype, the identified rules themselves could be helpful
in teaching high school students how to solve compass and
straight-edge construction problems.

By identifying precisely what it is that students must know
(i.e., one possible knowledge base), these rules provide an explicit basis for both diagnosis and instruction. In particular,
the methods of analysis formalized by Scandura (1973) and developed empirically by Scandura and Durnin (Chapter 8) and
Durnin and Scandura (Chapter 9) can be applied directly to assess
the behavior potential of individual subjects on the individual
rules, including the higher-order ones. Operationalizing the
knowledge of individual subjects in this way, and comparing this
knowledge with the initial competence theory (i.e., set of rules),
provides an explicit basis for remedial instruction (Chapter 9).
In effect, each subject can be taught precisely those portions
of each competence rule that testing indicates he has not
mastered.

Care was taken to help insure that the higher-order rules
reflect the kinds of ability individual subjects might have, or
use. To the extent that the identified higher-order rules are
unknown to high school students, instruction in these rules

---

[15]We realize, of course, that some computer specialists may not take our
suggestion very seriously. We, however, find the work in simulation and AI
highly suggestive for our own studies and hope, in the interest of interdisciplinary communication, that some readers may be moved more in this direction.

ought to facilitate problem-solving performance. A field test of the efficacy of these higher-order rules is now underway and will be reported in due time. (See Chapter 13.)

The above discussion of how knowledge is acquired through interaction of the learner with a problem environment also has educational relevance. Specifically, by assigning values to various objectives and costs to particular kinds of instruction (or rules), it should be possible to study the problem of instructional sequencing and optimization in a way that is both precise and relevant to meaningful education. We view this problem as critically important for future research. (See Chapters 14 and 15.)

REFERENCES

Amarel, S. On representations of problems of reasoning about actions. In D. Michie (Ed.), *Machine intelligence* (Series No. 3). New York: American Elsevier, 1968.

Bower, G. A selective review of organizational factors in memory. In E. Tulving & W. Donaldson (Eds.), *Organization of memory*. New York: Academic Press, 1972.

Chomsky, N. *Syntactic structures*. The Hague: Mouton Press, 1957.

Feigenbaum, E. A. The simulation of verbal learning behavior. In *Proceedings of the Western Joint Computer Conference*, 1961.

Gelernter, H. Realization of a geometry theorem proving machine. In E. Feigenbaum & J. Feldman (Eds.), *Computers and thought*. New York: McGraw-Hill Book Co., 1963.

Guzman, A. Decomposition of a visual scene into three-dimensional bodies. In *Proceedings of the Fall Joint Computer Conference*, 1968.

Minsky, M., & Papert, S. *Research at the laboratory in vision, language and other problems of intelligence* (Artificial Intelligence Progress Report, Memo 252). Cambridge, Mass.: M.I.T. Artificial Intelligence Laboratory, January 1972.

Newell, A., & Simon, H. A. *Human problem solving*. Englewood Cliffs, N.J.: Prentice-Hall, 1972.

Nilsson, N. J. *Problem-solving methods in artificial intelligence*. New York: McGraw-Hill, 1971.

Polya, G. *Mathematical discovery* (Vol. 1.). New York: Wiley, 1962.

Rumelhart, D. E., Lindsay, P. H., & Norman, D. A. A process model for long-term memory. In E. Tulving & W. Donaldson (Eds.), *Organization of memory*. New York: Academic Press, 1972.

Samuel, A. Some studies in machine learning using the game of checkers. *IBM Journal of Research and Development*, 1959, *3*, 211-229.

Scandura, J. M. Deterministic theorizing in structural learning: Three levels of empiricism. *Journal of Structural Learning*, 1971, *3*, 21-53.

Scandura, J. M. *Structural learning I: Theory and research*. New York: Gordon & Breach, 1973.

Scandura, J. M. The structure of memory: Fixed or flexible? *Catalog of Selected Documents in Psychology*, Spring, 1974, Abstract, pp. 37-38. Abridged version in F. Klix (Ed.), *Organismische Informationsverarbeitung*. Berlin: Akademie-Verlag, 1974.

Winston, P. H. Summary of selected vision topics (Flash 30). Cambridge, Mass.: M.I.T. Artificial Intelligence Laboratory, July, 1972.

4
Structural (Algorithmic) Analysis of Algebraic Proofs[1]

Joseph M. Scandura and John H. Durnin

One of the most difficult problems in mathematics education is teaching students how to prove theorems. Traditionally, two basic methods have been used in the classroom. One method involves presenting the student with a wide variety of proofs and explaining or having the student explain why they work, in the hope that the learner will extract general methods that he can then apply in other situations. Another school of thought would have the student construct his own proofs that are then subject to criticism by the teacher and/or his peers. An extreme form of this approach is the well-known method used by R. L. Moore at Texas, in which the student not only proves his own theorems but also decides on which conjectures to try to prove (or disprove).

The first method of proof instruction depends heavily on induction from example. Success in using this method depends both on the wise selection of sample proofs and precautions to ensure that students do in fact attempt to infer general methods of proof rather than to simply memorize the samples. The second method of proof instruction most likely depends on the self generation of semantic models (and counter examples) of the theorems (conjectures) in question, as well as on the generation of proofs per se (such models correspond to structures in the sense of Chapter 2; cf. Scandura, 1971). This method more nearly parallels the types of capabilities needed in research mathematics. On the other hand, the method may not work well with relatively unmotivated students, and the instructor must be prepared to cover less material, at least initially.

Although both methods have been used successfully by many

[1]This research was supported by National Science Foundation Grant GW-7901 to Research for Better Schools.

teachers, there are perhaps more who have experienced something less than complete success--either because they do not know themselves what goes into proof making, and/or because they are unable to effectively impart to students the necessary know-how. In either case, we believe that qualitative improvements in proof-making instruction will require more precise specification of what it is that students must learn in order to prove theorems, irrespective of whether the primary goal is to teach the general nature of proof or to produce creative research mathematicians. Without such knowledge, the only reasonable alternatives seem to be informal, trial-and-error instruction by example and/or lots of experience and practice in theorem production and proof generation. (Even here, of course, more complete specification of what is to be learned would make possible wiser and more efficient selection of appropriate activities.)

We do not believe, however, that it will ever be possible to fully specify all that an ingenious theorem prover needs to know or might acquire through long years of study and practice. Nor, do we even think that this would be desirable, since new, creative insights undoubtedly depend to some extent on individual idiosyncracies and capabilities. Nonetheless, we do believe that progress in this direction is possible and that the inability of many students to benefit from traditional instruction in proof making more than justifies attempts to develop alternative methods of instruction.

In recent years, a beginning has been made in this direction, primarily in computer-assisted instruction (e.g., Goldberg, 1971; Kane, 1972). For example, Suppes (1971) and his collaborators have provided students with an adaptive computer-controlled environment that checks each step in a proof as it is made to see if it is valid. To our knowledge, however, no one has attempted direct, systematic instruction in how to construct proofs. The primary reason is that no one has known exactly what it is that one should attempt to teach.

The purpose of the present study was to take a first step in this direction--to determine whether systematic, structural analyses of proof making are feasible. Specifically, our aim was to determine whether it is possible to construct algorithms that generate proofs of the theorems and exercises contained in Brumfiel, Eicholz, and Shanks' (1961) high school algebra text[2] and that accomplish this in the same general way as might competent ninth-graders. The formulation of conjectures for possible proof or disproof was not considered.

---

[2]We chose this text for analysis because it was one of the first to place heavy emphasis on proof in high school algebra. Also, because the text has become somewhat dated, our analysis is more likely to be viewed as a prototype (as we intend) rather than as a possible endorsement of one or another textbook.

1. BACKGROUND

In their analysis of geometry construction problems, Scandura, Durnin, and Wulfeck (Chapter 3) demonstrated the feasibility of systematic, rigorous structural (algorithmic) analyses of particular problem domains in mathematics. This research provided a general model for our analysis.

The geometry analysis of Chapter 3 was built on Polya's (1962) classification of straight-edge and compass construction problems in geometry and, in part, involved the precise formulation of three heuristics: The pattern of two-loci, the pattern of similar figures, and the pattern of auxiliary figures. After classifying the various construction problems (according to the heuristics involved in their solution), a sample of specific problems was identified within each class. Then, specific rules (procedures/algorithms) were devised whereby each of the sampled problems could be solved, one procedure for each type of problem. Next, parallels among these solution procedures were observed. Components of the solution rules and higher-order rules were identified that reflected these parallels (cf. Scandura, 1973), and from which the solution rules could be derived (by applying higher-order rules to component rules). The obtained set of component and higher-order rules was then checked with new problems to determine its adequacy (i.e., to see if the rules could be used to generate solution procedures for the new problems). The individual rules so identified were refined and modified as necessary. The resulting rules were sufficiently precise as to be programable on a computer.

In addition to the simplification afforded by Polya's (1962) preclassification of problems and identification of heuristics, the Scandura *et al.* (Ch. 3) analysis had several important limitations. First, the analysis was explicitly limited with regard to logical inference. At no point was an attempt made to show how various constructions might be logically justified. Second, some of the sampled tasks did not form "natural" units; no attempt was made to account for subproblems (cf. Chapter 2). This is an important limitation, since the identification of rules for constructing subproblem (goal) hierarchies (Newell & Simon, 1972) potentially could reduce the complexity of needed higher-order rules (cf. Chapter 3). Third, the only kinds of solution rules that could be generated using the identified higher-order rules were simple compositions (of component rules/inputs). In no case did a higher-order rule actually modify (e.g., generalize) an input rule. Clearly, other forms of derivation are also important in problem solving (e.g., solving problems by analogy).

In part, the present study was designed to overcome these limitations. Specifically: (1) logical inference formed the core of the analysis; (2) rules for breaking problems into more natural subproblems were included; (3) explicit attention was given to higher-order relationships other than composition.

2. METHOD OF ANALYSIS

As was done in Chapter 3 the first step in our analysis was to become thoroughly familiar with the problem domain. In the present case, this meant first of all to properly interpret the tasks from a behavioral point of view. In proving theorems, one might think that the inputs are the premises (antecedents) and that the outputs are the final steps in the proofs (which are frequently the consequents). In reality, the inputs are the theorems and the (final) outputs are the proofs themselves. This point is implicitly recognized in Polya's (1962) distinction between "problems to solve" and "problems to prove".

After generally familiarizing ourselves with the contents of Brumfiel *et al.* (1961), we went through the proofs of all 67 theorems and 35 proof exercises in the text. The theorems were also proved independently, paying close attention to the processes we used (i.e., the processes that might be used by someone generally familiar with the content but not necessarily with all of the given proofs). In almost all cases, the proofs we derived were roughly the same as in the textbook.

Unlike the previous geometry analysis, we gave more explicit attention to the distinction between breaking a problem down into subproblems, and rule derivation. In particular, we were especially cognizant, in proving the theorems, as to when we generated portions of a proof, before even considering the rest, and when we knew exactly how to generate an entire proof, before actually attempting to generate it.

Although this distinction is not important computationally (insofar as deriving the proofs), it is important psychologically. As described in Chapter 2, the former corresponds to breaking problems down into subproblems and the latter to deriving new solution procedures (for given subproblems). Allowing for both possibilities brings together the subgoal hierarchy notion proposed by Newell and Simon (1972) and the rule derivation notion proposed by Scandura (1973). In the former case, problems are presumed to be solved by forming a hierarchy of subgoals and solving each of them in turn by directly applying available operators (component rules). A selected operator is assumed to be applied before the next one is determined (i.e., the various subgoals are considered one at a time). In simple rule derivation, on the other hand, new solution procedures are presumed to be derived in their entirety (by application of higher-order rules to other available rules) before any part of them is applied. This latter view corresponds essentially to "insight", in which a puzzled organism often suddenly sees how to proceed.

In truth, it would appear that both systematic step-by-step

planning and insight may occur during problem solving, and our aim was to come up with a characterization of underlying competence (rules) that reflects each of them. Thus, in our search for parallels among the proof-generating procedures identified, we were concerned with: (1) how the various types of theorems-to-prove were broken down into subproblems, and (2) how solution procedures for solving various subproblems were derived. In the latter regard, we were particularly concerned with analogies among solution procedures in different algebraic systems (e.g., natural numbers and integers).

A total of 24 basic problem definition, higher-order and lower-order rules are identified and described in the following text. The adequacy of the rules was checked, not only with respect to the 67 theorems and 35 proof exercises in the book, but also with respect to additional sampled theorems concerning number systems that were not contained in the book.

As in the geometry construction analysis, however, only critical portions of the basic rules were detailed. Although all of these rules are potentially programable on a computer, our aim was to identify rules similar to those that a competent, idealized ninth-grader might reasonably be expected to use in proving the given theorems, and to describe them in terms of "natural" cognitive units rather than in some specific programming language.

Furthermore, the analysis does not consider the growth of knowledge over time, as would be expected to take place, for example, as a result of proving a variety of similar theorems of the same type. One of the first author's dissertation students (Wulfeck) has extended the geometry analysis of Scandura et al. (Chapter 3) to deal with the latter problem. Specifically, the underlying higher- and lower-order rules identified in the original geometry analysis were subjected to further analysis as described in Chapter 2 to identify still more basic rule sets (called *innate bases*). Wulfeck repeated this process until a base level (rule set) was reached (see Chapter 14).

In general, when such an analysis is performed, two important things happen: (1) the individual rules become simpler, but (2) the resulting rule set as a whole becomes more powerful (than the set from which it was derived). The latter obtains in exactly the same sense that a set of higher- and lower-order rules can be used to solve more problems than the solution rules from which the set is derived. As this chapter goes to press, Wulfeck's analysis has been largely completed and is being used as a basis for exploring questions of optimization in adaptive instruction with respect to various types of problem-solving objectives. An overview of the theoretical approach is described in Scandura (1977; also Chapter 14).

3. INITIAL SUBDIVISION OF COMPOUND THEOREMS

In Brumfiel *et al.* (1961) there was no categorization of problems (theorems-to-prove) comparable to that given by Polya (1962), only the usual classification by chapter (whole numbers, integers, rationals, algebraic extension Q ($\sqrt{2}$) over the rationals, and reals). Nonetheless, in our analysis it quickly became apparent that a number of the problems involved simpler subproblems; these compound problems did not form "natural units" in the sense described in Chapter 2.

Three general types of compound problems were identified. The corresponding (compound) theorems are listed in Table 1. (Note: "iff" means "if and only if.")

TABLE 1
Types of Compound Theorems

Biconditionals

Rationals:
$a/b > c/b$ $(b > 0)$ iff $a > c$
$a/b = c/d$ $(b,d \neq 0)$ iff $ad = bc$
$a/b = c/d$ $(b,d \neq 0)$ iff $a/c = b/d$
$a/b = c/d$ $(b,d \neq 0)$ iff $(a+b)/b = (c+d)/d$
$a/b = c/d$ $(b,d \neq 0)$ iff $a/b = (a+c)/(b+d)$

$Q(\sqrt{2})$:
$a + b\sqrt{2} = 0$ iff $a = 0$ and $b = 0$
$a + b\sqrt{2} = c + d\sqrt{2}$ iff $a = c$ and $b = d$
$r \cdot s = 0$ iff $r = 0$ or $s = 0$

Reals:
$a > b$ iff $a + c > b + c$

Existence and Uniqueness

Rationals:
For every a/b, $c/d \neq 0$ there exists a unique x such that $c/d \cdot x = a/b$
For every $a/b \neq 0$ there exists a unique x such that $a/b \cdot x = 1$
For every a/b, c/d there exists a unique x such that $a/b - c/d = x$

$Q(\sqrt{2})$:
For every $a + b\sqrt{2}$, $c + d\sqrt{2}$ there exists a unique x such that $x = (a+b\sqrt{2})/(c+d\sqrt{2})$ $(c+d\sqrt{2} \neq 0)$

Simple Antecedent, Compound Consequent

Wholes:
If $ca < cb$, then $a < b$ and $c \neq 0$

Integers:
If $x \cdot y = 0$, then $x = 0$ or $y = 0$

Rationals:
If $a/b \neq 0$, then $a/b > 0$ or $a/b < 0$

Perhaps the easiest compound theorems to detect were the biconditionals (e.g., in the system of rationals $a/b > c/b$ $[b > 0]$ if and only if $a > c$); next were theorems asserting both existence and uniqueness, for example, (rationals) for every a/b, $c/d \neq 0$, there exists a unique x such that $c/d \cdot x = a/b$; and third were theorems involving a compound consequent, where indirect proofs are required, for example, (whole numbers) if $ca < cb$, then $a < b$ and $c \neq 0$.

In proving compound theorems, the first thing to do, invariably, was to break them down into a pair of subproblems. This decomposition could be accomplished by applying the following problem definition rules:

Biconditional Problem Definition Rule:
If a theorem-to-prove is of the form "P if and only if Q" break it down into the following theorems-to-prove "If P, then Q" and "If Q, then P"

For example, application of this problem definition rule to
a/b > c/b (b > 0) if and only if a > c (rationals)
yields the pair of theorems:
If a/b > c/b (b > 0), then a > c
If a > c, then a/b > c/b (b > 0)
(Note: In the following sections, subproblems are often denoted as ordered pairs of givens and goals. For example, the theorem-to-prove "If P, then Q" might be denoted, If P, then Q; If P, then Q + Proof.)

Existence and Uniqueness Problem Definition Rule:
If a theorem involves "there exists a unique", or some equivalent statement, break the theorem down into two subproblems, the first involving existence and the second involving uniqueness.

For example, application of the above rule, to
For every a/b, c/d ≠ 0, there exists a unique x such that
c/d · x = a/b (rationals)
gives the following pair of theorems-to-prove:
For every a/b, c/d ≠ 0, there exists an x such that
c/d · x = a/b
For every a/b, c/d ≠ 0 such that c/d · x = a/b, x is unique
(Note: Although it would not be difficult to do, it is beyond the scope of this analysis to include the grammatical detail that would be required in any complete statement of these problem definition rules.)
In the case of theorems involving a simple antecedent and a compound consequent, two related problem definition rules were required.

Simple Antecedent - Compound Consequent Problem Definition Rule:
(1) If a theorem is of the form
    "If P, then Q and R",
  break it down into the pair
    "If not Q, then not P" and
    "If not R, then not P"
(2) If a theorem is of the form
    "If P, then Q or R",
  break it down into the pair

"If P and not Q, then R"
"If P and not R, then Q"

For example, application of the former rule to

If ca < cb, then a < b and c ≠ 0 (whole numbers)

gives the pair

If a ≥ b, then ca ≥ cb
If c = 0, then ca = cb (i.e., ca ≥ cb)

Similarly, application of the latter rule to

If x · y = 0, then x = 0 or y = 0

gives

If x · y = 0 and x ≠ 0, then y = 0
If x · y = 0 and y ≠ 0, then x = 0

Although more "elegant" proofs are possible in some cases
(e.g., with biconditionals, where proof steps are reversible),
the applicability of the above problem definition rules seems
universal. Breaking biconditionals into pairs of conditionals,
breaking theorems of existence and uniqueness into existence
theorems and uniqueness theorems, and breaking theorems involving compound consequents into pairs of theorems involving simple
consequents, is equally appropriate whether the theorems are
algebraic, geometric, or concerned with analysis. More important in the case of the theorems under consideration, this manner of formulating subproblems is consistent with the way a
knowledgeable theorem prover might be expected to proceed.

The remainder of our analysis is simplified accordingly.
We consider only those rules of competence necessary for proving
the simple/basic theorems that remain after the above problem
definition rules have been applied. (Insofar as teaching and
learning is concerned, this amounts to assuming that students
can successfully be taught how to break compound theorems into
simpler theorems, and that once problems have been so defined,
students will deal with each part separately [cf. Chapter 2].)

4.   KEY FIRST STEP SUBPROBLEMS--DEFINITION RULES

In attempting to prove the basic theorems (implicit or explicit) in Brumfiel *et al.* (1961) the importance of selecting
an appropriate first step became almost immediately apparent.
The first thing that had to be done in essentially every case,
was to identify a key first step. In effect, each basic problem
was broken down into a pair of subproblems, the first of which
was to determine the key first step. (The second subproblem,
of course, was to generate the remainder of the proof.) This
fact led us to introduce the following first approximation to
a new problem definition rule.

Key Step Problem Definition Rule (First Approximation):
Given a basic theorem-to-prove involving number systems
(the rule applies potentially to theorems other than just
those in Brumfiel *et al.*, 1961), break the theorem into a
pair of subproblems ⟨theorem, theorem + appropriately related expression⟩ and ⟨theorem + appropriately related expression, theorem + proof⟩. The first subproblem takes
the theorem as input and the first step, an expression
"appropriately related" to the theorem, as its goal.

As it stands, the statement of this problem definition rule contains a "hooker". Just what is meant by "appropriately related"?
On further analysis, it turned out that the key first step
(i.e., the solution to the first subproblem) depends directly,
and often simply, on the form of the given theorem statement.
In this regard, there are six relevant types of basic theorems
in Brumfiel *et al.* (1961). Complete categorization of all
theorems by type is given in Table 2. For example, in proofs
of theorems involving Type 1, a simple relational antecedent and
a simple consequent, the key first step is simply the antecedent
--in every case. In the system of whole numbers, for instance,
the theorem "If $x + a = a + b$, then $x = b$", has "$x + a = a + b$"
as its first step. It is important to emphasize that this relationship is obtained in all number systems, not only in the
system of natural numbers. The key first step in the proof of
the theorem "If $x > 0$, then $-x < 0$" (integers), for example,
is "$x > 0$".

The initial key step also follows directly from the theorem
statement in four other cases: Type 2, compound antecedent,
simple consequent; Type 3, existence of element denied; Type 4,
universally quantified statements of equality; and Type 5,
uniqueness of an element x satisfying a given equation. The
various types of key step subproblems and rules for generating
key first steps in these cases, along with examples, are given
in Table 3.

As can be seen from the table, the nature of the desired
output of the first subproblem (i.e., the subgoal/appropriately
related expression) can be specified in each of the above cases.
In Case 1, the appropriately related expression is the antecedent; in Case 2, the compound antecedent; in Case 3, the assumption of the existence of the denied element; in Case 4, the
assumption of the universally quantified equation, and in Case
5, the assertion of two distinguished elements satisfying the
given equation. [3]

In Case 6 (existence of elements), however, key first steps
could not be determined from theorem statements quite so easily.

---

[3]We were tempted in several cases to insert *relation* for *equation* but decided
to restrict ourselves to the latter in those Cases (4 and 5) where equations were
the only kinds of relations considered in Brumfiel *et al.* (1961).

TABLE 2
Categorization of Theorems and Proof Exercises (E)

System	Type 1 Simple Antecedent, Simple Consequent	Type 2 Compound Antecedent, Simple Consequent
Wholes	$x + a = a + b \supset x = b$ $a + x = a + b \supset x = b$ $a + x = b + a \supset x = b$ $c = 0 \supset ca = cb$ $r - x = r - s \supset x = s$ $x - a = 0 \supset x = a$ (E) $x - a = b - a \supset x = b$ $a > b \supset ca > cb$ $(c \neq 0)$ $a > b \supset a + c > b + c$	$a > b \wedge b > c \supset a > c$ $a > b \wedge c > d \supset a + c > b + d$ $a > b \wedge b > c \supset a - c > b - c$
Integers	$x \div a = y \div a \supset x = y$ $2\,|\,x \supset 4\,|\,x^2$ (E) $2 \nmid x \supset 2 \nmid x^2$ (E) $r > s \supset r + t > s + t$ (E) $r > 0 \supset r^2 > 0$ (E) $x > 0 \supset -x < 0$ (E) $a > b \supset a-b > 0$ (E)	$a > 0 \wedge b < 0 \supset ab < 0$ (E) $a > b \wedge c < 0 \supset ca < cb$ (E) $a > b \wedge b > c \supset a > c$ (E) $x\,|\,y \wedge y\,|\,z \supset x\,|\,z$ $x\,|\,y \wedge x\,|\,z \supset x\,|\,(y + z)$ (E) $x \cdot y = 0 \wedge x \neq 0 \supset y = 0$ $x \cdot y = 0 \wedge y \neq 0 \supset x = 0$
Rationals	$a/b = c/d \supset ad = bc$ $(b,d \neq 0)$ $ad = bc \supset a/b = c/d$ $(b,d \neq 0)$ $a/b = c/d \supset a/c = b/d$ $(c,b,d \neq 0)$ $a/c = b/d \supset a/b = c/d$ $(c,b,d \neq 0)$ $a/b = c/d \supset (a+b)/b = (c+d)/d$ $(b,d \neq 0)$ $(a+b)/b = (c+d)/d \supset a/b = c/d$ $(b,d \neq 0)$ $a/b = c/d \supset (a+c)/(b+d) = a/b$ $(b,d \neq 0)$ $a > c \supset a/b > c/b$ $(b > 0)$ $(a+c)/(b+d) = a/b \supset a/b = c/d$ $(b,d \neq 0)$ $a/b > c/b \supset a > c$ $(b > 0)$	$a/b \neq 0 \wedge a/b \not< 0 \supset a/b > 0$ $(b \neq 0)$ $a/b \neq 0 \wedge a/b \not> 0 \supset a/b < 0$ $(b \neq 0)$
$Q\;(\sqrt{2})$	$a \neq 0 \supset a + b\sqrt{2} \neq 0$ $b \neq 0 \supset a + b\sqrt{2} \neq 0$ $a \neq c \supset a + b\sqrt{2} \neq c + d\sqrt{2}$ $b \neq d \supset a + b\sqrt{2} \neq c + d\sqrt{2}$	$a = c \wedge b = d \supset a + b\sqrt{2} = c + d\sqrt{2}$ $a = 0 \wedge b = 0 \supset a + b\sqrt{2} = 0$ $r \cdot s = 0 \wedge r \neq 0 \supset s = 0$ $r \cdot s = 0 \wedge s \neq 0 \supset r = 0$
Reals	$ax^2 + bx + c = 0 \supset x =$ $\dfrac{(-b \pm \sqrt{b^2 - 4ac})}{2a}$ where $(a \neq 0)$ $a > b \supset a + c > b + c$ $a + c > b + c \supset a > b$ $a > 0 \supset 1/a > 0$ (E) $1/a > 1$ $(a \neq 0) \supset 1 > a$ (E) $r_1 = -r_2 \supset r_2 = -r_1$ (E) $a > 0 \supset -a < 0$ $b < 0 \supset -b > 0$	$x > 0 \wedge y < 0 \supset xy < 0$ $x < 0 \wedge y < 0 \supset xy > 0$ $a > b \wedge c > 0 \supset ca > cb$ $a > b \wedge c < 0 \supset cb > ca$ $a > b \wedge b > c \supset a > c$ $1/a > 1/c \wedge c > 0 \supset c > a$ (E) $a > b \wedge b > 0 \supset a^2 > b^2$ (E) $a \neq b \wedge a \not< b \supset a > b$ (E) $a \neq b \wedge a \not> b \supset a < b$ (E)

System	Type 3 Denial of Existence	Type 4 Universally Quantified Statements
Wholes		$\forall\ x,y,\ (0 + x) + y = y + x$ (E) $\forall\ x,y,\ (1 \cdot x) \cdot y = y \cdot x$ (E) $\forall\ a,b,c,\ a\,(b + c + d) = ab + ac + ad$ $\forall\ r,s,\ r\,(s + 1) = rs + r$ (E) $\forall\ x,\ 2x = x + x$ $\forall\ x,\ x \cdot 0 = 0$ $\forall\ a,\ a - 0 = a$ (E) $\forall\ a,\ a - a = 0$ (E) $\forall\ c,\ b > a,\ c\,(b - a) = cb - ca$ $\forall\ a,b,c,\ a + (b - c) = (a + b) - c$ $\forall\ a > (b + c),\ a - (b + c) = (a - b)$ $\forall\ a > b > c,\ (a - b) + c = a - (b - c)$ $\forall\ x,\ 0 + x = x$ (E) $\forall\ x,\ 1 \cdot x = x$ (E)

Integers

∀ x, (-1)x = -x
∀ a,b, (-a) · b = -(ab)
∀ a,b, (-a) (-b) = ab
∀ x, -(-x) = x
∀ a,b, -(a + b) = (-a) + (-b)
∀ x, -x = 0 - x
∀ x,y, x - y = x + -y
∀ a,b,c, a + (b - c) = (a + b) -c   (E)
∀ a,b,c, a - (b + c) = (a - b) -c   (E)
∀ a,b,c, a - (b - c) = (a - b) +c   (E)
∀ a,b,c, a (b - c) = ab - ac

Rationals

~∃ a/b, b ≠ 0, a/b · 0/1 = 1

~∃ r, r² = 2
~∃ r, r² = 3   (E)

∀ a/b, c/d ≠ 0, a/b ÷ c/d =
    a/b · d/c (b,c,d ≠ 0)
∀ a/b, -a/b = -(a/b)   (b ≠ 0)
∀ a/b, -(a/b) = a/-b   (b ≠ 0)
∀ a/b, c/d, a/b · c/d = ac/bd   (bd ≠ 0)
∀ a/b, c/d, a/b + c/d =
    (ad + bc)/bd (bd ≠ 0)
∀ a/b, c/b, a/b + c/b = (a + c)/b (b ≠ 0)
∀ a/1, a/1 = a
∀ a ≠ 0, a/a = 1
∀ a ≠ 0, 0/a = 0
∀ a/b ≠ 0, c/d ≠ 0,
    (a/b ÷ c/d) (c/d ÷ a/b) = 1   (E)
∀ r/s,t/u, r/s - t/u = (ru - st)/su   (E)
    (su ≠ 0)

Q (√2)

~∃ a + b√2, (a + b√2)² = 3

∀ x,y, x - y = x + -y   (E)
∀ x,y, x(-y) = -(xy)   (E)
∀ x,y, (-x)(-y) = xy   (E)
∀ a > 0, b > 0, √ab = √a √b

System	Type 5 Uniqueness	Type 6 Existence
Wholes		
Integers	∀ a, b, x = a ÷ b, x is unique (b ≠ 0)	
Rationals	∀ a/b, c/d, c/d · x = a/b, x is unique (b, d ≠ 0) ∀ a/b, a/b · x = 1, x is unique (b ≠ 0) ∀ a/b, c/d, a/b - c/d = x x is unique (b,d ≠ 0)	∀ a/b, c/d, ∃ x, c/d · x = a/b (b,d ≠ 0) ∀ a/b, ∃ x, a/b · x = 1 (b ≠ 0) ∀ a/b, c/d, ∃ x, a/b - c/d = x (b,d ≠ 0)
Q (√2)	∀ a + b√2, c + d√2, x + y√2 = (a + b√2) - (c + d√2), x + y√2 is unique (E) ∀ a + b√2, c + d√2, x + y√2 = (a + b√2)/(c + d√2), x + y√2 is unique (c,d ≠ 0)	∃ two x's, x² = 2 ∀ (a + b√2), (c + d√2), ∃ x + y√2, x + y√2 = (a + b√2) - (c + d√2) (E) ∀ (a + b√2), (c + d√2), ∃ x + y√2, x + y√2 = (a + b√2)/(c + d√2) (c,d ≠ 0) ∀ (a + b√2), ∃ x² + sx + t = 0, (a + b√2)² + s (a + b√2) + t = 0
Reals		

Note: Key to logical notation

∀ - For every
∃ - There exists
~ - Not
∧ - And
⊃ - Implies

TABLE 3
Key Step Subproblems and Rules for Generating Key Steps with Examples

---

Case 1. *Simple antecedent, simple consequent*
    Key Step Subproblem: ⟨Simple antecedent, simple consequent (theorem);
                             theorem + antecedent⟩
    Rule: Write the antecedent.
    Example: Subtheorem (wholes)--to-prove: ⟨If $x + a = a + b$ then $x = b$;
                                                 theorem + antecedent⟩
    Key Step (antecedent): $x + a = a + b$

Case 2. *Compound antecedent, simple consequent*
    Key Step Subproblem: ⟨Compound antecedent, simple consequent (theorem);
                             theorem + compound antecedent⟩
    Rule: Write each relation in the antecedent on a separate line.
    Example: Subtheorem (wholes)--to-prove: ⟨If $a > b$ and $b > c$ then $a > c$;
                                                 theorem + compound antecedent⟩
    Key Steps (compound antecedent): $a > b$
                                       $b > c$

Case 3. *Existence of element denied*
    Key Step Subproblem: ⟨ Existence denied (theorem); theorem + existence ⟩
    Rule: Assume the existence of the element.
    Example: Subtheorem (rationals)--to-prove: There does not exist a rational a/b,
                                                 $b \neq 0$ such that $a/b \cdot 0/1 = 1$
    Key Step (existence):   Assume there is a rational a/b, $b \neq 0$
                            such that $a/b \cdot 0/1 = 1$

Case 4. *Universally quantified statements of equality*
    Key Steps Subproblem: ⟨Universally quantified equation (theorem);
                              theorem + equation⟩
    Rule: Write the equation in the statement.
    Example: Subtheorem (wholes)--to-prove: For all whole numbers a, b, c, d,
                                              $a (b + c + d) = ab + ac + ad$
    Key Step (equation): $a (b + c + d) = ab + ac + ad$

Case 5. *Uniqueness of element satisfying given equation*
    Key Step Subproblem: ⟨Uniqueness theorem; theorem + 2 equations each with
                             different distinguished element⟩
    Rule: Assume two "distinguished" elements (x_1, x_2) satisfying equation.
    Example: Subtheorem (integers)--to-prove: Given x such that $x = a \div r$, x is unique
    Key Steps (2 equations): $x_1 = a \div r$
                               $x_2 = a \div r$

Case 6. *Existence of element(s) (equation) satisfying given equation (equation form)**
    Key Step Subproblem: ⟨ Existence theorem; theorem + solution/postulated element ⟩
    Rule: Solve the given equation using the real-number solution module and
           substitute. (Solve the given equation form [to determine unknown
           coefficients] using the real-number module and substitute.)
    Examples: Subtheorem (rationals)--to-prove: For all rationals a/b, c/d, there
                                                  exists an x such that $a/b - c/d = x$
    Key Step (solution):   Reason from $a/b - c/d = x$
                           via real-number module to get $a/b + {}^-c/d = x$;
                           substituting gives $a/b - c/d = a/b + {}^-c/d$
    Subtheorem (extension of rationals)--to-prove:
                           For every $a + b\sqrt{2}$ in $Q (\sqrt{2})$
                           where a and b are rational, there exists a quadratic
                           equation $x^2 + sx + t = 0$ with s and t unknown rationals,
                           such that $(a + b\sqrt{2})^2 + s (a + b\sqrt{2}) + t = 0$
    Key Steps (solution): Reason from $(a + b\sqrt{2})^2 + s(a + b\sqrt{2}) + t = 0$
                           $a^2 + 2b^2 + sa + t + (2ab + sb) \sqrt{2} = 0$
                           to get $2ab + sb = 0$
                           $s = -2a$
                           and $a^2 + 2b^2 + sa + t = 0$
                           $t = a^2 - 2b^2$
    Substituting gives $(a + b\sqrt{2})^2 + (-2a) (a + b\sqrt{2}) + (a^2 - 2b^2) = 0$

---

*The real-number solution rule plays a special role in generating key steps in
existence proofs. The rationale for its inclusion is described in the text.

In proofs of the Type 6 theorems in Brumfiel *et al.* (1961), as often occurs in mathematics texts emphasizing proofs, the key first steps typically appeared mysteriously, without apparent reason--the result presumably of immediate "insight" (or, prior and unspecified trial and error).

At least in the case of the Brumfiel *et al.* (1961) theorems, however, the nature of these key steps and their derivations can be specified. Although they often appear to come out of nowhere, the key first steps satisfy general goal requirements and can be generated algorithmically (i.e., by rule). In particular, the key first steps (postulated elements) involve real number solutions of given equations (or equation forms) involving one or more unknowns. These key first steps are not derived logically, but rather are generated via informal algebraic manipulation in which individual steps are not logically justified.

TABLE 4

Real-Number Solution Rule

---

1. Write the equation.
2. If the unknown is squared, transform the equation so that one side equals 0 and go to 19.
3. If the equation involves division, transform the equation, so that the divisors become the multipliers on the opposite side.
4. If subtraction is indicated change - to + and write the additive inverse in place of the expression behind the - sign.
5. If $\sqrt{2}$ is in the equation, go to 14.
6. If the designated x is by itself on one side of equation, go to 11.
7. Multiply both sides of the equation by the denominators, if any, distribute terms and simplify by adding like terms with numerical coefficients.
8. Transform the equation so that all terms involving x are added on one side of the equation and those not involving x are added on the other side; change signs of those terms moved from one side to the other.
9. Factor out x.
10. Multiply both sides of the equation by the multiplicative inverse of the coefficient of x, simplify both sides of the equation and go to 6.
11. If the expression opposite the designated x contains another unknown, consider the equation still unsolved; select the other equation obtained from 17, substitute the obtained value for x into this equation, consider the other unknown as the designated x and go to 7.
12. If the expression opposite the designated x contains no other unknown term, then consider it a real-number solution.
13. If all real-number solutions for the unknowns have been obtained, go to 21; otherwise substitute the real-number solution obtained into the other unsolved equation, designate the remaining unknown x and go to 7.
14. Multiply and square expressions so indicated.
15. Commute and associate terms so that all terms involving $\sqrt{2}$ are added together on both sides of the equation.
16. Factor out $\sqrt{2}$.
17. Set those expressions that are the coefficients of $\sqrt{2}$ on either side of the equation equal to each other, and set the expressions that are not the coefficients of $\sqrt{2}$ on either side of the equation equal to each other.
18. If one of the two equations obtained from 17 contains only one unknown, select it, and go to 6; otherwise select any one of the two equations, designate one of unknowns x and go to 6.
19. Apply the quadratic formula $ax^2 + bx + c = 0$ $x = (-b + \sqrt{b^2 - 4ac})/2a$ and $x = (-b - \sqrt{b^2 - 4ac})/2a$ for real solutions only.
20. Simplify by factoring, clearing squared values from the radical and dividing.
21. Substitute the simplified real-number solutions into the original equation and stop.

Although one would not want to automatically assume a priori mastery of proofs in the real number system (i.e., the ability to generate proofs of theorems in this system), it is quite reasonable to assume that our idealized subject (in view of eight or more years exposure to ordinary arithmetic) has intuitive mastery of manipulations that are legal in the system of real numbers. More specifically, we assume that the subject knows how to solve linear, quadratic, and simple rational equations. The real number solution rule, which represents this capability, is given in Table 4.

We illustrate below how this rule operates with respect to the theorem "For all $a + b\sqrt{2}$, $c + d\sqrt{2}$ (c, $d \neq 0$), there exists an $x + y\sqrt{2} = (a + b\sqrt{2}) \div (c + d\sqrt{2})$ $[Q(\sqrt{2})]$ ". Step by step derivation of the key first step,

$$x_0 + y_0\sqrt{2} = (a + b\sqrt{2}) \div (c + d\sqrt{2}),$$

where x_0, y_0 are known, goes as follows:

Step 1.	$x + y\sqrt{2} = (a + b\sqrt{2}) \div (c + d\sqrt{2})$
Step 3.	$(x + y\sqrt{2})(c + d\sqrt{2}) = (a + b\sqrt{2})$
Step 14.	$xc + yc\sqrt{2} + xd\sqrt{2} + 2dy = a + b\sqrt{2}$
Step 15.	$xc + 2dy + (yc\sqrt{2} + xd\sqrt{2}) = a + b\sqrt{2}$
Step 16.	$xc + 2dy + (yc + xd)\sqrt{2} = a + b\sqrt{2}$
Step 17.	$yc + xd = b$
	$xc + 2dy = a$
Step 18.	$yc + xd = b$
Step 8.	$xd = b + -yc$
Step 10.	$x = (b + -yc)/d$
Step 11.	$([b + -yc]/d)\, c + 2dy = a$
Step 7.	$bc + -yc^2 + 2d^2y = ad$
Step 8.	$-yc^2 + 2d^2y = ad + -bc$
Step 9.	$y\,(-c^2 + 2d^2) = ad + -bc$
Steps 10 and 12.	$y_0 = (ad + -bc)/(2d^2 + -c^2)$
Real Number Solution:	
Step 13.	$([ad + -bc]/[2d^2 + -c^2])\, c + xd = b$
Step 7.	$adc + -bc^2 + 2xd^3 + -xc^2d = 2bd^2 + -bc^2$
Step 8.	$2xd^3 + -xc^2d = 2bd^2 + -adc$
Step 9.	$(2d^3 + -c^2d)x = 2bd^2 + -adc$
Steps 10, 12, and 13.	$x_0 = (2bd + -ac)/(2d^2 + -c^2)$
Real Number Solution:	
Step 21.	$([2bd + -ac]/[2d^2 + -c^2]) +$ $([ad + -bc]/[2d^2 + -c^2])\sqrt{2} =$ $(a + b\sqrt{2}) \div (c + d\sqrt{2})$

To summarize, the phrase "appropriately related" in the above problem definition rule can be given a precise meaning for all six types of theorems. In the first five cases, the key first steps are identical or closely related to expressions in given theorem statements (e.g., antecedents). In Case 6, they are more indirectly related and must be derived.

In effect, the first of the subproblems obtained on appli-

cation of the above problem definition rule can be specified
precisely in each case. The given is the theorem statement,
and the goal (desired output) can be characterized in terms of
the specified "appropriate" relationship (i.e., key first steps).
Put somewhat differently, given a theorem-to-prove, the first
subproblem can be fully and precisely determined (via the problem definition rules) from the form of the theorem.

Because there are only six possibilities, it is easy to
see how the above "approximation" to the key step problem definition rule might be rigorized: Either represent the problem
definition rule in terms of six specialized definition rules
(with suitably restricted domains of applicability), one for
each case. Or, introduce internal decisions (e.g., Is the theorem of the form simple antecedent, simple consequent?) into a
single, more general definition rule that has the same effect.
One such key step problem definition rule is shown in Table 5.

TABLE 5

Key Step Problem Definition Rule

1-2.	If the theorem involves an antecedent and a simple consequent, go to (1-2).
3-6.	If the theorem involves existence, go to (3-6).
4.	If the theorem involves universally quantified statements of equality, go to (4).
5.	If the theorem involves uniqueness of an element, go to (5).
(1-2).	Define the subproblems: ⟨theorem, theorem + antecedent⟩ and ⟨theorem + antecedent, theorem + proof⟩ and STOP.
(4).	Define: ⟨theorem, theorem + equation⟩ and ⟨theorem + equation, theorem + proof⟩ and STOP.
(5).	Define: ⟨theorem, theorem + 2 equations⟩ and ⟨theorem + 2 equations, theorem + proof⟩ and STOP.
(3-6).	If the theorem involves denial, go to (3).
(6).	Define: ⟨theorem, theorem + real-number solution⟩ and ⟨theorem + real-number solution, theorem + proof⟩ and STOP.
(3).	Define: ⟨theorem, theorem + existence⟩ and ⟨theorem + existence, theorem + proof⟩ and STOP.

(For clarification of that part of Table 5 that deals with proof
completion subproblems ⟨ theorem + key step, theorem + proof ⟩
see the discussion in the next section.) Anyone moderately
skilled at constructing programs can devise others.

Although higher-order rules are important in many structural analyses, they do not seem to play a central role in the
above. Simple lower-order rules are sufficient for identifying
key first steps in 5 cases; in the sixth case the real-number
solution rule applies directly. Higher-order rules enter more
naturally in the next section.

5.   PROOF COMPLETION SUBPROBLEMS

So far, nothing has been said about the proof completion
subproblems generated by the above problem definition rule.
These subproblems take theorems, together with key first steps,
as inputs; and, roughly speaking, they take completed proofs as
outputs (goals). The exact form of the subgoals of the proof
completion subproblems, however, depends on the type of theorem

involved. In Cases 1 and 2, for example, the subgoals are the
consequents of given theorems and the steps leading up to them.
That is, to complete the proof of a given theorem, it is sufficient to generate the consequent from the given theorem/key
first step (antecedent) via logical operations.

In each Case 3 proof completion subproblem, the subgoal is
to find a contradiction (and the steps leading to it). Although
there is no subgoal criterion that is both simple and specific,
the general idea is to generate a proof statement that contradicts basic assumptions (e.g., $0 = 1$), or an earlier assumed
statement or part thereof (e.g., assume $\sqrt{2} = p/q$ where p and q
are relatively prime and show that 2 divides both p and q). In
all, there were only two different types of contradiction in
Brumfiel *et al*. (1961).

The Case 4 subgoals involve finding equations with identical
expressions on both sides (e.g., $a = a$, $0 = 0$, ab + ac + ad =
ab + ac + ad). In the example of Table 3, this involves manipulating the left side to make it identical with the right. In
other examples both sides are modified. In all cases, however,
each operation acts to reduce the difference between the two
sides in a manner not unlike means-ends analysis (Ernst & Newell,
1969). Furthermore, only reversible modifications are allowed.
The psychological significance of the latter restriction is that
of knowing, whenever reversible steps are used, that it is possible to start from equations having identical expressions on
both sides, and to generate the initial (assumed) equation by
applying the same steps in reverse order. A less sophisticated
way to characterize competence (sufficient to the task) would
be to introduce a problem definition rule that operates on Case
4 proof completion subproblems and generates a pair of subprob-
lems--one to generate equations with identical expressions on
both sides and the second to go in the reverse direction.

In Case 5, the subgoal of each proof completion subproblem
is to derive an equation showing explicitly that the two hypothesized "unique" elements are identical (e.g., $x_1 = x_2$). Each
subgoal in Case 6 also involves deriving an equation with identical expressions on both sides.

Although the above level of subproblem definition seemed
appropriate for the initial decomposition, further analysis was
often necessary in order to solve the proof completion subproblems. In particular, some of the relations and operations of
the key steps and goals were defined in terms of primitives in
Brumfiel *et al*. (1961).

Thus, the relation a > b was defined as a = b + k (with
special cases $a > 0 \rightarrow a = 0 + a$; $a < 0 \rightarrow a + -a = 0$) and a|b
(a divides b) was defined as b = ak ($2 \nmid b \rightarrow b = 2k + 1$). The
operations - and ÷ (/) were defined in terms of addition and
multiplication, respectively (i.e., $k + (a - b) = c \rightarrow k + a =
c + b$ and $k (a \div b) = c \rightarrow ka = cb$).

In attacking the proof completion subproblems, then, we checked first to see if the relations and operations were defined. If not, we transformed the first steps and goals (of proof completion subproblems) into corresponding first steps and goals in which the relations (> , |) and operations (-, ÷) were defined in terms of more primitive relations (=) and operations (+, x).

Redefinition of the proof completion subproblems was accomplished by the following:

Redefinition Rule:
Inputs: Proof completion subproblems ⟨Theorem + first step, goal⟩ that involve undefined relations and/or operations,

Outputs: Proof completion subproblems that involve corresponding defined relations and/or operations,

Rule:

1. If > is involved, apply $a > b \rightarrow a = b + k$ $(k > 0)$; $a > 0 \rightarrow a = 0 + a$; $0 > a \rightarrow 0 = a + -a$ $(-a > 0)$ and justify corresponding steps in proof "by definition".

2. If $a|b$ $(2 \nmid x)$ is involved, apply $a|b \rightarrow b = ak$ $(2 \nmid x \rightarrow x = 2k + 1)$ and justify corresponding steps in proof "by definition".

3. If - or ÷ (/) is involved, apply $k + a - b = c \rightarrow k + a = c + b$; $k \cdot (a \div b) = c \rightarrow k \cdot a = c \cdot b$ for $b \neq 0$ $(k \cdot a/b = c/d \rightarrow k \cdot a = b \cdot c/d$ for $b, d \neq 0)$ and justify corresponding steps in proof "by definition".

4. Reapply the above steps until all possible relations and/or operations are defined.

For instance, consider the proof completion subproblem associated with the theorem (rationals) "If $(a + b)/b = (c + d)/d$, then $a/b = c/d$" (i.e., consider the first step $(a + b)/b = (c + d)/d$ and the consequent $a/b = c/d$). Application of the redefinition rule to this subproblem yields the defined first step:

$(a + b) d = b (c + d)$ by definition of/

and the defined consequent:

$ad = bc$ by definition of/

Similarly, application of the redefinition rule with respect to the Type 4 theorem (whole numbers) "For all a, b > c, $a + (b - c) = (a + b) - c$" yields the defined first step:

$a + (b - c) + c = a + b$ by definition of -

The goal steps of Type 4 theorems are necessarily defined.

The redefinition rule, of course, only applies to certain proof completion subproblems, in particular to those involving >, | (divides) and/or - or ÷. For example, the proof completion subproblem corresponding to the theorem "For every x, $x \cdot 0 = 0$" is already defined in the above sense.

Since applying the redefinition rule to proof completion

subproblems always yields equivalent subproblems that are defined, the remainder of our analysis concerns the competence
necessary for solving defined proof completion subproblems.

Unlike key first step rules, proof completion procedures
depend on the number system involved, as well as on the type of
theorem. Some operations that would be allowed in proving theorems about rationals, for example, could not be used in proving
theorems about whole numbers. In general, the whole number
system is more restrictive in this sense than any of the other
number systems considered. Because of this type of restriction,
the theorem "For all a, b, c, a - (b + c) = (a - b) - c", for
instance, is a satisfactory statement about rationals but not
about whole numbers. For whole numbers, the stipulation must
be added that a > (b + c); otherwise subtraction is undefined.
Similarly, some of the operations associated with the reals
(and algebraic extensions of the rationals) cannot be used in
proving theorems about the rationals.

In view of present emphases in lower school mathematics
curricula, we assumed in our analysis that idealized ninth-
graders who are capable of proving the Brumfiel et al. (1961)
theorems have a greater intuitive feel for both the arithmetic
operations and the corresponding logical justifications associated with the rationals than for either the more restricted
operations on integers and whole numbers or the special operations associated with the reals and the algebraic extension
$Q (-\sqrt{2})$. For this reason, we selected the system of rational
numbers as the main basis for our analysis. (We were tempted,
initially, to build only on the positive rationals but decided
that most contemporary mathematics curricula give sufficient attention, by eighth-grade, to the basic operations with signed
numbers, to justify consideration of the rationals as a whole.)

TABLE 6
Proof Completion Rules for Rationals*

---

1. *Simple antecedent, simple consequent*
   Input: Theorem, defined antecedent (key step) and defined consequent
   Output: Completed proof
   Rule: 1. *If the consequent contains an undistributed term, distribute and give
             reason (i.e., distributivity) in proof; if it contains an additive
             term or additive inverse (identity) term(s) not in the first step,
             add the term(s) to both sides of the equation and indicate addition
             of equals in the proof.*
          2. *If the consequent contains a multiplicative term or multiplicative
             inverse (identity) term (or squared expressions) not in the first
             step equation, multiply the term to (square) both sides of the
             equation and indicate multiplication of equals in the proof. (If
             two different products = 0 • a, set the products equal to each other.)*
          3. *If the equation is the same as the consequent, stop; otherwise
             associate, commute, and distribute the terms where necessary and
             simplify the equation by applying one of the following as needed:
             a + b = c + b → a = c; a • b = c • b → a = c (for b ≠ 0);
             (a - b) + b → a; (a ÷ b) • b → a (for b ≠ 0); b • a/b → a (for b ≠ 0);
             a + ⁻a → 0, a + 0 → a • 1 → a and indicate in the proof which is used.*
          4. Reapply Step 3.

2. *Compound antecedent, simple consequent*
   Input: Theorem, defined antecedent and defined consequent
   Output: Completed proof
   Rule: 1. *If one term $\neq 0$ in the antecedent is not in the consequent and multiplication is not indicated in either the antecedent or consequent (or subtraction is indicated on both sides of relation in the consequent), apply substitution $a = b + k_1$, $b = c + k_2 \to a = c + (k_1 + k_2)$ or $a = bk_1$, $b = ck_2 \to a = c\ k_1 k_2$, and distribute, if necessary (or apply $b = c + k \to b - c = k$ for subtraction in the consequent, substitute again and reapply Step 1). Indicate substitution in the proof.*
   2. *If the consequent is a sum of terms in the defined key step equations add the equations, distribute terms as needed and indicate addition of equals (and distributivity) in the proof.*
   3. *If the consequent is a product (squared or a reciprocal of an element in the antecedent) elect from the key step the term > 0 or additive inverse of the term < 0, multiply it to (square) both sides of the defined key step obtained from the other key step and indicate multiplication of equals in the proof. Distribute terms, apply $a \cdot b/a \to b$, for $a \neq 0$, and indicate these in the proof, as needed. If the product was obtained by multiplying by the additive inverse, add the additive inverse(s) of the (nonconstant, k) product(s) to both sides of the equation, apply $a + {}^-a \to 0$ and $0 + a \to a$ and indicate these in the proof, until the equation is the same as the consequent.*
   4. *If the key step equation is $x \cdot y = 0$ and $x \neq 0$ set $x \cdot y = x \cdot 0$ apply cancellation and indicate this in the proof.*
   5. *If one relation in the antecedent is $\neq$ and the other is $\not>$ ($\not<$) apply disjunction to $a = b$ or $a > b$ or $a < b$ and indicate this in the proof.*

   Denial of Existence
   Input: Theorem, defined key step
   Output: Completed proof
   Rule: 1. *If the key step contains a multiplicative expression with 0 in it, take the product and simplify using $a \cdot 0 \to 0$ and indicate the rule in the proof.*
   2. *If the key step assumes there exists a rational r such that $r^2 = 2(3)$, redefine r as a/b where a, b are relatively prime.*
   3. *Through substitution of a/b for r and multiplication by b^2, show $2 | a^2$ ($3 | a^2$). Apply $2 | x^2 \to 2 | x$). ($3 | x^2 \to 3 | x$). Indicate at each step of the proof the rule used.*
   4. *If a contradiction is obtained, stop; otherwise substitute $2k$ ($3k$) for a in $a^2/b^2 = 2$ (3). Indicate this in the proof and apply step 3 to show $2 | b^2$ ($3 | b^2$).*

4. *Universally quantified equations*
   Input: Theorem, defined key step
   Output: Completed proof
   Rule: 1. *If the defined key step equation involves additive (multiplicative) inverses, add (multiply) the immediate inverse of the expression having the least notation to both sides of the equation. If $x \cdot 0 = 0$ is the key step add $x \cdot 0$ to both sides of the equation; if $2x$ is the first step apply $2 \to 1 + 1$. Indicate addition (multiplication) of equals in the proof.*
   2. *If the expressions on both sides of the equation are the same, stop; otherwise commute, associate and distribute terms (apply $x \to 1 \cdot x$, $-x \to ({}^-1)\ x$ **, ${}^-(ab) \to (-a)b$** as needed before distributing) and simplify the equation by applying one of the following as needed: $a + 0 \to a$, $a + {}^-a \to 0$, $a \cdot 0 \to 0$**, $a \cdot 1 \to a$, $a/a \to 1$ (for $a \neq 0$), $(a - b) + b \to a$, $(a \div b) \cdot b \to a$ (for $b \neq 0$), $b \cdot a/b \to a$ (for $b \neq 0$), $a/b + c/b \to (a + c)/b$ (for $b \neq 0$)**, and indicate in the proof which is used.*
   3. *Reapply Step 2.*

5. *Uniqueness*
   Input: Theorem, defined key step
   Output: Completed proof
   Rule: 1. *Set expressions equal to the same element equal to each other and indicate substitution in the proof.*
   2. *Apply $a + b = c + b \to a = c$ or $a \cdot b = c \cdot b \to a = c$ for $b \neq 0$ and indicate cancellation in the proof.*
   3. *If unique elements x_1 and x_2 are equal to each other, stop; otherwise reapply Step 2.*

6. *Existence*
    Input: Theorem, defined key step
    Output: Completed proof
    Rule: 1. Combine terms through multiplication as needed.
            2. *If the expressions on both sides of the equation are the same, stop; otherwise commute, associate and distribute terms in order to simplify the equation by applying one of the following as needed:*
               $b \cdot a/b \to a$ (for $b \neq 0$), $a + {}^{-}a \to 0$, $a + 0 \to a$, $a \cdot 0 \to 0$**,
               $a \cdot 1 \to a$, $(a - b) + b \to a$ and indicate in the proof which is used.
            3. *Reapply Step 2.*

---

      *The *italicized* parts of the rules are applicable in most cases; whereas the parts that are not italicized are applicable only in special cases. In the statements, *expressions* refer to one or the other side of an equation and *terms* to additive and multiplicative elements of an expression.

      **These rules are applicable only after they have been proven.

    The six proof completion rules for the rationals in Table 6 correspond to defined versions of the six types of proof completion subproblems given above. Each proof completion rule identifies the competence necessary for one to get from a defined first step to a defined goal (e.g., consequent).

    1. For example, application of the *simple antecedent, simple consequent* rule of Table 6 to the defined first step is sufficient to complete the proof of the above theorem (rationals) "If $(a + b)/b = (c + d)/d$, then $a/b = c/d$." Thus, starting with $(a + b)d = b(c + d)$, distributivity of Step 3 of the rule gives
    $ad + bd = bc + bd$
Step 3 also gives
    $ad = bc$ by cancellation.
Since $ad = bc$ is the same as the defined consequent, the proof is complete.

    Application of the proof completion rules in Table 6 for Cases 2 through 6 are illustrated below.

    2. *Compound antecedent, simple consequent*
        Theorem: If $a/b \neq 0$ and $a/b \not< 0$ then $a/b > 0$.
        Defined key steps: $a/b \neq 0$
                        $a/b \not< 0$
Applying Step 5 of the Case 2 proof completion rule of Table 6, the trichotomy law for rationals
    $a/b = 0$ or $a/b > 0$ or $a/b < 0$
is stated and we obtain
    $a/b > 0$ by disjunction
Since this result is the same as the consequent, the proof is finished.

    3. *Denial of existence*
        Theorem: There does not exist a rational r such that $r^2 = 2$.
        Defined key step: Assume there exists r such that $r^2 = 2$.
Step 2 of the Case 3 proof completion rule of Table 6 gives

```
r = a/b where a, b are relatively prime
a²/b² = 2                    by substitution and squaring
a² = 2b²                     by multiplication of equals
2|a²                         by definition of |
2|a                          by 2|x² ⊃ 2|x (cf. exercise,
                                Integers, Table 2)
2k = a                       by definition of |
(2k)² = 2b²                  by substitution
4k² = 2b²                    by squaring and multiplication
                                of equals
2k² = b²                     by multiplication of equals
2|b²                         by definition of |
2|b                          by 2|x² ⊃ 2|x
```

$2|a$ and $2|b$ contradicts the assumption that a and b are relatively prime. This completes the proof.

    4. *Universally quantified equations*

        Theorem: For all r/s, t/u, r/s - t/u = (ru - st)/su

        Defined key step: $r = s \left[(ru - st)/su + t/u\right]$

By distributivity of Step 2 of the Case 4 proof completion rule of Table 6 we get r = s (ru - st)/su + st/u. Application of Step 2 of the rule gives

```
r = (ru - st)/u + st/u      by b · a/b → a
r = [(ru - st) + st] /u     by a/b + c/b → (a + c)/b
r = ru/u                    by (a - b) + b → a
r = r · 1                   by a/a → 1
r = r                       by a · 1 → a
```

Since the expressions on both sides of the equation are the same the proof is finished.

    5. *Uniqueness*

        Theorem: For all a/b, c/d such that a/b - c/d = x, x is unique

        Defined key steps: $a/b = (x_1 + c/d)$
                          $a/b = (x_2 + c/d)$

Applying Step 1 of the uniqueness proof completion rule of Table 6 we obtain:

```
x₁ + c/d = x₂ + c/d         by substitution
x₁ = x₂                     by cancellation
```

Since $x_1 = x_2$, the proof is finished.

    6. *Existence*

        Theorem: For all a/b, c/d (b, d ≠ 0), there exists an x such that a/b - c/d = x

        Defined key step: $a/b = \left[a/b + -c/d + c/d\right]$

Application of Step 2 of the existence proof completion rule of Table 6 gives

```
a/b = [a/b + 0]             by -a + a → 0
a/b = a/b                   by a + 0 → a
```

Since the expressions on both sides of the equation are the same; the proof is finished.

    To summarize so far, the above analysis is based on the

assumption that proof completion subproblems are first redefined (so that initially given relations and operations are
defined). Subsequent analysis was restricted to the rationals,
and rules were identified by which the remaining steps in each
type of theorem could be generated. (Note: An alternative way
of completing the proofs would be to introduce a simple higher-
order composition rule similar to those in Chapters 2 and 3.
In those cases where relations and/or operations are undefined,
the composition rule would operate on a simpler version of the
redefinition rule and a proof completion rule, and generate composites of these two rules. In turn, the composite rule would
first redefine relations and operations in the key first steps,
and then generate the remaining steps in the proof. The ter-
mination of such proofs can be made explicit by applying the
inverse of the redefinition rule to the defined output gener-
by the above composite rule.)

Six proof completion rules, parallel to those given in
Table 6, can be devised for each of the other number systems.
In the case of the whole numbers and the integers, the corresponding operations and decisions (relations) are relatively
restricted. For example, the operations of subtraction (a - b)
and division (a ÷ b) in the whole number system may be applied,
respectively, only where $a > b$ and $b|a$ (b is a factor of a).
Furthermore, there are no additive or multiplicative inverses
in the system (except for 0 and 1). With the integers, the
only restrictions that are relevant involve division.

With the algebraic extension $\sqrt{2}$ over the rationals and the
reals, on the other hand, not only are all of the rational operations and relations applicable but, in addition, there are
other allowable operations/relations as well. For example,
addition and multiplication with $\sqrt{2}$ and corresponding relations
such as $\sqrt{2} > 0$ and $\sqrt{2} \neq$ rational are allowable in the algebraic
extension. In addition, operations such as $\sqrt[n]{x}$ (nth root),
$(\sqrt[n]{a})^n = a$ (exponential rules), and completion of the square
are allowable in the reals.

Knowledge of the former type (e.g., restricted operations)
may be represented in terms of the corresponding rational number
operators with suitably restricted domains. (In the case of the
inverse operators, the domains would be limited to one of the
single elements 0 or 1.) Knowledge of the latter type would be
represented simply in terms of new rules (operations) and relations.

More important for present purposes, it is easy to envisage
higher-order substitution (restriction) and generalization rules
by which the sets of proof completion rules, associated with the
various number systems, can be derived from the corresponding
proof completion rules associated with the rationals. Thus
given: (1) a theorem involving the whole number system/integers,
including the corresponding defined proof completion sub-

problem, (2) the corresponding restricted operations and decisions, and (3) that proof completion rule (rationals) associated
with the given type of theorem; the needed proof completion rule
(whole numbers or integers) can be derived by simply substituting
the restricted operations and decisions for the corresponding
ones in the proof completion rule for the rationals. For example, if applied to a Case 4 proof completion subproblem over
the whole numbers, and the fourth proof completion rule of Table
6, the higher-order substitution rule would generate the following proof completion rule for whole numbers.

1. If $x \cdot 0 = 0$ is the key step, add $x \cdot 0$ to both sides
   of the equation and indicate addition of equals in the
   proof; if $2x$ is the first step, apply $2 \to 1 + 1$.
2. If the expressions on both sides of the equation are the
   same, stop; otherwise commute, associate and distribute
   terms (apply $x \to 1 \cdot x$ where required before distributing) and simplify the equation by applying one of the
   following as needed: $a + 0 \to a$; $a \cdot 1 \to a$; $a \cdot 0 \to 0$
   (after proven); $(a - b) + b \to a$ (for $a > b$); $(a \div b) \cdot$
   $b \to a$ (for $b \,|\, a$) and indicate in the proof which is used.
3. Reapply Step 2.

The higher-order generalization rule would operate on similar inputs, but rather than substituting new operations and decisions for old ones it would simply add the new operations/de-
cisions allowable in the new system (i.e., the algebraic extension or the reals). For instance, application of the higher-
order generalization rule to a proof completion subproblem over
the algebraic extension Q ($\neg\sqrt{2}$) involving existence, and the
sixth proof completion rule of Table 6, would yield the following proof completion rule for the extension Q ($\neg\sqrt{2}$).

1. Combine terms through multiplication and squaring
   $\neg\sqrt{2}$ ($-\neg\sqrt{2}$) as needed.
2. If the expressions on both sides of the equation are the
   same, stop; otherwise commute, associate and distribute
   rational terms and $\neg\sqrt{2}$ terms in order to simplify the
   equation by applying one of the following, as needed:
   $b \cdot a/b \to a$ (for $b \neq 0$), $a + -a \to 0$, $a + 0 \to a$,
   $a \cdot 0 \to 0$ (after proven), $a \cdot 1 \to a$, $(a - b) + b \to a$
   and indicate in the proof which justification is used.
3. Reapply Step 2.

With regard to the reals, notice that there are two different real-number system rules, the real-numbers solution rule,
and the proof completion rule over the reals. Each rule plays
a distinct role in generating proofs. The reals solution rule
is used to generate "candidate" elements (equations) in existence
proofs of all types. In turn, these elements are systematically
checked via appropriate proof completion rules to see if they
satisfy the postulated existence conditions. The solution rule
for the reals is relatively more complex than the reals proof

completion rule[4] because the former applies in a wider variety
of computational situations. On the other hand, although it
applies in a more limited set of situations, the proof completion
rule generates reasons (justification) for steps in addition to
the steps themselves.

The fact that we have assumed the availability of the real-
number solution rule may raise some question in the reader's
mind as to why we based our analysis of the proof completion
subproblems on the rationals rather than on the reals. Our main
reasons were two in number:

1. As suggested in the preceding paragraph, there is a
    difference between simple intuitive computational
    ability without explicit understanding of why each
    operation/decision can be applied, and the ability
    not only to perform, but also to justify the use of
    such operations/relations. While others may disagree,
    we felt that it was reasonable to assume that capable
    ninth-grade students have the former capability but
    not the latter.

2. By basing our analysis on the rationals it was possible
    to illustrate two kinds of higher-order rules, one
    involving substitution (restriction) and the other
    generalization. If the reals had been used, only re-
    striction would have been required.

While on the subject of higher-order rules, we note parenthetically that the above higher-order restriction and generalization rules can be extended in a natural way to apply in a
broader range of situations than indicated. Perhaps the most
trivial generalizations, for example, would involve new number
systems (e.g., different algebraic extensions) in which the
higher-order rules might be used to generate proof completion
rules for the new systems. Further generalizations might involve
quite different areas of application that deal only indirectly
with number systems. For example, the above substitution rule
is directly analogous to, and could be generalized to include,
the substitution rules identified in Scandura et al. (1971; also
see Chapter 11). The latter were concerned with such things as
changing bases in numeration systems. Even in everyday life we
solve new problems by analogy to (substitution in rules for dealing with) familiar situations (e.g., by substituting a stone for
a hammer where the latter is not available), or by generalizing
learned rules (e.g., generalizing from one or two instances of
dishonest behavior to general distrust).

---

[4]This is over and above the complexity introduced simply because we spelled
out the individual steps in greater detail in Table 5 than in describing the
proof completion rules.

6. SUMMARY AND COMPUTATIONAL ADEQUACY OF THE RULE SET

By way of summary, we have identified a total of 24 rules in our analysis: 10 problem definition rules, 12 lower-order (proof-generating) rules, and 2 higher-order derivation rules. The 24 basic rules and their specific functions are summarized in Table 7.

TABLE 7
Summary of Rules and Their Functions

Type/Rule	Function
Problem Definition Rules	Each Reformulates or Breaks Down Given Theorems-to-prove (TTP) into Sub TTP
Compound Problem Definition Rules	Breaks Compound TTP into Simple TTP
D1 Biconditional (P if and only if Q)	Breaks compound biconditional TTP into pairs of conditional TTP (If P, then Q; If Q, then P)
D2 Existence and Uniqueness (There exists a unique....)	Breaks compound existence and uniqueness TTP into an existence sub TTP and a uniqueness sub TTP) (There exists an X; X is unique)
D3 Simple Antecedent-Compound Consequent (If P, then Q or R)	Breaks compound simple antecedent-compound consequent TTP into pairs of TTP (If P and not Q, then R; if P and not R, then Q)
Six Key Step Definition Rules	Each breaks simple TTP into pairs of sub TTP (key step subproblem and proof completion subproblem)
KD1 Simple antecedent-simple consequent	1. ⟨theorem, theorem + antecedent⟩ ⟨theorem + antecedent, completed proof (through consequent)⟩
KD2 Compound antecedent-simple consequent	2. ⟨theorem, theorem + compound antecedent⟩ ⟨theorem + compound antecedent, completed proof (through consequent)⟩
KD3 Existence denied	3. ⟨theorem, theorem + assumed existence⟩ ⟨theorem + assumed existence, completed proof (through contradiction)⟩
KD4 Universally quantified equations	4. ⟨theorem, theorem + equation⟩ ⟨theorem + equation, completed proof (through equation with identical expressions on both sides)⟩
KD5 Uniqueness of element	5. ⟨theorem, theorem + assumed two elements x_1 and x_2⟩ ⟨theorem + assumed two elements, completed proof (through $x_1 = x_2$)⟩
KD6 Existence of element	6. ⟨theorem, theorem + postulated element⟩ ⟨theorem + postulated element, completed proof (through equation with identical expressions on both sides)⟩
RD Redefinition Rule	Redefines proof completion subproblems involving *undefined* relations/operations in terms of corresponding proof completion subproblems involving *defined* relations/operations

Proof-Generating Rules	*Generate Key Steps or Completed Proofs*
Six Key Step Proof-Generating Rules	Generate Key Step for the Six Types of Theorems
KG1 Simple antecedent-simple consequent	1. generates antecedent
KG2 Compound antecedent-simple consequent	2. generates compound antecedent
KG3 Existence denied	3. generates assumption of existence
KG4 Universally quantified equations	4. generates given equation
KG5 Uniqueness of element	5. generates assumption of two elements
KG6 Existence of element (real-number solution rule)	6. generates postulated element
Six Proof Completion Rules for Rationals	*Generate completed proofs for the six types of theorems over the rationals*
CG1 Simple antecedent-simple consequent (rationals)	1. generates completed proof thru consequent (rationals)
CG2 Compound antecedent-simple consequent (rationals)	2. generates completed proof thru consequent (rationals)
CG3 Existence denied (rationals)	3. generates completed proof thru contradiction (rationals)
CG4 Universally quantified equations (rationals)	4. generates completed proof thru equation with identical expressions on both sides (rationals)
CG5 Uniqueness of element (rationals)	5. generates completed proof thru $x_1 = x_2$ (rationals)
CG6 Existence of element (rationals)	6. generates completed proof thru equation with identical expressions on both sides (rationals)
Higher-Order Rules	*Given proof completion rule (rationals) and restrictions or operations/relations in new system, generates corresponding proof completion for new system*
H1 Substitution (Restriction) Rule	Generates proof completion rules for wholes/integers (given restrictions in new system)
H2 Generalization Rule	Generates proof completion rules for algebraic extension/reals (given additional operations/relations in new system)

These rules, together with the special restrictions, operations, and relations associated with the various number systems, are computationally sufficient for proving all of the theorems and exercises in Table 2. In this regard, we implicitly assume an adequate control mechanism by which the rules may be appropriately combined (see Chapter 2). Furthermore, to the extent that these rules accurately reflect idealized competence with respect to some specifiable population, they collectively provide a potential basis for simulating individual human behavior. (The population compatibility requirement is necessary to insure that the rule set can be used effectively to assess the specific

knowledge available to individuals in the target population,
see Chapters 5, 8, and 9.)

In this section, we shall limit ourselves to illustrating
the computational sufficiency of the rule set. The reader may
want to check the rule set with respect to other theorems/exer-
cises in Table 2.

Example 1: Consider the theorem (rationals) "For every
a/b, c/d in the rationals, there exists a unique x such that
c/d $\cdot$ x = a/b." When presented with this theorem-to-prove, the
first rule that is applied is the Compound Existence and Uniqueness Problem Definition Rule (D2). This gives a pair of simple
theorems-to-prove. The first simple theorem involves existence
(i.e., For every a/b, c/d $\neq$ 0 there exists an x such that
c/d $\cdot$ x = a/b) and the second, uniqueness (i.e., Given x such
that c/d $\cdot$ x = a/b, x is unique).

Then the existence theorem-to-prove is broken down by the
Existence Key Step Problem Definition Rule (KD6) into a key step
subproblem and a proof completion subproblem. Next, the key step
subproblem is solved by applying the real-number solution rule
to obtain c/d $\cdot$ ad/bc = a/b (i.e., x = ad/bc). Since the proof
completion subproblem involves an undefined operation (i.e.,
division, /), Redefinition Rule (RD) is applied, giving a corresponding proof completion subproblem in which the operations/
relations are defined. Specifically, the defined key step is
c/d $\cdot$ ad = a/b $\cdot$ bc.[5] Finally, the Proof-Generating Rule (CG6)
is applied to the defined proof completion subproblem (key step)
and the existence theorem is proved.

The simple uniqueness theorem is proven in similar fashion,
only this time the Type 5 rules play the main role. The main
difference between the two proofs is that the uniqueness proof
involves a pair of elements x_1 and x_2 that are assumed in the
first step to satisfy the equation c/d $\cdot$ x = a/b. In this case,
the first step rule (KG5) generates the equations c/d $\cdot$ x_1 = a/b
and c/d $\cdot$ x_2 = a/b.[5] Then, the Proof-Generating Rule (CG5) is
applied to the proof completion subproblem completing the proof;
it begins by generating the equation c/d $\cdot$ x_1 = c/d $\cdot$ x_2 and
ends with the final step x_1 = x_2.

Example 2: In proving the theorem (whole numbers) "If
x + a = a + b then x = b," the Case 1 Key Step Problem Definition Rule (KD1) is applied first. This rule breaks the problem
into a key step subproblem and a proof completion subproblem.
The key step subproblem is solved by applying the Case 1 Key
Step Rule (KG1), giving x + a = a + b. The operations/relations
of the proof completion subproblem are already defined, so no
redefinition is needed. However, since this subproblem involves
the whole numbers rather than the rationals, a new proof comple-

---

[5]The redefinition rule applies only where / refers to the operation of
division.

tion rule is required.

An appropriate proof completion rule for the whole numbers can be derived by applying the Higher-Order Substitution Rule (H1) to the restrictions associated with the whole number system and the Case 1 Proof Completion Rule (CG1) for rationals. The result is a restricted simple antecedent--Simple Consequent (Case 1) Proof Completion Rule for the whole numbers. Finally, the newly derived rule is applied to the key step $x + a = a + b$, generating the remaining steps (and reasons) in the proof ending with $x = b$.

Example 3: In the case of the theorem (reals) "For every $a > 0$, $b > 0$, $\sqrt{ab} = \sqrt{a} \sqrt{b}$", the first rule applied is the Case 4 Problem Definition Rule (KD4). The obtained key step subproblem is solved by applying the Case 4 Key Step Rule (KG4), which gives $\sqrt{ab} = \sqrt{a} \sqrt{b}$ as the key first step.

Since the proof completion subproblem involves real numbers, the Higher-Order Generalization Rule (H2) is applied to the Case 4 Proof Completion Rule (CG4) for the rationals and the special operations/relations associated with the real-number system. Application of H2 has the effect of adding the operation of raising $\sqrt[n]{}$ to the nth power to Step 1 of rule CG4 and the operations $(\sqrt[n]{a})^n \rightarrow a$ and completion of the square to Step 2. As before, the final step involves applying the generalized proof completion rule (reals) to the key step $\sqrt{ab} = \sqrt{a} \sqrt{b}$. The final step in the proof is $ab = ab$.

Although we have not seriously attempted to define its outer limits, the rule set summarized in Table 7 is sufficient for proving many theorems and exercises not given in Brumfiel *et al.* (1961). Clearly, for example, any statement that is a theorem in one system (e.g., wholes) is necessarily also a theorem in any more constrained system (e.g., reals). The identified rule set can obviously be used to generate proofs of such theorems irrespective of whether or not they are made explicit in Brumfiel *et al.* (1961).

The following are just a few additional theorems not explicitly stated in Brumfiel *et al.* (1961) that can be proven via the rule set:

1. If $a \cdot x = a \cdot b$ then $x = b$ (whole numbers)
2. If $a \cdot b = b$, then $a = 1$ (whole numbers)
3. If $a \div x = b \div x$ ($x \neq 0$), then $a = b$ (integers)
4. There does not exist a rational r such that $r^2 = 5$ (rationals)
5. For every a/b, c/d, $a/b + (-c)/d = a/b - c/d$ (rationals)
6. For every pair of real numbers r_1, r_2, there exists a unique r such that $r_1 - r_2 = r$ (reals)

There are also some less trivial statements that can be proven using the identified rules. Consider the following theorem over the whole numbers "For all $a > b$, $c > d$, $(a - b) +$

$(c - d) = (a + c) - (b + d)$." In this case, application of the Universally Quantified Equations Problem Definition Rule (KD4), the Key Step Rule (KG4), the Redefinition Rule (RD), the Universally Quantified Equations Proof Completion Rule (CG4) and the Substitution Rule (H1) yields the following proof:

1. $(a - b) + (c - d) = (a + c) - (b + d)$
        key step
2. $(a - b) + (c - d) + b + d = a + c$
        by definition of -
3. $((a - b) + b) + ((c - d) + d) = a + c$
        by commutativity and associativity
4. $a + ((c - d) + d) = a + c$
        by $(a - b) + b \to a$ (Step 2 of CG4 whole numbers)
5. $a + c = a + c$
        by $(a - b) + b \to a$ (i.e., $(c - d) + d \to c$)

Another theorem that can be proved in a similar manner is, "For all a, b, $-(a - b) = b - a$" over the integers. In this case, rules KD4, RD, CG4, and H1 are required.

Furthermore, the addition of special restrictions and/or operations/relations associated with new systems (e.g., $Q\,(\sqrt{3})$) (which may be represented as rules) would make it possible to prove theorems over such systems. In this case, the same higher-order rules could be used. For example, the following are some statements about $Q(\sqrt{3})$ that are provable in the rule set:

1. There does not exist $a + b\text{-}\sqrt{3}$ such that $(a + b\sqrt{3})^2 = 2$
2. $a + b\sqrt{3} = 0$ if and only if $a = 0$ and $b = 0$
3. For all $a + b\sqrt{3}$ and $c + d\sqrt{3} \neq 0$, there exists a unique $x + y\sqrt{3}$ such that $(a + b\sqrt{3})/(c + d\sqrt{3}) = x + y\sqrt{3}$

The rule set does, of course, have its limitations, particularly as it stands. It cannot be used to prove such (relatively) deep theorems as the Fundamental Theorem of Arithmetic. This theorem was stated but left unproven in Brumfiel et al. (1961). In fact, the rule set fails even on some apparently easy theorems (e.g., If $2|ab$, then $2|a$ or $2|b$ [intergers]).

In some cases, however, the rule set can easily be extended so that it does work. For example, although the rule set fails with the compound theorem "If $2|ab$, then $2|a$ or $2|b$ (integers)," it does not fail by much. Without citing all of the rules involved, the identified rules are sufficient for generating the following proof steps for the associated simple theorem, "If $2|ab$ and $2\nmid a$, then $2|b$"

1. $2|ab$ $\Big\}$ key step
   $2\nmid a$
2. $ab = 2k_1$ $\Big\}$ by definition
   $a = 2k_2 + 1$
3. $(2k_2 + 1)\,b = 2k_1$ $\Big\}$ Type 2 proof completion rule
   $2bk_2 + b = 2k_1$ $\Big.$ for the integers

Only two steps remain to complete the proof, namely:

4. $b = 2k_1 - 2bk_2$
5. $b = 2(k_1 - bk_2)$ (i.e., $2|b$)

In particular, the existing Compound Antecedent, Simple Consequent Proof Completion Rule lacks two simple, but in this case, important operations. To overcome this limitation it would be sufficient to incorporate the inverse of the subtraction rule $a + b = c \rightarrow b = c - a$ and distributivity over subtraction.

Finally, we note that although all of the theorems in Table 2 can be proven via the rule set, some of them required the introduction of special-purpose operations. For example, the real number theorem, "If $ax^2 + bx + c = 0$, then $x = (-b \pm \sqrt{b^2 - 4ac})/2a$" is the only one that required the completion of the square procedure. In particular, this bit of knowledge (including both the domain and the operational aspect of the rule) would have to be available, as special knowledge about the reals, in order for the higher-order generalization rule to generate a proof completion rule sufficient for completing the proof (starting with $ax^2 + bx + c = 0$).

7. CONCLUSION AND IMPLICATIONS

As a result of our analysis, it would appear that the specific competencies necessary for proving relatively substantial classes of theorems can be identified. Moreover, given information concerning the procedures used to prove a representative sample of theorems, such competencies can be identified in a reasonably systematic manner.

A total of 24 rules (procedures) are sufficient for generating proofs of all 67 theorems and 35 exercises of Brumfiel *et al.* (1961), plus an undetermined number of other theorems about number systems. Among the theorems that cannot be so proved is the Fundamental Theorem of Arithmetic, which intuitively seems to require a different method of proof.

Of the basic 24 rules, 10 are relatively simple problem definition rules, 12 are proof-generating rules, and 2 are higher-order rules. The problem definition rules construct subproblems and are directly analogous to the subgoal hierarchies of Newell and Simon (1972).

There are two types of proof-generating rules (i.e., rules for solving problems): key step-generating rules and proof completion rules. The six key step generating rules are independent of particular number systems and correspond respectively to six types of theorems. All but one are extremely simple; this exception generates postulated elements (trick steps) to be tested in existence proofs.

The six corresponding proof completion rules, on the other hand, apply only with the rationals. Corresponding proof completion rules for each of the other number systems can be generated from the rationals' rules and specific information about the other number systems, by applying either the restriction or the generalization higher-order rule. Although the methods of representation differ, the proof completion rules operate as in means-ends analysis (Ernst & Newell, 1969) to reduce the differences between given and goal states.

In spite of the noted similarities, the overall analysis differs from those proposed by Newell and Simon (1972) and/or Ernst and Newell (1969) in at least two important ways:

1. In means-ends analysis, production systems, and state space methods generally (Nilsson, 1971), solution procedures are generated essentially by composing individual operations (rules, productions). In the structural learning theory (cf. Scandura, 1973; Chapter 2, this book), new rules also may be generated in other ways. The present research demonstrates this fact in the case of restriction and generalization of proof generating procedures.

2. The methods by which individual rules are assumed to interact in generating behavior (and learning) also differ. In production systems, for example, it is assumed that rules (productions) are tested one by one. If a state satisfies the domain condition of a rule, then it is applied. If not, the next rule is tested. This particular mechanism makes no specific provision for learning (other than to add new productions). In the structural learning theory, rules interact in a more general way. For example, allowance is made both for solving subproblems in turn, which corresponds to sequential application of rules, and for deriving/generating (i.e., learning) new solution rules, in a manner that corresponds to "insight" (see Chapter 2).

The major practical implications of the research fall into two major categories: (1) those involving the method of analysis generally and, (2) those involving the specific rule set identified. The general method of analysis is suggestive, for example, both for research in artificial intelligence and for curriculum development. In each case the major goal is to identify the competencies needed to perform satisfactorily on a given task domain; the proposed method of analysis provides a quasisystematic means of accomplishing this.

The specific results obtained also have obvious implications for artificial intelligence and education. Most good programmers, for example, would have relatively little difficulty in implementing the identified rule set and basic control structure. (Wulfeck has already done this with the geometry analysis of Chapter 3.) Moreover, in addition to their demonstrated value in proving theorems about number systems, the problem definition and higher-order rules identified might reasonably be expected to play a useful role in other proof-making domains.

A skilled mathematics educator could also use the present analysis to advantage, for example, in preparing instructional materials for teaching proof making. Just as the programmer would have to translate the present analysis into a form a

computer can compile, the text writer (or classroom teacher)
would have to translate the analysis into a form suitable for
the learner. In the latter case, for example, it is not necessary that any particular rule be learned in a particular way,
say either by exposition or by discovery. The important thing
is that the rules are learned. In this regard, it is our contention that if text writers and/or teachers knew exactly what
it is that must be learned in order to prove theorems, then
he or she would be able to do a more effective job of promoting
learning than otherwise.

It also is worth noting that a text based on the obtained
rule set would be quite different than the text by Brumfiel *et
al*. (1961), even though the present rule set was derived from
the latter. At a gross level, for example, proofs involving the
rationals would enter much earlier than in the Brumfiel text
and would provide a basis for comparison throughout. More
generally, the various types of proof and relationships among
theorems and systems would be made explicit for the learner
rather than left to chance discovery.

One final comment by way of conclusion: Some readers might
object to our analysis on the grounds that no apparent attempt
has been made to relate the identified rules to what is sometimes
referred to as general cognitive structure. This is true, however, only in a limited and unavoidable sense. There is no one
cognitive structure to which the present rule set might be related, in the sense that individual differences in knowledge
that do not directly involve the problem domain (say, the text)
are irrelevant insofar as explaining and predicting basic capabilities with respect to this domain. Relationships to broader cognitive structure make a difference only with respect to
problems beyond the given domain. In this case, however, structural analysis of a broader domain that includes such problems
would deal specifically with such relationships.

This is not to say, however, that structures (on which
rules operate) of the sort introduced in Chapter 2 may be ignored. In fact, they are implicit in the domains of the rules
identified. Several of the rules identified, for example the
higher-order rules, may be thought of as operating on entire
numbers systems (i.e., structures) and aspects thereof (cf.
Scandura, 1971, 1973, Chapter 5; also see Chapter 15, Section
3.5, this book). Although the central role such systems play
was not emphasized, a precise specification of these rules
would necessarily involve the properties which collectively
define such systems.

REFERENCES

Brumfiel, C. F., Eicholz, R. E., & Shanks, M. E. *Algebra I*. Reading, Mass.: Addison-Wesley, 1961.

Ernst, G. W., & Newell, A. *GPS (General Problem Solver): A case study in generality and problem solving*. New York: Academic Press, 1969.

Goldberg, A. *A generalized instructional system for elementary mathematical logic* (Technical Report No. 179). Palo Alto, Calif.: Stanford, University, Institute for Mathematical Studies in the Social Sciences, 1971.

Kane, M. J. *Variability in the proof behavior of college students in a CAI course in logic as a function of problem characteristics* (Technical Report No. 192). Palo Alto, Calif.: Stanford University, Institute for Mathematical Studies in the Social Sciences, 1972.

Newell, A., & Simon, H. A. *Human problem solving*. Englewood Cliffs N.J.: Prentice-Hall, 1972.

Nilsson, N. J. *Problem-solving methods in artificial intelligence.* New York: McGraw-Hill, 1971.

Polya, G. *Mathematical discovery* (Vol. 1). New York: Wiley, 1962.

Scandura, J. M. A theory of mathematical knowledge: Can rules account for creative behavior? *Journal of Research in Mathematics Education,* 1971, *2,* 183-186. (Also in Scandura, J. M. *Structural learning II: Issues and approaches.* New York/London: Gordon & Breach, 1976.)

Scandura, J. M. Structural approach to instructional problems. *American Psychologist,* 1977, *32,* 33-53.

Scandura, J. M. *Structural learning I: Theory and research.* New York: Gordon & Breach, 1973.

Scandura, J. M. Structural approach to instructional problems. *American Psychologist,* in press.

Scandura, J. M., Durnin, J. H., Ehrenpreis, W., & Luger, G. *An algorithmic approach to mathematics: Concrete behavioral foundations.* New York: Harper & Row, 1971.

Suppes, P. Computer-assisted instruction at Stanford (Technical Report No. 174). Palo Alto, Calif.: Stanford University, Institute for Mathematical Studies in the Social Sciences, 1971.

PART 3

Cognitive Mechanisms

The chapters in Part 3 attempt to explicate certain aspects of the problem solving process that are independent of any particular class of problems. In this sense, they are written from the perspective of the psychologist.

The experimental methods used, however, differ in fundamental ways from those which characterize much of contemporary experimental psychology. Although modern information processing psychology has a deterministic base, for example, the methods that have been used to test such theories have been essentially the same as those used to test probabilistic theories. In particular, the essential data have been means and variances and the basic variables themselves often have no clear relationship to deterministic theory itself.

Perhaps the major limitation in the latter case is the lack of adequate structural analysis (i.e., clear specification of the task domain and/or underlying competence). Thus, for example, the frequently stated aim of experimental questions is to find out such things as how people make size comparisons, or recognize and evaluate paraphrases, or remember narrative discourse. Yet, without careful prior analysis of the tasks involved, the variables chosen for study often fail to capture more than global aspects of cognitive processes. Consequently, when left unqualified, empirical relationships involving such variables have little chance of withstanding the test of time. Equally important, such research typically proceeds on the assumption that there are unique answers to the above kinds of questions, answers that hold for all individuals. The search for such answers takes place via successive refinements, based on intersecting programs of experimental research.

As argued in Chapters 1 and 2, I believe that this is a false assumption. Moreover, detailed *a priori* structural analysis may make it possible to "home in" on truth more efficiently, and thereby to minimize the need for redundant experimentation. Furthermore, by searching for prototypes in structural analysis, rather than common denominators (processes which provide best overall accounts), one can bridge the gap between studies of cognition and individual differences measurement (see Chapter 2, Section 5).

Although some of the research reported in Part 2 deals with the role of individual differences (e.g., Chapter 5, Experiments III and IV), the emphasis is on cognitive universals. Particular attention is given to the goal switching control mechanism proposed in Chapter 2, and processing capacity. As argued in Chapter 1, it is useful in this type of research (i.e., in dealing with universals) to make a sharp distinction between structural and incidental factors. In the case of the hypothesized control mechanism, specific higher- and lower-order rules (knowledge) are taken into account in the "memory-free" theory (of structural learning) and, hence, they constitute the structural variables. The degree of availability of such knowledge, processing capacity, and so on (e.g., processing speed, encoding capabilities) are not included in this (partial) theory and, thus, are the incidental variables.

Because experimental deviations from universality may be attributed to either type of variable and because the relevant deterministic theory deals with only one of these types, the studies have been conducted, where possible, under idealized boundary conditions. In effect, an attempt has been made to eliminate the effects of incidental variables. Where idealized conditions can be achieved, the Structural Learning Theory (e.g., hypothesized control and specific knowledge) generates deterministic predictions concerning individual behavior in specific situations. Where idealized conditions either cannot or have not been achieved, deviations from resulting predictions may be attributed to inadequacies either in the deterministic theory itself and/or in a complementary observation theory. (Observation theories, recall, deal with incidental variables and are invariably probabilistic in nature; e.g., see Chapter 7.)

In the context of the Structural Learning Theory, precise predictions concerning nonidealized behavior require theoretical systems that include both deterministic and probabilistic components. Such systems, therefore, are necessarily probabilistic. Nonetheless, as argued in Chapter 1, there are still important advantages in maintaining a sharp distinction between both types of variables. For one thing, the requirement of deterministic results under idealized laboratory conditions imposes severe constraints on meaningful experimentation. This requirement cannot easily be met on the basis of sheer empiricism; research is literally forced to rely on fundamental theoretical assumptions (that have the potential of universality). Equally important, this distinction allows direct inferences between laboratory findings and applications. Deterministic effects (in the laboratory) due to structural variables, unlike results attributable to confounded variables, *cannot* be eliminated in the real world. They necessarily apply in a weaker probabilistic sense (see Chapters 1 and 11, Section 4; also Hilke, Kempf, & Scandura, 1977).

In Chapter 5, the "first approximation" mechanism of Chapter 2 is summarized and tested in the context of rule derivation. Specific knowledge (rules) aside, this mechanism appeared to be universally available to (essentially) all individuals. No instruction in the control mechanism was given nor did it appear to be needed. Under idealized conditions, where memory, problem definition, motivation, etc. were not involved, subjects solved problems if and only if they knew all of the lower- and higher-order rules postulated in the theory to be sufficient.

Five experiments are reported. The data in Experiments I and II are consistent with the following assumptions: When confronted with a problem, subjects first search through their available rules to see if an appropriate rule is available. If so, the subject selects that rule and solves the problem. If not, control moves to a higher-level goal and the subject searches through his rule set for a higher-order rule (so-called because it acts on other rules) that can be used to derive a rule sufficient for solving the problem. Once a solution rule has been derived, control reverts to the original goal, and the rule is applied to solve the problem.

The experimental demonstrations take place with respect to two different kinds of higher-order derivation rules. Experiment I involves a higher-order composition rule that operates on pairs of compatible A → B, B → C rules and generates corresponding composite A → B → C rules. Experiment II involves higher-order generalization rules and demonstrates that generalization phenomenon also may be handled within this framework.

In Experiments III and IV, rather than experimentally manipulating instruction in higher-order rules, the subjects were tested to determine which, if any, (relevant generalization) higher-order rules they knew on entering into the experiments. This assessment of the subject's prior knowledge (and consequent potential for solving problems) was made possible by the knowledge assessment technique detailed in Part 4. Predictions concerning success on new problems were about 90 percent accurate.

Experiment V was conducted after the others and suggests that the "first approximation" mechanism is universally available to children as young as four years of age. It also demonstrates that insuring idealized test conditions involves attention to factors internal to subjects as well as to environmental ones. Specifically, conditions that are adequate to insure idealization with seven-year-olds, say, may not be sufficient with four-year-olds. The idea is directly analogous, in testing the inclined plane law in physics, to the fact that the same amount of "friction proofing" may have different effects with different materials (see Chapter 1).

Chapter 6 is a sequel to Chapter 5 and reports studies that deal with retrieval, problem definition (subgoal formation), rule selection, and multiple processes in problem solving. With the exception of the higher-order rules involved, retrieval (extraction) from memory (under "memory-free" conditions) requires no changes in the "first approximation" control mechanism.

The construction of subproblems may be accounted for by generalizing higher-level goals so that they may be satisfied by "plans" (e.g., sequences of subproblems) as well as by specific solution procedures. Otherwise, goal switching operates as before. In the experiment reported, subjects were presented with a problem identical to the one used in Experiment I, Chapter 5. Instead of composing compatible A → B and B → C rules, however, subjects were taught how to break A-C problems into A-B and B-C subproblems and to solve each in turn.

Study three was concerned with what the subject does when he has a task and two or more different ways of solving it. Why does he choose the procedure (rule) that he does rather than some other one? Clearly, such selections are an integral part of all serious problem solving and clarification of the underlying processes would be an essential part of any complete explanation (of problem solving).

To allow for motivation phenomena, the above mechanism must be modified slightly so that control moves to higher-goal levels until *exactly* one rule applies. To date, empirical research on this problem has barely begun; the research reported is limited to a simple demonstration that such selections are governed by selection rules that operate on pairs of rules, for example, and generate as outputs one of the rules. It was found that subjects used given selection rules in new situations in over 97 percent of the test cases. From the perspective of the Structural Learning Theory, selection rules are simply special kinds of higher-order rules.

The last study extends the analysis to deal simultaneously with multiple processes, specifically the processes of retrieval and rule derivation. In more complex situations of this sort, the mechanism must be enriched to allow for the derivation (retrieval/extraction) of knowledge (rules) *on which* higher-order rules may operate. If the need for new information becomes apparent during the course of solving a problem, control is assumed to move temporarily to a subsidiary (domain) goal for finding it. Once the needed information is retrieved and the domain goal is satisfied, control reverts automatically to the goal from which the derivation was initiated. Empirical support for the mechanism is reported.

To summarize, the "first approximation" mechanism, originally proposed to account for rule derivation in problem solving, can be generalized without essential change to deal with a wide variety of other psychological phenomena. This is not just a fortuitous circumstance. The required changes seem perfectly natural and do not have the ad hoc character that frequently results when theories are modified to account for unanticipated fact.

Although the memory-free theory has not in any real sense been pushed to its limits, it does appear to hold up quite well under a broad range of conditions. An essential limit of the theory, however, seems clear on a priori grounds. It does not in any way take into account the effects of other basic characteristics of the human organism that may place constraints on problem solving behavior. The reference here is to such things as the range of peripheral vision, the frequencies of aural stimulation which can be detected by the human ear, processing speed, and the limited capacity of human subjects to process information. Such constraints presumably are universally applicable, and, insofar as extensions of the theory are concerned, might be treated as empirically determined boundary conditions. In effect, physiological and developmental boundary conditions of this sort could serve as fixed parameters in extended theories of structural learning and might help to generate predictions in wider varieties of (nonidealized) situations. The theory itself, however, would provide no basis for identifying or explaining such boundary conditions.

Looking at the problem the other way around, not all data is idealized in the above sense. In the present case, for example, a given task may impose a memory load that exceeds the human processor's capacity. In order to deal with such data, the theorist may do one (or both) of two things: (a) he may enrich the given deterministic theory, so that it takes memory load into account, and/or (b) he may add a complementary observation theory (see Chapter 1). An extension of the Structural Learning Theory that deals with memory load (and processing speed) is proposed in Chapter 2 (Section 4). Among other things, this theory shows in outline form how the memory load imposed on a human information processor may be determined analytically. This theory applies at any given stage of processing, whether the control mechanism is effecting shifts among goals, a set of rules is being tested against a goal, or some rule is operating on data (possibly including other rules).

The analytic model summarized in Chapter 7 is restricted to the last case only. After reviewing some of the relevant literature, the deterministic model is described together with an experiment designed to test it. In this experiment, an attempt was made to partial out incidental factors (e.g., processing speed by allowing subjects to work at their own speed). This attempt, however, was only partially successful. The data were generally supportive of the model but not in the same deterministic sense as was the case in Chapters 5 and 6. The major difficulty appeared to be that of controlling the exact nature of the processing. Even after a considerable degree of training, extraneous elements apparently entered into individual processors and supposedly discrete elements were inadvertently "chunked". In the former case, for example, subjects frequently reported self-monitoring and other distractions. In the latter case, elements that were supposed to be processed as discrete entities were apparently recoded as units (e.g., 3-9 as one's office number).

Incidental random variables, α and β, were introduced to account for these sources of deviation (from idealized conditions) and were incorporated within the deterministic model. The result was a stochastic theory based on the random variables α and β and the deterministic parameters C_i, the processing capacity of subject i and L_j, the memory load imposed at stage j of the given process (rule). This stochastic theory provided a good fit, both of the original data and of new data collected under somewhat different boundary conditions. As hypothesized might be the case in Chapter 1, these boundary conditions appeared to be reflected in the parameter values.

In the near future, hopefully, the above research will be extended in a number of directions (e.g., see Chapters 2 and 15). (1) The general methodology should be applied to realistic problem domains of contemporary interest (e.g., conservation tasks, language comprehension). More detailed, prior structural analyses could be invaluable in "homing in" on generalizable answers. (2) The distinction between structural and incidental variables should be further exploited, possibly in the context of (1). (3) Basic assumptions of the theory should be subjected to further testing, both directly under idealized conditions and indirectly by systematically varying the effects of incidental variables (see Chapter 7, Section 5). The relationship between memory load and processing speed, proposed in Chapter 2, Section 4, is especially important.

5
Role of Higher-Order Rules in Problem Solving[1]

Joseph M. Scandura

One of the most crucial questions in problem-solving research is why some problem solvers succeed on problems for which
they have all of the necessary component skills, whereas others
do not. In dealing with this question, most studies of problem
solving have attempted to deal with the process in its full complexity (e.g., Dunker, 1945; Newell & Simon, 1972). That is,
most studies have employed problem situations that involve problem definition (the formation of subgoals), memory, the derivation of solution procedures, and the use of such procedures.
The situation is further complicated because existing theories
of problem solving are either extremely limited in scope (i.e.,
to specific kinds of problems) or, if general, are more like
overall schemas than strong theories (cf. Greeno, 1973).
    The present research has adopted a somewhat different
strategy. It seeks to deal separately with the various aspects
of problem solving (e.g., the derivation of solution procedures)
but in a way that generalizes over tasks. Specifically, this
research is not concerned with the role of memory or with problem definition. Precautions were taken to ensure that subjects
fully understood the problems (goals and given) presented, and
that they were understood in the way the experimenter intended.
Further, the ongoing research is concerned with a specific fal-

[1]Adapted from Scandura, J. M., "The Role of Higher-Order Rules in Problem
Solving", *Journal of Experimental Psychology*, 1974, *120*, 984-991 with permission
of the American Psychological Association. Major additions appear in *italics*.
This research was supported in part by National Science Foundation Grant GW 6796,
and U.S. Office of Education Grant OEG-3-71-0136. Experiment I was conducted
with Louis Ackler; Experiment II with Francine Endicott and John Durnin, and
Experiments III and IV with Durnin and Wallace Wulfeck. The author would also
like to thank Joe Karabinos and Diane Triman, who helped proctor the experimental
sessions. The research reported in Section 4 "Effect of Incidental Variables"
was supported by National Institute of Health Grant 9185.

sifiable theory (Scandura, 1973) concerning the behavior of
individual subjects in particular problem situations, and not
with either the performance of groups or of individuals averaged
over tasks. (As emphasized in Chapter 1 this requires testing
under idealized/near idealized conditions.)

The general point of view adopted is that rules underlie
all behavior (e.g., Scandura, 1970). More specifically, this
research is based on the assumption that, when the goal adopted
by a subject is known, a major portion of problem-solving ability
can be traced to the presence or absence of higher-order (h.o.)
rules. These rules may be used to combine constituent parts of
a problem solution into a coherent whole adequate for solving
the problem (cf. Saugstad, 1955) and/or to otherwise generate
solution procedures from known rules.

In this context, the question arises as to how known rules
interact in problem solving. It is hypothesized that in problem
solving (as in all learning) rules interact according to a fixed
mechanism that is presumed to be innate (or at least available
to people from the age of about seven without training) rather
than learned (Scandura, 1973). As a first approximation, this
mechanism is assumed to operate as follows: Given a goal situation $\langle S,G \rangle$, the subject tests to see if the problem solution
is immediately available (i.e., to see if he knows the solution).
If not, control shifts to the solution goal (SG = G2), consisting of the set of potential solution rules, and the subject
tests the rules available to him to see if any includes S in its
domain and the goal in its range.[2] If such a rule is available,
control reverts to the original goal and the rule is applied to
S. If not, control shifts to the higher-level goal (HG = G3),
consisting of h.o. rules that apply in the given goal situation
$\langle S, G \rangle$ and whose ranges contain a potential solution rule. With
this higher-level goal in force, the subject is assumed to test
his available rules as before. If one is found, control reverts
to the next lower-level goal and the h.o. rule is applied to
other available rules (domain elements), thereby generating a
potentially new solution rule. If the lower-level goal is satisfied by the new solution rule, control reverts to the original
goal, and the solution rule is applied to S. The problem is
solved if the (potential) solution so generated satisfies the
goal situation.

It should be noted that testing, goal shifting, and rule

---

[2]This condition is slightly different from that in an earlier formulation
(Scandura, 1973). Instead of requiring that the range of the rule contain the
goal, I had initially proposed that the range be contained in the goal. While
the latter condition works equally as well with initial goals, it is not fully
adequate. For example, in the trading-game experiment, requiring the range of a
composition rule to be contained in the higher-level goal is overly restrictive,
because this goal only contains A → Y → C rules (Y variable and A and C constants) whereas the range of the composition rule more naturally includes all
composite rules of the form X → Y → Z (where X and Z are also variables).

application are essentially the same at all goal levels (cf. Chapters 2 and 6). Furthermore, h.o. rules are formally identical to other rules and obey the same laws of behavior. The descriptor *higher-order* refers to the role of a rule in a particular instance of problem solving, not to its basic nature. In particular, any given rule may either serve as an operator (e.g., apply to other rules) or be operated upon. This differs from common usage. The term *higher-order rule* as used by Gagne (1970), for example, corresponds to the output of what is referred to here, by this term. (In computer science the type of control that allows this duality of usage is sometimes referred to as *unstratified control*.)

Suppose, for example, that a subject adopts goal G in situation S and has only the following rules available: r_1, r_2 (neither of which satisfy SG), and h, where $h(r_1, r_2) = p$ and p satisfies SG. What can we say about what the subject will or will not do? Given that a subject has adopted goal G in situation S, and only has rules r_1, r_2, and h available, Table 1 shows that the above mechanism provides a sufficient basis for predicting the subject's behavior. If we changed the situation by eliminating any one of r_1, r_2, or h, we could conclude that the subject would fail. In order to make predictions where training on rules is not a central variable, it is essential to determine what rules the subject knows. Indeed, the general importance of prior knowledge in research on complex human behavior is becoming increasingly clear (e.g., Bourne, Ekstrand, & Dominowski, 1971; Scandura, 1973).

The major purpose of this research was to test this mechanism empirically, under appropriate idealized conditions, both by manipulating h.o. rules and by testing to determine their availability prior to problem solving. Incidental comparisons also were made between this control mechanism and a commonly assumed alternative.

TABLE 1
Sequence of Events in Idealized Problem Solving

Event	Theoretical justification
SG = $\{r_i \mid S \in$ Domain r_i, G $\subset$ Range $r_i\} = \emptyset$ (is empty)	Assumption
∴ Control shifts to HG	Higher-level hypothesis
HG contains h ∴ Control reverts back to SG and S applies h to r_1, r_2 (to get p)	Assumption / Reversion and performance hypotheses
p satisfies SG	Assumption
∴ Control reverts to G and S applies p to S (to get R). R may satisfy G	Reversion and performance hypotheses

Note: See text for explanation of abbreviations used.

1.   TEST OF GOAL SWITCHING MECHANISM

Experiment I provided a test of the mechanism involving an h.o. composition rule.

1.1   METHOD

Materials and tasks: The experimental material consisted of tasks involving trading stimulus objects of one kind (e.g., red chips) for response objects of another (e.g., pencils). Each task can be characterized as a set of stimulus-response pairs in which n stimulus objects are mapped into (n + m) response objects (e.g., n red chips into n + 3 pencils). Throughout the experiment, $n + m \leq 10$, with $n \leq 7$ and $m \leq 4$.

There were two kinds of rules, *simple* and *composite,* for solving such tasks. Simple rules were represented on 5" x 8" cards. To represent the simple rule that maps n paper clips into n + 1 blue chips, for example, a paper clip was glued on the left and a blue chip on the right of the card. Composite rules generate trades in two steps. One composite rule, for example, first changes pencils into paper clips and then paper clips into white chips. Composite rules were represented by taping together two simple rule cards. (Pictures of simple and composite rule cards are shown in Figure 1 of Chapter 6, Section 1.1.)

A pair of simple rules was said to be *compatible* if the outputs of one of the rules were of the same type as the inputs of the other. Compatible rules can be combined to form composite rules (e.g., the rules denoted "n caramels → n + 1 toy soldiers" and "n toy soldiers → n + 2 pencils" can be combined to form a composite rule that maps n caramels into n + 3 pencils). The set of compatible pairs of simple rules comprises the domain of an h.o. rule that maps such pairs into corresponding composite rules. This h.o. rule was used to define a second, higher-level task in which, given a compatible pair (e.g., "n caramels → n + 2 white chips", "n white chips → n + 1 pencils"), the goal was to devise the corresponding composite rule (i.e., for converting caramels into pencils).

Subjects, design, and procedures: The subjects were 31 boys and girls between the ages of 5 and 9. They were run individually and given $.25 for participating. Seven subjects were excluded from the experimental comparison, six because they passed the pretest and the seventh because she failed to learn how to interpret the composite rule cards.

At the start of the experiment, each subject was told that he was going to play a trading game with the experimenter and was given several sets of objects to trade. The subject was then taught to interpret simple rule cards and to make trades using the rules represented by the cards. For example, the subject was shown a rule card for trading paper clips for blue chips and the experimenter explained "No matter how many paper clips I give you, you must give me the same number of blue chips

and then add one more". Practice was provided and, if necessary,
the experimenter showed the subject how to make trades of this
sort and asked him to repeat what he had been shown. The criterion was three consecutive successful trades. The experimenter
then gave the subject a set of objects not in the domain of the
rule (e.g., two pencils) and asked the subject if he could use
the rule to trade pencils for blue chips. Regardless of the
subject's response, the experimenter emphasized that the rule
could be used only to trade paper clips for blue chips.

The experimenter then showed the subject a different rule
card and asked him to interpret the rule, providing assistance
if necessary. Practice continued until the subject reached criterion. Again, the experimenter emphasized that the rule was
restricted to objects on the card. This procedure was repeated
using different rules until the subject was able to interpret
three consecutive rule cards and use them without assistance.
At this point, it was assumed that for the subject, simply seeing
a simple rule card was equivalent to knowing and being able to
apply the rule.

During Phase 2, the subject was taught to interpret and
use the composite rules. For example, the subject was presented
with a composite rule for trading pencils for white chips (via
paper clips) together with two pencils. He was told to use the
first rule (the experimenter pointed at the first card) to trade
the pencils for paper clips. The subject was required to place
the correct number of paper clips on the table. The experimenter
continued, "Now, use the second rule to trade these four paper
clips for white chips." This procedure was repeated with different stimuli until the subject performed three consecutive
trades correctly. Practice continued with similar rules until
the subject interpreted and correctly applied three consecutive
composite rules.

The subject was then given a pretest consisting of two
parts. First, the subject was presented with new cards representing a pair of compatible simple rules. (It was assumed that,
by virtue of the subject's earlier training, he knew what the
cards meant.) Then, the subject was asked to make three trades
requiring use of the corresponding composite rule. (The subject
was never shown this rule directly, either before or after
testing.) For example, a subject who was presented with the
rules "n pencils → n + 2 pieces of bubble gum" and "n pieces of
bubble gum → n + 1 paper clips" would be presented in turn with
various numbers of pencils (e.g., 2, 4, and 1) and asked to
trade the appropriate number of paper clips. No reinforcement
was provided on the pretest.

Those subjects who consistently failed on the pretest were
randomly assigned, in matched pairs, to one of two treatment
groups, Group HR, which received training on the h.o. rule, and
Group C, the control group. Those subjects who succeeded on two
or more instances of the pretest were given 5 minutes of irrele-

vant instruction (reading a comic book) and were given a posttest, that involved new rules but paralleled the pretest in
every other respect.

Each subject in Group HR was taught the h.o. rule.   The
subjects were first shown two compatible rule cards and asked
to interpret each.   The experimenter then demonstrated how to
combine the rules by sliding the rule cards together in the
appropriate manner.   The subject was then asked to interpret
this newly formed rule, and the experimenter emphasized that the
rules could be combined only because the output of one was the
same as the input of the other.   Next, the subject was presented
with several pairs of rules, some of which were not compatible.
For each pair, he was required to form the composite rule, if
possible, and to interpret the newly formed rule, but did not
actually make the trades.   For the randomly interspersed incompatible pairs, the subject had to indicate that the rules could
not be so combined.   After performing successfully on five consecutive (compatible and incompatible) pairs of rules, the subject was given the posttest.   The time required for training on
the h.o. rule was recorded.   Each Group C subject was asked to
read a comic book for the same amount of time as his matched
partner in Group HR required to learn the h.o. rule.   Finally,
the posttest was administered in the same manner as the pretest
to all subjects.

1.2   RESULTS AND DISCUSSION

The experimental results were relatively clear-cut.   Eleven
of the 12 HR subjects solved all three transfer problems.   The
one subject who failed after reaching criterion on the h.o. rule
was put through the experimental procedure a week later.   This
time he performed perfectly (only) on the posttest.   All 12 of
the control subjects failed uniformly on the posttest.   The
individual results are summarized in Table 2.

Although statistical comparisons between groups seem inappropriate, reliability of the percent correct predictions may
be expressed in terms of confidence intervals (for the HR Group).
Based on the assumption that correct and incorrect predictions
are binomially distributed and using the obtained mean of 91.7
percent to estimate the expected percentage of correct predictions in Group HR, the 68 percent confidence interval was between 83.9 percent and 99.5 percent.

*In effect, these results strongly support the hypothesis
that the above goal-switching mechanism is uniformly available
to children from about the age of 7 years.   This does not mean
that the results could not be explained in some alternative
manner.   On the basis of these results, however, it is possible to essentially rule out one major alternative, namely a
cyclical "stack type" mechanism in which available rules are
tested and applied consecutively.   According to this mechanism, rules are assumed to be stored in a list.   The rules are
tested in turn to determine their applicability.   If the current*

TABLE 2

Summary of Problem-Solving Results

Task	Experimental (HR) Ss										Control Ss												Disqualified Ss						
Age	8	8	9	7	8	8	8	8	9	8	8	7	8	9	8	8	9	8	8	8	7	8	8	9	8	8	9	5
Sex	G	G	B	B	B	B	B	B	B	G	B	G	G	B	B	B	B	G	B	B	G	B	G	B	B	B	B	G
Interpreting single rule cards	+	+	+	+	+	+	+	+	+	+	+	+	+	+	+	+	+	+	+	+	+	+	+	+	+	+	+	+
Interpreting composite rule cards	+	+	+	+	+	+	+	+	+	+	+	+	+	+	+	+	+	+	+	+	+	+	+	+	+	+	+	−
Pretest	−	−	−	−	−	−	−	−	−	−	−	−	−	−	−	−	−	−	−	−	−	−	+	+	+	+	+	−
Minutes on experimental (HR or irrelevant) instruction	6	5	4	5*	3	4	7	4	4	5	6	5	4	5	3	4	7	4	4	5	3	5	5	5	5	5	5	3
Transfer (Re) test	+	+	−*	+	+	+	+	+	+	+	−	−	−	−	−	−	−	−	−	−	−	−	+	+	+	+	+	−

Note: The + indicates that S reached criterion; −, that he or she did not. The Ss are identified according to age (5, 7, 8, and 9) and sex (B, G).

*On readministration of the HR treatment, this S required 2 minutes of instruction and reached criterion.

249

input is in the domain of a rule, the rule is applied and goes
to the bottom of the list. The obtained output serves as a new
input for testing by the next rule. If a rule is not applicable,
it is simply put at the bottom of the list and the next rule is
tested. In effect, available rules are applied consecutively
until the desired output is obtained or the system fails. This
mechanism corresponds directly to that used in current production
systems (e.g., Newell & Simon, 1972) and is equivalent to the
type of control implicitly assumed in all formal systems in
mathematics (including generative grammars).

As commonly assumed as this control mechanism is, however,
it is inconsistent with our data. Had such a control mechanism
been available to our subjects, they all would have succeeded
on our pretest. That 24 of 30 subjects failed would seem to
rule this assumption out, at least for 7-to-9-year-olds with
similar novel tasks. Clearly, the proportion of successful subjects may be expected to vary with population sophistication and
complexity of simple rules. Even universal availability of composition capabilities, however, would not eliminate the need for
other kinds of higher-order rules (see Experiment II) and, hence,
some alternative to stack-type control.

2. GENERALIZATION OF SOLUTION RULES

The purpose of Experiment II was to test the mechanism
proposed above with two different, and more complex, h.o. rules
of varying generality. Both involved generalization from a restricted rule to one more general. To help make it easier to
identify common and disparate features, the method description
parallels that of Experiment I.

2.1 METHOD

Tasks and materials: The experimental tasks involved responding, with appropriate numerals, to given stimulus numerals.
Each task can be characterized as a set of stimulus-response
pairs in which each number n is mapped into a number of the form
$an + d$, where a and d are whole numbers (e.g., n into $4n + 13$).
In addition to the above, the domains of the *restricted* tasks
contained exactly three numbers, 1 together with any two consecutive numbers (e.g., 8 and 9). Restricted tasks were represented as triples which also designated the underlying rules.
Triples were always presented to subjects together with the
three input numbers; the pairs were printed on the left of a
sheet of paper and the inputs on the right. The rules underlying the *unrestricted* tasks were of two types. The *(an)* rules
simply involved multiplying the input numbers by a (i.e.,
$d = 0$). The *(an + d)* rules involved both multiplication by a
and addition of d.

Two h.o. generalization rules were identified. Both h.o.
rules act on restricted rules (triples) and generate output

rules of types an and $an + d$, respectively. A flow diagram for the more general Finite Differences (F) Rule is given in Figure 1. The Division (D) Rule is similar. Both h.o. rules partition the class of restricted rules into two equivalence classes consisting of an rules and $an + d$ rules, respectively. The D Rule only generates an rules, whereas the F Rule generates $an + d$ rules as well. (The D Rule may also be viewed as having a limited domain consisting of only those restricted rules in which the output associated with the number 1 equals the quotient of the output in one of the other pairs divided by its input.)

Subjects, design, and procedure: The 80 subjects were students in Grades 5 to 12 of Catholic and public schools of Philadelphia. They were run individually. Eight were eliminated because they were unable to do simple arithmetic computations. The experiment was also terminated early (to insure

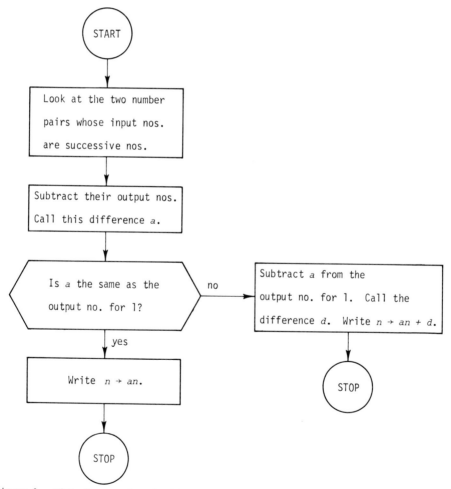

Figure 1. Flow diagram for the higher-order finite differences rule which acts on restricted rules and generates rules of the form $n \rightarrow an + d$.

equal numbers in experimental groups and save experimenter time)
with 12 more subjects who were able to solve *an* problems but not
an + d problems on the pretest (Phase 3 below).

Experiment II was also run in five phases. First, the
subject was presented with triples of number pairs and shown
how to interpret them. He was instructed "to write the output
that goes with each input according to the triple." The criterion was two correct solutions in succession. Second, the
experimenter introduced rules of the form $n \rightarrow an + d$, gave one
example of a general rule where $d = 0$ and one where $d > 0$, and
stated that for every triple there is a rule of the form
$n \rightarrow an + d$ that "fits" the triple. The subject was told: "A
general rule fits a triple if, when you use the rule on the
input numbers ... you get the same outputs as in the triple."
The subject was taught how to check whether a rule fits a triple
and practiced checking with four different rules, two *an + d*
and two *an*. Then the subject was presented in turn with six
pages, each containing a rule, a triple, and two to four inputs
not in the triple. He was told to "find what output goes with
each new input number according to the rule." This involved
first checking to determine whether the given rule fits the
triple and, if so, to use it to compute the output for each new
input. The criterion was four consecutive correct problems.

Just prior to the pretest the experimenter summarized for
the subject what he had learned. That is, there are two ways
to find the output for a given input of a triple: (1) look at
the triple to see what the output for that input is, and (2)
use a rule that fits the triple, to compute the output for the
input. The subject also was reminded how to check whether a
rule fit a triple; and, that, given a triple and a rule that
fits the triple, the outputs for new inputs can be computed via
the rule.

Third, the subject was given a pretest consisting of four
randomly sequenced transfer problems, two *an* and two *an + d*.
Each problem consisted of a triple and three new inputs (but no
rule). The subject was instructed to "find out what output goes
with each new input according to a rule ... that fits the triple." If the subject solved one but not both problems of type
an (an + d), he was given another problem of that type. If he
solved it, he was given the unsolved problem again. Under these
conditions, if he solved the original two problems, he was considered able to solve that type in general, otherwise not. When
a subject encountered difficulty on the pretest, the experimenter
explained that the task was difficult and provided encouragement.
Based on pretest results, subjects were categorized into three
classes: *None*--unable to solve either type of problem; *an*--able
to solve *an* but not *an + d* problems; and *an + d*--able to solve
both *an* and *an + d* problems. The *None* Class was randomly divided
into three groups: *Control* (C) (subjects receiving no h.o. rule

training), *Division* (D) (subjects taught the D Rule), and
Finite Difference (F) (subjects taught the F Rule). Class *an*
was randomly divided into treatment groups D and F. The *an + d*
subjects effectively knew the identified h.o. rules and were
unassigned.

Fourth, each subject assigned to Group D or Group F was
told, "I will teach you a procedure that can be used for some
kinds of triples to find a general rule ... that fits the
triple." On each h.o. task the subject was presented with a
triple and required to construct a rule that fit the triple.
A description of the appropriate h.o. rule was placed on a
stand in front of the subject and the experimenter worked through
two h.o. practice tasks with him. Then the subject was presented, in turn, with six more h.o. tasks and required to reach
a criterion of four correct solutions in a row. The Classes C
and *an + d* subjects received no h.o. training. (The latter
solved all pretest problems and effectively "tested out" of the
experiment.) Just prior to the posttest, the experimenter again
summarized what the subject had learned, adding for subjects in
the h.o. treatment groups: "You know a procedure that can be
used for some kinds of triples to find a general rule ... that
fits the triple ... refer to this procedure whenever you wish".
The h.o. rule remained in front of the subject during the posttest. Fifth, the posttest involved new transfer problems but
paralled the pretest in every respect.

2.2 RESULTS AND DISCUSSION
Of 60 subjects admitted, 40 received h.o. rules training.
The 10 subjects in Pretest Class *None* all failed both the *an* and
an + d problems on the pretest and the posttest. Those in Pretest Class *an + d* passed both types on both the pre- and posttests. The experimental results for the 40 other subjects also
were exactly as predicted. All 10 subjects in Groups D of Pretest Classes *None* and *an* were successful on the *an* problems of
the posttest but again failed the *an + d* problems. In addition,
all subjects in Groups F of these pretest classes were successful on both the *an* and *an + d* problems.

In short, subjects were successful on posttest problems if,
and only if, they knew how to solve the problems before entering
the experiment (given only the restricted rules) and/or they
were taught an appropriate h.o. rule.

3. DIAGNOSIS OF HIGHER-ORDER RULES

Experiments III and IV were conducted to determine the
feasibility of predicting the performance of individual subjects
on specific problems by assessing the subjects' knowledge relative to the h.o. generalization rules identified. Specifically,
could the algorithmic methods developed in Part 4 (Chapters 8

and 9) be used to determine which parts of the h.o. rules used
in Experiment II were available to individuals? And, could this
information be used to predict the performance of individual
subjects on new problems?

3.1 METHOD

The tasks and rules were as in Experiment II. The materials
were six booklets. Booklets 1 to 3 covered the same material as
Phases 1 and 2 of Experiment II. Materials for Phase 3, pretest
on criterion problems, and Phase 4, training on h.o. rules, were
eliminated. Booklets 4 and 5 were inserted in their place.
These booklets made it possible to assess knowledge relative to
the h.o. rules. Because outputs of h.o. rules are themselves
rules, Booklet 4 was used to provide instruction in how to write
rules of the form $n \rightarrow an + d$. Page 1 read, "to write a rule ...
in which we multiply the input number by 3 and add 4 to the
product, let n be the input number. To multiply n by 3, write
$3 \times n$. To add 4 to the product, write $3 \times n + 4$." Eight practice problems were given. Booklet 5 tested for the h.o. rules,
"On each page ... is a triple. Find and write ... a rule of the
form $n \rightarrow an + d$ that fits the triple." Four problems followed.
Two problems required use of an h.o. rule for deriving $n \rightarrow an$
rules and two problems for deriving $n \rightarrow an + d$ rules. Booklet
6 corresponded to Phase 6, the posttest.

Experiment III was run with 17 first-year algebra students
and Experiment IV, with 9 general math and 11 algebra students,
all from West Philadelphia. The students were enrolled in a
remedial mathematics class in summer school. In Experiment III,
Booklets 1 through 6 were administered during a 1-hour class
period. In Experiment IV, Booklets 1 to 4 were administered
on one day, and a short review booklet and Test Booklets 5 and
6 on the next. Both class periods were 40 minutes long. In
contrast to Experiment II, instructions were read to classes
instead of individuals. Each subject had to work at least four
problems correctly in each booklet. From 3 to 5 proctors were
available in each classroom. In scoring Test Booklets 5 and 6,
problems were divided into two categories, according to whether
an $an + d$ or an an rule was involved. If a subject got both
problems of one type in a booklet correct, he was considered
successful, otherwise not. Although Tests 5 and 6 both involved
h.o. rules, the difference between them is critical. Predictions
were based on the prior availability of appropriate h.o. rules.
A subject who could derive an, but not $an + d$, rules in Booklet
5, for example, was assumed able on Test Booklet 6 to solve only
transfer problems involving an rules.

3.2 RESULTS

The results of Experiments III and IV are summarized in
Table 3. In all cases, the number of correct, as opposed to

TABLE 3

Summary of Generalization Assessment Results

Group	No. successful on assessment Test (5)	Proportion correct predictions on transfer test (6)	No. of Ss not successful on assessment Test (5)	Proportion correct predictions on transfer Test (6)	Total no. of correct predictions	Overall percent correct predictions
Experiment III (Ns = 17)						
an problems	7	4/7	10	10/10	14	82
an + d problems	2	2/2	15	13/15	15	88
Experiment IV (Ns = 20)						
an problems	13	11/13	7	7/7	18	90
an + d problems	3	2/3	17	17/17	19	95
Combined (Ns = 37)						
an problems	20	15/20	17	17/17	32	86
an + d problems	5	4/5	32	30/32	34	92

Note: The numbers in parentheses refer to Booklets 5 and 6.

incorrect, predictions differed significantly from chance with
$p < .05$ for both an and an + d problems in Experiment III;
$p < .001$ and $p < .05$, respectively, for an and an + d problems
in Experiment IV; and $p < .001$ and $p < .005$, respectively, for
an and an + d problems in the combined study; exact probability,
Finney, 1948. Although the difference was not reliable, the
additional 20 minutes of study provided in Experiment IV appeared to increase precision of prediction on both an and an + d
problems (8 percent and 7 percent, respectively). Whether or
not the level of prediction could be further increased is not
clear, but this observation tends to support the notion that
results of such experiments may be expected to conform to prediction just to the extent that memory-free conditions are
realized (cf. Chapters 1 and 11).

3.3 DISCUSSION

Overall, the results of Experiments I and II provide strong
support for the postulated goal-switching control mechanism.
When the effects of memory are minimized, and a subject's goals
are known to the experimenter, availability of appropriate
higher- and lower-order rules appears to be both a necessary and
sufficient condition for solving transfer problems. Although
its importance was not emphasized, ability to determine whether
or not a given or derived rule satisfies a higher-level goal is
also crucial (Scandura, 1973).

*Moreover, as discussed above, the results of Experiment I
appear to rule out "stack-type" control mechanisms as viable
alternatives. Thus, in spite of the formal equivalence of goal
switching and stack-type mechanisms, there is an important psychological difference. Given the widespread adoption of stack-
type control mechanisms in psychological research (see Chapter
15), these results would seem to suggest the need for a careful
reappraisal of current theoretical assumptions.*

*The results of Experiments III and IV show further how
availability of h.o. rules may be determined through testing
(also see Chapters 8, 9, and 13) and used as a basis for explanation and prediction in problem solving. These results,
however, apply only in situations where memory and problem definition are not likely to be involved. Extension of the proposed mechanism to include memory, problem definition, etc.,
is given in Chapter 2 (cf. Scandura, 1973). Empirical testing
should be a first order of business.*

Another feature of this research which deserves mention is
the possibility of systematically identifying the basic rules
underlying a set of problems (cf. Chapter 3). In general, the
rules (including h.o. rules) underlying a set of problems may
be determined as follows:

1. Select a broad (finite) sample of problems in the set
and identify solution rules for each problem. These rules

provide a sufficient basis for solving not only the sampled problems but all other problems "like" them. The use of such rules corresponds to *reproductive* problem solving (Wertheimer, 1945) and, aside from relative complexity, to performance theories in computer simulation (e.g. Newell & Simon, 1972).

2. Identify parallels among the identified rules (e.g., successive applications of simple trading rules, or rules of the form *an + d*). These "parallels" indicate the presence of higher-order rules via which the solution rules may be constructed. The composite and simple-trading rules of Experiment I (from which the composite rules may be derived) and the generalization and restricted rules of Experiment II (from which the *an* and *an + d* rules may be derived) provide examples.

This type of analysis (of rule sets) may be repeated as many times as desired (cf. Chapters 2 and 14).

In general, the more basic rule sets obtained in this way make it possible, according to the postulated mechanism (Scandura, 1973), to solve a set of problems larger than originally envisioned and, thus provide a basis for *productive* problem solving (Wertheimer, 1945).

4.   EFFECT OF INCIDENTAL VARIABLES: AGE AND TRAINING CONDITIONS[3]

In one important sense, the traditional format used in the methods sections for Experiments I-IV was unfortunate. In reading them, one could easily lose sight of the fact that these studies (especially, Experiments I and II) are concerned first and foremost with the *universality* of the hypothesized control mechanism. As argued in Chapter 1, deterministic principles of this sort, which allow one to predict individual behavior in particular situations, can be demonstrated only under appropriate idealized conditions. Thus, in order to demonstrate universality of control it is essential that the subjects actually know and have available the requisite rules and that they actually try to solve the given problems. Training criteria, then, and conditions of testing, as used in these experiments, are not really independent variables in the usual sense. Rather, they are dependent in the sense that their values must be determined prior to the experiment proper.

Although pilot research is common throughout experimental psychology, and in many other areas of behavioral science, it plays a very special and unique role in deterministic research. It is an essential ingredient in ensuring appropriate idealized conditions. Recall, in Chapter 1, that there is an important distinction between structural or deterministic factors, which may be expected to hold universally under idealized conditions,

[3]The research reported in this section was conducted in collaboration with Ed Herman, Jasenka Pregrad, and Nancy Fox and was supported by National Institute of Health Grant 9185. The help of Diane Berson also is gratefully acknowledged.

and incidental factors, which may weaken deterministic effects
but which may not eliminate them entirely. The latter correspond to deviations from idealized conditions, and insofar as
human behavior is concerned, they fall into two general categories: environmental (e.g., training conditions) and internal
(e.g., degree of availability of rules).

Previous studies also leave open the question of whether
(some computational equivalent of) the hypothesized control
mechanism is innate, whether it is due to maturation, or whether
it is somehow learned. In either of the latter two cases, given
the results of Experiment I, the acquisition of goal switching
presumably takes place prior to about seven years of age. Obviously, however, there are many different facets to this difficult question and it will be a long time, if ever, before it can
be answered definitively.

The present study, which was conducted several years after
Experiments I-IV, had two major purposes. One purpose was to
determine whether the hypothesized control mechanism is available to children at ages 4, 5, and 6. These ages are especially
important in view of the well known changes in cognitive behavior
that take place within the age range 4-7 (e.g., the change from
Piaget's preoperational stage of development to concrete operations). The basic question is whether goal switching control
emerges gradually, along with other stage related changes, or
whether it is already available to four-year-olds.

The second major purpose of this research was to determine
the effects of an incidental variable, that corresponds to a
combination of deviations from idealized conditions. The inclusion of this variable was motivated by the possibility that what
is an appropriate level of idealization for one subject population may not be appropriate for another population. Thus, whereas the training criteria (corresponding to internal effects,
e.g., rule availability) and test conditions in Experiments I
and II may be adequate with children 7 years of age or older,
this may not be the case, say, with four-year-olds. Simply
showing a subject how "a higher-order rule can be used to derive
a solution rule" may be sufficient with a seven-year-old, for
example, but a four-year-old also may have to be reminded of the
kinds of problems to which solution rules apply (even though
they have previously learned how to solve such problems).

4.1 METHOD

Materials, rules, and tasks: The experimental materials,
rules, and tasks were similar but somewhat simpler than those
used in Experiment I. The tasks involved matching 2 x 3 inch
picture cards (of clowns, lions, bears, toys, etc.) with common
stimulus objects (e.g., rubber bands, pencils, bandaids, etc.).
Each picture card had a full color picture on one side and a
black and white xerox copy of the picture on the other side.

There were two kinds of simple (lower-order) tasks and solution rules, plain and fancy. Each solution rule was represented on a 5 x 8 inch white card with a black arrow in the center pointing from an input object on the left side (e.g., a rubber band) to an output picture card (e.g., lion) on the right. On the fancy rule cards, there was a star under the object on the left; on the right, the full color side of the picture card was face up. On the plain rule cards, only the object was present and the xerox side of the picture card was visible.

The experimental (lower-order) tasks consisted of a given (available) rule card with a matching object (with or without a star) below the rule card under the input object. The goal was to identify the appropriate picture card (by name or pointing), and to place it directly under the picture card on the rule card with the appropriate face up (e.g., xerox side up in the plain tasks).

The higher-order tasks involved changing given plain rule cards into corresponding fancy rule cards. The higher-order rule for accomplishing such tasks consisted of placing a given star under the stimulus object on the given rule card and turning the picture card over exposing the full colored side.

Subjects and design: The subjects were 46 four-year-old children, 57 five-year-olds, and 49 six-year-olds from day care centers and public schools in West Philadelphia. Within each age level, subjects were randomly assigned to idealized and nonidealized treatment groups. The children were run individually by three different experimenters (Diane Berman, Jasenka Pregrad, and Nancy Fox).[4]

After an intensive period of pilot research, we settled on two sets of training and test conditions and procedures. The procedures used in the nonidealized condition were similar (but not identical) to those used in Experiment I. (Note: Training and test conditions that are adequate for insuring idealized conditions with children 7 years of age or older may not be adequate with four- to six-year-old children.)

Nonidealized procedures: The subject was seated facing the experimenter at a right angle across a small, low table upon which the rule card rested. To help minimize distractions, all materials other than those actually presented for the subject's attention were kept on a higher table next to the experimenter, away from the subject.

Once seated at the game table, the subject was asked if he

---

[4]One experimenter tested 32 subjects in the idealized condition and 33 in the nonidealized condition, the second tested 32 and 33 children, respectively, and the third 12 and 10, respectively. All assignments were random, subject to both experimenter and subject availability, resulting in slightly unequal assignments to treatment groups. There were no significant differences attributed to experimenter so this factor is ignored in reporting the results.

or she wanted to play a game with the experimenter. Given the
subject's agreement, the experimenter presented a plain rule
card and explained how to use it. That is, stimulus objects
were placed on the game table below the rule card and the subject
was asked to tell the experimenter which picture went with the
"question" object and to place it beneath the rule picture card
on the game table, with the proper side facing up. This procedure was repeated, each time with a different rule card, until
the subject was able to use three consecutive rule cards to solve
corresponding problems without assistance. The number of rules
on which the subject required assistance was recorded.

After a subject reached criterion on the plain rules, the
same procedures and training criteria were used to teach him how
to interpret and use star rules. Next, the subjects were given
a pretest which consisted of a star question object and a plain
rule card, which the subject had never seen before. The starred
object was placed directly below the corresponding object on the
plain rule card. Each subject was given a star, that could be
used as desired, and also was told, "Even though the starred object is different (from that on the rule card) there is a way
to pick the picture card," that goes with the star object. The
subject then was asked which picture card he thought went with
the star object and was required, as before, to place the picture
card below the corresponding rule card, this time with the fancy
side up. In the 18 cases where the subject passed the pretest,
he was asked why he picked that picture card.

The subjects that failed the pretest were told, "We are
now going to learn how to change plain rules into rules with a
star and fancy picture. You can use this star. This rule shows
that (insert object name) goes with (insert xerox picture card
name). To change this rule into a rule with a star and a fancy
picture, you put the star under the (insert object name) and
turn the (insert picture name) over so that the fancy side is
showing."

After demonstrating how to make the change, the experimenter asked the subject to change the plain rule into a "rule
with a star and a fancy picture." New plain rules were presented until the subject was able to change three consecutive
plain rules into starred rules without assistance.

Finally, the posttest was administered in the same manner
as the pretest, again using a plain rule that the subject had
not seen before. In addition to the number of training trials
required and rights versus wrongs on the pre- and posttests, a
record was kept of the times needed for training and testing.
The procedures used by subjects in solving the pre- and posttests also were noted.

Idealized procedures: The materials and procedures used
in the idealized treatment were the same as the above with the
following exceptions: (1) The white rule cards were mounted on

an 8 x 11 inch piece of black construction paper that provided
a three inch black border on all sides. This border served as
a perceptual frame. To further concentrate the subjects attention, the experimenter said that "everything that matters in the
game happens here" (while outlining an imaginary circle on the
table with her hands). "You should only pay attention to this
space." Moreover, throughout the game, the experimenter closely
monitored the subject's activities during these and other instructions, and generally did everything within her capabilities
to ensure a high degree of attention. One subject had to be
eliminated from the experiments because he failed to cooperate.

(2) During the plain and star rule training, the subjects
were presented with negative as well as with positive instances.
In particular, during plain rule training it was emphasized that
plain rules "did not work" with star objects because the latter
were different from the rule object. Conversely, during starred
rule training, such rules were said not to work with plain objects. (This had the effect of more precisely identifying the
domains of the plain and star rules.) To achieve criterion,
subjects were required to respond correctly to three consecutive
positive and negative instances (i.e., they had to correctly
apply the rule to positive instances and to indicate that it
did not work with negative instances).

(3) The higher-order rule training was modified to take
advantage of the more prescriptive plain and star rule training.
Specifically, in addition to the plain rule card, a corresponding
star object was placed below the rule and the subject was asked,
"Does the rule tell you what picture goes with this (insert star
object name)?" Independent of what the subject said, the experimenter explained "You can change this rule into a rule with a
star and fancy picture that does tell you what picture goes with
this (insert star object name)." The remainder of the instruction
was as in the nonidealized condition.[5]

---

[5]On the posttest some subjects changed the plain rule into a star rule and
then stopped. (As far as we know no one stopped on the pretest.) In this case,
the experimenter would say "And?" or "And, what goes here?" (pointing to the spot
where the picture card was to go). There are at least two obvious reasons why a
subject might perform in this way. (1) The subject might simply misunderstand the
posttest question, confusing it with that given during the higher-order rule
training. In this case, restating the goal simple insures appropriate idealized
conditions. (2) The subject's processor may become overloaded in goal-switching
from the higher goal level. In this case again, the hint serves primarily to
insure memory-free conditions. Nonetheless, the latter possibility allows some
ambiguity in interpretation since it does not allow one to infer that control
automatically reverts to lower from higher level(s). (Where a cue is introduced,
only shifting up to a higher level goal need be fully automatic.) Unfortunately,
an exact record was not kept of how many times cues were introduced and/or needed.
Hopefully, future research will clarify the precise nature and importance of this
factor, and particularly whether or not idealized conditions can be arranged so as
to eliminate entirely the need for such cueing.

4.2 RESULTS AND DISCUSSION

The major results are summarized in Table 4. Notice especially that every one of the 65 subjects in the idealized condition who failed the pretest passed the posttest after receiving higher-order rule training. Where rules were both learned and available, and more generally where the effects of memory had been partialled out (of the experiment), age in the range from 4 to 6 had no effect on the ability to use these rules. In effect, four-year-olds as well as older children appear to use rules in a way that is consistent with the hypothesized control mechanism.

TABLE 4
Performance of Subjects by Age and Condition

Age	Performance on Pretest/Posttest	Idealized	Nonidealized
4	Fail/Pass	20	13
	Fail/Fail	0	8
5	Fail/Pass	24	16
	Fail/Fail	0	5
6	Fail/Pass	21	18
	Fail/Fail	0	4

In the nonidealized condition, on the other hand, 17 of 64 subjects failed the posttest even after higher-order rule training. The difference between idealized and nonidealized conditions in performance on the posttest was significant (χ^2 = 12.2, df = 1, p < .001). This difference suggests that conditions that are sufficient to insure idealization with one population of subjects (e.g., that of Experiment I) may not be sufficient with another population. In line with this expectation, the proportion of subjects in the nonidealized condition that passed the posttest decreased from 38 percent for four-year-olds to 24 percent and 18 percent, respectively, for five- and six-year-olds. Inspite of the better than two-to-one difference, however, this difference was not statistically significant.

On secondary measures, there was a small decrease with increasing age in the mean number of trials required to learn rules. These differences were significant in the case of the plain and higher-order rules ($F_{2, 126}$ = 4.98 and 4.50, p < .01 and .05, respectively). Similarly, as would be expected, training time was greater with the younger children and in the idealized condition (p < .01).

Insofar as the process of problem solving is concerned, all but 7 of the 112 subjects who received explicit overt training on the higher-order rules changed the plain rule into a star rule on the posttest before applying the rule to the given star object. Questioning after the posttest suggested that the others made the change mentally and did not bother to display the change overtly. Of those who passed the pretest, without the benefit of higher-order rule training, only 5 of 18 subjects changed the plain rule into a star rule. The others presumably used some computationally equivalent method to solve the pretest problem.

In addition, of the 17 subjects in the nonidealized condition who failed the posttest, after higher-order rule training, only one changed the plain rule into a star rule. In effect, almost all of the experimental subjects who actually learned and used the higher-order rule also solved the posttest problem. This is what one would expect if the hypothesized control mechanism were uniformly operative. Nonetheless, in some cases, the experimenter had to remind subjects of what the original posttest problem was after they had derived the star rule. Although the hint given (e.g., "And -") stopped considerably short of telling the subject what to do, the fact that one was needed at all leaves open the question of whether the control mechanism operates in an entirely automatic manner (cf. footnote 5). Given the well known and documented limitations on the ability of four- and five-year-old children to process information, we found it difficult to eliminate this cue entirely and to replace it with a methodology less subject to ambiguous interpretation. Hopefully this might be possible in future research.

REFERENCES

Bourne, L. E., Jr., Ekstrand, B., & Dominowski, R. *Psychology of thinking.* Englewood Cliffs, N.J.: Prentice-Hall, 1971.

Dunker, K. On problem-solving (L. S. Lees, trans.). *Psychological Monographs,* 1945, *58,* 198-311.

Finney, D. J. The Fisher-Yates test of significance in 2 x 2 contingency tables. *Biometrika,* 1948, *35,* 145-156.

Gagne, R. M. *The conditions of learning* (2nd ed.). New York: Holt, Rinehart, & Winston, 1970.

Greeno, J. G. The structure of memory and the process of solving problems. In R. Solso (Ed.), *Contemporary issues in cognitive psychology: Loyola symposium.* New York: Halsted-Wiley, 1973.

Newell, A., & Simon, H. A. *Human problem solving.* Englewood Cliffs, N.J.: Prentice-Hall, 1972.

Saugstad, P. Problem solving as dependent on availability of functions. *British Journal of Psychology,* 1955, *46,* 191-198.

Scandura, J. M. Role of rules in behavior: Toward an operational definition of what (rule) is learned. *Psychological Review,* 1970, *77,* 516-533.

Scandura, J. M. *Structural learning I: Theory and research.* New York: Gordon & Breach, 1973.

Wertheimer, M. *Productive thinking.* New York: Harper, 1945.

6
Retrieval, Problem Definition, and Rule Selection in Problem Solving[1]

Joseph M. Scandura

In experimental situations where memory, rule selection, and problem definition do *not* play a significant role, Scandura (Chapter 5) found that higher-order rules which operate on other rules, play an important role in deriving solution procedures for new problems. In any information processing system, however, whether human or otherwise, available knowledge (rules and higher-order rules) is not sufficient. Some type of executive control mechanism is also necessary in order to tell the processor what rules to use and when to use them. In effect, the rules presented to the experimental subjects during pretraining in the Scandura study tell only part of the story.

Fortunately, the results of this study show that the way in which children from about the age of 4 use the knowledge (rules and higher-order rules) available to them may be explained in terms of a simple "first approximation" goal-switching mechanism. On the other hand, the use of knowledge in that study could not be explained in terms of stack-type control mechanisms in which available rules are tested and applied consecutively. (The latter correspond to formal systems and to the type of production systems used in Newell & Simon, 1972; see Chapter 5.) It is possible, of course, that stack-type mechanisms might be uniformly available to older children and adults. But, the obtained results suggest that only the goal-switching mechanism (or some computational equivalent) can be assumed to be universally available to children above the age of about 4.

The adequacy of this control mechanism in other situations, however, remains untested (undemonstrated) in at least three senses. First, we do not know whether the first approximation goal-switching mechanism is sufficient *even in a generative/ computational sense* to explain the use of knowledge in situations

[1]This research was supported by the National Institute of Health Grant 9185.

265

where something other than simple rule derivation is involved
(e.g., where rule selection, retrieval, etc. enter). Second,
we do not know whether the first approximation mechanism can be
modified in a natural way so as to account for behavior in both
old (rule derivation) and new (e.g., rule selection) situations.
Further, we do not know whether or not there are other equally
viable (parsimonious) mechanisms that also could account for
such behavior. Third, even assuming a control mechanism that
is adequate in a generative sense, we would not know whether it
is behaviorally viable. While always crucial in psychological
research, the question of behavioral adequacy takes on added
import in the present case where we seek deterministic (universal) effects.

In this chapter, which is a sequel to Chapter 5, three
additional aspects of problem solving are considered:

1. What are the mechanisms by which subjects retrieve information in problem solving (under memory-free conditions)?

2. How do subjects come to understand problem statements
and define underlying problems (i.e., break them down into subproblems) before attempting to solve them?

3. Why is it, when a subject knows (and has available) two
or more rules for solving a given problem, he chooses the rule
that he does?

In dealing with each type of situation, we first determined,
on generative/computational grounds, whether the proposed first
approximation mechanism of Chapter 5 is adequate as it stands.
Where it was inadequate (or where there were questions concerning applicability), alternative mechanisms were proposed and
tested. This approach to the problem seemed advisable because
of the sequential nature of the three questions above. Furthermore, some of the required changes (in mechanisms) were subtle
and could easily have been overlooked had we skipped directly
to proposed experiments.

As in Chapter 5, all of the experiments were run under
memory-free conditions. That is, measures were taken to help
ensure, to the extent possible, that all of the information that
was supposed to be immediately available to the subject was indeed available. For example, mnemonics were introduced where
feasible and made readily available to subjects. In addition,
serious attempts were made to keep processing load within the
subject's capacity. This was important because processing
capacity otherwise could interact with proposed control mechanisms thereby confounding results and making them more difficult
to interpret. In this case, as a minimum, we could no longer
expect to obtain deterministic results. (Note: Recall from
Chapters 1 and 5, Section 4 that idealized conditions ordinarily
can only be approached in varying degrees, and thus constitute
independent, manipulable variables.)

In spite of whatever precautions might be taken, processing

capacity is almost certain to influence behavior in more complicated problem-solving situations. With this in mind, a fourth
study was conducted to help determine the limits of memory-free
research and to provide information concerning possible generalizations of the control mechanism that might be necessary in
more complex applications. This study involved problem situations in which more than one type of process was involved.

1. RULE RETRIEVAL

During the past several years, there has been an increasing
amount of research on memory generally (e.g., Anderson & Bower,
1973; Rumelhart, Lindsay, & Norman, 1972) and, to a lesser extent, on memory in problem solving (e.g., Greeno, 1973; Scandura,
1973, 1974; Voorhies, 1973). Most contemporary memory theorists,
with an information-processing orientation, believe that memory
units can be represented in terms of relational nets/structures,
and I am no exception (cf. Chapter 2). Retrieval from such nets
takes various forms, including searching through networks node
by node (Anderson & Bower, 1973), and reconstructing needed
elements (Rumelhart et al., 1972) from available properties.
On the other hand, the traditional distinction between
permanent and working memory disappears in my formulation. The
only memory units which are assumed to affect behavior are those
that are available in working memory. This alternative view is
accomplished by allowing working memory to contain rules/networks
of arbitrary complexity (cf. Scandura, 1973, Chapter 10; 1974;
Nahinsky, 1974), including what may otherwise be called retrieval
rules and (global) networks on which they operate.
The central aim of this research, stated simply, was to
determine whether the first approximation control mechanism is
sufficiently general to allow for retrieval. At a strictly
analytical level, the answer appears to be "yes". Retrieval in
the structural learning theory consists of extracting information (possibly itself a subnetwork/rule) which is embedded in
an available relational net/rule. In effect, instead of operating on structures (e.g., classes of available rules that are
often but not necessarily components) and generating (deriving)
new rules, the higher-order (retrieval) rule involved in retrieval operate on classes of available, more comprehensive struc-
tures/networks/rules and extract subportions of them.
Thus, in situations where one wants to retrieve an item
that is not immediately available, one can envisage checking
available (retrieval) rules to see if they apply to some comprehensive and available network, and contain the goal in their
range. Or, where needed, of course, control could go up additional levels to allow for the possibility of deriving new retrieval rules. (The reader may wish to check the first approximation mechanism described in Chapter 5 by applying it to the
rules described below.)

To summarize, the results of Chapter 5 demonstrate the
prior and universal availability of the first approximation control mechanism in the context of rule derivation (from about the
age of 4), in particular with respect to higher-order rules for
combining component rules and for generalization by means of
induction or analogy (Chapter 5). As argued above, this mechanism also appears to be analytically (computationally) sufficient for dealing with retrieval, the extraction of information
from more comprehensive wholes.

Nonetheless, it would be dangerous to assume without behavioral testing that the differences between rule derivation
and rule retrieval can safely be ignored. Although the only
analytic differences involve rules (and not the assumed mechanism), these differences are qualitative in nature (e.g., one
combines; the other extracts). It is not at all certain that
both types of rules may be assumed to interact *deterministically*
in the same way--especially with seven-year-old children.

The simple demonstration experiments described below were
designed to determine the prior availability and behavioral
adequacy of the first approximation mechanism in a retrieval
(extraction) context. Toward this end, the networks that include the to-be-recalled items were built into working memory.
This constitutes an essential part of the idealized conditions
required for a fair test of the hypothesis. (Note: The study
below on rule retrieval and derivation implicitly deals with the
process by which networks may be activated in working memory.)

1.1   EXPERIMENT I

Method, tasks, and materials: The experimental materials
were identical to those used in Experiment I of Chapter 5. As
before, the tasks involved trading stimulus objects of one kind
(e.g., red chips) for response objects of another (e.g., pencils). There also were two kinds of rules, *simple* A → B rules
and *composite* A → B → C rules, for solving such tasks.

In Chapter 5, the set of compatible (A → B, B → C) pairs
of simple rules comprised the domain of a higher-order rule that
mapped such pairs into corresponding composite A → B → C rules.
This higher-order rule was used to define a second, higher-order
kind of task in which the goal was to devise a composite
A → B → C rule for effecting a given kind of trade. For example,
the goal might be to construct a composite rule for converting
caramels into pencils given the rules denoted "n caramels →
n + 2 white chips" and "n white chips → n + 1 pencils."

In this study, the higher-order task and rule were just the
opposite. That is, given an A → B → C rule, the higher-order
task was to decompose the composite rule, in particular, to
retrieve the simple B → C rule embedded in it. The higher-order
rule takes composite A → B → C rules, like that shown at the
bottom of Figure 1, and folds the B → C cards under, thereby

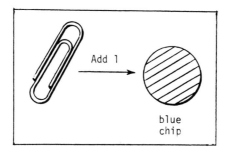

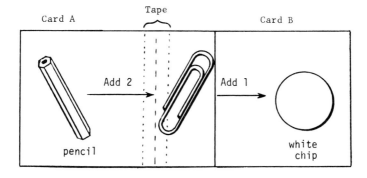

Figure 1. Sample of simple and composite rule cards used in trading game experiments.

exposing the corresponding simple A → B rules.

Subjects, design, and procedures: The subjects were 20 elementary school boys and girls in kindergarten and first grade at the Lea School in West Philadelphia who were trained and tested individually.

As in Experiment I of Chapter 5, each subject was taught to interpret the simple rule cards and to make trades using the rules represented by the cards. The subjects also were trained on the composite rule cards in a similar manner. They were shown how to make trades in two steps and were given practice in making them. As before, training continued until the subject was able to interpret three consecutive, arbitrary composite rule cards and to apply each rule in three instances.

Next came the transfer pretest. Each subject was presented with a composite A → B → C rule card he had never seen before and was told, "Here is a rule for trading ____(A) for ___(C), using ___(B)." The subject was then presented with some A objects and asked to trade them for B objects. (The subject had never before seen the required A → B card.) The subject was given all of the time he required (usually between 3 to 5 minutes). Then, the subject was presented with a second (new) task of the same type.

Seven subjects who failed at least one task on the pretest were then trained on the identified higher-order retrieval rule. Specifically, they were taught how to obtain an A → B rule from a composite A → B → C rule by folding the B → C card under. Retrieval rule training took only between 3 and 7 minutes, with an average of 5 minutes, much of which was spent giving the student instructions.

Finally, the seven failure subjects were given a transfer posttest, which involved new tasks, but otherwise was identical to the pretest.

Results and discussion: Thirteen of the 20 subjects tested solved both A-B transfer tasks on the pretest. Of the other 7 subjects, 4 succeeded on one pretest problem. (This was the only time, in any of our experiments, that more than a rare subject succeeded on one pre- or posttest problem and failed on the other. Whether this was due to personal idiosyncracies of the subjects--they were younger than usual, our instructions and procedures, and/or real sequence effects, I cannot say with certainty.)

After retrieval rule training, 6 of the 7 failure subjects were successful on both posttest tasks. The seventh subject succeeded on the first posttest trade but failed the second as he had originally done in the pretest.

1.2 EXPERIMENT II

The results of the above experiment suggested that the transfer tasks were too easy for a majority of the subjects.

Moreover, given the (small number of) inconsistencies during testing, there is some question as to whether the training or test conditions achieved the required degree of idealization. For one thing, these conditions were not nearly as exacting as those used with four-, five-, and six-year-olds in the study of incidental factors reported in Chapter 5, Section 4. Consequently, a second experiment was performed, this time using slightly older children (in the same age range as those used in Experiment I of Chapter 5) and a retrieval rule that was less likely to be already available to the subjects.

Method: The experimental materials involved simple A-B tasks and rules as in Experiment I. This time, however, a different letter was printed on the back of each rule card. This letter was called the *name of the card.* In addition, there was a 5 x 5 (row by column) chart in which the entries were names of rules for converting corresponding row labels (e.g., pencils) into column labels (e.g., paper clips). No element could be traded for itself so there were 20 entries; the main diagonal was blank.

The subjects were 16 elementary school children between the ages of 8 and 9 at the Lea Elementary School in West Philadelphia. They were run individually.

Training on how to interpret the simple A → B rule cards progressed as above. It was also emphasized that trades could not be made without using a rule. This was done, for example, by placing two blue chips on the table and asking the subject to trade them for rubber bands. Initially, most subjects responded by placing a random number of rubber bands on the table, so the experimenter emphasized that such a trade could not be made without a rule.

In addition, the subject was told that each rule card had a letter printed on the back. Then the subject was shown the chart and told, "This chart contains the names of all of the rule cards. If you ever want a rule card, tell me the name and I will give it to you." To make sure the subject understood, he was asked to pick a name; the experimenter gave the subject the corresponding rule card and told him what kinds of trades the rule could be used for. (This latter instruction was redundant since the subject had already been trained on how to interpret rule cards.)

Next, the subject was given a pretest, involving a new task. In the task, the subject was presented with some A objects and asked to trade for B objects. The experimenter added, "If you can figure out how to use the chart to find a rule you need to make the trade, you can ask me for it by saying its name." (In the one case where a subject was successful, she was given a new, second pretest task.)

As one might expect, all 16 subjects failed the pretest and were trained on how to use the chart. The experimenter taught each subject to identify the needed letter name by first placing one finger on the row label, corresponding to the given (input) A objects and moving it across the chart until he came to the column labeled with the goal B objects. The subject was required to state the name of the rule needed to solve five consecutive A-B tasks. Training took between 5 and 10 minutes.

The posttest involved two new tasks but, otherwise, was identical to the pretest.

Results: After training on the higher-order rule, all subjects passed both posttest tasks. These results suggest that although retrieval requires different kinds of higher-order rules than rule derivation (i.e., extraction rather than construction rules), the same control mechanism suffices for using both.

2.   PROBLEM DEFINITION (SUBGOAL FORMATION)

Subgoal formation plays a central role in most contemporary theories of problem solving (e.g., Newell & Simon, 1972; Greeno, 1973; also see Scandura, 1973, p. 348). Indeed, one of the main features of problem solving by individual subjects is the tendency to break given problems into subproblems and then to attack the subproblems in turn. Confronted with an A-C pretest, as in Chapter 5, for example, subjects might break it up into a pair of A-B, B-C subproblems, solve the A-B subproblem, and then solve the B-C subproblem. Although the data of that study did not address the point directly, it appeared that some of the subjects who were successful on the pretest may in fact have solved the A-C problem in this way. (This was suggested, for example, by children who paused for a moment before solving the A-B subproblem, and who paused *again* before solving the associated B-C subproblem.)

This was not true, however, of those subjects in the study who were initially unsuccessful on the A-C problems. It is unlikely that in attacking the problems they formed subproblems. If they had, they likely would have been successful. Since they had learned to solve simple A-B (B-C) problems, they would (according to the proposed control mechanism) be able to solve each subproblem directly. On the posttest problems, after training on higher-order composition rules, the initially unsuccessful subjects appeared to derive (learn) new composite A → B → C rules before attempting to solve the problems. That is, the subjects slid the A → B and B → C rule cards together before attempting to solve the A-C problem.

Why this apparent discrepancy? Do subjects automatically break problems into subproblems, or does subgoal formation, like the derivation of solution rules, depend on what the subject knows or has learned?

The present study was only a first attempt to help clarify the processes involved. In particular, I wanted to find out

simply whether young children, who were otherwise unable to do
so, could be successfully trained to break problems of a given
type into corresponding subproblems. And, if so, would they be
able to use such knowledge to solve new problems of this type
without explicit training (i.e., without being taught a control
mechanism for combining their available knowledge)? In effect,
problem definition rules were taught in lieu of higher-order
derivation rules.

Incidentally, there is an analogy between breaking problems
into subproblems and interpreting problem descriptions. Thus,
when presented with problem descriptions (the givens), most
people intuitively understand that they will have to first understand these descriptions and then solve the underlying problems. In each case the overall goal is to solve the problem
defined by the given description. In this type of problem
situation, with most school-age children (age 7 and up) it can
reasonably be assumed that the subjects will define a given
problem by breaking it down into a pair of subproblems: First
interpret the problem statement (description) and then solve the
subproblems so defined. (The inability of many young children
to properly understand problem descriptions may be one major
source of difficulty in running experiments with younger
children.)

Interpreting problem statements also is directly analogous
to the situation the scientist finds himself in when formulating
problems. The scholar is confronted with a complex of internal
stimulation and stimulation from the real world, and has the
goal of imposing order on this complex. In this case, the subject first identifies problems implied by the complex and only
then attempts to solve them.

2.1 EXPERIMENT III

Method, tasks, and materials: The experimental materials
were similar to those used in the retrieval study.

In addition to the rule cards, there were corresponding
problem statements. Statements of A-B problems consisted of the
names of the stimulus and goal objects, with an arrow drawn between them; they were printed on the backs of corresponding
A → B rule cards (e.g., "pencil → chip"). Statements of A-B-C
problems were printed on separate cards containing the names of
the stimulus (A) and goal (C) objects, with an arrow between
them, and the words "use B" over the arrow

(e.g., "pencil $\xrightarrow{\text{use B}}$ rubber band").

Subjects, design, and procedure: The subjects were 21
elementary school children in the fourth grade between the ages
of 8 and 10 at the Lea Elementary School in West Philadelphia.
They were run individually.

As before, the subjects were told that they were going to
play a trading game with the experimenter. Each subject was
first shown an A-B problem statement and a set of stimulus A

objects positioned directly below A on the statement card. The
subject was told, "This card means that you are to trade A for
B." The subjects were shown several A-B problem statement cards,
with corresponding stimulus objects, and were required to identify the underlying problems. Given the problem statement card
"Toothpicks → Erasers", and a set of toothpicks, for example,
the subject was required to describe the problem (trade erasers
for toothpicks), simultaneously pointing or otherwise indicating
that he understood the significance of what he was saying. The
criterion was at least three consecutive correct responses to
different problem statement cards without prompting by the
experimenter.

Then the subjects were taught how to solve A-B problems.
Given the toothpicks-to-erasers problem, for example, and after
the subject defined the problem as above, the experimenter said,
"To find out how to do any simple (A-B) problem, turn the card
over." The experimenter simultaneously turned the card, pointed
to the exposed A → B rule, described its meaning, and provided
the subject with practice in using it as in the previous study.
This included training on how to distinguish between problems
where a given rule could and could not be used. Training continued until the subject was able to define arbitrary A-B problem statements, turn over the statement cards (exposing the
corresponding rules), and use the rule to solve the A-B problem
without prompting by the experimenter. Criterion was set at
three consecutive successes. (In turning cards, the subject was
required to align the stimulus and response objects with the
input and output, respectively, on the rule card.)

Next came the pretest. The subject was presented with a
pair of compatible simple problem statement cards A-B and B-C
and a composite A-C (using B) problem statement card with a set
of A objects directly beneath A on the card. The A-B and B-C
cards were randomly placed on the periphery. The subject was
told, "Here is a new kind of problem, a long (composite) problem
card ... trade A for C using B. I have not shown you how to
solve long problems like this but perhaps you can figure out
how to solve it." The subject's strategy in attempting to solve
the problem was noted. Particular attention was paid to whether
the subject used a subgoal procedure (i.e., used one simple
A → B rule at a time) or some other method of attack--for example, turned both cards over and combined them to form a composite rule before using either simple rule.

The subjects who succeeded on the pretest, and half of
those who failed (randomly determined), were presented immediately with another pretest problem exactly as before. This data
was used to determine test reliability and, in the case of the
failure subjects, to provide a control group.

Following the pretest, all of the subjects were trained on
a procedure for defining composite (long) problem statements.

During training, the subject was presented with long problem statements and asked leading questions designed to help the subject learn how to break A-C (using B) problem statements into A-B, B-C statements. Progressively more help was provided until every subject eventually succeeded in replacing long problem statement cards with A-B and B-C statement cards and could explain that the latter statements were to be considered in order. Initially, the experimenter asked the subject if he could find the trick for solving the problem. Increasing numbers of successes were observed as the experimenter in turn: explained that composite problems can be broken down into two simple problems; replaced the composite problem card with the simple A-B problem card so that the A objects were directly below A on the card; asked, "What will you get after you solve it?" (B.) "Where will they be?"; made the trade in front of the subject but without turning over the cards or showing him the rule, placing the correct number of B under the B on the A-B card; asked what had to be done next. (Trade C for B.) Whenever the subject failed to answer a question correctly during training, the experimenter gave the correct response and went on to the next question. Additional long problems were presented in turn, with the subject being asked to tell how he could do the problem, until the subject defined three composite problem statements in a row in terms of A-B, B-C subproblems. The subject never actually solved a long problem, or saw an A → B or B → C rule.

After training, the experimenter reviewed what had been learned: (1) how to break long problem statements into two simple problem statements; and (2) how to solve easy A-B (B-C) problem statements--one practice problem on each was provided.

Finally, the subject was given a new posttest problem in the same manner as on the pretest.

Results and discussion: Of the 20 subjects who failed on the pretest, 18 succeeded on the transfer posttest after training on the higher-order subproblem rule, 9 from the single pretest group and 9 from the double pretest group. The double pretest group served as a control group; all 10 subjects in this group who failed the first pretest (long) problem also failed the second. Practice on long problems, without training, did not improve performance.

The one subject (of 21) who solved the pretest problem turned the A-B card over first, performed the trade, and then did the same with the B-C card. This sequence of events suggests that this subject spontaneously introduced B as a subgoal. In pilot studies using almost identical procedures during the pretraining, three other subjects (two fifth-graders) passed the pretest. Two subjects used strategies identical to the one above but the third turned both cards over before trading. The latter strategy is consistent with the hypothesis that the subject: (1) recognized the applicability of a higher-order composition

rule, (2) adopted the domain goal of retrieving a pair of compatible ⟨ A → B, B → C ⟩ rules and turned over the given cards
(cf. Section 4 on Multiple Processes), (3) used the higher-order
composition rule (perhaps implicitly) to generate an A → B → C
rule (cf. Chapter 5), and (4) applied the composite rule to solve
the problem. In short, rule retrieval and derivation, rather
than subgoal formation, may have played the primary role. This
observation is significant in that it suggests that both processes may play a role in spontaneous problem solving. As one
might expect, in view of their generally higher ability level,
the four subjects who succeeded on the pretest (even though they
too received training and the posttest) took an average of 20
minutes in the experiment, whereas the single and double pretest
failure subjects took 32 and 43 minutes, respectively.

On the posttest, all subjects who succeeded did so as expected. They (1) replaced the A-C composite problem statement
card with A-B and B-C problem statement cards, (2) solved the
A-B problem, (3) moved the B under the B-C problem card, and
(4) solved the B-C problem. The subject in the double pretest
group who failed, did not turn over the A-B card. Instead, she
replaced the A objects with an identical number of B. The experimenter said, "How do you know that's the right number of B?"
The subject then said, "Oh! Turn the card over," and proceeded
to solve the composite problem correctly. A reasonable interpretation is that, in spite of special precautions taken during
the experiment (e.g., reviewing what had been learned just prior
to the posttest), the subject initially misinterpreted the posttest problem to mean "Show me how you can solve... ."

The behavior of the other subject who failed was harder to
explain. This subject turned over the A-B card, traded correctly, moved the B under the B-C card, turned it over but seemed
confused as to what to do next. Furthermore, after she had
placed an arbitrary number of C on the table (and thereby failed), the experimenter reminded her that this was a simple problem, but the subject still did (or could) not finish the problem.

Concluding comment: This study represents only a simple
demonstration that subjects can solve (classes of) problems by
breaking them down into subproblems, and more specifically, that
otherwise naive young children can be taught rules for accomplishing this. The study says relatively little about the type
of control mechanism needed to effect problem solving in such
situations. In particular, the first-approximation mechanism,
as such, says nothing about forming subproblems. It tells what
happens once a problem has been defined and adopted but not how
or when given problems are broken down into subproblems. Given
that subjects use rules to break problems into subproblems, the
major question that remains is how such rules and others interact in problem solving.

As a minimum, any adequate control mechanism must address

itself to the question of why subjects sometimes solve problems
by deriving solution rules and sometimes by breaking problems
down into subproblems. Given an A-C problem situation, for example, where requisite (sufficient) higher-order derivation and
subproblem rules are both available, why does a person solve the
problem one way rather than the other?

Possible answers to this question would appear to fall into
three major categories: (1) people first attempt to derive solution rules, (2) people first attempt to break problems into subproblems, (3) what people do depends inextricably on the problem
situation and other knowledge that happens to be available.

In the first case, for example, the first approximation
mechanism could be generalized so that when goal switching fails,
the subject attempts to break the problem into subproblems. In
particular, suppose that a subject knows *all* of the relevant
rules, *including* both a higher-order composition rule and an
appropriate subproblem rule. How, given this generalized mechanism, would the subject solve a given A-C problem (assuming that
it is understood)? According to the goal switching mechanism
above, the subject would simply derive a higher-order A → B → C
rule, and then apply that composite rule to solve the A-C problem. This would be indicated as in Experiment I (Chapter 5),
for example, by a child who first slides together available
A → B and B → C rule cards before attempting to solve the A-C
problem. According to this mechanism, therefore, when a choice
is available, the subject will opt for deriving a solution rule.
(According to this view, subjects will break problems into subproblems *only* where subproblem rules are available and derivation rules are not.)

Another (parsimonious) control mechanism would have the
subject first break the A-C problem down into A-B and B-C subproblems. Then, and only then, would the first approximation
control mechanism take over, as the subject solves each subproblem in turn. This would be indicated, for example, by a
child who pauses for a moment or so, before solving the A-B subproblem, and who pauses *again* before solving the corresponding
B-C subproblem. Such a mechanism effectively would involve a
generalization of the first approximation control mechanism in
which problems are first broken down into subproblems (where
appropriate subproblem rules are available) before goal switching
comes into play (cf. Scandura, 1973, p. 348).

A third possibility would be to generalize the first approximation control mechanism to allow higher-level goals to be
satisfied by solution *plans,* consisting of sequences of subproblems, as well as by prospective solution rules. Where both
a higher-order derivation rule and a (higher-order) subproblem
rule are available, of course, the subject would still have to
make a choice. In this case, it would be necessary to further
modify the control mechanism, for example, as proposed in Section 3, to allow for selections among two or more available

rules at any given goal level. The generalized control mechanism proposed in Chapter 2 is based on the third possibility.

Most of the above, of course, is largely speculation and a good deal of further research will be needed both to refine the issues and to distinguish among the possible alternatives. Nonetheless, the results of the following study provide some indirect support for the third, and most flexible, type of control.

3. RULE SELECTION[2]

Previous research on preferences (e.g., Cason, 1975; Suchman & Trabasso, 1966; Wittrock & Hill, 1968) has involved probabilistic inferences. For example, Suchman and Trabasso (1968) found that younger children on the average prefer color whereas older children prefer form.

In line with the structural learning theory (Scandura, 1973), it is hypothesized here that selections among two or more applicable rules in problem solving are made via higher-order selection rules; deterministic predictions may be possible just to the extent that such selection rules are known or can be determined. Selection rules apply to pairs (or more) of rules, which apply in given problem situations, and select single rules. (As argued in Scandura, 1973, selections are based on internal and/or external criteria associated with task situations that are over and above those essential for a solution rule's applicability. For example, it is possible to sum arithmetic number sequences by both simple addition and via the formula $((A + L)/2)N$ where A is the first term, L the last, and N the number of terms. Yet, given the series $1 + 3 + 5 + \ldots + 99$, anyone who knew both would almost certainly prefer the latter, among other reasons, because it is faster.)

In comparison to the derivation of solution rules (Chapter 5), however, the study of rule selection poses two additional complications. First, empirical testing is more difficult because subjects almost invariably have learned some (idiosyncratic) selection rules that apply, irrespective of whether the experimental problems are familiar or novel. This prior availability of selection rules makes the presence or absence of crucial selection rules relatively difficult to manipulate in experimental settings since the manipulated rules must necessarily compete with previously acquired (perhaps idiosyncratic) selection tendencies (rules).

Second, on the theoretical side, the first approximation control mechanism (Chapter 5) is not (computationally) adequate to account for rule selection. Where two or more solution rules

[2]This experiment was conducted in collaboration with Francine Endicott.

are available, the mechanism says that one of the rules will be applied, but not which one. (Insofar as first approximation control is concerned, predictions are nondeterministic, rather than probabilistic, see Scandura, 1973, Chapter 8. This means that we know with a certainty that one of the two rules will be used but that no preferences beyond this are specified.)

There is, however, a very natural way to modify this mechanism so that it applies not only in the case of rule derivation and rule retrieval, but in rule selection as well. Specifically, the first approximation mechanism may be modified so that a rule is applied at a given goal level only where exactly one available rule applies (Scandura, 1973). In particular, if two or more rules apply, control is assumed to move to a higher-level goal just as when no rules apply. Otherwise, the mechanism is assumed to work as before.

Moreover, this modified mechanism may be substituted for the first-approximation mechanism in the third generalized mechanism hypothesized in Section 2. The result is a mechanism that applies in an analytic/computational sense in each of the situations considered (above). The behavioral viability of this, or of any of the other mechanisms, of course, must be determined empirically.

The more exacting selection control mechanism proposed here provides a potential basis for overcoming the empirical complication mentioned above. In particular, because two or more (i.e., manipulated and idiosyncratic) selection rules may apply at a higher-goal level, control may have to shift upward one additional level.

In order to test the above more exacting mechanism, therefore, it would be necessary to include, among the experimentally manipulated rules, a selection rule for selecting from among the selection rules. One such selection rule might be characterized by the simple instruction, "When possible, use the selection rule I taught you."

The purpose of the experiment described below was to determine the viability of the above modification of the first-approximation mechanism; the experiment was designed basically as a simple demonstration. (None of the alternative mechanisms that I have been able to devise are nearly as simple and general as that under consideration. If the data had turned out negative, it would nevertheless have been necessary to consider alternatives.) An incidental purpose of the experiment was to explore the feasibility of identifying via pretesting the selection rules used by individual subjects.

3.1 EXPERIMENT IV

Method, tasks, and materials: The experimental materials were based on the trading tasks used in the previous studies. For each task, two kinds of rules were identified; both were variants of the simple +m rules used earlier. One kind was called, "Match first, then add" (MA). MA rules involved: (1) using output objects to form a one-to-one correspondence with the n given input objects, and (2) adding m more output objects. In the other kind of rule, "Add first, then match" (AM), these steps were reversed. The two kinds of rules are illustrated in Figure 2 for a trading game task, with n = 3, m = 2. The ⊗ refer to given inputs, ◯ to added inputs, and — to outputs.

In addition to these two kinds of rules, four selection rules were introduced: (1) *Alternate beginning with MA* (Alt-MA). Description to the subject: "First use MA, then use AM, next use MA, next use AM, and so on;" (2) *Alternate beginning with AM* (Alt-AM); (3) If the input is candy, use MA; else use AM (C-MA); (4) If candy, use AM; else MA (C-AM).

Subjects, design, and procedure: The subjects were 12 individually tested second- and third-grade pupils in one private and one public school in West Philadelphia.

At the beginning of the experiment, the experimenter introduced the tasks as before, adding, "I'll teach you two ways to play the games." Then the experimenter taught the subject how to solve the tasks, first using one rule (AM or MA) and then the other. The order of presentation of the two kinds of rules was randomized over subjects. A sign (e.g., Match Add) was placed above a generalized command statement (e.g., Add 2) to indicate which rule was to be used on a given trial (see Figure 2).

Each subject worked several tasks using both kinds of rules. The experimenter helped the subject, by commenting and asking leading questions, to see that the same number of output objects was obtained, irrespective of whether rule AM or MA was used. This procedure was continued until the experimenter was satisfied that the subject could correctly use the rules indicated by the signs and that the subject was aware that both kinds of rules yielded the same number of output objects. At this point, additional practice was provided on several new trading game tasks. On each, the rule to be used was stipulated.

The pretest was given next. It consisted of 3 sets of new trading game tasks of 4, 3, and 2 tasks respectively. The subjects were told: "Each of the 2 kinds of rules you have just learned will work on these problems." Each task was presented together with 2 rule signs and the subject was required to indicate which rule he used (this was verified by observation).

Next, subjects were randomly assigned to one of 4 selection rule treatment groups. The experimenter presented a card describing the indicated selection rule and explained how to use it. The subject was required to indicate which of the two possible rules should be used (but not to work the task) on each of 3 sets of tasks consisting of 4, 3, and 2 tasks respectively.

The posttest involved new tasks, but was otherwise identical to the pretest, except that the selection rule card used during

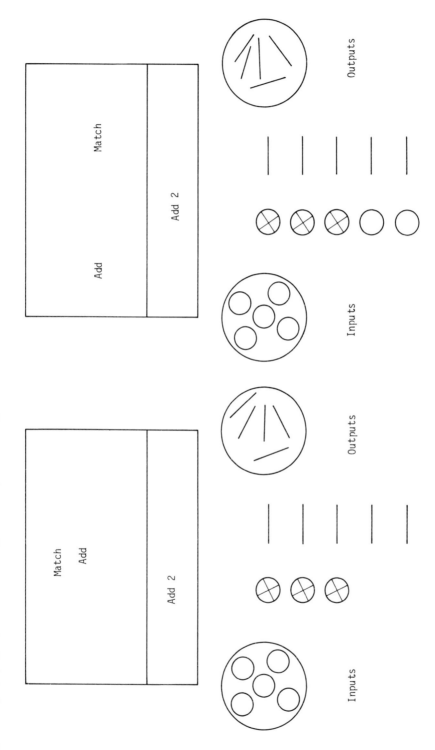

Figure 2. MA and AM rules employed in Rule Selection study.

training was made available.

The experiment was conducted over 2 sessions. The first session included the procedure up to the pretest. The second session began with a practice-review of the AM and MA rules.

Results and discussion: The results are summarized in Table 1, including selection rules that appeared to be operative during the pretest, the selection rules taught (treatment), and the selection rules that were operative during the posttest.

TABLE 1
Summary of Results

Subject	Pretest	Treatment	Posttest
1	?	C-MA	C-MA
2	AM	C-AM	C-AM
3	?	Alt-MA	Alt-MA
4	?	Alt-AM	Alt-AM 8/9
5	?	C-AM	C-AM
6	Alt	Alt-MA	Alt-MA
7	?	Alt-AM	Alt-AM Sets 1 and 2
			Alt-MA Set 3
8	?	Alt-MA	Alt-MA
9	?	C-MA	C-MA
10	MA	Alt-AM	Alt-AM
11	Alt-MA Set 1		
	AM Set 2		
	Alt-AM Set 3	C-AM	C-AM
12	Alt-MA Set 1		
	? Sets 2 and 3	C-MA	C-MA

Note: ? means that it was unclear what selection rules subjects were using.

Generally speaking, the results were consistent with the hypothesized control mechanism in all 12 cases. There were 105 or 97 percent correct predictions out of 108. Based on the assumption that correct and incorrect predictions are binomially distributed, the 87 percent confidence interval for correct predictions was between 94 percent and 100 percent.

It is instructive, nonetheless, to consider the deviations. During the selection rule practice and on the posttest, Subject 4 seemed to have difficulty remembering what problem she was on, and because she received the Alt-MA treatment, had some trouble determining which operation rule to use. On the fourth problem of the first set of posttest problems, it appeared that she had lost track of where she was, and she picked AM instead of MA. Subject 3, on the other hand, had no such difficulty; he seemed to simply note which rule sign was up from the last problem and chose the other sign. After Subject 4 had been run, the procedure was changed slightly to emphasize this method with the remaining subjects who were taught an "alternate" selection rule.

Subject 7, on the first problem of Set 3 on the posttest, chose MA instead of AM, as he was expected to. (In this case, notice, no rule sign was up from the last problem.) The problem involved erasers as input and flags mounted on toothpicks as output. This was the second time in the posttest that the erasers-flags situation had appeared. After the first such situation, Subject 7 discovered that he could stick the flags into the erasers. On problem one of Set 3, he seemed distracted by the prospect of sticking the flags into the erasers, and grabbed the wrong rule sign (i.e., instead of the problem and relevant rules, his processor seemed filled with incidentals).

Extensions: If the relevant lower-order rules and the selection rules (including rules for selecting selection rules) available to a subject are known, then the proposed control mechanism makes it possible, in principle, to predict his behavior perfectly. Unless these rules are built directly into the subject, however, one can never know for sure the full extent of his capabilities; and predictions, accordingly, become less certain. This circumstance is not as restrictive in practice as one might suspect--for many of the same reasons that it is not necessary in assessing behavior potential to know precisely which rules a given subject has available (cf. Scandura, 1973, Chapter 11).

Useful predictions also may be obtained in relatively unstructured situations by modifying the motivation mechanism to allow for probabilistic, rather than deterministic, selections. Consider, for example, the ordinary classroom, where one might want to make predictions concerning the various choices among activities that individual students continually have to make--choices, for example, between baseball and "bull" sessions during free play or painting and sculpture during art class. In situations of this sort it would appear to be overly ambitious to attempt completely definitive accounts.

Nonetheless, the probabilities involved in this type of situation may be sufficiently stable as to make useful predictions possible (e.g., Suchman & Trabasso, 1966). Furthermore, those who have worked with children, for example, know that they often have very definite preferences for the kinds of activities in which they participate; the kinds of choices they make often tend to fall into a regular and predictable pattern. The existence of such patterns of behavior is the source of such common remarks as, "George always takes the hard way" or "Vivian is always so cooperative." In the school setting, such tendencies might manifest themselves, for example, in the more-or-less ready acceptance of challenging, as opposed to routine, intellectual activities.

Assuming that such preferences tend to remain stable, at least over short periods of time, it may prove possible to predict, as in the present study, the kinds of choices students make in one type of choice situation on the basis of the kinds of choices made in different, but analogous situations. (For details, see Scandura, 1973, Chapter 8.)

Although the selection rules manipulated in this experiment were somewhat arbitrary, this will not be the case in real problem solving. Indeed, the kinds of distinctions that some problem solvers learn to make among problems can have important implications, not only regarding success but also problem-solving efficiency. Suppose, for example, in addition to the +n rules used in this study, that subtraction (-n) rules of the type $A^{-m}B$ were also allowed. In this case, the efficiency of corresponding MA and AM rules depends directly on whether or not the rules involve addition (+n) or subtraction (-n). For example, consider MA and AM rules for converting m erasers into m - 3 chips. In using the MA rule, the subject must match the m given erasers with chips and then remove three chips. Using the AM rule eliminates unnecessary steps because the subject would remove three erasers before matching. On the other hand, if MA and AM rules involve addition, say to convert from n erasers to n + 3 chips, the MA rule would be more efficient because this would eliminate the necessity of adding three erasers (before matching).

Rigorous theoretical analyses of the processes by which subjects learn to make such distinctions have not yet been attempted. The essential ingredients for such analyses, however, seem fairly clear (e.g., see Chapter 2, Section 2.4). For example, in analyzing alternative solution rules for sets of related problems, it would not (generally speaking) be especially hard to determine which rules work more efficiently with which problems. Moreover, one presumably could identify those properties that determine efficiency and use them as a basis for devising appropriate higher-order selection rules. Indeed, with the exception of the crucial role played by higher-order (selection) rules, the kinds of structural analyses required would not be unlike those used with discrimination learning tasks in Hypothesis Theory (e.g., Levine, 1969; Restle, 1962). In particular, subjects apparently remember how well various rules work on previous problems and make future selections so as to be consistent with this information. Changes in the selections subjects make on successive problems are typically understood in terms of feedback provided either by the experimenter or by the subject himself. There is no a priori reason, however, why selection rules could not be worked into the analysis. (For details, see Scandura, 1973, Chapter 8.) Because alternative rules are assigned equal probabilities, there probably would not be any great advantage to doing so within the context of Hypothesis Theory. In real world applications, however, where subjects tend to have specific preferences, higher-order selection rules could play a central role.

4. RULE RETRIEVAL AND DERIVATION (MULTIPLE PROCESSES)

The research reported above and in Chapter 5 involves a variety of different processes, processes ranging from rule derivation via combination and via generalization, retrieval (i.e., extraction of information from more encompassing wholes), breaking problems into sequences (more generally hierarchies) of subproblems, and rule selection (motivation). In searching for a control mechanism that would be adequate to account for

the use of all such processes a sequence of increasingly general
goal switching mechanisms was proposed and tested.

The empirical tests were all conducted under idealized
(memory-free) conditions (i.e., where all rules necessary for
problem solving were immediately available to the subject and
where the subject was not encumbered by his limited capacity
for processing information). In view of the arguments in Chapter
1 (also see the introduction to Chapter 7 and the last section
of Chapter 11), therefore, and the (near) deterministic results
reported above, the prior and *uniform* availability of the generalized, goal switching control mechanism (or some computational equivalent) would seem to be indicated--in effectively *any*
situation where it is called for. This is a strong statement
(about a simple mechanism) but one which follows from successful
deterministic tests under a representative sample of conditions.
The general impact of the statement becomes even clearer perhaps
if one takes into account the fact that the method of structural
analysis used to identify underlying competence is *independent*
of the subject matter. This method, together with the control
mechanism, provides a basis for predicting behavior with respect
to any problem domain. The trading game task, for example, is
only one such domain. Moreover, far more extensive structural
analyses have been completed of some rather complex problem
domains (e.g., the class of geometry construction problems, the
class of proofs of all theorems and proof exercises in a contemporary algebra text, Chapters 3 and 4) and used as a basis
for predicting human problem solving behavior (e.g., Chapters
13 and 14).

Nonetheless, the above studies all deal with problem-solving situations involving only a single process. The question
remains as to whether the generalized control mechanism (described above) is sufficient in principle to account for problem-
solving behavior in more complex situations. In particular,
what happens where two or more kinds of processes are involved?
Is the proposed control mechanism adequate to account for such
behavior, and if not, can it be generalized so that it is?

This study extends the previous research and is concerned
with how subjects solve problems where certain rules must be
retrieved before higher-order rules, which operate on them, can
be applied (e.g., to derive solution rules). Given an A-C trading task, for example, and assuming the availability of the
corresponding B → C rule and the higher-order composition rule,
subjects must somehow "retrieve" an appropriate A → B rule before the composition rule can be applied--and the A-C problem
solved. This corresponds to an examination problem, where a
student could convert 5 centimeters into inches, say, if only
he could remember some specific fact (e.g., how many centimeters
equal 1 inch).

In order to deal with such situations the proposed control
mechanism must be further modified and extended. In even the
most general of the mechanisms considered, it is assumed at each

goal level that the domains and ranges of rules are tested
simultaneously. In more complex situations, where needed information may have to be retrieved, analytic/computational provision
may be made by generalizing the generalized control mechanism
so that the tests are performed in series. Specifically, goals
are redefined to include only one kind of test, and the basic
control mechanism itself is enriched. Higher-level goals are
satisfied by rules whose ranges contain[3] next lower-level goals.
Given a rule that satisfies a higher-level goal, a corresponding
goal based on domain conditions (domain goals) is automatically
defined. The domain goal consists of elements that belong in
the domain of the identified (higher-order) rule.

In effect, once a higher-level goal has been satisfied
(i.e., a rule satisfying it has been identified), control is
assumed to revert to the corresponding domain goal. Control
here is assumed to shift to higher- and lower-level goals as
with any other initial goal. Once a domain goal has been satisfied, control reverts to the next lower-level, the identified
higher-order rule is applied (to the domain elements generated),
and the process continues. The composition rule introduced
above, for example, satisfies a higher-level goal in the sense
that its range contains composite $A \rightarrow Y \rightarrow C$ rules (Y unspecified) whose ranges in turn contain the desired output C. Hence,
control is assumed to shift to the domain goal satisfied by
pairs of compatible $A \rightarrow Y$, $Y \rightarrow C$ rules. Once the domain goal
is satisfied, the composition rule is applied, control moves to
the next lower-level goal, and the process continues.[4] (Notice
that this control mechanism reduces (essentially) to the earlier
one where needed domain elements are immediately available. In
this case, domain goals are satisfied directly; the needed elements do not have to be derived.)

Analytic/computational adequacy, of course, says nothing
directly about behavioral adequacy. We seek to identify a control mechanism that, in principle, is sufficient for all problem
solving and which can be assumed to be available to children
from (at least) the age of 7. Toward this end, the purpose of
this study was to determine the behavioral viability of the ex-

[3]See related discussion in Chapter 2.

[4]Note that, as in the above retrieval studies, no distinction is made
between elements generated for the first time and retrieval of elements that may
have been learned previously. The mechanism proposed is essentially the same in
both retrieval and derivation. The major difference is connotative and resides
in whether the to-be-generated element is embedded in some available relational
net or represents a discrete unit of knowledge (cf. Greeno, 1973). In the former
case, retrieval is not unlike that in many contemporary memory theories (cf.
Anderson & Bower, 1973; Kintsch, 1972; Pask et al. 1973; Rumelhart et al. 1972)
in that retrieval corresponds to generating and applying a rule (path) from some
given or available cue (in the network) to the to-be-recalled element. The major
differences are that the to-be-recalled element may itself be a network (equivalently, a directed graph or rule) and that the generation of a particular path is
presumed to be governed by the above goal-switching mechanism. (In the struc-
tural-learning theory [Scandura, 1973a] storing information is viewed as generating a network [rule] in which the to-be-retrieved element [e.g., rule] is
embedded.)

tended mechanism as a basis for explaining multiple-process problem solving, specifically that involving retrieval and rule derivation.

Because of the relatively large number of rules (and goals) involved, it should be emphasized that processing capacity could well become a major factor in this research, in spite of attempts to eliminate (minimize) its effects (e.g., by making desired rules and mnemonics directly available in the environment). Nonetheless, the previous experiments, together with those reported below, could help set upper limits on the complexity of the needed control mechanism; in fact, these experiments were selected precisely because they take into account most (or all) of the major types of goal switching that appear necessary in problem solving, goal switching as involved in rule derivation and retrieval, subproblem formation, rule selection and domain control. All further complications seem to involve simple recursions on these factors. For example, the generalized mechanism appears to provide an adequate basis for explaining the cognitive processes underlying such complex protocols as that described in Chapter 15.

4.1 EXPERIMENT V

Since pilot experimentation plays a rather special role in the present paradigm, where the behavior of individual subjects is of central concern, it is instructive to consider this research in some detail.

Method, materials, and tasks: The experimental materials were an extended version of those used in the retrieval experiment. In addition to the +n cards/rules, however, there were corresponding -m cards/rules that involved taking away. On the back of each card was a symbol designated as the "name" of the card.

There was also a 9 x 9 inch chart that could be used for locating rule cards by name for making specific trades. As before, the chart entries were names of rules for converting row elements (e.g., pencils) into column elements (e.g., paper clips). The main diagonal and all entries below and to the left of it were blank. Thus, no element could be traded for itself, and no rule had an inverse. For example, there was a rule for trading pencils for paper clips but none for trading paper clips for pencils.

The set of compatible pairs of simple rules comprised the domain of a higher-order composition rule that mapped each such pair into the corresponding composite rule (see Chapter 5).

Four tasks were used:

1. Direct trading tasks involving either simple or composite rules as in Experiment I.

2. Higher-order (H) tasks in which the subject was presented with a compatible pair of A → B and B → C rules and a set of

stimulus objects A, and was asked to trade the given A objects
for the output (C) of the simple B → C rule. The H tasks could
be solved by first deriving the necessary composite rule (as in
Chapter 5) and then applying it.

   3. Domain (D) tasks in which the subject was given a B → C
rule and a set of A items not represented on the card and was
asked to find a pair of compatible rules (including the given
B → C rule). The column on the chart that corresponded to C
was covered so that it was not possible to name the A → C rule
directly. The domain rule for solving D tasks involved locating
the name of the needed A → B rule in the chart (i.e., in that
row and column corresponding, respectively, to the domain and
range of the A → B rule).

   4. Combined (HD) tasks in which the stimulus situation was
identical to that in the domain task, but where the subject was
required to trade A for C. HD tasks could be solved by recognizing the adequacy of the composition higher-order rule, retrieving the needed A → B rule (by asking for it by name), forming the composite A → B → C rule, and finally applying the composite rule to solve the problem.

   Subjects, design, and procedure: The subjects were 30
nine- to twelve-year-old children at the Belmont Hills and Lea
Elementary Schools in Lower Merion, Pennsylvania, and West
Philadelphia, respectively. The experiment was conducted with
individual subjects during two separate sessions, usually a day
apart.

   The first session consisted of pretraining and a Transfer
Pretest. First, the subject was taught how to interpret the
A → B and A → B → C rule cards, how to make trades, and that
each simple A → B rule card had a name printed on its back. The
experimenter did not indicate how the chart was to be used.
Then the subject was given a Transfer Pretest consisting of three
tasks: an H task, a D task, and an HD task in that order.

   On the H task, the subject was presented with cards representing a pair of compatible A → B, B → C rules and a set of A
objects. The subject was asked to trade for C (which required
use of the corresponding composite A → B → C rule). (The subject was never shown this rule directly either before or after
testing.)

   On the D task, the subject was presented with a B → C rule
card and a set of stimulus A objects. The C column of the table
was covered so it was not possible to find the rule converting
A objects directly to C objects. The subject was told, "We want
to trade A (e.g., pipe cleaners) for C (e.g., rubber bands).
We need a pair of rules to let us do that. One of them is going
to be this (B → C) rule. Can you tell me what other rule I need
so I can trade A for C?" The experimenter also emphasized that
the subject could use the chart (but no training was given).

   Before testing on the HD task, the subject was reminded of

the kinds of relevant rules he knew or had learned up to that
point.

Each of the 22 subjects who failed at least one of the pretest tasks participated in the second session during which training was given on the H task and the D rule. The subjects were
trained first on the H task and then given Transfer Posttest I,
which was identical to the pretest. Next, they were trained on
the D task and given Transfer Posttest II. All 22 subjects were
given both H and D training, even if they were already competent
on a corresponding H or D task. No subject was trained on the
HD task.

In training on the H task, the experimenter demonstrated
how the rules could be combined by sliding the simple rules together. The subject was asked to interpret the newly formed
A → B → C rule, and to use it. (In effect, the training included
both the higher-order composition rule and what to do with the
derived A → B → C rule , i.e., the control mechanism .) New
pairs of rules were introduced until the subject made three successful trades with three consecutive, different pairs in a row.
Counterexamples were also given.

In the D training, the subject was shown how to use the
chart to find the needed A → B card. After the subject retrieved
each A → B rule by using the chart, the experimenter held the
rule against the given B → C rule so that the subject could see
that the output of the former matched the input of the latter.
(Note: Training was modified in later experiments to eliminate
unintended transfer to the H task.) Criterion was success in
finding the missing rule on three consecutive tasks.

Results and discussion: Of the 30 subjects given the
transfer pretest, 8 were successful on the H, D, and HD tasks.
Of the remaining 22, 9 failed on all three Transfer Pretests;
the other 13 succeeded only on the H Pretest.

After training on the H task, all 22 training subjects
succeeded on the H task on Transfer Posttest I. One subject
succeeded on both the D and HD tasks; the others all failed on
both the D and HD tasks. After training on the D task, all 22
subjects not only succeeded on the H and D tasks on Transfer
Posttest II but they also succeeded on the HD task.

With the exception of one of 44 posttest results, therefore,
these results appear to be consistent with the assumption that
elementary school subjects come "prewired" with the proposed
control mechanism. Before H and D training, there was no basis
for predicting performance on the H and D tasks because there
was no way of knowing whether or not the subject had already
mastered the requisite rules. According to the theory, the only
restriction on the Pretest is that if the subject is successful
on the H and D tasks, then he also should be successful on the
HD task. The data support this prediction in 8 of 8 cases. The
same pattern was obtained after the H and D training. In only 1

of 22 cases on Posttest I did H training lead to success on the
D task, and this subject was also successful on the HD task.

All in all, one might be tempted to report strong support
for the proposed mechanism. This would be inappropriate, however, because (as described above) the experimenter inadvertently
failed to restrict H training to the higher-order composition
rule. The subjects were not only taught how to generate composite rules from pairs of compatible simple rules, but also to use
the derived composite rules to solve H tasks. In effect, they
were taught both the H rule and the (first approximation) control
mechanism itself, thereby leaving unanswered the question of
whether the generalized mechanism itself is innate. (It must
be emphasized that although conceptually clear, the implied distinctions are not easy to realize experimentally. Even seasoned
experimenters must be wary.) In itself, however, this procedural
modification was not a serious problem since the uniform availability of the first approximation mechanism had been tested
previously with children from the age of about 4 (Chapter 5).

The problem came in interpreting performance on the HD task.
Our original intent was to determine whether training on the
composition rule and the D rule (together with the given B → C
rule) was sufficient for solving an A-C problem. Assuming that
the lower- and higher-level goals involved are available to the
subject, the enriched control mechanism postulated above (cf.
Scandura, 1973, Chapter 9, especially pp. 287 & 294) would provide the necessary control. Thus, given a set of A objects with
the goal of finding the appropriate number of C objects, control
would be assumed to go first to the higher-level goal satisfied
by (higher-order) rules that generate rules that apply to A objects and generate C objects. The only available rule for accomplishing this is the higher-order composition rule. Since
the composition rule operates only on pairs of compatible simple
rules, control is assumed to go to the domain goal, consisting
of such pairs. Because no such pair is available, control goes
to the next higher-level domain goal. At this level, the only
adequate and available rule is the D rule (which applies in
situations where a B → C rule and A objects are available).
Since the necessary domain elements are available, the rule is
applied and a compatible pair of A → B, B → C rules is generated.
This pair satisfies the domain goal so control reverts to the
next lower-level goal. Here, the composition rule is applied
(to the pair) and a composite A → B → C is generated. Because
the solution-level goal is satisfied, control goes to the
original goal, the composite A → B → C rule is applied, and the
problem is solved.

Unfortunately, this is not the only reasonable way to account for success on the HD task. Because of the unintended
nature of the H training, it is just as reasonable, perhaps more
so, to assume that the HD task was solved by simply composing

the rules actually taught during the D and H training. To see this, notice that application of the D rule taught during the D training generates the needed A → B, B → C pair. Subsequent application of the combined composition rule and control mechanism taught during H training not only generates the composite A → B → C rule but also applies it to solve the problem. (It is important to recognize that generating an A → B → C rule and then using it is not equivalent to simply generating the rule.)

After H training, then, assuming that the subject also knows the composition rule apart from the mechanism (something which seems reasonable given the results of Experiment I), success on the HD task can be explained as follows: After control goes to the higher-level goal, the composition rule is applied to the D rule and the combined H rule and mechanism. (These two rules are compatible since the output of the former serves as input for the latter. Notice, however, that the latter "rule" does not qualify as a rule in the restricted sense of Chapter 2.) The resulting composite rule satisfies the higher-level goal so control reverts to the original goal; the resulting composite rule is applied, and the task solved.

4.2 EXPERIMENTS VI-A AND VI-B

In pilot experimentation, there was a strong tendency for D rule training to transfer to the H task. Experiment VI-A was designed to see if D training could be purified, to avoid such transfer. Experiment VI-B was designed to eliminate the second interpretation above as a viable alternative. Except for order of training (H-D and D-H) and age level of subjects, the method was identical in each experiment.

Method: The materials, tasks, and procedures in Experiments VI-A and VI-B were identical to those of Experiment V except in training on the composition rule and in stating the subject's goal during D rule training.

Instead of training on the H transfer task itself (i.e., including the control mechanism), H rule training in Experiment VI was limited to the higher-order composition rule for forming composite rules from compatible simple A → B, B → C rules. (A set of stimulus A objects was included as part of the context.) The subject's goal was to find an A → B → C rule for trading the given A objects for C objects. The experimenter demonstrated how the simple rules could be combined by sliding them together in the appropriate manner. Then, the rules were separated, the number of stimulus A objects was changed, and the subject was asked to construct a composite rule. The subject did not perform any trades with the rule. This process was repeated with other pairs until the subject was able to form appropriate composite rules when this was possible, or to identify the simple rules as incompatible. In addition, the subject was given some pairs of compatible A' → B', B' → C' rules where A' ≠ A and C' ≠ C and, if necessary, instructed why the corresponding A' → B' → C' rule could not be used to trade A objects for C

objects. (This amounted essentially to training on the higher-
level goal.)

On the D task, the subject was given a simple B → C rule
and a set of A items, with the C column of the chart covered,
as in Experiment V. However, the goal was stated differently.
No reference was made to finding a pair of compatible rules for
making trades. Rather, the subject's stated task was to find
a pair of rules in which the output (B) of one rule (A → B) was
the same as the input (B) of the other (B → C), and so that the
input (A) of the first was identical to the given A objects and
the output (C) of the second was identical to the output of the
(given) B → C rule.

During D training, the subject was shown how to locate
needed rules by name (in the table). The subjects also were
taught to identify the given rule as one member of the needed
pair by giving the name on the back of the rule card. In short,
the D instruction involved identifying compatible pairs of rules
by name; references to possible uses of the rules in making
trades were eliminated.

Because pilot experimentation suggested that D rule training
may influence H test performance, second-grade subjects (aged
7 to 8) at the Lea School were used in Experiment VI-A (training
sequence D-H); they presumably were more sensitive to inadequacies in wording and less likely to enter the experiment with
extraneous competences which could result in transfer from D
training to H tasks. Four D-H subjects in Experiment VI-A were
trained on the D task as in Experiment V. Six other D-H subjects
were trained on this task as described above; one failed the
pretraining.

One second-grader, a seven-year-old boy, was unable to complete the pretraining successfully, and was not included in the
experimental comparison. Five of the younger subjects (aged 7
or 8 years) required three or more sessions to complete the experiment, depending on the subject's attention span and rate of
progress. A typical subject might participate in four 1-hour
sessions with the first consisting of pretraining, the second,
of further pretraining and the Pretest, the third, a review, D
rule training and Posttest I, and the fourth, another review,
H rule training and Posttest II. The mean experimental time per
subject was three hours and 45 minutes. The shortest time was
two hours and 25 minutes; the longest, seven hours and 55 minutes.

The subjects in Experiment VI-B were 10 fourth-graders
(aged 8 to 10 years) at the Lea School, trained in the order H-D.
These subjects all received the modified H and D training described above. The mean experimental time per subject was two
hours and 35 minutes. The shortest time was one hour and 55
minutes; the longest, four hours and 40 minutes.

Results and discussion: The results of Experiment VI-B
closely paralleled those of Experiment V. After training on the

H and D tasks, all 10 subjects on Posttest II not only succeeded
on the H and D tasks, but on the HD task as well. Also as expected, H training improved performance only with those 2 subjects who failed on the H Pretest. In no case did H training
transfer to success on the D task. In effect, these results
clearly tend to discount the alternative explanation of the
Experiment V data lending further support for the proposed
(enriched) theoretical mechanism.

The results of Experiment VI-A, involving the younger D-H
subjects, however, were less clear. All 4 subjects run under
the D training conditions of Experiment V failed uniformly on
the Pretest. After D training, 2 of the 4 subjects not only
succeeded on the D task, but also on the H task (and the HD
task). Under the new D training conditions, on the other hand,
none of the 3 subjects who uniformly failed the Pretest succeeded after D training on the H task of Posttest I.

However, whereas all 4 (Pretest failure) subjects run under
D training conditions of Experiment V succeeded uniformly on
Posttest II (after D and H training), the results under the D
conditions of Experiment VI were mixed. For the first time, 2
subjects succeeded on both the H and D tasks but failed on the
corresponding HD task, one on Posttest I and the other on Posttest II. The former subject had solved (only) the first H task
on the pretest; the latter had failed all three pretest tasks.

Although 2 out of 16 (ignoring H-D order) deviations is
small, the experimental effort that went into ensuring required
memory-free preconditions of the idealized theory is suggestive
of the difficulties in running such experiments with younger
(educationally disadvantaged) children. The greater load placed
on active memory by the increased number of higher-order rules
and goals and the inability of many such children to identify
crucial information, even when it is familiar and readily available in the environment (i.e., some such subjects may lack even
basic searching skills), may be especially critical. Among
other things, given rules may use up a larger number of chunks
in the working memories of developmentally less advanced subjects
than with older children, so that processing capacity in the
former case is more apt to be exceeded (cf. Scandura, 1973).

4.3 EXPERIMENT VII

The purpose of Experiment VII was to replicate the results
of Experiment VI-A under slightly refined D-H conditions.

Method: The method used in Experiment VII was identical
to that used in Experiments VI-A and VI-B, except in the D rule
training. The stimulus situation and statement of the task were
unchanged. After the subject used the chart to retrieve an
A → B domain rule, however, the experimenter never held the retrieved rule against the given B → C rule. As before, the experimenter did draw the subject's attention to the fact that the

input of the retrieved rule matched the stimulus A objects, and
that the output of the retrieved rule matched the input of the
given rule, but not in a manner that might also reveal how to
form the composite A → B → C rule. (Close scrutiny of tape re-
cordings from Experiment VI suggested that in one or two cases
the experimenter may inadvertently have shown the subject how
the A → B rules matched the given B → C rules. This activity
was not part of the instructions but evolved naturally in the
course of interacting with young children about rather subtle
ideas.)

     The scoring criteria for the H task also were modified
slightly. If the subject succeeded on an A-B-C problem but
failed on another involving the same A → B → C rule, he was
presented with an entirely new problem and allowed to try again.
(This apparently helped to avoid a potentially ambiguous scoring
problem observed in Experiment VI-A. Nonetheless, as the dis-
cerning reader may have noticed, the experiments reported in
Chapters 5 and 6 call for single test items. The only real
purpose served by having more than one test item is to demonstrate consistency cf. Chapters 8 and 9. In addition, since
some subjects in earlier studies were observed to try to use
the given B → C rule to trade A objects for C objects on the HD
task, the subject was reminded just prior to the HD task that
the given rule could be used only to trade B objects for C objects. All subjects had received such training earlier.)

     All 15 subjects were second- and third-graders from the Lea
School between the ages of 7 and 9 years. All subjects were
trained on the D rule first. Fourteen subjects required more
than two sessions in order to complete the experiment. The
average time per subject was four hours and 20 minutes. The
shortest time was two hours and 15 minutes; the longest time,
nine hours.

     Results and discussion: After training on the D tasks, all
8 +-- subjects (i.e., subjects who solved the H task on the Pretest and failed the others) succeeded on the D task of Posttest
I and uniformly on Posttest II. All but one subject also succeeded on the HD task. The one exception was a nine-year-old
girl, who failed the HD task on Posttest I and who succeeded on
Posttest II only after receiving special help. On Posttest I
she appeared to ask for cards randomly and then reject them because they did not "help". On Posttest II when the experimenter
asked "What would help?" she indicated that an A → C card would
(help) but that the C column on the chart was covered. When asked, "Can it be anything else?" the subject said she could use an
A → B card. She did not proceed to look for it until later reminded, while she was in the process of randomly selecting cards,
"What were the things you told me would help?" The subject looked on the chart for the A → B card and solved the HD problem.
Although hardly unambiguous, this dialogue suggests: The initial

search for an A → C rule may have been guided by a prelearned
selection rule (cf. Luchins, 1942; Scandura, 1973). Subsequent
rejection may have added to an apparent overload on working
memory.

Most of the 7 --- subjects performed as predicted. After
D training, all six subjects who succeeded on the D Posttest I
failed on the H Posttest, indicating success in separating the
two experimentally. The other subject, surprisingly, failed
the D Posttest I even after the D training. Five of 7 --- subjects also performed as expected on the HD task of Posttest II
after H training. The other two subjects, however, failed on
the HD task. One, a seven-year-old boy, seemed to have no idea
of how to proceed. After a number of apparently random guesses,
he became discouraged and unable to concentrate. The other, an
eight-year-old girl, moved through the pretraining relatively
quickly but on the HD task, as with the nine-year-old girl mentioned above, she refused to investigate any other possibility
after finding that the given A objects could not be traded
directly for C objects. Both deviations are consistent with
the interpretation offered above and in Experiment VI.

5.   SUMMARY AND CONCLUSIONS

Derivation of solution procedures, memory retrieval, subproblem definition, and rule selection all play an important
role in human problem solving. In most contemporary problem-
solving research (cf. Chapter 15) these processes have been involved in varying and usually unknown proportion. The research
reported in Chapter 5 and in the present sequel have followed
a somewhat different approach. In this series of studies an
attempt was made to isolate for study each of the above components, and particularly to determine the viability of a generalized control mechanism.

The results of Chapter 5 show that when the effects of
other processes are partialed out, the presence or absence of
relevant higher-order composition or generalization rules (and
associated goal related, decision-making capabilities) is critical. They show further that the first approximation, goal-
switching control mechanism provides a simple, explicit, and
reasonable way of accounting for and predicting such results.
Perhaps more impressive, this same control mechanism was shown
to provide an equally viable account of retrieval, and to allow
natural generalization to subproblem definition. Specifically,
in the latter case, goals are redefined so as to allow (i.e.,
be satisfied by) solution plans as well as solution rules.

In order to account for selection from among two or more
applicable rules, an additional natural constraint was added to
the control mechanism, specifically, that a rule is put to use

at a given goal level only where exactly one rule applies. In
effect, the structure of the control mechanism was enriched
without destroying its original character; the enriched mechanism
is equivalent to the original one in previous applications. Experimental subjects were shown to behave in accordance with this
mechanism and to use manipulatable higher-order selection rules
in choosing from among alternative rules.

It was possible to further enrich the mechanism in a natural way to account for the broader range of experimental conditions considered in the final study, which dealt with both retrieval and rule derivation. This time, instead of testing domains and ranges of rules simultaneously, these tests were performed in series, thereby making it possible to derive (retrieve)
needed domain elements. Moreover, up to recursion, this final
generalization appears potentially adequate (insofar as control
itself is concerned) to deal with most instances of problem
solving.

As was the case throughout, the data were generally consistent with the theoretical analysis. There were a few significant
deviations from the ideal in individual cases, however, and the
degree of explicitness required of the experimental conditions
is suggestive of increasing difficulties in obtaining deterministic results in more complex problem-solving situations.

In future research, if one is to obtain deterministic results, new paradigms may have to be developed to take into account the subject's limited capacity for processing information
and for exploring more fully the boundaries between the present
approach and others. Methods analogous to those introduced by
Sternberg, Knoll, & Naste (1969), for example, coupled with recently proposed analytic methods for determining memory loads
on arbitrary tasks (Scandura, 1973; Chapter 7; Voorhies, 1973),
might be used to manipulate the contents of active memory just
prior to or during problem solving. As we shall see in Chapter
7 (also see Chapter 1), it would also be possible in experimental
work to maintain a sharp distinction between deterministic
(structural) and observational (incidental) variables.

By way of conclusion, one major point deserves re-emphasis:
Availability of a set of rules is not equivalent to their appropriate use in human problem solving. In order to provide an
adequate basis for explaining all relevant facets of problem
solving, it is necessary to also assume (either implicitly or
explicitly as in the present study) some control mechanism which
is both sufficiently general to allow for these various facets
and universally available to human beings. This problem is not
critical in most current information-processing models of problem solving, either because they have not been formulated with
enough precision to make any difference in this regard and/or
because they deal primarily with adult performance (e.g., Newell
& Simon, 1972). In the latter case, for example, where the

emphasis is on relatively complex hierarchies of subgoals, a stack-type control mechanism has been quite adequate. Indeed, in accounting for the *performance* of adult subjects it most likely is behaviorally (but not necessarily cognitively) equivalent to goal switching (cf. Chapters 5 and 15). The present research is complementary in the sense that it deals with the question of how derivation, retrieval, subproblem definition, and rule selection are all interrelated, and specifically with how they may be governed by a common control mechanism.

REFERENCES

Anderson, J. R., & Bower, G. H. *Human associative memory.* New York: Halsted-Wiley, 1973.

Cason, G. J. Individual differences in dimension preference and saliency in concept identification. *JSAS Catalogue of Selected Documents in Psychology,* 1975, *5,* 318. (M.S. No. 1080)

Greeno, J. G. The structure of memory and the process of solving problems. In R. Solso (Ed.), *Contemporary issues in cognitive psychology: Loyola symposium.* New York: Halsted-Wiley, 1973.

Kintsch, W. Notes on the structure of semantic memory. In E. Tulving & W. Donaldson (Eds.), *Organization of memory.* New York: Academic Press, 1972.

Levine M. Neo-noncontinuity theory. In G. H. Bower & J. T. Spence (Eds.), *The psychology of learning and motivation: Advances in research and theory* (Vol. 3). New York: Academic Press, 1969.

Luchins, A. S. Mechanization in problem solving: The effect of Einstellung. *Psychological Monographs,* 1942, *54,* No. 6, (Whole No. 248).

Minsky, M., & Papert, S. *Research at the laboratory in vision, language and other problems in intelligence* (Artificial Intelligence Progress Report, Memo 252). Cambridge, Mass.: M.I.T. Artificial Intelligence Laboratory, 1972.

Nahinsky, I. D. Going by rules (A review of Scandura, J. M., *Structural learning I: Theory and research.* New York: Gordon & Breach, 1973). *Contemporary Psychology,* 1974, *19,* 414-416.

Newell, A., & Simon, H. A. *Human problem solving.* Englewood Cliffs, N.J.: Prentice-Hall, 1972.

Pask, G., Scott, B. C. E., & Kallikourdis, D. A. Theory of conversations and individuals (Exemplified by the learning process on CASTE). *International Journal of Man-Machine Studies,* 1973, *5,* 443-566.

Restle, F. The selection of strategies in cue learning. *Psychological Review,* 1962, *69,* 329-343.

Rumelhart, D. E., Lindsay, P. H., & Norman, D. A. A process model for long-term memory. In E. Tulving & W. Donaldson (Eds.), *Organization of memory.* New York: Academic Press, 1972.

Scandura, J. M. *Structural learning I: Theory and research.* New York: Gordon & Breach, 1973.

Scandura, J. M. The structure of memory: Fixed or flexible? *Catalog of Selected Documents in Psychology,* Spring, 1974, Abstract, pp. 37-38. Abridged version in F. Klix (Ed.), *Organismische Informationsverarbeitung.* Berlin: Akademie-Verlag, 1974.

Sternberg, S., Knoll, R. L., & Naste, B. A. Retrieval from long-term vs. active memory. Paper given at Psychonomic Society Meeting, St. Louis, Novermber, 1969.

Suchman, R. C., & Trabasso, T. Stimulus preference and cue function in young children's concept attainment. *Journal of Experimental Child Psychology,* 1966, *3,* 188-198.

Voorhies, D. J. *Human information-processing capacity.* Unpublished doctoral dissertation, University of Pennsylvania, 1973.

Wittrock, M. C., & Hill, C. E. *Children's preference in the transfer of learning* (Final Report, Project No. 3264, Contract No. OE-6-10-303). Washington, D.C.: Office of Education, Bureau of Research, 1968.

7
Determination of Memory Load in Information Processing[1]

Donald J. Voorhies and Joseph M. Scandura

Miller's (1956) classic "The magical number seven, plus or minus two" has inspired a considerable amount of experimental research on task memory load and its relation to human informa-tion-processing capacity. Until recently, however, relatively little has been done to clarify why, psychologically, a chunk is a chunk or, more generally, to develop methods for determin-ing memory loads on arbitrary tasks. As a first approximation, memory load clearly is a function of task complexity, and varies both across different tasks (e.g., memory span, addition, multi-plication) and over different instances of given tasks (e.g., mentally adding two- versus three-digit numbers). Although existing information theoretic (e.g., Posner, 1964) and regres-sion (Suppes, 1967) models provide general quantitative measures of task complexity in such cases, they seem to work better with some tasks than others, and deal only indirectly with underlying cognitive processes.

Scandura (1973) has proposed a more general, deterministic-analytic method for determining the memory load imposed at each stage of processing by any given procedure (rule) as applied to any specific task. Data collected by Voorhies and Scandura (reported in Scandura, 1973; Voorhies, 1973) using this method showed that there are individual differences in processing ca-pacity that are stable across different tasks (e.g., digit lists, addition). Not surprisingly, however, they also found that there were deviations from the deterministic ideal. For example, a subject with capacity of eight sometimes recalled seven digits correctly and sometimes nine.

The main purpose of this chapter is to introduce random

[1]This research was supported in part by Research Grant NSF GW-7901 from the National Science Foundation and in part by National Institute of Health Grant 9185.

variation into the Scandura (1973) theory as a means of accounting for obtained deviations. Rather than the standard procedure
of introducing a stochastic analog (of the deterministic theory),
however, this is accomplished by constructing a more general
theoretical system that incorporates both the deterministic
memory load theory and a complementary observation theory (see
Chapter 1). The observation theory, and hence the theoretical
system as a whole, is stochastic in nature. The observation
theory itself is based on two major sources of deviation from
idealized conditions. (Note: The major difference between
stochastic analogs and complementary, stochastic observation
theories is that the parameters in the former case correspond
directly to constructs in the deterministic theory. In the
latter case, they correspond to deviations from the ideal.)
The theoretical system is tested with respect both to previously reported and new data.

The chapter is organized as follows: (1) a review of the
relevant literature pertaining to processing capacity; (2) a
summary of the deterministic-analytic model proposed for determining memory loads, along with relevant data; (3) a stochastic
theory (system) proposed to account for deviations from ideal
performance (Scandura, 1973, Chapter 10); and (4) application
of the stochastic model both to existing data (Scandura, 1973)
and to new data (Voorhies, 1973) collected under somewhat different nonidealized conditions.

1.   RELATED RESEARCH

The distinction between primary and secondary (permanent)
memory has been with us since William James. It was not, however, until Miller's (1956) classic work that the notion of a
fixed processing capacity came into prominence. Synthesizing
research involving absolute judgements, span of attention, and
span of immediate memory, Miller showed that humans have a
definite limit in the amount of information they are able to
process at one time, and that generally speaking the limit is
seven plus or minus two elements.

Drachman and Zaks (1967) further demonstrate that there is
a rather sudden decrement in performance--a "memory cliff"--at
capacity. They administered the same task twice, using the data
from the first administration to account and adjust for individual variation on the second. After first determining individual
memory spans, they administered additional memoranda (strings
of digits) of various lengths. The dependent measure on the
second test was a function of the digits recalled by subjects
on strings of length span minus one (C-1), span (C), span plus
one (C+1), etc. Pooling the data across subjects, and adjusting
for individual spans in this way, there was a fairly sharp break

in performance beyond the estimated memory span.

This limit appears to be independent of whether or not the elements being processed are familiar. Crowder (1967) and Conrad (1960), for example, found that requiring subjects to prefix to-be-remembered lists at recall with an extra, redundant digit (e.g., "1") causes a decrement in the percentage of correct responses. Savin (1968) further showed that prefixing a given digit to an eight-digit list, for example, causes the list to act at recall as a nine-digit list. The extra digit, even though highly familiar to the subjects, apparently occupies as much processing space as any other.

Processing capacity, however, depends only indirectly on the number of elements. As Miller (1956) has shown, the essential factor is the number of effective units, which he called "chunks". In a similar vein, Bower (1969) has shown that the critical feature in recall is the number of functional units in memory, rather than the sheer number of units. He had subjects recall words from lists that included single words (one functional unit), three-word cliches (one functional unit), or three-word triples (three functional units). In all cases, although the number of words recalled varied, the number of functional units recalled was the same.

More important, in view of the approach adopted below, there are indications in the literature that the number of chunks depends on the procedures subjects use, as well as on the tasks themselves. Posner and Rossman (1965), for example, gave subjects number strings, and required them to transform the strings in various ways (e.g., add, give the highest number, give the lowest number, etc.). They found that both the number of transformations and their size had a significant effect on the amount of untransformed material that was lost from store. The more processing required of the subject, the less peripheral material he can continue to retain. This suggests that on the average the more complex a procedure, the more processing space is required to apply it. (In this regard, it should be noted that Posner and Rossman used an information theoretic measure of transformation difficulty [i.e., the size of reduction in "bits"], which on some tasks was not compatible with obtained difficulty. We comment on this again below.)

The dependence of memory load on procedures is clearly not a simple one; procedures can serve to decrease the number of chunks that must be retained, leave it unchanged, or even increase the number. The results of Miller (1956), for example, suggest that a subject can increase the absolute number of elements (e.g., strings of binary digits) that he can process by recoding them into a smaller number of chunks (e.g., into strings of decimal digits). In order to recover the original elements, of course, they must be recoded in a way that makes it possible to regenerate the original elements on demand.

Dalrymple-Alford (1967) overcame the highly variable and often idiosyncratic effects of rehearsal by building it (rehearsal) directly into his experimental procedure. Rather than attempt to prevent it, he tried to ensure that rehearsal was of a known type and magnitude, and was uniform across all subjects. He had his subjects rehearse all previous digits aloud before the experimenter added a new digit. For example, suppose the first four digits were 2, 7, 3, and 9. Then the subject had to say "two, seven, three, nine" before the experimenter presented the next digit. Following Brown (1958), Dalrymple-Alford reasoned that any increase in retention as a result of rehearsal is due to recoding and not rehearsal per se (i.e., the "strengthening of memory traces"). With this in mind, he also determined each subject's memory span in the conventional (Woodworth & Schlosberg 1954) manner. Surprisingly, the proportions of errorless repetitions were almost identical under both conditions indicating that no learning (recoding) occurred during rehearsal. Dalrymple-Alford further noted the absence of traditional serial position effects. First errors in repetition (breakdowns) tended to occur equally often at all positions of the number sequences. Meunier, Ritz, and Meunier (1972) have shown further that rehearsal is used primarily to maintain items in short-term memory.

The limited-capacity hypothesis (cf. Broadbent, 1958) also has considerable explanatory power. It has been used as a basis for explaining and/or predicting the effects of a number of variables in short-term memory experiments. Katz (1968), for example found that primacy and recency effects on the serial position curve for short-term free recall are due to the subject's selective use of attention and storage and retrieval strategies operating under the constraint of a fixed short-term processing capacity. He had his subjects repeat random lists of two-digit numbers, and instructed one group to give the last pair before recalling the others. The other group was allowed to give the digits in any order they wished. Although he found no overall difference between the two groups in correct recall, the former group showed a relatively strong recency effect and the latter, a relatively strong primacy effect.

The results of several other studies suggest that processing capacity underlies the opposing effects of certain pairs of factors. Murdock (1965), for example, reasoned that if memory capacity is constant, then it should be possible to "trade off" the number of times a stimulus is presented with the exposure time on each trial. He constructed a list of six pairs of common English words, and presented them for study for a period of 24 seconds. Three conditions were used: in the first condition, each pair was presented once, for a period of 4 seconds; in the second, each pair was presented twice for a period of 2 seconds (on each trial); in the third, each pair was presented four times for a period of 1 second (on each trial). Murdock found that

there was essentially no difference between the first and second
conditions, with the third only slightly better than the others.
In a study involving incidental learning, Somers (1967) obtained
basically the same result. Sitterly (1968) used various combinations of digit and interdigit duration and also found that retention depended on total presentation time.

Other studies have been of a primarily empirical nature.
Thus, for example, Williams and Fish (1965) showed that increasing the length of the individual items to be recalled, and increasing the number of symbols from which the items are constructed, both decrease the percentage of correct recall (of the
items). Corballis (1966) varied the speed at which strings of
nine digits were presented, as well as the duration of time each
digit was actually visible. He found that when stimulus durations were long, the number correct was higher the slower the
presentation speed, but when stimulus durations were short, there
was a tendency for this trend to be reversed. Although generally
compatible with the limited-capacity hypothesis, the results were
relatively complex and no theoretical explanation was offered.

Use of the limited-capacity hypothesis as a basis for explanation with more complex tasks has been limited largely to
correlational studies. Whimbey, Fischhof, and Silikowitz (1969),
for example, measured performance on a digit span task, a mental
addition task, a vocabulary task, and a test of general intelligence. They found a generally high correlation between the digit
span task and the mental addition task, suggesting that both are
influenced by a limited-processing capacity. Vocabulary and
general intelligence both showed little relation. Whimbey and
Leiblum (1967) found similar high correlations among simple
repetition, repetition preceded by "0", and repetition with interspersed verbal activity. Later, Whimbey and Ryan (1969) found
correlations between the digit span task and mental syllogistic-
reasoning problems.

By way of summary, three general conclusions may be drawn
from the available literature. First, there is a definite limit
on the number of effective units (chunks) that subjects may process at any one time; this limit is seven plus or minus two
chunks. (Note: Using slightly different methods of assessment,
some investigators have obtained lower estimates. However,
consideration of the issues involved is beyond the scope of the
present chapter.) Second, the memory load imposed by a task
depends, in a nonsimple way, on the procedure used by the subject as well as on the task itself. Third, the limited-capacity hypothesis provides a useful basis for explanation, and,
hence, it is not surprising that it plays a central role in
most contemporary theories of memory (e.g., Anderson & Bower,
1973; Rumelhart, Lindsay, & Norman, 1972; Scandura, 1973).

Although more might be gleaned from the available literature, there are two important limitations inherent in it. For

one thing, there is no way to specify precisely how a subject is to process given information, even with the simplest tasks. Savin (1968), for example, required his subjects to prefix a given digit at recall but did not specify how this digit was to be processed in relation to the others. Other investigators have instructed their subjects not to organize the given digits, but made no attempt to tell them what they should do. Under these conditions it is uncertain, for example, when information is in so-called permanent memory and when it is in the information processor (Waugh & Norman, 1965). Even on simple tests of memory span, recoding and rehearsal processes tend to be highly dependent on individual preference and susceptible, at best in only partly known ways, to even slight changes in experimental conditions. Indeed, in only one study reviewed (Dalrymple-Alford, 1967) was a serious attempt made to ensure that the subjects used a particular procedure (rehearsal).

For another thing, even if procedures were to be specified, there is no a priori way available to determine the processing load they (the procedures) impose on the subject. Under these conditions it has been impossible to compare different tasks (procedures) with regard to memory load, short of direct empirical testing. For example, as promising as the technique originally appeared, measures of information reduction (e.g., Posner, 1964) seem to work well only with certain tasks. Suppes (1967) proposed an analytic method for calculating memory loads that was used with some success in predicting latencies on simple addition problems. Suppes' (1967) regression model involved three structural variables: the magnitude of the sum (MAGSUM), the magnitude of the smallest addend (MAGSMALL), and the number of steps necessary to complete a problem (NSTEPS). In determining NSTEPS, specific account is taken of how many quantities must be kept in memory in the course of solving a problem. Although the predictions made by the model correlated .86 with the actual data of 24 fourth-grade students, the method used to determine memory load was too crude for present purposes (cf. Chapter 2, Section 4).

2.   DETERMINISTIC APPROACH TO MEMORY LOAD

2.1   THE MODEL

In information processing, new elements may be encoded, thereby adding to memory load, and old elements may be decoded, thereby reducing memory load. In addition, internal operations themselves may serve either to generate new memory elements and/or to eliminate (erase) others.

Scandura (1973) has proposed an analytic model for calculating memory loads at each stage of processing, with arbitrary tasks, and taking into account the particular procedures used.

In the model, memory load is characterized in terms of the number of *distinct data types* (called "substimuli" in Scandura, 1973, Chapter 10) that must be distinguished during the course of a computation.

Directed graphs are used to represent underlying processes, with the nodes labelled so as to indicate memory loads at each stage (state) of processing. In these directed graphs, nodes represent states, and arrows between nodes represent operations between states.[2] The model rests on the principle that, at any given state, each substimulus (data type) that must be processed as a distinct unit (by the next or a subsequent operation) imposes a memory load of one on the processor. The memory load at any given state, then, is the sum of such units, and the memory load for an entire computation (the sequence of states between the input and final output) is the maximum of the memory loads imposed at the various states of the computation.

The directed graph in Figure 1 represents Non-Carry Addition (NCA), a process for adding two n-digit numbers of the form

$$\begin{array}{r} a_n \ a_{n-1} \ \cdots \ a_2 \ a_1 \\ + \ b_n \ b_{n-1} \ \cdots \ b_2 \ b_1 \\ \hline s_n \ s_{n-1} \ \cdots \ s_2 \ s_1 \end{array}$$

where $a_i + b_i < 10$

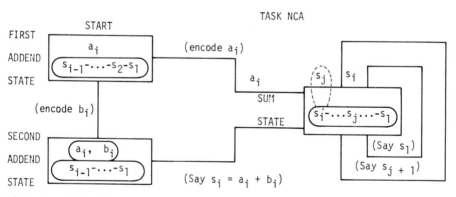

Figure 1. Node labelled directed graph for Task NCA showing states and transformations.

This process includes three nodes (states): FIRST ADDEND STATE, SECOND ADDEND STATE, and SUM STATE. The first addend a_i is presented and encoded prior to the FIRST ADDEND STATE and b_i is presented and encoded prior to the SECOND ADDEND STATE. The sum of the last two addends (less than 10) is determined prior to the SUM STATE. At each state, the processor must retain the

[2]It is possible to generalize directed graphs to include decision-making capabilities as well (see Gorn, 1973), but we have not done so here.

partial sum $(s_{i-1} \ldots s_2\ s_1)$ obtained prior to encoding the new
addends a_i and b_i. For example, just after the subject has
added the digits a_1 and b_1, he repeats the partial sum s_1 aloud
(at SUM STATE). Then, he encodes a_2 and is at the FIRST ADDEND
STATE. Next, he encodes b_2 and moves to the SECOND ADDEND
STATE. Finally, the subject adds a_2 and b_2, giving s_2, and
moves to the SUM STATE where the new partial sum $(s_2\ s_1)$ is repeated aloud. The process cycles through the three states each
time a new column is added.

In general, the maximum loads occur at the SECOND ADDEND
STATE. In adding two three-digit numbers, for example, the
maximum load of six occurs at the SECOND ADDEND STATE just before the third pair of digits (a_3, b_3) is added: two for the
column sums s_2 and s_1, one for the chunk (unit/data type)
$(s_2\ s_1)$, two for the new addends (a_3 and b_3), and one for those
addends as a distinct unit (data type). The rationalization for
counting $(s_2\ s_1)$ and $(a_3,\ b_3)$ as data types, over and above their
constituent elements, is that these units enter into subsequent
operations, $(s_2\ s_1)$ during recall at the SUM STATE and $(a_3,\ b_3)$
during addition between the SECOND ADDEND STATE and the SUM
STATE. Notice that after the sum is generated, the load is
four: one for the partial sum $(s_3\ s_2\ s_1)$, and three for the
column sums s_3, s_2, and s_1, which are subsequently repeated
aloud. The maximum load at the FIRST ADDEND STATE is also four:
two for the column sums s_2 and s_1, one for $(s_2\ s_1)$ and one
for a_3.

2.2 TEST OF THE ANALYTIC MODEL

The empirical viability of the proposed model was studied
by Voorhies and Scandura (reported in Scandura, 1973; more details are given in Voorhies, 1973). The method and results are
summarized below.

Method: Six tasks were used in the experiment: repeating
digit lists (L), repeating digit lists an extra time (XL), saying "1" before repeating digit lists (1L), noncarry addition
(NCA), carry addition (CA), and mixed addition (MA) with both
carrying and noncarrying.

In all three-list tasks, the digits were presented orally,
one at a time. After each digit was presented, the subject was
required to say the digit and then repeat every digit presented
up to that point. In Task XL, after hearing the instruction
"Repeat", the subject was required to repeat the last string of
digits an extra time. In Task 1L, the subject had to say "One"
before repeating the last string. The lists used in Tasks XL
and 1L were of predetermined length; in Task L, new digits were
added until the subject made a mistake.

The addition tasks were presented similarly. Each successive pair of digits corresponded to the digits in one column of
a column addition problem. After each such pair, the subject
was required to say the sum of the two digits. In the NCA task,
the next pair of digits was presented immediately thereafter,

and the process was repeated until the subject made a mistake. In the CA task, the subject verbally separated the tens and units digits of each column sum before continuing and added one to the first input digit from the next column. In the MA task, the tens digit of the sum was sometimes zero, so that no carrying was involved. In all addition tasks, the subjects were required to repeat each partial sum after adding the digits in a given column. This repeated overt responding on the part of the subject made it possible to both monitor progress during processing and help ensure that rehearsal was of a fixed, known variety.

The digits used in the individual problems were selected randomly, subject to constraints designed to minimize undesired chunking (see Voorhies, 1973). On each task, the subjects also were asked to evaluate the degree to which they followed the assigned processing procedure.

The subjects were six volunteer graduate mathematics students at the University of Pennsylvania who were tested individually. The subjects were trained both on the nature of the study and on the six tasks over a period of approximately three months prior to the experiment. Their cooperation in following each processing procedure to the best of their ability was strongly encouraged. In addition to extensive practice, a metronome was used to pace both the experimenter's presentation of digits and the subject's processing. The metronome speeds varied over subjects and were chosen so as to maximize the subject's "comfort" (cf. Chapter 2, Section 4.2). Preliminary training and practice continued until the experimenter was confident that the subjects were able to process the numbers automatically, under the experimental conditions and without errors or hesitations. During the experiment proper, each subject was tested within a ten-day period in a room as free of distractions as possible.

Each task was given on a different day with the order of tasks counterbalanced over subjects. After a brief review of the procedure in question, and being reminded of the need for cooperation, the subject was given five warm-up problems. Performance was evaluated on the twenty problems that followed. The main dependent variable was the percentage of criterion strings of a given length that were repeated correctly.

The analytic model described in the previous section was used to determine memory loads for each task at each stage of processing. Maximum loads of 7 and 8, respectively, were predicted for lists of length 6 and 7, noncarry addition with 4 and 5 digits per addend, carry addition with 3 and 4 digits per addend, and mixed addition with 3 and 4 digits per addend.

Results and Discussion: The data of the individual subjects were analyzed to determine sharp drops (over 40 percent in percentage correct from one load level to the next). The average of the base load levels (just prior to such drops), rounded to the nearest integer, was used to estimate each subject's processing capacity (C). Two of the six subjects had estimated capacities of 7 and four had capacities of 8.

Figure 2 summarizes the experimental results adjusted for capacity and averaged over subjects for each task (e.g., NCA). Although the differences between C-1 and C (t_{10} = 2.5, p < .02), C and C + 1 (t_{10} = 5.35, p < .001), and C + 1 and C + 2 (t_{10} = 1.9, p < .05) are all significant, the drop at capacity C from 65 percent correct to 27 percent correct at C + 1 is more than twice the drops of 17 percent between the other successive loads. (Note: The data at successive loads is conditional on success at the preceding loads. In effect, the probabilities of success at successive loads are statistically independent of the probabilities of success at the preceding loads so that simple t-tests provide an adequate basis for making essential comparisons.

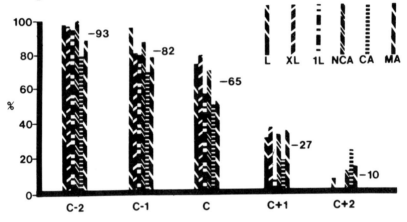

Figure 2. Performance at various capacity levels pooled over subjects, but adjusted for varying capacity levels.

In general, the analytic model seemed to provide reasonably good estimates of the memory loads involved in applying the assigned procedures to the various tasks. In the majority of cases (26 of 36) actual percentage drops in individual performance between successive loads on the various tasks were as predicted. That is, these drops tended to occur at the same, analytically determined (predicted) load level regardless of the task in question. Because all subjects were using essentially the same processing rules, this result suggests that information-processing capacity is not itself subject to short-term training (although task performance may be), and may have a physiological base. We agree with Miller (1956) that the "magic" of the number 7 (or 8) is one manifestation of being human.

Incidentally, rehearsal was observed to act just as any other processing procedure, and did not seem to improve performance. Although rehearsal may provide opportunity for recoding, where subjects inject rhythm or other process deviations into the procedure, rehearsal in and of itself does not seem to affect retention (cf. Dalrymple-Alford, 1967, in Section 1).

3. GENERALIZED, STOCHASTIC MODEL OF HUMAN INFORMATION-PROCESSING

In spite of the heuristic value of the deterministic model, actual predictions were something less than perfect. For example, at load C-1, 18 percent of the items were missed, while at load C+1, 27 percent of the items were repeated correctly. In spite of our efforts to minimize idiosyncratic variation, by intensively training subjects on particular procedures, such variation still existed. Undoubtedly, there were lapses in attention, unwanted chunking, and other deviations from the ideal that influenced performance.[3]

As suggested in Chapter 1, one way to account for such deviations is to introduce random variables that correspond to deviations from idealized conditions. There appear to be two major sources of such deviation, both involving extraneous processing. On the one hand, memory load may be increased because new, irrelevant information unintentionally becomes activated (e.g., via self-monitoring, thinking of things external to the algorithm). Such information may replace needed information and thereby hinder performance. On the other hand, extraneous processes may reduce memory load, for example, where two digits are recoded (chunked) as one unit.

Let α be the probability of an extraneous element (data structure) entering a fully utilized processor and displacing an element already present, and β, the probability of two critical elements being chunked into one unit. Assuming independence, α^n and β^n, respectively, are the probabilities of n extraneous elements entering the processor and n + 1 elements being recoded as one. For purposes of simplification, we also assume that errors occur only when the number of extraneous elements minus the reduction due to chunking is exactly one greater than the difference $C - L_j$ where C is the individual's capacity and L_j is the load at stage j. Accordingly, the probability of an error at the *j*th stage of processing is

$$P(E_j) = \alpha^{C-L_j+1} (1 - \sum_{i=1}^{\infty} \beta^i) + \sum_{i=1}^{\infty} \beta^i \, \alpha^{C-L_j+1+i}$$

which is equivalent to

$$P(E_j) = \alpha^{C-L_j+1} \left(\frac{1 - 2\beta}{1 - \beta} + \frac{\alpha\,\beta}{1 - \alpha\,\beta}\right) \tag{1}$$

where i + 1 is the number of critical elements reduced to one

---

[3]Although our training procedures were fairly intensive, our subjects were volunteers and hence not subject to the type of control that might have been possible had they been explicitly hired for purposes of the experiment, with attendant reward for good performance. To some extent, the algorithms taught could also have been somewhat ambiguous regarding memory load. For example, we did not attempt to formally represent distinctions stemming from whether items were to be stored or held in active memory.

chunk. Assuming that the subject never corrects himself once
an error is made, the probability of making an error in an n-
state computation is

$$P(E) = P(E_1) + (1-P(E_1)) \cdot P(E_2) + \ldots$$
$$+ (1-P(E_1)) \cdot \ldots \cdot (1-P(E_{n-1})) \cdot P(E_n) \tag{2}$$

Implicit in equation (1) are the assumptions that there is a
positive probability that no critical element is displaced

$(1 - \sum_{i=1}^{\infty} \alpha^i) > 0$ and that no chunking occurs $(1 - \sum_{i=1}^{\infty} \beta^i) > 0$.

These relations lead to the boundary conditions $0 < \alpha < 1/2$ and
$0 < \beta < 1/2$.

4. TESTS OF THE STOCHASTIC MODEL

4.1 STUDY ONE

In view of the complexity of the above equations, parameters
α and β cannot easily be estimated using standard maximum
likelihood methods. Instead, a computer program was constructed
which considered all possible $\langle \alpha, \beta \rangle$ pairs, representative of
intervals of size .01 (i.e., $\langle .01, .01 \rangle$, $\langle .01, .02 \rangle$, ..., $\langle .49,
.49 \rangle$). The estimated values of $\langle \hat{\alpha}, \hat{\beta} \rangle$ were the means of those
$\langle \alpha, \beta \rangle$ pairs for which the sum of the absolute differences between obtained and predicted data was minimal (e.g., less than
.1, see Voorhies, 1973, for details). (Such pairs were always
found to lie in relatively small convex, connected regions.)

The obtained $\langle \hat{\alpha}, \hat{\beta} \rangle$ estimates for each of the six subjects
on tasks L, NCA, and CA are shown in Table 1. Figure 3 shows
that these estimates provided a good fit of the data.

TABLE 1
$\langle \hat{\alpha}, \hat{\beta} \rangle$ Values at Critical Loads C-1, C, C+1

	L	NCA	CA	Mean
S_H	.04, .21	.17, .40	.46, .09	.22, .23
S_J	.46, .43	.42, .49	.46, .48	.45, .47
S_B	.33, .26	.41, .06	.47, .49	.40, .27
S_F	.14, .36	.26, .30	*	.20, .33
S_L	.30, .33	.30, .30	.37, .11	.32, .25
S_G	.38, .39	.26, .44	.16, .21	.27, .35
Mean	.28, .33	.30, .33	.38, .28	.32, .31

*None of the possible $\langle \hat{\alpha}, \hat{\beta} \rangle$ pairs met the required standard
suggesting that these two parameters were not adequate to account
for the data.

In general, the obtained estimates were relatively high, $\hat{\alpha}$ = .32, $\hat{\beta}$ = .31, and consistent with both the experimenter's informal observations and subject evaluations of their own performance (e.g., the use of rythmic patterns). (There were only five cases where $\hat{\alpha}$ or $\hat{\beta}$ was below .15.) This result suggests both that extraneous processing and chunking were involved and that these factors may be reflected in the $\hat{\alpha}$, $\hat{\beta}$ values.

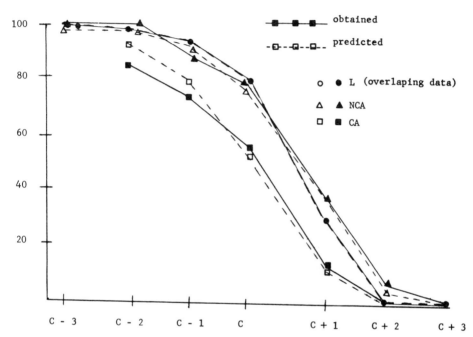

Figure 3. Obtained and predicted performance based on the stochastic model. Note: Obtained and predicted performance of L overlap.

Although the small number of cases precluded statistical tests, the parameters tended to vary more over subjects than over tasks. The respective means of $\hat{\alpha}$ and $\hat{\beta}$ over subjects ranged from .20 to .45 and from .23 to .47, while over tasks $\hat{\alpha}$ ranged from .28 to .38 and β, from .28 to .33. These results are generally consistent with the view that $\hat{\alpha}$ and $\hat{\beta}$ reflect internal deviations from the ideal that tend to remain constant over tasks for given subjects (i.e., where the presentation conditions are roughly equivalent).

4.2   STUDY TWO

To determine whether the degree of extraneous processing and/or chunking can be modified, a second study was conducted in which the subject was encouraged to bring visual and tactile processes into play.

Method: Four of the 6 subjects in the first study volun-
teered again to serve as subjects. Three of the six tasks (L,
NCA, and CA) were used and presented as in the first study with
the following differences:

1. Subjects were asked to "Bring a picture to mind" of each
digit presented but to eliminate the picture, if possible, before
processing the next digit. The analogue of an automatic slide
projector was used.

2. Subjects were required to move their arms in sharp up-
and-down movements as digits were spoken in cadence with the
metronome.
After each task instance (problem), the subjects also were required to respond to an explicit evaluation sheet concerned with
the extent to which they felt the problems had been processed
as planned. In addition, one-fourth of the 36 problems for each
task were presented on each of the four experimental days, instead of one task per day as in Study One. The reported results
are based on that two-thirds of the data, obtained where the
processes used were rated by both the experimenter and the subject as being most in conformance with the designated procedure.

Results and Discussion: Using the same criteria as Study
One to determine the individual capacities (C) of the individual
subjects, the obtained estimate for each of the 4 subjects was
one higher than in the previous study. For example, S_J's average capacity in Study One was 7 3/8 (rounded to 7), whereas in
Study Two, it was 8 1/4 (rounded to 8). Because of the higher
incidence of chunking reported by subjects in Study Two, and to
facilitate comparison, the lower estimates were used consistently.

The experimental results are summarized in Figure 4. The
drops between C and C + 1 ($p < .05$), C + 1 and C + 2 ($p < .05$),
and C + 2 and C + 3 ($p < .025$) are all significant.

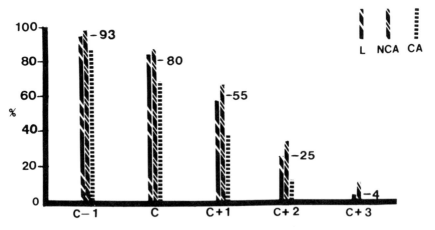

Figure 4. Performance at various capacity levels pooled over subjects, but
adjusted for varying capacities.

Overall, the obtained results differed in two ways from those in Study One: (1) the subjects performed at a generally higher level, and (2) the relatively sharp drop in performance that was previously found between C and C + 1 was replaced by a more gradual decline, spread over several load levels.

Although it was impossible to specify precisely the source of the generally improved performance, it is possible that the modified experimental procedure used in Study Two increased chunking. Indeed, subjects' comments on the *post hoc* evaluation form suggested that recoding was facilitated by images (cf. Paivio, 1971) of the digits. For example, subjects frequently reported that "pictures" of the digits often tended to linger and become superimposed on one another in memory, enabling them to "read" the digits off during recall. This observation, together with the possibilities for verbal, as well as visual, coding would lead one to expect a higher $\hat{\beta}$ than in Study One.

Application of the stochastic model tended to support this expectation; the suggested increase in chunking is reflected in the estimated values of $\hat{\beta}$. Using the individual estimates in Table 2 for prediction purposes, χ^2 tests revealed no significant differences between obtained and predicted performance. (In Study One, χ^2 was significant in only 1 of 30 cases.)

TABLE 2

$\langle \hat{\alpha}, \hat{\beta} \rangle$ Values at Critical Loads C-1, C, C+1

L	NCA	CA	Mean
S_J	.44, .49	.24, .45	.31, .44	.33, .46
S_B	.30, .43	.15, .43	.43, .48	.29, .45
S_F	.33, .45	NS	.43, .46	.38, .46
S_G	.12, .47	.21, .45	.33, .39	.22, .44
Mean	.30, .46	.20, .44	.38, .44	.30, .45

Note: NS means that the parameters $\hat{\alpha}$ and $\hat{\beta}$ did not provide a sufficiently close account of the data (Voorhies, 1973).

The obtained estimates of $\hat{\beta}$ averaged .14 above the corresponding mean (.31) in Study One. In only two cases did $\hat{\beta}$ decrease, and then only by .04. Although $\hat{\alpha}$ estimates for individual subjects and tasks differed from Study One, the average value ($\hat{\alpha}$ = .30) remained at approximately the same level (cf. $\hat{\alpha}$ = .32). Furthermore, whereas the variability of $\hat{\alpha}$ was approximately the same in both studies (σ = .13 in Study One and .11 in Study Two), the standard deviation for $\hat{\beta}$ was reduced from .14 in Study One to .03 in Study Two. The cause of this effect is not clear. One possibility is that directing the subjects to process digits simultaneously in multiple modes reduced the individual variation open to the subjects in Study One. (Another possibility is that the result was simply an artifact reflecting a boundary condition on $\hat{\beta}$.)

5. CONCLUDING COMMENTS

Basic theory and various results aside, perhaps the most important single contribution of this research is the new method it provides for studying a wide variety of memory and information-processing phenomena. Rather than having to rely exclusively on highly prescribed experimental conditions to control subject behavior, the proposed method of representing procedures (including processing loads) provides a feasible and psychologically meaningful way of manipulating the processes individual subjects use in dealing with such tasks. This possibility would appear to have important implications in a number of areas. For example, the proposed methodology could provide a useful way of dealing with such perennial experimental problems as ensuring that an item is in short-term store (or long-term memory) when that is what we want (cf. Waugh & Norman, 1965).

Research along these lines also could have important practical implications. In mathematics education, for example, considerable attention has been given to research concerned with the relative efficiency of various algorithms in arithmetic computation--between, say, the borrowing and equal additions methods for subtraction. The results of such research have traditionally been ambiguous. The proposed model not only provides a method for the explicit analytic determination of memory loads in using the respective algorithms but also a feasible method for obtaining definitive, empirical information. Such applications, of course, would imply some commitment to the deterministic model, and in turn to a sharp distinction between structural (deterministic) and incidental (stochastic) variables. (The latter correspond to deviations from the ideal, cf. Chapter 1.)

Because support for the deterministic model (Section 2) did not approach determinism, one might reasonably question the entire notion of a theoretical system based on a deterministic model--and, hence, reject the above distinction between structural and incidental factors. In this case, one might reasonably ask, for example, whether it is reasonable to postulate parameters, like α and β, that are independent of processor load. Indeed, it is reasonable to argue that α and β depend on processor load in two diametrically opposed ways. (1) the likelihood of extraneous processing and/or chunking could be a direct function of the availability of space for "turning around" on oneself, and (2) extraneous processing and/or chunking could vary directly with cognitive strain. Under these conditions, one also might reasonably ask whether C should have a fixed, integral value for each individual, as assumed here, or whether it should be estimated as a data parameter.

These alternatives would appear to be worthy of serious consideration. On the other hand, one could argue in favor of the deterministic model because the values of the parameters (especially β) appear to vary directly with degree of deviation from the ideal (cf. Studies One and Two, Section 4).

Admittedly, to argue so convincingly, far more extensive data would be needed than has been reported here. The main point, however, is that even where idealized conditions seem infeasible to realize (cf. Voorhies, 1973), one could conduct an experiment, in which deviations from the ideal are systematically varied. Thus, for example, were asymptotic values of α and β to approach 0 in such an experiment, one might reasonably infer deterministic results under idealized conditions. We know of no research, other than that reported, which bears even indirectly on this possibility but it would seem that some ought to be done.

REFERENCES

Anderson, J. R., & Bower, G. H. *Human associative memory.* New York: Halsted-Wiley, 1973.

Bower, G. H. Chunks as interference units in free recall. *Journal of Verbal Learning and Verbal Behavior,* 1969, *8,* 610-613.

Broadbent, D. E. *Perception and communication.* New York: Pergamon, 1958.

Brown, J. Some tests of the decay theory of immediate memory. *Quarterly Journal of Experimental Psychology,* 1958, *10,* 12-21.

Conrad, R. Serial order intrusions in immediate memory. *British Journal of Psychology,* 1960, *51,* 45-48.

Corballis, M. C. Rehearsal and decay in immediate recall of visually and aurally presented items. *Canadian Journal of Psychology,* 1966, *20,* 42-51.

Crowder, R. G. Prefix effects in immediate memory. *Canadian Journal of Psychology,* 1967, *21,* 450-461.

Dalrymple-Alford, E. C. Perception and immediate memory. *British Journal of Psychology,* 1967, *21,* 63-67.

Drachman, D. A., & Zaks, M. S. The "memory cliff" beyond span in immediate recall. *Psychological Reports,* 1967, *21,* 105-112.

Gorn, S. On conclusive validation of symbol manipulative processes: How do you know it has to work? *Journal of the Franklin Institute,* 1973, *296,* 499-518.

Katz, L. Limited-capacity hypotheses (?). *Journal of Verbal Learning and Verbal Behavior,* 1968, *7,* 942-944.

Meunier, G. F., Ritz, D., & Meunier, J. Rehearsal of individual items in short-term memory. *Journal of Experimental Psychology,* 1972, *95,* 465-467.

Miller, G. A. The magic number seven, plus or minus two: Some limits on our capacity for processing information. *Psychological Review,* 1956, *63,* 81-97.

Murdock, R. B. Test of the "limited capacity" hypothesis. *Journal of Experimental Psychology,* 1965, *69,* 237-240.

Paivio, A. *Imagery and verbal processes.* New York: Holt, Rinehart, & Winston, 1971.

Posner, M. I. Rate of presentation and order of recall in immediate memory. *British Journal of Psychology,* 1964, *55,* 303-306.

Posner, M. I., & Rossman, E. Effect of size and location of information transforms upon short-term retention. *Journal of Experimental Psychology,* 1965, *70,* 496-505.

Rumelhart, D. E., Lindsay, P. H., & Norman, D. A. A process model for long-term memory. In E. Tulving & W. Donaldson (Eds.), *Organization of memory.* New York: Academic Press, 1972.

Savin, H. B. On Conrad's prefix and grouping in short-term memory. *Quarterly Journal of Experimental Psychology,* 1968, *20,* 123-128.

Scandura, J. M. *Structural learning I: Theory and research.* New York: Gordon & Breach, 1973.

Sitterly, T. J. Short-term retention of sequentially presented digits as a function of interdigit interval, digit duration, and series length. *Journal of Experimental Psychology,* 1968, *78,* 174-178.

Somers, R. H. "Limited-capacity" hypothesis in incidental and intentional learning. *Psychological Reports,* 1967, *21,* 545-548.

Sternberg, S. The discovery of processing stages: Extensions of Donder's method *Acta Psychologica,* 1969, *30,* 276-315.

Suppes, P. Some theoretical models for mathematics learning. *Journal of Research and Development in Education,* 1967, *1,* 5-21.

Voorhies, D. *Information-processing capacity.* Unpublished doctoral dissertation University of Pennsylvania, 1973.

Waugh, N. C., & Norman, D. A. Primary memory. *Psychological Review,* 1965, *72,* 89-104.

Whimbey, A., & Lieblum S. Individual differences in memory span with and without activity intervening between presentation and recall. *Journal of Educational Psychology,* 1967, *58,* 311-314.

Whimbey, A., & Ryan, S. F. Role of short-term memory in solving reasoning problems mentally. *Journal of Educational Psychology,* 1969, *60,* 361-364.

Whimbey, A., Fischhof, V., & Silikowitz, R. Memory span: A forgotten capacity. *Journal of Educational Psychology,* 1969, *60,* 56-58.

Williams, J. R., & Fish, D. Effect of item length and number of different elements on immediate memory. *Psychonomic Society,* 1965, *3,* 353-354.

Woodworth, R. S., & Schlosberg, H. *Experimental psychology.* New York: Holt, 1954.

PART **4**

Individual Differences

In Part 2, we adopted the position of the competence theorist. Concern centered on the search for rules representing the competence underlying given problem domains. Rather than adopting the methods of generative scientists (e.g., in linguistics, artificial intelligence), however, two major additional constraints were imposed.

(1) Rules of competence were required to interact in a very specific way. This form of interaction (and other universal constraints) was assumed to be compatible with human cognition. Some justification for this assumption was provided in Part 3 where we adopted the perspective of the psychologist. There, attention was focused on cognitive universals--on discovering that which is common to human beings, rather than that which may be unique.

(2) The rules themselves were required to be "compatible" with the knowledge associated with idealized, prototypic individuals associated with particular subject populations.

Part 4 makes precise the intended sense of "compatible" in the context of simple problem domains. A major component in the analysis of any task domain is the identification of prototypic competence (solution) rules. In this regard, it matters little whether these rules are based on intuitive insights, systematic observation, or specific *a priori* information concerning the relevant culture of (i.e., competencies associated with) the population. The ultimate test of compatibility, of course, is empirical.

In effect, in Part 4 we take the role of the measurement (assessment) theorist, but not the traditional role based on normative testing. We are not interested in how different in-

dividuals perform relative to some group or to each other.
Rather, our approach falls within the criterion referenced philosophy. (The theory described in Chapter 2, Section 5, however,
is considerably more general and potentially more precise and
efficient.) The goal is to determine the kinds of behavior in
given problem domains that individual subjects are capable of
and the kinds that they are not capable of. In short, we want
to identify *individual behavior potential* (knowledge). In the
present context, this is equivalent to specifying what individual subjects know relative to the rules in the corresponding
competence theory.

Chapter 8 deals with knowledge assessment, relative to
simple problem domains, in situations where partial information
is available regarding what the subjects know; in particular,
where the atomic (component) rules are known. After training
on individual atomic rules, the subjects were given an opportunity to learn how to solve more complex, novel tasks by combining
and modifying the atomic rules in various ways. Then, sets of
test items were constructed, in a specific, theoretically prescribed manner. Next, the subjects were tested on two items of
each type. The use of two items made it possible to determine
both what the subjects had learned, and the reliability of the
assessment. Using a wide variety of tasks and subject populations it was possible, given performance on systematically
selected sets of items, to predict performance on (any) other
items in the respective domains with 96 percent accuracy. The
obtained phi coefficients, frequently used to measure test-
retest reliability, were unusually high (approximately .92).

Chapter 8 ASSESSING BEHAVIOR POTENTIAL: TEST OF BASIC THEORETICAL ASSUMPTIONS

Chapter 9 is concerned with knowledge assessment in regard
to ordinary subtraction, where judgements had to be made concerning the atomic rules. Various algorithms (rules) for solving
column subtraction problems were constructed so as to reflect
various likely ways in which the subjects might attack the prob-

lems. The intersection of the partitions imposed by these algorithms was used to divide the domain of subtraction problems
into equivalence classes. The domain was also partitioned by
two alternative technologies based on *item forms*.

In comparison with the item forms technologies, the algorithmic (structural) approach resulted in: (a) higher phi
coefficients, (b) significantly better prediction regarding
failures, (c) higher generalizability levels, (d) greater efficiency, and (e) higher validity indices on hierarchical ordering
of tasks. In addition, the close relationship in the structural
approach, between testing and what the subject does and does
not know, exposed an extremely close, parallel relationship between diagnostic testing and remedial instruction. (Note:
Experiments III and IV in Chapter 5 also can be thought of in
terms of diagnosis and remediation--in that case with respect
to higher-order generalization rules. For an additional example,
involving higher-order rules, see Chapter 13.)

Chapter 10 is concerned with certain statistical questions
that arise in evaluating rule-based theories. Specifically,
where several rules are equally feasible on *a priori* grounds,
how can one determine which one(s) are most compatible with
human knowledge? After briefly noting limitations of the reliability (consistency) measure used in Chapters 8 and 9, alternative information (entropy) measures and χ^2 tests are proposed.

In addition, the distinction between structural and incidental variables, first discussed in Chapter 1, is illustrated
in the context of simple observation theories (models) based on
the Poisson distribution. These models provide a convenient
method for distinguishing between knowers and non-knowers where
there are arbitrary numbers of test items associated with given
equivalence classes. Although the models were developed initially for dealing with simple concept learning, they are potentially applicable to assessment based on arbitrary rules.

It would appear that the research reported in Chapters 8,
9, and 10 represents a measurable advance in our ability to
assess behavior potential. Nonetheless, this progress is clearly
modest in comparison with the theoretical possibilities described
in Chapter 2. It falls short in two general ways.

First, the reported research pertains only to simple problem
domains where all problems may be solved via one or more (easily
identified) rules. Nothing was done or said with respect to
broader problem domains that can reasonably be accounted for only
in terms of (nondegenerate) rule sets. Such domains are characteristic of the hypothetical item populations on which normative
testing is based. Hence, among other things, research in this
direction could help to bridge the gap that currently exists
between normative and criterion-referenced testing. In view of
the theoretical progress that has already been made in structural
analysis (of nontrivial domains), empirical research on testing
is especially needed.

Second, the reported research deals only with success/fail-
ure data. Extensions to other types of equivalence (Chapter 2,
Section 5) are not dealt with in this part. Nonetheless, a
natural extension of this work in the context of stage equivalence (and to a lesser extent process equivalence) is provided
by the relatively large amount of literature on computer simulation. Insofar as the present theory is concerned, what needs
to be done is to demonstrate that protocol data, of the sort
used to evaluate simulation theories, can be explained in a way
that is consistent with the hypothesized cognitive universals
(see Chapter 2 and Part 3). (For an example based on a hypothetical protocol, see Chapter 15, Section 2.2.)

Perhaps even more important in this regard is the need to
bridge the gap between structural assessment and information
processing theories in cognitive psychology. On the one hand,
alternative rule-based theories in structural assessment have
been evaluated only up to success/failure equivalence. On the
other hand, the further requirements of process equivalence

exceed those in most contemporary information processing theories. Most contemporary research on skilled performance, for example, deals directly with latency measures, associated with component processes. But, to my knowledge, there have been few if any attempts to relate *component* processing speed with memory load (cf. Chapter 2, Section 4). Clearly, basic assumptions pertaining to process equivalence need to be tested and, if successful, they need to be more widely applied in information processing research.

8
Assessing Behavior Potential: Test of Basic Theoretical Assumptions[1]

Joseph M. Scandura and John H. Durnin

According to the theory described in Chapter 2, if one knows the rules available to a subject for achieving a given goal, then one can predict the subject's behavior perfectly. Ordinarily, however, one does not know this. Indeed, one of the main tasks to which the structural learning theory must address itself is that of how to determine what rules given subjects know.

Assessing what a subject knows is always relative to a given rule (procedure) set. Thus, given a potentially large and diverse problem domain, and a finite rule set that accounts for this domain, one major task of the behavior theorist is to determine which parts of which rules (procedures) in the set each given subject knows. This is equivalent to determining the subject's behavior potential (i.e., finding out which of the problems, associated with a given problem domain, that the subject can solve and which problems, he cannot solve).[2]

The precise nature of the problem and the current status

[1]The research reported herein was supported by U.S. Office of Education Grant GW 6796. This chapter is based on Scandura (1973, Section 3 of Chapter 7) which in turn was based on a more extensive paper by Scandura and Durnin (in press) which was originally published in 1971 as Technicap Report 62 in the Structural Learning Series. Support for the research was provided by the now defunct Basic Research Program of the U.S. Office of Education.

[2]Note that it is one thing to devise a procedure that accounts for a given class of rule-governed behaviors, and quite another to identify the subclass of these behaviors that a given subject can generate. The first problem is strictly analytical in nature and involves inventing a procedure(s) that accounts for the given class of rule-governed behaviors. No psychological assumptions are involved. Finding a solution to the latter problem, however, will necessarily depend on what can be assumed about the mechanisms that govern human behavior.

of directly related theory on individual differences measurement is described in Chapter 2. In this chapter, we sketch some
of the early developments that eventually led to this formulation. First, we sketch some of the earlier research that led
us to the question in the first place. This is followed by an
operational definition of "what (rule) is learned," and a discussion of its relationship to assessing behavior potential.
Next, we show how the simple theoretical assumption of Scandura
(1973) provides an adequate basis for assessing individual behavior potential, or equivalently, for finding out what a subject has learned, given the relevant prerequisite rules that
the subject knew before learning. Finally, a substantial amount
of supporting data is presented. In Chapter 9, we show further
that given a simple problem domain (where it is feasible to
identify one or more rules, each of which accounts for the domain in its entirety) it is possible both in principle and in
practice to determine which problems in the domain individual
subjects can and cannot solve. Given a performance profile on
a small selected sample of problems from the domain, it is possible (both below and in Chapter 9) to construct a rule that
accurately represents what the subject knows or has learned.

1.   THEORETICAL RATIONALE

1.1   RELATED RESEARCH

In his dissertation (1960-62), Scandura (1964) found that
the relative effectiveness of different modes of instruction
depended more on timing (i.e., what students knew relative to
the instruction being given) than on global differences in the
methods themselves. His interest in the problem of assessing
behavior potential increased during the summer of 1962, when
Greeno and Scandura (1966) found in an experiment on verbal concept learning that subjects either give the correct response the
first time they see a transfer stimulus or the transfer stimulus
is learned as its control. The thought later occurred to Scandura (1966) that if transfer obtains on the first trial, if at
all, then responses to additional transfer items, at least under
certain conditions, should be contingent on the response given
to the first transfer stimulus. In effect, a first transfer
stimulus could serve as a test to determine what had been learned during the original training. It would then be possible to
predict a subject's response to a second transfer stimulus.
During the middle and late 1960s, Scandura and some of his
students collected a fairly substantial body of data that provides strong support for this contention (Scandura, 1966, 1967,
1969; Scandura, Woodward, & Lee, 1967; Scandura & Durnin, 1968;
Roughead & Scandura, 1968). In these studies, the subjects were
presented with a rule statement or a number of instances of a
rule and required to learn the underlying rule. The subjects
were then presented with a test stimulus and instructed to re-

spond on the basis of what they had just learned. They were
told that they were correct no matter what the response. Then,
they were presented with a second test stimulus.

The results have generally been quite clear-cut. Whenever
the response given by a subject to the first test stimulus was
in accord with a particular given or derived rule, so was the
response to the second test stimulus. Generally speaking, it
was possible to predict second test behavior with anywhere between 80 and 95 percent accuracy.

The results of one study (Scandura & Durnin, 1968) on
extra-scope transfer further suggest that individual subject's
behavior potential can often be determined by the appropriate
selection of just two test instances. In particular, Scandura
and Durnin found that successful performance with two stimuli
that differ along one or more familiar dimensions implies successful performance with other stimuli that differ only along
these dimensions. This result suggests that success on well-
chosen test instances may be adequate to determine which S-R
instances (problems) in a given class a subject is potentially
capable of generating (solving) and which he is not. The question remains, of course, as to what is meant by a well-learned
dimension (or, well-chosen test instance).

Although our work progressed independently, and with somewhat different objectives, it was encouraging to note that
Levine (1966) and his collaborators (Levine, Leitenberg, &
Richter, 1964) also found this consistency notion useful in working with simple discrimination learning tasks. Levine, Leitenberg, and Richter, for example, used performance on nonreinforced
trials to predict performance on reinforced trials with a high
degree of success.

In general, it would appear that when a subject thinks he
is right and the new situation remains relevant, he will continue
to respond in a consistent manner.

Scandura originally thought that the entire notion of response consistency involved capitalizing on Einstellung (a mental set to perform) to ascertain what is learned and to predict
performance on future items. As it turned out, that hypothesis
was too restrictive (in memory-free research). It does not appear necessary to assume that a subject will (necessarily) continue to use the same rule on all test instances. Rather, one
can simply assume (Simple Performance Hypothesis): If a subject
has one or more appropriate rules available, in a given problem
situation, then he will use one of them. This allows a subject
to use one rule on one test instance and another one on a different instance. For example, in adding numbers, a subject might
apply the ordinary addition algorithm to a problem like 726 +
398, whereas a doubling technique of sorts might be used with a
problem like 250 + 250.

1.2   THE PROBLEM
With this in mind, let us turn more specifically to the

problem at hand: how to determine a subject's behavior potential, relative to a given class of rule-governed behaviors (simple
problem domain), on the basis of the subject's performance on
a (relatively small) finite number of test instances. The definition of "what rule is learned" in Scandura (1970), takes a
step in the right direction. The basic idea is that given a
performance profile, characterized by success on m of n problems
in a given class and failure on the remaining n-m problems, then
"what is learned" may be defined as the class of rules that
provides an adequate account of the data.

To see how this definition applies, consider the class consisting of arithmetic number series and their respective sums.
First suppose that a subject has demonstrated his ability to
find the sum (2,500) of the arithmetic series $1 + 3 + \ldots + 99$.
The definition tells us that the class "what is learned" includes
all and only those rules that provide an adequate account of
this behavior. In this case, the class would include, among
possibly other rules, each of the following: sequential addition (applied to arithmetic number series); the general rule
$([A + L]/2)$ N for summing arithmetic series; the rule N^2, which
applies to all arithmetic series of the form $1 + 3 + \ldots +$
$(2N - 1)$; the direct "association" between the series $1 + 3 +$
$\ldots + 99$ and its sum 2,500. Thus, "what is learned" might be
denoted by the class

> {direct association, N^2, $([A + L]/2)$ N,
>   sequential addition, ...}

As more test information is obtained about a subject's performance capability, it will generally be possible to eliminate
rules from this class. Suppose, for example, that a subject is
successful in determining the sum not only of the original test
series but also, say, of the series $1 + 3 + \ldots + 47$. Then the
size of the class "what is learned" is reduced accordingly to

> {N^2, $([A + L]/2)$ N, sequential addition, ...}

The direct association would no longer be allowed because
it does not apply to the second series. If the subject is successful on still another test instance, say, on the series
$2 + 4 + \ldots + 100$, then the class "what is learned" is further
reduced to the set

> {$([A + L]/2)$ N, sequential addition, ...}

(Note: In each case the class "what is learned" only characterizes individual behavior potential in terms of success/fail-
ure. It does not pinpoint the processes individuals use in order
to generate their responses, nor does it necessarily imply that
individuals use any of the rules in the class, or the same rule
on each problem. See Chapter 2 for a detailed discussion of

the theoretical issues involved.)

Suppose, on the other hand, that the subject is successful
on the first two test stimuli (i.e., $1 + 3 + \ldots + 99$ and
$1 + 3 + \ldots + 47$), but not the third (i.e., $2 + 4 + \ldots + 100$).
Then, according to the definition, not only would the direct
association be eliminated as a feasible rule, but so would the
more general rules ($[A + L]/2$) N and sequential addition. In
effect, the class "what is learned" would include only N^2, together with possible other unidentified rules which provide an
adequate account of the behavior.

As indicated, this definition provides a way for deciding
whether or not a rule is to be included in a class. It can also
be useful in making predictions about behavior potential. The
definition, however, says nothing about how rules in the class
are identified in the first place. More important, the definition provides no basis for identifying the test instances needed
to determine behavior potential. To specify the behavior potential of an individual relative to a given class of behaviors,
one must be able to specify a finite subset of test instances
that make it possible to predict the subject's performance on
all of the remaining items.

The traditional approach to this problem has been to resort
to probability statements of one sort or another (e.g., "On the
average, he should get eight out of ten items correct"). Thus,
predictions about behavior are made on the basis of past performance on a random sampling of test items. In this case we refer
to such statistics as expected values and variances in making
predictions.

The point of view taken here is that under memory-free conditions, there is no need to resort to probability in describing
the behavior potential of human beings. This does not imply perfect prediction, but only that uncertainty, rather than being
an explicit part of the theory or prediction model, has its
source elsewhere. Perfect prediction is impossible in principle
because there is always some residual uncertainty about the
capabilities and motivations that a subject brings to any given
task. And, we feel that this is exactly where this uncertainty
should be put.

Rather than make probabilistic predictions, based on a
random sampling of test instances, we propose an approach to
assessing behavior potential that makes deterministic predictions
possible. The basic idea involved in selecting an adequate set
of test instances is to partition the given class of problems
(and solutions) into a set of mutually exclusive and exhaustive
subsets so that each subset of problem instances is atomic. By
an atomic subset is meant an equivalence class in which success
on any one instance in the class is indicative of success on any
other instance in the class, and similarly for failure. Rule
learning studies conducted by Scandura and his students (for

reviews see Scandura, 1970, 1976) and others (e.g., Restle &
Brown, 1970; Suppes, 1976) over the past several years strongly
suggest the existence of such equivalence classes. Scandura
and Durnin's (1968) subjects, for example, almost always performed uniformly (well or poorly) on classes of similar items.
    Once such a partition has been found, of course, the next
step is obvious. One simply selects one test instance for each
equivalence class in the partition. Predictions on new instances,
then, are made in accordance with whether or not the subject
succeeds on the corresponding test instance--that is, the test
instance in the same equivalence class of the partition.
    Unfortunately, the problem of how to determine such a par-
tition in the first place is not trivial. Some idea of the difficulty may be seen by considering simple addition. Any attempt
to identify equivalence classes of addition problems, immediately
raises such questions as whether 25 + 30 is more like 5 + 30 or
more like 20 + 30. Clearly, some alternative to sheer guesswork
is needed.

1.3 A SOLUTION
    After mulling this problem over for some time, we concluded
that the most feasible way of identifying such a partition was
to tackle the problem intentionally--in terms of underlying procedures. (This does not rule out the possibility that extensional, cf. Scandura & Durnin, 1968, or dimensional analysis, cf.
Chapter 12, may also work.[3]) The problem here is one of reducing the number of possible procedures to reasonable proportions.
Theoretically, there are an infinite number of procedures that
might account for any given class of rule-governed behaviors/
simple problem domain (Rogers, 1967).
    Fortunately, this does not seem to pose undue difficulty
in practice. Given any familiar rule-governed class, it is
usually possible to determine those procedures that the subjects
in question are most likely to use. There are relatively few
basically different procedures for adding fractions, for example.
Furthermore, given any algorithm it is always possible to break
the procedure down into what might be called *atomic (sub)rules*.
By an atomic rule is meant a rule that is atomic with respect
to its domain (i.e., if use of the rule results in success on
one instance, it will result in success with the others, and
similarly for failure).
    To see this, it is sufficient to recall (e.g., Scandura,
1973), that, given any rule, it is always possible to break it

---

[3]Originally, we proposed that behavior potential might be defined relative
to certain (test) stimulus dimensions that were assumed to be well-defined for
the subject (cf. Scandura & Durnin, 1968). Although developed on more pragmatic
grounds, the item form method proposed by Hively, Patterson, & Page (1968) also
addresses itself to this problem. It now appears that both types of extensional
analysis are more naturally interpreted in terms of underlying procedures.

down far enough so that the constituent rules act in atomic fashion. This is trivially true in the case where the constituent rules are associations.

Furthermore, given even the barest minimum of information about a subject's capabilities, it is usually possible in practice to make intelligent guesses concerning whether or not a given subrule is apt to act in atomic fashion. Thus, for example, in adding whole numbers, most subjects either know how to carry, or they do not. There is no in-between. (Note: The question of atomicity is discussed in Chapter 2 in the context of "cultural" constraints; also see Scandura, 1973, 1976, Chapter 1.)

The precise nature of the relationship between a procedure and the atomic rules of which it is composed can perhaps be seen most easily by representing the former as a directed graph in which the arcs correspond to atomic rules in the procedure, and the nodes to branches. For example, consider the procedure for generating the "next" numeral in base three arithmetic. The atomic rules (numerals) and decisions (letters) are as follows.

1. Read (encode) rightmost (one's) digit of numeral.
A. If digit is "2", do operation 2; else go to operation 5.
2. Change "2" to "0," write it down.
B. If there are additional digits, do 3; else do 4.
3. Read next digit to left (and go to A).
4. Write "1" in next position to left of last "0" (and stop).
C. Stop.
5. Increment digit by 1, write it and remainder of numeral.

The problem-solution instances generated by this procedure are of the following sort: $0 \rightarrow 1$, $1 \rightarrow 2$, $2 \rightarrow 10$, $10 \rightarrow 11$, ..., $1022 \rightarrow 1100$, ... The procedure may be represented by the directed graph

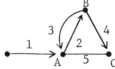

where the individual arcs of the graph correspond to atomic rules. Ignoring the number of times a "loop" is traversed (see Chapter 2, this book; Scandura, 1973), there are four distinct paths through the procedure.

(a)   (b)   (c)   (d)

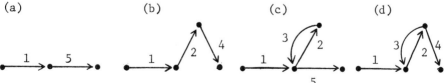

When looked at in this way it is easy to see that a person might master certain paths of a given procedure but not others. Furthermore, given that the rules in such a procedure (including the decision rules) are atomic, one can logically conclude that

each path in the procedure must also act in atomic fashion.[4]
From this it follows that each procedure effectively partitions
the original rule-governed class into equivalence classes of the
type mentioned earlier. In effect, an observer can determine
which paths a subject has learned, and which paths the subject
has not, by observing the subject's performance on a single instance from each equivalence class in the partition. In the
"next numeral" example, the numerals 101, 2, 112, and 222 provide an adequate set of test instances. Each is associated with
a distinct equivalence class.

Of course, more than one procedure may underlie the same
rule-governed class. Essentially the same approach applies here,
however, because the "intersection" of the partitions[5] that are
associated with the various procedures is also a partition (see
Chapter 9). In this case, it is the *intersection partition* that
we use to select the test instances--one test instance for each
element in the intersection partition.

The principle that underlies assessing behavior potential,
may be stated as follows: Given the simple performance hypothesis and assuming that the constituent rules of the procedures
associated with the rule-governed class all act in atomic fashion, then if a subject can solve any task in a given equivalence
class of the intersection partition, he should also be able to
solve any other task in the same equivalence class--and similarly
for failure.[6]

The intentional (structural) approach to testing provides
a systematic way of devising procedures that directly parallel
the behavior potential of individual subjects--that is, for constructing procedures that generate solutions to those and only
to those problems on which given individuals might be expected

[4]Durnin has found that the number of different paths through a procedure and,
hence, the number of elements in the partition, depends on the number of branches
in a very direct way. If a procedure has N binary branches, then it must have at
least $N + 1$ but no more than 2^{2N} different paths.

[5]More precisely, "intersection partition" refers to that partition that
consists of all n-fold intersections of equivalence classes involving one
equivalence class from each of the n partitions associated with the n non-
equivalent rules.

[6]The usefulness of this approach in future research, as well as practice,
requires more than just testing the theoretical hypothesis on which it is based.
With experimental confirmation of the simple performance hypothesis in the assessment situation, research can proceed in several directions. First of all, it
would be important to determine the value of this procedure in assessing the behavior potential of individuals at different developmental levels and with a
variety of different kinds of meaningful tasks. This could be particularly
important for research in various subject matter areas such as mathematics.
Second, it might be used to determine individual differences in computational
ability so that this might be taken into account in studies of problem solving
in which subjects have to compute. If the procedure can also be made to work
with such tasks as number conservation and the like, developmental psychologists
could have a valuable new tool for their research.
    Insofar as practice is concerned, there are also some fairly immediate
implications of such a procedure for diagnostic testing, sequential testing,
and computer-assisted instruction.

to succeed. This can be accomplished by deleting those atomic
rules of the original procedures that contribute only to the
generation of incorrect responses during testing.

Implicit in this process is the assumption that the paths
of a given procedure can be partially ordered according to difficulty. A path that contains all of the atomic rules of another
path plus some of its own would occupy, relatively speaking, a
higher position in the ordering. If a subject is successful on
an instance associated with a higher-level path, then the subject should also be successful on items associated with all
(relatively) lower-level paths. This provides a second hypothesis that can be tested experimentally.

1.4 TESTING THE HYPOTHESIS

The above principle rests on two major premises: (1) the
simple performance hypothesis of Scandura (1973) holds; (2) all
of the procedures that might possibly be used by a subject have
been identified, and have been represented so that each component subrule acts in atomic fashion. Given these premises, it
is possible both to predict the subject's behavior potential
relative to the given rule-governed class, and to determine which
of the identified procedures, or parts thereof, that individual
subjects know.

In testing the above principle, we implicitly assume that
the simple performance assumption holds--without formal empirical
testing. That is, we assume that if we somehow knew ahead of
time what relevant rules a subject had available, then we could
predict his behavior perfectly. Our concern is almost exclusively with the second premise, where we have less than complete information about what given subjects actually know.

A direct test of the second premise would involve situations
where one knows explicitly what procedures might be used and
that these procedures have been represented in terms of atomic
rules. Although this ideal can only be approximated in practice,
it can be approached in the laboratory by using novel tasks.
Here, the task solutions are defined in terms of arbitrarily
constructed procedures that the subjects could hardly be expected
to know ahead of time. Subjects, then, can either be trained
(to a high criterion), or not be trained, on individual components of these procedures so that each component subsequently
acts in atomic fashion. Next, the subject can be provided with
an opportunity to learn how to solve the tasks (presumably according to the mechanisms of Chapter 2). The above principle
can be tested after some degree of learning has taken place--
that is, after certain of the known atomic rules have been appropriately combined to form paths of a solution procedure.

A series of mini-experiments is reported in the next section
which demonstrate, the feasibility of the basic principle. Given
all of the solution procedures likely to be used, and after
training the subjects in the use of the atomic rules to a high

criterion, the subjects were provided with an opportunity to learn as much as they reasonably could be expected to learn with respect to the given task. A special (practical) problem in this regard was to devise tasks and procedures that were at an intermediate level of difficulty. If the procedures were too simple, the subjects learned all of the paths and, if they were too complex, they learned none. Then, the subjects were tested under nonreinforcement conditions on two items representative of each equivalence class in the associated partition. Performance on the first test item in each equivalence class was used to pinpoint what had been learned, and the second item to determine the adequacy of the assessment. These mini-experiments were conducted with a variety of tasks under different conditions and with different age populations.

To illustrate, again consider the procedure for generating the next numeral in base three arithmetic. (Assume that the task is unfamiliar to the subject [s] in question.) After identifying the paths of the procedure, and the four corresponding equivalence classes, two instances are arbitrarily selected from each. The numerals 101, 2, 112, and 222 are illustrative of the four equivalence classes.

In an actual experiment each subject would be trained on those atomic rules that one wants the subject to enter the testing situation with. Thus, in the "next numeral" example one might have the subject learn atomic Rules 1, 2, 3, and 4, but not, say, 5. The criteria used to ensure that the intended learning of the atomic rules has indeed taken place would necessarily be to some extent arbitrary but this should pose little problem in practice. The main thing to ensure is that the subject can perform perfectly on any instance of each atomic rule introduced during training. Consider, for example, atomic Rule 1. Only the most determined nonbeliever would be unwilling to admit that a subject had mastered Rule 1 if, after training, he is able to read correctly the rightmost digit of a wide variety of numerals such as: 2, 10, 110, 1010101, 112, 1111, 1012, 22222, etc.

Because the procedure is assumed to be unknown initially, the subject would then be provided with an opportunity to learn (parts of) the next numeral procedure. Although the mechanisms by which such learning takes place are not explained here the results of previous research provide a sufficient basis for defining appropriate learning and testing environments. Specifically, it has been shown (e.g., Levine, 1966) that learning only takes place on reinforced trials, where the subject is told or can otherwise determine whether or not his responses are correct (cf. Scandura, 1973, Chapter 7; also see Chapter 2; Part 3). After the subject is provided with an opportunity to learn, he is tested under nonreinforced conditions.

Experiments of this sort involve manipulating certain

aspects of prior learning of individual subjects, providing an opportunity for learning, testing each subject, and then, making predictions as to what they will do on additional test items. It is not a question of running groups of subjects or of averaging over different tasks. The following experiments were conducted with a number of different subjects on a number of different tasks under a number of different learning and test conditions. Our goal was to see if we could predict exactly what each subject could and could not do.

The predictions were tested by seeing in how many cases they held and in how many cases they did not hold. Questions of statistical inference did not enter, at least not in the usual sense. Of course, one cannot expect to be right all the time, but we did want to come as close to that ideal as possible. Our earlier research on response consistency (referred to in Scandura, 1969, 1976, Chapter 2) suggests that four correct predictions out of five would be a good standard to apply.

In view of the deterministic goal of this research, however, it was not our intention to simply attribute the fifth case to random error. Where possible, we sought to explain why the results did not turn out as expected. In this sense, our goals were much like the early physicist's. Where a law failed, he tended to attribute the results (where possible) to inadequate controls of one sort or another. His reasons typically ranged from unwanted friction or air resistance to an unknown additional force or forces acting on the body in question. In our case, the corresponding reasons might range from incomplete prior learning or inadequate test conditions to the influence of unidentified learning.[7] Nonetheless, in reporting actual results, we found it useful to compute confidence intervals concerning the percentage of "hits" and "misses".[8]

By combining this paradigm with that introduced and well-documented by Levine (e.g., 1966, 1969), it is possible to study the actual course of learning. Although Levine's research has dealt exclusively with simple discrimination learning, the basic ideas can apparently be extended to more complex situations as well. Stated in terms relevant to our purposes, the main ideas are as follows.

1. After pretraining on the atomic rules (hypotheses), the subject is provided with an opportunity to learn. That is, the subject is presented with test instances of the given rule-gov-

[7]These observations are but special cases of a discovery by philosophers of science (Ossorio, unpublished) that scientific laws cannot be demonstrated to be false. There is always an out. The point of experimentation is to determine how useful a scientific law is--that is, how widely applicable the law and how succinctly it summarizes the data to be explained.

[8]An interesting new approach to hypothesis testing that seems to be compatible with present requirements can be found in Hildebrand, Laing, and Rosenthal (1971).

erned class (simple problem domain) and given feedback (i.e., told whether he is right or wrong).[9]

2. Periodically during the course of learning, the subject is tested without reinforcement by a procedure that is directly analogous to the assessment procedure described above. (According to our own research findings and those of Levine's, a subject will not learn under the proposed conditions of nonreinforcement.)

Unlike Levine's procedure, however, ours is perfectly general. It should also be noted that whereas we introduced a second set of test items to determine the adequacy of the original assessment, Levine did not.

Although it is possible to gain information about the course of learning in this way, such information is necessarily probabilistic. Changes in learning from stage to stage, as in the research of Levine (1966) and Restle (1962), for example, have been essentially stochastic phenomena.

One further point is worth mentioning. Although the research of Levine, Restle, and others of that persuasion has included important elements of the type of analytical method we are proposing, they have not attempted to eliminate memory load. To the contrary, their theory (hypothesis theory, as it has been called) has been designed to take the subject's limited capacity to process information into account. This confounding of theorizing at the memory-free and memory-dependent levels has, in our opinion, led learning theorists to an almost complete reliance on stochastic theories.

It is one thing, of course, to test the assessment hypothesis directly, and quite another to determine what a subject knows on entering a situation. In the latter case, assumptions must be made not only about what procedures are viable, but also about the level of refinement required so that the components of these procedures act in atomic fashion.[10]

Where the tasks and procedures involved are familiar, what makes this feasible is the common culture shared by subjects in the target population (and the experimenter). To the extent that their backgrounds differ, the more difficulty one might reasonably expect in identifying viable procedures, and in representing them appropriately. As Piaget's research so clearly shows, for example, the rules that govern the behavior of young children are sometimes quite foreign to adults.

Durnin and Scandura (Chapter 9) not only demonstrated the

---

[9] There is, however, a major difference between the type of "learning" involved in the Levine studies and that proposed here.

[10] Assuming that all of the viable underlying procedures have been identified, the predictions should be adequate to the extent that the presumed atomic rules are indeed atomic. One would not expect good predictions and constituent rules that are not atomic, or poor predictions and constituent rules which are atomic.

feasibility of this algorithmic approach to assessing behavior
potential, but also compared it with two other approaches (item
forms, Hively, 1963, and hierarchical analysis) that have recently been proposed on more strictly pragmatic grounds.

2. EMPIRICAL STUDIES

2.1 GENERAL APPROACH

During 1969-71, we completed a number of experiments designed to test the above hypotheses. The approach was as follows.

1. A suitable class of rule-governed behaviors was selected,
together with an algorithm for generating each behavior in this
class. That is, given any problem in the class of problems, the
corresponding solution could be generated by following a path
of this algorithm. It was of particular interest to choose tasks
that were not so easy that the subjects, on their own, could
learn to be uniformly successful on the tasks, nor so hard that
they would be uniformly unsuccessful.

2. Each of the atomic rules included in the identified algorithm was then built directly into the subject in question in
the sense that he could correctly apply each of the constituent
atomic rules uniformly well. Where the number of instances of
an atomic rule was infinite, enough varied instances of the rule
were chosen to assure ourselves that the subject did have complete mastery.

3. Armed with these atomic rules as prerequisite knowledge,
the subject was presented with problems from the given rule-governed class and was asked to generate the corresponding solutions. After the subject proposed a solution, or indicated that
he did not know the answer, knowledge of results was provided
in either one of two forms--self-reinforcement or external reinforcement given by the experimenter. This procedure was continued with new instances until the subject seemed not to be
making any further progress on the learning trials. During the
learning period, care was taken to insure that the subject had
ample opportunity with problems (test instances) corresponding
to each path of the algorithm.

4. The subject was then tested on one arbitrarily selected
instance for each path. More accurately, the instances were
selected from the equivalence classes corresponding to the various paths through the algorithm.

5. Predictions were made as to the subject's performance
on future instances associated with these equivalence classes
(paths of the algorithm) on the basis of how the subject had
performed on the test instances. These predictions were checked
in the obvious way by simply testing the subject on another set
of representative instances.

According to our analyses, confirmation was expected with

all subjects on all tasks to the extent that the presumed boundary conditions were met--that is, to the extent that: the subject was actually trying to solve the problems, the presumed
atomic rules were indeed atomic, and the subject was unencumbered by memory or his limited capacity to process information.
Our aim was to run this basic experiment with a wide variety of
different tasks and with a wide variety of different subjects
at different developmental levels. In particular, subjects were
sampled from graduate school down to the preschool level. Notice
that each combination of task and subject constitutes a replication of the basic experiment.

The task and method used in Experiments 1 to 5 are described
in detail. The others are only summarized, except where we wish
to emphasize a particular point. (For details, see Scandura &
Durnin, in press.)

2.2 EXPERIMENTS 1 TO 5

The task used involved self-reinforcement. Whereas the
subjects were able to check their answers independently during
the learning period, however, this was not possible during
testing.

First, the class of rule-governed behaviors (problem domain) used in these experiments involved finding multiplicative
inverses of four-tuples (e.g., (0, 1, 2, 0)) of integers modulo
3 (mod 3), and was modelled on matrix multiplication. The system of integers mod 3, which consists of elements 0, 1, and 2,
may be defined by the addition and multiplication matrices in
Table 1. The subject was shown how to multiply two four-tuples
by using the definition $(a, b, c, d) \cdot (e, f, g, h) = (a \cdot e + b \cdot g, a \cdot f + b \cdot h, c \cdot e + d \cdot g, c \cdot f + d \cdot h)$ where + and
$\cdot$, respectively, are the operations of addition and multiplication in mod 3. For example, $(1, 0, 2, 1) \cdot (2, 0, 1, 2) = (1 \cdot 2 + 0 \cdot 1, 1 \cdot 0 + 0 \cdot 2, 2 \cdot 2 + 1 \cdot 1, 2 \cdot 0 + 1 \cdot 2) = (2, 0, 2, 2)$.

TABLE 1
Addition and Multiplication Matrices for Four-Tuples

(a) Addition				(b) Multiplication		
+	0	1	2	$\cdot$	0	1	2
0	0	1	2	0	0	0	0
1	1	2	0	1	0	1	2
2	2	0	1	2	0	2	1

A four-tuple A is said to have a *multiplicative inverse* if
there exists a second four-tuple B (possibly the same) such that
their product is (1, 0, 0, 1). For example, since A $\cdot$ B =
$(1, 0, 2, 1) \cdot (1, 0, 1, 1) = (1, 0, 0, 1)$, B is said to be the

multiplicative inverse of A.

The subject's goal in Experiments 1-5 was to find inverses for given problem four-tuples. If a four-tuple (a, b, c, d) has an inverse, then the flow diagram in Figure 1 presents one algorithmic procedure for finding it.

This flow diagram can be represented more simply as a directed graph where lines represent operations (atomic rules) and points, the decisions that need to be made in carrying out the algorithm. This graph, together with the six possible paths through it, and illustrative problems associated with these paths, is given in Figure 2.

Second, during the preliminary-training phase, the subjects were first taught how to add and multiply integers mod 3 and an operation * defined by *(0) = 0, *(2) = 1 and *(1) = 2. They were also given the definition for multiplying four-tuples and practice in applying the definition. In addition, the subjects were shown the identity (1, 0, 0, 1) and told what an inverse was. This information made it possible for the subject to check his answers.

Then, each subject was taught the following six atomic rules.

1. Form the products a · d and b · c (i.e., multiply a,d and b,c).

Example: Given (1, 0, 2, 1) then a · d = 1, b · c = 0.

2. Form *(b · c) and the sum a · d + *(b · c).

Example: Given b · c = 2, a · d = 1, then *(b · c) = 1, a · d + *(b · c) = 2.

3.a. Interchange a and d; i.e., (a, b, c, d) → (d, b, c, a)
   b. Multiply d, b, c, and a by 2; i.e., (2d, 2b, 2c, 2a)
   c. Change 2b to *(2b) and 2c to *(2c)

Example: (2, 2, 1, 0) $\overset{(a)}{\to}$ (0, 2, 1, 2) $\overset{(b)}{\to}$ (0, 1, 2, 1) $\overset{(c)}{\to}$ (0, 2, 1, 1)

4.a. Multiply a, b, c, and d by 2; i.e., (2a, 2b, 2c, 2d)
   b. Change 2b to *(2b) and 2c to *(2c)

Example: (2, 1, 0, 1) $\overset{(a)}{\to}$ (1, 2, 0, 2) $\overset{(b)}{\to}$ (1, 1, 0, 2)

5.a. Interchange a and d; i.e., (a, b, c, d) → (d, b, c, a)
   b. Change b to *(b) and c to *(c)

Example: (2, 1, 0, 1) $\overset{(a)}{\to}$ (1, 1, 0, 2) $\overset{(b)}{\to}$ (1, 2, 0, 2)

6. Change b to *(b) and c to *(c)

Example: (1, 1, 0, 1) → (1, 2, 0, 1)

The subject was trained on each rule to a criterion of at least three correct responses in a row and was allowed as much time in working with the rules as he required. The order of presenting these rules was randomized.

Third, after the subject had learned the six atomic rules to criterion, he was given a practice sheet consisting of 24 problem four-tuples from the rule-governed class. The problems presented were divided into four sets of six instances each, one instance from each of the six equivalence classes. Within each set, the instances were randomized. The subject was then told

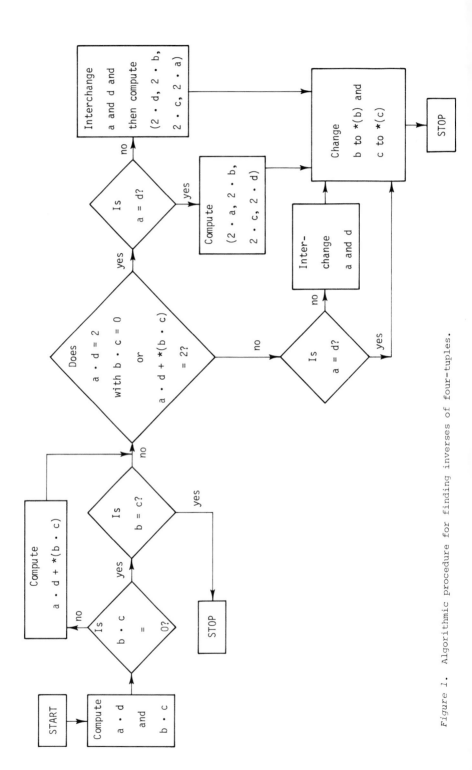

Figure 1. Algorithmic procedure for finding inverses of four-tuples.

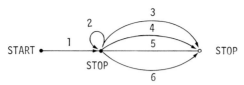

Paths[a]	Stimulus Instances from Corresponding Equivalence Classes
1.	(1, 0, 0, 2)
2.	(2, 1, 0, 1)
3.	(2, 0, 2, 2)
4.	(0, 1, 1, 1)
5.	(0, 1, 1, 0)
6.	(1, 2, 2, 2)

Figure 2. Sample paths through four-tuple algorithm and sample stimulus instance from each corresponding equivalence class.

[a]The numbers associated with the various arrows specify which atomic rules they represent.
The diagram indicates that there are several other paths through the procedure (e.g.,). No instances in the given rule-governed class require the use of these vacuous paths, however, so they may be discarded.

to find the inverse of each four-tuple using the (atomic) rules
he had just learned. He was told to do as many of the problems
as he could and to check his answers by multiplying the four-
tuple he derived with the one given. The subject knew he was
correct, if and only if the product was (1, 0, 0, 1). A printed
statement of the rule for multiplying four-tuples was available
to him at all times so that he did not need to commit the rule
to memory. The subject was allowed as much time as he needed
to complete the problems.

Fourth, after the subject had completed as many problems
as he could, the experimenter collected the problem sets and the
printed statement of the rule for multiplying four-tuples.

The first set of test problems consisted of six new problem
four-tuples, one instance from each equivalence class. During
the testing, as well as the pretraining, the subject had statements of the atomic rules available in case he forgot any of
them. He did not, however, have the rule for multiplying four-
tuples so that he could not check his answers. Indeed, the
subject was closely monitored so that he did not have time to
check his answers even if he had succeeded in memorizing the
rule. According to our earlier results, then, the subject was
unable to learn during testing; the test trials correspond to
Levine's (1966) nonreinforcement trials.

Fifth, the subject was given a second set of test problems
of the same type immediately following the first test. There
were no time limits on either test.

The results of Experiments 1 to 5 (five subjects using this
task) are given in Table 2. The "+" indicates a correct solution
while "-" indicates an incorrect solution. The encircled pair
indicates a result that went contrary to prediction. In this
case, there were 29 correct predictions and one incorrect.

TABLE 2
Results of Experiments 1 to 5

	1		2		3		4		5	
	Grad. Student w/background in Coll. Math		Grad. Student w/background in Coll. Math		Grad. Student w/background in Coll. Math		Coll. Grad. w/background in H.S. Math		Coll. Student w/background in H.S. Math	
Equiv. Class.	1st test in-stance	2nd test in-stance	1st test in-stance	2nd test in-stance	1st test in-stance	2nd test in-stance	1st test in-stance	2nd test in-stance	1st test in-stance	2nd test in-stance
1	+	+	+	+	+	+	+	+	+	+
2	+	+	+	+	+	+	-	-	-	-
3	+	+	+	+	+	+	+	+	-	-
4	+	-	+	+	+	+	-	-	-	-
5	+	+	+	+	+	+	+	+	-	-
6	+	+	+	+	+	+	-	-	-	-

2.3 EXPERIMENTS 6 TO 21

The second set of experiments involved tasks in which the reinforcement was external. Only on the practice trials, did the experimenter tell the subject whether or not he was correct.

The task used in *Experiments 6 to 9* was adapted from Polish notation used in logic to avoid the use of parentheses (cf. McCall, 1967). For example, subjects were given strings of symbols, like MA5,6A2,1, and asked to compute the result given that A meant add and M meant multiply. In accordance with the algorithm identified, the first step in this case would be to add 5 and 6, then add 2 and 1, and finally multiply the two sums 11 and 3, giving the result 33. Eight equivalence classes of stimuli were determined from the algorithm.

The subjects were two graduate and two undergraduate students at the University of Pennsylvania and the experimental procedure was identical to that described earlier. The results were as predicted in 31 of 32 cases. Ten of the correct predictions involved consistent failure (on tasks from given equivalence classes) and the remainder, consistent success.

In *Experiments 10 and 11,* the task was based on an array method for multiplication (cf. Eves, 1964). To illustrate the method, consider the task of finding the product 456 x 32. First, construct the array

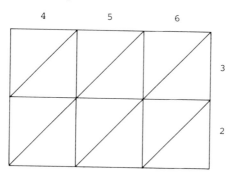

and record the individual products in the boxes as shown. The product 14,592 is determined by summing (within the large rectangle) along the diagonals.

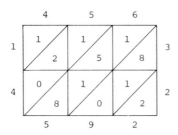

The specific procedure employed had eight paths.

Again the same experimental procedures were used, this time with two sixth-grade students in West Philadelphia. Fifteen of 16 predictions were correct. Five correct predictions involved (consistent) failure.

The task for *Experiments 12 to 15* was designed for use with preschoolers, and involved crossing out squares, circles, and combinations thereof from given displays of three circles and three squares (e.g., ◯ ◯ ☐ ◯ ☐ ☐). The subject was given a stack of 3 x 5 inch stimulus cards with a colored figure drawn on one side of each card. The figures varied along two dimensions: color (red, blue, and yellow) and shape (square and circle), with the relevant dimension being shape. The cards were turned face down. The subject was told to turn each card over and cross out on the display sheet whatever figure was shown on the card. The corresponding procedure had 5 paths.

Four children, aged 5, 4, 3, and 2 1/2, served as subjects. The results were as predicted in all 20 cases. Eight correct predictions involved failure.

During the course of Experiments 12 and 13 we observed that the two older subjects who could count used a slightly different procedure than the one we identified. Fortunately, the paths through the procedure they used partitioned the class of tasks into exactly the same equivalence classes. The hierarchical arrangement of the paths associated with these two procedures was different, however, and the effect of this on the hierarchy results is reported below.

The task used in *Experiments 16 to 19* also was designed for use with young children. In addition to crossing out squares and circles, as before, whenever two circles or three squares, respectively, were crossed out the subject was required to also draw a circle within a square or a square within a circle. Given the stimulus ◯ ☐ ◯ ☐ ☐ ☐ ◯ , for example, a correct response would be ◯ ☐ ⊘ ⊠ ⊠ ⊠ ⊘, ☐ ⊡ . One seven-year-old, one six-year-old, and two four-year-olds served as subjects.

Four equivalence classes of test instances were identified; 14 of the 16 predictions were correct. Eight correct predictions involved failure. The two inconsistencies were attributed to the six-year-old for whom single and repeated application of an atomic rule seemed to pose a different problem. Although the data do not speak to this point it seems reasonable to suspect that the decision-making capabilities employed by this particular child were not adequate.

In *Experiments 20 to 21,* the subjects were shown two cards containing one, two, or three congruent figures (circles, triangles, or squares) and were asked to identify which properties (number, shape) were common to both. This was indicated by turning over response cards indicating specific properties. The procedure for accomplishing this involved two atomic rules and four paths. One subject was five-years-old and the other was 6. Eight correct predictions were made out of 8. Six of the eight predictions involved failure.

2.4 EXPERIMENTS 22 TO 30

In the third set of experiments the subjects had no obvious way of knowing during practice whether their answers were correct or not. They were neither told when they were correct nor given an independent means for checking their answers. The main purpose was to determine whether the intrinsic structure of procedures may itself provide sufficient reinforcement for learning.

The task used in *Experiments 22 to 26* was based on forming products of two-cycle permutations (cf. Herstein, 1964). The procedure employed had eight paths.

The subjects were one undergraduate and four graduate students at the University of Pennsylvania. Correct predictions were made in 39 of 40 cases. Seven correct predictions involved failure.

The task used in *Experiment 27* was essentially a complication of that used in Experiments 16 to 19. The subject was an undergraduate at the University of Pennsylvania. The results were 7 predictions out of 8. No correct predictions involved failure.

The final task *(Experiments 28 to 30)* was adapted from an old method for adding Roman numerals (cf. Eves, 1964). There were eight paths through the associated algorithm.

The subjects were two high school students in West Philadelphia and one undergraduate at the University of Pennsylvania. Correct predictions were made in 24 of 24 cases. Five correct predictions involved failure.

2.5 DISCUSSION

The studies reported in the previous section provide strong support for the basic hypothesis. In a total of 194 cases, there were 187 or 96 percent correct predictions. The 95 percent confidence interval for this proportion (96 percent is between 93 percent and 99 percent).

The results also provide evidence in favor of an even stronger hypothesis. Not only does success on one instance of a given equivalence class imply success on any other instance in that class, but frequently it also implies success on instances in certain other equivalence classes. As suggested earlier, the equivalence classes associated with a given partition may be partially ordered as to difficulty.

The basis for this partial ordering, recall, resides in the nature of the corresponding paths. Thus, certain paths include others in the sense that the former contain all of the atomic rules of the latter, and in the same order, plus some

additional ones. For example, in the task used in Experiments
12 to 15, Path 5 is superordinate to Paths 4, 3, 2, and 1 and
Paths 4 and 3 are superordinate, respectively, to Paths 1 and
2. These relationships can be represented

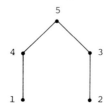

The data show that in all 12 cases where a subject was consistently successful on a superordinate path, he was also successful
on the subordinate paths. The converse was not always true.
Of the 8 cases where the subjects were successful on all of the
subordinate tasks, they were also successful on the corresponding superordinate tasks only 6 times. (Note: The interested
reader may derive corresponding relationships for Experiments
1-5 from the paths in Figure 2, e.g., Path 2 is superordinate
to Path 1. These may be checked in Table 2.)

     In all, there were 205 cases in which one path was super-
ordinate to another. In all but 7 or 3 percent of these cases,
success on a superordinate task implied success on the subordinate ones. The 95 percent confidence interval for the obtained
97 percent prediction level is between 95 percent and 99 percent.

     It should be noted that 4 of the 7 exceptions can be attri-
buted to the strong possiblity in Experiments 12 to 15 that two
of the subjects generated a procedure from the given atomic rules
that differed from that on which the analysis was based. This
possibility could not have had an effect on the within-equiv-
alence-class analysis because the same partition would have resulted. But, it would have affected the hierarchy analysis.

     Conversely, where subjects were successful on *all* subordi-
nate tasks (at the next lower level) they also were consistently
successful on the corresponding superordinate tasks, in 90 of
117 cases. These results are directly comparable to those obtained using the form of task analysis that was pioneered in
education by Gagne (1962) and his collaborators (e.g., Gagne,
Mayor, Garstens, & Paradise, 1962). There too, successful
performance on superordinate tasks is almost always indicative
of success on subordinate tasks, and success on all of the
subordinates frequently (about 80 percent of the time) implies
success on corresponding superordinate tasks (cf. Chapters 1
and 11).

     This should not come as a surprise, because the hierarchical
algorithmic analysis proposed roughly parallels task analysis.
The major difference is that our intentional analysis allows for
denumerably many different ways of solving a given class of tasks

whereas task analysis implicitly assumes that there is just one. Analysis in terms of procedures is also more precise and explicit in the sense that the analyst is forced to make his intuitions public. It is interesting to note that some task analysts have recently begun to move in this direction (Resnick, 1970). (Note: This study was conducted during 1969-71.)

As suggestive as they might be, our experimental results deal only indirectly with the problem of assessing individual behavior potential with respect to given classes of rule-governed behavior (simple problem domains). In these experiments, the subjects were trained in the atomic rules. To assess behavior potential, the observer must make intelligent guesses as to which procedures given subjects (i.e., populations of subjects) might reasonably use, including judgements concerning the component (i.e., atomic) rules. The feasibility of the algorithmic approach in the latter context was tested by Durnin and Scandura; the essentials are reported in the next chapter.

REFERENCES

Eves, H. *Introduction to the history of mathematics* (2nd ed.). New York: Holt, Rinehart, & Winston, 1964.

Gagne, R. M. The acquisition of knowledge. *Psychological Review*, 1962, *59*, 355-365.

Gagne, R. M., Mayor, J. R., Garstens, H. L., & Paradise, N. E. Factors in acquiring knowledge of a mathematical task. *Psychological Monographs*, 1962, *76*, Whole No. 526.

Greeno, J. G., & Scandura, J. M. All-or-none transfer based on verbally mediated concepts. *Journal of Mathematical Psychology*, 1966, *3*, 338-411.

Herstein, I. N. *Topics in algebra*. New York: Blaisdell, 1964.

Hildebrand, D. K., Laing, J. D., & Rosenthal, H. A measure for relating qualitative data to hypothesized forms of association. Mimeographed paper WP-48-70-1, GSIA, Carnegie-Mellon University, 1971.

Hively, W., II. Defining criterion behavior for programmed instruction in elementary mathematics. Cambridge Mass.: Harvard University, 1963.

Hively, W., II, Patterson, H. L., & Page, S. A "universe defined" system of arithmetic achievement tests. *Journal of Educational Measurement*, 1968, *5*, 275-290.

Levine, M. Hypothesis behavior by humans during discrimination learning. *Journal of Experimental Psychology*, 1966, *71*, 331-338.

Levine, M. Neo-noncontiguity theory. In G. Bower & J. T. Spence (Eds.), *The psychology of learning and motivation* (Vol. 3). New York: Academic Press, 1969.

Levine, M., Leitenberg, H., & Richter, M. The blank trials law: The equivalence of positive reinforcement and nonreinforcement. *Psychological Review*, 1964, *71*, 94-103.

McCall, S. *Polish logic 1920-1939*. London: Oxford University Press, 1967.

Resnick, L. B. Issues in the study of learning hierarchies. Paper read at the Annual American Educational Research Association Meeting, Minneapolis, March, 1970.

Restle, F. The selection of strategies in cue learning. *Psychological Review*, 1962, *69*, 329-343.

Restle, F., & Brown, E. Serial pattern learning. *Journal of Experimental Psychology*, 1970, *83*, 120-125.

Rogers, H. J. *Theory of recursiveness and effective computability*. New York: McGraw-Hill, 1967.

Roughead, W. G., & Scandura, J. M. "What is learned" in mathematical discovery. *Journal of Educational Psychology*, 1968, *61*, 581-591.

Scandura, J. M.   An analysis of expository and discovery modes of problem
    solving instruction. *Journal of Experimental Education,* 1964, *33,* 149-159.

Scandura, J. M.   Precision in research on mathematics learning: The emerging
    field of psycho-mathematics. *Journal of Research in Science Teaching,*
    1966, *4,* 253-274.

Scandura, J. M.   Learning verbal and symbolic statements of mathematical rules.
    Journal of Educational Psychology, 1967, *58,* 346-364.

Scandura, J. M.   New directions for theory and research on rule learning: II.
    Empirical research. *Acta Psychologica,* 1969, *29,* 101-133.

Scandura, J. M.   Role of rules in behavior: Toward an operational definition of
    what (rule) is learned. *Psychological Review,* 1970, *77,* 516-533.

Scandura, J. M.   *Structural learning I: Theory and research.*   New York: Gordon
    & Breach, 1973.

Scandura, J. M.   *Structural learning II: Issues and approaches.*   London/New York
    Gordon & Breach 1976.

Scandura, J. M., & Durnin, J. H.   Extra-scope transfer in learning mathematical
    strategies. *Journal of Educational Psychology,* 1968, *59,* 350-354.

Scandura, J. M., & Durnin, J. H.   Assessing behavior potential: Adequacy of basi
    theoretical assumptions. *Journal of Structural Learning,* in press (To
    appear in Volume 6, No. 1).   (Originally published as University of
    Pennsylvania, Structural Learning Series Report No. 62.)

Scandura, J. M., Woodward, E., & Lee, F.   Rule generality and consistency in
    mathematics learning. *American Educational Research Journal,* 1967, *4,*
    303-320.

Suppes, P.   Stimulus-response theory of finite automata.   In J. M. Scandura (Ed.)
    Structural learning II: Issues and approaches.   London/New York: Gordon &
    Breach, 1976.

9
Algorithmic Approach to Assessing Behavior Potential: Comparison with Item Forms[1]

John H. Durnin and Joseph M. Scandura

Recent research in individualized and computer-assisted instruction has led to an increasing awareness of the inadequacies of norm-referenced testing and the need for testing procedures that determine each individual's mastery on specific types of tasks (e.g., Coulson & Cogswell, 1965). Knowing how well a student has performed relative to some peer group, for example, says relatively little about the kinds of decisions that must be made if instruction is to be totally individualized. Ideally, mastery testing should (1) provide a sound basis for diagnosing individual strengths and weaknesses on each type of task, (2) require as few items as possible, and (3) provide a basis for generalizing from overall test performance to behavior on a clearly defined universe or domain of tasks. If, in addition, items can be ordered hierarchically to allow for conditional (sequential) testing, efficiency could be further increased.

Fortunately, a number of new technologies have recently been developed for constructing tests that have the above characteristics (e.g., Ferguson, 1969; Hively, Patterson, & Page, 1968; Scandura, 1971). The purpose of this study was to

[1]This chapter is adapted from "An Algorithmic Approach to Assessing Behavior Potential: Comparison with Item Forms and Hierarchical Technologies", by John Durnin and Joseph M. Scandura, *Journal of Educational Psychology*, 1973, *65*, 262-272 with permission of the American Psychological Association. This study, based on a doctoral dissertation submitted by the first author under the second author's chairmanship, was supported by U.S. Office of Education Grant 3-71-0136 and, in part, by the National Science Foundation Grant GW 6796, both to the second author. The authors thank Alfonzo Georeno and David Shore for their cooperation in providing subjects.

compare, with respect to these characteristics, three of the
technologies; the item forms technology (domain-referenced testing) of Hively *et al.* (1968), the hierarchical or stratified
item forms technology of Ferguson (1969), and the algorithmic
technology of Scandura (1971, 1973).

In domain-referenced testing, a defined universe or domain
of items (e.g., column subtraction problems) is subdivided into
classes of items or item forms on the basis of observable properties the items in each class have in common. Osburn (1968)
characterized an item form as having a fixed syntactical structure (e.g., x-y), one or more elements (e.g., 42-21, 28-16),
and explicit criteria for specifying which elements belong to
the form (e.g., $x = x_1x_2$; $y = y_1y_2$; $y_1 < x_1$; $y_2 < x_2$; x_1, x_2,
y_1, $y_2 \in \{0, 1, 2, \ldots, 9\}$). To assess pupil performance on a
given domain of problems a test is constructed by randomly
selecting one item from each of the identified forms.

It was felt by Hively *et al.* (1968) that item forms might
be used not only to assess a pupil's overall performance on the
domain of problems but also to predict his behavior on specific
problems in the domain. That is, if a subject were successful
on one problem belonging to an item form then he would be successful on any other problem of the same form, and, similarly,
if he were unsuccessful on a problem belonging to an item form,
he would be unsuccessful on any other problem of the same form.
Although Hively *et al.* (1968) obtained high coefficients of
generalizability (Cronbach, Rajaratnam, & Gleser, 1963) for
tests based on the item forms technology, their item forms, in
general, were not homogeneous in the sense that the problems
associated with individual item forms were not behaviorally
equivalent (regarding success-failure).

One criticism of the item forms technology has been that
the hierarchical relationships among item forms have not been
taken into account in testing. In a recent study by Ferguson
(1969), these relationships were dealt with explicitly. In this
study, item forms were generated for both terminal and prerequisite instructional objectives in a way analogous to task analysis
(e.g., Gagne, 1962). Starting with a terminal item form, corresponding to a terminal instructional objective, sub-item forms
(i.e., sub-objectives) were identified that were considered prerequisite to the terminal item form. The item forms so identified were then ordered according to the hypothesized hierarchical structure and a computer was programmed to make branching
decisions based on probabilistic evaluations of student performance on each of the forms. Clearly, a conditional testing
procedure of this sort could conceivably provide a highly efficient basis for assessing the behavior potential of individual
subjects.

Although the technologies for assessing mastery developed

by Hively *et al.* (1968) and Ferguson (1969) appear to be major steps toward improved mastery and diagnostic testing, they are subject to serious criticism if one adopts a cognitive, information-processing view. The technologies are based primarily on extensional analyses of item domains (i.e., analyses in terms of observable properties of items). With the possible exception of Ferguson's hierarchical ordering of forms that is based essentially on task analysis, there appears to be little basis other than (possible) sound intuitive judgement as to how items should be categorized. As a result, both technologies can be criticized on a priori grounds. For example, the item forms identified for subtraction by Hively *et al.* (1968) and those identified by Ferguson (1969), both failed to partition the domain of subtraction problems into mutually exclusive and exhaustive classes (i.e., equivalence classes). More specifically, some problems were associated with more than one item form and some problems were not associated with any item form. For example, the problem, 153 - 92, cannot be uniquely classified in terms of the item forms of Hively *et al.* (1968). This problem is compatible with both the "borrow" and "no borrow" item forms. This lack of strict partition in the mathematical sense may very well have contributed to Hively *et al.'s* (1968) finding that item forms did not represent homogeneous classes of items. In general, it is not an easy task to generate item forms that will partition a domain.

Furthermore, neither technology specifically takes into account the knowledge that makes it possible to solve problems belonging to a given domain. This is an important limitation because there can be any number of ways of solving problems within a domain. For example, there are several common rules a pupil may use to solve subtraction problems. His performance on such problems could be due to his mastery of any one of these rules. (Identifying what rules may be used on a domain of problems also has important implications for providing remediation; more is said on this below.)

Scandura's (1971, 1973) theory of structural learning provides a theoretical basis for an algorithmic technology for assessing behavior potential that deals directly with the above problems. This theory consists of three hierarchically related partial theories: a theory of competence, a memory-free theory of learning and performance, and a theory of memory. For present purposes, two basic assumptions of the memory-free theory suffice. Stated simply, they are that people use rules (procedures) to solve problems and if an individual has learned a rule for solving a given problem or task, then he will use it.

To see how these assumptions are involved, notice that if an observer knows what rule or rules a subject has available for solving a given domain of problems, then he can predict perfectly the subject's performance on problems in that domain. Unfortunately, the observer generally has no a priori way of knowing this. Nonetheless, with many familiar tasks (e.g., ordinary

subtraction) there is a limited number of rules that subjects
in a given population are most likely to use (e.g., the "borrowing" and "equal addition" methods for subtraction), and the
first step in assessing behavior potential is for the observer-
theorist to identify them.

It does not necessarily follow, of course, that every subject (or even any subject) will know any one of these rules
completely. Rules consist of operations and branching decisions
(i.e., subrules) that are performed in certain specified orders
(see Scandura, 1973). The branching decisions of the rule serve
to combine the operations in different ways for solving different
kinds of problems. Thus a subject may know part of a rule or
parts of several rules, and hence, may solve certain tasks
governed by the rule(s) but not others. The object of testing
is to determine from a subject's performance on a limited number
of problems what parts of the rule or rules he knows and what
parts he does not know.

The operations and branching decisions of a rule (algorithm)
can be represented as a computer program, flow chart, or directed
graph. From a flow chart representation one can see that there
are a finite number of ways in which the subrules may be composed
or sequenced to solve problems. These sequences of subrules,
ignoring repetitions, are called *paths,* and partition the domain
of tasks governed by an algorithm into equivalence classes (for
details, see Scandura, 1973, Chapter 9).

Consider, for example, the domain described by "Find sums
(less than 100) for column addition using two or more addends
of one digit." For illustrative purposes, it is convenient to
consider a rather mechanical algorithm governing this domain
(cf. Chapters 12 and 15, Sections 3.2 and 3.3). This algorithm
may be characterized by the following program: (1) add the top
two addends;   (2) if there are no other addends, go to 3, otherwise go to 4;   (3) write the sum and stop; (4) add the unit's
digit of the obtained sum to the next addend; (5) if the sum is
greater than 10, go to 6, otherwise go to 7; (6) add 1 to whatever is in the ten's place and return to 2; (7) return to 2.

This program can be represented by a directed graph (see
Figure 1) in which the numbered arcs correspond to the subrules
and points, to branching decisions (i.e., "if" statements).
From the graph it can be determined that there are four paths
through the algorithm:

1. Path 1 is used to solve problems having only two addends.
2. Path 2 is used to solve problems having more than two
   addends but with intermediate sums less than ten and the
   final sum less than nineteen.
3. Path 3 is used to solve problems having more than two
   addends, where successive sums increment the ten's place.
4. Path 4 is used to solve problems having more than two
   addends where the successive sums may or may not incre-

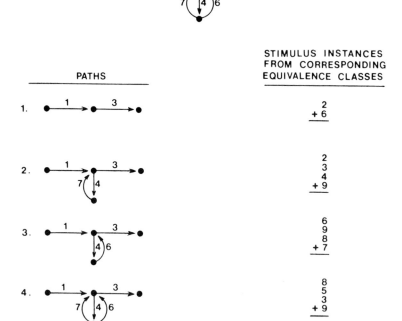

Figure 1. Directed graph of column addition algorithm.

ment the ten's place.

Each problem in the domain of an algorithm is solvable via exactly one of its paths. Hence, the paths partition the domain into equivalence classes (i.e., problems are equivalent if and only if they are solvable by the same path).

If the constituent subrules of an algorithm are atomic for a subject (i.e., if each is either "known" perfectly or not at all) then it follows logically that the paths of the algorithm will also act in atomic fashion. That is, if a subject is successful on any one item in an equivalence class, then he should also be successful on any other and similarly for failure. In effect, according to this theory, only one item is needed from each equivalence class in order to test for mastery of the algorithm (i.e., assess a subject's behavior potential).

There may, of course, be more than one feasible algorithm underlying a domain of tasks, each of which, in general, will

partition the domain differently. This slight complication can
be easily handled by forming what we shall call an *intersection
partition* on the given domain of tasks. The intersection partition is formed by selecting equivalence classes from one partition and taking their intersections with equivalence classes
of other partitions. The collection of all possible nonempty
intersections formed in this way generates the intersection
partition. Generally speaking, the intersection partition is
a finer partition of the domain than the partition associated
with any one algorithm. Thus, to assess behavior potential
simultaneously with respect to all of the identified algorithms,
it will suffice in theory to (randomly) select just one item
from each equivalence class belonging to the intersection
partition.

In order for this assessment procedure to be applicable to
a given population of subjects, the observer must assume that
he has refined the algorithms to a point where the subrules are
atomic for most of the subjects. According to the theory, this
is always possible in principle because the subrules of an algorithm may be decomposed into ever finer subrules (i.e., refined).
Indeed, rules can be reduced to associations such as 3 + 2 = 5
(Arbib, 1976; Scandura, 1970, 1976; Suppes, 1976), that, under
the present memory-free conditions, are necessarily atomic. It
should be kept in mind, however, that unnecessary refinement of
an algorithm results in a loss of testing efficiency. More test
items are needed. In practice the goal is to find some optimal
level of refinement.

The algorithmic technology also provides a basis for ordering equivalence classes of problems. Certain paths in an algorithm are superordinate to other paths in that they contain all
of the atomic rules of the subordinate path plus some of their
own. For example, Path 4 of the above algorithm is superordinate to Paths 1, 2, and 3, and both Path 2 and Path 3 are superordinate to Path 1. Since the branching decisions associated
with a superordinate path encompass those associated with its
subordinate paths, it follows that if a student can use a superordinate path, he should be able to use the subordinate paths.
Hence, success on problems associated (only) with a superordinate path should imply success on all problems associated with
relatively subordinate paths.

Empirical support for the above analysis is reported in
Chapter 8 (also see Scandura, 1971, 1973). In that study a
variety of tasks were used and the subjects ranged in ability
from preschool to the graduate level. The atomic rules of
each algorithm were "built in" (taught) to each subject. They
were then provided with an opportunity to put the rules together
to solve problems belonging to the domain of the algorithm. (The
theory of structural learning accounts for the combining of subrules through the use of higher-order rules, see Scandura, 1971.)

Each subject was then tested on one item from each equivalence class associated with a path of the algorithm. Based on first test performance, predictions were made concerning performance on individual second test items. The results of the study showed that prediction of combined success-failure on second test items was possible with 96 percent accuracy (ϕ = .92). Furthermore, it was found that in 95 percent of the cases where a subject was successful on a superordinate path he was also successful on all subordinate paths.

In summary, the algorithmic approach deals directly with all of the questions raised earlier. It provides a theoretical basis for categorizing classes of problems, and assures that this categorization partitions the domain of problems into equivalence classes. It also provides a theoretical basis for the hierarchical relationship between tasks and takes into account the different ways in which a domain of tasks may be solved. (The implication of this for task analysis is that there can be more than one way of hierarchically ordering problems within a given domain of tasks. In fact, there is a different hierarchy for each rule governing the domain.)

Granting the more rigorous theoretical foundations for the algorithmic technology, its pragmatic value relative to other existing technologies was still an open question. The objective of this study was to help clarify this issue. Specifically, we wanted to determine whether or not the algorithmic approach to partitioning, which is based on an intuitive analysis of intension (i.e., analysis in terms of underlying rules or procedures), provides any practical advantage in criterion referenced testing, relative to the extensional technologies of Hively et al. (1968) and Ferguson (1969). The domain of column subtraction problems was chosen for the comparison.

In effect, the different ways in which the various technologies subdivided the domain of subtraction problems constituted the independent variable. Item forms are based on extensional analysis of the kinds of problems involved. Ferguson's approach is essentially another version of item forms, in which more explicit attention is given to hierarchical relationships. (Here, however, some of the complex problems were left out of the analysis.) Algorithmic analysis, on the other hand, is based on what the subject has to do, that is, the processes he must go through in order to solve the problems. This form of intensional analysis sometimes combines classes that, on the surface, appear to be different; it may also distinguish classes that can otherwise be grouped on extensional grounds. For example, consider that path of the subtraction algorithm (Figure 2) shown in Figure 3. This path governs both problems shown in Figure 3 but according to item forms analysis the problems belong to two different classes.

For purposes of this study, practical advantage meant that one or more of the following criteria were met: (1) improvement in predictions concerning the performance of individual subjects

on particular kinds of test items, (2) improvement in the degree
of generalizability (from test items to a clearly specified
domain), (3) reduction in the number of test instances required
to determine behavior potential, and (4) improvement in the
hierarchical ordering of tasks (with its important implications
for conditional testing).

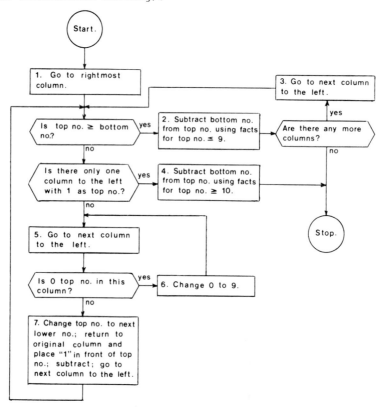

Figure 2. Subtraction algorithm.

1. METHOD

The algorithmic technology was used to construct four algorithms for column subtraction. Two algorithms were based on a
"borrowing" procedure for subtraction and consisted of 6 and 5
paths, respectively. The other two algorithms were based on an
"equal additions" procedure and consisted of 4 and 8 paths, respectively. The intersection partition with respect to all four
algorithms was then constructed. It contained 12 equivalence
classes. The flow chart of the subtraction algorithm shown in
Figure 2 was designed explicitly to have a path corresponding
to each and every equivalence class in the intersection partition. For example, the path of the algorithm in Figure 3 determines correct solutions for the class of subtraction problems

having more than one column and using facts $\leq$ 9.

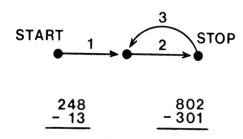

Figure 3. Sample path through subtraction algorithm and two stimulus instances from the corresponding equivalence class.

Hively et al. (1968) used an item forms analysis of subtraction problems to identify 28 subclasses of problems. Of these 28 subclasses, 22 pertained to column subtraction. With the exception of "Large numbers", which was omitted from consideration because it included several of the other categories (e.g., "Borrow one digit from large number", "Repeated borrows", "Separated borrows", etc.), the item forms were interpreted to represent mutually exclusive classes of problems.

By taking intersections of the 21 item forms with the 12 equivalence classes generated by the algorithmic approach, 37 distinct classes of subtraction problems were obtained. Prediction and criterion tests, parallel Tests A and B respectively, were constructed by generating two arbitrary items for each of the 37 classes in the intersection set obtained from item forms and equivalence classes, one for each test. The order of items was randomized within each test.

1.1 SUBJECTS AND PROCEDURES

The subjects were 34 ninth-grade general mathematics students attending summer school at Shaw Junior High School in Philadelphia. Tests A and B were administered to the subjects in their classrooms on consecutive days. The order in which the tests were given was counterbalanced over subjects. Of the 34 subjects, 25 were in attendance both days and received both Tests A and B.

1.2 ANALYSIS

Since Ferguson (1969) in his analysis identified hierarchical forms involving only simple subtraction problems (i.e, numbers with three or fewer digits), comparison of the assessment procedures was done in two parts: (1) for the entire domain of column subtraction problems, and (2) for a restricted domain of subtraction problems, comparable to Ferguson's hierarchical forms. The restricted domain consisted of classes of problems in the intersection set associated with 7 of the 12 equivalence classes and 13 of the 22 item forms.

In order to compare the item forms and algorithmic approaches on the unrestricted domain of subtraction problems, two imbedded subtests were designated for each technology, one from *Test A* and one from *Test B*. With the algorithmic technology, for example, this was done by randomly selecting one test item for each equivalence class from those items in *Tests A* and *B,* respectively, that belonged to that equivalence class. This was possible because the 12 equivalence classes partitioned the 37 items in each test into 12 mutually exclusive and exhaustive classes. The other *A* and *B Tests* were constructed similarly, using item forms.

To compare performance on the restricted domain, a pair of similar imbedded subtests was designated for each technology (restricted intersection, algorithmic, hierarchical forms, and item forms), from problems belonging only to the restricted classes of items in *Tests A* and *B.*

Performance on the unrestricted subtests provided the basic data for comparison of the algorithmic and item forms technologies for the unrestricted domain of subtraction problems. Performance on the restricted subtests provided the basic data for comparison of the algorithmic, item forms, and hierarchical forms technologies on the restricted domain of subtraction problems.

2.   RESULTS AND DISCUSSION

2.1   LEVELS OF PREDICTABILITY

Table 1 shows the levels of predictability and correlation between items belonging to the same class for each of the various types of tests on the unrestricted domain of subtraction problems.

In regard to the first criterion, the overall levels of predictability on individual items were approximately the same for all unrestricted tests. However, the correlation (Phi coefficient) of .53, between corresponding *Test A* and *Test B* items, involving the 2 x 2 success-failure matrix for the 300 equivalence class instances, was significantly greater ($p < .05$) than the correlation of .39 between corresponding items for item form instances. This correlation for equivalence classes was also higher, although not significantly so, than that for the intersection of equivalence classes and item forms (.49).

The difference in correlations between equivalence classes and item forms was due to the significantly higher ($p < .05$) levels of predictability for equivalence classes for those *Test A* items on which subjects were not successful. Furthermore, the level of predictability for those *Test A* items on which subjects were not successful was also significantly greater ($p < .05$) for equivalence classes than for the intersection of

TABLE 1

Number of Items, Percent Correct Predictions, and Correlations between Corresponding Items

Tests	Number of Items	Number of Test A instances on which Ss were successful	Percent correct predictions	Number of Test A instances on which Ss were not successful	Percent correct predictions	Total number of Test A instances	Percent correct predictions	Correlation between corresponding A and B test instances
Intersection	37	699	91%	226	55%	925	82%	.49
Item Forms	21	444	89%	81	51%	525	83%	.39
Equivalence	12	225	85%*	75	71%*	300	82%	.53*

* p < .05

357

item forms and equivalence classes. This latter result must be
tempered, however, because the difference in levels of predictability between the intersection and equivalence classes for
those *Test A* items on which subjects were successful was also
significant (p < .05). (The corresponding difference between
equivalence classes and item forms was not significant.)

In effect, the test constructed on the basis of the algorithmic technology with approximately 57 percent as many items
(12 as compared to 21) gave better predictions on individual
items than the corresponding test for item forms. Furthermore,
tests formed from the two algorithms based on "borrowing" had
65 percent and 75 percent levels of prediction where subjects
were unsuccessful on *Test A* items with overall levels of predictability at 78 percent. These levels of prediction were
obtained with only 6 and 5 items for the respective tests.
Hence, with considerably fewer items these tests were not only
as effective in overall predictability as the intersection and
item forms tests, but also had higher (and for the 5 item test
significantly higher, p < .05) levels of predictability than
the item forms test for those *Test A* items where subjects were
unsuccessful.

It is also worth noting, that of the four algorithms originally identified, the two based on "borrowing" had significantly higher (p < .05) levels of prediction than the two algorithms based on "equal additions" where subjects were unsuccessful on *Test A* items (65 percent and 75 percent as compared to
29 percent and 32 percent). The implication of this, of course,
is that for these subjects the tests formed from algorithms
based on "borrowing" were better predictors than the tests formed
from algorithms based on "equal additions". This difference
between the two types of subtraction appears to reflect the fact
that "borrowing" is the more common procedure taught in American
schools.

Components of variance analysis (Winer, 1962, pp. 184-191)
are also relevant to criterion one. For example, although the
interaction of subjects by items within classes contributed most
of the variance for each of the three types of test on the unrestricted domain, the contribution was lowest for equivalence
classes (40 percent versus 63 percent for item forms). Furthermore, the sources of variance due to classes and subjects by
classes were greater for equivalence classes than item forms
(22 percent versus 15 percent and 27 percent versus 15 percent,
respectively). These results tend to confirm the previous finding that even with fewer items, the algorithmic approach was
more sensitive than the item forms technology in pinpointing
strengths and weaknesses of individual students.

As regards the restricted domain, none of the obtained results concerning the levels of predictability or correlation was
significantly different. Restricting the domain, however, had

the effect of increasing overall predictability for each technology. The obtained levels of predictability were practically identical, ranging only from 89 percent to 91 percent. Since most of the problems in the restricted domain appeared to be relatively easy for the subjects, the levels of predictability for "success" items were even higher (93 percent - 95 percent). The relatively small number of errors involved overall suggests that the low levels of predictability for items on which subjects were not successful (22 percent - 41 percent) may have been due to careless mistakes.

Components of variance could not be obtained for most of the tests in regard to the restricted domain because estimates of variance due to items within classes were negative for all restricted tests except item forms. In that case, the contribution of variance due to persons by items within item forms was 77 percent.

2.2 GENERALIZABILITY RESULTS

In regard to the second criterion, Table 2 shows the coefficients of generalizability α' and α'_s for each type of test. The coefficient α' is a lower bound estimate of how well one can generalize from a subject's obtained score on a test to his performance on the stated domain of items (Cronbach et al., 1963), in this case column subtraction problems. It is also an intraclass correlation coefficient for estimating reliability (Winer, 1962, pp. 124-132). The coefficient α'_s (Rajaratnam, Cronbach, & Gleser, 1965) is an estimate of generalizability for stratified parallel tests, tests for which the domain of items is divided into different classes as was the case in this study.

TABLE 2
Coefficients of Generalizability α' and α'_s

Tests	α'	α'_s
Intersection	.85	.87
Item Forms	.62	.66
Equivalence Classes	.71	.74
Restricted Intersection	.39	.46
Hierarchical Forms	.15	.14
Restricted Item Forms	.29	.25
Restricted Equivalence Classes	.30	.21

The top half of Table 2 shows the coefficients of generalizability for the unrestricted domain of subtraction problems. Of these, the intersection test provided the highest estimates of generalizability; those for equivalence classes were next; and item forms last. Again, it is of interest to note that the two subtests formed from "borrowing" algorithms had levels of generalizability as high as the subtest formed from item forms. For the test with 6 items $\alpha' = .75$; $\alpha'_s = .60$, and for the test with 5 items $\alpha = .64$; $\alpha'_s = .62$.

On the restricted domain of subtraction problems, the coefficients shown in the lower half of Table 2 for the restricted intersection, restricted item forms, and restricted equivalence classes were greater than the coefficients for hierarchical forms.

The values of α' and α'_s obtained for the restricted tests were not the same as those obtained for the unrestricted tests ($\chi^2 = 20.6$, 6df, $p < .01$; $\chi^2 = 26.19$, 6df, $p < .01$). In effect, a subject's score on a restricted test and in particular on the test generated by hierarchical forms could not viably be generalized to the entire domain of column subtraction problems. Hence, although the overall levels of predictability for these tests were higher than those generated from the unrestricted domain, the above results indicate that this was accompanied by a significant loss in generalizability.

2.3 EFFICIENCY CRITERION

The data clearly show that the algorithmic approach was more efficient than the item forms technology. Only 12, as compared to 21, items were required to achieve an equivalent overall level of predictability, significantly better error predictions, a significantly higher correlation between corresponding A and B test instances, and somewhat better levels of generalizability. The increase in efficiency evident with the tests formed from the two "borrowing" algorithms is even more striking. With only 6 and 5 items, respectively, they had essentially the same levels of predictability and generalizability as the item forms test with 21 items.

Furthermore, although it seems reasonable to suppose that the intersection test with 37 items would produce the highest levels of predictability and generalizability, in general this was not the case. With a third (12 as compared to 37) as many items, the algorithmic approach maintained as high a level of overall predictability and only slightly (nonsignificantly) lower levels of generalizability. The item forms test, which had slightly more than half the number of items as the intersection test, also obtained as high a level of predictability although somewhat lower levels of generalizability. Overall, these results lead one to suspect under the testing conditions used, that the algorithmic approach for assessing mastery approaches asymptote. Further improvement would almost necessarily require more rigorous testing conditions (cf. Chapter 8; Scandura & Durnin, in press).

Even on the restricted domain the equivalence classes test appeared to be the most efficient. Overall levels of predictability were the same for all tests, while generalizability coefficients were somewhat higher for the equivalence class and item forms tests. These higher levels of generalizability, however, were obtained with half as many items in the case of the equivalence classes test.

2.4 HIERARCHICAL ANALYSES

The fourth criterion is concerned with the fact that efficiency may sometimes be increased through the use of conditional testing procedures, at least where the various items lend themselves to Guttman (1947) type scaling. In the present study, however, it must be noted that each of the technologies compared provides an explicit basis for ordering items that is independent of empirical data (cf. Ferguson, 1969; Hively et al., 1968).

The method of analysis used to determine the relative validity of the three hierarchies was similar to that used by Gagne (1962) to confirm relationships between higher- and lower-levels in task analysis. A hierarchy was validated when failure on at least one of the relatively subordinate classes implied failure on (at least one of the problems in) a superordinate class and success on a pair of problems associated with a superordinate class implied uniform success on all problems associated with relatively subordinate classes. A hierarchy was contradicted when success on a superordinate class failed to indicate success on all relatively subordinate classes. The proportion of verifying cases (i.e., the number of verifying cases divided by the number of verifying plus contradictory cases) was .82 for the equivalence classes hierarchy as compared to .74 for the item forms hierarchy (p < .01). None of the differences on the restricted domain were significant.

To summarize, then, the algorithmic approach not only provided the best and most efficient method for assessing behavior potential, but the hierarchy induced by the approach could be used to increase this efficiency even more (relatively speaking) through the use of conditional testing procedures that involve branching.

2.5 IMPLICATIONS

On almost all measures obtained the algorithmic approach to assessing behavior potential proved to be either better, or at least as good, as the technologies based on item forms or hierarchical analysis. Nonetheless, at first thought the item forms technology might appear to have a certain advantage over the algorithmic approach. Given an item form, it is a routine matter to generate an instance of that item form. This could be particularly useful in computer-assisted testing since the computer could be programmed to randomly generate test items within forms. (The item forms themselves, however, must be determined directly by the test constructor.)

In the algorithmic approach, this would have to be done indirectly. Nonetheless, the computer, once given an algorithm, could be programmed to automatically trace out the paths, identify the equivalence classes, and order the items for testing. That is, the computer should be able to generate not only the items but also the item forms (i.e., equivalence classes) themselves.

Moreover, on further reflection, it becomes apparent that the more circuitous route required for generating test items via the algorithmic approach has a further major advantage. It provides an explicit basis for remedial instruction. To see this, we assume in accordance with Scandura's theory that subjects actually use rules (algorithms) to generate their behavior. Then, because each equivalence class of items corresponds to a unique path of a rule, and because the steps in each such path are known explicitly to the instructor (or computer), each pupil can be given specific instruction to overcome his inadequacies. Put succinctly, he can be taught the needed paths. These ideas constitute the theoretical basis for a series of self-diagnostic and remedial workbooks developed by the Mathematics Education Research Group (e.g., Scandura, 1972) and could be extended for use in computer-assisted testing and instruction.[2]

---

[2]After this chapter was prepared, the second author had the pleasure of reading John Bormuth's (1970) fine book on test construction and was delighted to find so many compatible ideas in it. Bormuth argued that traditional methods of test construction suffer serious limitations and proposed a new approach in which test items are operationally defined in terms of instructional material. For example, an instruction like, "George Washington was the first president of the United States," can be converted into the "who" item, "Who was the first president of the United States?"

Bormuth's methods of operationally defining test construction is in some ways similar to that proposed by Scandura (1973) and developed here. Both methods provide a systematic way to construct (identify) test items, the former from verbal instruction and the latter from procedures. An even closer relationship becomes apparent if one accepts the view that the meanings of verbal instructions can be represented as to-be-learned procedures (e.g., Minsky & Papert, 1972; Scandura, 1973). This is not to say, however, that the two studies are equivalent. Indeed, Bormuth's main goal was to show how test construction can be operationally defined in terms of instruction. Scandura's concern was to show how human knowledge can be operationally defined in terms of the rules in a competence theory, and to incorporate the idea in a comprehensive theory of structural learning. The relationship between testing and instruction proposed here is viewed as just one application of these ideas.

REFERENCES

Arbib, M. A. Memory limitations of stimulus-response models. In J. M. Scandura
(Ed.), *Structural learning II: Issues and approaches*. London/New York:
Gordon & Breach, 1976.

Bormuth, J. R. *On the theory of achievement test items*. Chicago: University
of Chicago Press, 1970.

Coulson, J. E., & Cogswell, J. F. Effects of individualized instruction on
testing. *Journal of Educational Measurement*, 1965, *2*, 59-64.

Cronbach, L. J., Rajaratnam, N., & Gleser, G. C. Theory of generalizability: A
liberalization of reliability theory. *The British Journal of Statistical
Psychology*, 1963, *16*, 137-163.

Ferguson, R. L. *Computer-assisted criterion-referenced measurement*. Unpublished
doctoral dissertation, University of Pittsburgh, Learning Research and
Development Center, 1969.

Gagne, R. M. The acquisition of knowledge. *Psychological Review*, 1962, *59*,
355-365.

Guttman, L. The Cornell technique for scale and intensity analysis. *Educational
and Psychological Measurement*, 1947, *7*, 247-280.

Hively, W., II, Patterson, H. L., & Page, S. A "universe defined" system of
arithmetic achievement tests. *Journal of Educational Measurement*, 1968, *5*,
275-290.

Minsky, M., & Papert, S. *Research at the laboratory in vision, language, and
other problems of intelligence* (Artificial Intelligence Progress Report,
Memo 252). Cambridge, Mass.: M.I.T. Artificial Intelligence Laboratory,
1972.

Osburn, H. G. Item sampling for achievement testing. *Educational and
Psychological Measurement*, 1968, *28*, 95-104.

Rajaratnam, N., Cronbach, L. J., & Gleser, G. C. Generalizability of stratified-
parallel tests. *Psychometrika*, 1965, *30*, 39-56.

Scandura, J. M. Role of rules in behavior: Toward an operational definition of
what (rule) is learned. *Psychological Review*, 1970, *77*, 516-533.

Scandura, J. M. Deterministic theorizing in structural learning. *Journal of
Structural Learning*, 1971, *3*, 21-53.

Scandura, J. M. A plan for the development of a conceptually based mathematics
curriculum for disadvantaged children. Part I: Theoretical foundations;
Part II: Applications. *Instructional Science*, 1972, *2*, 247-262; 363-387.

Scandura, J. M. *Structural learning I: Theory and research*. New York: Gordon
& Breach, 1973.

Scandura, J. M. Theoretical note: S-R theory or automata? (A reaction to Suppes'
reaction). In J. M. Scandura (Ed.), *Structural learning II: Issues and
approaches*. London/New York: Gordon & Breach, 1976.

Scandura, J. M., & Durnin, J. H. Assessing behavior potential: Adequacy of
basic theoretical assumptions. *Journal of Structural Learning*, in press,
(to appear in Volume 4, No. 4). (Originally published as University of
Pennsylvania Structural Learning Series, Report No. 62, November 30, 1971.)

Suppes, P. Stimulus-response theory of finite automata. In J. M. Scandura (Ed.)
Structural learning II: Issues and approaches. London/New York: Gordon &
Breach, 1976.

Winer, B. J. *Statistical principles in experimental design*. New York: McGraw-
Hill, 1962.

10
Some Statistical Concerns in Structural Learning[1]

Joseph M. Scandura and Wolfram A. Reulecke

This chapter deals with some statistical issues directly
relevant to structural learning. In Section 1, we propose some
statistics and χ^2 tests for use in evaluating deterministic rule-
based theories. In Section 2, we comment further on the distinction between structural and incidental variables (see Chapter 1)
in the context of a particular class of Poisson-based observation
theories (cf. Chapter 7).

1. EMPIRICAL EVALUATION OF RULE-BASED THEORIES

As we have seen in Chapters 8 and 9, rules may provide an
adequate basis for assessing the behavior potential of individuals relative to success/failure on tasks in simple domains.
As emphasized in Chapters 2 and 15, however, rules assess individual behavior potential only up to some preset equivalence
relation defined on observables. Thus, a rule that adequately
accounts for success/failure, for example, may not adequately
account for latencies.

Conversely, a given rule, or combination of rules such as
that in Chapter 9, may provide an adequate basis for testing but
may not do so as efficiently as possible. For example, where
two or more rules are analytically adequate to account for the
behavior (e.g., borrowing and equal additions), the question
arises as to which rule is most compatible with the "culture"
of the population(s) in question--or, alternatively, whether

[1]This research was supported, in part, by National Institute of Health
Grant 9185. Sections 2.1-2.4 are based largely on W. A. Reulecke, "A statistical
analysis of deterministic theories," in H. Spada & W. F. Kempf (Eds.), *Formalized
theories of thinking and learning and their implications for science instruction*.
Bern: Huber, 1977.

one of the rules might do just as well as the two or more rules
collectively. A related question is: What are the most molar
subprocedures (in the sense of subroutines in computer programming) that might serve as atomic rules and still provide a
satisfactory basis for measuring individual behavior potential?
Recall, in this regard, that unnecessary partitioning of a task
domain decreases test efficiency.

There also are occasions where it might be of some interest
to compare the relative adequacy of various rules over different
populations or subpopulations of subjects. Although the borrowing method of subtraction appears to provide the preferred account for contemporary American children, for example, it is not
at all clear that this would be true in Europe (or even at an
earlier time in America). Such comparisons would provide a
measure of how well, relatively speaking, the competence associated with different subpopulations might be assessed on the
basis of given competence rules. Does borrowing do a better
job with American students, when the number of test items is
controlled, than does the method of equal additions, say, with
Europeans? What about our relative understanding of the rules
used by various ethnic, religious, and racial groups in dealing
with given social situations? Similar questions might be raised
concerning the production of speech (e.g., Carroll, 1975).

For these and related purposes, systematic statistical
methods for choosing among rules could have considerable value.
One such method is to simply compare the levels of predictability
made possible by the various rules considered individually.
Indeed, this is precisely what was done in Chapter 9 in comparing the efficacy of various methods of partitioning the domain
of subtraction problems (i.e., via borrowing and equal additions)

Unfortunately, this method is relatively inefficient and
limited insofar as applicability is concerned. The predictability measure used (proportion of consistencies within equivalence classes) applies directly only where there are exactly
two test instances per equivalence class (path). Where this is
not the case, the measure either breaks down (where there is
only one test item per equivalence class) or requires discarding
data or making undesirable simplifying assumptions (where there
are more than two test items). Consequently, statistical tests
based on this measure could loose considerable statistical power.
Furthermore, this measure is insensitive to the number of equivalence classes associated with a given rule, and so does not take
test efficiency into account. More general and efficient normative measures and statistical tests would be highly desirable.

The purpose of this section is to make a small beginning
in this direction. Specifically, we shall show how a measure
based on entropy (information) might be assigned to test profiles
associated with particular rules. This measure involves a
tradeoff between precision and efficiency and, therefore, may
be useful in identifying levels of rule atomicity that are op-

timal for test purposes. In addition, some "home grown" statistical tests are introduced, based on χ^2, that can be used to
help evaluate the reliability of test results associated with
particular rules. The need for additional statistical tests
also is noted.

1.1 ENTROPY OF TEST PROFILES

Rule Imposed Partitions: Let C be a class of tasks and
let r_1 and r_2 be two rules proposed to account for C. (It is
possible to generalize directly to n rules.) Denote the parti-
tions imposed on C by r_1 and r_2 by $P_1 = \{A_1, \ldots, A_n\}$ and $P_2 = \{B_1, \ldots, B_m\}$, respectively. The intersection partition then
may be represented by

$$P = \{C_{11}, C_{12}, \ldots, C_{nm}\}$$

where $C_{ij} = A_i \cap B_j$ for $i = 1, \ldots, n;\ j = 1, \ldots, m$. Finally,
let p_{ij} be the probability of event C_{ij}, so $p_i = \sum_j p_{ij}$ is the

probability of $A_i = \bigcup_j C_{ij}$ and $p_j = \sum_i p_{ij}$ is the probability of

$B_j = \bigcup_i C_{ij}$.

Before any observations are taken, we have no information
as to how a subject will perform on various items selected from
the class of tasks. In this case, the standard a priori assumption is that the probability of success on any one item is 1/2.
Given normative data on a random sample of tasks, the best that
can be done is to set the probability of success on any one item
at p_c, the overall probability of success on the class sample.

More intensive analyses, where account is taken of one or
another of the partitions imposed by rules, make it possible to
assign separate probabilities to the respective equivalence
classes (elements of the partitions). In general, such assignment provides a more exacting basis for predicting behavior just
to the extent that the rule or rules in question are compatible
with the relevant competence associated with the target population of subjects.

Finite Schemes: In probability theory, a complete system
of events $E_1, E_2, \ldots, E_n$ is a set of exclusive and exhaustive
events from some sample space such that one and only one of them
must occur on each trial. Given the events $E_1, E_2, \ldots, E_n$ of
a complete system, together with their probabilities $p_1, p_2, \ldots, p_n$ where $p_i \geq 0$, and $\sum p_i = 1$, the associated *finite scheme*
(Khinchin, 1957) can be represented

$$\begin{pmatrix} E_1 & E_2 & \cdots & E_n \\ p_1 & p_2 & \cdots & p_n \end{pmatrix}$$

In the present context, the pattern of success-failure on
any one element of a partition is a finite scheme. A finite

scheme corresponding to a priori knowledge, for example, is

$$
\begin{pmatrix} sC & fC \\ 1/2 & 1/2 \end{pmatrix}
$$

where sC and fC are events corresponding, respectively, to success and failure on tasks in Class C. (Note: The Set C itself
can be thought of as the only element in a one-element partition.) After obtaining performance on a sample, we get

$$
\begin{pmatrix} sC & fC \\ p & q \end{pmatrix}
$$

where p is the obtained proportion of successes on tasks from
C and q = 1 - p is the proportion of failures. Similarly

$$
\begin{pmatrix} sC_{ij} & fC_{ij} \\ p & q \end{pmatrix}
$$

is a finite scheme for the ij-th element of the intersection
partition P.

An Entropy Measure: The quantity

$$
H(p_1, \ldots, p_n) = - \sum_{k=1}^{n} p_k \ln p_k
$$

(where logarithms are to Base e) is a measure of the entropy,
or amount of uncertainty, of a finite scheme. For example, the
entropies associated with a priori and a posteriori knowledge
of performance on the Class of tasks C are

$$
H(1/2, 1/2) = -(1/2 \ln 1/2 + 1/2 \ln 1/2) = \ln 2 = .6931
$$

and

$$
H(p, q) = -(p \ln p + q \ln q)
$$

respectively.

For comparative purposes, notice that if p = .99, then

$$
\begin{aligned}
H (.99, .01) &= -(.99 \ln .99 + .01 \ln .01) \\
&= .99 (\ln 100 - \ln 99) + .01 (\ln 100) \\
&= .05605
\end{aligned}
$$

which is considerably smaller than the entropy associated with
a priori uncertainty. Indeed, it can easily be proven (e.g.,
Khinchin, 1957, p. 4) that for a fixed number of events the
finite scheme with the most uncertainty is one with equally
likely outcomes as in the former case. It is even easier to

see that uncertainty is a minimum, $H(p_1, p_2, \ldots, p_n) = 0$, if and only if exactly one of the probabilities $p_1, p_2, \ldots, p_n$ is one and the others are all zero. In regard to present concerns, this corresponds to the case where the subject is either successful or unsuccessful uniformly on each task in a partition element—$H(1, 0) = -(1 \cdot \ln 1 + 0 \cdot \ln 0) = 0$. This case is precisely what one would expect where the underlying rules, or components thereof, act in atomic fashion (Chapters 2, 8, or 9).

This measure of entropy has an important additional property that makes it particularly useful as a measure of the adequacy of particular rules. The entropy of two or more independent finite schemes is the sum of the entropies of the individual finite schemes. Thus, the collective uncertainty of any partition (imposed by some rule or rules) is the sum of the entropies of each of its elements (equivalence classes). Suppose, for example, that a Rule r partitions a Class of tasks C into the set of mutually exclusive and exhaustive equivalence classes $P = \{C_1, C_2, C_3, C_4\}$. Suppose further that a sample of test items from C, stratified according to the partition, is administered to a particular subject. Then, the resulting test profile may be represented by the set of finite schemes

$$\begin{pmatrix} sC_1 & fC_1 \\ p_1 & q_1 \end{pmatrix} \begin{pmatrix} sC_2 & fC_2 \\ p_2 & q_2 \end{pmatrix} \begin{pmatrix} sC_3 & fC_3 \\ p_3 & q_3 \end{pmatrix} \begin{pmatrix} sC_4 & fC_4 \\ p_4 & q_4 \end{pmatrix}$$

where $p_1, p_2, p_3,$ and p_4 represent the percentages of successes on the sampled tasks in $C_1, C_2, C_3,$ and $C_4,$ respectively, and $q_1, q_2, q_3,$ and q_4 similarly represent failures. The entropy of this partition (P) is

$$\begin{aligned} H(P) &= H(C_1) + H(C_2) + H(C_3) + H(C_4) \\ &= H(p_1, q_1) + H(p_2, q_2) + H(p_3, q_3) + H(p_4, q_4) \\ &= -\sum_{i=1}^{4} (p_i \ln p_i + q_i \ln q_i) \end{aligned}$$

The minimum entropy of a partition is obtained as one might expect, when each of the p_i (q_i) is either 0 or 1. For example, when $p_1 = 0, p_2 = 1, p_3 = 1, p_4 = 0,$ then $H(P) = 0 + 0 + 0 + 0 = 0.$

The entropy is maximum prior to testing, where the best guess, in the absence of any information to the contrary, is that $p_i = 1/2$ for all i. Here, $H(P) = -4 \ln 1/2 = 4 \ln 2 = 2.772.$ All other possible values of $H(P)$ lie between these two extremes. For example, if $p_1 = .2, p_2 = .8, p_3 = .2, p_4 = .8,$

$$\begin{aligned} H(P) &= -4(.2 \ln .2) - 4(.8 \ln .8) \\ &= .8 \ln 5 + 3.2(\ln 10 - \ln 8) = 2.004 \end{aligned}$$

whereas, if $p_1 = .1$, $p_2 = .9$, $p_3 = .1$, $p_4 = .9$

$$H(P) = .4 \ln 10 + 3.6 \ (\ln 10 - \ln 9) = 1.6628$$

and if $p_1 = .01$, $p_2 = .99$, $p_3 = .01$, and $p_4 = .99$, then

$$H(P) = .04 \ln 100 + 3.96 \ (\ln 100 - \ln .99) = .2238$$

In interpreting these entropy measures, it is important to emphasize that the precise interpretation given to a success or failure depends on whether the measure pertains to individual performance or to group performance. The above applications pertain to individual subjects. There, a "success" is simply correct performance on a particular task. With groups of subjects, however, this unit is not appropriate. In this case, the overall probabilities of success and failure on each equivalence class are of minimal concern.

What is needed is a unit that taps the extent to which, for each subject, the equivalence class acts in atomic fashion. That is, the extent to which the proportion of successes is sufficiently close to either one or zero. For these purposes, "sufficiently close" may conveniently be defined to mean (assuming a uniform distribution) that the proportion of successes for each subject is either over .75 or below .25. (More exact methods for distinguishing between subjects who know a path [or equivalence class], subjects who do not, and subjects who are responding on the basis of partial [non-atomic] knowledge may be derived by extending the methods described in Sections 2.3–2.5.) The probabilities used in computing entropy measures, then, are based on the proportions of subjects who score sufficiently close to one or zero. These are the "success" probabilities. Proportions of successes in the middle range (e.g., between .25 and .75) are termed *failures*. In what follows, unless stated to the contrary, *probability of success* (failure) refers to groups of subjects.

1.2 STATISTICAL TESTS

It is all well and good to have a normative measure that uses all of the data and that summarizes the uncertainty remaining after testing. But, this is not sufficient for deciding among alternative rule accounts. Tests of statistical inference are needed to determine whether observed differences are (statistically) significant (irrespective of whether they are practically significant).

Although statistical tests based on information measures have been proposed (e.g., Kullback, 1959), they are all based on the χ^2 distribution. In the following discussion, only the latter are considered because they are more familiar to most behavioral scientists. (Clearly, this discussion is not intended as a statistical treatise.) Although far from elegant, the "homemade" tests that are proposed seem adequate to deal with certain important comparisons. These tests are all based on

$$\chi^2 = \sum_{i=1}^{n} \frac{(O_i - E_i)^2}{E_i}$$

where O_i is the observed frequency of successes on an equivalence class and E_i is the corresponding expected frequency of successes. Since the distribution of this statistic is only approximately χ^2, it is usually required that $E_i \geq 5$ for each i.

In evaluating a particular rule, one of the first things that one wants to do is determine whether its use adds significantly to a priori knowledge--that is, whether performance within equivalence classes is sufficiently homogeneous (sufficiently near one or zero) relative to a priori expectation that the proportion of successes will be 1/2. For example, suppose we administer a sample of test items, stratified into four equivalence classes A_1, A_2, A_3, and A_4 according to Rule r, to a sample of 20 subjects. Of the 20 subjects, suppose that 16 subjects score sufficiently close to one or zero on items from each of A_1, A_2, A_3, and A_4. Then,

$$\chi^2_4 = 4 \left[\frac{(16 - 10)^2}{10} \right] = 14.4$$

this result is significant at the .01 level. (Note: This is actually a one-tailed test since the rule could not add to a priori knowledge if fewer than half of the subjects scored sufficiently close to one or zero.)

It also is natural to inquire whether a rule adds significantly to overall knowledge after testing. Assuming independence of performance on the equivalence classes, it is reasonable for the sake of argument to suppose, say, that 8 of the subjects scored sufficiently close to one or zero on the task domain taken as a whole, giving

$$\chi^2_4 = 4 \left[\frac{(16 - 8)^2}{8} \right] = 32$$

In addition, it is reasonable to ask whether the rule provides a reasonably "good fit" of the test data. That is, do the obtained results differ significantly from what would be predicted on the basis of the rule, assuming perfect atomicity (i.e., that all 20 subjects score sufficiently close to one or zero)? In this case, we get

$$\chi^2_4 = 4 \left[\frac{(16 - 20)^2}{20} \right] = 3.2$$

which is *not* significant. It is reasonable, therefore, to entertain the hypothesis that Rule r provides a reasonable account of the knowledge had by subjects in the population.

Finally, where two or more rules may be used in assessing behavior potential it is of considerable interest to know whether the addition of a second rule, say, reduces uncertainty beyond that realized by the first rule. (Notice that the number of subjects who perform in atomic fashion [i.e., score sufficiently close to one or zero] with respect to equivalence classes associated with an (nontrivial) intersection partition (Chapters 2 and 9) will necessarily be at least as large as with corresponding classes associated with individual rules that contribute to the intersection partition. This follows because the equivalence classes associated with the intersection partition are necessarily more homogeneous. On the other hand, the number of equivalence classes in the case of intersection partitions will be greater than the number associated with any one rule. The latter fact would be reflected in the associated information measure.) Suppose, for example, that the intersection partition in the present case contains six equivalence classes with 20, 16, 18, 18, 20, and 16 subjects, respectively, who perform in atomic fashion (i.e., who score sufficiently close to one or zero). Using 16 (the number of atomic subjects per equivalence class associated with the base rule used for comparison purposes) as the expected value(s)

$$\chi_6^2 = \frac{2(20 - 16)^2}{16} + \frac{2(16 - 16)^2}{16} + \frac{2(18 - 16)^2}{16} = 2.5$$

which is not significant. (Notice that a similar test could have been applied in Chapter 9, to determine the relative contributions of the equal additions and borrowing methods of subtraction.)

In cases such as this, one can reasonably ask whether testing the rule provides as good (or bad) an account as can reasonably be expected in the given circumstances (i.e., whether there is a ceiling effect).

There are, of course, other types of relationships that might be of interest. It is hoped that the above discussion may be suggestive and will encourage others to develop alternative and more sophisticated methods. For example, one might be concerned with measures of association between the partitions associated with various rules. Although consideration of such issues is beyond the scope of this chapter, appropriate tests based directly on information measures, using likelihood ratio tests, may be formulated along the lines described in Hayes (1963, Chapter 17). More complete treatments, tailored to the needs of psychologists, are given in Garner (1962) and Attneave (1959). The development in Kullback (1959) is more mathematical Suffice it to say here that such tests provide a measure of strength of association, as well as determining whether or not an association exists, and are preferred by many statisticians.

1.3 CONCLUSIONS

Standard measures of entropy can be assigned to performance data on given problem domains (stratified according to some underlying rule), because of the additivity property. All other things being equal, entropy decreases with the homogeneity of individual equivalence classes (associated with paths of an algorithm) and increases with the number of paths. Because homogeneity tends to vary directly with the number of paths, an increase in the latter results in both increased test precision and reduced test efficiency. In addition, simple statistical tests based on χ^2 can be used to evaluate certain aspects of given rule based theories. For other purposes, however, statistical tests based directly on information measures may be preferable and should be considered.

2. STATISTICAL ANALYSIS OF DETERMINISTIC TESTS

2.1 STRUCTURAL VARIABLES AND INTENSITY VARIABLES

As shown in Chapter 1, observable behavior can be thought of as being influenced by two types of factors, namely, structural variables, and intensity (incidental) variables.

Structural variables refer to clearly delineated, qualitative determinants of behavior. In the study of cognition, for example, the main structural variables involve particular higher- and lower-order rules, operations, decisions/goals, solution strategies, and so on. Such variables have binary values: they are, at any given moment, available or not (i.e., a person either knows or does not know a certain rule). Given the results reported in Chapters 5 and 6, especially, structural variables can be thought of as acting in deterministic fashion (also see Scandura, 1971, 1973).

Intensity (incidental) variables can be regarded as influencing behavior in a probabilistic fashion; their values vary randomly (over time, over tasks, over individuals). Examples of intensity variables include: level of attention and activity, speed of performance, motivation, neuroticism, and so on.

The introduction of intensity variables naturally raises several questions: How many and what types of intensity variables should be considered? How do they relate to one another? In what way and under which conditions do they affect behavior?

2.2 INTEGRATED AND COMBINED THEORIZING

Attempts to coordinate the effects of structural and incidental variables have generally taken one of two forms, integrated theorizing and combined theorizing.

Integrated Theorizing: Structural/process theories, in which deterministic and probabilistic sources of behavior are viewed as indistinguishable (as a consequence of the empirical fact that real world behavior usually is not predictable in a deterministic sense), are inherently probabilistic and based on intensity assumptions concerning underlying structures/processes. As observed in Chapter 1, such theories may (e.g., Suppes & Morningstar, 1972; Hilke, Kempf, & Scandura, 1977) or may not be analogous to the structural learning theory.

In the latter case, for example, theories that are formalized in terms of the linear logistic test model (e.g., Fischer, 1974; Scheiblechner, 1972; Spada & Kempf, 1977) consist of an a priori defined set of operations (lower-order rules), that are assumed to be necessary for solving problems in a prespecified domain, and a corresponding set of operation-specific (and individual) intensities, expressed as parameters. (The values of the latter are determined empirically.) Typically, perfect (deterministic) behavior is not allowed in such theories. Where it is, as is true of the related dynamic test theory (Kempf, 1974), the statistical models turn out to be so complex that it becomes somewhat impractical to test them empirically (see Chapter 1).

Integrated theories of this type represent a compromise and typically result in confounding structural and intensity variables. Consequently, important restrictions are imposed on the theoretical statements that can be made (e.g., one can not infer that just because parameters associated with given operations provide a good fit of the data that any cognitive equivalent of these operations was actually used). Presumably, the most important advantages of such theories are that they have desirable statistical properties which lend themselves to precise empirical tests.

Combined Theorizing: An alternative theoretical strategy is to maintain a sharp separation between structural and incidental variables. This can be accomplished in the case of the Structural Learning Theory by introducing a complementary probabilistic theory that deals specifically and solely with needed incidental variables (see Chapters 1 and 7, this book; cf. Scandura, 1971). In accounting for actual behavior in nonidealized situations both theories must be combined and treated as a unit. In this combination the deterministic theory plays the essential role and is, theoretically speaking, strictly separated from the probabilistic theory. To make this point clear, recall that structural variables (e.g., presence or absence of rules) account for behavior perfectly, but only under idealized test conditions.

To predict test behavior under nonidealized conditions, (proven) structural variables must be complemented with intensity variables that correspond to one or more sources of deviation from idealized conditions. Where the primary goal is to understand the structural foundations of behavior, the intensity

variables serve a largely incidental role that makes it possible
to deal with a broader variety of observations (hence the term
"observation theory", see Chapter 1, this book; cf. Scandura,
1977). Because of their primarily service function, observation
theories should be as simple as possible, and clearly related
to the corresponding deterministic theories. Undoubtedly, the
simplest way to accomplish this is to lump all intensity factors
together.

According to the Structural Learning Theory, for example,
a student who knows a rule should succeed on any task to which
the rule is applicable, at least under idealized test conditions.
In the subsequent discussion such a student is said to be in the
Known State (K). Similarly, a student who does not know a certain
rule should fail, except by chance, on any item where that specific rule is needed. Such a student is said to be in the Unknown State (U). Whether or not he is positively motivated,
whether or not he is working quickly, whether or not he is fully
concentrating on the problem: He still should fail. In state
U, therefore, it is sufficient to assume that the probability
of a correct response on any item equals the probability of
guessing.

2.3 AN OBSERVATION THEORY

Where idealized conditions are not satisfied (i.e., where
intensity variables are involved), behavior may be expected to
deviate from deterministic predictions just to the extent that
the test conditions deviate from the ideal.

A class of simple observation theories, that complement
the above deterministic (knowledge) assumptions (it would be
presumptuous to call them a theory), can be formulated on the
basis of the following assumptions:

1. In the known state K, deviations from expected response
patterns are relatively rare and not systematic. (Consequently,
the observation theories may be expected to apply only where
test conditions do not differ significantly from the ideal.)

2. The deviation effects can be represented by a single
stochastic parameter.

3. In the unknown state U, the congruence between actual
and expected behavior is random; it follows the laws of guessing.

4. Each subject is in either state K or state U and stays
there throughout testing.

Given these assumptions, a class of simple distribution
models can be derived that provides a basis for: (1) explaining
and predicting distributions of response deviations, and (2)
deriving critical deviation scores for distinguishing between
knowers (K) and nonknowers (U). Two sample models in this class
are described below.

Poisson-Binomial Model (PB-Model): The two-state Poisson-
Binomial Model (PB-Model) is applicable to knowledge assessment
situations involving binary responses where there is a high

probability of guessing correctly. This model is based on assumptions A and B.

A. In state K, deviations are assumed to be poisson-distributed with parameter k

(1) $p(m \mid K) = \dfrac{k^m e^{-k}}{m!}$

where m is the number of deviations from perfect prediction.[2]

B. In state U, deviations are binomially-distributed with
the guessing probability, p = .50.

(2) $p(m \mid U) = \binom{n}{m} 2^{-n}$

where n is the total number of predictions and $\binom{n}{m}$ is the number
of combinations of n things taken m at a time.

The unconditional probability of m deviations, which corresponds to the observable relative frequency of m deviations, is

(3) $p(m) = p(m \mid K) \cdot p(K) + p(m \mid U) \cdot p(U)$

where $p(K)$ and $p(U)$ are the unconditional a priori state probabilities. The parameters k and $p(K) = 1 - p(U)$ must be estimated from the data.

To the extent that this model provides a good fit of the
data, a critical deviation score can be derived based on Bayes
inference theorem. Since

(4) $\dfrac{p(K \mid m)}{p(U \mid m)} = \dfrac{p(K) \cdot p(m \mid K)}{p(U) \cdot p(m \mid U)}$

one possible decision rule would be to classify a person with m
deviations as a being in state K, if

(5) $c < \dfrac{p(K) \cdot p(m \mid K)}{p(U) \cdot p(m \mid U)}$

where c corresponds to a ratio of educational/psychological
costs associated with each kind of decision, namely: hit, false
alarm, miss, and correct rejection. With c = 1 we have the
equal-weights condition. Substituting the assumed distribution
functions yields

(6) $1 < \dfrac{b \, k^m \, 2^n}{m! \, e^k \binom{n}{m}}$

---

[2]The Binomial distribution b(m; n,p) approaches this Poisson distribution
as n → ∞, p → o, and np = k, where n is the number of predictions, m is the
number of deviations from correct predictions, and p is the probability of
incorrect predictions. Thus, the Poisson distribution approximates the binomial
distribution where p is small and may be preferred because it is independent of
n (also see Reulecke & Rollett, 1976; Reulecke, 1977).

or

$$(7) \quad e^k k^{-m} \; < \; \frac{b \, 2^n}{\prod_{j=0}^{m-1} (n-j)}$$

where $b = \dfrac{p(K)}{p(U)}$

For better computability the ln-transformation gives

$$(8) \quad k - m \, \ln k \; < \; \ln b + n \, \ln 2 - \sum_{j=1}^{m-1} \ln(n - j)$$

The largest value of m (m = 1, m = 2, ...), for which (8) holds, is the critical deviation score. Subjects with fewer deviations are assumed to be in state K; the others in state U. An example is given in Section 2.4.

Poisson-Poisson Model (PP-Model): The two-state Poisson-Poisson Model (PP-Model) is a variant of the above that is applicable to test situations involving arbitrary kinds of items (equivalence classes) where the probability of guessing correctly is small. The basic assumptions (C and D) are:

C. In state K, deviations are poisson-distributed with parameter k

$$(9) \quad p(m \mid K) = \frac{k^m \, e^{-k}}{m!}$$

D. In state U, deviations are poisson-distributed, also, but in the opposite sense, with parameter u.

$$(10) \quad p(m \mid U) = \frac{u^{n-m} \, e^{-u}}{(n-m)!}$$

In this case, a checking formula for calculating critical deviation scores also can be derived

$$(11) \quad m > \frac{\sum_{i=1}^{m} \ln i - \sum_{j=m}^{n-1} \ln(n-j) + n \, \ln u - g}{\ln(uk)}$$

where $g = \ln m_0 - \ln m_n$

where m_0 is the number of subjects with no deviations and m_n is the number, with n deviations (n is the number of items).

2.4 AN EMPIRICAL EXAMPLE

Ninety-nine seventh-graders were asked to solve a generalized concept learning problem. Each instance (exemplar/nonexemplar) contained 4 geometric figures, each of which varied over

the binary dimensions of color, form, and size. Initially, a
sample of 4 exemplars and 3 nonexemplars was presented simultaneously. The subject's task was to identify a solution strategy
(i.e., to verbalize a concept) for distinguishing between the
examplars and nonexemplars. Then, each subject was confronted
with 32 test instances. In each case, the subject had to decide
whether or not the instance was an exemplar. No reinforcement
was given.

There were two different types of strategies that could be
empirically identified. One type of solution strategy was based
on sequential relationships. For example, in "form alternation"
the geometric figures change their form successively (e.g.,
triangle-circle-triangle-circle). Another sequential concept
was "size double alternation" (e.g., small-small-large-large).

The other type of solution strategy consisted of simply
checking for the existence of certain dimension values. A typical existence checker might verbalize his hypothesis: "All correct compositions have a small and a large triangle, and a small
and a large circle." (Incidentally, one finding was that the
percentage of existence checkers decreases as the age of subjects
increases. Moreover, subjects were consistent in the type of
solution strategy they used. It was possible to predict the
strategies selected by individual subjects on a related task
almost perfectly.)

Eight of the 32 test instances were constructed so that
they could be correctly classified by any subject who had learned one of the acceptable strategies (i.e., a strategy that worked with the original sample). (Four of the instances were exemplars, and 4 were nonexemplars.) Table 1 shows the number of
subjects with m (= 0, 1, ..., 8) deviations from error-free
performance (i.e., deviations from what would be expected if
the subjects had learned and used one of the acceptable strategies). In particular, 65 subjects evidenced no deviations, 11
subjects evidenced 1, and 23 evidenced 2 or more. Obviously,
the distribution of deviations differs from what would be expected if the subjects either had merely guessed or had all used
an acceptable strategy consistently. It was hypothesized that
the deviations were distributed according to the Poisson-Binomial model.

Table 1
*Absolute Number of Subjects with m Deviations
from the Error-Free Performance*

m =	0	1	2	3	4	5	6	7	8
No. of Subjects =	65	11	7	2	9	3	2	0	0

Estimating Parameters of the PB-Model: In this section a
simple procedure for estimating the parameters k and p(K) is
suggested that seems to have some practical value.

First, because we assume that knowers should perform perfectly or nearly perfectly (i.e., $k = np = 8p$, where p is assumed to be small) k may be estimated using only the data for $m = 0$ and $m = 1$. In particular, the ratio

$$(12) \quad \frac{p(1 \mid K)}{p(0 \mid K)} = \frac{k\,e^{-k}}{e^{-k}} \approx \frac{11/99}{65/99}$$

may be computed, giving the estimate

$$\hat{k} = 11/65 = .17$$

More generally, $\hat{k} = p(1)/p(0)$. This estimation is biased, because the Binomial effect is not taken into account (i.e., some subjects in state U may guess correctly on all or almost all test instances). But, the bias is so small that it can be ignored. For example, the probability of guessing correctly 8 out of 8 times is .003. The actual influence is even smaller because only a certain portion of the total number of subjects is assumed to be in the unknown state U.

Without taking the data into account, the best guess for the unconditional state probabilities $p(K)$ and $p(U) = 1 - p(K)$ would be to set them equal to .50. Given the estimate $\hat{k}$ of the Poisson parameter k, however, the probability of state K, $p(K) = v/n = v/99$, and in turn the number of knowers, v, can be determined by substituting $\hat{k}$ for k in (3), with $m = 0$.

$$p(0) = e^{-\hat{k}}p(K) + \left[2^{-99}(1 - p(K))\right] = e^{-\hat{k}}p(K) + [A]$$

Again, ignoring the small Binomial effect due to A (when $m = 0$), and solving for $p(K)$ (and in turn v), we get

$$p(K) = v/99 = p(0)\,e^{\hat{k}} = (65/99)e^{.17} = .777$$

so

$$v = .777 \times 99 = 76.9$$

The simple estimation procedure outlined above is based on just two events, namely, the observed number of subjects with no deviations and with one deviation (from an "idealized" behavior pattern). The estimated parameters, then, can be substituted in Equation (3) to obtain expected frequencies for the entire deviation distribution (i.e., for $m = 0, 1, 2, \ldots, n$). As shown in Table 2, there is good agreement between observed and expected deviation frequencies.

Table 2
Observed and Expected Deviation Frequencies

m =	0	1	2	3	4	5	6	7	8
Observed =	.66	.11	.07	.02	.09	.03	.02	.00	.00
Expected =	.66	.11	.06	.04	.06	.04	.02	.01	.00

Substitution of the obtained parameter estimates in Equation (8) for successive values of m indicates that subjects with 0 or 1 deviations from error-free performance should be classified as being in state K. All other subjects are assigned to state U (unknown). This splitting technique effectively involves a sequence of binary branching decisions and is analogous to the blank trials technique used by Levine (1975) in studying discrimination learning.

2.5 CONCLUDING COMMENTS

In most of the tasks considered in this book, the probability of guessing correctly is quite low. In this case, then, the Poisson-Poisson (PP) model could be used to distinguish between those subjects who do and do not know a path of a given rule of competence (see Chapters 8, 9, and 2, Section 5). Owing to their simplicity of application, techniques similar to those described above could be useful in determining mastery (i.e., appropriate cutting scores) where several test items are given for each equivalence class and where testing is conducted under less than idealized conditions. In particular, splitting techniques of this type could be useful in determining whether or not the proportion of successes by individual subjects on given equivalence classes of tasks is "sufficiently close" to either zero or one (see Section 1.1). (Similar models have been developed for use in criterion-referenced testing, Reulecke, 1977.)

Some important issues are more uncertain at this time. For example, in view of our assumption to the effect that test conditions do not deviate significantly from the ideal, and our use of this assumption in estimating the parameters k and p(K), it is not clear whether k provides a useful measure of degree of deviation from idealized conditions. As argued in Chapter 1, and illustrated in Chapter 7, parameters that lend themselves to this interpretation may ultimately provide a basis for independent prediction in completely new situations (e.g., on new tests). That is, the new parameters required might be estimated directly from values of independent variables associated with the test conditions in question. In effect, the parameters might be estimated on an a priori basis and used to truely predict the data (before it is collected).

REFERENCES

Attneave, F. *Applications of information theory to psychology*. New York: Holt, 1959.

Carroll, J. B. Towards a performance grammar for core sentences in spoken and written English. *Journal of Structural Learning*, 1975, *4*, 189-198.

Fischer, G. H. Linear logistic test models: Theory and application. In H. Spada & W. F. Kempf (Eds.), *Formalized theories of thinking and learning and their implications for science instruction*. Bern: Huber, 1977.

Garner, W. R. *Uncertainty and structure as psychological concepts*. New York: Wiley, 1962.

Hayes, W. L. *Statistics for psychologists*. New York: Holt, Rinehart, & Winston, 1963.

Hilke, R, Kempf, W. F., & Scandura, J. M. Deterministic and probabilistic theorizing in structural learning. In H. Spada & W. F. Kempf (Eds.), *Formalized theories of thinking and learning and their implications for science instruction*. Bern: Huber, 1977.

Kempf, W. F. A dynamic test model and its use in the microevaluation of instructional material. In H. Spada & W. F. Kempf (Eds.), *Formalized theories of thinking and learning and their implications for science instruction*. Bern: Huber, 1977.

Khinchin, A. I. *Mathematical foundations of information theory*. New York: Dover, 1957.

Kullback, S. *Information theory and statistics*. New York: Wiley, 1959.

Levine, M. *A cognitive theory of learning: Research on hypothesis testing*. Hillsdale, N.J.: Erlbaum, 1975.

Reulecke, W. A. A statistical analysis of deterministic theories. In H. Spada & W. F. Kempf (Eds.), *Formalized theories of thinking and learning and their implications for science instruction*. Bern: Huber, 1977.

Reulecke, W. A. Ein Modell fur die kriteriumsorientierte Testauswertung (A model for evaluating criterion-referenced tests). *Zeitschrift fur Empirische Padagogik*, 1977, *1*, 49-72 (with an English summary).

Reulecke, W. A., & Rollett, B. Padagogische Diagnostik und lehrzielorientierte Tests. In K. Pawlik (Ed.), *Diagnose der Diagnostik*. Stuttgart: Klett, 1976.

Scandura, J. M. Deterministic theorizing in structural learning: Three levels of empiricism. *Journal of Structural Learning*, 1971, *3*, 21-53.

Scandura, J. M. *Structural learning I: Theory and research*. London/New York: Gordon and Breach, 1973.

Scandura, J. M. A deterministic theory of teaching and learning. In H. Spada & W. F. Kempf (Eds.), *Formalized theories of thinking and learning and their implications for science instruction*. Bern: Huber, 1977.

Scheiblechner, H. Das Lernen und Losen komplexer Denkaufgaben. *Z. exp. angew. Psychol.*, 1972, *19*, 476-506.

Spada, H., & Kempf, W. F. *Formalized theories of thinking and learning and their implications for science instruction*. Bern: Huber, 1977.

Suppes, P., & Morningstar, M. *Computer-assisted instruction at Stanford: Data, models, and evaluation of arithmetic programmes*. New York: Academic Press, 1972.

PART 5

Instructional Application and Extensions

In Parts 2, 3, and 4, the emphasis, respectively, has been on content (structural analysis), cognitive universals, and individual differences measurement. The chapters in Part 5 tend to be less focused and yet more comprehensive. More specifically, the emphasis is on instructional applications of the Structural Learning Theory, including (in Chapter 14) the essentials of an important theoretical extension that has direct educational implications.

The research reported in Chapter 11 was the first to demonstrate the feasibility of representing curriculum content in terms of rules and higher-order rules. A preliminary form of structural analysis was used to analyze and prepare a workbook to accompany the author's text *Mathematics: Concrete Behavioral Foundations* (Scandura, 1971). In this study, the introduction of just 5 higher-order rules made it possible to reduce the total of 303 solution rules by over 40 percent. Unlike the analyses in Part 2, however, second order rule sets were derived by simply eliminating redundant lower-order solution rules. No attempt was made to identify more basic lower-order rules as was done in Chapter 3, for example.

The study also shows that the resulting set of higher- and lower-order rules provides a viable basis for instruction. Two rule-based curricula were compared: one curriculum consisted of the original 303 lower-order rules; the other consisted of 169 of these lower-order rules and the 5 higher-order rules. Both groups achieved a mastery level of about 95 percent on the lower-order rules on which they were trained. More important, subjects in the higher-order rules curriculum did as well on problems involving the eliminated rules as did the subjects who were

taught these rules directly.   In addition, they were better able
to solve problems beyond the scope of either curriculum than
were subjects in the lower-order rules group.

Finally, in an addendum to the original study it is shown
that the degree of rule availability is reflected directly in
the degree of transfer.   This observation is closely related to
the distinction between structural and incidental variables
(Chapter 1).

The research reported in Chapter 12 demonstrates that useful competence analyses are not necessarily restricted to the
identification of rules.   Where identifying rules that underlie
given classes of tasks would be overly difficult or time consuming, or would otherwise require more time and effort than
could reasonably be expended, rule-based analyses may be approximated by certain types of extensional analysis.   In some cases,
for example, tasks may be classified according to difficulty
along predetermined sets of independent dimensions (e.g.,
Scandura, 1968, 1969; Scandura & Durnin, 1969).   Increasing
levels of difficulty along such dimensions tend to parallel
hierarchies of paths inherent in underlying rules (e.g., see
Chapters 2 or 9).

In Chapter 12, *dimensional analysis* was used to classify
reading passages in which individual statements were related by
logical rules.   Five (presumably) mutually exclusive and exhaustive dimensions (e.g., "complexity of context") were identified over which passages could vary.   For any rule of logical
inference, reading passages can be constructed with predetermined levels of difficulty along each dimension.   In the study,
however, only two rules of inference were considered: "or"
elimination (A or B, not A; therefore, B) and "all" elimination

(All A are B, x is an A; therefore, x is a B).

Individualized materials were developed, involving two of the five dimensions and the above two logical rules. These materials were designed for children reading at the third- and fourth-grade levels and above. They included sequential pretests and posttests, based on dimension levels, and instruction, designed to aid the learner in progressing from level to level. The pretests provided efficient and reliable bases for identifying the entering levels of individual children. In addition, the instruction resulted in significant gains on the posttests.

In the addendum, structural analysis (cf. Chapter 2 and Part 2) is discussed in relation to the method of dimensional analysis.

Chapter 13 is based on an empirical evaluation of the heuristics (higher-order rules) identified in the geometry construction analysis of Chapter 3. The major concerns were to determine whether: (1) these higher-order rules are consistent with human knowledge--that is, whether they can be used to reliably determine the heuristic capabilities that are available to individual subjects in a typical high school or college; (2) training on the higher-order rules (heuristics) facilitates solving geometry construction problems. Testing showed that the higher-order rules are compatible with human knowledge; the paths of these rules acted (essentially) in atomic fashion. The higher-order rules also were shown to be highly effective in facilitating problem solving. Furthermore, not only did instruction help, but the effects appeared to be cumulative. Training on initial higher-order rules made it easier to learn subsequent ones.

The basic theory described in Chapter 2 details the nature of the interaction between subject and environment at any given state of learning. In this sense, the theory is static and does not deal directly with the dynamic, ongoing interaction that is characteristic of everyday life, in general, or of instruction, in particular.

In the first half of Chapter 14, an extension of the Structural Learning Theory to ongoing instruction is described, together with some of the open questions pertaining to such extension. In addition to the general problem of how knowledge may grow over time, attention is given to the question of instructional optimization--how to maximize educational value relative to instructional costs.

The second half of the chapter describes a first step toward computer implementation of the theory and an empirical evaluation with respect to ongoing instruction. (1) Structural analysis was (re)applied recursively to the previously analyzed domain of geometry construction tasks (Chapter 3). This analysis reduced underlying competence to such simple rules as using a straight-edge to draw a line and setting a compass to a given radius. (2) The basic rules, together with the universal goal switching control mechanism, were implemented using the SNOBOL language to create a system that takes sets of geometry construction problems as input and arranges them in a learnable order (i.e., according to the theory). (3) Two theoretically derived sequences of problems were compared empirically both with each other and with random and learner-controlled sequences. The data showed that the theoretically derived sequences resulted in better learning than either the random or learner-derived sequences, by a factor of about two. The only exceptions were a few learners who demonstrated nearly equal facility in selecting at each stage problems that they could solve. Moreover, in the theoretically derived sequences, there was a close relationship between level of derivation (problem complexity) and solution times.

Chapter 14 THEORY OF ADAPTIVE INSTRUCTION WITH APPLICATION TO
            SEQUENCING IN TEACHING PROBLEM SOLVING   459

REFERENCES

Scandura, J. M. *Problem-solving ability in school mathematics--
    Its nature and measurement* (Philadelphia: University of
    Pennsylvania, Structural Learning Series, Report 57). 1968.
Scandura, J. M. New directions for theory and research on rule
    learning: II. Empirical research. *Acta Psychologica*,
    1969, *29*, 101-133.
Scandura, J. M. *Mathematics: Concrete behavioral foundations*.
    New York: Harper & Row, 1971.
Scandura, J. M., & Durnin, J. Extra-scope transfer in learning
    mathematics strategies. *Journal of Educational Psychology*,
    1968, *59*, 350-354.

11
Algorithmic Approach to Curriculum Construction:
A Field Test in Mathematics[1]

Walter Ehrenpreis and Joseph M. Scandura

Curriculum construction has traditionally been an artistic endeavor. Even today, the vast majority of texts and new curricula are developed almost exclusively on the basis of the curriculum constructor's subject-matter knowledge and professional know-how.

During the 1960s, a strong technological counterforce developed under the leadership of behavioral scientists. The basic position taken was that objectives must be stated in behavioral (operational) terms so as to make it possible to determine, through testing, whether or not learners have achieved individual objectives. As a result, a healthy debate developed between proponents of behavioral objectives (e.g., Gagne, 1970; Lipson, 1967; Mager, 1962; Popham, 1969; Tyler, 1964) and others who raised cautions concerning their use (e.g., Atkin, 1968; Ebel, 1970; Eisner, 1967; MacDonald & Wolfson, 1970).

In recent publications, the positions taken have become increasingly more flexible (e.g., Glaser, 1973; Resnick, 1972; MacDonald-Ross, 1973). A statement by Scandura (1971) summarizes much of the current view: "It is felt that complete reliance on operationally defined objectives has led some to fragmented curricula, curricula based on discrete bits of knowledge ... nonobjectivists have not gone as far as possible in pinning down the vague and nonoperational aims of education" (p. 4). Elaborating on this view Scandura (1972) has identified two basic inadequacies of the behavioral objectives approach considered in its simplest form: (1) The approach deals only with observable behavior and says nothing about how that behavior

[1]Adapted from "Algorithmic Approach to Curriculum Construction: A Field Test", by W. Ehrenpreis and J. M. Scandura, *Journal of Educational Psychology*, 1974, *66*, 491-498 with permission. This study was supported, in part, by National Science Foundation Grant GW-6796 to the second author.

is to be generated and, (2) it provides no systematic way of dealing with interrelationships among the identified objectives, or equivalently, of building transfer into a curriculum.

Regarding the first point, the distinction between the behavior of a subject and the knowledge (rule) that makes that behavior possible is fundamental. It can easily be proven mathematically that if just one rule exists for generating a class of behaviors, then there is a countably infinite number of other rules that will do the same thing (e.g., see Rogers, 1967). This fact is important in curriculum planning, because in practice there is almost always more than one viable way of approaching a task. The subtraction methods of "borrowing" and "equal additions", for example, are both widely used.

Regarding the second point, it is clearly an impossible task with any but the most trivial curricula, to explicitly teach the learner all that the curriculum constructor wants him to know. The limitations imposed by time and the capacity of the learner to absorb and retain information make this impractical. Some attention to interrelationships would seem almost essential.

One approach to this problem is based on learning hierarchies (e.g., Gagne, 1970; Resnick, Wang, & Kaplan, 1970). As is well known, this approach makes use of task analysis (e.g., Miller, 1962) as a means of determining subordinate tasks. Subordinate tasks are prerequisite to *type I* higher-order tasks (Gagne, 1970) in the sense that transfer to type I higher-order tasks frequently occurs once all of the prerequisites are learned. (It may be noted parenthetically that implicit in any specific task analysis is a specific underlying rule that is not necessarily, and often is not, explicit in the analyst's mind. Different rules may underlie the same task, as indicated above. Hence, it follows that any given task, theoretically speaking, may be task analyzed in any number of different ways, e.g., consider task analyses of subtraction based on borrowing and equal additions.)

In the present study, we have adopted a second (algorithmic) approach to the problem of transfer (Scandura, 1972). This approach bears some relationship to learning hierarchies but it includes an important conceptual generalization that has often gone undetected because of the common use of the descriptor "higher-order".

This approach is based on a recent theory of structural learning in which *type II* higher-order rules (Scandura, 1973a) may operate on classes of other rules (e.g., subordinate ones) to generate what, in task analysis, are type I higher-order rules. More generally, the meaning of "higher-order" is a relative one. A rule that operates on another rule is said to be of higher-order (type II) relative to it. (Mathematically speaking, type II higher-order rules correspond to functions defined on functions. Type I higher-order rules simply correspond to composite functions.)

In this sense, type II higher-order rules correspond roughly to the "directions" that are sometimes necessary in moving
from one level in a hierarchy to another. Unlike such directions, however, type II higher-order rules normally would not
be limited to operating between particular levels of given hierarchies. They typically would operate between various levels
of any one of a class of hierarchies, including hierarchies that
superficially appear quite different. Consider, for example,
the following two higher-order type I tasks: (1) given a certain number of yards, find the equivalent number of inches and
(2) given an airplane (on the ground), get it up in the air and
then back down safely. One way to analyze these tasks is to
break them into component parts: (1) subordinate tasks that involve converting yards into feet and feet into inches and (2)
subordinate tasks that involve "taking off" and "landing". Although involving quite different rules, the hierarchies have a
common structure (form). In particular, the type I higher-order
tasks (more exactly, the rules for solving the indicated type I
higher-order tasks) can be generated from the respective subordinate tasks (rules) by applying a type II higher-order composition rule (see Scandura, 1973a, pp. 213-218). (Note: In
structural analysis, type II higher-order composition rules
would be indicated where learning hierarchies share common forms.
A single type II higher-order rule, then, could take the place
of a potentially infinite class of separate "instructions".)

Further, type II higher-order rules are not limited in their
application to traditional hierarchies. For example, given a
rule for converting inches to centimeters (1 in. = 2.54 cm.) it
is a simple matter to envision a type II higher-order inverse
rule that applies to such rules and generates a new rule for
converting centimeters to inches (1 cm. = in./2.54). This inverse rule, of course, might apply to any conversion rule. (For
a discussion of these and other differences between type I higher-order rules and type II higher-order rules, see Scandura,
1973b; also see Chapter 2, Section 2.4 and Chapter 15, Section
3.4, this book.) In this chapter, all subsequent references to
"higher-order" are of type II.

It should perhaps be added in passing that the structural
learning theory is designed to be comprehensive in scope. It
deals explicitly with the role of the teacher (as an observer-
competence theorist) as well as the learner, and provides a
unified theoretical system that incorporates content, cognition,
and individual differences, and their relationships. The algorithmic approach to curriculum construction may, we think, best
be thought of as just one of several technologies (e.g., Scandura, 1972; Chapters 9, 12, and 15, this volume) based on this
theory.

In particular, the algorithmic approach to curriculum construction is based on the observation that every behavioral objective corresponds to a class of tasks that can be computed
(solved) by applying a rule or algorithm. It is further assumed

that curricula (i.e., what is to be learned) can be represented
in terms of finite sets of rules, including higher-order rules
that operate on rules. In effect, the task of curriculum construction may be viewed as one of identifying a finite set of
rules that provides an efficient account of the desired behavior. The algorithmic approach is basically a method for constructing curricula based on behavioral objectives and characterized in terms of rules and higher-order rules.

The first step in this method is to select text materials
to analyze. This, of course, involves making value judgements
concerning the type of material to be considered. All of the
tasks implicit in the text material are then identified and
stated as behavioral objectives. Next, rules are written for
solving each of the tasks and parallels among these rules are
identified. Such parallels are indicative of common structure
and provide a basis for devising higher-order rules. Finally,
those rules that are derivable by application of the higher-
order rules to other rules in the characterizing set may be
eliminated. (For details, see Chapter 2, Section 2.)

To summarize, the algorithmic approach provides a potential basis for overcoming the two aforementioned major limitations of the simple behavioral-objectives approach. First, it
makes specific how the desired behaviors are to be generated,
and thus might provide a viable basis for instruction. Second,
it makes explicit provision for the inclusion of higher-order
relationships among objectives. Indeed, it provides a systematic way for possibly building transfer potential into a
curriculum.

Two studies are reported. The first study was strictly
analytical in nature and was designed to determine the general
feasibility of the algorithmic approach. Specifically, we wanted to determine the practicality of characterizing the knowledge
inherent in a given mathematics text in terms of a finite set
of rules, including higher-order rules.

The second study was contingent on the success of Study I.
The purpose of Study II was to determine: (1) whether making
rules explicit provides a viable basis for instruction in the
classroom and, (2) whether the introduction of higher-order rules
provides an adequate basis for improving the ability of students
to transfer.

1. STUDY I: CONTENT ANALYSIS

1.1 FEASIBILITY OF THE ALGORITHMIC APPROACH TO CURRICULUM CONSTRUCTION

In order to judge the feasibility of the approach, the
following criteria were established:
1. A subjective appraisal of:
    a. the ease with which the tasks (behavioral objec-
        tives) inherent in the given text material could

be identified,
b. the ease with which rules associated with each of
   the respective tasks could be written,
c. the extent to which the tasks and rules identified
   were compatible with the approach taken in the text.
2. The extent and ease with which the higher-order rules
   inherent in the text could be:
   a. identified,
   b. used to eliminate those rules (and their corre-
      sponding tasks) that were derivable by application
      of the higher-order rules to other rules identified.

Consideration was also given to the sheer numbers of tasks
and rules involved, and particularly to the extent these numbers
could be reduced by the introduction of higher-order rules.

Method: Part 3 of *Mathematics: Concrete Behavioral
Foundations (M:CBF)* (Scandura, 1971) was chosen for analysis.
(This book was later analyzed in its entirety and published
as a workbook--Scandura, Durnin, Ehrenpreis, & Luger, 1971.)

The first step was to identify the individual tasks (behavioral objectives) inherent in the text. This was accomplished by going through the text paragraph-by-paragraph and
asking what performance capabilities might reasonably be expected of a student who had studied the material. For example, the
following tasks were identified on pages 182 and 191 respectively.

Task A: Given a whole number m, determine whether or not
         X is an additive identity for m.
Task B: Given a whole number m, determine whether or not
         Y is a multiplicative identity for m.

The second step was to identify and eliminate redundancies
in the tasks identified. Very few (less than eight) such redundancies were found in the text aside from prerequisites to
other tasks. Prerequisite tasks were not eliminated because
it was felt desirable to maintain the original sequencing of
ideas in the text.

Third, one efficient rule was constructed for each task.
The rules were written so as to be compatible with the text
materials. The rules written for the illustrative Tasks A
and B were as follows:

Rule A: Find the sum m + X and then the sum X + m. If
         m + X = X + m = m, then X is an additive identity
         for m; if m + X $\neq$ m or X + m $\neq$ m, then X is not
         an additive identity for m.
Rule B: Find the product m x Y and then the product Y x m.
         If m x Y = Y x m = m, then Y is a multiplicative
         identity for m; if m x Y $\neq$ m or Y x m $\neq$ m, then
         Y is not a multiplicative identity for m.

The fourth step was to look for higher-order relationships
among the rules. These relationships were stated as tasks to
be performed and higher-order rules underlying these higher-
order tasks were then constructed. For example, *Rules A* and
B are obviously related. The nature of this relationship can

be illustrated by the following task and its underlying rule.

   Task H: Give a rule for demonstrating that a given set of
             numbers provides an instance of a property (e.g.,
             commutativity) under some operation, generate a
             corresponding rule involving another set and/or
             another operation.

   Rule H: In the given rule, replace the original operation
             by the new operation and any "special" elements
             (e.g., the identity) by its counterpart.

Fifth, the higher-order rules identified in Step four were
used to eliminate those tasks and corresponding rules that are
derivable by application of the higher-order rules to other
rules identified. Thus, for example, *Rule B* was eliminated
inasmuch as it could be generated by applying *Rule H* to *Rule A.*

   Results and Discussion: The chapters analyzed lent themselves very naturally to a task-rule type of analysis. The
major requirements found necessary for such analysis were a
thorough familiarity with the subject matter and a good working
knowledge of the algorithmic approach.

   Upon completion of Step three, a list of 303 tasks and
their corresponding rules (one rule for each task) had been
identified. A list containing 174 rules, five of which were
higher-order rules, was obtained upon completion of Step five.

   Although the process of identifying the tasks inherent in
the text was time consuming, it was felt that the list of 303
tasks gave almost complete coverage of the material. Once the
tasks were identified, there was little difficulty encountered
in writing rules compatible with the approach taken in the text.
This was partly due to the fact that the narrative and illustrative examples provided adequate guidance. The identification
of the higher-order rules and the subsequent reduction of the
list of 303 rules to the final list of 174 rules was the most
difficult step. Some of the higher-order rules were easier to
identify than others and the analysis was pursued just far
enough to demonstrate the feasibility of the approach. Doubt-
less, a more intensive analysis would have resulted in a larger
number and variety of higher-order rules. Overall, based on
the criteria established, it was concluded that the algorithmic
approach is feasible.

2.   STUDY II : EMPIRICAL TEST

   The second study, in contrast to the first, was experimental
and involved a comparison of two rule-based curricula. The
first curriculum *(D)* was characterized in terms of a list of
discrete tasks and rules for solving these tasks, one rule for
each task. The second curriculum *(H)* included the higher-order
rules and all *Curriculum D* tasks and rules except those derivable
by application of the higher-order rules to other rules in

Curriculum D (as described in Step 5, Study I).

The degree of learning evidenced by students trained in *Curriculum D* provided evidence concerning the hypothesis that making rules explicit provides a viable basis for classroom instruction. This hypothesis was tested directly in terms of mastery rather than by comparison with some arbitrarily defined control.

Comparative performance of the students trained in *Curricula D* and *H* pertained to the question of transfer. We hypothesized that students trained in the higher-order rules *(Curriculum H)*, would perform as well on those *Curriculum D* tasks that had been eliminated from *Curriculum H* as the subjects who were trained on these *D* tasks directly. This was expected (according to the theory) because these tasks could be solved by using higher-order rules to derive solution rules. Furthermore, we predicted that the *Curriculum H* students would perform significantly better on tasks, not in *Curriculum D,* that could be solved in the same way (i.e., by use of the higher-order rules). No difference in performance was expected on tasks included in both curricula.

Method and materials: The experimental materials were based directly on the analyses reported in Study I. The discrete rules curriculum *(D)* resulted on application of Steps 1 to 3 of the algorithmic approach. The higher-order rules curriculum *(H)* included Steps 4 and 5 as well. *Curriculum D* consisted of 303 tasks and rules, and *Curriculum H* of 174 tasks and rules, including five higher-order tasks and rules. Although experimental materials were prepared for Chapters 5 to 9 of *M:CBF*, only those materials pertaining to Chapters 5, 6, and 7 were actually used in the experiment.

The two curricula were reproduced in the form of workbooks with the following format: In the beginning there is a statement of the task, and then, a rule statement in simple terms. Next, three to five worked examples are presented (depending on the experimenter's judgement as to task difficulty), and finally, ten exercises. In addition, a set of task exercises for review purposes was selected on the basis of the apparent difficulty subjects encountered during learning. All higher-order tasks were included in the *Curriculum H* review.

Pretests and posttests were also constructed. The pretest consisted of a sample of 40 exercises (stated exactly as they appeared in the workbooks) that (1) tested applications of rules found in *both* treatments and, (2) in the judgement of the experimenter, were most likely to discriminate among subjects. The posttest consisted of a stratified sample of 32 task exercises from each of the following categories: (1) tasks found in *Curricula D* and *H,* (2) tasks found only in *Curriculum D,* (3) higher-order tasks found only in *Curriculum H,* and (4) tasks found in neither treatment but that theoretically could be derived from rules found in *Curriculum H.* The exercises were selected randomly from each of these categories--10 each from categories (1) and (2), and 6 each from categories (3) and (4). Kuder-Richardson formula 20 was used to obtain reliability coefficients of .86 for both the pretest and the posttest. High curricular content validity (Cureton, 1951) was assured by the method of construction used.

Subjects: The subjects were 48 (16 male, 32 female) Trenton State College Summer School students enrolled in two sections of a course on teaching modern mathematics in the elementary grades. The first author was the instructor for both sections of the course.

Design and procedure: The pretest was administered to each section during the first class meeting. The highest score on the pretest was 24 exercises correct out of the possible 40. The mean was 11.2. Forty-five of the 48 subjects had pretest scores below 20, and 26 had scores of 10 or below.

The pretest scores were used to assign 24 subjects to a high group and 24 subjects to a low group. Within each group, 12 subjects were randomly assigned to each curriculum.

Each subject purchased a notebook at the beginning of the term; all work was done in these notebooks. The instructional workbooks and student notebooks were distributed at the beginning of each class period and collected at the end. The *Curriculum D* and *H* subjects were in separate classrooms for three class periods per week. Each subject was permitted to go on to the next task as soon as he had demonstrated success on a number of consecutive exercises equal to the number of illustrative examples constructed for that task. A daily record of each subject's performance was kept, as well as anecdotal records indicating particular difficulties or problems that arose.

During the first meeting of each week (beginning with Week two) subjects were given a set of review exercises that were individualized so that each subject was given review exercises involving tasks he had completed during the preceding two weeks. The tasks chosen for review were those that caused the greatest difficulty. The subjects were required to work these exercises without the use of the workbook or their notebooks. On the final class meeting of each week the review exercises and solutions were returned to the subjects. They were told to check their solutions, using their workbooks and notebooks, and to correct any errors. As soon as this had been completed, the review materials were collected.

During the final three weeks, class time was set aside to enable subjects to review and study the rules they had learned up to that time (45 minutes during Weeks 4 and 5; 3 hours during Week 6). The amount of time spent working on the tasks and on review was the same for all subjects. In those few cases where the subject missed a class, he was required to make up the time missed.

At the end of the term, 14 of the 24 subjects in Group D were working in Chapter 7, with the farthest advance to Task 36. Two of the 24 Group H subjects completed Chapter 7, and 16 others were working in Chapter 7. All *Curriculum H* subjects completed the five higher-order tasks.

The posttest was given during the next-to-last meeting. The subjects were given all of the time they needed and encouraged to do their best.

Results and Discussion: The *Curriculum D* subjects were successful on 339 of the 362 posttest tasks on which they were trained, for a mastery level of 94 percent. The number of test items on which each subject had been trained was determined by examination of his class workbook. The *Curriculum H* subjects were successful on 183 of the 190 lower-order tasks (96 percent) on which they were trained. It would appear that making rules explicit does provide a viable basis for instruction.

On the higher-order tasks, *Curriculum H* subjects performed as expected at a significantly higher level ($F = 7.37$; $df = 1$, 44; $p < .01$) than the *Curriculum D* subjects. The overall means were 3.2 *(Curriculum D)* and 4.3 *(Curriculum H)* with a maximum score of 6. The data of the individual subjects showed that the *Curriculum H* subjects were successful on 103 out of the 144 posttest exercises (71.5 percent), whereas the *Curriculum D* subjects were successful on 77 out of 144 (53.4 percent) exercises. The proportions differed significantly (arcsine transformation, $Z = 2.9$; $p < .01$--cf. Baggaley, 1957).

It is of interest, nonetheless, that the *Curriculum D* subjects, although not trained on the higher-order tasks, did perform successfully 53.4 percent of the time. This suggests that some of the *Curriculum D* subjects may have known these relatively simple higher-order rules prior to the experiment, while others may have been able to induce them as they worked through *Curriculum D*. In any case, the performance level did not approach that of the *Curriculum H* subjects and it can safely be concluded that training on higher-order rules had a positive effect. This gap undoubtedly would have been even greater had more complex higher-order rules been introduced.

Transfer: The hypotheses pertaining to transfer were equally conclusive. As expected, *Curriculum H* subjects performed just about as well on tasks found only in *Curriculum D* as did the *Curriculum D* subjects who were trained on these tasks directly. The *Curriculum D* subjects were successful on 168 out of the 181 posttest tasks (93 percent) in this category and the *Curriculum H* subjects were successful on 167 out of the corresponding 190 tasks (88 percent). The difference between these two proportions was not significant (arcsine transformation, $0 < Z < .5$; $p > .05$). The overall means were 8.3 *(Curriculum D)* and 8.0 *(Curriculum H)* with a maximum score of 10 ($F = 1.02$, $df = 1.44$; $p > .05$).

In addition, the *Curriculum H* subjects, as predicted, performed at a significantly higher level ($F = 30.03$, $df = 1$, 44;

p < .01) than the *Curriculum D* subjects on tasks beyond the
scope of either curriculum. On the six tasks, where solution
rules could be derived from given rules via the higher-order
rules, the obtained means were 3.1 *(Curriculum D)* and 4.1
(Curriculum H). The *Curriculum H* subjects were successful on
98 of the 144 transfer opportunities provided (68 percent) and
the *Curriculum D* subjects on 74 of the 144 (51.3 percent).
These proportions differed significantly (arcsine transformation, Z = 2.9; p < .01).

Notice also that the difference in group performance of
about 17 to 18 percent on the higher-order tasks was directly
reflected in performance on the six transfer tasks that were
neither in *Curriculum D* nor *Curriculum H*. There too the difference was about 17 to 18 percent. This observation suggests that
subjects who had directly or indirectly learned a higher-order
rule were able to apply it successfully to transfer tasks. In
effect, it would appear that the availability of a suitable
higher-order rule, together with appropriate lower-order rules,
provides a sufficient basis for transfer to new tasks. (See
Section 4.3.)

A more detailed analysis showed that: (1) of the 235
cases where subjects were successful on a higher-order task,
they were successful on 166 of the corresponding transfer tasks
giving 71 percent correct prediction, (2) of the 101 cases where
subjects were unsuccessful on a higher-order task, they were unsuccessful on 72 of the corresponding transfer tasks again giving 71 percent correct prediction. These findings are generally
compatible with a number of related "laboratory" experiments
(Scandura, 1973a). Although predictability did not approach the
levels obtained there (86 percent to 100 percent accuracy), these
results do demonstrate the robustness of the theory.

Nonetheless, the *Curriculum H* subjects did better on those
transfer tasks, on which the *Curriculum D* subjects had been
trained, than on those which were new to both groups. According
to the author of the book, it is likely that the former (which
were derived directly from the book) were simpler. Although
both types were solvable via the same higher-order rules, unless
these rules were atomic (in the sense of Chapters 2, 8, and 9),
they might well involve two or more hierarchically related
paths--with the subordinate paths more likely to be associated
with the former (simpler) transfer tasks. Unfortunately, however, the precision of the (structural) analysis employed does
not allow definitive resolution of this possibility.

Other data showed that transfer was not affected by the
direct presentation on the transfer tasks of the necessary
lower-order rules. (The rules to which the higher-order rules
applied were presented directly on four of the six transfer
tasks.) The *Curriculum D* subjects were successful on 48 out of
96 transfer problems (50 percent) where the needed lower-order
rules were presented, and 28 out of 48 transfer problems (54 percent) where the subjects were trained on the needed lower-order

rules but were not formally presented with them on the test. Correspondingly, the *Curriculum H* subjects were successful on 66 out of 96 transfer problems (69 percent) and 32 out of 48 transfer problems (67 percent). Neither pair of proportions differed significantly. ($Z = .59$; $p > .05$ for the *D* differences and $Z = .29$; $p > .05$ for the *H* differences.) This suggests that memory was not an essential factor, at least under the present conditions where the level of mastery on the lower-order rules was about 95 percent.

3. SUMMARY AND IMPLICATIONS

In summary, these results clearly show that rules provide a viable and explicit basis for instruction and transfer. The *Curriculum H* subjects not only had fewer rules to learn than did the *Curriculum D* subjects, but they were also able to solve tasks that the latter could not. The strong transfer effects were obtained even though the six-week course came to an end just as many of the *Curriculum H* subjects were reaching that portion of the workbook where the higher-order formulation had made it possible to eliminate large numbers of *Curriculum D* tasks (cf. Table 1). If time had permitted some of the subjects to complete Chapters 8 and 9, it seems quite possible that an even greater difference might have been obtained in favor of the *H* subjects in amount of material covered per unit of time.

TABLE 1
Number of Tasks in Chapters 5 to 9

Chapter Number	5	6	7	8	9
Curriculum D	47	22	79	72	83
Curriculum H	32	17	46	44	35

These results suggest that the algorithmic approach should be given serious consideration in planning future curriculum development. Curricula that are characterized in terms of rules and higher-order rules provide an explicit basis for instruction and, even more important, make specific provision for remote transfer, something that many subject matter specialists feel is lacking in current curricula based on operational objectives.

It should be emphasized, however, that while knowledge can be rigorously characterized in terms of rules, this does not imply that knowledge must be imparted to students (e.g., young children) in this manner. As was true of this study, rules can be acquired by telling, or by discovery from instances, or by symbol juggling or concrete manipulation--the choice is up to the teacher and depends on factors other than the particular knowledge in question. Instructional formats other than the workbooks, of course, should also be explored. The important point is that if we know precisely what rule it is that we want a child to learn then we can facilitate learning far better than if we do not.

There is no reason, of course, to restrict the algorithmic approach to analyses of available texts. The approach is perfectly general and provides, for example, an explicit basis for improving existing curricula based on "operational objectives". By providing an explicit basis for instruction, the algorithmic approach may be particularly helpful in training low-ability and/or disadvantaged students (e.g., Scandura, 1972). Furthermore, some of our recent research and development (Chapters 9 and 13) has shown how the algorithmic approach can be extended to provide a natural basis for detailed diagnosis and remediation

4.   ADDENDUM: DETERMINISTIC APPROACH TO RESEARCH IN INSTRUCTIONAL SCIENCE[2]

With the possible exception of testing and psychometrics, which drew at least part of their inspiration from educational needs, educational research traditionally has relied on other disciplines for its methodologies. Experimental research in education, for example, has drawn from a Fisherian experimental design and statistics that was developed initially to evaluate crop yields in agriculture (Fisher, 1935). This methodology has led over the years to many-fold increases in *farm production*. (In education, and I would propose also in psychology, the results have been equivocal.)

As noted in Chapter 1, traditional behavioristic and educational theories and hypotheses have been inherently probabilistic. Thus, for example, we have theories which indicate that certain behavior will occur with some probability in given situations and theories which refer to average behavior in given classes of situations. In the literature, for example, we frequently read, on the one hand, such things as "the probability of behavior A is a function of the number of reinforcements" or "each subject learns on each trial with probability c" and, on the other hand, such things as "discovery learning (on the average) leads to more transfer than does expository learning."

In testing probabilistic theories and hypotheses, the essential data have been means and other group statistics. This works fine, and is appropriate, where the emphasis is on external, manipulable variables, or even where the reference is to diffuse underlying cognitive constructs. Modern information processing psychology however, has a different theoretical base, one that is inherently deterministic. Theories and hypotheses of this type provide a potential basis for stating what individual subjects will do in particular experimental situations.

[2]This addendum was written by the second author and is based on J. M. Scandura, "A deterministic approach to research in instructional science," *Educational Psychologist,* in press. Preparation of this summary was supported by National Institute of Health Grant 9185 and in part by the MERGE Research Institute.

To date, however, the methods and experimental paradigms that have been used to test such theories, have been essentially the same as those used to test probabilistic theories. Suppose, for example, we want to test alternative information processing theories, each of which consists of some hypothesized rule (process/procedure). In this case, experiments are set up to determine which rule best accounts for *average* group behavior. In experimental psychology, we often use response latencies for this purpose. Related work in education generally deals with more complex tasks but uses less refined response measures.

There is a serious problem with this approach to theory verification. Just because a rule or process provides a viable account of average, group behavior, this does not say anything necessarily about how *individuals* perform--in particular, it does not say anything definitive about individual processes. Perhaps the clearest example of this goes back to the old controversy over whether learning is incremental or all-or-none. Essentially the same group predictions can be made using either assumption about individual processes. For the most part, the data were simply inadequate to answer the question.

Deterministic behavior theories cannot be tested in the same way as probabilistic theories. Whereas probabilistic theories can be tested under actual behavior conditions, because the presence of random error is always assumed, this is not the case with deterministic theories. Deterministic theories must be tested under *idealized* conditions which pertain to individual subjects in particular environmental situations. Thus, for example, the deterministic laws of mechanics in physics--involving say the inclined plane--hold only where friction, and other *peripheral* factors are *not* involved. One could, of course, devise alternative stochastic theories of such phenomena under nonidealized conditions, but the resulting theories would be far more complex and *ad hoc* than the relatively unified, simple, and aesthetic mechanics developed by Newton.

One wonders in contemporary cognitive psychology and instructional science whether specific laws (rules/information processing theories) introduced to account for unconstrained average behavior could in the long run have far less generality than simpler deterministic laws determined under idealized behavior conditions.

4.1 TESTS OF DETERMINISTIC BEHAVIOR THEORIES UNDER IDEALIZED CONDITIONS

It is my contention that deterministic theorizing in behavioral science is not only possible, but that it is also feasible to realize idealized conditions in many behavioral situations. Indeed, much of the Gagne (1962) inspired work pertaining to learning hierarchies makes this assumption implicitly. Consider, for example, the generalization that students who fail on subordinate tasks will also fail on relatively superordinate tasks. This generalization is a deterministic statement, moreover, one that frequently holds in a near deterministic sense. The generalization, moving in the opposite direction, is more fallible. Thus, students who learn all of the prerequisites of a given task, as determined through a standard hierarchical task analysis, are not always able to solve the superordinate task. More accurately, standard hierarchical task analyses do not identify all important prerequisites. (The missing prerequisites relate to higher-order rules/processes by which relatively lower-order prerequisites may be combined and/ or modified to provide a basis for solving the superordinate task.)

The important thing for present purposes is to clarify the methodological underpinnings of deterministic research. Recall that the experiments reported in Chapters 5 and 6 were run under idealized, memory-free conditions, conditions designed to eliminate the effects of memory, processing capacity, and response latency. The latter were effectively factored out of the experiments.

Let us review briefly Experiment I of Chapter 5. In this experiment, recall, children were taught A → B and B → C rules and were asked to solve A-C problems, both before and after training on a higher-order rule.

The results of the experiment showed the following. (1) Knowing the components of a solution (rule) for a task is not sufficient. The subject must know how to put the components together appropriately. (2) Integrating components is accomplished by applying higher-order rules to lower-order ones (e.g., component rules). Indeed, higher-order rules seem to be both a necessary and a sufficient condition for solving problems where needed components are available. (3) Component rules and higher-order rules, although behaviorally sufficient for problem solving are not logically sufficient. Human beings must have some prior and presumably universal capability, equivalent to the proposed goal switching control mechanism, which tells them how and when various rules are to be used in attacking problems.

The central issue here pertains to the internal/external conditions under which the experiment was run. In running this experiment we took every feasible precaution to insure that the subjects were indeed attempting to achieve the stated goals, that the requisite to-be-learned rules really were learned, and, perhaps most important, that the learned rules were available to each subject at the time of testing. The subjects were also given physical mnemonics to help them remember the critical rules, and all the time they needed. Under these "memory-free" conditions, the deterministic theory was shown to account almost perfectly for the performance of individual subjects on specific problems.

Now, of course, not all data is idealized. Most real world

data comes from nonidealized situations. This is certainly true,
for example, in the classroom and in the experiment reported in
this chapter.

4.2 PROBABILISTIC GENERALIZATION OF DETERMINISTIC FINDINGS

Perhaps surprisingly, deterministic theories, and parallel
data collected under idealized conditions, have an important
advantage over probabilistic theories and corresponding group
data. This advantage has to do with the generalizability of
laboratory results to the real world of education.

Consider, first, the situation with regard to group data.
In this case, results obtained in the laboratory may be generalized to the population from which the experimental samples
have been drawn. Usually, this population is poorly defined
and one can never be sure whether or not an obtained finding
will hold up in a new situation or not. It is this fact, above
all, which has made so many educators skeptical of basic behavioral research and its applicability to education. Hence, the
well known clarion call for lots of expensive "field testing".

Although representativeness of experiments is necessary to
insure generalizability of results, in testing both probabilistic and deterministic theories, the situation in the latter case
is quite different. In testing deterministic theories, results
do not refer to average effects. The results pertain to what
individual subjects will do in specific situations. We are essentially replicating an experiment every time a new subject is
tested in a given situation, or, for that matter, every time the
same subject is tested in a new situation. Accordingly, it is
far easier to obtain representative data in the case of deterministic theories than in the case of probabilistic ones. (On
the other hand, of course, deterministic theories only apply
deterministically under idealized boundary conditions.)

By way of analogy, for example, consider the inclined plane
law I mentioned earlier. Suppose we pull a given cart up a
given inclined plane and measure the force needed. Each time
we do this, we are obtaining a critical data point that may be
compared directly with predictions from the inclined plane law.
If the inclined plane were perfectly smooth, and the cart were
frictionless, this law would allow us to determine the needed
force (almost) perfectly. Of course, there is no perfectly
smooth inclined plane, or frictionless cart. But, under laboratory conditions, one can approximate the ideal so closely that
the error of measurement may be ignored for all practical
purposes.

For present purposes, the important point is that while
deviations from the ideal may cloud experimental comparisons,
they cannot eliminate differences. Thus, given any inclined
plane, bumpy or otherwise, and given any cart, frictionless or
otherwise, the force required to move the cart up the plane will

depend directly on the angle of inclination. This dependence, however, is no longer deterministic but rather is probabilistic. Although the measurements themselves may be equally precise, they must be treated as random variables because of uncontrolled variation from "boundary conditions".

An analogous thing happens with respect to human behavior. As we have seen, subjects will uniformly succeed on simple problems if they know both the components of a solution and a higher-order rule by which these components may appropriately be combined. If any of these essentials is missing the subjects will fail. This basic result has been replicated in the laboratory with different tasks and different kinds of rules, with individuals ranging in age level from preschool through junior high school. (This is like checking the inclined plane law in the laboratory at different angles of inclination.)

In the behavioral situation I have described, then, what corresponds to friction and bumpiness of the inclined plane? A large part of the answer essentially concerns the availability in working memory of the requisite rules. To the extent that the needed rules have been learned and are available in a given test situation, to that extent, and only to that extent, will a subject succeed. If any one of these rules is missing the subject should fail.

In the real world of education, we cannot be sure, without prior testing, which rules are and are not known. Hence, any advantages of instruction will accrue just to the extent that the instruction results in the student learning a critical rule that he or she did not know before.

To summarize, whereas valid deterministic theories only apply deterministically under idealized boundary conditions, they necessarily also apply probabilistically in nonidealized situations. They lend themselves to generalization from the laboratory to the real world in a way that probabilistic theories do not. (The latter is a direct consequence among other things of the relative expense, in the sense of both time and money, involved in obtaining representative data.)

4.3 TEST OF AN ANALOGOUS PROBABILISTIC THEORY UNDER "REAL WORLD" CONDITIONS

The (experimental) study reported in this chapter directly parallels Experiment I of Chapter 5 but was conducted under "real world" conditions. For present purposes, the key results were as follows. (1) Both the D and H subjects performed at a high level on the lower-order tasks (about 95 percent correct). (2) The H subjects had 71.5 percent success on the H tasks after training and the D subjects had 53 percent success without training (difference, $p < .01$). (3) The H and D subjects, respectively, had 68 percent and 51 percent success ($p < .01$) on the transfer problems, on which neither group had been trained.

These results can be summarized without serious distortion by saying that the H subjects were taught less but learned more. Notice, however, that the higher-order rules training was considerably less than perfect (71.5 percent success after training), especially considering the fact that many (53 percent) of the trainees apparently could use these relatively simple higher-order rules before training. This suggests that many simple higher-order rules have already been acquired by the time people reach adulthood, and that, one can normally expect less than perfect acquisition unless special precautions and extended and carefully detailed training are undertaken. Put differently, the training and transfer tests were conducted under something less than idealized conditions.

It is of special interest in the latter regard, that the degree of deviation from the ideal, in terms of higher-order rule availability (H = 71.5 percent, D = 53 percent), is closely paralleled by the obtained degrees of transfer (H = 68 percent, D = 51 percent). An even better fit is obtained when one takes into account the fact that the availability of both higher- and lower-order rules was necessary for success on the transfer problems. Thus, for example, ignoring rounding error, 95 percent (the average lower-order rules availability) of 71.5 percent (H group, higher-order rules success) is 68 percent (H group, transfer success). Similarly for the D group, 95 percent x 53 percent closely approximates 51 percent.

4.4 CONCLUSIONS AND EPILOGUE

By way of conclusion, I would like to reiterate three main points. (1) There are alternatives in instructional research to the usual probabilistic paradigm. Direct tests of deterministic theories are demanding but they are not only possible but, in many cases, they are quite feasible. The main requisite is that of realizing suitable idealized test conditions. (2) Deterministic behavior theories do exist. The structural learning theory has been tested under idealized conditions with strong empirical support; a level of support which goes far beyond what is normally found in behavioral research (cf. Part 3). (3) Such empirical support implies the applicability of the results in real world situations.

The implications of this last point are potentially far reaching. They could affect the very way in which instructional scientists look at the relationship between research and practice. Specifically, it may be possible to by-pass a good deal of expensive field testing. My argument purports to show that direct empirical support for a deterministic theory is sufficient alone to insure applicability. The only requirement is that the theory be tested in a representative number of specific situations under suitable idealized conditions.

In view of this conclusion, one might wonder whether the

converse also holds.   That is, since deterministic support under idealized conditions necessarily implies probabilistic support under real world conditions, it is natural to ask whether probabilistic support for a theory or hypothesis necessarily implies deterministic support under idealized conditions.

In general, the answer is no. Although this is not the context in which to dwell on what is basically a complex issue, consider probabilistic laws of the form $P(R) = f(x_1, x_2, \ldots, x_n)$. In particular, consider the following simple theoretical law: The probability of getting an "A" in a course is a direct function of I.Q. and grades in prerequisite courses. In this and similar cases, it is assumed (implicitly or explicitly) that we do not yet know enough to make perfect predictions—but that, in principle, if we added enough (of the right) predictor variables, or equivalently, if we could specify appropriate idealized conditions, we could predict things perfectly. (Identifying an extended and suitable list of predictors is equivalent to being able to specify appropriate idealized conditions.)

In fact, of course, no one really believes that we would succeed in accomplishing this. Even if we did succeed, the number of predictors would almost certainly be so large (even countably infinite) that the result would hardly be worthy of the name "theory".

The essential point is that if one wants a deterministic theory that lends itself to empirical testing, it is essential that one start with appropriate variables. It is just not possible to start with diffuse variables such as I.Q. and prior grades, just because they happen to be convenient, and reasonably expect that they might be extended to a deterministic theory.

REFERENCES

Atkin, M. J. Behavioral objectives in curriculum design: A cautionary note. *The Science Teacher,* 1968, *35,* 27-29.
Baggaley, A. R. A table to facilitate comparison of proportions by slide rule. *Psychological Bulletin,* 1957, *54,* 250-252.
Cureton, E. E. Validity. In E. F. Lindquist (Ed.), *Educational measurements.* Washington, D.C.: American Council on Education, 1951.
Ebel, R. L. Behavioral objectives: A close look. *Phi Delta Kappan,* 1970, *52,* 171-173.
Eisner, E. W. Educational objectives: Help or hindrance? *School Review,* 1967, *75,* 250-266.
Fisher, R. A. *The design of experiments.* Edinburgh: Oliver & Boyd, 1935.
Gagne, R. M. The acquisition of knowledge. *Psychological Review,* 1962, *59,* 355-365.
Gagne, R. M. *The conditions of learning* (2nd ed.). New York: Harper & Row, 1970.
Glaser, R. Educational psychology and education. *American Psychologist,* 1973, *28,* 557-566.
Lipson, J. The development of a mathematical curriculum for individualized instruction. In J. M. Scandura (Ed.), *Research in mathematics education.* Washington, D.C.: National Council of Teachers of Mathematics, 1967.

MacDpnald, J. B., & Wolfson, B. J. Case against behavioral objectives. *Elementary School Journal*, 1970, *71*, 119-128.

MacDonald-Ross, M. Behavioral objectives--a critical review. *Instructional Science*, 1973, *2*, 1-52.

Mager, R. F. *Preparing instructional objectives*. Palo Alto, Calif.: Fearon, 1962.

Miller, R. B. Task description and analysis. In R. M. Gagne (Ed.), *Psychological principles in system development*. New York: Holt, Rinehart, & Winston, 1962.

Popham, W. J. Probing the validity of arguments against behavioral goals. In G. W. Faust, M. C. Roderick, D. J. Cunningham, & R. C. Anderson (Eds.), *Current research on instruction*. Englewood Cliffs, N.J.: Prentice-Hall, 1969.

Resnick, L. B. Open education: Some tasks for technology. *Educational Technology*, 1972, *12*, 70-76.

Resnick, L. B., Wang, M. C., & Kaplan, J. Behavior analysis in curriculum design: A hierarchically sequenced introductory mathematics curriculum (Monograph 2). Pittsburgh: University of Pittsburgh, Learning Research and Development Center, 1970.

Rogers, H. J. *Theory of recursive functions and effective computability*. New York: McGraw-Hill, 1967.

Scandura, J. M. *Mathematics: Concrete behavioral foundations*. New York: Harper & Row, 1971.

Scandura, J. M. A plan for the development of a conceptually based curriculum for disadvantaged children: Part I: Theoretical foundations; Part II: Applications. *Instructional Science*, 1972, *2*, 247-262; 363-387.

Scandura, J. M. *Structural learning I: Theory and research*. New York: Gordon & Breach, 1973. (a)

Scandura, J. M. On higher-order rules. *Educational Psychologist*, 1973, *10*, 159-160. (b)

Scandura, J. M., Durnin, J., Ehrenpreis, W., & Luger, G. *Algorithmic approach to mathematics: Concrete behavioral foundations*. New York: Harper & Row, 1971.

Tyler, R. W. Some persistent questions on the defining of objectives. In C. M. Lindvall (Ed.), *Defining educational objectives*. Pittsburgh: University of Pittsburgh Press, 1964.

12
Development and Evaluation of Individualized Materials for Critical Reading[1]

George F. Lowerre[2] and Joseph M. Scandura

Many children know how to read in the sense that they can assign sounds to symbols on a page, and they may even be able to assign meanings to individual phrases and sentences; but they often are unable to combine these meanings in a logically consistent way. In particular, they may be unable to draw simple inferences from material they read, detect inconsistencies in various parts of a literary message, or determine whether additional new material is logically independent of what they have already read.

The present study was designed to develop, apply and evaluate a systematic, conceptually based method for producing diagnostic and instructional materials in this one area of critical thinking.[3] Specifically, we:

1. Developed a systematic procedure (systematic dimensional analysis) for constructing diagnostic tests and instructional materials dealing with specific logical inference rules.

2. Applied this procedure to develop prototype materials for use in the elementary school.

3. Evaluated these prototype materials and tested the assumptions on which the development was based.

---

[1]Adapted from "Development and Evaluation of Individualized Materials for Critical Thinking Based on Logical Inference", by G. Lowerre and J. M. Scandura, *Reading Research Quarterly*, 1973, *9*, 186-205 with permission. The school materials described herein have been expanded by members of the MERGE Research Institute and published by Ann Arbor Publishers, Worthington, Ohio 43085.

[2]Now at Northern Virginia Community College.

[3]Logical reasoning, as used here, is meant to include deductive reasoning only. It does not include inductive reasoning.

1. BACKGROUND AND RELATED RESEARCH

Many writers and researchers have attempted to list the skills involved in *critical thinking* (including critical thinking while reading).[4] Some have developed long lists of skills (see, for example, McCanne, 1969; Williams, 1959; Wolf, King, & Huck, 1968), and others have reduced their lists to a more modest length (for example, see Ennis, 1962; Spache & Spache, 1969). Although these lists contain a wide variety of skills, all of them include skills involving the ability to reason deductively. Thus, while experts in the field of critical thinking (and critical reading) cannot agree on a definition of exactly what it is, they do agree that logical reasoning skills are an important part of critical thinking.

Fortunately, the number of basic logical inference rules is relatively small; the others are all combinations of inference rules from the basic set. Corcoran (1968), for example, has identified 24 logical inference rules that are sufficient for all proofs in first-order logic.[5] While it may not be desirable pedagogically to teach each of these rules in the form in which Corcoran presents them, they demonstrate the relatively small size of the basic set of logical inference rules.

Experimental testing has shown that many children have not mastered all of the basic inference rules. Scandura and McGee (1972), for example, found that 12 out of 16 kindergarten children could not use simple rules of inference governing the words "some" and "all".

Other research has tested the use of logical rules by somewhat older children. Suppes (1964, 1965) cites a study by Hill in which she found that a group of eight-year-olds averaged 86 correct responses on a 100-item test requiring the use of logical rules.[6] Her test, however, excluded items where no valid conclusion could be drawn. O'Brien and Shapiro (1968) made her test more difficult by including "Not Enough Clues" as a possible response to each item, and by making that the correct response for one-third of the items. They found that the average score

---

[4]Some writers speak of *critical thinking;* others use the term *critical reading.* We agree with Moffett (1968) that critical reading is actually critical thinking about written discourse. The ability to read per se is a prerequisite to the ability to read critically.

[5]First-order logic includes the logic of propositions (sentential logic) and the use of quantifiers ("for all" and "there exists") applied to members of the relevant universe. It was not felt that second-order logic, in which quantifiers are applied to relations and functions, is relevant to the elementary school. Corcoran's (1968) list of 24 logical inference rules can be shortened by eliminating some of the logical connectives and defining them in terms of other logical connectives.

[6]Hill (see Suppes, 1965) and O'Brien and Shapiro (1968) also included younger children in their studies. Only the results for the 8-year-olds are quoted here.

dropped to 56 out of 100 for their group of eight-year-olds. For items whose correct response was "Not Enough Clues" the average score dropped to approximately the chance level.

Ennis, Finkelstein, Smith, and Wilson (1969), using only conditional statements, obtained results similar to those of O'Brien and Shapiro. They found that 62 percent of their third-grade subjects had mastered the rule for contrapositives of conditional statements.[7] But only 45 percent of their third-grade subjects had mastered the rule for transitivity of conditionals, 31 percent had mastered the rule for using inverses of conditionals,[8] and 7 percent had mastered the rule for using converses of conditionals.

It appears that Hill's data result (partly) from the type of test item she used, rather than from real mastery of logical rules by most third-graders. The evidence is that most eight-year-olds have not mastered the common rules of logical inference in a reading context, even when the circumstances in which the rules are applied contain no distracting or irrelevant information.

On the other hand, several earlier studies have demonstrated that it is possible to teach logic to elementary school children. Although Ennis *et al.* (1969) were not successful in teaching specific rules for conditional logic to elementary school children, Hyram (1957), Suppes and Binford (1965), and Wolf *et al.* (1968) were all successful to some extent in improving overall performance on a general logic test.

None of the studies in which logic was successfully taught, however, combined teaching and diagnostic testing in a unified way. Subjects were not tested before training to determine exactly which logical rules they knew and in what contexts they could use them. Similarly, the posttests in these studies gave only a single overall score; no indication was given as to which inference rules each subject had or had not mastered. For example, the posttest scores in these studies did not distinguish between the use of logical inference rules involving the quantifiers "for all" and "there exists", and the use of logical in-

---

[7]Ennis *et al.* (1969) also included younger children in their study. Only the results for the third-graders are quoted here.

[8]A conditional statement is one of the form: "If Fido is a dog, then Fido has a tail." The converse is "If Fido has a tail, then Fido is a dog." The inverse is "If Fido is not a dog, then Fido does not have a tail," and the contrapositive is "If Fido does not have a tail, then Fido is not a dog." If a conditional statement is true, then its contrapositive must also be true. But the converse and inverse of a true conditional statement may be either true or false. (For the example given, they are both false since Fido may be a cat with a tail.)

ference rules not involving quantifiers.[9]

The prototype materials developed and evaluated in the present study were designed to avoid these limitations by:

1. Including a pretest for each rule to determine whether and in which reading contexts each child can use it.

2. Basing the initial instruction for each child directly on his performance on the pretest.

3. Permitting each child to study the use of each rule in a more difficult setting only after he had mastered its use in simpler settings.

4. Generating posttest scores that indicate the contexts in which each child can use each rule tested.

2.   SYSTEMATIC DIMENSIONAL ANALYSIS

The systematic procedure used to develop the prototype diagnostic testing and teaching materials was adapted from ideas set forth in Scandura (1968). Each logical rule determines a class of stimulus-response pairs, where the stimuli consist of reading materials in which the logical rule can be applied, and the responses are logical implications of these reading materials. Adaptation of Scandura's ideas further required the identification of dimensions over which such reading materials may vary, together with levels of difficulty along each dimension. The difficulty levels depend on the amount of information that must bè processed and how consistent the information is with what is commonly known.

Five dimensions were identified, and levels of difficulty along each of them were determined. These are given in Table 1. A serious attempt was made to make these dimensions exhaustive and essentially independent. It should be emphasized that these dimensions were determined by strictly analytical means. There was no use of factor analysis or other statistical procedures.

For each logical inference rule it is possible to construct reading passages at predetermined levels of difficulty along each dimension. For example, a passage might be at Level 2 of Dimension A, Level 3 of Dimension B and so on. The testing procedure depends on the assumption that success in using a logical rule at any level of difficulty along any dimension implies suc-

---

[9]An example of use of a logical inference rule involving the quantifier "for all" is the following:

               All dogs have tails.
               Fido is a dog.
               Therefore, Fido has a tail.

An example of use of a logical inference rule not involving use of a quantifier is the following:

               Fido is a dog or a cat.
               Fido is not a dog.
               Therefore, Fido is a cat.

TABLE 1
*Dimensions Over Which Reading Settings May Vary,
With Difficulty Levels Along Them*

A. *Relation of statements in message to reality*

| 1. Statements that agree with facts known by reader | 2. (Neutral) Statements that neither agree nor contradict facts known by reader | 3. Statements that contradict facts known by reader |

B. *Complexity of context (including length)*

| 1. Simple: single implication; message contains only relevant statements | 2. More than 1 implication; message contains only relevant statements | 3. More than 1 implication; message contains 3 to 5 extra statements, 1 or 2 of which may appear to be relevant |

C. *Availability of premises in message*

| 1. All relevant premises present and clearly stated | 2. Nuance; premise determined from context | 3. Some premise is missing but implied by the context |

D. *Required length of chain of inference*

| 1. Single rule application | 2. Two rule applications | 3. Three rule applications | 4. Four rule applications |

E. *Terminology used*

| 1. Most common English terminology (e.g., If A, then B) | 2. Variations from common terminology (e.g., A only if B, or B is necesssry for A) |

---

cess at the less difficult level(s). Conversely, failure at any level of difficulty along a dimension is assumed to imply failure to use the logical rule correctly at the more difficult level(s).

Studies by Scandura, Woodward, and Lee (1967) and Scandura and Durnin (1968) lend support for these assumptions. They studied rules (that define classes of tasks) that may be thought of as varying in generality along ordered dimensions. In these studies, success in generalizing to one new instance of a more general rule implied success in generalizing to other instances of the rule. Similarly, failure in generalizing to one instance implied failure to generalize to others.[10]

It seems reasonable to expect similar results with logical rules where the reading contexts (which define classes of tasks) vary in difficulty along ordered dimensions. Part of the experimental procedure involved specific testing of the assumptions on which the testing procedure was based.

[10]See Scandura (1973) for a more rigorous analysis based on rules.

Given these assumptions, the most difficult level at which a child can use a logical rule along one dimension was determined by testing in the following order:

1. Test for use of the logical inference rule at the least difficult level on that dimension.

2. Test for use of the logical rule at the most difficult level on that dimension.

3. Test for use of the logical rule at successively less difficult levels along that dimension.

For a single dimension with n levels of difficulty, this testing procedure may be diagramed as shown in Figure 1. When a child can solve test items at one level, the first assumption allows us to conclude that he can do all of the problems requiring use of the logical rule at less difficult levels along the dimension being tested. Hence, when one tests in the sequence above and a child succeeds on the test items at any level beyond the simplest one, further testing along that dimension is unnecessary. Also, failure on the test items at the simplest level implies, on the basis of the second assumption, that the child cannot use the logical rule at the other levels, so that testing stops. Finally, success on the test items at the simplest level, followed by failure on the test items at all other levels, implies that the child can use the logical rule only in the simplest setting along that dimension. (Although this testing procedure is not the most efficient when the number of difficulty levels is large, it was roughly as efficient in the present study and appeared to have certain pedagogical advantages.)

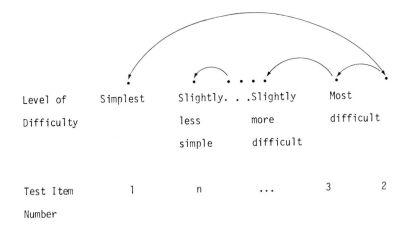

Figure 1. Determination of most difficult level at which subject could use a logical rule.

This procedure works well with any logical inference rule, and may be extended to test for use of the rule along two or more dimensions. To determine the most difficult levels at which a child can apply a rule along several dimensions, the following procedure was used:

1. Hold the level of difficulty on all dimensions fixed but one, and test as just described to find the maximum level of difficulty at which the child can apply the logical rule along that dimension.

2. Hold the level of difficulty on the first dimension fixed at the level just determined, and repeat the procedure with the second dimension. (The level of difficulty on the first dimension is held fixed at the level just determined because the dimensions may not be independent for a given child. As noted above, an attempt was made to identify dimensions that are independent for purposes of classifying reading materials, but no definitive claim can be made regarding their behavioral independence.)

3. Repeat the process, one dimension at a time, to determine the maximum level at which the child can apply the logical rule on succeeding dimensions.

Instruction on a logical inference rule begins after the most difficult levels at which a child can use a logical rule have been determined. The prototype instructional materials developed for this study, like the testing materials, also were based on the dimensional analysis. Specifically, the instructional materials were designed to start at the levels at which the child can use a logical rule, and gradually to increase the difficulty of the material along one dimension at a time.

A child may be said to know how to use a logical rule when he can: (1) use the rule to make or recognize a valid inference, (2) use the rule to detect logical incompatibilities, and (3) know when *not* to use the rule (i.e., to recognize invalid uses of the rule). The prototype materials were designed to test and teach all three aspects of each logical rule.

3.   PROTOTYPE MATERIALS

The prototype materials were based on two logical rules, and the stimulus reading materials were allowed to vary over only two of the five dimensions. The two logical inference rules may be represented:

Rule for "Or" Elimination[11]

From the premise	P or Q
and the premise	not P (or not Q)
we conclude	Q (or P)

[11]The names used for different logical rules vary among authors. These names are a variation of the relatively simple naming system used by Corcoran (1968).

Rule for "All" Elimination

From the premise	All P's are Q's (have property Q)
and the premise	x is a P
we conclude	x is a Q (has property Q).

The materials developed for the "all" elimination rule included sentences using a pattern that appears similar to the valid one above.

All P's are Q's (have property Q)
x is a Q (has property Q).

But in this case, no valid conclusion is possible. Any child who drew the invalid conclusion, "x is a P," will be said to have used the fallacy of "all" conversion.[12]

These two rules were chosen because they are common logical inference rules, and because one of them ("all" elimination) involves the use of a quantifier and the other does not. The materials were designed for use by children reading at the third- or fourth-grade levels.

Dimensions B (Complexity of Context) and C (Availability of Premises) were allowed to vary. Dimension A was held fixed at Level 2 (the "neutral" level) and Dimensions D and E were held fixed at Level 1 (the simplest level).

All test items were of the multiple choice variety. The child was to circle TRUE if the statement must be true (based on the preceding paragraph), and to circle FALSE if the statement must be false (based on the preceding paragraph), and to circle DON'T KNOW if the paragraph did not give enough information to determine whether the statement is true or false.

A sample item follows:

All pro football linemen weigh over 200 pounds. Tom Smith weighs over 200 pounds. Fred Jones is a pro football lineman. Paul Franks is a pro football lineman, too.

A. Tom Smith is a pro football lineman.	TRUE FALSE DON'T KNOW
B. Paul Franks weighs over 200 pounds.	TRUE FALSE DON'T KNOW
C. Fred Jones weighs less than 200 pounds.	TRUE FALSE DON'T KNOW
D. Tom Smith lives near Paul Franks.	TRUE FALSE DON'T KNOW
E. Fred Jones weighs over 200 pounds.	TRUE FALSE DON'T KNOW

Such an item tests a child's ability to deal with all three

[12]This name is adapted from Ennis, Finkelstein, Smith, and Wilson (1969). They consider conversion (of a conditional statement) to be a separate case. In these materials, the fallacy of "all" conversion is considered to be an invalid application of the rule for "all" elimination.

aspects of a logical rule as follows:

1. Sentences that should be marked TRUE (B and E in the sample item) test his ability to make or to recognize a valid inference.

2. Sentences that should be marked FALSE (C in the sample item) test his ability to detect statements that are incompatible with the rest of the message.

3. Sentences that should be marked DON'T KNOW (A and D in the sample item) test his ability to recognize statements that, while not incompatible with the rest of the message, do not follow from it by use of the logical rule.[13] (All of the test items were written so that such sentences did not follow from the use of any other logical rule.)

Two tests were written for each rule with 12 to 16 items at each pair of difficulty levels. They were made as nearly equivalent as possible. Both used essentially the same stories, but names, colors, dates, and order of sentences were changed. Each test was 20 pages long, including two practice pages. The pages were grouped in pairs, with all problems on each pair of pages being at the same level along both dimensions. At each level on the "all" elimination tests there were at least three sentences (responses) that could be marked using the similar appearing, but invalid fallacy of "all" conversion. Mastery, or criterion, at each level was set at a maximum of two errors out of a total of 12 to 16 responses.[14]

The instructional materials consisted of 10 workbooks for each logical rule, with a prerecorded cassette tape accompanying each workbook. The tapes provided hints and diminishing amounts of help as the instruction progressed, together with answers for checking. The workbooks were between 5 to 7 pages long, and they required from 37 to 62 student responses. The workbooks were sequenced as shown in Table 2. The even-numbered workbooks were used as backups, where the child had not mastered use of the rule at the higher level by the time he had completed the preceding odd-numbered workbook. For example, a child used Workbook 6 only if he had not mastered use of the rule at Level 3 - 1 by the end of Workbook 5. (The first number represents the level of Dimension B; the second number represents the level on Dimension C.)

---

[13]It must be recognized that this response may be chosen not only in the case where a child recognizes an invalid application of the logical rule, but also in the case where he does not know whether a logical rule applies or not. Complete inability to use a logical rule will result in correct responses in cases where DON'T KNOW is the correct answer.

[14]It was felt that this would allow a large enough number of careless mistakes for a child who could really use the rule at the given level. It was also small enough that any child who systematically used the invalid fallacy of "all" conversion, and who therefore did not fully understand the rule for "all" elimination, would not meet criterion.

TABLE 2
Workbook Sequence and Content Level

Workbook Number	Entering Level	Level After Completing
1, 2	0 - 0*	1 - 1
3, 4	1 - 1	2 - 1
5, 6	2 - 1	3 - 1
7, 8	3 - 1	3 - 2
9, 10	3 - 2	3 - 3

*The first number represents the level on Dimension B; the second number represents the level on Dimension C.

The starting workbook for each child was determined by the pretest. These were as shown in Table 3. The child then progressed through the workbooks in numerical order, skipping the even-numbered workbooks whenever possible.

Notice that some of the starting workbooks were grouped (for Levels 1, 2, and 3 of Dimension C). This was done in order to keep the number of workbooks relatively small. Although it would have been possible to provide a separate starting point for each pair of levels of Dimensions B and C, this would have increased the total number of workbooks to a level that was felt to be impractical for school use.

The instructional materials utilized a guided discovery format. Each workbook contained marked examples. Spoken com-

TABLE 3
Determination of Starting Workbook

Maximum Levels at Which Child Demonstrated Mastery on Pretest	Beginning Workbook
0 - 0*	1
1 - 1	
1 - 2	3
1 - 3	
2 - 1	
2 - 2	5
2 - 3	
3 - 1	7
3 - 2	9
3 - 3	NONE

*The first number represents the level on Dimension B; the second number represents the level on Dimension C.

ments on the corresponding tape explained the examples and gave
relevant ideas. Then the child worked some examples. These
were explained on the tape. More examples were worked and the
answers explained and so on. The tapes were completely self-
contained. They included directions for marking sentences, when
to stop and start the tape player, and what workbook to use next.
Once a child knew how to operate the tape player, he received
all of his directions, as well as explanations of the correct
responses for the workbook sentences, from the tape and had no
need for outside help.

All of the written materials, both the tests and the workbooks, were tested for readability using the Spache (1953) readability formula with the Stone (1956) revised word list. Because
these materials were designed for children reading at the third-
or fourth-grade level, a cut-off level of 2.5 was used. Any
test items that gave a reading level higher than 2.5 were re-
written or deleted.

No formal method was used to evaluate the language used on
the tapes, although an effort was made to keep the vocabulary
as simple as possible.

4. EMPIRICAL TEST: SUBJECTS, EXPERIMENTAL DESIGN, AND PROCEDURE

The empirical study was designed primarily to test the efficacy of the prototype materials. In addition, it was used to
test the basic assumptions underlying the testing procedure,
namely, that success in using a logical rule at Level 3 along
either dimension implied success at Level 2, and that failure
at Level 1 along both dimensions implied failure at all higher
levels.

A simple pretest-posttest control group design was used.
The pretests for both rules were first administered to 45 children from 9 different classrooms in the second, third, and
fourth grades in the Henry C. Lea School in West Philadelphia.
All of the children were volunteers reading at the third- or
fourth-grade level. The reading levels had been determined by
their teachers using a group informal reading inventory, following procedures outlined by the School District of Philadelphia
for that purpose.

The pretest was given to groups ranging from 3 to 6 subjects each. There was no time limit for taking the test. First,
the maximum levels along both dimensions, at which a child could
use each logical rule, were determined. Then, additional items
from the test, that had not been required to determine the maximum levels along dimensions, were assigned in order to test the
basic assumptions regarding difficulty levels.

Each child took the pretest for the "or" elimination rule
first, and took the "all" elimination pretest between one and

five days later.

Five of the original children were excluded from further participation for technical reasons. This left 40 subjects for the experiment. Of these, 17 scored at Level 3 of both dimensions on the test for the rule for "or" elimination; none of the subjects scored at Level 3 on both dimensions on the test for the rule for "all" elimination.

The 40 subjects were randomly assigned to experimental and control groups, without constraints on group size, because of scheduling limitations at the Lea School. The experimental group turned out to be slightly smaller (n = 19) than the control group (n = 21). All of the experimental subjects who had not scored at Level 3 on both dimensions received instruction for the "or" elimination rule. All but three experimental subjects received instruction for the "all" elimination rule. (One of those three moved out of the school district; the other two were absent for an extended period of time.) No instruction was provided to any of the control subjects.

The experimental subjects received the instruction two at a time (except when one subject scheduled for a given time was absent). Each was furnished with a cassette tape player and workbook, and proceeded at his own pace. Most subjects received instruction two times per week, although a subject occasionally worked with the materials either one or three times in a given week. All instruction took place in carrels in the Instructional Materials Center at the Lea School.

The subjects worked by themselves. The experimenter was available to handle unforeseen difficulties. Any subject who failed to meet criterion at any level both on the original (odd-numbered) workbook and on the back-up (even-numbered) workbook, used the original workbook again. If he met criterion on that try, he continued in the usual manner.[15] If he again failed to meet criterion, instruction on that rule was halted.[16]

Those experimental subjects who did not score at Level 3 on both dimensions on the pretest for the "or" elimination rule, received instruction on that rule first. Then they received the corresponding posttest. Next they received instruction on the rule for "all" elimination, followed by the posttest for that rule. All posttests were given on separate days. Those in the experimental group who scored at Level 3 on each dimension on the "or" elimination pretest, went directly to instruction on the rule for "all" elimination.

The subjects in the control group were given the posttests at the same time as the last members of the experimental group were completing the posttest on the "all" elimination rule.

[15]This happened twice (both times on the "all" elimination rule).

[16]This happened three times (two times with the "or" elimination rule and one time with the "all" elimination rule).

The elapsed time between pretests and posttests for the control group varied from 50 days to 64 days, with a median of 54 days.

5.   TEST VALIDATION RESULTS

The test data were first analyzed to determine whether the assumptions on which the testing procedure was based were valid. In general these hierarchical assumptions were supported. Subjects who met criterion at Level 3 along a dimension, also tended to meet criterion at Level 2 along that dimension. And subjects who failed at Level 1 - 1, also tended to fail at all other levels tested.[17]

There was one exception. In 10 out of 51 tests (counting pretests and posttests together) on the rule for "or" elimination, a subject succeeded at Level 3 of Dimension C but failed at Level 2. Reexamination of the test items at Level 3 of Dimension C (regardless of the level of Dimension B) showed that these items required the child to find a missing premise, but did not require him to use the "or" elimination rule after finding the missing premise. Therefore, all materials related to Level 3 of Dimension C for "or" elimination were discarded.

With Level 3 of Dimension C discarded, the testing assumptions were upheld in a total of 68 out of 72 instances (94 percent) on the "or" elimination pretest and in 30 out of 33 instances (91 percent) on the "or" elimination posttest. The testing assumptions were upheld on the "all" elimination pretest in a total of 128 out of 152 instances (84 percent), and, on the "all" elimination posttest, in 78 out of 83 instances (94 percent).[18]

Because the pretests and posttests each involve what is essentially a series of subtests, it is not appropriate to compute ordinary reliability coefficients. Indeed, there is, to our knowledge no accepted method for calculating such reliabilities on sequential tests. Nonetheless, for comparative purposes, reliability coefficients were computed for each subtest that was taken by at least 10 subjects. For this purpose, use was made of the Livingston (1972) criterion-referenced re-

---

[17]Because of time limitations, the only additional levels tested in this case were Levels 1 - 2, 1 - 3, 2 - 1, and 3 - 1. For subjects who failed to meet criterion at all of these levels it seems safe to assume that they would also fail to meet criterion at Levels 2 - 2, 3 - 2, 2 - 3, and 3 - 3.

[18]Most of the cases where the testing assumptions were not upheld on the "all" elimination pretest involved Level 3 of Dimension C. However, at Level 3 of Dimension C on the pretest, the child had only to find the missing premise; he did not have to use the "all" elimination rule. This was changed on the posttest. All items at Level 3 of Dimension C on the posttest required the child to find the missing premise and then to use the "all" elimination rule to find a conclusion (or to recognize that no valid conclusion was possible). This accounts for the higher percentage on the "all" elimination posttest.

liability formula, based on norm-referenced reliabilities determined by Kuder-Richardson formula 20.   Twenty reliability
coefficients were computed.   Eight ranged from .84 to .90; seven
from .77 to .81; three from .73 to .75; and two from .52 to .53.
The last two reliabilities were unusually low because almost all
of the subjects scored at the criterion level.   (This resulted
from an artifact of the formula used.)   Although quite high,
considering the lengths of the subtests, such reliabilities in
sequential tests are of secondary importance relative to the
above percentages concerned with hierarchical validity.

G.   INSTRUCTIONAL RESULTS

The results of the instruction are summarized in Tables 4
and 5.   Table 4 compares the number of subjects in the experimental and control groups who improved their scores between the
pretest and posttest (i.e., who learned or "expanded" use of a
rule).   For the "or" elimination rule, the differences in number
of subjects who improved their scores approaches significance
(.05 < p < .10).   For the "all" elimination rule, the differences are highly significant (p < .0001).

Table 5 compares the changes in performance between pretest
and posttest.   The change in performance for each subject was
obtained by adding the changes along both dimensions.   For example, a change from Level 2 - 1 on the pretest to Level 3 - 2
on the posttest is a change of +2.[19]   According to this criterion, too, the experimental subjects learned significantly more,
both for the "or" elimination rule (p < .05) and for the "all"
elimination rule (p < .0001).

The differences associated with "or" elimination are not
as large as those for "all" elimination.   Many of the control
subjects did better on the "or" elimination posttest than they
did on the pretest, while very few control subjects did better
on the "all" elimination posttest than they did on the pretest.
"Or" elimination seems to have been a relatively easy rule, and
apparently many subjects learned to use it while taking the pretest.   "All" elimination was distinctly harder, probably because
of the fallacy of "all" conversion, and the effects of instruction were more apparent.

In summary, all of the experimental results favored the
experimental group.   Perhaps most important, every experimental
subject scored better on both posttests than on the pretests
(excepting, of course, those 9 subjects who scored at the top
level (3 - 2) on the "or" elimination pretest).   This clearly
was not true for the control subjects.

_____

[19]Because Levels 0 - 1 and 1 - 0 do not exist (Level 0 - 0 indicates
complete inability to use the rule, and Level 1 - 1 means the child can use
the rule at the lowest level along each dimension), a change from Level 0 - 0
to Level 1 - 1 was considered a change of +1.

TABLE 4

Relative Gains in Expanding Use of Rules

Pretest Level	Posttest Level	"Or" Elimination			"All" Elimination		
		n			n		
		Exper.	Control	P*	Exper.	Control	P*
0 - 0	Higher	6	4	.23	13	3	.0001
	Same or lower	0	2		0	14	
1 - 1 or higher*	Higher	4	5	.38	3	2	.29
	Same or lower	0	2		0	2	
All levels**	Higher	10	9	.08	16	5	.00001
	Same or lower	0	4		0	16	

*Using the Fisher-Yates (Finney, 1948) exact test
**Any S who was able to use the rule at the highest level on the pretest was not included here.

TABLE 5

Comparison of Change of Levels (Gain) from Pretest to Posttest

	"Or" Elimination		"All" Elimination	
	Exper.	Control	Exper.	Control
n*	10	13	16	21
mean	2.50	1.23	3.44	0.43
S. D.	1.12	1.25	1.75	1.00
sum of ranks	86.5	189.5	153.5	549.5
p**	.025		.0001	

*Any S who was able to use the rule at the highest levels on the pretest was not included here.
**Using a one-tailed Mann-Whitney U test.

7.   DISCUSSION AND IMPLICATIONS

Within the bounds set for these prototype materials (they dealt with only two of five dimensions and with only two logical rules), dimensional analysis appeared to be a useful technology. The testing assumptions were shown to be valid, and the tests were shown to be efficient instruments for measuring the reading contexts in which children can use a logical rule. Basing instruction directly on pretest performance and sequencing instruction systematically by expanding reading contexts along one dimension at a time appears to be a sound procedure.

It would appear, therefore, that further materials development based on the above dimensional analysis seems justified. Specifically, such development should involve all five dimensions and a wider variety of logical inference rules. Besides additional materials on general topics, as in the prototype materials, tapes and workbooks also could be developed to accompany curriculum materials in particular subject matters, such as mathematics or social studies.

Answers to the following questions could aid such development.

1. How should logical rules be matched with grade or reading level for teaching purposes? For example, "or" elimination seems less appropriate for third- and fourth-graders than does "all" elimination.

2. What is the role of fallacious rules, such as the fallacy of "all" conversion? Should fallacious rules be taught as misapplications of valid rules, or should separate materials be devoted just to them? Comparing the results of this study with the results of Ennis *et al.* (1969), where invalid converses and inverses of conditionals were taught as separate rules, it would appear that it is better to teach fallacious rules as misapplications of valid ones. But this is not clearly established.

3. More basically, what are the cognitive procedures (rules of competence), corresponding to rules of inference, that allow children to draw inferences and to detect logical inconsistencies? How do children distinguish between situations where a rule (e.g., "all" elimination) may validly be used and apparently similar situations where it cannot (e.g., the fallacy of "all" conversion)? Further, how if at all do the underlying procedures depend on the target population? (In short, can structural analysis, as described say in Chapter 2, be usefully applied to critical reading? And, if so, what is the relationship between extensional dimensional analyses and intensional competence?)

4. What can be done to make materials of this kind more interesting? Although only a subjective observation, it appeared that some of the experimental subjects found the workbooks tedious at times. If different types of responses, or different

instructional formats (e.g., workbooks) might improve motivation and/or interest, what form should they take? In any case, simple scoring would appear essential in order to maintain the self-instructional feature.

5. How can one be sure that a child will use a logical rule, which he has mastered in a paper-and-pencil test situation, in nontest situations? Out-of-class use of what is learned in class is, of course, a major goal of all education. Can methods be developed for measuring the use of logical rules in other classroom subjects and in nonschool reading and other activities?

6. Finally, it should be noted that use of the discovery method to teach the use of logical rules with written materials requires a wide variety of stories. If efficiency is to be increased further, it will be necessary to identify more precisely the various underlying rules of competence. Specifying the general form of each logical rule is just a first step in this direction. To the extent that such specification can be achieved, the present inductive approach might be replaced by more direct instruction. (The following addendum is concerned largely with this issue. It was added primarily to show how the above chapter might be related to the structural/process orientation of this book.)

8.   ADDENDUM: STRUCTURAL FOUNDATIONS (A PROPOSAL FOR FUTURE RESEARCH)[20]

Along with the general renewal of interest in reading in schools, there has been an increasing amount of basic research on language comprehension and an increasing concern with the role of logical inference (e.g., Bormuth, 1970; Williams, 1971; Carroll & Freedle, 1972; Davis, 1971; Olson, 1970; Rothkopf, 1972; Frase, 1969; Kintsch, 1972; Rumelhart, Lindsay, & Norman, 1972). Most of the recent research in this area is based on the information-processing view (e.g., Miller, Galanter, & Pribram, 1960), although there also have been a large number of studies involving the use of multiple-regression or factor-analysis techniques (Holmes, 1948; Davis, 1967, 1968; Holmes & Singer, 1966) to identify predictor variables or variance components in reading. (For a more detailed review of the psychometric literature see Davis, 1971.)

Even among scientists of the former persuasion, however, there are important differences of opinion regarding the extent to which theory development should be specific to language comprehension (e.g., Freedle & Carroll, 1972) or apply generally to all knowledge and understanding (e.g., Scriven, 1972;

[20]This section was prepared by the second author after the original paper was published. Preparation of the section was supported in part by National Institute of Health Grant 9185.

Scandura, 1973). The research also has differed with regard to
the complexity of the prose studied; the materials used have
ranged from simple sentences (e.g., Trabasso, 1972) to topical
paragraphs (e.g., as in this chapter). Although useful scientific research can and should be done at all levels, our approach
to the problem favors the use of realistic content.

In view of our concern with general theory, which includes
language as a special case, it is interesting to note what
Thorndike said on the matter in 1917. "Understanding a paragraph is like solving a problem in mathematics. It consists
in selecting the right elements of the situation and putting
them together in the right relations, and also with the right
amount of weight or influence or force for each" (1917, p. 329).

The following discussion is included in the hope that it
may encourage further research on critical reading; particularly
relating to Questions 3 and 6 of the preceding section. Attention is focused primarily on the identification of competence
in critical reading and the assessment of individual knowledge
(relevant to that competence).

8.1 STRUCTURAL APPROACH TO CRITICAL READING

Although direct empirical support for the structural-
learning theory with respect to critical reading is lacking, the
work of Lowerre and Scandura described earlier in this chapter
is relevant. In particular, the dimensional approach used
approximates the type of diagnosis made possible by algorithmic
means (see Chapter 9). Although the above results are reasonably clear-cut, and were of sufficient practical value to warrant commercial publication of a series of critical reading
workbooks for schools, the dimensional approach has an important
limitation. It does not identify the actual rules (processes
subjects go through) in critical reading. For example, characterizing competence solely in terms of external stimulus (paragraph) dimensions, makes it difficult (at best) to compare
individuals or populations—for example, to determine whether
there are systematic differences in the way different subjects
engage in critical reading.

There has been a growing amount of research aimed at identifying procedures (rules) involved in the reception and production of natural language, but I do not know of any such procedures designed explicitly for critical reading. In the former
regard, for example, Carroll (1975) has developed a computer
program that generates a surprisingly large variety of sentences
given the intentions of the speaker. Although less sophisticated insofar as connotation and nuance are concerned, Winograd
(1971) has devised a more general computer program for answering
questions about blocks of various shapes and sizes. This program
both interprets and responds to questions within its "block's
world". Unlike the former program, Winograd's must necessarily

take into account the prior knowledge of the listener (computer) about the block's world. It is this aspect of comprehension that makes it more difficult to analyze than speech production (e.g., see Olson, 1970).

In addition to identifying underlying rules of competence, it is necessary to find out how they relate to human behavior. Some investigators have used computer-simulation studies with individual subjects for this purpose (e.g., Newell & Simon, 1972). In structural learning studies, this is accomplished by determining the compatibility of various procedures with the behavior of individuals in given populations of subjects. Specifically, a procedure that accounts for a given set of tasks partitions that set into subclasses of equivalent tasks (i.e., into equivalence classes, Scandura, 1973). The procedure provides a viable account of the behavior of individuals in a given population to the extent that success on one task within an equivalence class implies success on others, and similarly with failure. When success-failure profiles are obtained with respect to two or more procedures, choices can be made between alternative theories (rules/strategies/procedures/algorithms) (see Chapters 9 and 10).

In principle, the profile of successes and failures obtained for each subject not only pinpoints what the subject can and cannot do, but it also effectively tells which parts of the underlying rule(s) the subject needs to learn in order to overcome his inadequacies. The algorithmic approach, thereby, provides an explicit basis for remediation as well as diagnosis. Theoretical details are given in Scandura (1973; Chapters 2 and 9, this volume).

It is important to emphasize that the structural approach to measuring individual differences is *not* limited to highly structured tasks. Thus, although the precise specification of competence in terms of algorithms is usually accomplished via some formal, relatively low-level (i.e., detailed) algorithmic language, this does not mean that rules necessarily must be represented with this precision or in this degree of detail. Thus, whereas rules (procedures/algorithms) in computer programming are typically represented in terms of fixed computer languages, the linguistic elements used to represent rules of human competence/knowledge are more varied. Specifically, the units (operations and decisions) of which rules of competence are constructed, and correspondingly the linguistic elements used to represent these units, vary in scope according to the intended population of human information processors. The more sophisticated the population, in general the larger and more varied are the linguistic elements that can properly be understood (as units). In turn, the larger and more varied the units, the easier it is to represent competence. It is this characteristic flexibility that leads to the broad applicability of structural

representations, including applicability to what initially might
appear to be intractable tasks (cf. Chapter 15).

8.2 REPRESENTATION OF INFERENCE RULES
    On the surface, the ability to read critically--that is,
the ability to detect logical (or other) relationships among
statements in a paragraph might not seem suitable for structural
analysis. Indeed, it would be extremely difficult to detail
all of the operations and decisions involved in encoding and
interpreting individual morphemes as well as in determining
grammatical and logical interrelationships. Given that subjects
can properly understand individual statements, however, the task
becomes much easier. The individual meanings, for example, can
be represented as regions in Venn diagrams and the interrelationships, as set membership and inclusion, and intersections,
unions, and complements of such regions.
    In experimental research that is designed to deal with
interrelationships, therefore, the influence of extraneous factors might be eliminated by chosing appropriately sized units.
Thus, in critical reading the experimental discourse might be
constructed so that the individual statements can be successfully interpreted by essentially all of the subjects in question.
    In fact, these same considerations enter into the analysis
of any problem domain (see Chapter 2). One must always assume
some minimal unit of analysis, even in simple subtraction for
example. In critical reading, however, rather than subtraction
problems and numerical differences, the inputs consist of written discourse and key statements pertaining to the discourse.
The outputs consist of the response options: TRUE, FALSE, NOT
SURE. In this case, for example, individual statements in extended discourse correspond roughly to the digits used to construct subtraction problems (cf. Chapter 9, this volume).
    In order to deal with logical interrelationships among
statements, any adequate rule of competence must as a minimum:
(1) generate meanings of the individual statements (including
key statements) and represent these meanings in an appropriate
way, (2) combine the meanings of statements in the main discourse, (3) compare combined meanings with the meanings of key
statements, and (4) generate appropriate responses on the basis
of such comparisons. In order to devise critical reading rules,
therefore, a suitable way to represent meanings must be found.
Fortunately, Venn diagrams (e.g., see Chapter 2 of Scandura,
1971) provide a convenient way to accomplish this in the case
of (simple) logical inference. Furthermore, as Erickson (1973)
has shown, Venn diagrams can be used in syllogistic reasoning
to represent inaccurate, though common, interpretations (given
by real subjects) as well as veridical ones. For example, consider the following task:

Main Discourse:
    "Bonnie Bookworm was very excited about her new house.
Her father said, 'If the new house is finished before the
end of August, then you may have a party in September.'
Bonnie knew she was going to miss her friend Karen who liv-
ed next door. The new house was finished in August."
Key Statement:
"Bonnie had a party in September."
Response Options:
    TRUE   FALSE   NOT SURE
In this case, the meaning of "If (A) the new house is finished
before September, then (B) you may have a party in September
(if A, then B)" is accurately represented by the shaded area in
Figure 2. That is, the shaded area represents that subset of
real world events (U) that can be truthfully described by the
statement "If A, then B."

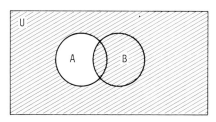

Figure 2. Correct Venn diagram for "If A then B."

    Not all subjects, however, necessarily assign correct mean-
ings to logical statements, even when they can accurately interpret all of the component parts (e.g., A and B). Thus, for example, statements of the form "If A, then B" may be variously
misinterpreted as in Figure 3.

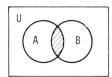
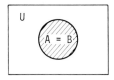
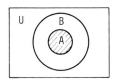

Figure 3. Incorrect Venn diagrams for "If A then B."

    Furthermore, the meanings of individual statements may be
combined by forming intersections of Venn diagrams for the individual statements. In the above discourse, for example, the
meaning of the minor premise "(A) The new house was finished
in August" might be represented by adding dots, say, within Set
A in Figure 2. The combined meaning then, would be that part
of the figure common to A and the shaded portion of Figure 2
(i.e., the intersection of A and B).
    More generally, a complete rule for solving critical read-
ing tasks would assign meanings to individual statements of the

paragraph, form set intersections of the various statements, assign a meaning to the key statement, and compare the meaning of the key statement with various set intersections to generate a TRUE, FALSE, or NOT SURE response. (The correct response depends on whether the key statement meaning is contained in the intersection, the two are distinct, or they overlap, respectively. It also should be noted that generating TRUE responses, when correct, indicates inference-generating ability; generating FALSE responses, when correct, indicates the ability to detect inconsistencies; and generating NOT SURE, when correct, indicates the ability to determine logical independence.)

Complete specification of any particular cognitive rule, of course, also requires making explicit the bases used for making decisions (i.e., the nodes or diamonds in flow diagrams) and for directing the flow of control within the rule. Among other things, this may involve specifying the order in which various statements are interpreted and the ways in which form or context affect the particular meanings assigned (cf. Landa, 1974).

The question arises in this context as to how rules of competence relate to dimensional analysis. Although detailed consideration here would take us too far afield of present concerns, the major points can be summed up as follows. (1) Dimensional analysis (like item forms) is concerned with the nature of the inputs. (Unlike item forms, however, they are not restricted to paper and pencil format, cf. Chapter 15, Section 3.) Rules of competence are concerned with underlying competence. (2) The "inference rules" referred to in our discussion of dimensional analysis basically identify only a *type* of competence rule. Complete specification of the latter requires detailing the internal operations and decisions that must be made in applying an inference rule (viewed as a rule of competence) to specific written discourse. (3) The various difficulty levels, along dimensions in dimensional analysis, correspond to "loops" in the procedural (flow diagram) representations of rules of competence. In general, the less difficult the level, the fewer loops are apt to be required in the corresponding path of the associated competence rule, and conversely.

Anyone with a modicum of programming experience can devise rules that perform as indicated above. To help ensure behavioral viability, however, prototypic rules should probably be based on informal observations of actual subjects. Since different people might well attack such problems in various ways, it might be useful to observe skilled readers (and some not so skilled for comparison) from various populations (e.g., educationally disadvantaged and educationally advantaged populations).

The purpose of such observations would be analogous to those of Bruner, Goodnow, and Austin (1967) in their now classical studies of thinking. As a result of their observations, Bruner

et al. (1967) determined that their subjects tended to use one
of several different cognitive processes (e.g., simultaneous
scanning, successive scanning, and conservative focusing) in
solving concept learning problems. These processes varied in
terms of the amount of information the subject had to retain in
memory at one time, the complexity of the decision rule required
and so forth. Each of these processes, however, was sufficient
to learn the intended concept. They were all equally valid;
each, if properly applied, would lead to the same (valid) result.

In critical reading, then, a variety of rules might be devised to reflect all reasonable possibilities. Observation of
individual behavior could help in refining the various processes
used by skilled readers in drawing inferences from printed
statements. As in the Bruner *et al.* investigations and in the
case of "borrowing" and "equal additions" algorithms for subtraction, the identified alternative processes might be equivalent in terms of result (i.e., they might lead to valid inferences). Presumably, they also would be consistent with the
above general requirements for drawing valid inferences (e.g.,
consistent with Venn diagrams). They might, however, differ in
internal form and/or detail, form and/or detail that could have
important implications for both diagnosis and instruction in
critical reading skills.

8.3 FURTHER DISCUSSION

The alternative rules might be evaluated empirically using
the methods detailed in Chapters 9 and 10. That is, the identified procedures could be used to partition corresponding
domains of critical reading tasks into equivalence classes, both
individually and collectively. In order to allow full use of
the data, in cases where there are only one or more than two
tasks in each equivalence class, use might be made of the information measures and Chi Square (χ^2) tests described in Chapter
10.

Consider, for example, one possible study that might be
conducted along these lines. The subjects might be from inner-
city schools in low-income, educationally disadvantaged neigh-
borhoods and from suburban schools in an affluent, educationally
advantaged areas. I would estimate a need for about 25 to 30
subjects from each population. To be included in the study, of
course, all experimental subjects would have to be able to read
and interpret individual statements in the critical reading
paragraphs. This ability could be determined via pretesting.

A main point of such a study would be to identify which of
the various strategies (rules) identified provide the "best"
account of individual behavior. Please keep in mind that one
strategy might provide the "best" account with one subpopulation,
and another strategy with the other. Although it is impossible
a priori to set strict limits on what will constitute an accept-

able level of consistency of performance within equivalence classes (homogeneity), judging from previous results with other tasks, a 75 percent to 80 percent level of predictability would seem both minimally acceptable and within expectation. Rules that satisfy this criterion would compare favorably with the results reported in the present chapter and, hence, would provide a useful foundation on which to build both testing and *expository* instruction.

In order to achieve the objectives of the suggested research, individual statements would have to be constructed so that they are equally understandable to all subjects. Otherwise, the obtained results would be hard to interpret. They would depend on an unknown combination of processes dealing with individual statements.

Parenthetically, it may be useful to comment on the "different language explanation" of differential language abilities in different American subcultures. As summarized by Cazden (1970), this hypothesis holds that the nonstandard English dialects (e.g., Negro Nonstandard English, NNE, Labov, 1967) used by some students are sufficiently different from Standard English (SE) to seriously impair these students' ability to communicate in Standard English (SE). Although demonstrable differences exist in speech production, however, Hall and Turner (1974) concluded in a recent review that: "In general, no acceptable, replicated research has found that NNE presents black children with unique problems in comprehending SE." This suggests that individual sentences commensurate with the NNE user's ability to read should pose no special problems if stated in SE. Although the possibility exists that different individuals use different processes to understand individual statements, this possibility would only be important where not all individuals are able to understand the statements and where one is interested in diagnosing individual strengths and weaknesses. In this case, the process differences would play a role similar to the "borrowing" and "equal additions" methods of subtraction.

The research cited by Hall and Turner, however, did not address itself to the logical relationships between individual statements. It is believed that skilled members of both educationally advantaged and disadvantaged subgroups draw the same (valid) inferences from SE text. What is uncertain, however, is whether these inferences are necessarily obtained in the same manner (i.e., through the application of identical cognitive procedures). Nor, is it known whether various valid alternative procedures are distributed similarly among both groups of students. Irrespective of whether such differences do or do not exist, in fact, the information could be very useful in constructing "culture fair" tests of critical reading.

Pushing this line of inquiry further one might also explore the question of how critical reading processes are learned.

Toward this end, one might seek to identify and evaluate the higher-level processes involved. The research described in Chapters 3 and 4 of this volume could provide a basic model for analysis. In particular, the analyst would seek out relationships among the strategies used by idealized prototypic individuals in dealing with various logical rules. Although normally different, these strategies, judging from our previous work with other task domains, may be expected to parallel one another in various ways. These parallels might be converted into higher-order rules by which the various strategies themselves may be derived (i.e., learned).

Although I have not exhaustively searched the literature, the only study that I know of that bears directly on the issue of learning in a reading context is one of my own (Scandura, 1967). It was found that knowing the meanings of component symbols or words, together with the semantic rules by which such meanings are combined, were both necessary and sufficient conditions for the correct comprehension of new statements composed of those components. Since the subjects had never seen the new statements before and had never been explicitly taught how to interpret such statements, it seems reasonable to suppose that they had somehow figured out (and thereby learned) how to interpret them.

REFERENCES

Bormuth, J. R. *On the theory of achievement test items.* Chicago: University of Chicago Press, 1970.
Bruner, J. S., Goodnow, J. J., & Austin, G. A. *A study of thinking.* New York: Wiley, 1967.
Carroll, J. B. Towards a performance grammar for core sentences of spoken and written English. *Journal of Structural Learning,* 1975, *4,* 189-198.
Carroll, J. B., & Freedle, R. O. (Eds.) *Language comprehension and the acquisition of knowledge.* Washington, D.C.: Winston & Sons, 1972.
Cazden, C. The situation: A neglected source of social class differences in language use. *Journal of Social Classes,* 1970, *26,* 35-59.
Corcoran, J. *Super natural deductive system for first order logic.* Mimeographed notes, 1968.
Davis, F. B. (Ed.) *The literature of research in reading with emphasis on models.* New Brunswick, N.J.: Graduate School of Education, Rutgers University, 1971.
Davis, F. B. Research in comprehension reading. *Reading Research Quarterly,* 1968, *4,* 499-545.
Davis, F. B. *Identification and measurement of reading skills of high school students* (Cooperative Research Project, No. 3023). Philadelphia: University of Pennsylvania, 1967.
Ennis, R. H. A concept of critical thinking. *Harvard Educational Review,* 1962, *32,* 81-111.
Ennis, R. H., Finkelstein, M. R., Smith, E. R., & Wilson, N. H. *Conditional logic and children.* Ithaca, N.Y.: Cornell Critical Thinking Project, 1969.
Erickson, J. R. A set analysis theory of behavior in formal syllogistic reasoning tasks. In R. Solso (Ed.), *Contemporary issues in cognitive psychology: The Loyola Symposium.* Washington, D.C.: Winston, 1973.

Frase, L. T. Cybernetic control of memory while reading connected discourse. *Journal of Educational Psychology*, 1969, *60*, 49-55.

Freedle, R. O., & Carroll, J. B. Language comprehension and the acquisition of knowledge: Reflections. In J. B. Carroll & R. O. Freedle (Eds.), *Language comprehension and the acquisition of knowledge*. Washington, D.C.: Winston & Sons, 1972.

Hall, J. C., & Turner, R. R. The validity of the "different language explanation" for poor scholastic performance by black students. *Review of Educational Research*, 1974, *44*, 69-81.

Holmes, J. A. *Factors underlying major reading disabilities at the college level*. Unpublished doctoral dissertation, University of California, Berkeley, 1948.

Holmes, J. A., & Singer, H. *Speed and power of reading in high school students* (Cooperative Research Monograph, No. 14). Washington, D.C.: U.S. Government Printing Office, 1966.

Hyram, G. An experiment in developing critical thinking in children. *Journal of Experimental Education*, 1957, *26*, 125-132.

Kintsch, W. Notes on the structure of semantic memory. In E. Tulving & W. Donaldson (Eds.), *Organization of memory*. New York: Academic Press, 1972.

Labov, W. Some sources of reading problems for Negro speakers of nonstandard English. In National Council of Teachers of English (Ed.), *New directions in elementary English*, 1967, pp. 140-167.

Landa, L. N. *Algorithmization of learning and instruction*. Englewood Cliffs, N.J.: Educational Technology Publications, 1974.

Livingston, S. A. Criterion-referenced application of classical test theory. *Journal of Educational Measurement*, 1972, *9*, 13-26.

Lowerre, G., & Scandura, J. M. Conceptually based development of individualized materials for critical thinking based on logical inference. *Reading Research Quarterly*, 1973, *9*, 186-205.

McCanne, R. Use of a checklist of reading skills with migratory children. Quoted in G. D. Spache & E. B. Spache, *Reading in the elementary school*. Boston: Allyn & Bacon, 1969.

Miller, G. A., Galanter, E. H., & Pribram, K. H. *Plans and the structure of behavior*. New York: Holt, 1960.

Moffett, J. *A student-centered language arts curriculum, grades K-13: A handbook for teachers*. Boston: Houghton-Mifflin, 1968.

Newell, A., & Simon, H. A. *Human problem solving*. Englewood Cliffs, N.J.: Prentice-Hall, 1972.

O'Brien, T. C., & Shapiro, B. J. The development of logical thinking in children. *American Educational Research Journal*, 1968, *5*, 531-542.

Olson, D. R. Language and thought: Aspects of a cognitive theory of semantics. *Psychological Review*, 1970, *77*, 257-273.

Rothkopf, E. Z. Structural text features and the control of processes in learning from written materials. In J. B. Carroll & R. O. Freedle (Eds.), *Language comprehension and the acquisition of knowledge*. Washington, D.C.: Winston & Sons, 1972.

Rumelhart, D. E., Lindsay, P. H., & Norman, D. A. A process model for long-term memory. In E. Tulving & W. Donaldson (Eds.), *Organization of memory*. New York: Academic Press, 1972.

Scandura, J. M. Learning verbal and symbolic statements of mathematical rules. *Journal of Educational Psychology*, 1967, *58*, 356-364.

Scandura, J. M. *Problem-solving ability in school mathematics--Its nature and measurement* (Philadelphia: University of Pennsylvania, Structural Learning Series, Report 57). 1968.

Scandura, J. M. *Mathematics: Concrete behavioral foundations*. New York: Harper & Row, 1971.

Scandura, J. M. *Structural learning I: Theory and research*. New York: Gordon & Breach, 1973.

Scandura, J. M., & Durnin, J. H.   Extrascope transfer in learning mathematical
    strategies.   *Journal of Educational Psychology,* 1968, *59,* 350-354.
Scandura, J. M., & McGee, R.   An exploratory investigation of basic mathematical
    abilities in kindergarten children.   *Educational Studies in Mathematics,*
    1972, *4,* 331-345.
Scandura, J. M., Durnin, J. H., & Wulfeck, W. H., II.   Higher-order rule
    characterization of heuristics for compass and straight-edge constructions
    in geometry.   *Artificial Intelligence,* 1974, *5,* 149-183.
Scandura, J. M., Lowerre, G., & Scandura, A. M.   *Critical reading series manual*
    (Workbooks A, B, C, D).   Worthington, Ohio: Ann Arbor Publishing, 1974.
Scandura, J. M., Woodward, E., & Lee, F.   Rule generality and consistency in
    mathematics learning.   *American Educational Research Journal,* 1967, *4,*
    303-320.
Scriven, M.   The concept of comprehension: From semantics to software.   In
    J. B. Carroll & R. O. Freedle (Eds.), *Language comprehension and the*
    acquisition of knowledge.   Washington, D.C.: Winston & Sons, 1972.
Spache, G. D.   A new readability formula for primary grade materials.   *Elementary*
    School Journal, 1953, *53,* 410-413.
Spache, G. D., & Spache, E. B.   *Reading in the elementary school.*   Boston:
    Allyn & Bacon, 1969.
Stone, C. R.   Measuring difficulty of primary reading material: A constructive
    criticism of Spache's measure.   *Elementary School Journal,* 1956, *57,* 36-41.
Suppes, P.   On the behavioral foundations of mathematical concepts.   *Monographs*
    of the Society for Research in Child Development, 1965, *30,* 90-93.
Suppes, P.   The ability of elementary school children to learn the NEW
    mathematics.   *Theory into Practice,* 1964, *3,* 57-61.
Suppes, P., & Binford, F.   Experimental teaching of mathematical logic in the
    elementary school.   *Arithmetic Teacher,* 1965, *12,* 187-195.
Thorndike, E. L.   Reading as reasoning: A study of mistakes in paragraph reading.
    Journal of Educational Psychology, 1917, *8,* 323-332.
Trabasso, T.   Mental operations in language comprehension.   In J. B. Carroll &
    R. O. Freedle (Eds.), *Language comprehension and the acquisition of*
    knowledge.   Washington, D.C.: Winston & Sons, 1972.
Williams, G.   Critical reading in basal readers.   *Elementary English,* 1959, *41,*
    323-330.
Williams, J. P.   Learning to read: A review of theories and models.   In F. B.
    Davis (Ed.), *The literature of research in reading with emphasis on models*
    (U.S.O.E. Project Report OEC-0-70-4790).   Washington, D.C.: U.S. Government
    Printing Office, 1971.
Winograd, T.   *Procedures as a representation for data in a computer program for*
    understanding natural language (Report No. AI-TR-17).   Cambridge, Mass.:
    M.I.T. Artificial Intelligence Laboratory, 1971.
Wolf, W., King, M. L., & Huck, C. S.   Teaching critical reading to elementary
    school children.   *Reading Research Quarterly,* 1968, *3,* 435-498.

13
Diagnosis and Instruction of Higher-Order Rules for Solving Geometry Construction Problems[1]

Joseph M. Scandura, Wallace H. Wulfeck II,
John H. Durnin, and Walter Ehrenpreis

The feasibility of systematic structural analyses of real
problem domains (in terms of rules and higher-order rules) has
been demonstrated in a number of recent studies (e.g., Chapters
3 and 4 of this book). In the Scandura, Durnin, and Wulfeck
(Chapter 3) study, for example, a quasi-systematic form of
structural analysis was applied to three specific classes of
compass and straight-edge construction problems in geometry:
two-loci, similar figures, and auxiliary figures. A set of
rules, consisting of lower-order rules (component operations involved in problem solutions) and higher-order rules (precise specifications of problem-solving heuristics), was identified. Application of the higher-order rules to lower-order rules and
given problems (i.e., givens plus goals) results in the selection, ordering, and concatenation of the lower-order rules into
new solution rules, adequate for solving the given problems.[2]

[1]Adapted from "Diagnosis and Instruction of Higher-Order Rules for Solving
Geometry Construction Problems", by J. M. Scandura, W. H. Wulfeck II, J. H.
Durnin, and W. Ehrenpreis in *1974 Proceedings: Fifth annual interdisciplinary
conference on structural learning* by J. M. Scandura, J. H. Durnin, and W. H.
Wulfeck II (Eds.), ONR Technical Report (MERGE Research Institute, 1249 Greentree
Lane, Narberth, PA 19072), 1974, pp. 209-221. The research reported in this
chapter was supported in part by National Science Foundation Grant GW-7901 and
in part by National Institute of Health Grant 9185.

[2]The terms *lower* and *higher order* do not refer to the level of a rule in a
fixed hierarchy (e.g., Gagne, 1970), or to a rule's complexity or difficulty;
they refer to the use to which a rule is put in a particular problem-solving
situation (cf. Scandura, 1973). A rule that is operated on by another is of lower
order relative to the latter (which is relatively of higher order in the given
situation). For any given problem and rule set, then, there are three problem
solving possibilities:
   1. There may exist a rule in the set that solves the problem directly (i.e.,
applying the rule to the given information generates an output which satisfies
the goal). (con't)

437

Although the rule sets resulting from the Scandura *et al.* (Chapter 3) analysis are adequate in a strictly generative sense, the psychological relevance of such rule sets was still an open question. In particular, although an attempt was made to devise rules (particularly higher-order rules) that reflect human behavior, it was not demonstrated there that they do. Rigorous tests of this thesis require experimental data. Furthermore, even if the higher-order rules turn out, in fact, to be compatible with human behavior, it is not clear whether, and to what extent, instruction in the higher-order rules will result in improved problem-solving performance.

The purpose of the present research was to determine the extent to which: (1) the basic higher-order rules identified in the geometric analysis are compatible with the knowledge had by a group of average-ability teenagers (i.e., can be used to identify what higher-order rules individuals in that population do and do not know), (2) instruction on missing higher-order rules, or paths thereof,[3] facilitates transfer to new geometry construction problems, and (3) instruction in some higher-order rules facilitates or hinders the learning and/or use of subsequent ones. In effect, the main goal of the research was to determine, with a realistically complex and previously analyzed subject matter, the feasibility of individualized diagnosis and instruction with higher-order rules (cf. Chapter 5, Experiments III and IV), and to explore some potentially important sequence effects. Although restricted here to only one content domain (geometric construction), it should be emphasized that the methods used for diagnosis and training in higher-order rules are perfectly general and apply universally (cf. Chapters 8 and 9 and 5 and 6, respectively).

According to the analysis given in Scandura (1973), the central question in determining behavioral compatibility, Purpose 1, is whether the identified rules (or paths) act in (near) atomic fashion. Although most of our existing data (e.g., Chapters 8 and 9) pertain to lower-order rules only, the basic theory

(con't)2. There may be no direct solution rule, but there may exist several (lower-order) rules in the set that are involved in the problem solution (i.e., are components of a solution process). For a solution process to be derived, however, a (higher-order) rule that operates on those (lower-order) rules to arrange a suitable solution process is also required (i.e., must also be in the rule set).

3. The problem may not be solvable by composition of available rules (e.g., the solution rule may be a generalization of an available rule or the problem may not even be solvable via the given rule set).

The present study is concerned with possibility (2).

[3]Rules (of any order) may be represented in terms of directed graphs (or the familiar flow diagrams of computer science) in which the nodes (hexagons) correspond to decisions and the arrows (rectangles) correspond to operations. If one ignores loops, there is at most a finite number of paths (ways of proceeding) through any given rule (directed graph, flow diagram). For example, there are two paths through the flow diagram of Figure 2. Throughout this chapter, when a rule has exactly one path, the terms *path* and *rule* are used interchangeably; in other cases, different paths are numbered.

applies to higher-order rules as well (cf. Chapter 5, Experiments III and IV): Briefly, the paths of any rule partition the associated class of tasks into disjoint (nonoverlapping) and exhaustive subclasses (equivalence classes). A behavioral test of atomicity (of paths), then, consists of determining whether subjects' performance reflects the partition imposed by the paths. In particular, a path (rule) is said to act in atomic fashion if subjects uniformly succeed (or fail) on all tasks in the equivalence class corresponding to that path.

The major task in this study, then, since it involves higher-order rules in geometry, is to determine whether the ability, or lack thereof, to appropriately combine available lower-order rules in one problem situation is reflected in transfer to other problem situations of the same type (in the same equivalence class). This ability can be determined either directly in higher-order task situations, where the subject is required to derive solution procedures for given problems, or indirectly, as we have done below, by asking the subject to actually solve problems (i.e., derive solution procedures and then use them).

In theory, when paths of a rule act in atomic fashion, with respect to a given population of subjects, inadequacies determined through testing can be overcome through direct instruction on the paths involved (see Purpose 2). If a person can solve problems whose solution rules require one path of a two-path higher-order rule, but not problems involving the other path, for example, then instruction presumably would be required only on the latter path (cf. Chapter 5, Experiments III and IV).

In effect, previous research provides more or less definitive guidelines on how to proceed and what to expect with regard to the first two questions. The research reported in Chapter 9 of this book, for example, suggests that introspection and informal observation of successful children as they attempt to solve problems in a given class may result in the identification of prototypic procedures that appropriately partition the class into equivalence classes.

With regard to Purpose 3, very little can be said on the basis of available evidence. The fact that various paths of the higher-order rules share many steps in common suggests that there might be positive transfer from one path to another. Thus, having learned one path, there is apt to be less to learn on subsequent ones so that learning them will require less time. On the other hand, one could argue that similarities among higher-order rules and paths could result in interference. In attempting to generate solution procedures to given problems, subjects might use the wrong rules or paths.

1. METHOD

Three paths of two higher-order (HO) rules provided a basis
for diagnosis and instruction in the study. Figure 1 depicts
the (one-path) two-loci (TL) rule and Figure 2, the two paths
of the similar-figures (SF) rule from Chapter 3. Path 1 (SF1)
involves steps A, J, K, L, and M of Figure 2, and Path 2 (SF2)
involves steps A, B, C, D, F, G, H, and I. The operation of
these HO rules, and the form in which they were presented to
subjects, is described below. The experimental tasks were 13
geometry construction problems (see Table 1) taken from Chapter
3. Twelve of these problems may be categorized according to
which of the three paths of the HO rules may be used to generate
an appropriate solution rule. The thirteenth problem was used
to test for "far transfer" and was solvable via an auxiliary-
figures (AF) rule given in Chapter 3. The higher-order solution
path for each problem is indicated in Table 1.

All of the lower-order (LO) rules needed (in addition to
the HO rules) in solving the experimental problems are shown in
Table 2. Only a few of these rules are required for any particular problem.

To illustrate the operation of the HO TL path (Figure 1),
consider Problem 1 of Table 1. In this case the stimulus situation (S_0) consists of a given point, line, and radius. The goal
(G) is a circle satisfying certain tangency and incidence conditions. First, an arbitrary representation or "sketch" ($\langle S_1,$
$R_1 \rangle$) analogous to the solved problem is constructed. Note that
constructing such a sketch is not the same, either as solving
the problem, or as constructing a solution rule for the problem.
In this case, a sketch may be generated by first drawing an
arbitrary circle, then drawing an arbitrary line tangent to it
and an arbitrary point on it, and indicating the given radius.
The first decision (Hexagon 1 of Figure 1) asks whether there
is: (1) a missing point x in $\langle S_1, R_1 \rangle$ that satisfies two of the
specified conditions, and (2) a goal rule (r_g), such that x (and
some other element) can serve as an input to the goal rule
(Dom r_g) and the goal is contained in the range of the goal rule
(Ran r_g). In this case, there is a missing point x, the center
of the required circle, and it satisfies two specified conditions
(i.e., one condition twice): it is a given distance (the radius
R) from the given point, and from the given line. Further, there
is, in Table 2, an appropriate goal rule, 1. Circle Rule, which
operates on points, and distances to generate circles. (Note:
the Goal G consists of circles satisfying certain conditions.)
The second operation (2 of Figure 1) reserves the selected goal
rule (Rule 1 of Table 2) for later use. The third step (3 of
Figure 1) asks essentially whether there are two locus rules
(r_L, $r_{L'}$) that operate on given information ($S_1 \in$ Dom r_L) and
generate loci (L $\in$ Ran r_L) that contain the missing point x.

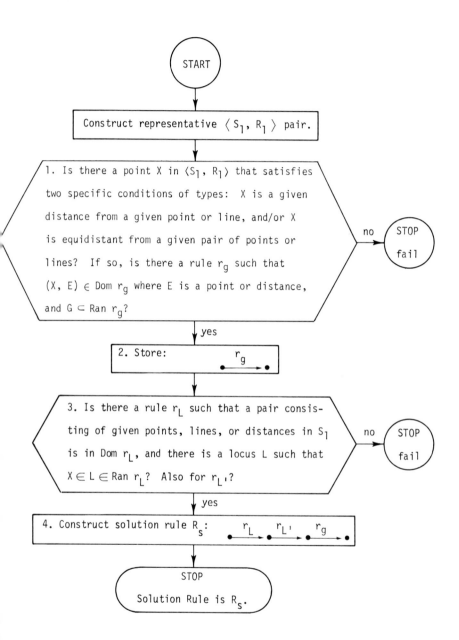

Figure 1. Two-loci higher order rule.

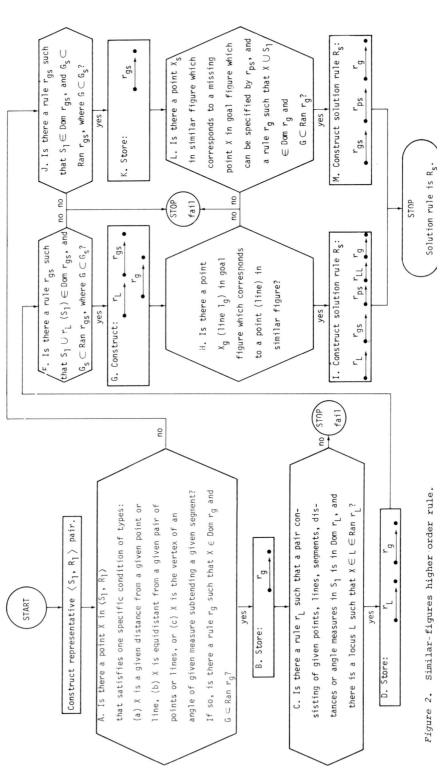

Figure 2. Similar-figures higher-order rule.

TABLE 1

Geometry Construction Tasks

Test	Problem Number	Solution Type	Problem Statement
Pretest I	1	Two-loci	Given a line and a point not on the line, and a radius R, find a circle having the given radius R, which is tangent to the line, and passes through the given point.
Pretest I	2	Path 1, similar-figures	Given angles B and C and the altitude H_a, construct the triangle.
Pretest I	3	Two-loci	Given side a, the median M_a, and the height H_a, construct the triangle.
Pretest I	4	Path 1, similar-figures	Given angles B and C and the angle bisector D_a, construct the triangle.
Posttest I	5	Two-loci	Given sides a and b and the median M_a, construct the triangle.
Posttest I	6	Path 1, similar-figures	Given angles B and C and side b opposite angle B, construct the triangle.
Posttest II	7	Two-loci	Given two intersecting lines and a radius R, construct a circle with radius R tangent to the two given lines.
Posttest II	8	Path 1, similar-figures	Given angles B and C and the median M_a, construct the triangle.
Choice test	9	Two-loci and Path 1, similar-figures	Given right triangle ABC with right angle at B, inscribe a square in it such that two sides of the square lie on the legs (AB and BC) of the triangle and the fourth vertex of the square (the intersection of the other two sides) is on AC.
Pretest II	10	Path 2, similar-figures	Given two intersecting lines m and n and a point A not on either line, construct a circle tangent to lines m and n that passes through point A.
Pretest II	11	Path 2, similar-figures	Given two intersecting lines m and n and a point P on line m, construct a circle whose center is on line m, which passes through point P and is tangent to line n.
Posttest III	12	Path 2, similar-figures	Given line m and points A and B on the same side of line m, construct a circle tangent to line m that passes through points A and B.
Posttest III	13	Auxiliary-figures	Given sides a and c and the altitude H_b, construct the triangle.

443

TABLE 2
Lower-Order Rules

1.	*Circle rule*	Construct the locus of points at a given distance from a given point.
2.	*Median-locus-circle rule*	Construct the locus of points at a given distance from the midpoint of a given segment.
3.	*Point-line circle rule*	Determine the distance between a given point and a given line and then construct the locus of points at the obtained distance from the given point.
4.	*Parallel-line rule*	Construct the locus of points at a given distance from a given line.
5.	*Angle-bisector rule*	Construct the locus of points equidistant from two given intersecting lines.
6.	*Triangle rule*	From a point not on a given line segment, draw segments to the endpoints of the given segment (i.e., construct a triangle given a side and an opposite vertex).
7.	*Perpendicular bisector rule*	Construct the locus of points equidistant from two given points.
8.	*Similar-triangle rule*	Construct an arbitrary triangle from a pair of given angles, and construct on it parts corresponding to other given segments.
9.	*Goal triangle rule*	Construct a triangle having some part of given length similar to a given triangle with a corresponding part.
10.	*Point-of-similarity rule*	Select a point of intersection of two lines through corresponding points of goal and similar figures as the point of similarity, then construct a line through the point of similarity and a point on the similar figure, to intersect the goal figure at a corresponding point, from which the goal figure may be constructed.
11.	*Similar-square rule*	Construct an arbitrary square in a right triangle with two of its sides contained in the legs of the triangle.
12.	*Goal-square rule*	Given a right triangle and a point on its hypotenuse, construct a square with that point as one vertex, such that its two opposite sides are contained in the legs of the triangle.
13.	*Similar-circle rule*	Construct an arbitrary circle with its center on one line and tangent to another line.

The present problem requires LO rules 1 and 4 of Table 2. The final step (4 of Figure 1) forms a solution rule for the problem, consisting of Rules 1, 4, and 1 (of Table 2) in that order. Note that the HO rule itself does not solve any problems; no constructions are performed. If correctly applied, however, the HO rule generates solution procedures that may be used to solve such problems.

Similarly, Path SF1 (Figure 2) assembles a solution rule for problem 2 (Table 1) using LO rules 8, 10, and 9 in that order, and similarly, Path SF2 (Figure 2) generates a solution rule for Problem 10 (Table 1), which consists of LO rules 5, 13, a variant of 10, 4, and 1 (Table 2) in that order. The operation of these paths is detailed in Chapter 3 of this book.

For instructional purposes, the decisions (hexagons) and operations (rectangles) of each HO path (in Figures 1 and 2) were written, respectively, as simple lists of questions and imperative statements. The only essential differences from Figures 1 and 2 were that notation was replaced by descriptive terms as in the above description (e.g., *goal rule* for "r_g", *sketch* for "$\langle s_1, R_1 \rangle$").

Also, for purposes of instruction, the LO rules were refined to the level of actual compass settings and placements. Each consisted of a sequence of operations to be performed; the inputs and outputs (Domains and Ranges) of each rule were indicated. Accompanying sketches illustrated the result of each operation. Descriptions of all problems and rules were reproduced on 21.59 cm x 27.94 cm (8 1/2" x 11") paper. Each problem appeared on a separate page so that constructions could be done on that page. The 13 problems were arranged into six separate tests as shown in Table 1.

The instructional materials were arranged into seven training booklets. Booklet 1 contained LO rules 1-10 and a sample task for each. Booklet 2 contained 10 review tasks for the rules of Booklet 1. Booklet 3 contained the TL HO rule (path) and two practice problems (the two Pretest I, two-loci problems). In parallel fashion, Booklet 4 contained the SF1 path of the similar figures HO rule with the Pretest I, similar figures problems as practice. Booklet 5 contained LO Rules 11 and 12 of Table 2 with corresponding practice tasks and Booklet 6 contained LO Rule 13 from Table 2 with a practice task. Booklet 7 contained the SF2 path of the similar figures HO rule along with the two problems from Pretest II as practice.

Pencils, compasses, and straight-edges were available where subjects did not provide their own.

Subjects, design, and procedure: The subjects were 30 Trenton State College students enrolled in an undergraduate college geometry class. Twenty-six subjects completed the entire experiment. Partial data for the other 4 subjects are reported in the results section.

A repeated measures design was used. Figure 3 depicts the experimental design, including all the training and testing sessions, and the number of subjects in each session of the experiment.

The first phase of the study involved LO rule training Booklets 1 and 2 and Pretest I. Its main purpose was to obtain information regarding the adequacy of the two-loci HO rule and Path 1 of the similar figures rule as a basis for assessing the (higher-order) behavior potential of subjects. A secondary purpose was to obtain success or failure profiles, so that subjects could be stratified before assignment to experimental groups.

The first meeting with the subjects occurred during a regu-

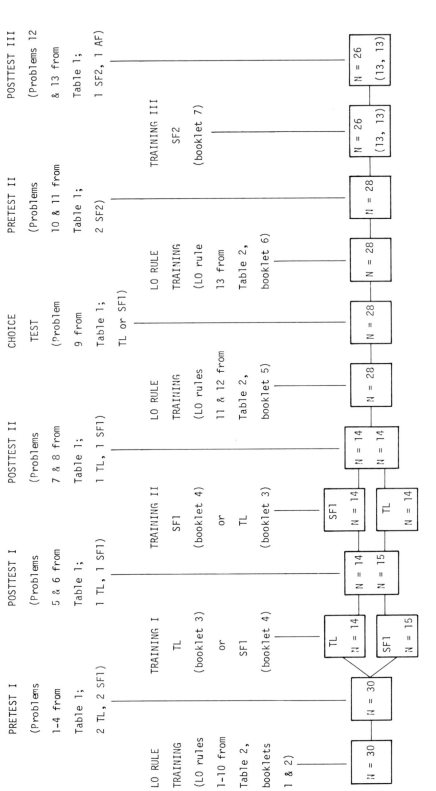

Figure 3. Experimental design.

larly scheduled 75-minute class period. One instructor and two experiment assistants were available to help subjects and to evaluate their work. They were given Booklet 1 and instruction on lower-order Rules 1-10 contained in it. The steps of each rule were read aloud and the corresponding constructions were performed on the blackboard. Each subject then completed the corresponding practice problem.

During a second regular class meeting, subjects were given the practice problems in Booklet 2 and were required to perform at least one correct construction for each of Rules 1-10. Achievement of this criterion level was verified by one of the experimenters. As soon as they reached criterion, individual subjects were given Pretest I. All subjects were instructed to attempt all problems in Pretest I before the period ended; no subject "ran out of time". Pretest problems were scored "passed" if a correct solution figure was constructed. Minor deviations ("compass errors") were allowed. Each pretest was scored individually by three experimenters; there was no disagreement. The pretest results were used to stratify subjects as shown in Table 3.

TABLE 3
Pretest Results

Similar-Figures Problems	Two-Loci Problems			
	Passed Both	*Passed One*	*Passed None*	*Sum*
Passed Both	6	1	0	7
Passed One	2	1	2	5
Passed None	2	6	10	18
Sum	10	8	12	30

On the basis of the pretest results, subjects were randomly divided into two groups of 15 each, the two-loci-then-similar figures (TS) group and the similar-figures-then-two-loci (ST) group, with the constraint that each of the cells in Table 3 was split evenly. (The two "singleton" subjects were placed in different groups.) Individual or small group sessions were arranged with each subject for all subsequent training and testing. Throughout the experiment, each subject retained all instructional materials, but not completed tests.

During the remainder of the study, instruction was provided on the three HO paths (TL, SF1, SF2) and performance was measured on both within and extrascope problems. At the third meeting, the TS subjects were given Booklet 3, the TL HO rule (path) as described above, and instruction in how to apply the rule. Specifically, they were shown how to determine whether particular LO rules from Booklet 1 (which was available) were relevant to

the solution (cf. Steps 1 and 3 of Figure 1), and if they were,
how to combine them (Steps 2 and 4) so as to generate solution
rules for the Pretest I, two-loci problems (1 and 3). No actual
constructions were performed. (One TS subject failed to attend
this or any other instructional session and was dropped from the
study.) The subjects in group ST received Booklet 4, the SF1
path of the similar figures HO rule, and instruction on the application of that path using Problems 2 and 4 from Pretest I.
(After 3 subjects had been trained, the instruction was modified
slightly so that additional emphasis was given to stop condi-
tions--i.e., conditions indicating that an HO rule did not apply.)

Immediately following instruction each subject was given
Posttest I. The subjects in both treatment groups received exactly the same problems. Notice that on Posttest I, each training group (ST or TS) served as the other's control. Booklet 1,
containing statements of Rules 1-10, was available throughout.
Also Booklets 3 and 4 containing the TL and SF1 paths were available to the subjects in Groups TS and ST, respectively. Following Posttest I, one subject in the ST group became ill and dropped out of school. (The two subjects dropped from the study had
both failed all pretest problems, and had been assigned to different training groups.)

At the fourth meeting, those subjects who had received the
TL training received SF1 training and vice versa. Instruction
was given exactly as before. Posttest II paralleled Posttest I
and followed immediately after training. Booklets 1, 3, and 4
were available to the subjects throughout the testing.

At each subject's fifth meeting, he was given Booklet 5
containing two new LO rules (11 and 12). Training proceeded
as with Booklet 1. With all previous training booklets available, the subjects then took the choice test problem. This
problem could be solved by either of the two HO paths, TL or
SF1, on which the subjects had been trained.

Next, at the sixth meeting, subjects were trained on LO
rule 13, in Booklet 6. With this rule and all previously learned rules also available, the subjects then took Pretest II.
The purposes of Pretest II were similar to those of the first
Pretest, but dealt with the SF2 path of the similar-figures HO
rule. (At this point, two additional subjects who were failing
the course, dropped out of the study. The remaining 26 subjects
completed the experiments, 13 in each group.)

Finally, at the seventh meeting, each subject was trained
as before on the SF2 path of the similar-figures HO rule (Booklet 7), using the problems in Pretest II. After training, subjects were given Posttest III. One problem of Posttest III was
within the scope of the SF2 path; the other was an auxiliary
figures problem not solvable via any of the three HO paths on
which instruction was provided.

Approximate times required by each subject were recorded

for each session of the experiment.

2. RESULTS AND DISCUSSION

2.1 ASSESSMENT RESULTS

Pretests I and II contained a total of six problems grouped on an a priori basis according to their solvability via the three HO paths on which training was provided. To test the behavioral atomicity of the identified HO rules, contingencies among within-class (path) problems were examined. Table 4 presents the Pretest I and II results on the three classes of problems. On Pretest I, performance on the first two-loci problem (Problem 1 from Table 1) was significantly correlated with performance on the second two-loci problem (Problem 3) (Fisher's exact probability = .00485; one-tailed), and similarly for the Path 1, similar-figures problems (2 and 4) (exact probability = .00165; one-tailed) and, on Pretest II, for the Path 2 problems (10 and 11) (exact probability = .00794; one-tailed).

TABLE 4
Results of Pretests I and II

	Pretest I				Pretest II	
	Two-loci		Path 1 of similar-figures		Path 2 of similar-figures	
	Problem 2		Problem 2		Problem 2	
Problem 1	Pass	Fail	Pass	Fail	Pass	Fail
Pass	10	1	7	3	2	1
Fail	7	12	2	18	0	25

If "success" on a pretest problem class is defined as correct solution on one or both problems in the class, then it can be seen from Table 3 that only 2 subjects succeeded on the Path 1 similar-figures class but not the two-loci class. In contrast, 10 subjects succeeded on both the two-loci and Path 1 similar-figures classes; 8 subjects succeeded on the two-loci class but failed the Path 1 similar-figures class; and 10 subjects failed both. The low probability of obtaining this pattern of results (exact probability = .03802), suggests that subjects who can solve similar-figures problems generally also will be able to solve two-loci problems, but not vice versa. In effect, the tasks of generating solution rules for similar-figures and two-loci problems appear to be hierarchically related. The data do not, of course, necessarily imply causality.

These results suggest that the identified paths, both collectively and individually, acted in atomic fashion for the experimental subjects. Some of the deviant cases, furthermore, are due to two particular subjects who initially were overtly

uncooperative but who later applied themselves. Nonetheless,
the relatively large number (5) of remaining "fail-pass" cases
(Table 4) on the two-loci problems requires some discussion.
In particular, this result suggests the possible desirability
of further refinement of the two-loci HO rule into a larger number of distinct paths (cf. Scandura, 1973). This would require
refinement of the assumed atomic operators and decisions and
their representation in terms of (flow diagram) subroutines.
Correspondingly, a number of paths would be substituted for the
original path.

Because the goal rules (r_g) required in solving Problems 1
and 3 were different, as were the test requirements (e.g., Decision 1 of Figure 1) for deciding which of the two goal rules
to use, a basis for such refinement follows directly. Decision
1 of the TL rule (Figure 1), for example, involves disjunctions
(A or B) of properties. Specifically, in order to determine
that the Circle (goal) Rule (1) satisfies Decision 1, a subject
must recognize that some point (X)-distance (E) pair in $\langle S_1, R_1 \rangle$
is in its domain. In the case of Triangle (goal) Rule 6, E is
another point. Just because a person is able to do the latter
does not mean that he can do the former. Both our data and intuition would suggest that the latter capability is easier.

The question of whether the TL rule of Figure 1 provides
an adequate basis for assessing individual behavior potential
depends on the level of homogeneity (atomicity) desired. On
the one hand, one could opt for the present relatively molar
level of representation, thereby maintaining the advantage of
test efficiency. On the other hand, should one be willing to
forgo such efficiency, one could improve test precision (reliability) by employing a refined version of the TL rule of Figure
1, and thereby increase the required number of test items. (For
further discussion of the level of refinement issue as it pertains to assessing behavior potential see Scandura, 1973, also
see Chapters 2 and 15 of this volume.)

2.2   INSTRUCTIONAL EFFECTIVENESS

Over the entire experiment there were 51 cases where subjects failed all pretest problems from a given class prior to
training on the path corresponding to that class. On posttests
immediately following such training, new problems from the same
classes were solved in 45 (88.2 percent) of the 51 cases. (The
95 percent confidence interval for this percentage is 79.3 percent to 97.1 percent.) In addition, there were 14 cases where
subjects had solved only one pretest problem in a given class.
The new posttest problems were solved in 13 of those cases.

Table 5 summarizes the results from Posttests I, II, and
III on problems for which training immediately preceded testing,
arranged according to the number of pretest problems passed.
After training on either the TL or SF1 paths, 11 of the 14 sub-

jects who failed both Pretest I problems in a given class succeeded on the corresponding Posttest I problem. In effect, the
training effect with naive subjects was highly significant (exact probability = .00109). Furthermore, training on the appropriate HO path was significantly (exact probability < .05) better
than training on the other HO path. Five of 14 subjects, who
failed Pretest I problems in one class and were trained on the
other path (i.e., the path inappropriate for that class), nonetheless solved the Posttest I problem in that class. (Not surprisingly, all 6 subjects who solved one Pretest I problem and
all 9 subjects who had solved both Pretest I problems also
solved the Posttest I problem.)

In interpreting data from the remaining posttests, one
should bear in mind that the observed behavior is conditional
on training (and testing) that is indirectly related to the
training in question. Nonetheless, these data provide two useful sources of information. First, they demonstrate the robustness of the training effects under various initial conditions
(judged in absolute rather than comparative terms). Second,
they provide information concerning sequence effects. In this
section, we consider only the former. (Sequence effects are
considered in the next section.)

TABLE 5
Results on Posttest Problems Within Scope of Immediately Preceding Training

	Number of pretest problems within scope of training passed prior to training	N	Number of subjects passing within scope problem after training
Posttest I	0	14	11
	1	6	6
	2	9	9
Posttest II	0	13	12
	1	7	6
	2	8	8
Posttest III	0	24	22
	1	1	1
	2	1	1
Total Cases	0	51	45
	1	14	13
	2	18	18

On Posttest II, 12 of 13 subjects who failed both pretest
problems in a given class succeeded after training on the HO
rule for that class. Of 7 subjects who solved one pretest problem, 6 solved the corresponding Posttest II problem after training. All 8 subjects who solved both pretest problems succeeded
following training. On Posttest III, 22 of 24 subjects who
failed both Pretest II problems succeeded following training.
Two other subjects, who had solved one or both Pretest II problems, also succeeded on the Posttest III problem.

Overall there were seven cases of posttest failure out of
83 cases where success was expected. Five of the seven discrepancies occurred on Posttests I and II. After failure, these 5
subjects were retrained on the respective HO paths, and retested.
All five succeeded on the second trial, suggesting that the subjects failed originally because they had not learned the relevant path during the initial training.

Inspection of the seven cases where individuals failed
showed that, in six of those cases, mistakes occurred at points
corresponding to disjunctive decision points in the TL or SF2
paths. These training results, therefore, provide further support for the above contention that refinement of the HO rules
might have reduced even the small number of inconsistencies noted.

In summary, it seems safe to conclude that explicit instruction on the HO rules can be effective. Less than three hours
of actual instruction was required to enable the subjects to
solve relatively complex construction problems. Instruction on
the component LO rules took an average of about 100 minutes; HO
rule training took an additional 75 minutes.

2.3 SEQUENCE EFFECTS

In addition to the positive assessment and instruction results, a number of interesting sequence effects were found. On
Posttest I positive transfer to problems, for which training
had not been provided, occurred in approximately 35 percent of
the cases. Of 14 subjects who had failed both Pretest I problems
in the class for which no training was given, five solved the
corresponding Posttest I problem. (Two subjects solved the two-
loci problem; three solved the Path 1, similar-figures problem.) Three of 7 subjects who had solved one of the untrained
problems on Pretest I solved the Posttest I problem. (All three
solved the two-loci problem after SF1 training.)

It is theoretically possible, of course, that these transfer results may have derived wholly or in part from practice in
working the pretest problems. We do not believe that this happened, however. Although testing progressed under similar conditions, the relatively extensive data of Chapters 5 and 6 suggest that practice alone does not improve problem solving ability. There was not a single case where unsuccessful practice
on one problem resulted in later success without training.

On the other hand, one subject who had previously solved both Pretest I two-loci problems failed the Posttest I two-loci problem after being trained on the SF1 path. Apparently, this negative transfer was due to his misunderstanding of the posttest instructions; the subject thought he was required to use the trained HO rule (which was inadequate). After this misapprehension was corrected, the subject was retested and he passed the problem. (After this subject was run, somewhat more emphasis in instruction was given to when a HO rule would not work--i.e., when to stop.)

The results on Posttest II, restricted to the problem for which training had been given prior to Posttest I, suggests that training on the second HO path did not interfere with earlier training. Twenty-seven of the 28 subjects who completed Posttest II solved the problem corresponding to the first-trained path, after training on the second path. The remaining subject passed the problem on a second trial.

This lack of interference was also reflected in performance on the choice problem, which could be solved using either the TL or SF1 paths. All 28 subjects solved the problem. There were 17 two-loci solutions and 11 Path 1 similar-figures solutions; this difference was not significant. Furthermore, there were no significant differences as to solution preference due to order of training. Group TS had 9 two-loci solutions and 5 similar-figures solutions; Group ST had 8 and 6, respectively. This suggests that when two (or more) rules are immediately available at the time of problem solving (as they were), selections do not depend on when the rules were originally learned.

Positive transfer was also found from training on one HO path to the next. When given first, the TL training required an average of about 32 minutes (25 to 60 minute range) and the SF1 training, 31 minutes (20 to 65 minute range). When the training came second, the corresponding times were 23.5 minutes (15 to 45 minute range) and 27.5 minutes (18 to 60 minute range). The third training session on the SF2 path required an average of only 18 minutes (10 to 30 minute range), even though the relatively large number of failures on the corresponding Pretest II problems suggests that the problems corresponding to this path may have been more difficult than the others.

Overall, then, ignoring the particular training involved, first training took an average of 32 minutes; second training, 25 minutes; and third training, 18 minutes. Differences among these means were highly reliable ($F_{2, 44} = 34.5$, $p < .005$). Individual comparisons of first and second training and second and third were equally reliable ($p < .001$). (It may be worth noting that others, e.g., Bourne, 1970, have found a similar systematic decrease in "instructional time" in experiments, e.g., on conceptual rule learning.)

Frankly, we were surprised by the results on the auxiliary

figures problem, which could not be solved using any of the
three trained HO paths. In this case performance depended on
the sequence in which the HO paths were learned ($\chi^2 = 7.58$,
df = 1, p < .01). Eleven of the 13 TS subjects solved the auxiliary figures problem while only 3 of the 13 ST subjects succeeded. No other relation was observed between the results on
this problem and those on any of the previous ones.

It is impossible to identify the source of this rather
striking sequence effect with any certainty. One possibility
is that, in attacking the problem, subjects may have tended to
select the first HO path on which they were trained. In this
case, the TS subjects could have had an advantage because the
auxiliary-figures problem can be solved by repeated application
of a variant of the TL rule. Equivalently, it is possible that
the subjects combined the HO paths into more encompassing rules
(see the combined two-loci similar-figures rule in Chapter 3)
as they were learned. If so, those subjects who tried the TL
path of the combined rule first, most likely the TS subjects,
would again have an advantage, especially if the effects of
limited memory are taken into account (cf. Chapter 7).

Both of these explanations, however, would imply differen-
tial-solution-type preferences on the choice test problem. Since
no such effect occurred, some alternative account seems necessary. One plausible explanation stems from the fact that the
similar-figures and auxiliary-figures HO rules may be regarded
as progressive generalizations of the two-loci rule. That is,
all of the HO rules begin by identifying some constructible elementary figure on which further operations may act to generate
a goal figure. In the TL rule, the elementary figure is "the
missing point X". In the SF rule, the elementary figure is more
general; it is no longer a "degenerate" point. It is, however,
still constrained by similiarity. Finally, in the AF rule, the
elementary figure is arbitrary. (For details, see Chapter 3.)

Because the TS subjects were taught the procedures in a
"natural" order of generalization, while the ST subjects were
not, the former may have been more likely to have "induced" a
generalization procedure. (The fact that subjects rarely solved
SF1 problems on the pretest without also solving TL problems,
whereas TL success was fairly often paired with SF1 failure,
lends some further credence to this interpretation.) More
specifically, the TS subjects may have discovered a "higher,
higher-order rule" for making generalizations. Such a rule
could have been used to derive some form of auxiliary figures
HO rule, which in turn would have allowed derivation of an
adequate solution rule.

3. CONCLUSIONS, RELATIONS TO RECENT PROBLEM-SOLVING RESEARCH, AND PRACTICAL IMPLICATIONS

In conclusion, it would appear that the identified higher-order rules can be used effectively and efficiently both to diagnose difficulties learners are having with geometry construction problems, and to provide instruction in how to solve such problems. Furthermore, as judged by learning times, higher-order rule training facilitated the learning of later ones.

This is not the first time, of course, that beneficial effects have been found for instruction in heuristics. In a normative study, for example, Wilson (1968) found that training subjects in general heuristics, such as means-ends analysis and planning, improved mathematical problem solving. Moreover, Polya's (1945) early classic on "How to solve it" is predicated on the assumption that general problem solving ability can be improved via training on heuristics. What the present study does is to demonstrate with a realistic subject matter the possibility of individualized diagnosis and instruction, and of problem specific behavioral predictions, based on precisely formulated heuristics (as well as other rules). In this sense, this research may be viewed as a sequel to that reported in Chapter 5 (Experiments III and IV).

Since a good deal of contemporary research on problem solving derives from state-space formulations (Nilsson, 1971), some discussion of important similarities and differences might be useful (also see Chapter 15). For one thing, there are no formal or behavioral distinctions in the Structural Learning Theory between rules and higher-order rules. The use of all rules is assumed to be governed by a universal control mechanism. Rules and higher-order rules correspond, respectively, to transitions between states in a problem state space, and to mappings between different state spaces. Whereas state spaces may themselves be viewed as states in higher-level state spaces they are not normally viewed in this way.

For another thing, (lower-order) solution rules of competence refer to idealized performance and, hence, correspond (roughly) to (collections of) paths through state spaces. All individual differences (in problem-solving ability) are measured relative to such rules. In contrast, state-space formulations give equal attention to all logical possibilities (i.e., all possible paths). Consequently, extraneous detail may obscure *important* relationships. In particular, state-space formulations do not appear to lend themselves naturally to assessing individual differences, at least not in a way that has direct instructional implications.

Moreover, problems may be solved, according to the Structural Learning Theory, in two basically different ways: by breaking problems into subproblems and by deriving new solution

rules. Although attempts have been made to provide for learning
in artificial intelligence, the state-space formulations favored
in psychology emphasize subgoal hierarchies (i.e., breaking
problems into subproblems). For example, GPS (Ernst & Newell,
1969) solves problems by establishing subgoals, and selecting
operators for reducing differences between present states and
desired subgoals. Also working within the state-space tradition, Greeno (1974) and Thomas (1974), for example, found
behavioral evidence for intermediate levels of organization in
problem solving. In examining behavior on the "missionaries
and cannibals" problem, where the state-space involves 11 states,
they found only three or four identifiable "cognitive changes"
(i.e., subsequences of state transition moves rather than individual moves were the behavioral norm).

Results such as these would be interpreted similarly in the
present context (i.e., in terms of subproblem solution plans;
see Chapter 2). The Structural Learning Theory, however, also
provides a potential basis for studying the processes by which
subjects derive solution rules for the three or four "cognitive
changes" that they apparently make. Presumably, they use higher-
order rules to compose simple state transition moves. In effect,
there are potentially important behavioral differences that can
be attributed to higher-order rules as opposed to subgoal hierarchies (cf. Chapter 2). Furthermore, unlike simple state-space
formulations, not all higher-order rules involve the simple composition (concatenation) of rules (cf. Banerji, 1974). Three of
the first four experiments described in Chapter 5, for example,
involve generalization rules.

Irrespective of these differences, one can always establish
a formal equivalence between the two formulations, at least when
viewed at the level of scientific languages (i.e., ignoring explicit theoretical assumptions such as goal switching control,
etc.; in this regard, see Chapter 5). In another recent study,
for example, Reed, Ernst, and Banerji (1974, Experiments I and
III) observed positive transfer between different embodiments
of the "missionaries and cannibals" problem that had similar
problem space structures. This transfer was attributed to
heuristic instruction in the homomorphism relating the two problem spaces. This homomorphism is nothing more than a general,
incompletely specified type of higher-order rule (see Scandura,
1973, Chapter 6). In addition, the observed transfer was asymmetric, and proceeded in the direction of increasing generalization. In this sense, the explanation given by Reed *et al.* (1974)
is analogous to that proposed above for the asymmetric sequence
effect involving the auxiliary-figures problem.

Nonetheless, although a considerable degree of transfer
was evident in the present study from training on one higher-
order rule to another, it is still an open question as to how
this transfer came about. Specifically, in what way does train-

ing on (some) higher-order rules help the learner to develop
new "heuristics" on his own? According to the Structural Learning Theory, any complete answer to this question would involve
the precise specification of a higher-order rule for deriving
needed heuristics (a higher higher-order rule). Earlier, for
example, Roughead and Scandura, 1968, found that "what is learned" in making simple discoveries can be presented in expository
form with equivalent results. The task of identifying "what
must be learned" in order to generate new heuristics, however,
is far from trivial.

In spite of the positive nature of the reported results,
it should be emphasized in conclusion that they deal primarily
with the question of how subjects perform in particular problem-
solving situations--given the rules they know on entering into
the situation. Any complete prescription for problem-solving
instruction must deal, in addition and in detail, with the
course of problem solving over time. Our preliminary findings
concerning the sequential effects of instruction on higher-order
rules demonstrate the importance of such study, but they are
just one small step in this direction. Chapter 14 deals with a
more dynamic situation in which the set of lower-order rules
continually changes as learning progresses.

REFERENCES

Bourne, L. E., Jr. Knowing and using concepts. *Psychological Review*, 1970, *77*,
    546-556.
Banerji, R. A formal approach to knowledge in problem solving. In J. M.
    Scandura, J. H. Durnin, & W. H. Wulfeck II (Eds.), *1974 Proceedings: Fifth
    .annual interdisciplinary conference on structural learning* (ONR Technical
    Report, 1974). MERGE Research Institute, 1249 Greentree Lane, Narberth, PA
    19072.
Ernst, G. W., & Newell, A. *GPS (General Problem Solver): A case study in
    generality and problem solving*. New York: Academic Press, 1969.
Gagne, R. M. *The conditions of learning* (2nd ed.). New York: Holt, Rinehart,
    and Winston, 1970.
Greeno, J. G. Hobbits and Orcs: Acquisition of a sequential concept. *Cognitive
    Psychology*, 1974, *6*, 270-292.
Nilsson, N. J. *Problem solving methods in artificial intelligence*. New York:
    McGraw-Hill, 1971.
Polya, G. *How to solve it*. Princeton: University Press, 1945.
Reed, S. K., Ernst, G. W., & Banerji, R. The role of analogy in transfer between
    similar problem states. *Cognitive Psychology*, 1974, *6*, 436-450.
Roughead, W. G., & Scandura, J. M. "What is learned" in mathematical discovery.
    Journal of Educational Psychology, 1968, *59*, 283-289.
Scandura, J. M. *Structural learning I: Theory and research*. New York:
    Gordon and Breach, 1973.
Scandura, J. M., Durnin, J. H., Wulfeck, W. H. II, & Ehrenpreis, W. Diagnosis
    and instruction of higher-order rules for solving geometry construction
    problems. In J. M. Scandura, J. H. Durnin, & W. H. Wulfeck II (Eds.),
    *1974 Proceedings: Fifth annual interdisciplinary conference on structural
    learning*. (ONR Technical Report, 1974). MERGE Research Institute, 1249
    Greentree Lane, Narberth, PA 19072.
Thomas, J. C., Jr. An analysis of behavior in the hobbits-orcs problem.
    Cognitive Psychology, 1974, *6*, 257-269.
Wilson, J. W. Generality of heuristics as an instructional variable. *Dissertation
    Abstracts International*, 1968, *28*, 2575.

14
Theory of Adaptive Instruction with Application to Sequencing in Teaching Problem Solving[1]

Wallace H. Wulfeck II and Joseph M. Scandura

The general problem of how to sequence subject matter content has never been satisfactorily resolved. Thus, whereas many teachers are convinced that when content is presented is just as important as what is presented, research on the issue has been equivocal. Most earlier studies of instructional sequencing have been either conflicting or inconclusive (e.g., Payne, Krathwohl, & Gordon, 1967; Roe, 1962). It is not even clear from such research that sequence really makes a difference, and if so under what circumstances and to what effect.

Theoretically based approaches to sequencing typically fall into two general categories. One class of approaches has been based on the structure of the discipline (e.g., Gagne, 1970; Resnick, Wang, & Kaplan, 1973; Heimer & Lottes, 1973). In this case, content is normally sequenced according to analytically determined hierarchical relationships among various "concepts". (The word *concept* is placed in quotes because the technical use of the term in psychology is different from the broader intuitive sense implied here.) A major problem with hierarchies (or heterarchies, see Chapter 15) is that they do not take into account the fact that some people can skip levels whereas others cannot. As a consequence, approaches to sequencing based on simple hierarchies have not proved entirely successful.

A second class of approaches is less closely related to that proposed here and is based largely on learner characteristics (estimated from response histories). Although based for

[1]The first half of this chapter is based on Scandura (1977) and a research proposal of his to ARPA. Section 2 is based largely on the first author's (1975) dissertation and Wulfeck (1977), and was prepared jointly. The research was supported in part by a Dissertation Year Scholarship from the University of Pennsylvania, in part by a grant from the Office of Computing Services, University of Pennsylvania, and in part by a grant from the National Institute of Health (9185) to the second author.

the most part on simple learning models (e.g., Markov models), such investigations have frequently proven to be successful in dealing with such things as learning German vocabulary (e.g., Atkinson, 1972). At the present time, however, it is at best unclear whether the learning models on which they are based will prove adequate for complex learning and problem solving where structure plays a more important role.

Any really adequate approach to sequencing and instructional optimization, in our opinion, almost certainly will require attention to content structure, (general) cognitive processes, and individual differences, as well as to their interrelationships (e.g., including the assignment of values to objectives and costs to instruction, cf. Atkinson, 1972). Clearly, an approach that satisfies these requirements could have both theoretical and practical value. In particular, we believe that the incorporation of higher-order rules into training programs will require more sophisticated and flexible sequencing methodologies.

1. STRUCTURAL APPROACH TO CONTENT ANALYSIS AND TO INSTRUCTIONAL SEQUENCING

With the exception of highly restricted task domains, it is impossible to teach students directly everything they need to know. In fact, contemporary training programs have usually been developed and carried out without even an adequate specification of just what it is that must be learned. The problem basically is that there is no general consensus on exactly how to represent the competence underlying given task domains (content), and even less on how to go about identifying such competence.

As an alternative to static relational nets, and to independent competencies associated with discrete behavioral objectives, competence in the structural learning theory is represented in terms of sets of processes (rules), which interact in prescribed, well defined ways (see Chapters 2 and 15). Among other things, structural analysis places considerable emphasis on (higher-order) rules/processes that act on other rules/processes. In effect, heuristics and other higher-level processes play a central role in the theory. Such processes should, in our opinion, play a more important role in instruction than is presently the case.[2]

---

[2]Although higher-order processes may have broad generality, it would be a mistake to think that any process, higher- or lower-order, is completely independent of content. Logical rules of inference, for example, perhaps come as close as any to universality of application but, psychologically speaking, even they have restricted scope. In effect, the question of generality of processes is always one of degree relative to some problem domain--broad though it may be.

Since there are indefinitely many different content domains of potential interest (e.g., domains of knowables) a really adequate solution to the problem of higher-order rules/processes will involve more than just a way to represent them (e.g., as higher-order rules), or just illustrations of how they might be used.[3] As emphasized in Chapter 2, any general solution to the problem must also include some systematic method for identifying the processes underlying *any* content domain of interest.

The problems of content analysis (higher-order rule identification) and instructional sequencing are closely related in the structural learning theory (Scandura, 1977; cf. Chapters 3 and 13, this book). Even more generally, the theory provides a basic model of the teaching-learning process, one that gives explicit attention to content structure, cognitive processes, and individual differences, all in the context of an interactive teaching-learning system. Among other things, the theory includes: (1) a way of identifying competence (i.e., rule sets consisting of higher- and lower-order rules) underlying any given content domain, and associated with a given population of trainees, (2) an explicit basis for determining individual knowledge based on such competence, with the potential of adapting instruction to individual needs, and (3) general cognitive constraints (e.g., control processes, limitations on processing capacity) which determine how individuals can and do use the knowledge they have available. In this chapter, an extension of the theory is outlined that deals with the dynamic interaction between learner and teacher in ongoing instructional situations.

1.1 STRUCTURAL ANALYSIS

Given a class of problems, structural analysis (for identifying underlying competence) involves: (1) selecting a representative sample of problems, (2) identifying a solution rule for solving each of the sampled tasks (these solution rules are designed to reflect the way in which prototypic subjects in a given target population might solve the sampled problems--the initial set of solution rules is denoted R), (3) identifying higher-order rules that reflect parallels among the initial solution rules, together with the relevant lower-order rules on which they operate, (4) eliminating lower-order rules made unnecessary by the higher-order rules, and/or otherwise constructing a second order rule set, containing both the higher-order rules and lower-order rules, that collectively make it possible to derive every rule in R, (5) testing and refining the result-

---

[3]It is rarely clear from isolated illustrations, for example, where a higher-order rule may be useful and where not. Decisions as to which rules to use and when, particularly with respect to higher-order rules, are increasingly recognized as being at the heart of understanding complex cognitive behavior. Moreover, restricting oneself to giving only examples avoids the hard and more basic problem of identifying rule sets which are sufficient for solving all problems in given content domains (not just those used for illustrative purposes).

ing rule set on new problems, and (6) extending the rule set
where necessary so that it accounts for both familiar and novel
problems in the domain.   (For details, see Chapter 2 and Part 2.)
    Consider, for example, step (1): two sample problems from
the domain of geometry construction problems, and step (2):
their corresponding solution rules.

> *Sample Problem 1:*   Using only a straight-edge and compass,
> construct a point x at a given distance d from two given
> points A and B.
> *Solution Rule 1:* [Set (the radius of) the compass to dis-
> tance d, put the point of the compass on point A, and draw
> a circular arc (i.e., the "locus" of points at distance d
> from point A)]; [place the compass point on B and draw
> another circular arc]; [label the point(s) of intersection
> of the two circles x].

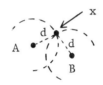

> *Sample Problem 2:*   Given a point A, a line l and a distance
> d, construct a circle with radius d which goes through
> point A and is tangent to line l.
> *Solution Rule 2:*   [Construct a circle with center at A and
> radius d]; [construct a locus of points at distance d from
> line l (i.e., parallel line at distance d from line l)];
> [construct a circle with center x (the intersection of the
> circle and the parallel line) and radius d].[4]

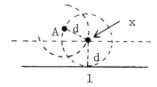

    Step (3): Notice that the two solution rules have the same
general structure ([set off by brackets]). Although the component rules of these solution rules differ substantially, each
solution rule involves two independent "locus" constructions,
with the intersection x of the two-loci playing a critical role.
In the first problem, x is the solution. In the second problem,
it is the center of the desired goal circle. In effect, both
solution rules can be derived by applying a higher-order "two-

----

[4]Each step in Solution Rule 2 can be detailed in terms of the more molecular
operations of setting a compass, using a fixed compass to construct a circular
arc, and using a straight-edge to construct a line segment.

locus" rule to the respective component rules. Roughly speaking (this can all be made quite precise--see Chapter 3), a higher-order two-locus rule operates on simple locus rules (e.g., for constructing circular arcs and parallel lines) and generates solution rules (i.e., combinations of the simpler locus rules). It is important to emphasize, that the two-locus higher-order rule can be used to derive solution rules for a wide (potentially infinite) range of problems, not just for the two sampled problems.

Step (4): Given the higher-order two-locus rule and the lower-order component rules, the solution rules themselves may be eliminated as redundant since they can be derived from the former rules acting collectively. Illustrating Steps (5) and (6) of structural analysis here would require more space than would be desirable, but the general intent is clear. More detail is given in Chapter 3.

It should perhaps be emphasized that structural analysis can and has been applied to several rather complex content areas (see below). Moreover, structural analysis may be applied recursively. Given an initial set of solution rules, one need not stop by deriving a more basic set (e.g., a set including both higher- and lower-order rules). The derived rule set, in turn, can be subjected to precisely the same type of analysis with the result being a rule set that is still more basic. In general, structural analysis may be reapplied as many times as desired, each time yielding a rule set which is more basic in two senses: (1) individual rules tend to become simpler and (2) the new rule set as a whole has greater generating power (i.e., it provides a basis for solving a greater variety of tasks (see Scandura, 1973, pp. 114-117)). Ultimately, reapplication of structural analysis yields rules that are atomic with respect to (all) individual learners.

1.2 INSTRUCTIONAL SEQUENCING

Structural analysis, as described above, is a crucial first step in dealing with the problem of instructional sequencing. Let us assume, for example, that we have applied structural analysis recursively to an initial set of solution rules, denoted by R.

Once such a sequence of rule sets R_1, R_2, ... , R_m has been generated, the knowledge available to individual students can be determinated by the methods described in Chapter 2 (and, in part, empirically tested in Chapters 8 and 9). In particular, sequential testing can be used with respect to the various hierarchically related rule sets and paths (in individual rules).

Learning may be assumed to take place as the learner interacts with the teaching environment according to the proposed control mechanism (see Chapters 2, 5, and 6). Since this mechanism makes no provision for processing capacity, however, reasonable limits must be placed on goal switching. Ideally, according to the present theory this should be done in accord-

ance with computed memory loads (Scandura, 1973; Chapters 2 and
7, this book) but other approximations may be more practical in
real world applications. In the research described in Section
2, for example, only a fixed number of levels of derivation is
allowed.

In line with the above let the final result of structural
analysis be a basic rule set B (=R_m). Without loss of generality, B can be thought of as the knowledge available to some subject on entering a course. Suppose B includes, for example,
such simple rules as: setting a compass to a given radius,
using a fixed compass to draw an arc, using a straight-edge to
draw a line segment and, perhaps, a higher-order rule that applies to pairs of available rules and forms their composites.

Given such a set, it is possible to determine by algorithmic
means (e.g., by computer) whether or not given problems might
be solved by applying available rules to other available rules,
and correspondingly which rules might be learned (derived) as
a result. Because of cognitive limitations on the learner (the
number of levels of derivation that he can successfully execute,
processing limitations, time), only certain problems may be
solved at each stage of learning. Thus, for example, whereas
the first sample problem (of finding a point at a given distance
from two given points) might be solved using the rules in set B,
the second sample problem would almost certainly be too complex.

We can denote the set of rules that might be learned by a
person who knows exactly the rules in B by B^2. In general, set
B^2 will include the original rules in B plus those rules that
may be derived from them directly (i.e., within the operating
cognitive constraints). In general then, set B^2 will include
rules that are more complex, including more complex higher-order
rules, than those that are contained in the initial basic rule
set B. In turn, the rules B^2 can be used to solve more complex
problems. In general, we can think of learning progressing from
stage to stage. Each time learning occurs (as a result of problem solving) new and more powerful rules (which can be used to
solve new and more complex problems) are added to the subject's
knowledge. In general, B^n may be used to denote the rules
learnable directly given the rules in B^{n-1}.

Ordinarily, B^n will be a far more encompassing (powerful)
rule set than the initial sample set R from which it ultimately
is derived. It is this feature which allows for "creative"
problem solving potential.

What does all of this have to do with sequencing? To
understand this, notice that the ability to solve problems associated with B^n comes about gradually as a result of solving
sequences of simpler problems associated with B, B^2, ..., B^{n-1}.
(In effect, each rule in B^n represents a unit of knowledge that
might be acquired as a result of solving problems, by a learner
who on entering a curriculum knows only the rules in B.) Hence,
given any random selection of problems from the problem domain

(e.g., geometry construction problems), it is possible to determine algorithmically which of the problems might be learned at
any given stage and which problems require further instruction
(e.g., in the form of prior problem-solving experience). In
turn, this makes it possible to algorithmically arrange the
problems in a learnable order(s).

In general, of course, it would be impossible and/or impractical to teach directly all of the solution rules contained
in B^n. With any real non-trivial content domain, they would
almost certainly be too large in number.

In order to talk about the optimization of instruction, two
additional things must be done. First, educational goals must
be identified, and (relative) values assigned to them. Since
testing is based on underlying rules (and not goals), however,
it would not be sufficient to simply assign values to educational goals. In general, achievement of an educational goal does
not specify what rules are learned. Consequently, philosophical-
ly determined values assigned to educational goals, must be
convertable into numerical values for rules associated with these
goals. (Note: Such rules correspond to those that would be
acquired by students who have mastered the curriculum. Compare
this situation to that in structural analysis where the desired
(atomic) rules correspond to entering capabilities that are
tailored to the weakest students.)

In general, a rule will be valued just to the extent that
it is involved in accounting for tasks associated with the corresponding educational goal(s). One problem for research will
be to determine suitable ways of measuring degree of involvement.
One requirement, for example, might be that a rule enter directly
into the solution of tasks associated with some educational goal.
In this case, one would rule out subordinate or source rules
that are only indirectly involved. Values need not, however,
be assigned to particular solution rules or particular higher-
order rules, but may be assigned to classes of same (e.g., including relational nets/structures; see Chapters 2 and 15).
Specifically, at one extreme, relatively high weight might be
placed on especially important rules (as is often the case in
technical training). At the other extreme, classes of higher-
level rules, which correspond to complex structures and thereby
insure broad transfer potential, might be given the highest
weights.

The second major addition concerns the various costs of
instruction. The time required to teach various types of rules,
by various types of instruction, would provide one natural
measure. In general, the cost (e.g., time, money) of testing
and instruction will vary directly with task complexity relative
to what the individual knows at the time. Hence, any really
adequate measure will have to deal with relative complexity;
complexity in the abstract can be no more than normative.

Given (1) a rule set B which represents the knowledge

available to a learner on entering a course, (2) constraints on
student behavior (e.g., number of levels of allowed goal switching), (3) the values assigned to the rules in B^n, and (4) the
time "costs" of (experience in solving) various problems and/or
of expository rule instruction (which in principle can be calcu-
lated relative to what each learner knows at each point in the
instruction), it is possible to determine the total cost and
instructional value associated with any given sequence of instruction. Moreover, the number of possible instructional sequences will necessarily be finite. In principle, therefore,
associated values and costs can all be determined and compared
to determine sequences that are optimal in some desired sense
(e.g., maximum value/unit cost, minimum cost/fixed value).

As a very simple example, suppose B = $\{r_{ab}, r_{bc}, r_{cd}, *\}$
where r_{ab} is a rule for converting from measure a (e.g., yards)
to measure b (e.g., feet); r_{bc} from b to c; r_{cd} from c to d;
and * is a higher-order composition rule that operates on pairs
of compatible rules (e.g., r_{ab} and r_{bc}) to generate their composites (i.e., r_{ac}, a rule that converts a to c).

If a subject is presented first with the task of converting
a given measure a to the appropriate number of d units, and
second the task of converting from a to c, the learner will
(according to the theory) fail on the first task and succeed on
the second. According to the theory, the solution to the first
problem (i.e., a to d) requires composing all three component
rules simultaneously whereas the available higher-order rule
can compose only two at a time.[5] The subject would succeed on
the second task, of course, because it requires composing only
a pair of rules. In the process, the subject would acquire a
rule for solving any a-to-c task. However, if the learner is
first presented with the a-to-c task, and then the a-to-d task,
he will succeed on both and in the process learn one rule for
converting from a-to-c, and another for converting from a-to-d.
(Once r_{ac} is learned, r_{ad} can be generated by applying * to r_{ac}
and r_{cd}.) If each learned rule is given a value of one and the
time cost for each task is assumed to be 5 minutes, then while
the time required for each sequence would be 10 minutes, the
educational value of the second instructional sequence would
be twice the first.

Although direct comparison of alternative sequences is
possible in principle (where reasonable assumptions can be made
as to the entering capabilities of learners or where the cost
of testing is either known or minimal), such comparison will
rarely be feasible via brute force evaluation of all possible
sequences. Practical considerations will ordinarily require
the use of more efficient, heuristic methods.

(Note: In Wulfeck's dissertation (summarized in Section

[5]In actuality, the postulated rules may be used collectively (in other ways
to solve the a-to-d problem but not in accordance with the "first approximation"
control mechanism assumed in the theory (Chapter 2).

2), which was an important first step in this direction, the sequencing problem was limited to rearranging random sequences of tasks into learnable sequences [i.e., sequences of tasks that can be solved in turn according to the postulated mechanisms]. In this case, it was possible to determine learnable sequences by strictly algorithmic means.)

In general, optimization will involve a far more complex balancing of gains versus costs. The case of testing versus instruction is particularly interesting, because it poses qualitatively different problems. The theory provides a strictly deterministic account of what can be learned only where sufficient information is available (via testing) concerning the learner's available knowledge. On the other hand, expending the costs necessary to get sufficient information could be counterproductive. In some cases, the teacher might do better by proceeding on the basis of partial information. Thus, ideally, the automated teacher (it is hard to imagine a human being with this much flexibility) must continually decide between testing and instruction. Does the information gained (about the learner's knowledge) via testing, and the subsequent prediction (via the theory) that this testing makes possible, justify the costs, when compared with the value that might be gained through instruction?

In the case of partial information, the teacher would necessarily have to content himself with nondeterministic judgements (cf. Chapter 8 of Scandura, 1973), or with probabilistic approximations (e.g., Hilke, Kempf, & Scandura, 1977).

To summarize the current situation briefly, the area of optimization poses a veritable gold mine of unanswered and, in many cases, unexplored problems. For example, a major open question of great theoretical and potential practical importance concerns the conditions under which local optimization will ensure overall optimization.

2. APPLICATION OF THE THEORY

This section describes an empirical study concerned with the problem of task sequencing. In this study: (1) The method of structural analysis was applied recursively to the geometry construction analysis described in Chapter 3. The resulting rule set was taken as basic (i.e., it was assumed to contain only rules that are atomic or correspond to entering capabilities available to all subjects in the target population). (2) A computer program was devised and implemented which takes as input arbitrary (random) sequences of geometry construction problems and arranges the problems in a (hypothesized) learnable sequence. In order to accomplish this, the problems and basic rules were represented in a form suitable for coding in SNOBOL

4 and learning was assumed to take place according to a programmed version of the "first approximation" control mechanism described in Chapters 2, 5, and 6. (3) In order to evaluate the learnability of the derived problem sequences, four groups of subjects were asked to solve the problems. Two groups received the problems in the theoretically derived order. In a third group, the problems were presented in random order. Sequencing in the fourth group was learner-controlled; individuals selected problems as they saw fit.

2.1 EXTENDED COMPETENCE ANALYSIS OF THE GEOMETRY CONSTRUCTION PROBLEMS

In extending the geometry construction analysis of Chapter 3, the method of structural analysis was applied recursively. Analysis continued until the rules identified could reasonably be assumed to be atomic or uniformly available to (essentially) all students working at the seventh-grade level. The identified basic rules included: (1) lower-order rules for constructing a circle (C) given the center point (P) and radius (D) (i.e., a preset compass), denoted $C(P,D)$; (2) drawing a line (L) or segment (S) through (between) two given points (P, P'), denoted $L(P,P')$ or $S(P,P')$; (3) finding points of intersection (PX) of intersecting lines (L) or circles (C), denoted $P(L,L')$, $P(L,C)$, $P(C,C')$, or simply PX; (4) measuring (setting a compass to) the distance (D) between given points (P,P'), denoted $D(P,P')$; and (5) choosing arbitrary points (P) or distances (D). Also included were higher-order rules for concatenating pairs of simple lower-order rules in which the output of one was a required input of the second *(composition)*, and combining pairs of independent rules to form a single rule having the same effect *(conjunction)*. Letting $Y(X)$, $Z(Y \times Y')$, and $Y'(X')$ be lower-order rules, these higher-order rules can be represented as follows.

Composition: $Y(X)$, $Z(Y \times Y') \rightarrow Z(Y(X) \times Y')$ and
Conjunction: $Y(X)$, $Y'(X') \rightarrow Y \times Y'(X \times X')$

Since the essentials of structural analysis have already been illustrated, we shall present here a few specifics and, in the process, hopefully, help the reader to better understand the method we used. For illustrative purposes, consider two geometry construction problems,

1. Given point P, line L, and distance D, construct a circle with radius D which passes through P and is tangent to L, and
2. Given triangle ABC, construct (circumscribe) a circle which passes through points A, B, and C.

In the analysis of Chapter 3, solution rules for these and other tasks were specified, parallels were identified and a two-locus

higher-order rule was constructed to reflect these parallels.
Solution rules for Problems 1 and 2, as well as other two-loci
problems, could be derived by applying the two-loci higher-order
rule to the following lower-order rules.

R1: Construct a circle (C) with a given point (P) as cen-
     ter, and a given distance (D) as radius. Denote it
     C(P,D).

R2: Construct a line (L') parallel to a given line (L) at
     a given distance (D) from the given line. Denote it
     L'(L,D).

R3: Construct the locus of points (a line, L') equidistant
     from two given points (P,P'). Denote it L'(P,P').

R4: Construct a circle (C), with a given point (P) as
     center, which passes through another given point (P').
     Denote it C(P,D[P,P']).

The above higher-order rule (essentially) concatenates pairs of
rules, each of which constructs a locus, and then adds a rule
for constructing the goal figure from an intersection point (PX)
of the two-loci. The solution rules generated for Problems 1
and 2 can be represented, respectively, in terms of the following sequences of component rules: C(P,D), L'(L,D), C(PX,D) and
L'(A,B), L"(B,C), C(PX,D(PX,A)).

Rule R1 above is basic enough so that it need not be further analyzed. However, the others (including the higher-order
rule) can be further analyzed. For example, Rule R4 can be
generated by applying a simple composition higher-order rule to
the following lower-order rules:

R5: Set a compass to the distance between two given points.
     Denote it D(P,P').

R6: Construct a circle given a center point and a preset
     compass. Denote it C(P,D).

Thus, application of the higher-order rule generates solution
Rule R5, R6, which is equivalent to R4.

The two-loci higher-order rule also can be further analyzed.
This rule (essentially) involves forming the conjunction of two
locus rules and, then, concatenating the conjunction rule with
a goal figure rule. In effect, the higher-order two-loci rule
can be generated by concatenating higher-order conjunction and
concatenation rules. To complete the analysis, the above ideas
were reapplied both recursively and exhaustively as required.
(For details, see Wulfeck, 1975.)

From the above, it might appear that learnable sequences
of problems might be determined by simply tracing backward
through the analysis that yielded the basic rule set. However,
this strategy is insufficient because there are many other
learnable sequences. More importantly, there also are learnable
sequences that include problems not even considered during the
analysis, but that are solvable via the identified rules. There
is only a small probability, for example, that the problems explicitly selected (e.g., by a teacher) will be the same as those
determined via structural analysis.

It is, of course, possible to enumerate all problems for which solution rules are generable from any given set of basic rules; one simply lets the higher-order and lower-order rules interact in all possible ways according to the hypothesized control mechanism (cf. Chapter 2). However, given a non-trivial, initial rule set, such a procedure would rapidly become unmanageable in practice. The point is that structural analyses do not yield strict hierarchies from which it is possible to simply "read" all learnable sequences. Instead, one gets an incomplete lattice of rules/tasks that, generally speaking, includes only a small portion of the possible (learnable) sequences. Given any set of problems, then, our basic task was to develop a systematic way to arrange them in a learnable order.

2.2 COMPUTER IMPLEMENTATION

SNOBOL 4 was used in the computer implementation because of its powerful pattern matching capability, which was essential in testing rules, and because newly constructed strings of characters can be added to, compiled, and executed by the program itself during its own operation. The latter feature made it possible to derive new rules during the course of problem solving and, then, to turn around and use them without reprogramming.

The learning control mechanism lies at the core of the computer implementation. Specifically, the mechanism depicted in Figure 1 was implemented in SNOBOL 4 so as to parallel the "first approximation" mechanism, as described, for example, in Chapter 5.

Given a problem represented in a suitable format (as a string) this portion of the program: (Step 1) checks each available rule to see if the problem goal is contained in its range and if there are given elements and/or available rules in the domain of the rule. If not, (Step 2) control moves to the next level goal (provided a preset goal limit has not been reached). That is, the current goal level (CG) is increased by one (CG + 1) and control returns to Step 1.

If the conditions of Step 1 are satisfied, (Steps 3) the rule is applied to the given elements. Where the output is a new rule it is added to the available set of rules, the current goal level (CG) is decreased by one (CG - 1) and control returns to Step 1. The problem is solved whenever a new output is generated and the current goal is equal to one. (In the context of the program, this is equivalent to testing a potential solution against the problem goal.) The program fails to solve a problem whenever the current goal exceeds the preset goal limit (GLIMIT).

Notice that limits on processing capacity are imposed indirectly (by a preset goal limit). At some point we hope to extend the implementation to deal with processing capacity directly as well as to generalize the mechanism itself along the lines described in Chapter 2.

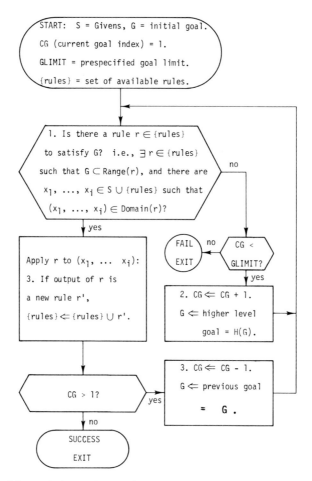

START: S = Givens, G = initial goal.
CG (current goal index) = 1.
GLIMIT = prespecified goal limit.
{rules} = set of available rules.

1. Is there a rule $r \in$ {rules}
to satisfy G? i.e., $\exists\, r \in$ {rules}
such that $G \subset$ Range(r), and there are
$x_1, \ldots, x_i \in S \cup$ {rules} such that
$(x_1, \ldots, x_i) \in$ Domain(r)?

no

yes

Apply r to $(x_1, \ldots x_i)$:
3. If output of r is
a new rule r',
{rules} $\Leftarrow$ {rules} $\cup$ r'.

FAIL
EXIT

no

CG <
GLIMIT?

yes

2. CG $\Leftarrow$ CG + 1.
G $\Leftarrow$ higher level
goal = H(G).

CG > 1?

yes

3. CG $\Leftarrow$ CG - 1.
G $\Leftarrow$ previous goal
= G .

no

SUCCESS
EXIT

Figure 1. Problem solving and learning mechanism.

The overall operation of the program is described in Figure 2. The program takes as input initial sets of rules and arbitrary lists of problems represented in a suitable format. (In the program both kinds of input were represented similarly with domains and ranges of the rules being interpreted as patterns and the goal and givens of problems, as objects to be matched.) The set of geometry construction rules, the only rule set considered, was the only part of the program specific to a particular problem domain. The program attempts the given problems in turn. Solved problems are added to a (learnable) sequence and rules derived while solving them are added to the rule set. Failed problems are retained on a failed problem list, and reattempted after all problems have been tried once. The process continues until all problems are solved, or until the number of failed problems reaches some prespecified failure

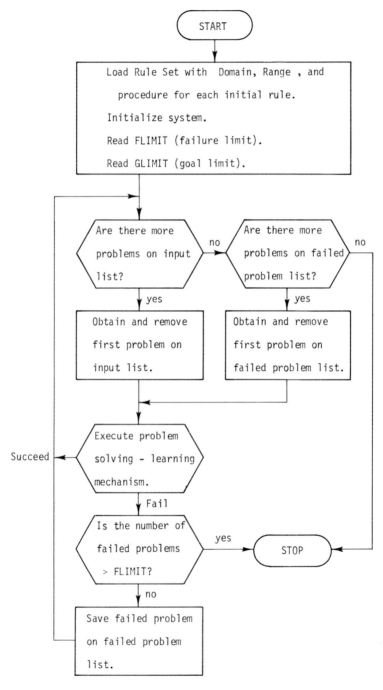

Figure 2. Overall program operation.

limit. This process has the effect of reordering presented
problems so that each problem (that is potentially solvable via
the rule set and control assumptions) is solvable on its first
presentation. (Further details are given in Wulfeck, 1975.)
More generally, program outputs may be used to discard redundant
problems, to rearrange problems, or to add intermediate problems
so that unsolved problems become solvable.

Notice also that the highest-level goal reached in solving
a problem provides a reasonable measure of the difficulty level
of individual problems. Problems for which a solution rule already exists in the current rule set, for example, are solvable
at the initial goal level (CG = 1 in Figure 1). Problems whose
solution rules are derivable from rules in the set via an available higher-order rule are solvable at the second goal level
(CG = 2), etc. This measure of difficulty summarizes (but is
not perfectly or linearly related to) the amount of processing
required in solving problems and provided a useful basis for
predicting problem solving latencies (see Section 2.3).

The central point here, however, is that there is no fixed
a priori difficulty level for any problem. Difficulty is always
relative to the knowledge base--the rule set--available at the
time a problem is presented. (Note: Setting the goal limit
[GLIMIT in Figure 1] to some whole number N restricts program
outputs [sequences of problems] so that each problem in the
sequence is solvable at CG $\leq$ N. Sequenced problems are thus
restricted to a maximum level of difficulty.)

2.3 EMPIRICAL EVALUATION[6]

This section summarizes relevant results from an experiment
conducted by Wulfeck (1975). According to the above discussion
concerning relative difficulty level and amounts of processing,
one would expect (with human subjects) direct relationships between difficulty levels and failure frequencies and between
difficulty levels and solution latencies. In effect, problem
sequences in which relative difficulty is kept small should lead
to better overall performance than those in which difficulty is
uncontrolled. In addition, solution latencies should increase
with level of difficulty.

Four groups of 10 seventh-grade subjects each, were given
different sequences of 20 geometric construction problems:
Group X_1 received the 20 problems arranged by the computer program so that the difficulty levels for Problems 18 and 20 were
three, and for all others, two. Group X_2 received a sequence
obtained from the first by deleting Problems 8, 10, 12, and 16.
This increased the relative difficulty levels for Problems 9
and 13 to three, and decreased the difficulty level for Problem
20 to two. (The higher-order rule derived at CG = 3 in solving

[6]The authors wish to thank Jonathon Baron for his helpful suggestions con-
cering certain aspects of the design of this experiment.

Problem 9 facilitated solving Problem 20. Although affected by
the deletions, Problem 11 had an alternate solution so that
relative difficulty was unchanged; similarly, Problem 17 used
the higher-order rule derived in solving Problem 13.)

Groups R (random) and L (learner-controlled) received the
original 20 problems with the first 6 problems in the same order
as the other groups. After Problem 6, the problem order in Group
R was random. In Group L, the individual subjects were allowed
to choose which (of 7 through 20) to attempt next.

Method: Subjects were run individually (under nonidealized
conditions). The problems were presented to the subjects on
separate sheets of paper one at a time (except to Group L after
Problem 6). Subjects were given a compass, straight-edge (not
a ruler), and pencil and were required to show their work on
the problem sheet.

To help insure correct interpretation of the problems, each
problem statement (when presented) was read aloud by the experimenter, given elements were pointed out, relational terms (e.g.,
parallel) were explained, and a sketch of the goal figure (in
required relationships to given elements) was drawn. If a problem was failed, the subject was shown a solution rule for it,
and was required to execute the rule correctly on the problem
page. To help ensure continued availability of derived solution
rules, subjects retained the problem pages and were allowed to
refer to them as desired. (In effect, differences among the
treatment groups may be attributed to differences in the *higher-
order rules* learned.)

Problems 1 through 6 were used to pretest subjects' prior
knowledge. All subjects were initially given Problem 6; no
subject solved it correctly on its first presentation. Subjects
then were given Problems 1 through 6 in that order. All subjects
solved Problems 1 through 6. (These results supported our initial knowledge assumptions; the basic rules seemed to be at an
appropriate level of detail.)

Results and Discussion: Mean percent success, on problems
attempted after Problem 6, for Groups X_1, X_2, L, and R were 85
percent, 73 percent, 47 percent, and 38 percent, respectively.
All differences were significant ($p < .05$) except X_1-X_2, and
L-R. Evidently, under these experimental conditions, problem
sequences in which problem difficulty is kept relatively low,
as was the case with sequences X_1 and X_2 (determined by the
program), lead to significantly better performance than do random or learner-controlled sequences. Furthermore, subjects must
have used previously derived rules in generating solutions to
later problems. If this were not so, that is if sequence played
no role in determining success or failure on given problems,
then all groups would have performed similarly.

Mean times to solution on problems common to Groups X_1 and
X_2 were in complete agreement with predictions from the structural learning theory. The only significant differences in
(mean log) solution times across Groups X_1 and X_2 occurred in

predicted directions on Problems 9 ($X_1 < X_2$), 13 ($X_1 < X_2$), and 20 ($X_1 > X_2$). These differences are consistent with what one would expect if goal switching had been used during problem solving, and therefore provide additional support for such a mechanism. Moreover, X_2 subjects evidently were able to retain and use higher-order rules derived on some problems (9 and 13) on later problems (20 and 17), even though they were not given memory support with respect to higher-order rules.

As expected, there also was a significant positive relationship between (relative) problem difficulty and frequency of failure. No subject ever solved a problem where the required goal level (difficulty level) was greater than three (72 cases). Presumably, memory load approximates subjects' processing capacities at step sizes around three.

In addition, a significant interaction (on percent success) was found between problem difficulty (2 or 3) and experimental groups. Subjects in Group L, and particularly in Group R, performed differentially more poorly on difficulty-level-three problems than did X_1 or X_2 subjects. Although other factors may be involved as well (e.g., motivation), we note that the Group X_1 and X_2 sequences had a "chaining" property, such that solution rules for problems were often derived using (composite) rules derived in solving immediately preceeding problems. The L and R problem sequences were less frequently chained in this way. Hence, memory may have had a differentially greater negative effect with the R and L subjects.

(Note: Chaining is only indirectly related to problem difficulty. However, when a relatively small set of problems is given to the program to be sequenced (as was the case in this study), restrictions on goal levels tend to force a moderate degree of chaining. With a larger set of problems, on the other hand, where there are many different intermediate problems between basic and terminal problems, restricting problem difficulty would tend not to force as much chaining. To the extent that rule recency, or *Einstellung,* is involved in subjects' processing, an even closer coordination between predictions and theory would have been obtained had limitations on processing capacity been built into the program. In this case, closer attention would have to be given to exactly what rules each subject had available at each stage of problem solving. For discussion of these issues, see Chapters 2 and 7 of this book, and Scandura, 1973, Chapter 10.)

Finally, it is worth noting that there was a fairly wide range of problem solving success over Group L subjects. Some L subjects apparently had bases for choosing next problems, that were related to problem difficulty, and correspondingly to success on the problems. Three subjects stated that they chose on the basis of similarity (of problem statement and display) to previous problems. The problems they chose tended to be chained

and of low difficulty (most often level two); about 73 percent
of these problems were solved. By way of contrast, two subjects
chose dissimilar problems, where the relative difficulty levels
were never as low as two; these subjects solved none of their
chosen problems. (The remaining subjects indicated no particular basis for selection, and solved about half of the problems
they chose.) These results and others (e.g., Pask & Scott,
1971) suggest that some subjects may have useful problem selection skills (rules), toward which additional research might be
directed.

3. DIRECTIONS FOR FURTHER RESEARCH

In addition to the extensions previously discussed, and
the need to consider other types of rule acquisition (e.g., by
exposition, cf. Scandura, 1973), we would like to underline two
particularly important directions for future research. As discussed in Section 1 of this chapter, (1) more consideration
should be given to the problems of individualization. The
balancing of gains and costs associated with testing seems to
provide an especially challenging area of inquiry. In this
regard, the assignment of values and costs will not be an entirely straightforward matter; both values and costs will be relative, and will depend on what individual subjects know at particular points during the course of learning. General characteristics, such as processing capacity, may also vary over subjects and a way should be found to incorporate them into a
working system.

(2) The second problem, which we just mention, concerns
the need to "automate" the method of structural analysis. We
believe that structural analysis could play a crucial role in
instructional design (as it does in much of our own work) but,
as yet, the method is neither fully general nor fully objective
or systematic. For one thing, it requires an analyst who is
thoroughly conversant with both the content and the underlying
theory. Making the method more objective and systematic would
appear to be a necessary prerequisite to its widespread use.

References

Atkinson, R. C. Ingredients for a theory of instruction. *American Psychologist,* 1972, *27,* 921-931.

Banerji, R. A formal approach to knowledge in problem solving. In J. M. Scandura, J. H. Durnin, & W. H. Wulfeck II (Eds.), *1974 Proceedings: Fifth annual interdisciplinary conference on structural learning* (ONR Technical Report, 1974). MERGE Research Institute, 1249 Greentree Lane, Narberth, PA 19072.

Bourne, L. E., Jr. Knowing and using concepts. *Psychological Review,* 1970, *77,* 546-556.

Ernst, G. W., & Newell, A. *GPS (General Problem Solver): A case study in generality and problem solving.* New York: Academic Press, 1969.

Gagne, R. *The conditions of learning.* New York: Holt, Rinehart, & Winston, 1970.

Heimer, R. T., & Lottes, J. J. The theoretical model and a synopsis of the first two years of the research program. *Journal of Research in Mathematics Education,* 1973, *4,* 85-93.

Hilke, R., Kempf, W. F., & Scandura, J. M. Deterministic and probabilistic theorizing in structural learning. In H. Spada & W. F. Kempf (Eds.), *Formalized theories of thinking and learning and their implications for science instruction.* Bern: Huber, 1977.

Nilsson, N. J. *Problem solving methods in artificial intelligence.* New York: McGraw-Hill, 1971.

Pask, G., & Scott, B. C. E. Learning and teaching strategies in a transformational skill. *British Journal of Mathematical and Statistical Psychology,* 1971, *24,* 205-229.

Payne, D. A., Krathwohl, D. R., & Gordon, J. The effect of sequence on programmed instruction. *American Educational Research Journal,* 1967, *4,* 125-132.

Polya, G. *How to solve it.* Princeton: University Press, 1945.

Resnick, L. B., Wang, M. P., & Kaplan, J. Task analysis in curriculum design: A hierarchically sequenced introductory mathematics curriculum. *Journal of Applied Behavioral Analysis,* 1973, *6,* 679-709.

Roe, A. A comparison of branching methods for programmed learning. *Journal of Educational Research,* 1962, *55,* 407-416.

Scandura, J. M. *Structural learning I: Theory and research.* New York: Gordon & Breach Science, 1973.

Scandura, J. M. A deterministic theory of learning and teaching. In H. Spada & W. F. Kempf (Eds.), *Formalized theories of thinking and learning and their implications for science instruction.* Bern: Huber, 1977.

Wulfeck, W. H., II. *An algorithmic approach to curriculum construction: Development, computer implementation, and evaluation of a method for identifying instructional content sequences.* Unpublished Ph.D. Dissertation, University of Pennsylvania, 1975.

Wulfeck, W. H., II. A structural approach to instructional sequencing. In H. Spada & W. F. Kempf (Eds.), *Formalized theories of thinking and learning and their implications for science instruction.* Bern: Huber, 1977.

PART 6

Conclusions

In Chapter 15 an attempt is made: (1) to summarize our progress; (2) to show how the Structural Learning Theory provides a basis for reinterpreting, explaining, and extending a variety of other kinds of problem solving research; (3) to outline various instructional implications of the research; and (4) to summarize limitations and discuss future directions designed to overcome these limitations.

Among the potentially important theoretical and research
contributions of the book are the following:　(1) clearer philosophical justification for testing deterministic behavior theories under idealized conditions, (2) explicit attention to systematic *methods* of content analysis (rather than just to the
type of competence that should result from such analyses) and

the application of such methods to realistic problem domains,
(3) empirical support for an extension of a previously hypothesized control mechanism to include a wider variety of complex
human behavior, (4) the introduction of specific, illustrative
"observation theories", that complement the Structural Learning
Theory, and that make it possible to explain and to predict human behavior in real (nonidealized) situations, (5) extension
of the theory to include the operation definition of individual
knowledge with respect to nonsimple problem domains (as well as
to just simple domains as in our earlier research), (6) concrete
suggestions for extension of the theory to dynamic interactions
between subject and environment, including adaptive instruction,
and for possible generalization to interactions among various
cultures, (7) computer implementation and empirical verification
of the theory in situations where subjects learn how to solve
problems, as a result of prior problem solving experience, that
they could not solve initially, and (8) more complete specification of similarities and differences with respect to other problem solving theory and research, including use of the theory to
analyze the problem solving process (e.g., as exemplified in
protocols).

15
Summary, Relationships
to Other Problem Solving Research,
Instructional Implications, and Future Directions[1]

Joseph M. Scandura

We set out in this book to shed light on the question, "Why is it that some people succeed in solving problems, whereas others do not?" Toward this end, we worked under the assumption that content, cognition, and individual differences all play a crucial role in problem solving--and that any complete understanding of the problem-solving process would require a synthesis of all three aspects. In the preceeding chapters, a refined and extended version of the structural learning theory was described, together with a wide variety of supporting behavioral research, including educational applications.

At this point, it seems appropriate to ask what we have accomplished and what remains to be done. In the following sections, we shall: (1) summarize the basic theory and results; (2) discuss relationships to other problem-solving research, including general relationships to other structural/process approaches, explanations of results of other problem-solving research and possible resolutions of some current issues in the area; (3) show how the theory might be used to deal with and/or to resolve open issues in education, and (4) list some directions in which the present work might be extended.

1. SUMMARY

1.1 GENERAL NATURE OF THE THEORY
The structural learning theory provides a unifying theoretical framework within which to view the concerns of the competence

[1]This chapter is based on research supported by National Institute of Health Grant 9185.

researcher (e.g., the artificial intelligence, linguistics, subject matter specialist), the cognitive psychologist, and the individual differences specialist (see Figure 1).

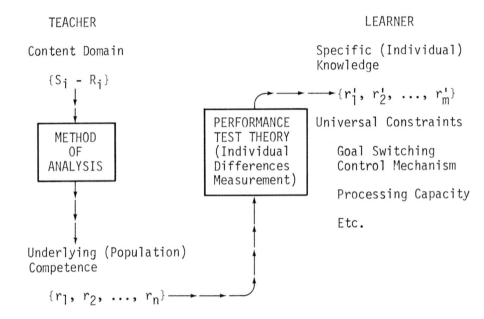

TEACHER   LEARNER

Content Domain   Specific (Individual)
                                        Knowledge

$\{S_i - R_i\}$

                                        $\{r_1', r_2', \ldots, r_m'\}$

METHOD   PERFORMANCE   Universal Constraints
OF   TEST THEORY
ANALYSIS   (Individual   Goal Switching
               Differences   Control Mechanism
               Measurement)
                                        Processing Capacity

                                        Etc.

Underlying (Population)
Competence

$\{r_1, r_2, \ldots, r_n\}$

Figure 1. Schematic representation of major components of the Structural Learning Theory; $S_i - R_i$ denotes a set of stimulus situations and responses, and $\{r_1, r_2, \ldots, r_n\}$ and $\{r_1', r_2', \ldots, r_m'\}$ denote sets of rules.

It would be presumptuous, of course, to suggest that the theory described provides a satisfactory account of all such phenomena. It does not. First and foremost, the theory emphasizes the overall architecture of human problem solving, the logical necessities for *any* theory of problem solving. In some respects, the theory provides only a sketchy map and a hunting license with the promise of plentiful game. Nonetheless, the degree of rigor, precision, and broad empirical support which characterizes the theory would seem to justify serious study by scientists interested in complex human behavior, including potential critics.

The theory is basically a relativistic one. What individual subjects know and what they are able to do is always judged relative to the cognitive structures and processes underlying some predetermined content (problem domain) and associated with idealized, prototypic members of some subject population. The prototypic processes that collectively make it possible to solve problems in a problem domain are referred to as *rules of competence.* (Structures are the entities on which rules operate and may consist, e.g., of cognitively meaningful subsets of rules, cf. Chapter 2 and Section 3.) Collectively, the set of competence rules is called a *competence account of the problem domain*.

In the theory, the term *problem domain* is used in a broad sense, and, in principle, may encompass anything from simple arithmetic to language or moral behavior. Similarly, the subject population might be either "multicultural" or highly homogeneous. Depending on the problem domain and target population, then, the underlying competence might provide a detailed account of highly prescribed behavior (e.g., borrowing in subtraction) or a *molar* account of a broad range of phenomena (e.g., concrete operations). In most applications to date, both the problem domains and the subject populations have been relatively well delineated but, in principle, this is not an essential limitation.

In theory, any given problem can be solved in any number of ways. In practice, however, only a small number of alternatives will normally be compatible with how a knowledgeable member of the target population might solve it. The subject population places definite constraints on the processes (rules) that may be introduced. For example, German children are taught the equal additions method of subtraction, whereas American children are taught borrowing. Such constraints severely limit the theoretically infinite number of competence accounts associated with any given problem domain.

Idealized competence, of course, is not the same as individual rules of knowledge. It is assumed in the theory that what an individual does and can learn depends directly and inextricably on what is already known. More particularly, it is assumed that the human information processor may be adequately characterized in terms of: (1) universal characteristics of the processor, and (2) individual knowledge that is judged relative to the competence associated with given problem domains (and subject populations to which the individuals belong).

Control mechanisms are among the most important universal characteristics. Control mechanisms serve to tell the organism which processes (rules) to use and when to use them. They are essential in all information-processing systems, whether man or machine. Whereas all complete information-processing theories make a distinction between process (rule) and control, control in most cases either plays a subordinate role (e.g., Newell & Simon, 1972), or is distributed among a variety of different control mechanisms whose coordination, in turn, is often left unspecified (e.g., Pascual-Leone, 1970).

In contrast, the structural learning theory postulates a single goal-switching control mechanism that makes minimal assumptions about the processor but that, nonetheless, has been shown adequate to account for many different kinds of behavior. This mechanism is hypothesized to be common to all humans and to govern all cognition, irrespective of the specific knowledge involved.

A second general characteristic of the theory, that has been empirically tested, is processing capacity. Again, almost all contemporary information-processing theories assume in one form or another that "working memory" has a limited capacity. In the structural learning theory, working memory is assumed to hold not only data (the stuff on which rules operate) but rules themselves. While capacity per se is assumed to be fixed (although it may vary over individuals), the memory load associated with any given task depends directly on the process used in attacking it. Thus, for example, whereas it may be impossible to multiply large numbers in one's head using the standard algorithm, many people know short-cut processes that enable them to perform successfully. The theory also allows for the inclusion of other general constraints, such as processing speed, but this part of the theory has been only partially developed.

Each universal characteristic of the human information processor says something about behavior but not all. Accordingly, one can conceive of a succession of deterministic partial theories, each of which in turn says progressively more about human behavior. Each partial theory is deterministic, in the sense that it deals with the behavior of given subjects in particular situations (see Chapter 1).

Deterministic predictions may be expected to hold, however, only in situations that satisfy appropriate boundary conditions. For example, the "memory-free" (partial) theory fully accounts for behavior only in situations where all relevant knowledge may be assumed to be readily available. (This partial theory involves only the control mechanism and does not take processing capacity into account.) To the extent that processing capacity is involved, for example, theoretical predictions can be expected to deviate from obtained results. The idea is directly analogous to the situation with the inclined plane law of elementary classical physics. This law allows one, for example, to calculate the force needed to move a given cart up an inclined plane but only where the inclined plane is perfectly smooth and the wheels on the cart are frictionless. Deviations from prediction may be expected just to the extent that the inclined plane is bumpy and/or that friction otherwise plays a role.

In effect, the structural theory of cognition is a "top-down" theory. Progressively more structure may be added to the theory by adding more and more (possibly universal) constraints. Thus, adding processing capacity to the "memory-free" theory, which involves only the control structure, makes it possible to account for behavior under a wider variety of conditions.

The possibility of adding more structure implies a particular (structural) approach to theory construction that is an essential aspect of the structural learning theory. In turn, this aspect of the theory has important implications for empirical testing. By way of summary, suffice it to say that each

partial theory must be tested under appropriate idealized conditions in the same sense that the inclined plane law must be
tested using smooth inclined planes and frictionless wheels.

In contrast to general cognitive constraints, specific
knowledge is assumed to vary over individuals. The theory shows
how competence, corresponding to the knowledge had by idealized,
prototypic members of given populations, may be used to operationally define the knowledge had by actual individual members
of such populations. The rules of competence serve effectively
as "rulers" or standards against which individual knowledge may
be measured.

Originally, the structural learning theory was primarily
schematic insofar as competence was concerned (Scandura, 1973b).
Illustrations and general requirements as to how such competence
should be represented were provided, but, along with other contemporary theories of knowledge, little was said about how to
identify such competence. In this sense, the theory was not
fully operational because predictions in the theory depended directly on the competence associated with given problem domains
and subject populations, and because the number of different
domains and populations is indeterminately large. In effect, it
is essential that a fully operational structural learning theory
include a theory (systematic method) for identifying arbitrary
competence. (Contrast this requirement with linguistics where
competence is more sharply prescribed.) Although a complete
solution to this important problem is beyond current reach, the
constraints imposed on competence by universal characteristics
of the human information processor make it possible, apparently,
to proceed in a quasi-systematic manner (called *structural
analysis*).

1.2 SUMMARY OF ACCOMPLISHMENTS

The research reported in Part 2 demonstrates the practicability of structural analysis when placed in the hands of a
skilled analyst who is familiar with the content in question.
The utility of the results of such analyses (i.e., the rule sets
identified) has been demonstrated in part in Chapters 11, 12,
and 13. Moreover, the expected advantages of applying structural
analysis recursively have been at least partially demonstrated
in Chapter 14. As a result of such analysis, the individual
rules became much simpler, while the generative potential of the
rule set as a whole became much greater.

In many respects, however, current empirical achievements
fall considerably short of theoretical prospects. These limitations fall into two basic categories. First, no attempt has been
made to take such things as rule selection or memory into account,
or to encompass more complex relational nets (sets of rules) as
inputs and outputs (however, see Chapter 4). Second, the method
of analysis at present is largely intuitive. In order to extend

its utility, more systematic, formal and automatic formulation of the method will be essential.

The research reported in Part 3 had a quite different purpose. Instead of being concerned with specific content or competence, the emphasis was on general cognitive constraints that affect the way people use the specific knowledge they have available. Foremost among these constraints was the goal-switching control mechanism.

The results of experiments reported in Chapters 5 and 6 strongly suggest the prior and universal availability of some form of this mechanism to all human beings, at least from about the age of four years. Although most of the data pertain to the derivation of new rules during problem solving, the studies reported in Chapter 6 show how the basic mechanism can be generalized analytically to account for such processes as problem definition, breaking down problems into subproblems, storage and retrieval in memory, and rule selection. Although preliminary in form, the results generally support the assumption of universality.

Perhaps the major innovation in these studies concerns the basic paradigm--the direct test of deterministic hypotheses under idealized behavior conditions. As argued in Chapter 1, such tests are essential if we are to identify truly *universal* characteristics of human information processors. This type of testing may be difficult to carry out in many cases, however, and in any case the vast bulk of behavioral data is nonidealized.

The theory and research reported in Chapter 7 shows how nonidealized data also may be treated within the structural framework. A deterministic theory of memory load is described that is more detailed, but less general, than that in Chapter 2. In testing the theory, however, it was not possible to fully realize appropriate idealized conditions. (The data were strongly supportive but only in the usual normative sense.) Nonetheless, in accord with our earlier argument (Chapter 1), it was possible to devise a complementary *observation theory,* which, together with the deterministic theory of memory load, provided a rather good account of the (nonidealized) data (also see Voorhies, 1973)

More generally, the implied distinction between *structural* and *incidental* variables (see Chapter 1) is a basic one, one that could fundamentally affect the way in which behavioral research is conducted. Much remains to be done even with respect to the present theory. For one thing, little has been done by way of integrating control and processing capacity, and specifically with regard to conducting appropriate tests. For another thing, relatively little has been done theoretically, and almost nothing empirically, with regard to latency measures and the like. The latter limitation is an important one, since latency is the primary dependent measure in much of the current research in information processing psychology (however, see Chapter 2, Section 4.2).

The studies in Part 4 demonstrate the feasibility of operationally defining individual knowledge in terms of population competence. In Chapter 8, given fairly complete information concerning the rules of competence, including the atomicity of their components, the results were highly encouraging. Testing made it possible to identify rules that summarized individual behavior potential with a high degree of validity and reliability. The results of Chapter 9 are generally compatible and further suggest that rules of competence will be adequate for "measuring" individual knowledge just to the extent that the rules are consistent with how knowledgeable members of the target population might solve the problems in question. Further, the results of Experiments III and IV of Chapter 5 and Chapter 13 indicate that these same methods may be used effectively with higher-order rules.

To date, however, these studies have been severely limited relative to the theoretical prospects described in Chapter 2. For one thing, no serious attempt has yet been made to apply the structural approach to diagnostic testing with respect to non-trivial problem domains--taken as wholes. This is a particularly important area of concern, especially since work in this direction could help to bridge the current gap between normative and criterion-referenced testing. For another thing, the completed research deals exclusively with "rights" and "wrongs". Almost nothing to date has been done by way of taking into account alternative wrong answers, latency, or more generally the different levels of behavioral data discussed in Chapter 2.

In addition to demonstrating the practical potential of the structural learning theory, the results of the studies reported in Part 5 serve to illustrate the fact that deterministic support for a theory under idealized conditions necessarily implies probabilistic support in the real world (e.g., in education; see Chapter 11). The research in Chapter 12 further demonstrates that the approach encompasses much more than just mathematics and other structured content.

The research reported in Chapters 13 and 14 demonstrates the applicability of the structural learning theory beyond "slices" of behavioral reality. More important, although couched primarily in terms of teaching and learning, the first part of Chapter 14 shows how the theory might be extended to deal with the dynamic ongoing interaction between subject and environment. Such interaction might properly be viewed as constituting the proper concern of human psychology (cf. Pask, 1975).

2. RELATIONSHIPS TO PROBLEM-SOLVING RESEARCH

The proposed theory provides an intuitively simple, empirically viable mechanism by which individuals may be assumed to bring the knowledge they have to bear in problem solving. In addition, it provides a basis for analyzing the specific competencies underlying given problem domains and for using such competencies to determine (i.e., operationally define) the relevant knowledge available to individual subjects. Practical applications and extensions of the theory also seem evident.

Nonetheless, it is still fair to ask how the theory fits into the current zeitgeist of problem-solving research. In turn, we shall consider: (1) general relationships to other structural/process approaches to the study of problem solving, (2) relationships to other problem-solving research, and (3) current issues in the study of human problem solving.

2.1 RELATIONSHIPS TO OTHER STRUCTURAL/PROCESS APPROACHES

Most structural and information-processing theorists would agree that problem content and individual differences must be considered in any complete account of the problem-solving process. Most also are generally agreed that problem definition (subgoal formation), the derivation of solution procedures, rule selection, and memory are all involved to some extent in the cognitive aspects of problem solving. Although there are many similarities, however, there are a number of important differences between the present theory and most other structural/process theories. Some of these relationships are important and some not so important; some subtle and some not so subtle. Unfortunately, many of the differences are both important and subtle.

Content: Understanding any problem domain requires identification of the underlying competence--specifically, an answer to the question, "What competencies are needed to solve problems in the given domain?"

In artificial intelligence, for example, a major goal has been to identify procedures that are sufficient for solving problems in the given domain efficiently (e.g., Minsky & Papert, 1972). Like theories in artificial intelligence, the structural learning theory is concerned, in part, with identifying procedures for solving problems in given problem domains. Unlike most theories in artificial intelligence, however, the structural learning theory is not just concerned with performance (cf. Newell & Simon, 1972). Cognitive restructuring (e.g., learning, storage and retrieval in memory) is given equal weight as is a particular fixed mode of interaction (control) by which such restructuring is assumed to take place.

The structural learning theory also is centrally concerned with the identification of objective and systematic methods for identifying the competence underlying arbitrary content domains and for combining competencies associated with two or more different and previously analyzed domains. The theory, in effect, also has goals analogous to theories of automatic programming. The major difference is one of emphasis. In the case of structural learning the search is for methods of analysis that yield competence accounts that are compatible with human cognition and behavior (e.g., with goal switching).

Perhaps the most important difference, in this regard, is that the level of representation is not fixed by some given computer language. Rather, the level and type of representation (including restrictions on the form of individual rules) is tailored to given subject populations and response measures (i.e., to atomicity assumptions). Although this requirement tends to complicate life in that there is no uniquely appropriate set of competencies associated with given problem domains, it also simplifies matters with regard to assessing individual behavior potential.

In effect, the two approaches differ mainly in emphasis. When viewed strictly within the context of "content" analysis, they are formally equivalent. When viewed from the broader perspective of behavioral science, however, they are not. The requirements of (hypothesized) cognitive universals and individual differences measurement place important constraints on competence and its representation.

Cognition: The structural/process commitment to explanation in terms of cognitive processes implies that human problem solving behavior depends on what the subject knows and has available at the time of problem solving. In part, therefore, the study of problem solving is concerned with identifying the specific processes (i.e., rules/procedures) used by subjects in solving problems. In computer simulation, for example, the identification of processes that simulate human problem-solving behavior is a central concern.

The study of cognition also is concerned with identifying more universal characteristics of the human information processor, ones that effect the way in which known structures and processes interact in problem solving. These characteristics include such things as control/executive processes, the limited capacity of humans to process information and the time typically required to encode discrete new information.

A variety of similarities and subtle but important differences exist between the structural learning theory and more traditional theories in cognitive psychology. Thus, both the structural learning theory and information processing theories in psychology are concerned with structures and processes that account for human problem-solving behavior. However, the structural learning theory is concerned with the structures and processes used by individuals (both idealized and actual) rather than with "amalgam" processes that best account for group (average) behavior. This difference is fundamental.

Equally if not more important, the structural learning theory and most information-processing theories work from opposite directions. The former emphasizes overall architecture, subject to specified boundary conditions, whereas the latter deals exclusively with nonidealized data and builds from the bottom up. At their best, the two approaches might be complementary. Thus, for example, specialized theories in contemporary information-processing psychology might be viewed as providing detailed specifications within the structural learning framework. Answers to such questions as whether certain kinds of information are stored as discrete propositions or iconically, or how subjects solve particular classes of problems, might help to flesh out the overall theoretical structure.

One should resort to direct integration of such findings, however, only with extreme caution. In the structural learning theory, structures and processes (rules) of competence refer to idealized members of given populations who perform tasks in specified, prototypic ways. These (idealized) rules serve as standards for measuring individual knowledge. There can be no guarantee that the average rules identified by standard experimental methods will be identical either to the prototypic rules of competence or to the rules of individual knowledge.

The structural approach is generally compatible with contemporary research on computer simulation of human performance; both are concerned with individual processes underlying problem solving. The structural learning theory, however, also is concerned with the problem of measuring individual differences. In addition, heavy emphasis has been given to developing a theoretical framework that also incorporates a variety of cognitive phenomena: learning, motivation, problem definition, and so forth, as well as performance.

In contrast, most computer simulation theories have emphasized performance primarily. Although programs have been devised to simulate motivation and other processes, most such programs tend to retain a performance-like character. To my knowledge, no one programming system lends itself *simultaneously* and naturally to the variety of processes that characterize man. This limitation may be due in part to the self-imposed requirement of developing working programs. Due to the complexities involved, and the sometimes undesirable constraints imposed by even the best high-level computer languages, it is often possible to get tangled in details and to lose sight of the whole. Hence, although computer implementation serves a useful and in many cases indispensible purpose, I believe that premature implementation may actually impede progress by drawing attention to peripheral issues. (The present bias in favor of prior analysis of architectural form should be clear.)

As a result of the above differences in emphasis, many simulation theories tend to mix specific competencies and cognitive universals in ways that would not be allowed in the structural learning theory. In part, this may derive from the need in computer simulation to rely on processing constraints that have been determined via standard experimental methods. This is perfectly understandable, given the lack of choice available, and in many cases may prove to be valid. Nonetheless, it leaves one open to criticism because of the possible confusion mentioned above between individual and group processes.

Furthermore, as discussed in Chapter 1, individual differences in simulation theories are largely idiosyncratic. Simulations of different individuals, even on the same problems, may share only postulated universals (e.g., means-ends analysis, Ernst & Newell, 1969). Consequently, similarities and differences in specific knowledge may be relatively difficult to detect. In principle, population-constrained competence in the structural learning theory provides a common basis for comparing individual knowledge.

Although different problem spaces (e.g., Nilsson, 1971; Newell & Simon, 1972) play a role roughly analogous to the competencies that characterize different subject populations, they do not serve the same purpose. Problem spaces deal with logical possibility not cognitive ideals. They do not, therefore, lend themselves naturally to individual differences measurement.

Individual differences: For the above, among other reasons, individual differences measurement is a relatively neglected aspect of human problem-solving, at least within the procedural and/or criterion-referenced tradition.[2] Put simply, what are needed are diagnostic methods for identifying the problem-solving processes available to individual subjects.

Traditionally, criterion-referenced testing has been applied primarily to classes of simple tasks such as adding in arithmetic or decoding in reading (e.g., Glaser, 1963). Such testing provides an overall measure of the extent to which a given class of tasks has been mastered and leads to such statements as, "On the average, he ought to get 8 out of 10 items correct" (Scandura & Durnin, in press). But, criterion-referenced testing does not specify which kinds of tasks (in the class) have been mastered and which have not.

Various extensions of criterion-referenced testing have been limited in other ways. Thus, item forms (e.g., Hively, Paterson, & Page, 1968) have been used in order to obtain more precise measures of mastery (see Chapter 9 for details). As noted by Gagne (1974), however, the use of item forms is limited to paper-and-pencil tests where the test items may all be represented in one of a finite number of different forms. They have

---

[2]One should, of course, at least acknowledge the well known and extensive body of normative research aimed at determining statistical correlates of human problem solving (e.g., Guilford, 1967; Speedie, Treffinger, & Feldhusen, 1973).

intrinsic limitations with regard to nonpaper-and-pencil applications such as job analysis. The structural approach (to testing) is not limited in this way. The direct relationship between molarity of atomic rules and sophistication of population allows for broader applicability. More is said on this point in Section 3 on educational applications.

Moreover, in applying the item forms technology to more complex tasks, learning hierarchies (e.g., Gagne, 1970) have sometimes been used to specify prerequisites (Hively *et al.*, 1968). (Note: The "complex" tasks considered have included such things as ordinary subtraction and have been relatively simple in comparison with problem domains of the sort considered in Part 2 of this book.) Criterion-referenced tests, then, are used to determine which prerequisites are and are not available to individuals (e.g., Hively *et al.*, 1968).

As pointed out previously (e.g., Scandura, 1974), however, the prerequisites identified via traditional task analysis do not include higher-level processes of the type considered in the structural learning theory. That is, the term *higher-order* is used differently in task analysis and in the structural learning theory (see Chapter 11).

The omission of higher-order rules in such analysis has been hypothesized to be a major reason why learning does not automatically progress up a learning hierarchy even after all of the identified prerequisites have been acquired. Thus, although the absence of just one prerequisite is always sufficient to eliminate transfer to a higher-level prerequisite, (lower-order) prerequisite availability is not always sufficient (e.g., Scandura, in press).

Like all criterion-referenced testing, then, individual differences measurement based on the structural learning theory involves judging behavior against predetermined standards. In the theory, however, the selection of test items is based on underlying rules (of competence) rather than on the form of the stimulus or the type of task. In addition, the structural approach has been successfully applied to higher-order (e.g., Chapters 5 and 13) as well as to lower-order task domains, and extensions of the approach can be applied even to complex problem domains whose limits are specified only implicitly (see also Chapters 2, 3, 4, and 14).

Creativity: In view of its close relationship to problem solving, I would like to comment briefly on how creativity is accounted for in the structural learning theory. In this view, creativity depends on two factors: (1) the availability of rules, particularly higher-order rules (including selection rules, problem definition rules, etc.); (2) pre-existing, possibly innate characteristics of particular individuals (i.e., capacity for processing information and processing speed).

In this regard, also consider the speculative hypothesis that the well-known distinction between convergent and divergent thinking may parallel the two factors outlined above. In par-

ticular, the ability to think convergently could vary directly
with the number and power of the higher-order rules; the ability
to think divergently could vary directly with processing capacity.

Although both factors undoubtedly enter into creative behavior, in one sense (and to some extent) the two might be
mutually exclusive. All other things being equal, for example,
those with a low processing capacity would have relatively
greater need and, therefore, over time might develop relatively
more and more powerful higher-order rules. According to the
present theory, higher-order (as well as other) rules are acquired gradually over the years as the need arises. Those with
relatively large processing capacities, given the relative ease
with which they might solve a greater diversity of problems,
could fail to develop the higher-order powers of analysis and
synthesis required for creative convergence.

Summary: Although generally compatible with contemporary
structural/process approaches to content, cognition, and individual differences, the structural learning approach to human problem solving includes a number of important extensions and, most
important, provides a new synthesis--a way of relating these
three concerns within a unified theory of human problem solving.
Equally important, the constraints, imposed on theory in any one
area by the requirements of theory in other areas, help to avoid
certain long-standing criticisms of other approaches. For example, like computer simulation, the structural learning theory
deals with the behavior of individual subjects in particular
problem-solving situations. But, it is not open to the criticism, often directed at computer simulation, to the effect that
a separate theory is required for each individual. In addition,
the theory allows for prediction as well as explanation, and it
is sufficiently precise that it has been partially mathematized
and, in part, also programmed on a computer.

Global Theories: As stressed repeatedly, the present theory is comprehensive in scope. Where time and working energy
have forced choices in its formulation, overall structure has
been selected for emphasis rather than detail, architecture
rather than bricklaying. This "structural approach" to theory
construction differs from that which has guided most work in
American psychology in that the former works largely from the
"top-down".

In late 1973, I was pleased to discover that this approach
was apparently shared to some extent by the British cyberneticist
Pask (1975). (Piaget's well-known views on structuralism, obviously, are also generally compatible but as indicated in Chapter
1, there are some important differences.) Although each of us
had been working independently for over a decade before becoming
more than vaguely aware of each other's work, the theories we
have developed share a number of important features, although,
as one might reasonably expect, the scientific languages used
and the specific mechanisms differ considerably. The first
translation into English (1974) of Landa's work in Moscow on

algorithmization in education suggests that it too is generally compatible at a global level. The emphasis here, however, is not so much with theory as with the use of algorithms as a scientific language for describing various aspects of teaching and learning. In this sense, it is a close scientific cousin to the Set/Function Language (Scandura, 1967, 1968, 1970) used to formulate a wide range of early studies on rule-governed behavior. (Many of these studies are summarized in Scandura, 1969, 1976.)

Let us consider Pask's (1975) major work in somewhat more detail. Like the present work, Pask has been as concerned with the general requirements of theory construction and verification as with specific theories and results. His book on the subject is devoted primarily to: a description of his theory of conversations, concrete realizations of this theory mostly in the area of teaching and learning, and philosophical justifications for his theory and its relationships to other theoretical work.

A proper understanding of Pask must take into account the general cybernetic and systems principles that have guided his thinking. Among other things, Pask has ignored neurophysiological processes and is concerned instead with that partial behavioral reality that falls under the rubric of awareness. On the other hand, his view of cognition transcends that of the typical cognitive psychologist. Pask's theory is concerned with processes that may go on in nonspecific processors, living and nonliving. The human being is only one of many. To quote, for example, "Cognition may occur (also) at the level of groups of people." Correspondingly, Pask tends to pass over characteristics of particular information processors, such as man, in favor of what he views as more general properties.

Given this all-pervasive concern for generality, it is surprising perhaps that Pask argues that there can be no theory of learning apart from teaching, and vice versa. There can be only a theory of learning and teaching (although Pask's conception of what may count as a learner or teacher is considerably broader than what is normally meant by these terms). Pask's theory of conversations adheres to this principle and is both dynamic and relativistic in nature. The theory is concerned primarily with the ongoing interaction between two participants, with special reference to that between a learner (student) and the environment (teacher). Such interaction always is judged relative to some predetermined conversational domain (topic), all in the context of an external observer/experimenter who may be allowed to influence the interaction indirectly by altering the environment or via a "teacher" (who effectively acts as his agent).

In the theory, Pask makes a number of important distinctions such as that between the object language L, in which the participants communicate, and the metalanguage L*, which the observer uses to instruct and communicate with the participants. The procedures, which characterize the knowledge of each parti-

cipant, also are partitioned. Level 0 (L_0) procedures bring
about relations (achieve goals) or explain them, and level
1 (L_1) procedures bring about procedures for bringing about relations, otherwise called *learning*. Pask calls classes of the
former *concepts*. The term *memory* is used to denote classes of
L_1 procedures that reproduce previously learned concepts.

In addition to these largely linguistic distinctions, the
author introduces a number of related theoretical assumptions.
For example, some classes of procedures are assumed to be incompatible in the sense that both cannot exist in the same
(human) processor. Pask's wholist-serialist distinction regarding learning styles provides the focus for considerable discussion and empirical work.

Although Pask describes several conversational domains at
length, his concern clearly is with task/conversational domains
in general. In this regard, he describes a quasi-systematic
method for constructing conversational domains with respect to
arbitrary subject matters. Step by step, Pask shows how one
can proceed from an informally understood subject matter to a
relatively precise conversational domain.

In general, conversational domains are similar to the relational nets commonly used in cognitive psychology with some
important additions. Among other things, Pask explicitly considers second-order relations (relational operators) between
relations (arcs in relational networks) and allows for the
"pruning" of redundant relations that can be derived from others.
(In Pask's terms, the others "entail" the relations.) In this
sense, conversational domains are very much like our "structures"
(cf. Section 3.3).

In general outline, the present approach and, particularly,
the theory of structural learning have much in common with that
developed by Pask. The languages used, the emphases, and the
basic mechanisms, however, are different.

1. Whereas Pask has concentrated on processor independent
procedures, the structural learning theory includes specific
mechanisms (e.g., control mechanisms, and processing limitations)
that pertain directly to human beings. As a result, critical
properties in Pask's theory apply more broadly but say less
about the behavior of individuals in particular situations. In
this same vein, empirical tests of Pask's theory utilize more
or less standard stochastic methods, whereas the structural
learning theory has evolved largely on the basis of direct deterministic tests.

2. Whereas both theories take the role of the observer into
account, and hence are relativistic theories, the emphases have
been quite different. Conversation theory emphasizes the dynamic relationship between two participants, whereas the structural learning theory initially dealt primarily with detailing
what happens at any given stage of such interaction. Current
extensions to ongoing instruction build on this detail (Chapter
14) although it is too early to say just how this work relates,

for example, to Pask's wholist-serialist distinction.

3. Pask views the distinction between higher- and lower-level procedures as a fixed, although merely convenient device. In the structural learning theory, the distinction also is one of use rather than substance, but with use dependent on a presumably universal control mechanism (something that is apparently disallowed in conversation theory).

4. Whereas both theories include prescriptions for how to construct conversational/problem domains, conversation theory gives more explicit attention to the role of language and the structural learning theory deals more specifically with performance capabilities.

To recapitulate, theories and approaches like Pask's, Landa's, and my own are concerned largely (but not necessarily exclusively) with the overall architecture of human reality. Although it tends to operate at a somewhat more global (less specific) level, Piaget's theory also is of this type. Specific mechanisms and emphases aside, these theories/approaches all reject the philosophical view in science that it is better to build from the ground up--brick by brick. Indirectly, as a result of the common acceptance (implicitly or explicitly) of this view, behavioral science research and theorizing has been directed largely toward relatively narrow problems where one has a greater probability of identifying and coping with variables that yield reliable results. (Whether the results are significant is more problematical.) In rejecting this view, structural/process theorists take a more global view. They would argue that the former approach is short-sighted; one cannot, simply for purposes of convenience, confine oneself to the "trunk", but hope to describe the "elephant".

On the other hand, it also is important to be as precise as possible and, where possible, to make contact with potentially compatible but more molecular problems and specialized theories (cf. Scandura, 1973b, 1974a). Fortunately, there appears to be a growing recognition of the importance and feasibility of developing global theories of cognition. A recent unpublished paper by Hunt, for example, makes this position explicit.[3] Hopefully, the future will bring forth greater understanding and appreciation for the potentially complementary roles of both kinds of theory and research.

2.2 RELATIONSHIPS TO OTHER PROBLEM-SOLVING RESEARCH

Obviously, if a theory is to have general rather than just parochial significance, it should provide reasonable explanations for the results of available psychological research. Preferably, such a theory also should provide a basis for generating new questions and more precise predictions than would otherwise be possible. In the case of the structural learning theory, specifically, let us ask:

[3]Earl Hunt, Imageful thought, Mimeograph, 1976.

1. Does the structural learning theory provide reasonable explanations for the results of well-known phenomena associated with psychological research on problem solving?

2. Does the theory provide a basis for explaining subject protocols obtained during the course of problem solving?

In answering these questions, our goal is not to attempt an exhaustive review or discussion of the literature. Rather, it is to illustrate by example how one might go about analyzing such research in structural learning terms and what additional insights such analyses might yield.

Early Problem-Solving Research: Consider first a general type of result common to a number of problem-solving studies. Given a problem for which all of the components of a solution (procedure) are available, some subjects succeed on the problem whereas others do not. In the case of Gagne's (1962) learning hierarchies, for example, all components are necessary conditions for solving what he calls *higher-order tasks.* However, they are not always sufficient. (Note: Gagne's higher-order rules/tasks correspond to outputs of higher-order rules, as used in this book. The latter operate on and generate other rules-- see Scandura, 1974b; Chapter 11, this book.) To the extent that memory is not a factor, explanation follows directly from the idealized theory. Those subjects who succeed can be distinguished from those who fail by the availability of appropriate higher-order rules (cf. Chapter 5). Unlike the rationales that motivated these earlier studies, notice, the structural learning theory makes it possible to identify and to independently test for the a priori presence of such higher-order rules.

In another well-known study, Luchins (1942) found, after solving a series of water jar problems using one solution procedure, that subjects strongly tended to use the same procedure on a subsequent problem even though the problem also could be solved by a simpler method. In particular, for each problem, the subjects in Luchins' study were presented with three jars (A, B, C) of varying capacities and were required to obtain a predetermined amount of liquid by pouring liquid among the three containers. The initial problems in Luchins' experiment could all be solved by a common rule: Fill Jar B, remove an amount equal to A, and then remove an amount equal to C twice. On initial problems in the series, although Luchins' data do not address the phenomenon, the subjects presumably had to derive the solution procedure in order to succeed. (It is reasonable to assume that this took place in stages, partial learning on one problem leading to more complete learning on the next.)

Once derived, however, the solution procedure could be assumed to be directly available (i.e., active) in the processor on subsequent problems. Since the procedure applied in all of the subsequent problem situations, including the one potentially solvable by a simpler rule (fill A and pour out C), the theory would predict that the former procedure would be used. According to the structural learning theory, subjects are assumed to derive new solution procedures only where some previously learned solution procedure is not available. Of course, the experimenter, or the subject, can place prior constraints on a problem (e.g., "Don't use the previous rule.") so as to require a new procedure for solution. To some extent, this may be what happened when Luchins told his subjects, "Don't be blind."

Dunker's (1945) findings regarding "functional fixedness" may be interpreted similarly. He found that use of an object or an idea in one situation made it difficult to solve later problems that required a new use of the object or idea as, for example, where use of a gimlet to bore holes in a board interfered with use of the gimlet as a hook (fastened in the board). Since all knowledge is assumed to consist of rules (a triple consisting of a domain, operator, and range), each of Dunker's "uses" (of an object or idea) corresponds, in effect, to a different rule. The operation of using a gimlet to bore a hole and then removing it is operationally distinct from using the gimlet to bore in only part way and leaving it (in the board). Similarly, the domains of applicability might differ. As in interpreting Luchins' results, then, subjects will try on new problems to use available rules (uses) first, thereby interfering with the required one.

When viewed in terms of the structural learning theory, the traditional distinction between productive and reproductive problem solving also takes a somewhat different form. It is not so much a question of insightful versus rote problem solving as it is differences in the knowledge that is available to a subject being confronted with a problem. Wertheimer's (1945) well-known problem of finding the area of a parallelogram provides an illustration. A person who did not have a readily available formula (rule) for solving the problem would be forced to figure one out. The strategy Wertheimer describes is just one such solution rule: Draw a diagram of the parallelogram; construct a perpendicular from a bottom vertex; notice that the (right) triangle obtained in this way is congruent to another whose area precisely compensates for it; superimpose one triangle on the other so as to transform the parallelogram into a rectangle whose area can be determined by the (presumably) learned rule b x h.

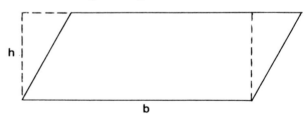

Figure 2. Finding the area of a parallelogram.

There is no question but that a person solving the problem in this way has demonstrated some degree of insight. Our form of analysis, however, suggests that this insight resides in the availability of appropriate information (e.g., a rule for changing parallelograms into rectangles, a rule for finding areas of rectangles), and appropriate higher-order rules for utilizing such knowledge to devise a solution plan and/or procedure. A possible solution plan, for example, might be to convert the parallelogram into a familiar figure with an equal area and then to find the area of the familiar figure.

In this view, reproductive problem solving while it may be "rote" is not necessarily uninsightful. Indeed, a person who knew the area formula for a parallelogram (b x h), and when to use it, would be foolish not to do so--unless, of course, the problem goal involved something more than just finding the area (e.g., if the subject was required to solve the problem using "first" principles only).

The creative restructuring of a problem (Wertheimer, 1945), as evidenced for example in Maier's (1930) hatrack problem, also can easily be interpreted in structural learning terms. (In artificial intelligence, restructuring a problem corresponds to using a different problem space to represent the problem.) In Maier's (1930) problem, the subject's goal is to construct an object from which an overcoat can be hung, given two boards and a C-clamp. Most subjects begin by attempting to use the sticks to make an inverted T or an inverted V. Such efforts invariably fail. According to Greeno (1973), critical insight into the problem is achieved when the subject realizes, or is told with a "hint" (Burke, Maier, & Hoffman, 1966) that the ceiling can be used in supporting the desired structure. "This idea provides a new interpretation of the problem, and it is usually quite easy for the subject to complete the construction after this insight is achieved" (p. 120).

A structural learning analysis would be generally compatible with the above but potentially more specific. That is, restructuring takes place because new information (e.g., the hint) enters active memory. This new information not only adds to but alters what is already there, effectively redefining the given problem (i.e., the information adds a new relation to those defining the given goal situation). In particular, in Maier's problem the given was broadened to include the ceiling as well as the two sticks and the clamp. Once redefined in this way, the problem more readily yielded to the knowledge available to the subjects. (Maier's hint played a role quite analagous to Luchins' "Don't be blind.")

Due largely to uncertainties as to exactly what the subjects learned, these analyses are only schematic in form. This is unavoidable in view of the nonidealized conditions under which the experiments were run. Two important points should be stressed, however.

1. The results of a significant number of earlier problem-

solving studies can be explained simply in terms of factors
(e.g., availability of higher-order rules) that are critical in
the structural learning theory.

2. The deterministic support reported in this book (and in
earlier research reports on rule learning, e.g., Scandura, 1969,
1976) for some of these factors necessarily implies their probabilistic applicability under nonidealized conditions--without
field testing (cf. Chapters 1, 5, and 11). To the extent, therefore, that these same factors play a crucial role, further
studies (along these lines) would appear to have limited value
in generating basically new information. (They could, of course,
tend to increase confidence in the rationale underlying these
two points.)

Recent Problem-Solving Research: In a more recent experiment (Mayer, reported in Greeno, 1974), subjects were required
to learn how to perform steps in a calculation in a fixed order
to solve problems involving binomial probabilities. Two major
kinds of steps were involved: (1) identifying values of variables in computational formulas from the text of a problem, and
(2) computational steps involving factorials, multiplying
numbers, etc.

Prior to learning the criterion task, subjects were given
one of two kinds of pretraining. One group of subjects was provided with general, conceptual background. Explanations were
given as to the nature of trials, outcomes, probabilities of
events, etc. The other group of subjects was trained directly
on the binomial probability formula. The various steps in writing out the formula were treated as items in a serial list.

After pretraining, the subjects were required to learn to
compute binomial probabilities, with training given by a method
of serial anticipation. Mayer found that the identification
steps were easier for those subjects given general conceptual
training, whereas the reverse was true for the computational
steps. Those subjects trained on the formula made an average
of only 3.8 errors on the computational steps before criterion,
whereas those trained on the concepts had a mean error rate of
17.2. On the identification steps, the corresponding means were
7.0 and 5.2. Parallel differences between discovery and expository learning have been studied by Egan (in Greeno, 1974) with
similar results.

These results are more situation specific, but otherwise
compatible, with those obtained by Scandura during the early-
mid-1960s in a series of studies on the problem-solving effects
of timing and meaningfulness of expository and discovery instruction (e.g., 1962, 1963, 1964a, 1964b, 1966).

Greeno (1973) interpreted these results in terms of the
degree to which knowledge is "internally" and "externally" connected. Thus, it was proposed that near transfer was enhanced
by direct expository training because the latter favors internal

connectedness. Similarly, far transfer purportedly was enhanced by conceptual and discovery training because this type of training increases external connectedness. This explanation is simple and intuitively appealing. (Although the critical variable of timing, or what the learner knows at the time new information is presented, was not considered in the Mayer and Egan studies, the general "rule of thumb" proposed as an explanation is otherwise generally compatible with the interpretation proposed in my earlier studies.)

As one might expect, these results also follow directly from the structural learning theory. In fact, interpreting many of the results requires only reference to the solution rules involved. For example, in the Mayer study, the formula subjects were effectively pretrained on the computational portion of a solution rule for the criterion task (i.e., the computation of binomial probabilities given the appropriate inputs). During criterion learning, all the subjects had to do was to learn how to identify (values of) variables and to use these appropriately as inputs on the computational portion of the task.

The results favoring the conceptual group on the identification portion of the task follow similarly. In this case, it is sufficient to point out that the pretraining essentially involved learning how to distinguish between exemplars of needed concepts and nonexemplars (e.g., distinguishing between a trial and something that is not). Although the authors' procedures were not sufficiently detailed to be certain, it seems that at least some of the training was more or less directly related to the task of identifying values of variables in given problem statements (i.e., elements in the domain of a solution rule).

Although they represent an important advance over many earlier studies in the degree of emphasis on task variables, a major limitation of such experiments (including my own) is that the tasks involved, and in particular the competencies necessary and sufficient for successful performance, are not fully specified. Compare the above with the degree of rigor required, for example, in the production systems of Newell and Simon (1972) and the rule competencies of Part 2, or with the tasks and underlying competencies in the experiments reported in Parts 3, 4, and 5.

Given this relative lack of precision, which obtains equally if not more so in the Maier and Luchins' studies above, it is impossible to provide a completely definitive interpretation of the above studies in structural learning terms. In effect, much of power and potential precision of prior competence analysis goes unused in studies of this type. As we have seen, however, rigorous structural analysis extracts a methodological price. It is far easier methodologically, although not as definitive empirically, to rely on informal task analyses in conducting problem solving research. The approach to be prefer-

red will necessarily depend on what one is trying to do. If one
is satisfied with normative information about problem solving,
then more definitive structural analyses may be unnecessary
(although the dangers of overgeneralization will always be
present). On the other hand, if one wants generalizable information about what individuals will and will not do on specific
problems (in arbitrarily large domains), then there would seem
to be no viable alternative to more rigorous structural analysis
(or some behavioral equivalent).

The problems of task analysis are relatively straightforward in simpler concept (e.g., Bruner, Goodnow, & Austin, 1956)
and discrimination (e.g., Levine, 1966) learning studies. Hence,
it is not surprising that they have long been favored by psychologists. Since such tasks are of a rather special type, however,
psychologists have been wary in interpreting experimental results
not to overgeneralize. Accordingly, theories in the area have
tended to be of a rather restrictive nature and often confound
specific task features with cognitive phenomena having more
general significance. Such confounding has, on occasion, obscured more general implications. It is shown in Scandura
(1973b), for example, that the "probe" technique developed by
Levine (1966) is a special case of the more general structural
approach to "assessing behavior potential" (cf., Scandura, 1964b,
1971c, 1973b; and Chapters 8 and 9, this book).

Another source of difficulty involving task structure derives from the fact that what are often called *rules*, formulas,
and algorithms do not necessarily refer to what we have in mind
in using the term *rule*. In the sense used here, *rules* refer to
procedures (algorithms) that may operate on inputs and generate
outputs (or that may themselves be operated on). Thus, for example, the rules referred to by Wason and Johnson-Laird (1972,
Chapter 10) are descriptions of the outputs of rules in our
sense. The rules (in our sense) involved in the Wason and
Johnson-Laird studies were not made explicit. The results, correspondingly, were more ambiguous than they might have been if
more definitive structural analysis had been used.

In this regard, I should emphasize that, although there
are relationships between the structural methods of "task analysis" used in Chapters 3, 4, and 11, for example, and those described by Gagne (1970), there also are important theoretical
differences. Among other things, rules that are higher in a
hierarchy obtained via traditional task analysis are not higher-
order rules in the sense described here. They correspond more
directly to the outputs of such rules (see Chapter 11, this book;
also Scandura, 1973a).

Consider next a series of as yet unpublished studies by
Morris and Resnick, Mulholland, and Pellegrino and Schadler at
the University of Pittsburgh (Resnick & Glaser, 1976). In
studying a Wertheimer type parallelogram task (see above),

Morris and Resnick found that of 24 children trained on component routines (rules) of a solution rule, 5 succeeded spontaneously and rather quickly. (Notice that this result is consistent with the pretest results of Experiment I of Scandura, 1974a, reported in Chapter 5.) All of the others attempted to use an inapplicable procedure. When told, "That's wrong, you can't do that," 7 children restarted the problem from scratch (indicated by clearing blocks that were to be used) and succeeded. The other 12 persisted on the same general track and failed.

According to the structural learning theory, what I think happened here is as follows:

1. Five children not only knew but had immediately available a higher-order rule (either of the rule derivation or planning variety) and used it. This hypothesis could be checked, as in Experiments III and IV of Chapter 5, by teaching the subjects the components needed to solve a new (but parallel) problem and asking them to solve the problem. In order to provide a valid test, of course, both the original and the new problem would have to be analytically solvable via the same higher-order rule.

2. The 7 children who succeeded on the second try apparently had the wrong (rectangle) rule available and used it (as would be predicted via goal-switching principles). In addition, however, they seemed to know the higher-order rule as well. When the incorrect solution rule was eliminated, goal switching led to the correct solution. Checking this interpretation, of course, would be impossible without detailed identification of the relevant and available rules and specification of the training conditions. It would appear, however, that applying a known rule inappropriately might be induced by context just as in the classic Luchin's (1942) experiments.

3. The 12 subjects who persisted with the incorrect procedure apparently did not know and could not derive an appropriate higher-order rule.

The study by Mulholland is interesting because it tends to reinforce the interpretation given in 2 above. Twelve of 24 subjects were given both a rectangle problem (with blocks) and a parallelogram problem. The others were given an "invention" task where only a parallelogram was presented. In the joint presentation, the theory would predict that the subjects who knew or learned the rectangle rule, based on blocks, might apply it inappropriately on the parallelogram problem. They could fail even where they might otherwise be able to derive an appropriate solution rule. Subjects in the single presentation condition, on the other hand, would succeed just to the extent that they had available appropriate higher-order rules. As the structural learning theory would predict, Mulholland found that the problems were solved by 2 and 6, respectively, of the 12 subjects in each group. Availability of the blocks apparently induced many of the subjects to use a filling-in-with-blocks

procedure (one of the available components of the other experiment) that was inappropriate for finding the area of the parallelogram.

The study by Pellegrino and Schadler adds another dimension
to the explanation. Again, the parallelogram task was used but
this time, the experimenters confronted the children with what
effectively were a pair of higher-level goals. First, the
children were asked what they thought the experimenter wanted
them to do (a problem definition subgoal); next, they were asked
how they would do it (a higher-level solution rule/plan goal);
finally, they were allowed to actually solve the problem.

In addition to relieving the subjects of having to have
available a basic (higher-order) problem definition rule (cf.
Chapters 2 and 6), this process of introducing a sequence of
higher- and lower-order goals effected a substantial reduction
in memory load in accordance with the discussion in Chapter 2.
The subjects did not, for example, have to remember the initial
problem goal while trying to figure out how to solve the problem.
Under these "look-ahead" conditions, therefore, it is not surprising that 14 of 16 subjects solved the problem, whereas only
6 succeeded of the 16 who were simply asked to solve the problem.

These and other studies out of the same laboratory (e.g.,
Holzman, Glaser, & Pellegrino, 1976) are interesting in several
respects. First, although the authors apparently did not recognize the relationships to our earlier work on rule learning
(e.g., Scandura, 1968, 1969) and problem solving (e.g., Scandura,
1971c, 1973b, 1974a), they too seem to have adopted a variant of
the "memory-free" paradigm. In this paradigm, subjects were
trained on (lower-order) components (rules) of problem solution
rules prior to testing on the problems. Also, similarly, the
major goal was to see if the subjects could "invent" a way
(i.e., assemble or compose the components) to solve the problems. In addition, the sequence of "look-ahead" conditions used
in the Pellegrino and Schadler study directly parallels the
order of occurrence of higher- and lower-level goals predicted
by the postulated goal-switching mechanism.

One major difference between their studies and ours is that
they did not identify or teach higher-order rules explicitly.
(Note: All of the studies reported by Resnick and Glaser (1976)
appear to involve rule composition in one form or another.) As
noted, however, their introduction of hints, instruction and
modified task environments often served a related role. Another
difference is that they did not attempt to control for memory
load. When these two factors (higher-order rules and memory
load) are taken into account, the results of the reported studies
are easily explained in terms of the structural learning theory.

Suggestions for Research: In view of the relative ease with
which the above studies can be explained and predicted, together
with the basic and in some cases deterministically supported

principles on which these explanations and predictions are based, future research might well be directed toward establishing the empirical limits of the structural learning theory, and where possible toward refining and extending it. Although the full potential of the theory has yet to be determined empirically, many possibilities appear to exist for generating problem-solving research. The research reported in this book barely begins to tap the potential of (quasi-systematic) methods for analyzing arbitrary problem domains, distinctions between specific higher- and lower-order knowledge (rules), universal principles of cognitive control, specific models for computing memory loads, methods for assessing individual knowledge, etc. The problem is not one of being able to generate new behavioral predictions but of deciding which of the many possibilities are worth testing.

In the case of the Mayer and Greeno (1972) study, for example, the results appear to follow directly from an analysis of what was taught. To the extent that content is a primary variable in future studies, therefore, more detailed structural analysis would seem to be almost mandatory.

In the studies reported by Resnick and Glaser, specific content (lower-order rules) is held more nearly constant by prior training, much as in our research. Here, the major underlying variables appear to involve unspecified higher-order rules and memory loads (which correspond to incidental variables in the sense of Chapter 1). Correspondingly, future research ought to give more explicit attention to the identification, training and/or testing of higher-order rules and to the role of memory load.

Sociological, Philosophical, and Methodological Comments: It is well-known that behavioral science, at least in the contemporary American context, tends to progress within informal circles determined by a variety of sociological, philosophical, and methodological factors. In the pluralistic American Society various orientations compete for attention with varying degrees of success based largely, but not exclusively, on intrinsic scientific worth. Normally, in fact, new developments, particularly of a theoretical or methodological nature, are accepted within a given circle only when they are either developed or rediscovered from within. Thus, for example, the pioneering work of Newell, Shaw, and Simon (1958) was not accepted for years by many experimental psychologists. It was only after experimentalists belatedly discovered that people have minds and really do think, together with continuing attempts by computer simulation researchers to incorporate the results of ongoing psychological research in their work, that an uneasy coalition began to form. In any case, beginning somewhere around 1970, the simulation approach came to be accepted by members of the experimental community as a viable (if not preferred) way to study cognitive processes. Even more important, younger scientists are now beginning to emerge with training in both areas. Other scientific orientations have tended to maintain their independence, for example, the operant conditioning and behavior modification movement under the titular leadership of B. F. Skinner.

Structural/cybernetic/systems approaches to complex human behavior have developed more slowly on the local scene (although not necessarily internationally). They presently share a position that is intermediate between the above two extremes. On the one hand, for example, the present approach to structural learning shares much in common with other approaches to cognitive science. On the other hand, much of its motivation derives from an attempt to understand overall interrelationships. Given the emphasis on "top-down" analysis, structural learning deals with a number of concerns that have not been seriously considered in cognitive science (cognitive psychology and artificial intelligence). This is particularly true of those concerns involving interrelationships among the various fields that are relevant to the study of teaching and learning. (In this sense, the field of structural learning has much in common with instructional science, at least those parts of it that deal with basic issues in the study of teaching and learning within the structural/process tradition. Its primary goal is to add to a store of fundamental knowledge, that both makes contact with basic psychological phenomena and upon which more pragmatic, engineering technologies in instructional design may be based.)

In view of the more prescribed concerns of much of the work in cognitive science, it is not surprising that the general significance of much of the research in structural learning has not always been understood. Although reference has frequently been made in the literature to structural learning research, for example, as often as not the references have been made in a context that obscures much of what it has to offer. As basic concepts are gradually rediscovered this could change. Thus, for example, most of the recent studies reviewed above were formulated after our own directly related research had been reported at numerous professional meetings, circulated and distributed as technical reports, and published in the scientific literature. Yet, the significance of this research was apparently not appreciated at the time and only recently have some experimental psychologists begun to build on our earlier findings.

Nonetheless, fundamental differences of opinion still exist. Let me try to clarify what seem to be some of the major issues. The comments below deal primarily with views that have been expressed to me by a number of former S-R psychologists who have recently turned their attention to the study of human cognition.

Although arguments have been either lacking, or rest on basic misunderstandings, some have suggested that the structural learning theory is either too abstract, and thereby presumably not applicable to "real" psychology, or that it presents an overly simplistic view of human behavior. Ironically, some of these same individuals have commented on the "interesting and instructive" empirical research (that has been stimulated directly by the structural learning theory), and/or the applicability of the research findings to education. What seems to bother such critics most, apparently, is that in formulating the structural learning theory sufficient attention was not given to traditional theories and data. The latter criticism is true in the sense that most of our empirical research (experimental and otherwise) has been designed primarily to determine the adequacy of the structural learning theory itself, rather than to contrast it with alternative theories (see Chapter 5 for a major exception). In large part this has been unavoidable because alternative theories (e.g., of problem solving) simply have not dealt with many of the issues with which my collaborators and I have been concerned (e.g., individual differences measurement). Relative to our concerns, the alternative theories have been either incomplete and/or unnecessarily restrictive. For example, consider the proposition that discovery and/or propositional learning leads to "external connectedness" and expository and/or algorithmic learning, to "internal connectedness". Although generally true in many cases, the hypothesis itself is imprecise and counterexamples are easy to find. More to the point, why should one take such a proposition seriously when similar theories had years before been considered, and later rejected as unsatisfactory--and, especially when alternatives exist (including the structural learning theory) that are both broader in scope and more precise?

Regretably, some investigators of the aforementioned persuasion have even suggested in the literature a number of purportedly open questions (e.g., the "invention" problem, the need for performance test theories, indefinite goals) and proposed, at best, incomplete resolutions, completely ignoring the fact that the phenomena appears to find, or have found, easy resolution within the structural learning theory. In some cases, rather extensive and relatively definitive empirical research has been completely overlooked.

A major part of the problem, I believe, derives from basically different views as to what constitutes the goal of our science. Like the blind men and the elephant, each of us sees something slightly different; these differences are magnified in the scientific realm by theoretical orientation. But, then, it would seem that these issues ought to be dealt with fully and openly in the scientific literature. To withdraw into the safe confines of established tradition, as we often do, may make one feel secure but it does not settle the really difficult and interesting issues, and may retard progress. [4]

[4] I hope that the discussion here may help to initiate dialogue and to break down artificial barriers between cognitive psychology, artificial intelligence, and structural learning (including instructional science). In my capacity as co-editor of the recently revamped *Journal of Structural Learning,* I plan to provide a convenient outlet for such dialogue.

Perhaps the most pervasive difference between structural learning and cognitive psychology derives from the way we are attacking the problem, from the top-down versus from the bottom-up--architecture versus bricklaying. I have commented on this issue in Chapter 1, earlier in this Section, and elsewhere in this book. In the present context, I would like to make one further point. With some notable exceptions, and in spite of serious criticisms of the approach (e.g., Kuhn, 1962), most experimental/cognitive psychologists still seem committed to the view that the primary role of experiments is to distinguish among competing theories. The idea, presumably, is to have everybody join in the game playfully contrasting in a variety of contexts whatever theories the game makers happen to propose.

The fact that many of the theories are extremely narrow in scope and could not possibly be true in the broader context of behavioral reality dissuades few adherents. The "critical" experiments go on, the theories are gradually modified, and sometimes they even improve. This is called progress. (Even when things get hopelessly complicated, as with the Markov models of mathematical psychology, this is still called progress. After all, it is reasoned, we could not possibly have known the limitations of such theories until we pushed them as far as we could go.)

I am amused by such contentions. Why is it that proponents of such theories rarely subject them to the "grandmother test". That is, describe the essentials of the theory in very simple terms to a naive, but wise and otherwise intelligent nonpsychologist (no correlation intended) and ask her whether she can come up with a counterexample. It is amazing how many psychological theories can be shot down in this way. More interestingly, the theories that most often fail the grandmother test are the highly restricted theories that say a lot about nothing of interest to grandmother.

Clearly, I am exaggerating just a bit. But, the argument illustrates an important, and basic difference in viewpoint. Structural learning adherants too want a theory that is precise, and that lends itself to falsification. A growing number of us have been working in that direction for well over a decade now, and the reader will have to judge whether the progress that has been made to date warrants further development of the approach. First and foremost, however, we want a theory that makes sense to grandmother. If it does not have a serious chance of being correct in the broad compass of complex human behavior, then in our opinion it is not worth pursuing.

The fact that many behaviorists failed in their early attempts at synthesis (Hull is often cited in this connection) gives testimony to the dangers of pursuing a theoretical policy that seeks to build a grand design from the bottom up. Having become disillusioned by these early failures, many contemporary

academic psychologists have responded by lowering their theoretical aspirations. I am not sure that that is where the problem
is. In spite of the so-called paradigm shift to information
processing, perhaps even because of it, it appears that many are
still trying to lay bricks (i.e., to aggregate a theory without
first having an adequate, integrating conceptual framework).
To be sure, a cognitive point of view has been adopted but few
seem to have questioned the basic approach, in which the emphasis
is placed on theories of limited scope, with little attention
to global requirements. Hopefully, the future will see more of
the bricklaying tied together with a better developed architecture. In spite of the differences, they are complementary in
principle and potentially have much to contribute to one another.

A more specific problem derives from the commitment in the
structural learning theory toward a general method for identifying competence underlying *arbitrary* problem domains. The fact
that we have analyzed some problem domains (e.g., Chapters 3 and
4) apparently rests well with some potential critics. But, some
of the same critics become unhappy when we introduce very simple
rules, or rules in the abstract *(because in principle we know
how to find them in any specific case)*, for example, to talk
about cognitive universals (e.g., control mechanisms) or individual differences measurement. In this case, the critics try to
argue that the theory is too abstract, or even vacuous. Although
most such critics recognize the difficulties inherent in generalizing experimental results across different content domains
(this is rarely referred to in the literature but nonetheless
is part of the scientific lore), most apparently are unable, or
unwilling, to come to grips with the problem. A major reason
for this failure, in my opinion, is that there is no way in
which this can be done without altering fundamentally certain
aspects of a research methodology (see Chapter 1) which has become almost sacrosanct (e.g., by focusing attention on idealized,
rather than average, competence).

Another major problem derives from the, I believe, false
hope that we can ever fully learn how subjects *really* solve
problems. As argued throughout this book, I believe that we
can only understand complex human behavior *relative* to some a
priori standard (i.e., relative to a competence account of a
problem domain that prespecifies the effective environment, including the level of observable behavioral detail). (In this
context, please bear in mind that a problem domain is not the
same as a problem space as the term is used in artificial intelligence, e.g., Newell & Simon, 1972.) As showed in Chapter 2
(also see Scandura, 1968, 1970, 1973b, Chapter 8), for example,
subjects may attack problems in a given domain in any number of
equivalent ways, and insofar as success or failure (or any other
predetermined behavior criterion) is concerned one will not be
able to tell the difference. Thus, subjects may use only (parts
of the) competence rules associated with the problem domain, or
they may use unidentified, though computationally equivalent,

ones. In either case, the observer will not be able to tell the
difference by testing the subject on problems within the domain
(i.e., that portion thereof that the rules account for).

In order to distinguish among behaviorally equivalent rule
accounts one must either introduce test problems, that lie outside the original domain, and/or introduce more exacting response measures (e.g., latency). These two possibilities are
equivalent in the sense that they both amount to redefining the
effective problem domain (see Chapter 2, Section 5). Generating
a solution to a problem within given (e.g., predicted) time
limits, for example, is behaviorally distinct from generating a
solution irrespective of time. Exactly the same type of redefinition is involved in placing constraints on the kinds of
solutions that are acceptable. In proving *existence theorems*
in mathematics, for example, instead of allowing any proof that
a postulated entity must exist, one might require a proof that
actually shows how to construct one (see Kleene, 1967, pp.
191-198 for a discussion of axiomatic versus intuitive, construc-
tivist thinking in mathematics). In this context, what Greeno
(1976) calls "indefinite goals in well-structured problems"
basically amounts to allowing structural learning type goals
(i.e., criteria which may be satisfied by any number of possible
solutions, not just one as in existing state-space theories of
problem solving, see Banerji, 1974). This question of indefinite
goals was dealt with fairly extensively and related to nondeterministic theorizing in Scandura (1973b, especially Chapter 8;
also see Chapter 2, Section 4.2, *Rule Selection*).

The above observations also are relevant in interpreting
the results of studies in which prior knowledge is manipulated.
In this case, there are two basic ways one might go. First, one
can build in part of the relevant knowledge (e.g., lower-order
component rules as in the studies reported by Resnick and Glaser,
1976) and determine the (incidental) conditions under which
various types of subjects are able to solve corresponding problems (e.g., by assembling the components). In this case, the
presence or absence of the manipulated rules are structural
variables in the sense of Chapter 1. The incidental/observa-
tional variables include the other experimental conditions (e.g.,
hints pertaining to higher-order rules), together with deviations from the ideal due to generative inadequacies in the
manipulated rules and/or their relative unavailability to the
subjects at the time of testing.

Recall from the discussion in Chapter 1 (also see Chapter
7) that incidental variables serve to fill the "gap" between
idealized conditions, where structural variables alone would
fully account for the data, and the nonidealized conditions
under which data have been collected. Moreover, recall that in
order to provide a useful and efficient basis for generalization
to new situations, these incidental variables should be kept as
basic and small in number as possible. In this regard, notice
that the incidental variables introduced in the studies reported

by Resnick and Glaser are largely symptomatic of the more fundamental variables mentioned above, namely processing capacity and the availability of higher-order rules (i.e., assuming goal switching control).

Second, after pretraining (e.g., on A → B and B → C rules), as in the studies reported in Chapters 5 and 6, one can use new problems from the domain (e.g., A-B-C problems) for pretest purposes only. Thus, after building in part of the knowledge necessary for dealing with problems in a given domain only the subjects who fail on the critical pretest problems are retained in the experiment proper. These failure subjects either are trained or not trained on the missing knowledge (usually but not necessarily of the higher-order variety). This experimental paradigm makes it possible either to study interactions among rules (e.g., as in the control mechanism studies of Chapters 5 and 6) and/or to determine the behavioral adequacy of (usually higher-order) rules identified as a result of applying structural analysis to more complex problem domains (e.g., as in Chapters 11 and 13). Subjects who succeed on the critical pretest problems presumably do so because they have learned some behavioral equivalent of the missing knowledge. Their data must be treated as in the first paradigm (discussed above).

To the extent that the originally missing knowledge (e.g., a postulated higher-order rule) fails to account for the posttest data (of the pretest failure subjects), and just to that extent, will it be possible to distinguish (within the given problem domain) between that (missing) knowledge and whatever extra-domain knowledge the pretest-successful subjects brought to bear. To demonstrate such distinctions where the identified (missing) knowledge is adequate, as noted above, one must effectively redefine the problem domain, either by changing the criteria for success (e.g., by including latency or other process considerations) or by introducing extra-domain problems. Consider, for example, the "A → B, B → C, then A-B-C" paradigm. The subjects who are successful on the A-B-C pretest may simply know and have available a higher-order composition rule of sufficient generality, comparable to the higher-order rule introduced in Experiment I of Chapter 5. Alternatively, they may be able to generalize a known composition rule so as to incorporate in its domain the kinds of A → B, B → C component rules used. The simpler the component rules, presumably, the more likely is a subject to know a higher-order composition rule which includes them in its domain. Moreover, all other things being equal (e.g., in the absence of extreme precautions to insure that processing capacity is not exceeded), the simpler the component rules and the more sophisticated the subject population, the more likely would it be that a subject could operate successfully at a higher-level of derivation (see Chapter 14) and thereby succeed on the A-B-C pretest.

One might argue that the above formulation always gives one

a way out whenever data deviate from theoretical predictions. This is true, however, only in the sense that the statement is true of any theory. Latencies aside (admittedly, we have reported little research in this regard; however, see Scandura, 1973b, Chapter 8), the structural learning theory allows predictions that are far more precise, and hence easier to reject, than the *normative* theories of complex human behavior with which it must compete.

The important point is that the "way out" is natural and consistent with intuition. Whatever precautions are taken, the possibility always exists that a subject may not perform as he is expected to--it is impossible to guarantee that unidentified or extraneous knowledge will not enter into a situation. Indeed, the primary rationale for using novel tasks in cognitive research is to minimize this possibility. It is relatively easy to accomplish such exclusion, via prior analysis, with regard to lower-order competencies, because of their typically content-specific nature. This is relatively more difficult, however, with higher-order competencies, because they tend to cross content boundaries.

The impossibility of a priori elimination of extraneous knowledge is directly analogous to the situation regarding forces in classical physics. Thus, in any new environment, it is impossible to know beforehand that all of the forces involved have been identified, especially where the environment may involve unfamiliar forces. Nonetheless, within the realm of Newtonian physics no one would call the force law $F = ma$, or the parallelogram law for combining forces, vacuous just because some unidentified force turns out to influence an empirical result. The critical test comes later. Does the theory correctly predict what will happen after the force has been identified (from observations of mass (m) and acceleration (a)) and preferably manipulated independently in a new experiment (e.g., compare Scandura, 1964b, and 1966)?

In the present case, individual knowledge is determined via testing relative to rules of competence (Chapter 2, Section 5). The latter in turn are defined in terms of finite samples of (observable) problems (Chapter 2, Section 2).

Concept Identification in Children: Related questions have arisen in other lines of research. For illustrative purposes consider children's hypothesis-testing behavior in concept identification (CI) problems. For example, it is well documented that five-year-old children, unlike older children, perform poorly on traditional CI problems as well as on modified and simplified CI tasks--in particular, on the two-trial CI task (Huttenlocher, 1964). Perhaps five-year-olds have not acquired the logical operations to infer solutions on the basis of stimulus and feedback information. Alternatively, it is possible that five-year-olds do possess the necessary inferential competence, but that they are unable to use it effectively, due to information-processing constraints such as memory overload or exclusive attention to a preferred stimulus dimension (e.g.,

Johnson, Warner, & Silleroy, 1971; Scholnick, 1970).

Toppino (1974) employed an extremely simple one-trial CI task and used materials that varied on only one dimension (e.g., geometric form) and thereby minimized the effects of memory load and dimensional preference respectively. Experimental procedures were adapted from Huttenlocher's (1964) two-trial CI task. On each problem, the subject was told that the experimenter was thinking about one of two specified pictures or dimension values (e.g., triangle or circle) and that the subject had to figure out which one (the experimenter was thinking about). The experimenter presented a stimulus that contained either one dimension value or two dimension values (e.g., only a triangle or a triangle and a square). In the latter case, one of the values (i.e., the square) was irrelevant. Before the subject was asked to guess which picture the experimenter was thinking about (on each trial), the subject was told that the stimulus did (positive feedback information) or did not (negative feedback information) contain the attribute/dimension value the experimenter was thinking about.

When the one-attribute stimuli were employed, five-year-olds performed nearly perfectly in both conditions of information feedback, indicating that they do possess at least minimal inferential competence. However, the addition of a second (and irrelevant) attribute to the stimuli seriously impaired performance. The obvious next question is why the addition of an irrelevant attribute should impair performance. The added attribute may simply increase the memory load to a point beyond the childrens' processing capacity. However, an alternative possibility is that many children have not acquired the logical competence to utilize irrelevant information appropriately. Unfortunately, the competencies (e.g., rules) required for utilizing various forms of logical information in CI tasks have never been specified in sufficient detail to allow an empirical test of the above question. Detailed structural analysis (e.g., Scandura, 1974b) might be useful in this regard.

Problem-Solving Protocols: As noted in a previous section, one can never be sure whether subjects actually solve problems in given domains as hypothesized. In principle, it is always possible to devise more than one competence account/theory (e.g., rule) that generates behaviorally-equivalent predictions with respect to any given problem domain. In addition to testing on extra-domain problems, finer (but never complete) distinctions among theories may be made by redefining the observables/problem-solutions (and, in turn, the corresponding problem domains). Thus, for example, some rules may be distinguished because the solutions they generate satisfy particular additional criteria (e.g., consider solutions that consist of axiomatic, mathematical proofs that merely demonstrate the existence of postulated entities versus proofs that are intuitionist, and which show in addition how to actually construct such entities.

Other rules may be distinguished because different latencies are associated with the solutions they generate. Introducing latencies is especially important in distinguishing between
rules used by unskilled performers and more efficient rules used
by skilled practitioners. Research on the arithmetic processes
used by children, by Groen and his associates (e.g., Suppes &
Groen, 1967; Groen, 1967), is generally compatible with this
view. Very little of the data reported in this book, however,
deals with skilled performance so further discussion here seems
inappropriate. (For details, see Scandura, 1973b, Chapter 8.)

Although we can never know (as behavioral scientists) exactly what processes are used in solving problems, it clearly
is possible to obtain more definitive information than success
or failure. Moreover, as demonstrated over the years by Newell
and Simon (1972) and their associates, verbal protocols, generated by subjects during the course of problem solving, often
provide a useful basis for evaluating theories of complex human
performance.

Granting, then, that the results of many problem-solving
experiments can be interpreted within the structural learning
theory, questions remain as to the theory's adequacy as a means
of accounting for more detail concerning the course of problem
solving--for example, accounting for problem-solving protocols.
In its strongest sense, this requirement is more stringent than
in most experimental studies in that it requires numerous con-
tacts during the course of each problem episode between the theory and experimental fact. For example, although some degree
of protocol viability is inherent in our Chapter 3 analyses of
geometry construction problems, providing an explicit theoretical account of the actual steps taken by an individual in problem solving is considerably more demanding.

Consider the following problem and its related protocol.
The problem is to "circumscribe a circle about a given triangle
using straight-edge and compass." The (edited) protocol goes
as follows:

What does this mean? Ah yes, we have a certain tri-
angle--and we want to construct a circle that goes through
the three vertices of the triangle. What should I do
first? ... If I knew the center of the circle it would be
easy. Let me see (if I can find the center). How can I
do this? Let's see, the center is equidistant (from the
three vertices of the triangle). I don't know (a procedure) off-hand. But perhaps I can figure it out.

(What would happen) if I bisected two of the angles?
... The bisectors would meet (at a point). Let's try it.
Too bad! The intersection isn't (necessarily) equidistant
(from the three vertices).

What else can I do? Let's see--I know (how to find)
the locus of points equidistant from two points. So! I

can do this twice (each time with a different pair of vertices). Yes, that might work. Good! (I have the center.)
Now I need to construct the circle. That's easy. I can measure the distance from the center to one of the vertices and then I can use that distance as a radius to construct the circle. (The subject carries out the construction and solves the problem.)

Without attempting to detail the underlying competence, and placing the emphasis on the postulated control mechanism, this particular protocol might be explained in structural learning terms as follows. When confronted with the problem statement and asked to solve the problem, the subject apparently interpreted the task as a series of subproblems: (1) Find a representation of the problem (i.e., identify the given, the goal, and any information about the solution) and then (2) solve the problem so defined. (This method of breaking a problem down into subproblems appears to be broadly applicable and undoubtedly is learned very early. See Chapters 2 and 6: The presentation of almost any problem statement together with the direction "solve the problem" is almost universally interpreted to mean: "First interpret the statement, i.e., identify the problem involved, and then solve the problem.")

Once broken down in this way, according to the theory, control went to the first subproblem, where the stimulus is the statement and the goal is to understand the statement. As noted in Chapter 2, Section 4.1 *(Problem Definition)*, just what constitutes understanding a problem statement depends to a great extent on the individual subject and particularly on his familiarity with the kinds of problems involved. The protocol subject, however, seems to adequately understand the problem. For one thing, he seems to know what triangles and circles are, that the term circumscribed refers to the vertices of the triangle, and the necessary semantic grammar. More generally, the subject appears to have available a learned rule that might be used to interpret similar statements. (It is beyond the scope of this analysis to get into the linguistic intricacies involved but it seems reasonable to suppose that "question-and-answer" analyses such as that of Winograd [1972] and Schank [1973] might be adapted for these purposes.) Let us represent the problem so identified by (S_o, G).

Once understood, control went to the problem itself. In this case, the subject appeared to break problem (S_o, G) into the following pair of subproblems:

1. Find the center of the goal circle (which the subject notes is equidistant from the three triangle vertices), denoted (S_o, G_1).

2. Construct the circumscribing circle, denoted $(f(S_o), G)$, where $f(S_o)$ is the stimulus resulting from the solution of subproblem (S_o, G_1). (In actuality, Subproblem 2 is not fully defined until after the first has been solved.)

The subject apparently does not know a procedure for solving the first subproblem off-hand, so control shifts to the higher-level goal of deriving one. The next statement in the protocol suggests that a rule for bisecting an angle is available in the subject's processor (presumably, along with an appropriate higher-order rule, S_o, and G_1 among possibly other elements). It is impossible to say why this is so, without more information, but one possibility is that the subject may in the recent past have been confronted with a similar problem (e.g., inscribe a circle in a triangle) in which this rule was required for solution.

The protocol becomes sketchy at this point. It appears, however, that a higher-order two-loci rule, which generates conjunctions (pairs) of rules (i.e., construct Locus 1 and then Locus 2) that apply to the same stimulus, may be either available or directly accessible to the subject. In this case, the conjunction rule would be applied and the resulting, combined rule would be tested to see if it applies to S_o and has a range that contains G_1. Indeed, the subject seems according to the protocol to be checking to see whether the point of intersection of the two bisectors is equidistant from the vertices. Rather than using a logical argument for this purpose, the subject's comments suggest that a quick sketch (or image) convinced him that the intersection so obtained is not equidistant from the three vertices.[5] (Note: The structural learning theory is not constrained to discrete entities.)

At this point, according to the theory, the subject's processor is cleared of the angle bisector rule and the subject starts subproblem (S_o, G_1) over. Although the protocol again is not explicit, it seems reasonable to suppose that the subject retained the higher-order rule and searched for a domain rule that applies to the triangle (twice) and has a range that contains the goal (i.e., the point equidistant from the three vertices).

This time, the subject recalls (retrieves or generates) a

---

[5] Normally, goals are defined as sets or, equivalently, as propositions (Scandura 1973a). Nonetheless, checking to see whether or not a goal is satisfied involves using the proposition as an operator. For example, checking the proposition "is a triangle" involves the operation of distinguishing between exemplars (triangles) and nonexemplars. It may also be noted that a proposition (n- any relation), strictly speaking, defines a class of algorithms (Scandura, 1970, 1973a Landa, 1974) (n-l any function), rather than a unique algorithm. Landa uses the term "rule" to refer to such a class whereas I have used the term "rule" as equivalent to the notion of a procedure (algorithm), with the specific connotation that the internal structure (steps) of the algorithm is not of immediate concern. I see no reason to use a separate term to replace the universally understood "class" of algorithms but then this is largely a matter of personal preference. The important thing is that these two different usages of the term "rule" are kept clearly in mind.

Formal distinctions between algorithms and procedures, while important mathematically and in computer applications, enter into psychological theorizing only incidentally (e.g., in computer implementations).

rule for constructing the locus of points equidistant from a
pair of points, and generates a composite of the rule with itself
(i.e., apply it twice, each time to a different pair of points).
This composite rule satisfies the higher-level goal, so control
goes to the original goal and the subject actually uses the rule
to construct the center point. The superimposition of this point
on the given triangle yields the elaborated stimulus $f(S_o)$.

Next, control goes to the second subproblem $(f(S_o), G)$,
which appears to have been solved more directly. In this case,
it would almost seem that the subject broke the second subproblem into even simpler subproblems. First, the subject measured
the distance from the center to one of the vertices and, then,
used that distance and center point to construct the goal circle.
The solution to each subproblem appears to have been direct.

Although this interpretation illustrates the potential
flexibility of the structural learning theory, it leaves open
the question of whether the competence theory of Chapter 3, say,
or Chapter 14, could be used successfully to account for the
processes used in solving other geometry construction problems
(or by other individuals in solving the same problem). This is
an important limitation. All protocols, even this relatively
explicit one, have frequent gaps and provide only suggestions
concerning the processes actually used in problem solving. Even
where an explicit theory of problem solving is available, it may
be difficult to distinguish between alternative explanations
without a variety of independent checks (i.e., various protocols).

The latter observation, of course, is in no way restricted
to the use of protocol analysis. It applies more broadly to all
clinical/observation approaches to the study of complex human
behavior (something that has become popular of late in mathematics education research, for example). Such research can serve
a very useful purpose where scientific understanding is limited,
thereby helping to identify important problems requiring scientific attention. When used in connection with knowledgeable or
otherwise prototypic subjects, such observation may also constitute an essential first step in identifying rules of competence.

2.3 CURRENT ISSUES

It is increasingly recognized by cognitive scientists that
the problem of representation is fundamental to any adequate
understanding of complex human behavior (e.g., Anderson & Bower,
1973; Kintsch, 1974; Minsky, 1975; Pask, 1975; Paivio, 1969;
Pylyshyn, 1973). This is certainly true of the present theory.
In addition to having some very definite opinions on how knowledge should be represented, we have applied (some) of these
ideas in a variety of more or less realistic contexts, ranging
from informal curriculum analyses for instructional purposes
(e.g., Chapter 11) to more intensive analyses that might serve
as a basis for computer implementation (e.g., Chapters 3 and 4).

In contrast, a significant part of the contemporary research in the area has been limited to arguing by illustration for one or another form of representation. While much of this work is inspirational, it avoids the really hard problems connected with representing the competencies associated with nontrivial and diverse problem domains. Moreover, little has been done by way of coming to grips with the basic methodological problems of having to invent a new competence theory for each new problem domain, or of how to represent individual differences (except in the self-defeating sense of having to introduce a separate theory for each individual, see Chapters 1 and 2).

Obviously, the proposed method of structural analysis for accomplishing these ends is neither completely objective nor systematic, nor is it sufficiently general that it can be applied in its still embryonic form to arbitrary content. (If it were, the extremely complex problem in computer science of automatic programming would be largely solved.) This is, nonetheless, our immediate as well as ultimate goal.

Consequently, the structural learning theory is largely schematic insofar as representing competence/knowledge is concerned. Although relatively more attention has been given to questions of overall form and method of analysis than in most work on human problem solving, the theory has been relatively neutral with regard to a number of contemporary issues: Should knowledge be represented in terms of propositions or algorithmically (e.g., Greeno, 1973; Minsky & Papert, 1972)? Should knowledge be represented in terms of discrete entities or (continuous) images (e.g., Paivio, 1969; Pylyshyn, 1973)? How should implicit knowledge be represented? Should incorrect knowledge be represented in the same way as correct knowledge?

Since much of the research pertaining to these important issues lies outside the domain of problem solving, we shall not attempt a detailed discussion or exhaustive critical review of the pertinent literature. The discussion that follows is intended primarily to help clarify my position on the issues.

Algorithmic and Propositional Knowledge in Cognitive Psychology: In a recent discussion, Greeno (1973) refers to the relatedness of specific knowledge required in problem solving to the subject's general cognitive structure (cf. Ausubel, 1968). Specific reference is made to an unsolvable problem taken from Paige and Simon (1966): If a board is cut into two pieces with the first equal to two-thirds the length of the original board, and the second four feet longer than the first, how long is the original board? According to Greeno, the subject is proceeding "algorithmically" if he solves the problem algebraically. Letting L represent the length of the board and L_1 and L_2, the lengths of the two pieces, we get $L_1 = 2/3\ L$ and $L_2 = L_1 + 4$. Because $L_1 + L_2 = L$, this leads to the equations $L_2 = 1/3\ L$ and $L_2 = 2/3\ L + 4$, which are contradictory (if one assumes $L > 0$).

According to Greeno (1973, p. 119), human subjects often avoid this kind of difficulty "because they do not necessarily proceed in such a mechanical, algorithmical way." In particular, problem solvers sometimes use images (or draw pictures) to represent important relationships in a problem. In this case, the inconsistency in the information given in the problem can be detected relatively easily. Greeno refers to diagrammatic representation as relating the problem situation directly to the subject's "propositional" knowledge about the world.

It is certainly true that drawing a diagram can be helpful. But, this in no way contradicts the idea that all knowledge can be represented in terms of rules, or the entities (structures) on which they operate. As we saw in our analysis of geometry construction problems, solving (as well as representing) a problem by means of a diagram may involve application of a rule (algorithm) just as surely as does solving the problem via algebraic equations. Furthermore, detecting an inconsistency in a diagram (or insuring that the inconsistency can be detected by drawing the diagram to scale) involves applying some algorithm no less than does the manipulation of algebraic symbols. (Simple drawing algorithms probably are more likely to be learned as a result of interacting with the everyday world than in the mathematics classroom. But, such knowledge certainly could be taught in school.)

The commonly made distinction between propositional and algorithmic (rule) knowledge does exist in fact but it has nothing to do with the nature of knowledge per se. In the present view, all knowledge, whether algorithmic or propositional (relational nets), may be represented in terms of rules, or the structures on which they operate (cf. Scandura, 1973a, 1973b, 1974a). The question of whether knowledge is to be considered as propositional or algorithmic depends not on any of its properties as such, but rather on the use to which the knowledge is being put by the subject at any given point in time. Knowledge that is actively being used, as an operator, corresponds roughly to the term *algorithmic,* although, as noted, a false distinction is sometimes made between ongoing operations involving symbol manipulation and, say, manipulation of a geometric figure. Knowledge (a structure) that is being acted on, or that is (to be) generated (e.g., an entity that satisfies a goal), acts as a state, and corresponds to propositional knowledge. Again, however, because of differences in terminology used in the literature (e.g., see Brown & Burton's 1975 discussion of multiple representation), the correspondence is not rigorous.

Much of the confusion, apparently, stems from the fact that the rules needed in problem solving may not stand alone but may be embedded in more encompassing relational nets of the sort discussed by Bower (1972), Kintsch (1972), Rumelhart, Lindsay, and Norman (1972), and Quillian (1968), or otherwise integrated in some psychologically meaningful unit (cf. Miller's, 1956, chunks, and Minsky's, 1975, frames). In the former case, entire subnetworks may have separate psychological status; it is not just a question of the individual nodes and relations but of collections of such nodes and relations, including the network itself. For example, although the rules involved in most of the studies reported in this book were available as distinct units, needed rules in the retrieval study of Chapter 6 were embedded in broader networks. (Also, the restricted higher-order generalization [division] rule of Experiments II to IV in Chapter 5 is embedded in the more general [finite differences] rule, but our experimental manipulations did not consider this possibility.)

Equally important, although they are absent from most relational nets used in behavioral science, higher-order relations between relations in networks correspond to higher-order rules and also may have psychological significance. (For examples, see that part of Section 3 dealing with content versus performance analysis.)

In the structural learning theory all relational nets, whether or not they involve higher-order relations, correspond to psychologically meaningful units, or structures (see Chapter 2, this book; also Scandura, 1973b, especially Chapter 6, p. 239). Indeed, relational nets are essentially equivalent but behaviorally less precise than what we have called *structures* in this book. (Relational nets are less precise, because the relations do not distinguish among the rules/procedures relating the various nodes, nor do they generally speaking include higher-order relations or rules. For some purposes, such distinctions may be ignored, but not for others. Again, see Section 3 for further discussion.)

The basic question, of course, is what is a psychologically meaningful unit, or *structure,* and how does one know one when one sees one? No one to my knowledge has a completely satisfactory and proven answer to this question and neither do I. Nonetheless, according to the structural learning theory, an entity is a structure if it is distinguished as an input element by some rule of competence (see Chapter 2; also the Glossary). In effect, what may serve as a structure, as with competence rules, depends ultimately on the population of subjects and on the level of behavioral detail in question. Structures (defined by arbitrary rules of competence) could have significance, say, for systems in artificial intelligence. In this regard, also, a number of relevant issues have been discussed at length in Scandura (1973b, Chapters 6 and 7), especially as this involves the representation of meaning.

Structures impose a fixed unit of memory load on the human processor (i.e., serve the same role as chunks) only with respect to latency/processing-capacity-sensitive rules of competence (i.e., *process atomic* rules, see Glossary). Thus, for example, competence rules that distinguish only between success and failure are memory-free and by definition do not take processing capacity into account. A direct analogy is intended here between

such structures and the chunks, or substimuli, of Chapter 7
(also see Scandura, 1973b, Chapter 10).

Furthermore, as shown in Chapter 2 (Section 4.2), what
(structures) are chunks, may be operationalized in terms of the
memory load model described in Chapter 7 generalized along the
lines indicated in (the main theoretical) Chapter 2. In particular, chunks might be operationalized in terms of behavior
in much the same way as (success-failure) behavior potential.
This was accomplished, recall, in terms of a hypothesized relationship between memory load and processing speed. In effect,
behavior constitutes the final test of whether or not a postulated chunk is a chunk, in fact, just as it determines whether
or not an atomic rule is atomic, or a competence rule is compatible with a given population (cf. Chapters 9 and 10). Further details as to how this should be done need to be worked
out, of course, and the amount of directly relevant research is
much too small to warrant definitive statements.

*Procedural and Declarative Knowledge in Artificial Intelli-
gence:* Although detailed discussion is beyond the scope of this
treatment, no discussion of procedural (algorithmic) and declarative (propositional) knowledge would be complete without
at least mentioning the currently intensive research on representation, based largely on mathematical and/or computational
(computer) methods, by workers in artificial intelligence.
(For a reasonably up-to-date treatment, see Bobrow & Collins,
1975. The discussion below draws heavily on Winograd, 1975.)

As in cognitive psychology, the basic debate centers on
the distinction between declarative and procedural knowledge
(cf. Minsky & Papert, 1972; McCarthy & Hayes, 1969). (In one
sense, of course, there is no distinction. As in the structural
learning theory, procedures may serve as data; they may be acted
upon. And, data may be defined in terms of procedures.) According to Winograd (1975), the basic issues in the debate center
on the relative epistemological advantages of the two views.
Declaratives are believed to offer greater economy of representation (for some purposes) and ease of understanding and use,
particularly as this involves natural language. Other kinds of
knowledge, on the other hand, are most easily described in procedural terms. This is especially true in talking about how to
do things, and especially with regard to higher-order heuristic
(nonlogical) knowledge of the sort that has played so central
a role in the present development.

Rather than being seduced into simply asserting that both
kinds of representation are needed, Winograd (1975) correctly
emphasizes that the basic issue is not just one of formalisms,
but also of how declarativists and proceduralists approach the

duality between modularity and interaction (cf. Scandura, 1974a).
Declarativists (in artificial intelligence) appear to have been
most heavily influenced by mathematics and logic. In the latter
areas modularity enters globally, in the sense that there is a
clear distinction between axioms (propositions) and rules of inference (procedures). Given a suitable logic, any mathematical
system can be completely characterized in terms of a set of axioms. Conversely, methods of proof can be understood independently of the elements on which they act. They are universally applicable (cf. Scandura, 1971b; 1973b, Chapter 6, especially
p. 151).

In formulating specific theories, mathematicians also take
great pains to ensure that axioms are logically independent.
As long as logical consistency is maintained, new axioms may be
added without altering the generative capacity of the original
axioms. Anything that could be proven before is still valid.
As put by Winograd (1975, p. 192), "Locally, axioms represent
the ultimate in decomposition of knowledge....All changes are
additive--we can only 'know different' by 'knowing more'."

In programming, on the other hand, from which proceduralists have drawn their inspiration, interaction is primary.
There is no separation between data and process and local interactions are strong. Consequently, one cannot understand a program by looking at the parts.

According to Winograd (1975), the basic question is how to
take advantage of decomposability without sacrificing the possibilities for interaction. Put somewhat differently, is it possible to identify a universally applicable mode of interaction
that is both (interactionally) richer than logic and at the same
time consistent with how people use their available knowledge?

I very much agree that this is (if not "the" then) certainly
one of the, most important problems of representation. I am not
fully convinced, however, by any of the solutions to this problem
that have been proposed to date. Thus, for example, while recent programming languages developed for use in artificial intelligence have achieved some degree of modularity (for a good
review, see Bobrow & Raphael, 1974) I doubt very much that anyone, particularly the developers, would seriously argue that the
modes of interaction that have been built into the languages
(e.g., pattern-directed call, backup search strategies) are universally characteristic of people (cf. Scandura, 1974b).

Consider, for example, the programming language that seems
most likely to meet this requirement--the "production systems"
of Newell and Simon (1972; cf. Scandura, 1973b, Chapter 6). In
this language, all interaction is highly restricted. Individual
productions (which consist solely of initial conditions and operations and which do not include internal decisions) interact
according to a fixed ordering coupled with a limited-capacity
short-term memory. (As noted previously, in Chapter 5, this

type of interaction has much in its favor. It is simple and it
parallels the way in which inference and grammatical rules, respectively, are applied successively in formal mathematical
systems and simple grammars.) The basic question here is whether
or not people naturally use productions (or rules) in a fixed
order (i.e., whether the human information processor works in
this way).

Although it is impossible to answer this question in a definitive way on the basis of available evidence (there are a
large number of possible static orders), the data reported in
Chapters 5 and 6 would seem to argue strongly against the simple,
linear, stack-type orderings that have been explored most extensively (e.g., Newell, 1973). Indeed, although goal switching
of the sort proposed in this volume may be simulated by production systems (or by almost any other programming language for
that matter), there are important differences.

Among the more important differences are the following:

1. Unlike productions, individual rules may involve internal decisions. In effect, each rule corresponds to a restricted
type of production system (without productions that operate on
other productions).

2. Working memory (STS) in the structural learning theory
contains all of the information that matters (including nonsimple
rules, higher-order rules, and structures. Thus, rather than
switching back and forth (conceptually speaking) between working
memory and a fixed long-term memory, as with production systems,
the contents of long-term memory are not fixed and, in fact, are
implicit in the rules available in working memory. The contents
of working memory, in this case, change over time in an as yet
only partially specified way that depends on the state of the
environment and what the subject has and is trying to do (at the
time) (see Chapter 10 in Scandura, 1973b; 1976, pp. 315–316).

3. The postulated order in which goal switching takes place
is fixed, but it depends in a nonsimple way on the rules and
higher-order rules available in working memory. This order is
definitely nonlinear, and strong interactions exist among the
individual rules. Moreover, goal switching derives from intuition to the effect: "If you don't know how to solve a problem,
try to figure out how to do it." Production systems seem to
have been motivated by the General Problem Solver (Ernst &
Newell, 1969), which is based on a special case of the above:
"Try to reduce the difference between the current state and the
goal."

In an attempt to incorporate advantages of both declarative
and procedural formulations, a new representational format called
frames has recently been proposed by Minsky (1975) and elaborated by Winograd (1975) and others. At the present time, there
is no completely general agreement on exactly what frames are,
and as this book goes to press those working on the problem in-

dicate that we are a long way from agreeing on how to formalize
the notion; furthermore, no one seems to have actually implemented the scheme on a computer (e.g., see Winograd, 1975, pp.
195-196).

It would, therefore, be premature for me to make any firm
statements about the ultimate value of frames. Nonetheless,
from what I have seen, frames appear to be nothing more than
structures in the sense described above and in Chapter 2 (also,
cf. meaningful units, Scandura, 1973b). The major difference
in our case is that structures are incorporated in a reasonably
well-specified psychological theory. It seems to me, however
the formal issues are ultimately resolved, that the basic psychological problem is how to operationally define structures/
frames in behaviorally meaningful terms. (As indicated above,
the operational definition proposed in this book might be useful
in this regard.)

To summarize, the issue of declarative/propositional versus
procedural/algorithmic representation has two major facets: (1)
Can all knowledge be represented in either format? Or, more
exactly, what are the relative *formal* advantages of representing
knowledge in one way or the other, and (2) How is knowledge best
represented in people? Although various aspects of knowledge
can be represented more or less easily in one or the other form,
the structural learning theory appears to provide one reasonable
basis for synthesis. In particular, structures are the entities
on which rules operate and are defined by them. Moreover, structures, including complexes of higher- and lower-order rules,
which act as psychologically meaningful units (on which rules
operate), may be represented in summary form as propositional
networks.

Discrete Representation versus Imagery: There is a parallel, but nonetheless orthogonal, controversy in cognitive psychology over how visual information is represented in memory--
whether in terms of discrete elements (as required in digital
computers) or as continuous images (as in analog computers).
As in the propositional/algorithmic issue, this controversy has
both a mathematical and a psychological aspect.

It is widely accepted in the former regard that the intuitive force behind classical geometry is largely visual and based
on continuity; that behind algebra is symbolic and discrete.
There is, nonetheless, a close relationship between the two.
In particular, the calculus, which was first developed by Newton
and Leibniz provides a crucial link between continuous and
discrete quantities. The former can be represented in terms of
the latter (via limits). Thus, for example, the real numbers,
which form a continuous set can be represented in terms of infinite sequences of rational numbers, which do not. At first
thought, this observation might lead one to suspect that digital
representation alone may be adequate. Relying exclusively on
digital representation, however, may extract a high price. The

representation of continuously varying quantities can become extremely cumbersome, and, at asymptote, requires reference to an infinite number of discrete entities. (For an informal discussion of some of the issues involved, see Scandura, 1971a, especially pp. 341-342.)

The psychological debate is somewhat different and has centered on the question of how people actually do represent visual information. Pylyshyn (1973), for example, rests his argument against imagery largely on the assumption that images are stored in memory as originally perceived (i.e., in an uninterpreted form). Accordingly, he argues that the direct storage of sensory information necessarily implies information overload. A major counterargument has been led by Paivio (1974), who has rejected this contention, and who has relied instead on a large amount of experimental evidence that demonstrates the positive advantages of imagery. The results of Shepherd and Cooper (Cooper & Shepherd, 1973; Cooper, 1975) have frequently been cited as specific support for the analog position. When subjects were asked to compare a rotated figure with one in a standard position, they found that the time required to make the comparison was a linear function of the amount of rotation. Moreover, as Cooper (1975) later showed, this relationship is independent of the complexity of the figures (line drawings).

Although there may be (short-term) advantages to using a single mode of representation, it is far from clear that psychologists should restrict themselves to one mode just because it might be convenient in computer implementations. (The entire issue seems much like the now discredited question of whether language is necessary for thought. The answer is sometimes yes and sometimes no. The real questions are why and when.) Indeed, everyday observations of human behavior, as well as simple introspection, suggest rather strongly that people use both discrete and continuous representations with respect to most of our senses. For a reasoned argument to this effect see Spence (1973).

In this regard, I see no inconsistency in any of the previous discussion concerning rules (algorithmic representation), or complexes of same (i.e., structures, propositional representations). Although most of the examples considered in this book may be handled in terms of a discrete type of representation this distinction has never been critical in structural learning formulations. As argued in Scandura (1970, 1973b, pp. 236-254), for example, both symbolic and iconic representation may play an important role in human cognition, and, moreover, both can be incorporated within the structural learning theory without affecting the mechanisms assumed to govern human cognition. In addition to being cognizant of the mathematical relationships mentioned above, I have been adamant in trying to separate psychological from computer requirements. Thus, while differences in hardware requirements (i.e., digital versus an-

alog computers) make the issue critical in artificial intelligence, this is not necessarily the case with humans. Whatever
hardware there is, is already there. We need only to discover
its effects on human behavior and to find some suitable way to
represent those essentials of this hardware that effect observable behavior. Indeed, increasing evidence suggests that human
physiology, particularly the right-left brain distinction, may
lend itself admirably to dual (i.e., discrete and continuous)
representation. (Note: Some theorists, including myself,
believe that dual representation may play an important role in
the distinction between formulating goals and procedures for
achieving them, cf. Pask, 1975. Based on his presentation at
the 21st International Congress in Psychology in Paris (1976),
Klix and his associates apparently are also pursuing research
that is based in part on this assumption.)

Moreover, the discussion in Scandura (1970, 1973b) shows
that the related distinction between symbolic and iconic (tem-
plate-type) representations in human knowledge is largely a
matter of degree (cf. Bobrow, 1975). The units used to represent human knowledge may involve both iconic and symbolic
aspects, both globally and locally. If computer implementation
(of human cognition) calls for both digital and analog hardware,
so be it. The very fact that humans can so easily encode certain
types of visual information (e.g., global patterns), in comparison to the complexities involved in computer implementation,
suggests that really successful, or at least humanlike, artificial intelligence systems may require something along this line.
(The fact that many icons can be represented in terms of discrete
entities is immaterial. The point is that in some cases, as in
the old Chinese proverb, one picture may be worth 10,000 words,
cf. Spence, 1973.) If this is the case, perhaps we should ac-
cept the challenge directly (in spite of the difficulties involved) rather than to try to force the problem into a digital
mold, irrespective of efficiency or human requirements.

Additional Issues: Current work on the problem of representation is intense and the previous discussion hardly exhausts
the issues under investigation. There is, for example, a growing
consensus among both cognitive psychologists and scientists in
artificial intelligence that *heuristics* (higher-order rules),
as well as logical inference, should play a central role in
problem-solving research. There are, however, some important
differences in outlook within various camps. In artificial intelligence, logical inference is typically viewed in its mathematical, or universal sense (see also Bobrow, 1975). If something can be deduced within efficiency constraints imposed on
the computation, then it will be. Individual differences have
been ignored, and even more basically, little explicit consideration is given to the fact that people frequently reason in an
imperfect manner.

Cognitive scientists, for obvious reasons, have been more concerned with the latter. Collins, Warnock, Aiello, and Miller (1975), for example, have argued that people often make erroneous inferences because their real-world knowledge is incomplete. (They have utilized, in this regard, a computer program [SCHOLAR] based on this assumption to successfully simulate aspects of human reasoning.) They also have begun to give increasing attention to humanlike, higher-order heuristic knowledge and, in this sense, appear to be moving toward our higher-order rules (cf. Scandura, 1971b, 1971c, 1973b). With the aforementioned exception of production systems, perhaps the major omission to date appears to be concern for a behaviorally viable and universal control mechanism.

In constructing real-world knowledge, the tendency in both artificial intelligence and cognitive theorizing has been to build in directly the knowledge one wants and to allow for various kinds of extensions. In some cases, the extensions are basically the result of logical inference whereas, in other cases, heuristic strategies also are involved.

In the present book, we have adopted a quite different approach. Rather than building in knowledge and then seeing what it can do for us, we begin by delineating some (arbitrarily large) problem domain (e.g., by providing some means of deciding whether or not a given task belongs) and systematically go about identifying the competence necessary to account for it (i.e., via *structural* analysis). Specifically, a finite but representative sample of tasks is drawn from the domain and used to generate prototypic rule sets from which solutions to many if not all of the problems in the original domain may be derived. This "core" competence includes both higher- and lower-level rules and corresponds to the (prototypic) knowledge available to idealized members of some target population of subjects.

This difference in approach is crucial in determining the nature of the resulting psychology. The former approach, for example, is closely tied to specific content domains. Theories of this sort are incomplete and nonoperational, in the sense that one must begin anew with each new body of content.

Also recall in this regard the previously mentioned epistomological issue as to whether competence should be attributed to individuals or to groups (Chapter 1). On the one hand, deterministic information-processing theories correspond most naturally to individual knowledge. As we have seen, however, the processes (theories) introduced to account for data in cognitive psychology, properly refer to groups (i.e., they are designed to provide accounts of average behavior).

This issue poses a dilemma for the psychological theorist. On the one hand, attributing knowledge to individuals poses the potential problem of having to invent a separate theory for each individual. The second alternative, however, forces the scientist into using group/average data in order to make inferences about what are essentially individual processes.

It seems sufficient here, to simply reiterate the present position. Rules of competence correspond to knowledge had by idealized members of the target population. This idealized knowledge may come in multiple forms (see the following discussion), and, in particular, any finite number of different rules (processes) may be introduced to account for the same subclasses of problems. This would correspond, for example, to a multiculture population (e.g., a population of fourth-graders, some of whom are being taught an equal additions method of subtraction and others, the method of borrowing). Prototypic rules of competence, in turn, are used to measure individual knowledge within the population. In effect, although the competence associated with a given problem domain and subject population is assumed to be fixed, knowledge may vary over individuals in the population. What avoids the basic dilemma is that individual knowledge is measured relative to (a finite number of) prototypic rules of competence. Furthermore, the level of molarity at which competence rules are represented is inversely related to the number of behaviorally equivalent equivalence classes of test items (and, hence, to the number of needed test items). In turn, of course, the more molar the representation (of rules) the smaller the variety of individual differences that may be distinguished (relative to the given level of behavioral detail).

Another potentially major issue concerns the possibility of *multiple representations*. Thus, whereas knowledge is represented uniformly in many artificial intelligence systems and cognitive theories, there is no a priori reason why algorithmic and declarative (e.g., Brown & Burton, 1975), discrete and continuous (e.g., Paivio, 1974), or semantic and episodic (e.g., Tulving, 1972; Abelson, 1975) knowledge may not be incorporated in the same system.

Indeed, a number of cognitive theories, including my own, are relatively neutral in this regard. The formal foundations of the structural learning theory (Scandura, 1973b, Chapters 5 and 9), for example, are largely limited to rules. Available applications of the theory, such as those described in Part 2, also deal primarily with procedural competence. Nonetheless, it appears possible at a theoretical level to incorporate declarative/propositional knowledge (competence) as well. For example, consider the discussion of semantic knowledge, which consists (in part) of distinguished subsets of rules (structures), to characterize meanings (see Chapter 2, this book; also Scandura, 1973b, Chapter 6).

Although many details would need to be worked out in any formal treatment, I also see no reason why both discrete and continuous knowledge, or episodic and semantic knowledge for that matter, might not be incorporated within this framework. In the latter case, for example, the distinction appears to derive largely from empirical rather than formal (theoretical) considerations. The first step in integrating episodic S-R-type knowledge with procedural knowledge would seem to be that of recognizing associations as degenerate rules (e.g., Scandura, 1970). Practical considerations aside, regarding the sheer numbers of associations that humans appear to store, the important point is that no new theoretical mechanisms appear necessary to maintain an operational theory. For example, choices among multiple representations of the same knowledge (e.g., direct S-R associations and procedural derivations) may be accounted for in terms of the hypothesized goal switching, together with appropriate higher-order selection rules (Chapters 2 and 6).

The further one moves from the computer, as simply a metaphor in psychological theorizing, toward the computer, as an integral part of such theory, this neutrality tends to break down. Thus, the question of what kinds of representations may be useful will depend not only on the tasks involved but also on hardware characteristics of the information processor itself. As noted earlier, for example, many psychologists believe that humans use visual images directly. Digital computers cannot do this (cf. Spence, 1973). Indeed, whether or not people actually do use images as such, it seems reasonably clear that what may be an efficient representation for one information processor (e.g., the computer), might be an extremely inefficient one for another (i.e., the human). The ease with which humans can perceive visual information (that may be extremely difficult if not impossible for computers to perceive) and, conversely, the relative ease with which computers can search through large data bases attest to such differences.

While recognizing (and arguing about) relative advantages, scientists in artificial intelligence have tended in their research toward uniform representations, even where different alternatives have been feasible. Given the state of the programming art, it is apparently easier to program exclusively, for example, in either procedural or declarative form. As shown by the work of Brown and Burton (1975), however, the use of multiple representations of knowledge may result in more efficient programs and I suspect that we will see increasingly more of this in the future.

Finally, I should like to comment parenthetically on *incorrect knowledge*, and its nature. There is a basic difference between knowing a rule or process and knowing when to use it. This distinction is an essential part of any complete characterization of any rule or process. As a minimum, one must be able to specify both the operations to be carried out and the domain of applicability of those operations. Neither alone is sufficient.

In psychology, it is often easier to identify the operations associated with a rule than the domain of applicability. This is particularly true of higher-order rules/heuristics. Consider, for example, the flow diagram depicted below (i.e.,

Figure 1 of Chapter 5). This higher-order finite differences

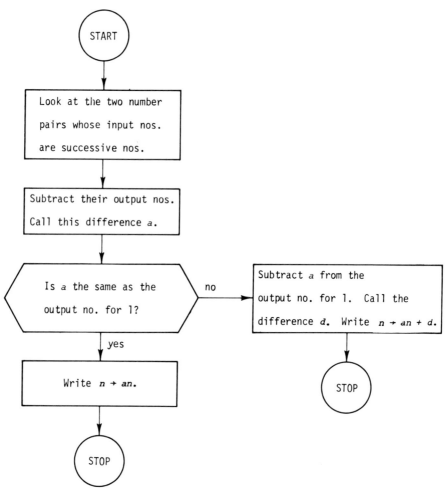

rule acts on restricted rules like

    1 → 5
    4 → 14
    5 → 17

and generates rules of the form n → an + d. Although the internal operations and decisions are appropriately specified in the
flow diagram, the domain strictly speaking is not. Thus, whereas the higher-order rule operates on every triple of number
pairs and generates a rule of the form n → an + d, the outputted
rule will not satisfy all such triples. For example, consider
the following:

    1 → 1
    4 → 16
    5 → 25

Application of the higher-order rule in this case yields n →
9n - 8 which clearly does not, for example, satisfy 4 → 16 (e.g.,
(9 x 4) - 8 = 28 and not 16).

In order for this higher-order rule to succeed uniformally,
the domain must be limited to triples of the form:

$$1 \to a + d$$
$$m \to am + d$$
$$m + 1 \to am + a + d$$

Whereas it is possible to devise a correct rule in this case,
and in others even more complex (e.g., see Part 2), I do not
believe for the most part that human knowledge is that algorithmic. In general, I believe that human knowledge, especially of
the higher-order variety, consists of rules with only more or
less accurate domains.

This does not mean, however, that one cannot have a theory
of how people use and acquire "imperfect" as well as perfect
knowledge. Indeed, psychologically speaking, this entire book
is predicated on the belief that there is no significant difference between the two. In the structural learning theory, it
makes no difference whether the rules of competence, or of knowledge, are perfect or imperfect. Their use and acquisition is
governed by the same principles. This results in a considerable
economy of explanation. For example, where both correct and
incorrect knowledge exist simultaneously, which certainly occurs,
rule selection may provide a possible basis for explaining unre-
liable behavior (e.g., the careless mistakes children often make
in arithmetic).

There is another kind of generative imperfection that is
often confused with the above. This imperfection is mathematical in nature and follows directly from a well-known theorem by
the logician Church (1936). Namely, there are classes of tasks
(problem domains) that cannot be solved (accounted for) by any
algorithm.

The major point here is that there is an important difference between mathematical constraints and psychological relevance. No serious psychologist ever thought that anyone knew
everything that there is to know. It is, in fact, the introduction of imperfect as well as perfect higher- and lower-order
rules that makes it possible to account for problem domains of
often unclear scope. The nonalgorithmic and often unpredictable
nature of such knowledge is what gives structural accounts a
lifelike creative character. On the other hand, it is important
to know that some task domains are sufficiently complex that no
strictly algorithmic account is possible. In such cases, as
with most realistic domains, one must rely, in evaluating alternative rule accounts, on empirical comparisons of relative generative power.

Further Methodological Comments: The fact that the structural learning theory seems adequate to explain existing problem-
solving data tells only part of the story. As observed previ-

ously, the inherent methodology is equally important. In this section, I would like to simply reemphasize a few points.

In structural analyses of problem domains attention is focused not only on generative adequacy, but also on compatibility with target populations and hypothesized cognitive universals. In addition, rather than dealing with population averages, structural analysis deals with idealized competence that may be used as a standard against which to measure individual knowledge. The representations chosen also are constrained by the requirement that they lend themselves to efficient operationalization. Interestingly enough, rather than making it more difficult to identify underlying competence, these constraints tend to simplify and to make structural analysis at least partly systematic.

Our experimental methodology draws directly on prior structural analysis and differs in other important ways from what has been the norm. In order to demonstrate deterministic effects, experiments must be run under idealized conditions. Rather than randomizing over incidental variables (including subjects), incidental effects (both external and internal to the subjects) must be effectively removed from the experiments. Where this seems infeasible, a sharp distinction still can be maintained between structural (deterministic) factors and incidental ones; the latter are treated probabilistically.

Individual differences are either eliminated or manipulated via prior training or they are determined via testing. In the former case, the major difference between our research and most contemporary research in experimental psychology is the insistence on absolute mastery relative to given standards. (Arbitrary criteria such as number of training trials are of secondary concern.) In effect, there is a need for different levels of empirical research. In the latter case, major differences between structural and other forms of criterion-referenced testing include explicit attention to cognitive processes, including higher- as well as lower-order rules, and to level of behavioral detail. More generally, specific attention must be given to constraints imposed by theory at any one level on theory and research at other levels.

These characteristics contrast sharply in several respects with other contemporary approaches to the study of problem solving. In most contemporary problem-solving research, for example, no sharp distinction is made between the competence, cognitive, and measurement aspects of problem solving, much less between deterministic (structural) and incidental factors. Even studies motivated by structural/process theories typically incorporate these three aspects in unspecified proportion.

As a result of such confounding, it has often been difficult to distinguish between those aspects of problem solving due to specific (or nonspecific) knowledge and those parts due to individual differences and the nature of the human information processor. Egan and Greeno (1973), for example, have elaborated on the general view that learning how to solve problems consists primarily of learning how to construct subgoal hierarchies (cf. Newell & Simon, 1972). In an experiment dealing with the Tower of Hanoi problem, they reported little evidence that subjects learned sequences of transformations (procedures consisting of composites of simple atomic operations) or that subjects determined subsequent transformations strictly in terms of the then current state (cf. Klix, 1967; Klix & Sydow, 1968).

Do these findings reflect specific tasks and knowledge or basic characteristics of the human information processor? There is no question that subgoal formation plays an important role in problem solving and there is certainly no reason to question the central importance of forming goal hierarchies in solving Tower of Hanoi tasks. A truly comprehensive theory, however, will necessarily have to allow not only for goal hierarchies but, as we have seen throughout Part 3, many other types of cognitive interactions as well.

Without prior and detailed structural analysis, research on specific tasks may lead to misleading or what might appear to be contradictory evidence. Any one type of problem is apt to differ from others as to which kinds of processes are most critical. The Tower of Hanoi, as with many other tasks used in computer simulation studies, is well defined in the sense that the initial goal situation and all of the allowable transformations (moves/atomic rules) are predetermined. Furthermore, the only new rules that can be derived during the course of solving such problems are simple compositions of the given transformations. With the intellectually advanced subject population used in the above study, it is quite likely that the subjects had well learned one or more appropriate higher-order composition rules (i.e., how to compose pairs of moves) before entering the experiment. The number of possible compositions is relatively large, however, so it is unlikely that such knowledge would be helpful on the initial (global) problem per se.

There is little reason to believe, on the other hand, that the otherwise naive subjects would automatically have known much about how to break Tower of Hanoi tasks down into "bite size" subgoals. Hence, it is not surprising that both Klix and Sydow (1968) and Egan and Greeno (1973) found evidence to suggest that experience in solving the Tower of Hanoi problem resulted in the subject's learning how to construct appropriate goal hierarchies.

Given the relatively complicated nature of the problems and the experimental data, however, the possible significance of certain other data with regard to basic psychological processes may have been overlooked. For example, Egan and Greeno's (1973) finding that subjects took more time in making the first move in identifiable sequences of moves, is consistent with the hypothesis that, in the course of solving subproblems, subjects may derive new solution rules. It takes extra time to derive such rules (sequences of moves) and, once derived, it takes time

to retrieve them, so that in either case a delay would be expected before the first move in a derived sequence is actually
applied. Similarly, their finding that subjects tend to group
moves into larger and larger sequences as they obtain more experience with the problems is also consistent with the notion
that subjects can derive (and learn) increasingly complex solution rules.

In less well-defined problems, such as Maier's (1930) hatrack problem, rather than subgoals, what becomes central is the
process whereby the subject understands the basic problem in
the first place. Maier's problem, as originally presented to
the subjects, was in an important sense misleading. The experimenter might just as well have said, "Use only these objects
to ...." Once the experimenter admonished the subjects not to
be "blind", many of them apparently interpreted the given in the
problem to include the ceiling as well as the implements specifically provided. In effect, although subgoal formation, rule
derivation, rule selection, and memory undoubtedly play a role
in Maier's hatrack problem, as in other problems, they were not
of central importance in Maier's study just because the subjects
in question probably already had the necessary knowledge. Unless this observation is made explicit ahead of time, however,
one could easily be misled into thinking that an explanation
for Maier's hatrack problem is an explanation for problem solving in general.

3. EDUCATIONAL IMPLICATIONS

In this section, we consider some educational implications
of the structural learning theory.

3.1 RELATIONSHIPS BETWEEN INSTRUCTIONAL SCIENCE, DESIGN AND PROFESSIONAL "KNOW-HOW"[6]

The different levels of theory in structural learning,
(e.g., Scandura, 1971c), together with Simon's (1969) conception
of *The Sciences of the Artificial* provide a useful basis for
understanding the relationship between educational theory and
development. Simon distinguishes between natural science (knowledge about natural objects), and engineering science where products of one sort or another are designed to meet given requirements. In order to synthesize or engineer something, according
to Simon, the scientist must have a purpose or goal. He must
synthesize the elements at his command so as to achieve that
goal, while taking into account the natural laws governing the
operation of these elements and the relationships between them.
As an example of what Simon has in mind, consider the task

---

[6]This section is based on Scandura (1972b).

of constructing a curriculum based on structural learning principles. In particular, consider the task of identifying the
content and basic processes (Scandura, 1971a, Chapter 1) to be
included in an idealized preelementary and elementary school
mathematics curriculum. Suppose further that the goal is to
devise a curriculum that is optimal in the sense that it provides maximum transfer potential, given the time limitations,
say, of a mathematics program for disadvantaged youth, ages
three to twelve (Scandura, 1972b). The task of the curriculum
engineer (designer) is to devise a systematic way of achieving
the goal within the constraints imposed by the (natural) theory.

An important point, which is only implicit in what Simon
says, is that it is the goal that determines how much of a given
natural theory need be taken into account in the (scientific)
engineering of any particular product. In this regard, the
partial theories pertaining to content, cognition, and individual
differences measurement have direct implications for curriculum
design. In fact, these levels of theory were initially motivated
largely by the need to provide information for dealing with the
various aspects of curriculum construction (Scandura, 1971c).
For example, in designing a curriculum (e.g., in identifying
the content and processes to be included in a curriculum), it
is sufficient to consider only those conceptualizations that
pertain to competence. Other conceptual information provided
by the structural learning theory, such as that dealing with individual performance and learning, may be ignored for this purpose. In fact, such information would be entirely irrelevant.
On the other hand, if one wanted to deal, in addition, with the
assessment of individual knowledge, or individually adapted instruction, say, then other aspects of the theory also would need
to be taken into account. In the latter case, the engineering
would be constrained not only by the structural competence theory (i.e., structural analysis), but by the mechanisms presumed
to govern learning, performance or motivation, as the case may
be.

The notion of partial theories (levels of theorizing) is
also helpful in another way. It makes explicit the fact that
development can never be entirely systematic. Although science
and technology (design principles) can encroach on professional
"know-how", there will always be some residual. At any given
stage in the advance of science, no matter how adequate a conceptualization, or associated technology, is available, there
always will be certain things that need to be dealt with on
intuitive grounds.

Specifically, the levels of partial theories in structural
learning make it easier to specify which aspects of curriculum
development can be engineered, based on available conceptualizations. The residual must be dealt with on the basis of professional "know-how". Thus, for example, given the method of
structural analysis, the curriculum constructor may systematical-

ly engineer (identify) the content and processes to be included in a curriculum. Those aspects of the curriculum with which a given technology does not deal must be dealt with intuitively (for example, the form of structural analysis used in Chapter 11 does not deal with testing or motivation). The relationships among basic science, technology, and professional "know-how" and their relative contributions to product development, are summarized in Table 1.

TABLE 1

Summary of Relative Contributions to Development and Relationships Between Basic Science, Technology and Professional "Know-How"

Development

A goal-oriented process which employs both available technology and professional "know-how."

Basic Science. Theory (conceptualization) provides basic constraints within which a technology must operate.

Technology. A goal-oriented process constrained only by available theory. Technology may be defined in terms of a natural theory plus a goal.

Professional "Know-How." The complement of technology relative to development.

Being explicit about such matters in large-scale development efforts could result in greater efficiency, especially in view of the direct implications deterministic results have for the real-world of education (Chapter 11). To the extent that the conceptualizations used adequately reflect that aspect of reality to be engineered, the resulting curricula should not only be better, but they should require relatively less revision than would otherwise be necessary. (For a more detailed and operational analysis of the basic relationship see Hilke, Kempf, & Scandura, 1977.)

3.2   BEHAVIORAL OBJECTIVES AND KNOWLEDGE[7]

As is well-known, specifying educational objectives in behavioral terms tells what it is that the learner must be able to do after learning. On the other hand, the term knowledge in structural/process theories refers to an underlying (rule/procedure/algorithm/relational net) construct that reflects a potential for behavior.

Perhaps the most basic inadequacy of traditional behavioral approaches to education is that *specifying behavioral objectives does not tell what the learner must learn or what the teacher must teach.* Specifying only behavioral objectives themselves leaves the "guts" out of learning. For example, consider an observation made in an individually prescribed learning environ-

---

[7]Sections 3.2-3.6 draw heavily on an invited address to Division 15 of the American Psychological Association, 1974, entitled "Structural Approach to Instructional Problems." A more complete published version is scheduled to appear in the American Psychologist.

ment by Bob Davis,[8] a well-known innovator in mathematics education. Davis became interested in a child who had learned to
place the decimal point in adding numbers according to his own
system. Given ".4 + .3", for example, the child would respond
".7". Similarly, he could correctly add ".2 + .7". His system
works fine where the decimal point is to the left. But, when
asked to add "3. + .2", for instance, the child would respond
".5.".

Why? Not surprisingly, answering this question requires
more than knowing the behavior to be expected in adding decimals.
It is necessary also to specify what (competence) a person must
know in order to add them. In particular, in this example, one
must specify what rule would lead a child to respond correctly
to the first two instances and incorrectly to the third.

To argue that the behavioral objective observed by Davis
may have been poorly formulated would miss the main point. Specifying underlying competence is important for several reasons:

1. Given any class of tasks (e.g., a behavioral objective),
if there is one rule that will generate a solution for each task,
then there are any (countably infinite) number of other rules
that will do the same thing.

2. In practice, there often is more than one feasible rule
for generating behavior associated with a behavioral objective.
Which rules are feasible depends on the "culture" in question.
For example, borrowing is the preferred method of teaching subtraction in American schools, whereas in German schools the
method of equal additions is used.

3. The selection of one or another (or all) feasible
rule(s) has important and direct implications for instruction
and for performance testing.

In teaching logical reasoning in reading (e.g., Chapter
12), for example, it is possible to emphasize syntax (e.g., "All
A are B," "x is an A." "Therefore x is a B.") and/or semantics
(e.g., Venn diagrams). Whereas syntactic rules of inference are
perfectly adequate within their assigned domains, however, there
is little basis for positive transfer to other inference rules
as is the case with inference rules based on meaning. In the
latter case only, the processes (e.g., using Venn diagrams) by
which one combines meanings of individual premises and checks
to see if conclusions follow from them, are the same irrespective of the particular inference rules involved (see Chapter
12; also Scandura, 1971a, Chapter 3).

In short, unlike behavioral objectives qua behavior objectives, which are devoid of underlying competence, competence
and behavior are intimately tied in the structural learning
theory--indeed, in most of the newer structural-algorithmic approaches to education (e.g., Bormuth, 1970; Gagne, 1970; Landa,

[8]Bob Davis, personal communication.

1974; Pask, 1975). Specifying behavior alone is not sufficient; the competence (rules) that makes that behavior possible must also be specified.

To minimize misinterpretation of the intended scope, or applicability of the rule construct, three cautions seem in order.

First, although the precise specification of competence in terms of rules is usually accomplished via some formal, relatively low level (i.e., detailed) algorithmic language, this does not mean that rules necessarily must be represented with this precision or in this degree of detail. Furthermore, competence need not always be represented in terms of discrete entities. Continuous quantities and operations may be required as well (e.g., coordinating pressure on the gas pedal in driving an automobile with a stick shift; making use of kinesthetic feedback in wrestling; and mentally rotating objects in space; see Spence, 1973, and Section 2.3 in this chapter).

In effect, whereas rules (procedures/algorithms) in computer programming are typically represented in terms of fixed computer languages, with discrete referents, the linguistic elements used to represent rules of human competence/knowledge are more varied. Specifically, the units (operations and decisions) of which competence/knowledge rules are constructed, and correspondingly the linguistic elements used to represent these units, vary in nature and scope according to the intended population of human information processors. The more sophisticated the population, in general, the larger and more varied are the linguistic elements that can properly be understood as units. In turn, the larger and more varied the units, the easier it is to represent competence. It is this characteristic flexibility that leads to the broad applicability of structural representations, including applicability to what initially might appear to be intractable tasks.

Consider, for example, the ability to read critically--that is, the ability to detect logical (or other) relationships among statements in a paragraph. It would be difficult indeed to detail all of the operations and decisions involved in encoding and interpreting individual morphemes as well as in determining grammatical and logical interrelationships. However, given that subjects can properly understand individual statements, the task becomes much easier. The individual meanings, for example, can be represented as regions in Venn diagrams and the interrelationships, as set membership, intersections, unions, and complements of such regions (cf. Chapter 12, this book; Scandura, 1971a, Chapter 3).

Second, the representation of competence in terms of rules is quite independent of how competence is to be imparted to children. The same competence frequently can be acquired by telling or by self-discovery, by symbol juggling or by concrete manipulation. In general, the way in which information is presented to the child depends on factors other than the particular competence in question. For example, it may depend on whether the teacher during the course of learning wants the student also to gain experience in discovery, and thereby to learn how to make discoveries in related situations, Scandura, 1971a, 1973b. (Choices regarding method of instruction are usually made on other grounds; see Scandura, 1977, Section 7.) *The main point is that if one knows precisely what it is that one wants a child to learn* (and not just the behavior the child is to evidence as a result of learning), *then one can facilitate learning far better than if one does not.*

Third, knowing the subject matter content involved is not equivalent to specifying the relevant competence. The former refers to an intuitive understanding and ability to use the content, whereas the latter refers to the ability to suitably describe or illustrate such understanding and ability. This distinction between knowing something and describing that competence is quite analogous to that, for example, between being able to solve mathematical problems and being able to tell someone else how to solve them.

It would appear, in summary, that specifying behavioral objectives is not equivalent to specifying underlying competence. The former tells only what the learner is supposed to be able to do; the latter tells in addition what the learner must know or learn in order to do it. Moreover, there is an important difference between specifying competence so that humans can understand it and specifying competence in a form that can be interpreted by computers. In the former case, competence is specified in terms of units at whatever level is appropriate to the target population. As noted below, the level of representation has important implications for performance testing.

3.3 PERFORMANCE TEST THEORY--WHAT FORM SHOULD IT TAKE?

Consider next the widely recognized need for better measures of specific behavioral competencies (e.g., see Resnick, 1972), and especially for better measures based on a sound theory of performance testing (e.g., see Glaser, 1973).

Mastery testing (e.g., Bloom, 1973) represents an important advance over normative testing insofar as instruction is concerned. It provides information not only concerning the relative capabilities of two or more individuals, but also concerning the specific capabilities of individuals. Criterion-referenced testing represents a refinement of mastery testing in which the conditions of testing and of mastery are defined more precisely. The introduction of item forms into criterion-referenced testing by Hively and his collaborators (e.g., Hively, Patterson, & Page, 1968) goes further in this direction, as does their later development at Pittsburgh (e.g., Ferguson, 1969). Item forms make it possible with paper-and-pencil tests to pinpoint, more precisely than in simple criterion-referenced testing, just what kinds of items within a given task domain a person can deal with effectively and what kinds he cannot.

None of the above forms of criterion-referenced testing, however, deal with the relationship between behavior and competence. The structural learning theory, on the other hand, provides an explicit way of dealing with this relationship. As we have seen, rules of competence introduced to account for performance on given behavioral objectives provide an instrument of sorts with which to measure human knowledge. The theory tells how, through a finite testing procedure, one can identify which parts of to-be-taught rules individual subjects know. The rules in a very real sense serve as rulers of measurement, and provide a basis for the operational definition of human knowledge.

Let us briefly review how this may be accomplished (for details, see Chapters 2, 8, 9, and 10 of this book). Consider, for example, the flow diagram in Chapter 9, which depicts a rule (procedure/algorithm) for subtracting numbers. This rule is broken down into steps that are so simple that each individual subject may be assumed able to perform either perfectly on each step or not at all. We say that each component step acts in atomic fashion (i.e., acts as a unit). In line with the above discussion, note that what are atomic units relative to one population may not be atomic units with respect to another (e.g., less sophisticated) population.

Because success on any path of a procedure depends on success on all atomic components, each path through the procedure also acts in atomic fashion. Furthermore, there are only a finite number of behaviorally distinct paths. We do not distinguish paths according to the number of repetitions of loops because the same cognitive operations and decisions are required regardless of how many times a given loop is traversed in carrying out a given "cognitive computation".

Collectively, the paths of any rule (e.g., subtraction) impose a partition on the domain of problems to which it applies (e.g., column subtraction problems); that is, they define a set of distinct, exhaustive, and homogeneous equivalence classes of problems such that each problem in any given class can be solved via exactly one of the paths.

The fact that each path is associated with a unique subclass of column subtraction problems, makes it possible to pinpoint through a finite testing procedure exactly what it is that each subject knows relative to the initial rule. It is sufficient for this purpose to test each subject on one item selected randomly from each subclass. Success on one such item, according to our assumptions, implies success on any other item drawn from the same equivalence class, and similarly for failure.

Individual knowledge (or behavior potential), then, may also be represented in terms of rules, specifically in terms of

subrules of the given rules of competence. The knowledge attributed to different individuals, however, may vary even where
only one rule of competence is used to assess behavior potential.
For example, suppose a subject succeeds on only one path, and
fails on the others. Then, his knowledge would be represented
by that path (which is a subrule of the initial one). Where two
or more paths are involved, a combination of the paths would be
used to represent the knowledge.

As we have seen, this discussion is not just a theoretical
exercise. Although the variety of task domains considered is
limited, a significant amount of supporting data has been collected over the past several years with subjects ranging from
preschool children to Ph.D. candidates. Given a class of tasks,
the general form of each study went as follows:

1. One or more rules were identified that were both adequate
for generating solutions to each of the tasks and compatible
with the way a knowledgeable/idealized member of the target population might be expected to solve them.

2. These rules singly and/or collectively were used to
partition the class of tasks into equivalence classes.

3. Subjects in the target population were tested on two
items (tasks) from each equivalence class.

4. Performance on one item from each equivalence class was
used as a basis for predicting success or failure on the other,
second, item.

With highly structured tasks run under carefully prescribed
laboratory conditions, it has been possible to predict performance on new (second) items--given performance on initial items,
with over 96 percent accuracy (Scandura, 1973b; Chapter 8, this
book). When testing took place under ordinary classroom conditions, with the subjects run as a group, the predictions were
accurate in about 84 percent of the cases (Chapter 9, this book).

In this latter case, the equivalence classes determined
via the structural/algorithmic approach were compared with item
forms identified by Hively et al. (1968) and Ferguson (1969).
Whereas the levels of prediction on success items were approximately the same, the equivalence classes led to significantly
better prediction of failures. Equally important, this level
of prediction was obtained with approximately half as many test
items--with an even greater increase in efficiency possible
through the use of conditional testing.

Moreover, the use of item forms has been limited to paper-
and-pencil tests. And, as noted by Gagne in his 1974 Thorndike
Award Address to Division 15 of the American Psychological Association, item forms have intrinsic limitations with regard to
nonpaper-and-pencil applications such as job analysis. The
structural approach is not limited in this way. The direct relationship between molarity of atomic rules and sophistication
of population allows for broader applicability. In job analysis,

for example, it would make little sense to attempt a molecular analysis of arithmetic skills in order to judge accounting skills, or of writing syntax in evaluating professorial capabilities. Although the impatient reader may have some doubts, minimal capabilities can reasonably be assumed of all bona fide professionals. Thus, all trained accountants presumably can add a column of figures and all experienced Ph.D.'s have at least minimal writing capabilities. Hence, it is sufficient to consider only those molar competencies (atomic rules) that distinguish among individuals in the target population--for example, the ability to set up and administer efficient accounting systems for companies of various types.

There is one further major advantage of the structural approach to assessing behavior potential: It fills an important need in making individualized instructional decisions. Quoting Glaser, "techniques need to be developed for analyzing properties of individual performance frequently enough and in enough detail for individualized instruction decisions" (1973, p. 563). Or, as suggested by DiVesta (1973), we need a deeper understanding of the relationships between objectives and what individuals do and do not know relative to these objectives.

It is clear from our examples that the algorithmic/structural approach makes it possible to identify precisely not only what individuals can and cannot do, as is the case with item forms, but also what the learner does and does not know relative to the particular rules involved. A simple basis for instructional decision making follows directly: Assume the paths the learner already knows and concentrate on those that he or she does not.

In summary, it would appear that any viable theory of performance testing must take into account underlying competence. Rules of competence associated with populations of subjects not only provide a basis for measuring individual knowledge and for providing remedial instruction but also for selecting appropriate test items. Furthermore, since the appropriate level of rule representation varies directly with population sophistication, it is often practicable to analyze even complex task domains (at a level of analysis that is sufficient for assessing the behavior potential of individuals in the population).

As noted previously in more technical discussions, additional implications may be derived from the available theory and/or research on: (a) the consolidation of knowledge (Chapter 2), (b) hierarchical relationships among paths and the conditional testing this makes possible (Chapter 9; Scandura, 1973a), (c) the use of sets of rules for assessment purposes (Chapter 2 of this book), and (d) the assessment of skilled performance in which response measures (e.g., latencies) more refined than success/failure are required (see Chapter 2 and Section 2.3 of this chapter).

3.4 SKIPPING PREREQUISITES (HIERARCHICAL TRANSFER)

The importance of prerequisites in learning is widely recognized (e.g., Gagne, 1970). Teaching, however, is not just a question of presenting prerequisites according to a predetermined hierarchy. For example, as Resnick (1972, p. 9) has noted, "Individuals appear to vary widely in their ability to 'skip' over prerequisites." Why is this so? Can we develop ways of determining ahead of time whether and which prerequisites individuals can skip? Further, is it possible to teach people how to transfer? If the ability to transfer not only can be taught, but can be tied in with problem solving and "generative skills" (Bruner, 1964), so much the better.

Stated simply, one fundamental question underlying these concerns is the following. When subjects are presented with a task where they know rules corresponding to all (lower-order) components of a solution, why is it that some of them succeed whereas others fail? Consider, for example, two children who know or who have been taught one rule for converting yards into feet (e.g., multiply by three) and another rule for converting feet into inches (e.g., multiply by 12). Suppose these children are presented with the task of converting yards into inches--and one child succeeds but the other fails. Why? Clearly, the yards to inches problem can be solved by combining the two known rules, the rule for converting yards into feet and the rule for converting feet into inches. But, how does the child know how to combine the given rules? Knowing two component rules is surely not logically equivalent to knowing when and how to use them.

As we have seen, a basic assumption in the structural learning theory is that new rules are derived by application of certain rules to other rules. Presumably, then, the child who succeeds on the yards-to-inches task does so because he knows something that the other child does not. He might, for example, know a higher-order composition rule, which includes in its domain (of rule pairs) the yards-to-feet and feet-to-inches rules.

Recall from previous discussions in Chapters 2, 5, and 6 that higher-order rules correspond roughly to plans (e.g., Miller, Galanter, & Pribram, 1960), heuristics (e.g., Polya, 1962), and higher-level strategies and not to a popular use of the term "higher-order" to indicate tasks and rules that are higher in learning hierarchies (e.g., Gagne, 1970); or to Miller *et al.'s*, (1960) TOTE hierarchies (cf. Scandura, 1973b). All rules, higher- and lower-order alike, are represented in the same way (e.g., as flow diagrams, labeled directed graphs). The descriptor *higher-order* is not a property of rules per se, but rather of the use to which they are being put at a given point in time. If rules are operating on other rules they are referred to as being of *relatively higher-order;* if they are being acted on, they are said to be of *relatively lower-order.*

While knowing both requisite higher-order rules and requisite lower-order rules is a necessary condition for solving composite tasks, this is not sufficient. In order to effectively use available rules to derive solution rules and to solve problems, some type of control mechanism also is needed to determine how each rule is to be used and when.[9]

As shown in Part 3, the simple goal-switching control mechanism appears to provide an adequate basis for explaining a wide variety of complex human behavior. Furthermore, although the empirical tests of this mechanism were conducted under idealized conditions (where all of the requisite higher- and lower-order rules were learned nearly perfectly and were active in "working" memory), the (near) deterministic results obtained have direct implications for the real world of education (cf. Chapters 1 and 11). Ehrenpreis and Scandura (Chapter 11), for example, found that higher-order rules underlying a college course for teachers could be identified in a systematic manner and that instruction on such rules had a highly positive effect on prespecified kinds of "far transfer". In addition, the degree of transfer was directly related to the degree to which the training conditions deviated from the ideal (i.e., the effectiveness of the training conditions, see Addendum to Chapter 11).

To summarize, learners who are able to skip prerequisites appear to do so because they have already learned higher-order rules by which they can solve higher-level tasks without instruction. In effect, higher-order rules, heuristics, or strategies, whichever term might be preferred, correspond to Gagne's (1962) instructions by which learners may progress from one level in a learning hierarchy to a higher-level. Single higher-order rules, however, generally operate in large classes of different hierarchies (cf. Chapter 11).

The significance of higher-order rules can be seen in another way. Whereas failure on a superordinate task (as used by Gagne, 1970) invariably implies failure on one or more prerequisites, success on all prerequisites in traditional learning hierarchies does not necessarily imply success on superordinates. Whereas the former is a deterministic effect, the latter is not. In the latter case, higher-order rules appear to provide the missing link toward determinism.

3.5 CONTENT VERSUS PERFORMANCE ANALYSES

Although the proposed theoretical formulation allows for both process and structure, the empirical work reported in Chapters 3, 4, and 11 emphasize the former. In instructional

---

[9]In many contemporary information processing theories no unique control mechanism is assumed (e.g., Pascual-Leone, 1970; the heterarchical artificial intelligence models of the Massachusetts Institute of Technology school). Such theories, however, suffer from the disadvantage of being either idiosyncratic and/or of moving effective control to a higher level. In the former case, there may be as many mechanisms as programmers and theory becomes a very individualistic enterprise. In the latter case, where there is more than one control mechanism, some control mechanism is needed to tell the others what to do and when.

science, process considerations usually fall under the rubric
of *performance analysis;* structural representations correspond
to *content analysis.*

On the surface, these two approaches appear quite different.
The aim of performance analysis is to specify in terms of behavior the instructional objectives associated with particular content. As we have seen, one may also identify the competencies
necessary to perform the behavior in question (see also Landa,
1974; Gerlach, 1975). In addition, given a particular behavioral
objective, and the desired competency underlying it (at least
implicitly), task analysis may be used to derive a learning hierarchy of prerequisite competencies. This can be accomplished
by asking Gagne's (1962) now familiar question, "What must a
learner know/be able to do in order to ...?"

In general, however, subject matter concepts cannot be
fully represented in terms of single behavioral objectives, or
learning hierarchies associated with same. Even such a relatively simple concept as "number" has a variety of interrelated
aspects (e.g., assigning numbers to sets, counting, relations
between adding elements and counting). Moreover, the prerequisite relation is not the only important way in which concepts
may be related (e.g., consider the relation between the cardinal
and ordinal aspects of number). It is not surprising, therefore,
that, whereas the behavioral emphasis of performance analyses
has appealed to behavioral scientists, the approach has frequently been criticized by subject matter specialists as leading to
fragmented curricula (e.g., see Chapter 11; Scandura, 1971a).

Content analysis, on the other hand, is concerned primarily
with identification of the major "concepts", and relationships
among these concepts, that are characteristic of particular subject matter units. In content analysis, prerequisite relationships among concepts are typically represented in a heterarchical manner (Merrill & Gibbons, 1974). Thus, instead of having
the most basic concepts at the bottom, as in learning hierarchies (Gagne, 1970), with progressively more complex concepts as
one moves toward the apex, there are in heterarchies a variety
of entry points and exits (e.g., see Figure 3).

Whereas content analysis reflects conceptual relationships
in a relatively simple manner, however, it also has important
limitations. It does not, for example, lend itself to individual differences measurement in the same direct way that performance analysis does. The apparently complementary advantages and
disadvantages of performance and content analyses have not gone
unnoticed. Indeed, the two forms of analysis have been combined
in a variety of ways, both on theoretical (e.g., Pask, 1974) and
pragmatic (e.g., Merrill & Boutwell, 1972) grounds. Thus, for
example, content analysis may be used to map out general relationships, with performance analysis used to operationalize
critical concepts in behavioral terms.

Simply combining content and performance analysis, however, has some major limitations:

1. Relationships among sets of paths of relational nets, which correspond to higher-order rules, are not usually or easily represented. For example, relationships among the parallel operations

$$a^{\pm 1}, \ b^{\pm 1}, \ c^{\pm 1}$$

in Figure 3 are left unspecified. The same can be said of the more complex relation expressing the fact that the paths

$$SIN^{\pm 2}, \ COS^{\pm 2}, \ \text{and} \ TAN^{\pm 2}$$

in Figure 3 can be derived in the same way, respectively, from paths

"substitute 1 o $c^{\pm 1}$ o $a^{\pm 1}$ o substitute 2,"
"substitute 1 o $c^{\pm 1}$ o $b^{\pm 1}$ o substitute 3," and
"substitute 2 o $a^{\pm 1}$ o $b^{\pm 1}$ o substitute 3."

(Note: "o" means "followed by".) In effect, parallel operations/relations are often scattered throughout relational nets with nothing specifically to indicate their relationships.

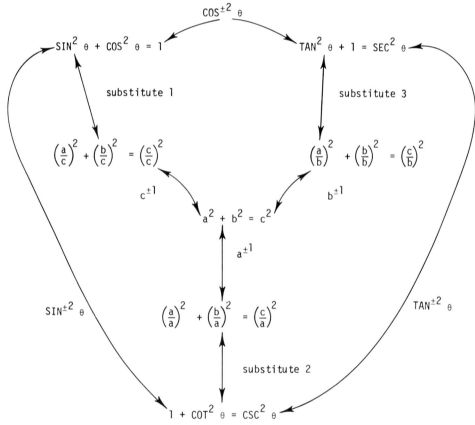

Figure 3. Relational net representing the Pythagorean Theorem, some basic trigonometric identities, and their relationships.

2. Representing knowledge (solely) in terms of comprehensive relational nets essentially eliminates the need for any nontrivial, superordinate control mechanism. Aside from questions pertaining to working memory and attention, there is no question as to how units of knowledge interact since there is only one unit of knowledge. This is an important limitation since the theoretical analyses and data reported in this book strongly suggest that control mechanisms may play a crucial role in learning.

3. The fact that one can represent higher-order concepts and relations in behavioral terms, after they have been identified, says little about how to do it. Representation in terms of relational nets does not direct the analyst's attention in this direction so that representation in terms of behavioral objectives normally has an ad hoc character. For similar reasons, potential relationships to other content (such as can be represented by higher-order rules) are never represented until, and rarely after, the new content has been made explicit.

Difficulties 1 and 2 stem, I believe, from representing knowledge/content in terms of unified but largely static relational nets, and minimizing, if not ignoring, the operational aspects of knowledge. As an alternative to this type of representation, knowledge/content in the structural learning theory is represented in terms of discrete units, called *rules,* and of the entities on which they operate (i.e., structures).

It is worth noting parenthetically that different operations, including different parallel operations, constitute different rules even where they have the same domains (e.g., consider
$$a^{\pm 1}, \ b^{\pm 1}, \text{ and } c^{\pm 1},$$
all of which operate on $a^2 + b^2 = c^2$). Conversely, a single operation may be attached to more than one domain, each combination of which constitutes a different rule. Such differences allow considerable flexibility and detail in representing knowledge. For instance, incorrect knowledge can be represented just as well as correct knowledge (e.g., in school mathematics one can represent the fact that many algebra students allow division by all numbers, even though division by zero is meaningless in ordinary arithmetic). Whereas the above kinds of distinctions are sometimes incorporated in relational net representations, however, this is rarely the case with higher-order relationships. Higher-order rules are especially convenient for this purpose.

Nonetheless, the simplicity provided by relational nets is an important advantage that should not be overlooked. The relational net of Figure 3, for example, corresponds to a subset of rules which could serve as a unitary psychological entity (i.e., structure). Such nets, and subsets thereof, may be operated on as units by other rules. In this sense, they come to play a role analogous to that of Miller's (1956) "chunks", or Minsky's (1974) "frames". (They are directly compatible with the "substimuli" of Scandura, 1973b, Chapter 10 and the "semantic knowl-

edge" of Scandura, 1973b, Chapter 6. In this book, in their
most general sense, they have been called "structures".) In
effect, as commonly used, relational networks may be viewed,
psychologically speaking, as restricted kinds of structures
(i.e., structures that do not include higher-order rules or
relations).

In regard to limitation 3, and especially in view of the
(partly) content specific nature of task domains, it is fortun-
ate that there are general, quasi-systematic methods (Chapter 2)
for identifying the higher-order and other rules underlying given
task domains (e.g., Chapters 3 and 4). Let us briefly summarize
a basic form of structural analysis and illustrate its use in
the analysis of (a portion of) the simple unit on trigonometric
identities depicted in Figure 3. The first step is to select a
representative sample of tasks from the indicated domain. For
illustrative purposes, we shall consider only relationships between trigonometric identities and the Pythagorean Theorem
$(a^2 + b^2 = c^2)$. In this case, suppose we choose the following
tasks:

1. $a^2 + b^2 = c^2$ -- $\sin^2 + \cos^2 = 1$
2. $\sin^2 + \cos^2 = 1$ -- $a^2 + b^2 = c^2$
3. $a^2 + b^2 = c^2$ -- $1 + \cot^2 = \csc^2$

The second step is to identify rules for solving each sampled task, keeping in mind the constraints mentioned in Section
3.3. This gives:

Rule 1. Divide by c^2 o $x^2/y^2 \rightarrow (x/y)^2$ o substitute 1
Rule 2. Substitute 1 o $(x/y)^2 \rightarrow x^2/y^2$ o multiply by c^2
Rule 3. Divide by a^2 o $x^2/y^2 \rightarrow (x/y)^2$ o substitute 2

Although this rule set accounts for the sampled tasks (i.e.,
there is a rule in the set that can be used to generate the desired output to each input), there are other tasks associated
with the domain that cannot be accounted for. For example,
consider

4. $1 + \cot^2 = \csc^2$ -- $a^2 + b^2 = c^2$

The third step is to identify parallels/patterns among the
rules in the initial rule set. In particular, notice that the
steps in Solution Rules 1 and 2 are reversed (including the
inverse operations of multiplication and division).

Such parallels almost invariably reflect the presence of
higher-order rules. In turn, the identification of higher-order
rules together with more basic lower-order rules, often makes
it possible not only to derive the initial solution rules, but
also to derive additional rules as well. For example, consider
the second-order rule set consisting of a higher-order rule, h,
which reverses steps (in rules to which it is applied), together
with Solution Rules 1 and 3.

Collectively, these rules can be used to derive solution
rules for both Tasks 2 and 4. Thus, application of h to rules
1 and 3, respectively, yields Solution Rules 2 and

Rule 4. Substitute $2 \circ (x/y)^2 \to x^2/y^2 \circ$ multiply by a^2.
The rule set, thereby, is said to account for Tasks 2 and 4, as well as Tasks 1 and 3. Hence, Solution Rule 2 may be eliminated as redundant.

Moreover, this rule set may be extended to account for a much broader range of tasks including such tasks as

$$\sin^2 + \cos^2 = 1 \quad -- \quad 1 + \cot^2 = \csc^2$$
$$a^2 + b^2 = c^2 \quad -- \quad a^2/c^2 + b^2/c^2 = c^2/c^2$$

This may be accomplished, for example, by decomposing the solution rules into their components and introducing a higher-order composition rule (which composes pairs of compatible rules, e.g., see Chapter 5). In the process, even Solution Rules 1 and 3 may be eliminated as redundant. As we have seen in Part 2, it is this almost incidental (typically large) gain in generative power, from which structural analysis derives its power.

To summarize, structural analysis provides a potential basis for bridging the gap between current forms of content and performance analysis.

1. The representation of knowledge/content in terms of rules and structures appears to retain the advantages of both performance and content analyses and to overcome the aforementioned limitations. In particular, relationships may be represented, as in content analysis, and in a way that retains the possibilities for individual differences measurement that is characteristic of performance analysis.

2. Rule sets are compatible with the control mechanism described above. They thereby reflect the close interdependence between competence (content) and cognitive theories.

3. There are quasi-systematic methods of structural analysis that make it possible to represent concepts and relations, including higher-order ones, in behavioral terms. These methods may in principle be applied to any content.

The possibility of such analyses alone, of course, does not solve real educational problems. Although detailed structural analyses may be possible in principle and hopefully will become increasingly available through future research, as we have seen in Part 2, rigorous and comprehensive analyses require considerable time, effort, and resources. For many purposes, it may be sufficient to use less sophisticated methods, which nonetheless are compatible with the general approach (cf. Chapters 11 and 12; Scandura, Durnin, Ehrenpreis, & Luger, 1971). For example, in helping teachers to see the need for introducing higher-order rules in their teaching, it may not be necessary to detail such rules. For example, it might be sufficient initially to simply introduce a variety of illustrative tasks whose solutions involve higher-order rules (cf. Scandura 1971a).

3.6 DEVELOPMENTAL STAGES

Current stage theories of human development are often suggestive regarding education, but they have not been sufficiently
developed to provide anything close to an adequate basis for
making specific instructional decisions concerning individual
children. Nonetheless, initial steps have recently been taken
in this direction. In 1972, Scandura showed how failure to
identify competencies underlying number conservation has led to
incorrect interpretations of data addressed to the task of
"proving Piaget wrong". Klahr and Wallace (1973) have shown
further how the competencies underlying conservation of quantity
can be represented in terms of (computerized) production systems.
Siegler's (1975) analysis of balance beam tasks at the 1975
Structural Learning Conference is analogous to the performance
test theory described earlier.

To date, however, competence analyses of developmental
phenomena have been limited to performance and restricted to
particular (usually conservation) tasks. In contrast, many
important developmental phenomena are more global in nature,
and involve a variety of tasks. Consider, for example, the
Piagetian notion of horizontal decalage. The term *horizontal
decalage* refers to the irregular performance that is frequently
observed across different task domains during transitions to new
developmental stages (e.g., number vs. length conservation
tasks). As Beilen (1973) states, "The issue of so-called horizontal decalage, or generalization across concept domains, has
been extensively discussed in the Piagetian literature, and a
number of studies by non-Genevans are addressed to this issue.
As the data show, there is both generalization and variability;
sometimes variability within a stage takes a consistent form,
sometimes not. The issue is a difficult one for stage theory
and investigations sympathetic and unsympathetic to stage theory
will be dealing with it for a long time."

The question here is whether horizontal decalage can be
usefully analyzed in structural learning terms. Unfortunately,
no hard answers to this question can be given in the absence of
relevant empirical information (i.e., serious attempts at and
behavioral evaluation of such analyses). On the other hand,
there are no a priori reasons why analysis along the lines described would not work.

As outlined in Section 3.5, structural analysis would involve drawing a representative sample of conservation tasks and
devising competence accounts consistent with the target populations. In particular, such accounts ought to be consistent with
how a conserver (in the target population) might be expected to
deal with the tasks. (If there is more than one possibility,
of course, each could be included and evaluated behaviorally.)
Thus, for example, a child who conserves both length and area
would be presumed either to have acquired a general rule applic-

able to both conservation tasks, and/or to have available a higher-order rule by which relationships among areas can be generalized from linear relationships.

The competence account, in turn, might be used to identify the relevant knowledge available to individual children. For example, a child who conserves length but not area might be found not to have available either a generalized conservation rule, or a higher-order rule relating linear and two-dimensional quantities. Conversely, once having pinned down the availability of specific higher- and lower-order source rules, it would be possible to make predictions concerning performance on new conservation tasks (derivable via the source rules).

In short, the theoretical machinery is available for guiding the analysis of developmental phenomena in structural learning terms, and for evaluating such analyses behaviorally. Whether or not structural analysis, in its present form, would prove sufficient to derive behaviorally valid accounts of horizontal decalage remains to be seen.

3.7   IMPLICATIONS FOR TEACHERS AND TEACHER EDUCATORS

In spite of continuing attention to CAI, computer-based curricula, and other technological approaches to education, most school and college instruction still takes place in the classroom. Instructors rely for the most part not on theories of learning, problem-solving, or instruction but rather on professional "know-how". Insights acquired over the years, either directly by the instructor or indirectly through someone else, constitute the primary basis for decision-making in the classroom.

Nonetheless, I believe that a generalized understanding of problem solving, as provided by the structural learning theory, may help the teacher/teacher educator in at least two ways:

1. Such understanding may generally sensitize the teacher as to what to look for as sources of student difficulty in problem solving. Is the inadequacy likely to reside in specific knowledge? Higher-order rules? Problem definition? Memory? Problem sequence? These are all questions on which the theory provides general guidance.

2. The structural learning theory and related technologies might be particularly helpful in instructional planning. They provide systematic methods for analyzing content (classes of problems), for detecting student inadequacies, and for overcoming such inadequacies.

Teacher-educators, especially, might benefit from a thorough understanding of the theory and skill in its application. The teacher, on the other hand, will have relatively little time to undertake detailed instructional analyses of the type provided by the theory. For most teachers, a more general understanding may be sufficient.

3.8 IMPLICATIONS FOR MATERIALS DEVELOPMENT AND EDUCATIONAL
TECHNOLOGY AND RELATIONSHIPS TO CLINICAL RESEARCH (WITH
SPECIAL REFERENCE TO SCHOOL MATHEMATICS)

Materials Development: During the 1930s, 1940s, and 1950s,
most school mathematics texts were written by individuals whose
mathematics backgrounds were somewhat dated. Later, at the beginning of the "new math" revolution, much greater weight was
given to contemporary mathematics (in some cases with too little
attention to learning capabilities of the students). Until very
recently, however, materials development in mathematics education has been based almost exclusively on mathematical knowledge
and "professional know-how".

In the middle 1960s, we began to see a new movement emerging in which new behavioral technologies were introduced into
the process. Because this movement was led largely by psychologists who were unfamiliar with mathematics or mathematics education, the resulting materials, at least initially, were often
inadequate and/or outdated mathematically. The methods used
(e.g., behavioral objectives, task analysis) were felt by many
mathematics educators to lead to fragmented curricula with little
attention to either interrelationships or basic learning processes (e.g., Scandura, 1971a).

In retrospect, it seems safe to say that the major difficulties with the use of such technologies resulted not so much
from the technologies themselves, but from the fact that too
little attention was given to mathematics and professional know-
how. Fortunately, that is beginning to change. Respected mathematics authors (e.g., Allendoerfer, 1971; Jansson & Heimer,
1973) are becoming increasingly aware that such technologies
should be the handmaiden of the materials developer, not the
foreman. They provide guidance as to materials development,
not prescriptions to be followed blindly.

Even in this limited role, there is much regarding materials development with which behavioral objectives and task analysis either do not deal or do not deal with adequately. Most are
agreed, for example, that some form of mastery (as opposed to
normative) testing will be required but there has been little
rigorous theory on which to base and improve mastery testing.

The algorithmic/structural approach to criterion-referenced
testing helps meet this need. As we saw in Chapter 9, both diagnostic precision and test efficiency can be improved using
this method. Further, the general theory makes explicit the
relationship between testing and instruction (with regard to
particular tasks). Testing identifies, in greater detail than
traditional mastery testing, not only what the student can and
cannot do but also what the student must learn in order to overcome inadequacies. Future developments hopefully will see the
extension of these ideas to the measurement of basic mathematical processes (cf. Chapter 13; Scandura, 1971a). The structural

learning theory also provides a clear basis for building transfer into curricula--in a way that far transcends traditional task analysis (e.g., Chapter 11).

More to the point, in addition to serving as prototypes, the specific results of available competence analyses (Chapters 3, 4, 11, and 12) have already been or could be useful in the development of instructional materials. An analysis of Scandura's (1971a) text *Mathematics: Concrete Behavioral Foundations* (Chapter 11), for example, was developed as a commercially available workbook to complement the text and has been used in various teacher education classes (Scandura *et al.*, 1971). Less extensive analyses of arithmetic computation (Chapter 9) also have been used effectively in ongoing instruction (Scandura, 1971c, 1972c). In addition, our analysis of geometry construction problems (Chapter 3) has been used as a basis for experimental instruction (Chapter 12) and could be useful as a first step in materials development. The analysis of algebraic proofs (Chapter 4) could be useful in still another way, as a basis for text revision. Restructuring the content of the *Ball State Algebra I Text* (Brumfiel, Eicholz, & Shanks, 1961), in ways consistent with the analysis, could result in more efficient and effective instruction in algebraic proof making (see Chapter 4).

In the future, hopefully, related technologies also may be developed to deal with motivation, problem definition, sequencing, and the like. Any such technologies, of course, should be viewed as helpful tools, not as replacements for common sense, subject matter knowledge, or professional "know-how".

Computer Assisted Instruction (CAI): CAI and other forms of computer usage in mathematics education (e.g., Papert & Solomon, 1972) call even more strongly for deeper understanding of the teaching-learning process. Because of the continuous monitoring of students' progress and the detailed specifications required to make a CAI system work, for example, inadequacies in intuitive judgement are difficult to hide. It is increasingly being recognized (cf. Suppes, 1967) that the major current problems in CAI are not due to hardware, or even to inadequate software, but rather to the lack of sufficient, specific information concerning the instructional process.

While I am well aware of its current limitations, it is nonetheless my considered opinion that the structural learning theory provides one of the most comprehensive and reliable foundations on which one might build a CAI system. Pask's (1974) conversation theory and Landa's (1974) algorithmic approach provide potentially compatible conceptual components for this purpose. Kopstein and Seidel's Project IMPACT was one early attempt to implement a number of potentially compatible ideas. A variety of more normative approaches to CAI also have been developed (e.g., Atkinson, 1972; Suppes, 1971), of course,

but in many cases they tend to derive from quite different basic
assumptions. Whether the present approach has greater potential
for computer-assisted instruction in higher-level processes is
as yet largely an unproven conjecture (however, see Chapter 14).

Clinical Research: As a result of recent research findings
showing a decline in computational and other mathematical skills,
the public and a growing number of mathematics educators have
become disenchanted with the so-called new mathematics. Many
apparently feel that the new curricula have been too abstract
for the broad middle range of mathematics students. Although
this has not necessarily been a result of the new curricula
themselves (e.g., the way they have been taught is probably more
important), many mathematics educators have begun to give increasing attention to concrete, manipulative experiences in more
open classroom settings. Implicit in such suggestions is the
continuing belief that teaching is to be treated primarily as
an art (cf. Polya, 1962). Given this milieu, it is natural that
in their search for adequate conceptualizations, many mathematics
educators have turned to Piagetian theory and the clinical approach to research on which it is based (Piaget, 1965).

In line with Piaget's and other arguments against S-R behaviorism and behavioral objectives (see above), many mathematics
educators have come to feel that any systematic approach to instruction must be diametrically opposed to the clinical, devel-
opment-oriented approaches they favor--and, more important, that
they must be inadequate.

It is undoubtedly true that the structured, more or less,
systematic approaches to curriculum construction that are being
used today have many limitations--as is also true of clinical
methods, I might add. As argued throughout Section 3, however,
this is not necessarily a characteristic of structural approaches
in general. To the contrary, the structural learning theory,
for example, provides a potential basis not only for extending
and generalizing the behavioral objectives approach in mathematics education but possibly also for parts of the more clinical-
ly-oriented Piagetian research (see Section 3.6; also Chapter 2).

Since there are various opinions in education, and particularly in mathematics education, concerning the proper role of
"clinical research", I should like to comment parenthetically
on the relationship between clinical observation and scientific
research in education. In my opinion, clinical observation is
one good source of insight and ideas concerning educational
problems. For one thing, in modified form, such observation may
play an essential role in the method of structural analysis (cf.
Chapter 2). Clinical observations, however, are subject to
varying interpretations (usually in the form of imprecise theories) and, therefore, should be considered only as a prelude
to more rigorous theory and carefully designed research. Once
a problem area is well understood scientifically, then the most

effective role of clinical activity is more analogous to that
of development. Although its importance as a possible source
of new ideas and insights may be expected to diminish, clinical
activity (and engineering) still may serve a useful purpose in
devising practical ways of using scientific knowledge.
   Conclusion: The educational potential of the structural
learning theory and related design principles has been demonstrated in a number of prototype projects (e.g., see Part 5).
More important, the number and variety of possible applications
mentioned above, and scattered throughout this book, would seem
to warrant further attention by educational researchers and
developers.

4. FUTURE DIRECTIONS

   Considerable ground has been covered in this book; in the
view of some perhaps we have attempted to do too much. The reported studies have ranged from analyses of rather complex problem domains, through experimental studies with human subjects
and the measurement of individual differences, to educational
applications and the cumulative effect on learning of interacting with a problem solving environment over time. Still, all
fall within the scope of the structural learning theory.
   Even the broad range of research reported, however, hardly
begins to tap the potential of the theory proposed (primarily)
in Chapters 1, 2, and 14. More research is needed to help fill
some significant gaps. In addition, the theory itself constitutes only a beginning and leaves many questions unanswered,
both as regards further refinement and extension to more global
phenomena.
   Among the more obvious and pressing problems are the
following.

4.1 STRUCTURAL ANALYSIS
   The area of structural analysis has a number of important
gaps, both as regards theory and empirical research. Although
general guidelines have been developed, much of what goes into
an adequate structural analysis is intuitive and heavily dependent on the perspecuity of the analyst. The method of analysis
must be made more objective so that it can be carried out by
less skilled personnel--ideally, one might want to automate the
method (e.g., implement it on a computer). In addition, structural analysis needs to be generalized, for example, so that
higher-order problem definition and selection rules may be identified (as well as higher-order derivation and subproblem rules).
The same applies to nontrivial structures (e.g., to structures
similar to the propositional nets commonly studies in language
comprehension).

Although several problem domains have been analyzed in structural terms (e.g., geometry construction, algebraic proofs, critical reading), they represent a fairly limited range of content. Very little, for example, has been done by way of dealing with content having a significant perceptual component. Analyses of global competencies, such as those concerned with values, morality, and motivation also are badly needed. Although there are rich scientific literatures in each of these areas, it is not at all clear whether or how existant research might relate to structural analyses of such domains.

4.2   COGNITIVE RESEARCH

Rule derivation, problem definition, rule selection, etc., as well as processing capacity and processing speed, are all involved in problem solving. Most of the research reported, however, deals with single processes under idealized conditions. To date, in fact, most of the directly related research has been directed toward the foundations of the theory--toward determining whether the basic assumptions of the theory are valid. Given the progress that has been made in this direction, it seems appropriate at this point to move beyond this level. Problem solving research concerned with the dynamic interaction of the proposed control (goal switching) mechanism and fixed processing capacity is especially needed. More generally, a greater variety of theoretical implications of the theory need to be derived and tested empirically.

In order to bear on the proposed theory, of course, it is not necessary that every experimental study be conducted under idealized conditions. In many cases, this may not be possible, or at least not feasible. The main requirement is that a clear separation be maintained between structural variables (those which have deterministic effects under idealized conditions, Chapter 1) and incidental variables which correspond to deviations from the ideal. Whereas effects of the former may be expected to hold in all contexts, even if in a weaker probabilistic sense, results associated with incidental variables will have strict limits. Consequently, to help insure generalizability of results, attention also should be given to the problem of how to map (real-world) empirical situations onto fundamental sources of deviation from the ideal (see Chapter 1).

All this is not to say that there are no further foundational concerns. Many theoretical details remain unclear. For example, although the proposed control mechanism appears generally viable, its exact nature is still open. When control shifts from lower- to higher-level goals, are the latter actually *constructed* from the former or does the higher-level goal depend to some extent on what knowledge is available (active in the processor) at the time? Precise specification of this mechanism as well as of the principles governing the activation and deactiva-

tion of information in the processor, and processing speed, will
require considerable interplay between theory and research. A
particularly intriguing conjecture in this regard is that processing speed may be directly related to processing capacity.
If true, this relationship, could have far reaching consequences.
Combined with the nonstandard conjecture made in Section 2.1
(Creativity) concerning reasoning ability, for example, such a
relationship could upset common notions as to what counts as
intelligence.

In some cases, distinguishing between theoretical alternatives may not be easy and new experimental methods may have to
be developed. Where processing capacity is a primary concern,
for example, it may be important to develop efficient techniques
for introducing (sometimes complex) cues at specified points
during the problem solving process. Generally speaking, the
effect of cues in problem solving may depend critically not only
on the content of a given cue but also on when the cue is given.
This was perhaps the major tentative conclusion of my very first
piece of serious research (Scandura, 1964a.)

4.3 MEASURING INDIVIDUAL DIFFERENCES
In the area of individual differences, available research
has been limited to the assessment of particular lower- (Chapter
8 and 9) and higher- (Chapters 3 and 13) order rules. As described in Chapter 2, it is clear schematically how one might
go about testing for mastery of broader domains, but whether it
would be feasible to actually do this remains to be seen. Research along these lines could have both theoretical and practical importance and should be encouraged. In the theoretical
vein, more exacting analyses could help to clarify relationships
between traditional normative testing and the structural (criterion-referenced) approach proposed in this book. Insofar as
testing itself is concerned, one has only to consider the possibilities that structural analysis of the commonly used SAT or
GRE tests might provide. If successful, such analyses not only
could provide more definitive measures of what testees are and
are not capable of but also what they need to know in order to
do better.

Although some research along these lines has already been
done (e.g., Groen, 1967), further developments in assessing
skilled performance also are badly needed in a wide variety of
areas, both academic and otherwise. Moreover, although the
effects of context in testing have received increasing attention
over the past few years, the obtained results to my knowledge
bear at best indirectly on underlying theoretical issues. Tying such work in more closely with underlying theory could have
both theoretical and practical value.

4.4 SEQUENCING

The research reported in this book has been limited largely to single problem-solving episodes; with the exception of Chapters 13 and 14, relatively little attention has been given to the growth of knowledge as it takes place over time (i.e., over sequences of problem solving episodes).

Nonetheless, undoubtedly the single most important ingredient of problem-solving ability is *experience*. As the successful mathematical problem solver, Murray Klamkin, has put it, "If you want to get good at solving problems then you must (attempt to) solve lots of them."[10] As true as this simple prescription is, however, it is not sufficient. Surely, a person who continually fails in his attempts to solve problems is not going to gain very much. Indeed, there is reason to believe that he may get worse (Scandura, Barksdale, Durnin, & McGee, 1969).

Providing problems that challenge the student but do not overwhelm him seems to be the key. But, exactly what does this mean? The kind of analysis we have proposed provides a partial answer: A problem should require a level of derivation that is commensurate with the processing capacity and (especially higher-level) rules available to a subject at any particular time.[11]

Most substantial improvements in problem-solving ability, however, take place over relatively long periods of time. As the subject interacts with a problem solving environment, his capabilities change and these new capabilities, in turn, affect how he will react in the future. As we saw in Chapter 14, the sequence in which problems are presented can have a critical influence on what the problem solver learns and can do.

Clearly, better understanding of how knowledge develops, and how to sequence problem-solving experiences to have desired effects, would be highly desirable. In this regard, I should mention that the growth of knowledge over time is basic, not only to education, but to human cognitive development generally. There are few problems that are more important, and every reasonable course towards its solution should be pursued.

4.5 THEORETICAL EXTENSIONS

Although the general nature of the structural learning theory has been reasonably well established, its ultimate scope is yet to be firmly established. As it stands, the theory is limited in its application to an observer and one subject inter-

---

[10]Personal communication.

[11]It is important to reemphasize in this regard that higher order rules are learned just as are other rules. In general, higher order rules are not themselves innate. Presumably, only the proposed control mechanism and other inborn/physiologically determined capabilities fall in this category. All other knowledge might be assumed to derive from such basic capabilities as a result of the organism's interaction over time with an ever-changing environment.

acting with a given environment. In a particular application, of course, the observer might serve simultaneously as a teacher who controls the subject's environment.

Group Problem Solving: Since much problem solving takes place in groups, it is natural to inquire as to the possibility of generalizing the theory in this direction. At a schematic level, it is relatively easy to see how this might be accomplished. Thus, suppose an observer is overseeing a pair of subjects interacting competitively in a problem situation. To fully understand the pair's behavior, the observer would not only have to assess the relevant knowledge had by the individuals but also to make judgements regarding what each individual knows concerning what the other person knows (and wants). Possibly, the latter type of information might be determined through suitable generalization of the assessment (observation) methods described in Chapter 2 and Part 4. If interactions among pairs of subjects could be handled in this way, it would be a small step conceptually to generalize further to include any finite number of interacting individuals. Presumably, some such framework could be made sufficiently broad to encompass both groups of subjects working in opposition and groups working toward a common goal.

Detailed analysis of any realistic situation, of course, could get quite complex and, in practical situations, it would almost certainly be necessary to impose restrictions of various kinds. In cooperative problem solving, for example, it might be sufficient to consider only the competence theory used to measure individual knowledge. In this case, notice that group activity might either facilitate or interfere with problem solving. In the latter case, for example, more capable members of a group might find themselves distracted by vocal but less-insightful individuals. Such vocalizations (potentially explicable in terms of less-insightful subjects' motivational tendencies--e.g., selection rules to speak or not to speak) could tend to overload more productive processors during critical periods, thereby hindering performance. Clearly, this entire scenario is intimately involved with decision-making. Since I am not familiar with the current state of decision theory it would be presumptuous to offer any opinions as to what, if anything, the above scheme might add. I suspect, however, that such judgements will only be possible after someone seriously looks into the question.

A Social/Cultural Example: Why is it that some immigrant groups have been more easily absorbed into the American melting pot than others? I do not pretend to have an answer to this complex question and could not present one here even if I did. Nonetheless, some speculations in this regard may be suggestive as regards possible extension of the present approach.

In order to answer this type of question it is important

to emphasize, one additional point. Although the Structural Learning Theory provides a basis for dealing with what individual subjects will do in particular situations, the basic unit of analysis need not be the individual, or for that matter, specific situations. One can conceive, for example, of a generalized problem solving environment in interaction with a population of subjects treated as a population. In the simplest case, the problem solving environment might be classified as to the types and varieties of rules and higher-order rules involved in their solutions. The corresponding subject population, in turn, would be classified according to the kinds of relevant knowledge which characterize the population. In some cases, obviously, there will be a closer fit between the requirements for successful problem solving in the problem environment and the kinds of knowledge characteristic of the population than in other cases. The closer the fit, obviously, the better, overall a population might be expected to fare in that problem environment.

Analogous reasoning may be applied in the case of immigrant groups, viewed as populations relating to the American social structure. While the individual differences involved, of course, are much greater than those that can be attributed to groups, it also is true that there are various cultural traits that tend to be generally characteristic of entire populations. These characteristics do not allow detailed prediction of individual behavior, nor for that matter do they refer to group averages. They may, however, allow one to predict the general "cultural chemistry" resulting from the mixture of two or more cultures.

To wit, at the risk of great oversimplification, some validity may be attributed to certain national stereotypes. Thus, German society is a formal one. It is a society of laws and regulations, laws for almost every conceivable purpose--and, moreover, everyone lives by them. English society does not seem to have as many laws but they seem to live by them anyway. Anyone who has observed English society first hand cannot fail to be impressed by its orderliness. In short, it is a society that substitutes in many cases custom for law.

In French society, law is not revered in the same sense-- laws are made by men and, hence may be good or bad. Laws are meant to make sure that nobody opts for more than his or her fair share. Bad laws not only are bad but, in the eyes of the French, should be broken. Italian society carries this view a step further. Because laws over a period of many centuries were made by outsiders, society developed in large part independently of formal law. In its place was substituted strong family ties, in the extended sense, coupled with a Catholic sense of morality that was understood and respected by all, if not always followed. As long as certain taboos were not violated, the superficialities of formal law were largely irrelevant.

American society, originally, was largely an informal mix-

ture of English/German culture that evolved gradually as a result of interaction with a vast continent. The major feature
of man-made (English/German) law prevailed, while personal
relationships tended to become at once more informal and, in
many ways, more superficial than on the European continent.
Later, American society became more pluralistic with the result
that various views and subgroups have vied for control. In
many ways, it is not an overstatement to say that the subgroups
who control various aspects of American society tend to make the
laws that are good for them, and to expect the others to live
by them. During the current cultural transition within American
society, indeed, we see new laws being made at an unprecedented
rate. In large measure, these laws are reflective of a shift
in power from traditional power segments of society to new ones.

In this context, let us consider the extent to which the
above analysis might be useful in explaining the continuing pre-
dominance, albeit a weakening one, of individuals of English/
German heritage in leadership positions of American society.
(The increasingly pluralistic character of American society
makes it even more important to achieve and/or maintain control
than it has been traditionally.) In traditional English/German
culture, it is well accepted that some people make the laws and
that they must be obeyed by all. Given this orientation, one
might say the presence of these higher-order rules, it is
natural that the leaders within this subculture have aspired
to positions of overall social control.

Americans of Latin origins, in contrast, are more influenced by intent, whether something is good or bad. Prejudice
aside, for the early immigrants faced a good deal of it, the
majority of newcomers from these countries found greater opportunities in their new home. They came to think of American
society and its laws as good ones. In many ways, for example,
judging in terms of the percentage of its sons who fought in
the major World Wars, they became among the most patriotic of
Americans. To some extent this has changed in recent years,
possibly due in part to the rapid changes that have taken place
in American society. Since the new laws have tended to indirectly but disproportionately penalize members of this group,
and since many of the new mores as well as laws, conflict with
their basic values, it should come as no surprise that there
has been a growing ethnic awareness in recent years.

Relationship to More Specialized Theories: As reemphasized
in Section 1 of this chapter, the structural learning theory
works from the top-down. Accordingly, although comprehensive
in scope, the theory is not as detailed, in some cases, as restricted theories designed especially to deal with particular
phenomena.

Fleshing out the structural learning theory, to fill in
missing detail, could be helpful in several ways. First, theo-

retical development along this line would help to establish empirical limits of the theory as a strictly deterministic enterprise (cf. Chapter 7). (Where determinism is no longer possible, one would have to decide between complementary observation theories or alternative, most likely probabilistic theories, cf. Chapter 1.) Second, the theory could help to provide psychological/cognitive substance to replace theoretical constructs (e.g., statistical parameters, information measures) in other structural/process theories that serve a primarily formal role and that are closely tied to empirical data (e.g., Rasch, 1960; Kempf, 1974; Weltner, 1973; cf. Hilke, Kempf, & Scandura, 1977).

Finally, because of its broad, empirically proven scope, the structural learning theory could help to identify modifications needed in more restricted theories in order to insure their generalizability (to new phenomena). To some extent, this has already been accomplished with respect to criterion-referenced testing (Chapter 9) and experimental studies of human problem solving (Section 2). Whether it might serve a similar purpose with specialized memory and/or information processing theories remains to be seen (cf. Chapter 2, Section 4.2).

REFERENCES

Abelson, R. P. Representing mundain reality in plans. In D. G. Bobrow & A. Collins (Eds.), *Representation and understanding: Studies in cognitive science.* New York: Academic Press, 1975.

Allendoerfer, C. B. Evaluation of elementary textbooks. *American Mathematical Monthly,* 1971, *78,* 189-192.

Anderson, J. R., & Bower, G. H. *Human associative memory.* Washington, D.C.: Winston & Sons, 1973.

Atkinson, R. C. Ingredients for a theory of instruction. *American Psychologist,* 1972, *27,* 921-931.

Ausubel, D. P. *Educational psychology: A cognitive view.* New York: Holt, Rinehart, & Winston, 1968.

Banerji, R. B. A formal approach to knowledge in problem solving. In J. M. Scandura, J. H. Durnin, & W. H. Wulfeck II (Eds.), *1974 Proceedings: Fifth annual interdisciplinary conference on structural learning* (Office of Naval Research Technical Report, 1974). MERGE Research Institute, 1249 Greentree Lane, Narberth, PA 19072.

Beilen, H. Future research in mathematics education: The view from developmental psychology. Symposium paper presented at "Cognitive Psychology and the Mathematics Laboratory," School of Education, Northwestern University, Chicago, February, 1973.

Bloom, B. S. Recent developments in mastery learning. *Educational Psychology,* 1973, *10,* 53-57.

Bobrow, D. G. Dimensions of representation. In D. G. Bobrow & A. Collins (Eds. *Representation and understanding: Studies in cognitive science.* New York: Academic Press, 1975.

Bobrow, D. G., & Collins, A. (Eds.). *Representation and understanding: Studies in cognitive science.* New York: Academic Press, 1975.

Bobrow, D. G., & Raphael, B. New programming languages for artificial intelligence research. *Computing Surveys,* 1974, *6,* 153-174.

Bormuth, J. R. *On the theory of achievement test items.* Chicago: University of Chicago Press, 1970.

Bower, G. H.   A selective review of organizational factors in memory.   In E.
    Tulving & W. Donaldson (Eds.), *Organization of memory*. New York: Academic
    Press, 1972.
Brown, J. S., & Burton, R. R.   Multiple representations of knowledge for tutorial
    reasoning.   In D. G. Bobrow & A. Collins (Eds.), *Representation and under-
    standing: Studies in cognitive science*. New York: Academic Press, 1975.
Brumfiel, C. F., Eicholz, R. E., & Shanks, M. E.   *Algebra I*. Reading, Mass.:
    Addison-Wesley, 1961.
Bruner, J. S.   Some theorems on instruction illustrated with references to
    mathematics.   In *Theories of learning and instruction, sixty-third yearbook
    of the National Society for the Study of Education, Part I*. Chicago:
    National Society for the Study of Education, 1974.
Bruner, J. S., Goodnow, J. J., & Austin, G. A.   *A study of thinking*. New York:
    Wiley, 1956.
Burke, R. J., Maier, N. R. F., & Hoffman, L. R.   Functions of hints in individual
    problem solving.   *American Journal of Psychology*, 1966, *79*, 389-399.
Carroll, J. B.   Towards a performance grammar for core sentences in spoken and
    written English.   *Journal of Structural Learning*, 1975, *4*, 189-197.
Church, A.   An unsolvable problem of elementary number theory.   *American Journal
    of Mathematics*, 1936, *58*, 345-363.
Collins, A., Warnock, E., Aiello, N., & Miller, M.   Reasoning from incomplete
    knowledge.   In D. G. Bobrow & A. Collins (Eds.), *Representation and under-
    standing: Studies in cognitive science*. New York: Academic Press, 1975.
Cooper, L. A.   Mental rotation of random two-dimensional shapes.   *Cognitive
    Psychology*, 1975, *1*, 20-43.
Cooper, L. A., & Shepard, R. N.   Cronometric of the rotation of mental images.
    In W. G. Chase (Ed.), *Visual information processing*. New York: Academic
    Press, 1973.
DiVesta, F.   Theory and measures of individual differences in studies of trait
    by treatment interaction.   *Educational Psychologist*, 1973, *10*, 67-75.
Dunker, K.   On problem solving.   Translated by L. S. Lees from the 1935 original.
    Psychological Monographs, 1945, *58*, 198-311.
Durnin, J. H., & Scandura, J. M.   An algorithmic approach to assessing behavior
    potential: Comparison with item forms and hierarchical analysis.   *Journal
    of Educational Psychology*, 1973, *65*, 262-272.
Egan, D. E., & Greeno, J. G.   *Theory of rule induction: Knowledge acquired in
    concept learning, serial pattern learning, and problem solving* (Human
    Performance Center, Technical Report No. 44). Ann Arbor: University of
    Michigan, 1973.
Ernst, G. W., & Newell, A.   *GPS (General Problem Solver): A case study in
    generality and problem solving*. New York: Academic Press, 1969.
Ferguson, R. L.   *Computer-assisted criterion-referenced measurement*. Unpublished
    doctoral dissertation, University of Pittsburgh, 1969.
Frey, K.   *Theorien des curriculum*. Beltz Verlag: Weinheim und Basel, 1971.
Gagne, R. M.   The acquisition of knowledge.   *Psychological Review*, 1962, *59*,
    355-365.
Gagne, R. M.   *The conditions of learning* (2nd ed.). New York: Holt, Rinehart,
    & Winston, 1970.
Gagne, R. M.   1974 Thorndike Award Address to Division 15 of the American
    Psychological Society. New Orleans, September 1, 1974.
Gerlach, V. S.   Instructional design: Beyond behavioral objectives and criterion-
    referenced assessment.   In B. Blai & J. Kornfeld (Eds.), *Proceedings of the
    sixth structural learning conference*. Narberth, Pa. 19072: MERGE Research
    Institute, 1975.
Glaser, R.   Instructional technology and the measurement of learning outcomes:
    Some questions.   *American Psychology*, 1963, *18*, 519-521.
Glaser, R.   Toward a behavioral science base for instructional design.   In R.
    Glaser (Ed.), *Teaching machines and programmed learning II*. Washington, D.C.:
    National Educational Association, 1965.
Glaser, R.   Educational psychology and education.   *American Psychologist*, 1973,
    28, 557-566.

Greeno, J. G. The structure of memory and the process of solving problems. In
    R. Solso (Ed.), *Contemporary issues in cognitive psychology: The Loyola
    Symposium*. Washington, D.C.: Winston, 1973.
Greeno, J. G. Processes of learning and comprehension. In L. W. Gregg (Ed.),
    Knowledge and cognition. Potomac, Md.: Erbaum, 1974.
Greeno, J. G. Indefinite goals in well-structured problems. *Psychological
    Review*, 1976, *83*, 479-491.
Groen, G. J. *An investigation of some counting algorithms for simple addition
    problems* (Technical Report No. 118). Stanford, Ca.: Institute for Mathema
    tical Studies in the Social Sciences, 1967.

Guilford, J. P. *The nature of human intelligence*. New York: McGraw-Hill, 1967.

Hilke, R., Kempf, W. F., & Scandura, J. M. Deterministic and probabilistic
    theorizing in structural learning. In H. Spada & W. F. Kempf (Eds.),
    *Formalized theories of thinking and learning and their implications for
    science instruction*. Bern: Huber, 1977.

Hively, W., Patterson, H. L., & Page, S. A "universe defined" system of
    arithmetic achievement tests. *Journal of Educational Measurement*, 1968,
    5, 275-290.

Holzman, T. G., Glaser, R., & Pellegrino, J. W. Process training derived from a
    computer simulation theory. *Memory and Cognition*, 1976, *4*, 349-356.

Huttenlocher, J. Development of formal reasoning on concept formation problems.
    Child Development, 1964, *35*, 1233-1242.
Jansson, L. C., & Heimer, R. T. On behavioral objectives in mathematics educatior
    American Mathematical Monthly, 1973, *80*, 930-933.
Johnson, P. J., Warner, M. L., & Silleroy, R. S. Factors influencing children's
    concept identification performance with nonpreferred relevant attributes.
    Journal of Experimental Child Psychology, 1971, *11*, 430-441.
Kempf, W. F. A test-theoretical approach to structural learning. In J. M.
    Scandura, J. H. Durnin, & W. H. Wulfeck II (Eds.), *1974 Proceedings: Fifth
    annual interdisciplinary conference on structural learning* (Office of Naval
    Research Technical Report, 1974). MERGE Research Institute, 1249 Greentree
    Lane, Narberth, PA 19072.
Kintsch, W. Notes on the structure of semantic memory. In E. Tulving & W.
    Donaldson (Eds.), *Organization of memory*. New York: Academic Press, 1972.
Kintsch, W. *The representation of meaning in memory*. New York: Wiley, 1974.
Klahr, D., & Wallace, J. G. The role of quantification operators in the develop-
    ment of conservation of quantity. *Cognitive Psychology*, 1973, *3*, 301-327.
Kleene, S. C. *Mathematical logic*. New York: Wiley, 1967.
Klix, F. Remarks on relationships between the algorithmic and the stochastic
    approach in mapping human thought processes. *Publications of the National
    Center of Scientific Research*, 15 Quai Anatole-France, Paris, 1967.
Klix, F., & Sydow, H. The organization of information processing in problem
    solving behavior. *Publications of the National Center of Scientific Researcl*
    15 Quai Anatole-France, Paris, 1968.
Kuhn, T. S. *The structure of scientific revolutions*. Chicago: University
    Press, 1962.
Landa, L. N. *Algorithmization of learning and instruction*. Englewood Cliffs,
    N.J.: Educational Technology Publications, 1974.
Levine, M. Hypothesis behavior by humans during discrimination learning. *Journa*
    of Experimental Psychology, 1966, *71*, 331-338.
Luchins, A. S. Mechanization in problem solving: The effect of Einstellung.
    Psychological Monographs, 1942, *54*, No. 6 (Whole No. 248).
Maier, N. R. F. Reasoning in humans. I. On direction. *Journal of Comparative
    Psychology*, 1930, *12*, 115-143.
Mayer, R. E., & Greeno, J. G. Structural differences between learning outcomes
    produced by different instructional methods. *Journal of Educational
    Psychology*, 1972, *63*, 165-173.
McCarthy, J., & Hayes, P. Some philosophical problems from the standpoint of
    artificial intelligence. In B. Meltzer & D. Michie (Eds.), *Machine
    intelligence 4*. New York: American Elsevier, 1969.

Merrill, M. D., & Boutwell, R. C. *Instructional Development: Methodology and research* (Working Paper No. 33). Provo, Utah: Brigham Young University (Division of Instructional Services), May 31, 1972.

Merrill, M. D., & Gibbons, A. Heterarchies and their relationship to behavioral hierarchies for sequencing content in instruction. In J. M. Scandura, J. H. Durnin, & W. H. Wulfeck II (Eds.), *1974 Proceedings: Fifth annual interdisciplinary conference on structural learning* (Office of Naval Research Technical Report, 1974). MERGE Research Institute, 1249 Greentree Lane, Narberth, PA 19072.

Miller, G. A. The magical number seven, plus or minus two: Some limits on our capacity for processing information. *Psychological Review,* 1956, *63,* 81-97.

Miller, G. A., Galanter, E., & Pribram, K. H. *Plans and the structure of behavior.* New York: Holt-Dryden, 1960.

Minsky, M., & Papert, S. *Research at the laboratory in vision, language and other problems of intelligence* (Artificial Intelligence Progress Report, Memo 252). Cambridge, Mass.: Massachusetts Institute of Technology, Artificial Intelligence Laboratory, 1972.

Minsky, M. A framework for representing knowledge. In P. Winston (Ed.), *The psychology of computer vision.* New York: McGraw-Hill, 1975.

Newell, A. Production systems: Models of control structures. In W. G. Chase (Ed.), *Visual information processing.* New York: Academic Press, 1973.

Newell, A., Shaw, J. C., & Simon, H. A. Elements of a theory of human problem solving. *Psychological Review,* 1958, *65,* 151-166.

Newell, A., & Simon, H. A. *Human problem solving.* Englewood Cliffs, N.J.: Prentice-Hall, 1972.

Nilsson, N. J. *Problem solving methods in artificial intelligence.* New York: McGraw-Hill, 1971.

Papert, S., & Soloman, C. Twenty things to do with a computer. *Educational Technology,* 1972, *12,* 9-18.

Paige, J. M., & Simon, H. A. Cognitive processes in solving algebra word problems. In B. Kleinmuntz (Ed.), *Problem solving: Research method and theory.* New York: Wiley, 1966.

Paivio, A. Mental imagery in associative learning and memory. *Psychological Review,* 1969, *76,* 241-263.

Paivio, A. *Images, proposition, and knowledge.* London, Ontario: Western Ontario University, Psychology Department, Report 309, 1974.

Pascual-Leone, J. A mathematical model for the transition rule in Piaget's developmental stages. *Acta Psychologica,* 1970, *63,* 301-345.

Pask, G. Practical methods for building extendable knowledge structures based on the idea that concepts are procedures for reconstructing relations and that memories are procedures for reconstructing concepts: Empirical data and theoretical discussion. In J. M. Scandura, J. H. Durnin, & W. H. Wulfeck II (Eds.), *1974 Proceedings: Fifth annual interdisciplinary conference on structural learning* (Office of Naval Research Technical Report 1974). MERGE Research Institute, 1249 Greentree Lane, Narberth, PA 19072.

Pask, G. *Conversation, cognition, and learning.* Amsterdam: Elsevier, 1975.

Pask, G., Scott, B. C. E., & Kallikourdis, D. A theory of conversations and individuals (Exemplified by the learning process on CASTE). *International Journal of Man-Machine Studies,* 1973, *5,* 443-566.

Piaget, J. *The child's conception of number.* New York: Norton, 1965.

Polya, G. *Mathematical discovery* (Vol. 1). New York: Wiley, 1962.

Pylyshyn, Z. W. What the mind's eye tells the mind's brain: A critique of mental imagery. *Psychological Bulletin,* 1973, *80,* 1-24.

Quillian, M. R. Semantic memory. In M. Minsky (Ed.), *Semantic information processing.* Cambridge, Mass.: Massachusetts Institute of Technology Press, 1968.

Rasch, G. *Probabilistic models for some intelligence and attainment tests.* Copenhagen: Nielsen & Lydiche, 1960.

Resnick, L. B. Open education: Some tasks for technology. *Educational Technology,* 1972, *12,* 70-76.

Resnick, L. B., & Glaser R. Problem solving and intelligence. In L. B.
Resnick (Ed.), *The nature of intelligence*. Hillsdale, N.J.: Erlbaum, 1976.

Rumelhart, D. E., Lindsay, P. H., & Norman, D. A. A process model for long-term memory. In E. Tulving & W. Donaldson (Eds.), *Organization of memory*. New York: Academic Press, 1972.

Scandura, J. M. The teaching-learning process: An exploratory investigation of exposition and discovery modes of problem solving instruction. Ph.D. dissertation, Syracuse University, 1962. *(Dissertation Abstracts*, 1963, *23*, No. 8.)

Scandura, J. M. Abstract card tasks for use in problem solving research. *Journal of Experimental Education*, 1964, *33*, 145-148. (a)

Scandura, J. M. An analysis of exposition and discovery modes of problem solving instruction. *Journal of Experimental Education*, 1964, *33*, 149-159. (b)

Scandura, J. M. Prior learning, presentation order, and prerequisite practice in problem solving. *Journal of Experimental Education*, 1966, *34*, 12-18.

Scandura, J. M. The basic unit in meaningful learning--association or principle? *The School Review*, 1967, *58*, 356-364.

Scandura, J. M. New directions for theory and research on rule learning: I. A set-function language. *Acta Psychologica*, 1968, *28*, 301-321.

Scandura, J. M. New directions for theory and research on rule learning: II. Empirical research. *Acta Psychologica*, 1969, *29*, 101-133.

Scandura, J. M. Role of rules in behavior: Toward an operational definition of what (rule) is learned. *Psychological Review*, 1970, *77*, 516-533.

Scandura, J. M. *Mathematics: Concrete behavioral foundations*. New York: Harper & Row, 1971. (a)

Scandura, J. M. A theory of mathematical knowledge: Can rules account for creative behavior? *Journal for Research in Mathematics Education*, 1971, *2*, 183-196. (b)

Scandura, J. M. Deterministic theorizing in structural learning: Three levels of empiricism. *Journal of Structural Learning*, 1971, *3*, 21-53. (c)

Scandura, J. M. What is a rule? *Journal of Educational Psychology*, 1972, *63*, 179-185. (a)

Scandura, J. M. A plan for the development of a conceptually based mathematics curriculum for disadvantaged children. I. Theoretical foundations. *Instructional Science*, 1972, *2*, 247-262. (b)

Scandura, J. M. A plan for the development of a conceptually based mathematics curriculum for disadvantaged children. II. Applications. *Instructional Science*, 1972, *2*, 363-387. (c)

Scandura, J. M. On higher order rules. *Journal of Educational Psychology*, 1973, *10*, 159-160. (a)

Scandura, J. M. *Structural learning I: Theory and research*. New York: Gordon & Breach, 1973. (b)

Scandura, J. M. The structure of memory: Fixed or flexible? *Catalog of Selected Documents in Psychology*, 1974 (Abstract pp. 37-38). Abridged version in F. Klix (Ed.), *Organismische Informationsverarbeitung*. Berlin: Akademie-Verlag, 1974. (a)

Scandura, J. M. Role of higher order rules in problem solving. *Journal of Experimental Psychology*, 1974, *120*, 984-991. (b)

Scandura, J. M. *Structural learning II: Issues and approaches*. London/New York: Gordon & Breach, 1976.

Scandura, J. M. Structural approach to instructional problems. *American Psychologist*, 1977, *32*, 33-53.

Scandura, J. M. A deterministic approach to research in instructional science. *Educational Psychologist*, in press (to appear in Volume 12, No. 2). (a)

Scandura, J. M., Barksdale, J., Durnin, J. H., & McGee, R. An unexpected relationship between failure and subsequent mathematics learning. *Educational Studies in Mathematics*, 1969, *1*, 247-251; also in *Psychology in the Schools*, 1969, *4*, 379-381.

Scandura, J. M., & Durnin, J. H.   Assessing behavior potential: Adequacy of basic theoretical assumptions.   *Journal of Structural Learning,* in press (to appear in Volume 6, No. 1).   (Originally published as University of Pennsylvania Structural Learning Series, Report No. 62, November 30, 1971.)

Scandura, J. M., Durnin, J. H., Ehrenpreis, W., & Luger, G.   *Algorithmic approach to mathematics: Concrete behavioral foundations.*   New York: Harper & Row, 1971.

Schank, R. C.   Identification of conceptualizations underlying natural language.   In R. C. Schank & K. M. Colby (Eds.), *Computer models of thought and language.*   San Francisco: Freeman, 1973.

Scholnick, E. K.   Inference and preference in children's conceptual performance.   *Child Development,* 1970, *41,* 449-460.

Siegler, R. S.   Issues in studying developmental change.   In B. Blai & J. Kornfeld (Eds.), *Proceedings of the sixth annual structural learning conference.*   Narberth, Pa. 19072:   Structural Learning Society and MERGE Research Institute, 1975.

Simon, H. A.   *The sciences of the artificial.*   Cambridge, Mass.:   Massachusetts Institute of Technology Press, 1969.

Speedie, S. M., Treffinger, D. J., & Feldhusen, J. F.   *Teaching problem solving skills: Development of an instructional model based on human abilities related to efficient problem solving* (Final Report, (OEG-5-72-0042(509)).   West Lafayette, Ind.:   Purdue University, 1973.

Spence, D. P.   Analog and digital descriptions of behavior.   *American Psychologist,* 1973, *28,* 479-488.

Suppes, P.   *Computer-assisted instruction at Stanford.*   Stanford University: Institute for Mathematical Studies in the Social Sciences, Report 174, May 19, 1971.

Suppes, P., & Groen, G. J.   Some counting models for first-grade performance data on simple addition facts.   In J. M. Scandura (Ed.), *Research in mathematics education.*   Washington, D.C.:   National Council of Teachers of Mathematics, 1967.

Toppino, T. C.   *The inferential component of children's hypothesis testing behavior.*   Unpublished doctoral dissertation, University of New Mexico, 1974.

Tulving, E.   Episodic and semantic memory.   In E. Tulving & W. Donaldson (Eds.), *Organization of memory.*   New York: Academic Press, 1972.

Voorhies, D.   *Information-processing capacity.*   Unpublished doctoral dissertaiton, University of Pennsylvania, 1973.

Wason, P. C., & Johnson-Laird, P. N.   *Psychology of reasoning: Structure and content.*   Cambridge, Mass.:   Harvard University Press, 1972.

Weltner, K.   *The measurement of verbal information in psychology and education.*   New York: Springer-Verlag, 1973.

Wertheimer, M.   *Productive thinking.*   New York: Harper, 1945.

Winograd, T.   *Procedures as a representation for data in a computer program for understanding natural language* (Report No. AI-TR-17).   Cambridge, Mass.:   Massachusetts Institute of Technology, Artificial Intelligence Laboratory, 1971.

Winograd, T.   Frame representations and the declarative/procedural controversy.   In D. G. Bobrow & A. Collins (Eds.), *Representation and understanding: Studies in cognitive science.*   New York: Academic Press, 1975.

COMPLETE LIST OF REPORTS BY NUMBER*

1. Scandura, J. M. An exceptionally rare athlete. *The Mentor Magazine*, 1959, *10*, 30-31.

TR1 Scandura, J. M. The teaching-learning process; an exploratory investigation of exposition and discovery modes of problem solving instruction. *Dissertation Abstracts*, 1963, *23*, No. 8., 2798.

2. Scandura, J. M. Abstract card tasks for use in problem solving research. *Journal of Experimental Education*, 1964, *33*, 145-148.

3. Scandura, J. M. An analysis of exposition and discovery modes of problem solving instruction. *Journal of Experimental Education*, 1964, *33*, 149-159. (Reprinted in P. C. Burns & A. M. Johnson (Eds.), *Research on elementary school curriculum and organization*. Rockleigh, N.J.: Allyn and Bacon, 1969.)

4. Scandura, J. M. The other role of schools of education. *Western New York Study Council Journal*, 1964, *15*, 11-13.

5. Scandura, J. M. Fraction-names and numbers. *The Arithmetic Teacher*, 1964, *11*, 468.

6. Scandura, J. M. Probability theory—basic concepts. *New York State Mathematics Teachers Journal*, 1965, *15*, 112-118.

7. Scandura, J. M. & Nelson, J. L. The emerging research role of the subject matter educator. *Journal of Research in Science Teaching*, 1965, *3*, 51-53.

8. Scandura, J. M. Educational research and the mathematics educator. *The Mathematics Teacher*, 1965, *58*, 131-138. (Reprinted in *The Mathematics Education*, 1967, *1*, 1-14.)

9. Scandura, J. M., Johnson, D. A., & Thomason, G. M. Federal funds for the improvement of mathematics education. *The Mathematics Teacher*, 1965, *58*, 551-554. (Also in *The Arithmetic Teacher*, 1965, *12*, 496-499.)

10. Scandura, J. M. Familiarization and cue selection. *Psychological Reports*, 1965, *16*, 19-22.

11. Scandura, J. M. Familiarization and one-trial learning: A positive interaction. *Psychological Reports*, 1965, *17*, 27-38.

12. Scandura, J. M. Problem solving and prior learning. *Journal of Experimental Education*, 1966, *34*, 7-11.

*As of March 1977. Reports can be ordered by number directly from the author.

13. Scandura, J. M. Algorithm learning and problem solving. *Journal of Experimental Education*, 1966, 34, 1–6.

14. Scandura, J. M. Prior learning, presentation order, and prerequisite practice in problem solving. *Journal of Experimental Education*, 1966, 34, 12–18.

15. Scandura, J. M. & Behr, M. Prerequisite practice and criterion form in mathematics learning. *Journal of Experimental Education*, 1966, 35, 54–55.

16. Scandura, J. M. Problem solving and prior learning. *The Reporter* (Central New York School Study Council, Education School, Syracuse University), 1966, 17(3), 1–5.

17. Scandura, J. M. Teaching--technology or theory. *American Educational Research Journal*, 1966, 3, 139–146. (Reprinted in *NIE Journal* (National Council of Educational Research and Training, New Delhi, India), 1966, 1, 11–17. French translation by Berengere de Senarclens, *Scientia Paedegogica Experimentalis*, 1967, 4, 231–243. Also reprinted (in German) in F. Loser (Ed.), *Theories of learning*. Stuttgart, Germany: Ernst Klett, 1977.)

18. Scandura, J. M. Precision in research on mathematics learning: The emerging field of psycho-mathematics. *Journal of Research in Science Teaching*, 1966, 4, 253–274.

19. Greeno, J. G. & Scandura, J. M. All-or-none transfer based on verbally mediated concepts. *Journal of Mathematical Psychology*, 1966, 3, 388–411.

20. Scandura, J. M. & Roughead, W. G. Conceptual organizers in short-term memory. *Journal of Verbal Learning and Verbal Behavior*, 1967, 6, 679–682. (Also in APA *Proceedings*, 1966.)

TR2 Scandura, J. M. *Problem solving and prior learning* (Project S-097). Washington, D.C.: U.S. Office of Education Mimeograph, 1966.

TR3 Scandura, J. M. *Rule generality and consistency in mathematics learning* (Project 6-8013). Washington, D.C.: U.S. Office of Education Mimeograph, 1966.

21. Scandura, J. M. A new doctoral program in mathematics education research. *The Mathematics Teacher*, 1966, 8, 729. (Also in the *American Mathematical Monthly*, 1967, 74, 72–74.) (The latter provides more background.)

22. Scandura, J. M. Concrete examples of commutative non-associative systems. *The Mathematics Teacher*, 1966, 59, 735–736. (Reprinted in *The Mathematics Education*.)

23. Scandura, J. M. Training leaders in mathematics education: A contrast with science education. *Journal of Research in Science Teaching*, 1966, 4, 227–229.

TR4 Scandura, J. M. *Precision in research on complex learning and teaching--the mathematical formulation of educational research questions* (Project 6-8002). Washington D.C.: U.S. Office of Education Mimeograph, 1967.

TR5 Scandura, J. M. *Teaching college students how to learn mathematics ("What is learned" in mathematical discovery)* (Project 6-8798). Washington, D.C.: U.S. Office of Education Mimeograph, 1967.

24. Scandura, J. M. Research in mathematics education: An overview and a perspective. In J. M. Scandura (Ed.), *Research in mathematics education*. Washington, D.C.: A Special Publication of the National Council of Teachers of Mathematics, 1967.

25. Scandura, J. M. The nature of research in mathematics education. *The High School Journal*, 1967, *50*, 227-237. (A special issue on mathematics education.)

26. Scandura, J. M. An alternative approach to research on mathematics learning--a reaction to Suppes' paper. *Journal of Research & Development in Education* (National Conference on Needed Research in Mathematics Education), 1967, *1*, 33-43.

TR6 Scandura, J. M. Critique of "Research in the Improvement of Verbal Problem Solving." Report for Department of Public Instruction, Commonwealth of Pennsylvania, Box 911, Harrisburg, Pennsylvania 17126 (Mr. Emanuel Berger), December, 1967.

27. Scandura, J. M. Training in mathematics education: A proposal for action. *The Mathematics Teacher*, 1967, *60*, 714 and 719.

28. Scandura, J. M. & Wells, J. N. Advance organizers in learning abstract mathematics. *American Educational Research Journal*, 1967, *4*, 295-301.

29. Scandura, J. M., Woodward, E., & Lee, F. Rule generality and consistency in mathematics learning. *American Educational Research Journal*, 1967, *4*, 303-319.

30. Scandura, J. M. The basic unit in meaningful learning--association or principle? *The Proceedings, APA*, 1967. (Also in *The School Review*, 1967, *75*, 329-341.)

31. Scandura, J. M. Learning verbal and symbolic statements of mathematical rules. *Journal of Educational Psychology*, 1967, *58*, 356-364.

32. Scandura, J. M. Learning principles in paired-associate lists. *Psychological Reports*, 1967, *20*, 329-330.

33. Scandura, J. M. Concept dominance in short term memory. *Journal of Verbal Learning and Verbal Behavior*, 1967, *6*, 461-469.

TR7 Scandura, J. M. (Ed.) *Report of a conference on elementary mathematics education and the Pennsylvania State Department of Public Instruction*. Harrisburg, 1968.

34. Scandura, J. M. & Satlow, J. *An analysis of existing curricular materials in mathematics. Phase one: (K-G)*. Philadelphia: Research for Better Schools, 1968.

35. Scandura, J. M. Con Ebel (Ebel's "Straw Man"). *Phi Delta Kappan* (Backtalk Section), 1968, *49*, 286.

573

36. Scandura, J. M. Research in mathematics and science education. *School Science and Mathematics,* 1968, *58,* 185-192.

37. Scandura, J. M. Research in psycho-mathematics. *The Mathematics Teacher,* 1968, *61,* 581-591. (Reprinted in *The Mathematics Education,* 1968, 3. Also reprinted in R. B. Ashlock & O. W. L. Herman, *Current research in elementary school mathematics.* New York: Macmillan, 1970.)

38. Roughead, W. G. & Scandura, J. M. "What is learned" in mathematical discovery. *Journal of Educational Psychology,* 1968, *59,* 283-289.

39. Scandura, J. M. Expository teaching of hierarchical subject matters. *Psychology in the Schools,* 1969, *6,* 307-310. (Also in *Journal of Structural Learning,* 1969, *2,* 17-25.)

40. Scandura, J. M. The formulation of research on subject matter learning. *Psychology in the Schools,* 1968, *5,* 330-341.

41. Scandura, J. M. & Durnin, J. H. Extra-scope transfer in learning mathematical rules. *Journal of Educational Psychology,* 1968, *59,* 350-354.

42. Scandura, J. M. & Anderson, J. L. Educational research and the science educatory. *Science Education,* 1968, 185-192.

43. Scandura, J. M. New directions for theory and research on rule learning: I. A set-function language. *Acta Psychologica,* 1968, *28,* 301-321.

44. Scandura, J. M. New directions for theory and research on rule learning: II. Empirical research. *Acta Psychologica,* 1969, *29,* 101-133.

45. Scandura, J. M. New directions for theory and research on rule learning: III. Analyses and theoretical direction. *Acta Psychologica,* 1969, *29,* 205-227.

46. Scandura, J. M. Federal control and basic research in education. *School & Society,* 1969, April, 227-228.

47. Scandura, J. M., Barksdale, J., Durnin, J., & McGee, R. An unexpected relationship between failure and subsequent mathematics learning. *Psychology in the Schools,* 1969, *6,* 379-381. (Also in *Educational Studies in Mathematics,* 1969, *1,* 247-251.)

TR8. Scandura, J. M. *Rule-governed behavior in mathematical structures.* University of Pennsylvania, Mathematics Education Research Group Report Series, February 2, 1969.

TR9. Scandura, J. M. *Mathematics and structural learning* (U.S.O.E. Project). Washington, D.C.: Mimeograph, 1970.

48. Scandura, J. M. *Problem solving ability in elementary mathematics--its nature and measurement.* Structural Learning Report 57, February 8, 1968.

574

264–280. (Also in *Educational Studies in Mathematics*, 1971, *3*, 229–243; and *Journal of Structural Learning*, 1970, *2*, 1–18.)

50. Scandura, J. M. The role of rules in behavior: Toward an operational definition of what (rule) is learned. *Psychological Review*, 1970, *77*, 516–533.

51. Scandura, J. M. & McGee, R. An exploratory investigation of basic mathematical abilities of kindergarten children. *Educational Studies in Mathematics*, 1971, *4*, 331–345. (Reprinted in *Journal of Structural Learning*, 1972, *3*, 79–99.)

52. Scandura, J. M. & Voorhies, D. Effect of irrelevant attributes and irrelevant operations in rule learning. *Journal of Educational Psychology*, 1971, *62*, 352–356.

53. Scandura, J. M. A theory of mathematical knowledge: Can rules account for creative behavior? *Journal of Research in Mathematics Education*, 1971, *2*, 183–196. (In *Structural Learning II*; see B–4.)

54. Scandura, J. M. What is a rule? *Journal of Educational Psychology*, 1972, *63*, 179–185.

55. Scandura, J. M. Deterministic theorizing in structural learning: Three levels of empiricism. *Journal of Structural Learning*, 1971, *3*, 21–53. (In *Structural Learning II*; see B–4.)

56. Scandura, J. M. A reply to Wittrock. In *Structural Learning II*; see B–4.

57. Scandura, J. M. Theoretical note: S–R theory or automata? September 10, 1970. (S–R Theory or Automata, A Final Word. In *Structural Learning II*; see B–4.)

58. Scandura, J. M. Plan for the development of a conceptually based mathematics curriculum for disadvantaged children. Part I: Theoretical foundations. *Instructional Science*, 1972, *2*, 247–262.

59. Scandura, J. M. Plan for the development of a conceptually based mathematics curriculum for disadvantaged children. Part II: Applications. *Instructional Science*, 1972, *2*, 363–387.

60. Scandura, J. M. An algorithmic base for curriculum construction in mathematics (A theory of mathematical knowledge). In W. E. Lamon (Ed.), *Learning and the nature of mathematics*. Chicago: Science Research Associates, 1971.

61. Scandura, J. M. On the value of status studies in education. *Journal for Research in Mathematics Education*, 1971, *2*, 115–117.

62. Scandura, J. M. & Durnin, J. H. Assessing behavior potential: Adequacy of basic theoretical assumptions. *Structural Learning Report 62*, November 30, 1971.

63. Durnin, J. H. & Scandura, J. M. An algorithmic approach to assessing behavior potential: Comparison with item forms and hierarchical analysis. *Journal of Educational Psychology*, 1973, *65*, 262–272. (Also to appear in *Journal of Structural Learning*, 1977, *6*, in press; and *Problem Solving*; see B–6.)

575

64. Ehrenpreis, W. & Scandura, J. M. Algorithmic approach to curriculum construction: A field test. *Journal of Educational Psychology*, 1974, *66*, 491-498. (To appear in *Problem Solving*; see B-6.)

65. Lowerre, G. & Scandura, J. M. Development and evaluation of individualized materials for critical thinking based on logical inference. *Reading Research Quarterly*, 1973, *IX*, 185-205.

66. Scandura, J. M. Mathematical problem solving. *American Mathematical Monthly*, 1974, *81*, 273-280. (Also in F. Klix (Ed.), *Organismische Informationsverarbeitung*, Bericht uber ein Symposium, September 11-14, 1973. Berlin: Akademie-Verlag, 1974.)

67. Scandura, J. M. The role of higher-order rules in problem solving. *Journal of Experimental Psychology*, 1974, *120*, 984-991. (To appear in *Problem Solving*; see B-6.)

68. Scandura, J. M. Structured knowledge: Static or dynamic? *Contemporary Psychology*, 1973, *18*, 23-24.

69. Scandura, J. M. Competence, knowledge, and their relation to human behavior. *Catalog of Selected Documents in Psychology*, 1974, *Summer*, Abstract on p. 72.

70. Scandura, J. M., Durnin, J. H., & Wulfeck, W. H., II. Higher-order rule characterization of heuristics for compass and straight-edge constructions in geometry. *Artificial Intelligence*, 1974, *5*, 149-183. (Also in *Problem Solving*; see B-6.)

71. Scandura, J. M. Structural learning and open education. Revision in *The Clearing House*, 1976, in press. (Also in *Educational Digest*, 1977, in press.)

72. Scandura, J. M. Structural learning and the design of educational materials. *Educational Technology*, 1973, *August*, 7-13.

73. Scandura, J. M. The structure of memory: Fixed or flexible? *Catalog of Selected Documents in Psychology*, 1974, *Spring*, Abstract on pp. 37-38. (Abridged version in F. Klix (Ed.), *Organismische Informationsverarbeitung*, Bericht uber ein Symposium, September 11-14, 1973. Berlin: Akademie-Verlag, 1974.)

74. Scandura, J. M. On higher-order rules. *Educational Psychologist*, 1973, *10*, 159-160.

75. Scandura, J. M. On conceptual foundations for mathematical education. *The Mathematics Education* (in India), 1975, *9*, 13-16.

76. Scandura, J. M. A book review of O. Milton's, *Alternatives to the traditional* (San Francisco: Jossey-Bass, 1972). *Educational Studies*, 1974, *5*, 85-86.

77. Scandura, J. M. The resolution of instructional problems: Rhetoric, research, or theory? Printed address, Division 15, APA, 1974.

78. Scandura, J. M. A short review of Arthur R. Jensen's, *Educability and Group Differences* (New York: Harper & Row, 1973). *Choice*, 1974, February, 1919.

79. Scandura, J. M. Problem definition, rule selection, and retrieval in problem solving. In *Problem Solving*; see B-6.

80. Scandura, J. M., Wulfeck, W. H., II, Durnin, J. H., & Ehrenpreis, W. Diagnosis and instruction of higher-order rules for solving geometry construction problems. In *1974 Proceedings*; see B-5. (Also in *Problem Solving*; see B-6.)

81. Scandura, J. M. On hiring and promotion. *The Almanac of the University of Pennsylvania*, February 5, 1974, *20(21)*.

82. Scandura, J. M. Empirical evaluation of rule-based theories. In *Problem Solving*; see B-6.

83. Scandura, J. M. Reaction to symposium: The learning research laboratory and the classroom. *Educational Psychologist*, 1974, *11*, 127-128.

84. Voorhies, D. & Scandura, J. M. Determination of memory load in information processing. In *1974 Proceedings*; see B-5. (Also in *Problem Solving*; see B-6.)

85. Scandura, J. M. Human problem solving: A synthesis of content, cognition, and individual differences. In *1974 Proceedings*; see B-5.

86. Scandura, J. M. How does mathematics learning take place? Invited talk given at General Session, NCTM meeting, Bozeman, Montana, June 14, 1974. (*Educational Studies in Mathematics*, 1975, *11*, 375-385.)

87. Scandura, J. M. & Durnin, J. H. Algorithmic analysis of algebraic proofs. In *Problem Solving*; see B-6.

88. Wulfeck, W. H., II & Scandura, J. M. The nature of mathematical genius? A review of *Mathematical talent: Discovery, description, and development* by J. C. Stanley, D. P. Keating, & L. H. Fox (Eds.). *The Review of Education*, 1975, *1*, 103-107.

89. Scandura, J. M. Structural approach to instructional problems. *American Psychologist*, 1977, *32*, 33-53.

90. Scandura, J. M. Creative problem solving. Talk given at APA, August, 1974.

91. Scandura, J. M., Lowerre, G. F., Scandura, A. M., & Veneski, J. *Mathematics curricula based on the electronic calculator? A feasibility study, grades K-2*. Texas Instruments: Technical Report, 1974.

92. Scandura, J. M., Scandura, A. M., & Lowerre, G. H. *Mathematics curricula based on the electronic calculator? A feasibility study, grades 3 and 4*. Texas Instruments: Technical Report, 1975.

93. Scandura, J. M. A deterministic theory of teaching and learning. In H. Spada & W. F. Kempf (Eds.), *Formalized theories of thinking and learning and their implications for science instruction.* Bern: Huber, 1977.

94. Hilke, R., Kempf, W. F., & Scandura, J. M. Deterministic and probabilistic theorizing in structural learning. In H. Spada & W. F. Kempf (Eds.), *Formalized theories of thinking and learning and their implications for science instruction.* Bern: Huber, 1977. (Ten-page summaries of 93 & 94 have already appeared in L. Hoffman & M. Lehrke (Eds.), *Formalisierte theorien des denkens und lernens und ihre anwendung in naturwissenshaftlichen unterricht.* Kiel, West Germany: IPN Technical Report 14, 1975.)

95. Scandura, J. M. IPN symposium discussion. In H. Spada & W. F. Kempf (Eds.), *Formalized theories of thinking and learning and their implications for science instruction.* Bern: Huber, 1977.

96. Scandura, J. M. The architecture of bricklaying (A review of G. Pask's, *Conversation, cognition, and learning.* Amsterdam: Elsevier, 1975). *Contemporary Psychology,* 1976, *21,* 630–631.

97. Scandura, J. M. A deterministic approach to research in instructional science. *Educational Psychologist,* 1977, in press.

98. Scandura, J. M. Structural approach to behavioral objectives and criterion-referenced testing. *Educational Technology,* 1977, in press.

99. Scandura, J. M. Cybernetic control of adaptive algorithms in instruction (A review of L. N. Landa's *Instructional regulation and control (cybernetics, algorithmization, and heuristics in education).* National Society of Programmed Instruction, 1977, in press.

Books

B-1. Scandura, J. M. *Mathematics: Concrete behavioral foundations.* New York: Harper & Row, 1971.

B-2. Scandura, J. M., Durnin, J. H., Ehrenpreis, W., & Luger, G. *An algorithmic approach to mathematics: Concrete behavioral foundations.* New York: Harper & Row, 1971.

B-3. Scandura, J. M. *Structural learning I: Theory and research.* London/New York: Gordon & Breach Science Publishers, 1973.

B-4. Scandura, J. M. (Ed.) with contributions by Arbib, M., Corcoran, J., Domotor, Z., Greeno, J., Lovell, K., Newell, A., Rosenbloom, P., Scandura, J., Shaw, R., Simon, H., Suppes, P., Wittrock, M., & Witz, K. *Structural learning II: Issues and approaches.* London/New York: Gordon & Breach Science Publishers, 1976.

B-5. Scandura, J. M., Durnin, J. H., & Wulfeck, W. H., II (Eds.). *1974 Proceedings: Fifth annual interdisciplinary conference on structural learning* (ONR Technical Report). MERGE Research Institute, 1249 Greentree Lane, Narberth, Pa., 1974.

B-6. Scandura, J. M. (with the collaboration of others). *Problem solving: A structural/process approach with instructional implications.* New York: Academic Press, 1977.

Curriculum Materials

C-1. Scandura, J. M., Lowerre, G. F., & Scandura, A. M. *Critical reading series (A self-diagnostic and instructional series of workbooks for teaching critical reading based on logical inference).* Worthington, Ohio: Ann Arbor Publishers, 1973. (Workbooks A, B, C, D, and Teachers' Manual)

Published Reviews of Books

Rising, G. R. Review of *Mathematics: Concrete behavioral foundations. Arithmetic Teacher,* 1972, *February,* 110-111.

Nahinsky, I. Going by rules (Review of *Structural learning I: Theory and research*). *Contemporary Psychology,* 1974, *19,* 414-416.

Krulee, G. K. Review of *Structural learning I: Theory and research. American Journal of Psychology,* 1975, *88,* 345-351.

AUTHOR INDEX

SUBJECT INDEX

A

Accounted for, *see* Competence account
Algorithm (rule), 46, 152, 167, 335, 350–352, 504
Algorithmic approach, 329, 347, 348, 353, 392, 427
Artificial intelligence, 10, 12–14, 31, 165, 197–198, 490, 528
Assessing behavior potential, 41, 80, 146, 323–324, 327, 345, 544
Assessment of individual knowledge, 426
Atomic goal, *see* Goal, Unitary/Atomic
Atomic rule, 25, 51, 73, 114, 153, 351–352
Atomic (structure), 51, 57, 58, 70, 72, 145
Atomic subset, 327
Atomic tests, 99, 145
Atomic unit, 44, 57, 105, 106, 146
Atomic (unitary), 51, 69, 70, 72, 95, 96, 99, 145
Atomicity (equivalence)
  behavioral (behavior
      equivalence/success–failure), 105, 106, 125, 145
  latency, 108, 128, 146
  process, 106, 130, 131, 146, 151
  rule, *see* Rule, Atomic
  stage (latency), 128, 146
  transfer, 122, 146
Auxiliary capabilities, 51, 53, 120, 146, 148

B

Behavior equivalence, *see* Atomicity
Behavior potential, 41, 80, 146, 153, 323, 325, 328
Behavior profile, 125, 146

Behavioral objective, 54, 146
Branching decisions, 350, 352

C

Chaining, 475
Chunk (substimulus), 28, 44, 57, 105–107, 146, 301, 303, 309, 311–314, 522, 549
Coefficient of generalizability, 359
Cognition, 9, 14, 34, 40
Cognitive constraints (universal), 50, 146
Cognitive mechanisms, *see* Control mechanism
Cognitive processing, 104, 147
Cognitive unit, *see* Structure
Combination, 284
Compatible (pairs of) rules, 55, 147, 168
Competence, 40–42, 167, 426, 460, 490
Competence account, 43, 49, 50, 53, 64, 147, 485
Competence global/molar, 43, 49, 147
Competence rule (prototypic/idealized rule), 50, 63, 147
Competencies (content), 9, 11, 17, 33, 35, 147
Complementary observation theory, Chapter 1, 150
Composition, 55, 149, 203, 244, 468
Composition rule (higher-order), 55, 149, 468
Computable function, 46, 147
Computation (associated with a rule), 108, 147
Compound problems (proofs), 206
  biconditional, 206, 207
  existence and uniqueness, 206, 207
  simple antecedent, compound consequent, 206–208
Computer-assisted instruction, 555
Computer-assisted testing, 361